# Contents

Introduction, acknowledgments and author

## chapters

# Introduction to the third edition

This updated third edition of Business Accounts provides a practical study of the principles of accounting. It covers courses in accounting such as Higher National, first year of Business Studies and Accounting degrees, National Vocational Qualifications (NVQ) and Scottish Vocational Qualifications (SVQ). The earlier chapters are also suitable for advanced book-keeping courses.

Business Accounts is a user-friendly text which shows the how and why of accounting. It contains progressive sections covering:

- the basics of double-entry book-keeping and the use of financial documents

- accounting concepts, the trial balance and the preparation of final accounts

- advanced accounting techniques, such as control accounts, suspense accounts, incomplete records

- final accounts of different types of organisations, such as clubs and societies, sole traders, partnerships and limited companies

- interpretation of accounts

- cash flow statements

This revised third edition provides a greater emphasis on the use of computer accounting. Chapter 11 explains the use of computers in accounting and Chapters 29 to 32 provide a 'hands-on' guide to the use of a Sage accounting system.

The book also contains two Case Studies which consolidate major sections of work:

- Case Study 1 is a fully-worked example of a handwritten book-keeping system and follows a month's routine business transactions through to the production of final accounts.

- Case Study 2 uses material from Case Study 1 and incorporates the year-end adjustments to the final accounts.

Each chapter is complete in itself and contains a variety of questions which have been carefully graded to ensure that the first ones develop basic principles, and the later questions test more advanced techniques. Answers to selected questions – those marked with an asterisk (*) – are given in Appendix 2. Answers are given in fully displayed form, showing the correct layouts – which is important in accounting. Answers to the remaining questions are given in a separate Tutor Pack available direct from Osborne Books (please telephone Customer Services on 01905 748071 for further information).

There are also ten sets of multiple choice questions placed throughout the book. Answers to multiple choice questions are given in Appendix 2 . Appendix 3 contains additional questions to reinforce learning. Answers to these questions are available in the Tutor Pack.

The Osborne Books website www.osbornebooks.co.uk continues to be very popular. Free downloads of blank documents and other material are available from the Resources Section. Please log on.

David Cox, June 2004

# Acknowledgments

In writing and updating this book I have been helped by a number of people. In particular, I would like to thank: Roger Petheram, Senior Lecturer in Accounting at Worcester College of Technology, for reading the text, commenting upon it, checking answers, and always being prepared to discuss any aspect of the book; Michael Fardon, of Osborne Books, for his continued assistance and editorial support; Jean Cox, my wife, who keyed in the original text; Mike Gilbert and Claire McCarthy of Osborne Books for technical support.

Thanks are also due to the following for permission to reproduce material: The Sage Group plc, and the Controller of Her Majesty's Stationery Office for reproduction of the VAT 100 form produced by HM Customs & Excise.

Questions from past examination papers at the end of the chapters are reproduced by kind permission of London Chamber of Commerce and Industry (LCCI), OCR Examinations, and Pitman Qualifications. Where answers are given to past examination questions, they are the responsibility of the author, not the examining board.

# The Author

David Cox is a Certified Accountant with more than twenty years experience teaching accountancy students over a wide range of levels. Formerly with the Management and Professional Studies Department at Worcester College of Technology, he now lectures on a freelance basis and carries out educational consultancy work in accountancy studies. He is author and joint author of a number of textbooks in the areas of accounting, finance and banking.

# 1 WHAT ARE BUSINESS ACCOUNTS?

Accounting – known as 'the language of business' – is essential to the recording and presentation of business activities in the form of business accounts. Accounting involves:

- recording business transactions in financial terms
- reporting financial information to the owner of the business and other interested parties
- advising the owner – and other parties – how to use the financial reports to assess the past performance of the business, and to make decisions for the future

We will see how the three main elements of the definition – recording, reporting and advising – are often carried out by different types of accounting personnel. First, though, we will look at an outline of the accounting system.

## THE ACCOUNTING SYSTEM

Businesses need to record financial transactions in the form of business accounts for very practical reasons:

- they need to quantify items such as sales, expenses and profit
- they need to present these figures in a meaningful way to measure the success of the business

Business financial records can be very complex, and one of the problems that you face as a student of business accounts is having difficulty in relating what you are learning to the accounting system of the business as a whole. In this chapter we will summarise how a typical business records and presents financial information in the form of accounts. The process follows a number of distinct stages which are illustrated in full in the diagram on the next page.

# the accounting system

## SOURCE DOCUMENTS

invoices – issued and received

credit notes – issued and received

debit notes – issued and received

bank paying-in slips

cheques issued

other banking documents

*sources of accounting information*

## PRIMARY ACCOUNTING RECORDS

day books

journal

cash books (also used in double-entry – see below)

*gathering and summarising accounting information*

## DOUBLE-ENTRY BOOK-KEEPING

**sales ledger** – accounts of debtors

**purchases ledger** – accounts of creditors

**general (nominal) ledger**

- 'nominal' accounts for sales, purchases, expenses, capital, loans etc

- 'real' accounts for items, eg fixed assets

**cash books**

- cash book for bank and cash transactions

- petty cash book

*recording the dual aspect of accounting transactions in the accounting system*

## TRIAL BALANCE

a summary of the balances of all the accounts at the end of the accounting period

*arithmetic checking of double-entry book-keeping*

## FINAL ACCOUNTS

- manufacturing account
- trading and profit and loss account

*and*

- balance sheet

*statement measuring profit (or loss) for an accounting period*

*statement of assets, liabilities and capital at the end of an accounting period*

The accounting system can be summarised as follows:

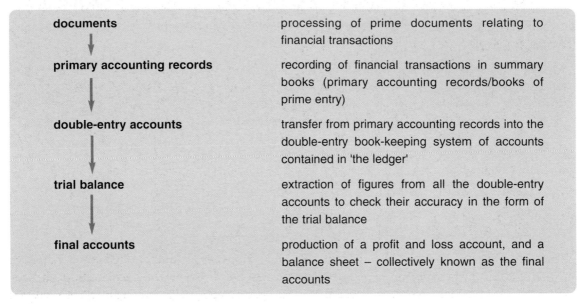

| | |
|---|---|
| **documents** | processing of prime documents relating to financial transactions |
| ↓ | |
| **primary accounting records** | recording of financial transactions in summary books (primary accounting records/books of prime entry) |
| ↓ | |
| **double-entry accounts** | transfer from primary accounting records into the double-entry book-keeping system of accounts contained in 'the ledger' |
| ↓ | |
| **trial balance** | extraction of figures from all the double-entry accounts to check their accuracy in the form of the trial balance |
| ↓ | |
| **final accounts** | production of a profit and loss account, and a balance sheet – collectively known as the final accounts |

The rest of this book covers these stages – the accounting system – in detail. If you should at any time lose sight of where your studies are taking you, refer back to this chapter, and it should help to place your work in context.

Before summarising each stage in the accounting system we will first examine what form accounting records can take.

## ACCOUNTING RECORDS

Accounting records are usually kept in one of two forms: handwritten records or computer records.

### written accounting records

This is the traditional form of keeping 'the books', particularly for the smaller business. The main record is the ledger which, at one time, would be a large leather-bound volume, neatly ruled, into which the book-keeper would enter each business transaction in immaculate copperplate handwriting into individual accounts. In modern times, the handwritten ledger is still used, and stationery shops sell ledgers and other accounting books, designed especially for the smaller business.

### computer accounting records

Nowadays, computers are relatively cheap so that they can be afforded by all but the smallest business. With computer accounting, business transactions are input into the computer and stored on disk. The major advantage of computer accounting is that it is a very accurate method of recording business transactions; the disadvantage is that it may be cumbersome and time-consuming to set up, particularly for the smaller business. Interestingly, the word 'ledger' has survived into the computer age but, instead of being a bound volume, it is represented by data files held on a computer disk.

Whether business transactions are recorded by hand, or by using a computer, the basic principles remain the same. The first few chapters of this book concentrate on these basic principles, and Chapter 11 shows how computers can be used in accounting.

## practical points

When maintaining business accounts you should bear in mind that they should be kept:

- accurately
- up-to-date
- confidentially, ie not revealed to people outside the business

Maintaining business accounts is a discipline, and you should develop disciplined accounting skills as you study with this book. Your study of business accounts will involve you in working through many questions and practical examples. These will require you to apply logical thought to the skills you have learned. In particular, when attempting questions you should:

- be neat in the layout of your work
- use ink (in accounting, the use of pencil shows indecision)
- not use correcting fluid (errors should be crossed through neatly with a single line and the correct version written on the line below)

The reason for not using correcting fluid in handwritten accounts is because, in practice, the accounts will often be audited (checked by accountants): correcting fluid may hide errors, but it can also conceal fraudulent transactions.

# BUSINESS DOCUMENTS

Business transactions generate documents. You will already be familiar with many of these. In this section we will relate them to the type of transaction involved and also introduce other accounting terminology which is essential to your studies.

## sale and purchase of goods and services – the invoice

When a business buys or sells goods or a service the seller prepares an invoice stating

- the amount owing
- when it should be paid
- details of the goods sold or service provided

An invoice is illustrated on page 47.

## cash sales and credit sales – debtors and creditors

An invoice is prepared by the seller for

- **cash sales** – where payment is immediate, whether in cash, by cheque, by debit card or by credit card (Note that not all cash sales will require an invoice to be prepared by the seller – shops, for instance, normally issue a receipt for the amount paid.)
- **credit sales** – where payment is to be made at a later date (often 30 days later)

    A debtor is a person who owes you money when you sell on credit.

    A creditor is a person to whom you owe money when you buy on credit.

## return of goods – the credit note

If the buyer returns goods which are bought on credit (they may be faulty or incorrect) the seller will prepare a credit note (see page 49 for an example) which is sent to the buyer, reducing the amount of money owed. The credit note, like the invoice, states the money amount and the goods or services to which it relates.

## banking transactions – paying-in slips, cheques, BACS transfers

Businesses, like anyone else with a bank account, need to pay in money, and draw out cash and make payments. Paying-in slips, cheques and BACS transfers are used frequently in business as source documents for bank account transactions. 'BACS' stands for Bankers Automated Clearing Services which provide electronic transfer of amounts from one bank account to another.

## further reading

The subject of business documents is covered in detail in Chapter 4, which you should read if you are unfamiliar with the documents mentioned so far.

# RECORDING OF TRANSACTIONS – PRIMARY ACCOUNTING RECORDS

Many businesses issue and receive large quantities of invoices, credit notes and banking documents, and it is useful for them to list these in summary form, during the course of the working day. These summaries are known as primary accounting records or books of prime (original) entry.

These include:

- **sales day book** – a list of sales made, compiled from invoices issued
- **purchases day book** – a list of purchases made, compiled from invoices received
- **sales returns day book** – a list of 'returns in', ie goods returned by customers, compiled from credit notes issued
- **purchases returns day book** – a list of 'returns out', ie goods returned by the business to suppliers, compiled from credit notes received

- **cash book** – the business' record of the bank account and the amount of cash held, compiled from receipts, paying-in slips, cheques and BACS documents
- **petty cash book** – a record of small cash (notes and coin) purchases made by the business, compiled from petty cash vouchers
- **journal** – a record of non-regular transactions, which are not recorded in any other primary accounting record

The primary accounting records are explained in detail in Chapter 6. The point you should bear in mind is that they provide the information for the double-entry book-keeping system.

## DOUBLE-ENTRY ACCOUNTS: THE LEDGER

The basis of the accounting system is the double-entry book-keeping system which is embodied in a series of records known as the ledger. This is divided into a number of separate accounts.

### double-entry book-keeping

Double-entry book-keeping involves making two entries in the accounts for each transaction: for instance, if you are paying wages by cheque you will make an entry in bank account and an entry in wages account. The reasoning behind this procedure and the rules involved are explained in detail in Chapters 2 and 3. If you are operating a manual accounting system you will make the two entries by hand, if you are operating a computer accounting system you will make one entry on the keyboard, but indicate to the machine where the other entry is to be made by means of a code.

### accounts

The sources for the entries you make are the primary accounting records (books of prime entry). The ledger into which you make the entries is normally a bound book (in a non-computerised system) divided into separate accounts, eg a separate account for sales, purchases, each type of business expense, each debtor, each creditor, and so on. Each account will be given a specific name, and a number for reference purposes (or input code, if you use a computer system).

### division of the ledger

Because of the large number of accounts involved, the ledger has traditionally been divided into a number of sections. These same sections are used in computer accounting systems.

- **sales ledger** – personal accounts of debtors, ie customers to whom the business has sold on credit
- **purchases ledger** – personal accounts of creditors, ie suppliers to whom the business owes money
- **cash books** – a cash book comprising cash account and bank account, and a petty cash book for petty cash account (small purchases). Note: the cash books are also primary accounting records

- **general (or nominal) ledger** – the remainder of the accounts: nominal accounts, eg sales, purchases, expenses, and real accounts for items owned by the business

## trial balance

Double-entry book-keeping, because it involves making two entries for each transaction, is open to error. What if the book-keeper writes in £45 in one account and £54 in another? The trial balance – explained in full in Chapter 5 – effectively checks the entries made over a given period and will pick up most errors. It sets out the balances of all the double-entry accounts, ie the totals of the accounts for a certain period. It is, as well as being an arithmetic check, the source of valuable information which is used to help in the preparation of the final accounts of the business.

## FINAL ACCOUNTS

The final accounts of a business comprise the profit statement and the balance sheet.

## profit statement

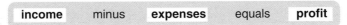

| income | minus | expenses | equals | profit |

The profit statement of a business includes the trading and profit and loss account, and if the business manufactures goods, a manufacturing account. The object of these statements is to calculate the profit due to the owner(s) of the business after certain expenses have been deducted from income:

- manufacturing account shows the costs of producing a quantity of finished goods
- trading and profit and loss account shows the profit (or loss) after the deduction of cost of goods sold to give gross profit, and also after the deduction of all expenses to give net profit

The figures for these calculations – sales, purchases, expenses of various kinds – are taken from the double-entry system. The layout of profit statements is explained in Chapter 12.

## balance sheet

The double-entry system also contains figures for:

**assets**    items the business owns, which can be
- fixed assets – items bought for use in the business, eg premises, vehicles, computers
- current assets – items used in the everyday running of the business, eg stock, debtors (money owed by customers), and money in the bank

**liabilities**    items that the business owes, eg bank loans and overdrafts, and creditors (money owed to suppliers)

**capital**    money or assets introduced by the owner(s) of the business; capital is in effect owed by the business to the owner

The balance sheet is so called because it balances in numerical (money) terms:

| **assets** | minus | **liabilities** | equals | **capital** |
|---|---|---|---|---|
| *what a business owns* | | *what a business owes* | | *how the business has been financed* |

The layout of balance sheets is explained in Chapter 12.

## the accounting equation

The balance sheet illustrates a concept important to accounting theory, known as the accounting equation. This equation is illustrated in the diagram above, namely

$$\text{Assets} - \text{Liabilities} = \text{Capital}$$

Every business transaction will change the balance sheet and the equation, as each transaction has a dual effect on the accounts. However, the equation will always balance.

Consider the following transactions made through the business bank account:

| | Transaction | Effect on equation |
|---|---|---|
| 1. | Business pays creditor | decrease in asset (bank) |
| | | decrease in liability (money owed to creditor) |
| 2. | Business buys computer* <br> (*VAT is ignored) | increase in asset (computer) |
| | | decrease in asset (bank) |
| 3. | The owner introduces new capital by paying a cheque into the bank | increase in asset (bank) |
| | | increase in capital (money owed by business to owner) |

How is the equation affected by these particular transactions?

1. Assets and liabilities both decrease by the amount of the payment; capital remains unchanged.
2. Assets remain the same because the two transactions cancel each other out in the assets section: value is transferred from the asset of bank to the asset of computer.
3. Both sides of the equation increase by the amount of the capital introduced.

In short, the equation always balances, as will the balance sheet of a business.

In conclusion, every transaction has a dual aspect, as two entries are involved: this is the basis of the theory of double-entry book-keeping, and will be described in detail in Chapters 2 and 3.

## ACCOUNTING CONCEPTS

Accounting concepts are broad assumptions which underlie the preparation of all accounting reports. For the moment, we will consider two very important aspects:

- business entity
- money measurement

**Business entity** means that the accounts record and report on the financial transactions of a particular business: for example, the accounts of J Smith Limited record and report on that business only. The problem is that, when a business is run by a sole trader, the owner's personal financial transactions can be sometimes mixed in with the business' financial transactions: the two should be kept entirely separate.

**Money measurement** means that the accounting system uses money as the common denominator in recording and reporting all business transactions. Thus, it is not possible to record, for example, the loyalty of a firm's workforce or the quality of a product, because these cannot be reported in money terms.

## WHO USES ACCOUNTS?

Before answering the question of who uses the accounts, and why, it is important to draw a distinction between the two processes of book-keeping and accounting.

**Book-keeping** is the basic recording of business transactions in financial terms – literally 'keeping the books of account'. This task can be carried out by anyone – the owner, or by a full-time or part-time book-keeper. The book-keeper should be able to record transactions, and extract a trial balance (see Chapter 5).

**Accounting** involves taking the information recorded by the book-keeper and presenting it in the form of financial reports to the business owners or managers. Such reports are either retrospective:

- profit statement and balance sheet

or forward looking:

- forecast, or budgeted, accounts

In each case, these reports help the owners or managers to monitor the financial progress of the business, and to make decisions for the future.

### information for the owner(s)

The accounting system will be able to give information on:

- purchases of goods (for resale) to date
- sales/turnover to date

- expenses to date
- debtors – both the total amount owed to the business, and also the names of individual debtors and the amount owed by each
- creditors – both the total owed by the business, and the amount owed to each creditor
- assets owned by the business
- liabilities owed by the business
- profit made by the business during a particular time period

The owner will want to know how profitable the business is, and what it may be worth.

## information for outside bodies

Other people interested in the accounts of a business include:

- the bank manager, if the business wants to borrow from the bank
- the Inland Revenue – tax will have to be paid on the profits of the business
- HM Customs and Excise (the VAT authorities) if a business is registered for Value Added Tax
- financial analysts who may be advising investors in the business
- official bodies, eg Companies House, who need to see the final accounts of limited companies
- creditors, who wish to assess the likelihood of receiving payment
- employees and trade unions, who wish to check on the financial prospects of the business

# ACCOUNTING PERSONNEL

If you are studying business accounts you will encounter references to different types of professional accountant. It is important to have a general idea of who does what in the accounting world – see the diagram on page 12.

## financial accountant

The function of the financial accountant is to take further the information prepared by the book-keeper. This will involve the preparation of final accounts, ie trading and profit and loss account, and balance sheet. The financial accountant may be also required to negotiate with the Inland Revenue on taxation matters.

Where the business is a limited company, the financial accountant will be also involved in preparing final accounts which comply with the requirements of the Companies Act 1985 (as amended by the Companies Act 1989). This Act requires the directors of a company to report annually to shareholders, with certain minimum financial accounting information being disclosed. The financial accountant of a limited company will usually report to the finance director.

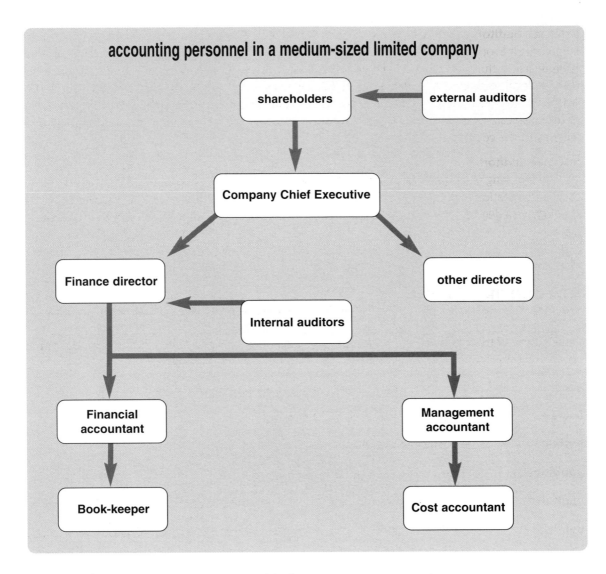

accounting personnel in a medium-sized limited company

## cost and management accountant

The cost accountant obtains information about the recent costs of the business, eg raw materials and labour, and estimates costs for the future. Often the cost accountant reports to the management accountant who prepares reports and makes recommendations to the owner(s) or managers of the business. The management accountant will usually report to the finance director.

## auditors

Auditors are accountants whose role is to check that accounting procedures have been followed correctly. There are two types of auditors:

- external auditors
- internal auditors

**External auditors** are independent of the firm whose accounts are being audited. The most common type of audit carried out by external auditors is the statutory audit for larger limited companies. In this, the auditors are reporting directly to the shareholders of the company, stating that the legal requirements laid down in the Companies Acts 1985 (as amended by the Companies Act 1989) have been complied with, and that the accounts represent a 'true and fair view' of the state of the business. External auditors are usually appointed by the shareholders at the Annual General Meeting of the company.

**Internal auditors** are employees of the business which they audit. They are concerned with the internal checking and control procedures of the business: for example, procedures for the control of cash, authorisation of purchases, and disposal of property. The nature of their work requires that they should have a degree of independence within the business and, in a limited company, they will usually report directly to the finance director.

## ACCOUNTING TERMS

In the course of this chapter a number of specific accounting terms have been introduced. You should now study this section closely to ensure that you are clear about these definitions:

| | |
|---|---|
| **accounts** | financial records, where business transactions are entered |
| **ledger** | the set of accounts of a business |
| **assets** | items owned by a business |
| **liabilities** | items owed by a business |
| **capital** | the amount of the owner's (or owners') stake in the business |
| **debtors** | individuals or businesses who owe money in respect of goods or services supplied by the business |
| **creditors** | individuals or businesses to whom money is owed by the business |
| **purchases** | goods bought, either on credit or for cash, which are intended to be resold later |
| **credit purchases** | goods bought, with payment to be made at a later date |
| **cash purchases** | goods bought and paid for immediately |
| **sales** | the sale of goods, whether on credit or for cash, in which the business trades |
| **credit sales** | goods sold, with payment to be received at an agreed date in the future |
| **cash sales** | goods sold, with immediate payment received in cash, by cheque, by credit card, or by debit card |
| **turnover** | the total of sales, both cash and credit, for a particular time period |

# CHAPTER SUMMARY

● Accounting is known as 'the language of business'.

● The accounting system comprises a number of specific stages of recording and presenting business transactions:
  • prime documents
  • primary accounting records
  • double-entry system of ledgers
  • trial balance
  • final accounts

● Accounting records call for the development of skills of accuracy and neatness.

● The balance sheet uses the accounting equation:

$$\text{Assets} - \text{Liabilities} = \text{Capital}$$

● Two basic accounting concepts which apply to all business accounts are:
  • business entity
  • money measurement.

● Business accounts are used both by the managers of the business and also by outside bodies.

● There are several different types of accounting personnel, including:
  • book-keeper
  • financial accountant
  • cost and management accountant
  • auditors, external and internal

● Accounting involves the use of very specific terminology which should be learned.

In the next chapter we will look at some financial transactions that are to be found in most business accounts. By studying these we will begin to understand the principles of double-entry book-keeping.

# QUESTIONS

NOTE: an asterisk (*) after the question number means that an answer to the question is given in Appendix 2.

**1.1\***   Fill in the missing words from the following sentences:

(a)   The set of double-entry accounts of a business is called the ........................................

(b)   A ........................................ is a person who owes you money when you sell on credit.

(c)   A ................................ is a person to whom you owe money when you buy on credit.

(d)   The ................. .................. ................... is a list of sales made, compiled from invoices issued.

(e)   The business' record of bank account and amount of cash held is kept in the

.............................. ..............................

(f)   Accounts such as sales, purchases, expenses are kept in the ...................................

...................................

(g)   The accounting equation is:

................................... minus ........................................equals ...................................

(h)   Accounts record and report on the financial transactions of a particular business: this

is the application of the   ................................. ................................. concept.

(i)   ................................. are accountants who check that accounting procedures have been followed correctly.

**1.2**  Describe the main stages in the accounting system. State five pieces of information that can be found from the accounting system that will be of interest to the owner of the business.

**1.3**  What types of accounting jobs are advertised in your local paper? Classify them in relation to accounting personnel described in this chapter. What tasks do the jobs involve?

**1.4**  Explain the accounting concepts of:

    (a)  business entity

    (b)  money measurement

**1.5**  Distinguish between:

- assets and liabilities
- debtors and creditors
- purchases and sales
- credit purchases and cash purchases

**1.6**  Show the dual aspect, as it affects the accounting equation (assets – liabilities = capital), of the following transactions for a particular business:

- owner starts in business with capital of £8,000 in the bank
- buys a computer for £4,000, paying by cheque
- obtains a loan of £3,000 by cheque from a friend
- buys a van for £6,000, paying by cheque

**1.7\***  Fill in the missing figures:

| Assets | Liabilities | Capital |
|---|---|---|
| £ | £ | £ |
| 20,000 | 0 | .......... |
| 15,000 | 5,000 | .......... |
| 16,400 | ......... | 8,850 |
| .......... | 3,850 | 10,250 |
| 25,380 | ......... | 6,950 |
| .......... | 7,910 | 13,250 |

**1.8\*** The table below sets out account balances from the books of a business. The columns (a) to (f) show the account balances resulting from a series of transactions that have taken place over time.

You are to compare each set of adjacent columns, ie (a) with (b), (b) with (c), and so on and state, with figures, what accounting transactions have taken place in each case.

(Ignore VAT).

| | (a) | (b) | (c) | (d) | (e) | (f) |
|---|---|---|---|---|---|---|
| | £ | £ | £ | £ | £ | £ |
| **Assets** | | | | | | |
| Office equipment | – | 2,000 | 2,000 | 2,000 | 2,000 | 2,000 |
| Van | – | – | – | 10,000 | 10,000 | 10,000 |
| Bank | 10,000 | 8,000 | 14,000 | 4,000 | 6,000 | 3,000 |
| | | | | | | |
| **Liabilities** | | | | | | |
| Loan | – | – | 6,000 | 6,000 | 6,000 | 3,000 |
| | | | | | | |
| **Capital** | 10,000 | 10,000 | 10,000 | 10,000 | 12,000 | 12,000 |

# 2 DOUBLE-ENTRY BOOK-KEEPING: FIRST PRINCIPLES

As we have seen in Chapter 1, book-keeping is the basic recording of business transactions in financial terms. Before studying business accounts in detail it is important to study the principles of double-entry book-keeping, as these form the basis of all that we shall be doing in the rest of the book.

In the previous chapter we looked briefly at the dual aspect of accounting – each time there is a business transaction there are two effects on the accounting equation. This chapter shows how the dual aspect is used in the principles of book-keeping. In particular, we shall be looking at accounts for:

- bank
- cash
- capital
- fixed assets
- expenses
- income
- drawings
- loans

## LEDGER ACCOUNTS

Double-entry book-keeping, as its name suggests, recognises that each transaction has a dual aspect. Once the dual aspect of each transaction has been identified, the two book-keeping entries can be made in the ledger accounts of the accounting system. An account is kept in the ledger to record each different type of transaction. In a handwritten book-keeping system, the ledger will consist either of a bound book, or a series of separate sheets of paper – each account in the ledger will occupy a separate page; in a computerised system, the ledger will consist of a computer file, divided into separate accounts. Whether a handwritten or computerised system is being used, the principles remain the same.

A commonly-used layout for an account is set out on the next page. Entries in ledger accounts always include dates. Please note that dates used throughout the book, for the sake of simplicity, are expressed as 20-1, 20-2, 20-3, etc, unlike in a real business where the actual year date is shown (ie 2001, 2002, 2003 etc). Occasionally in this book 20-9 is followed by 20-0, ie when the decade changes.

| Debit | | | | Name of the account, eg Wages Account | | | Credit |
|---|---|---|---|---|---|---|---|
| **Date** | **Details** | **Folio** | **£ p** | **Date** | **Details** | **Folio** | **£ p** |
| date of the trans-action | name of the other account | page or reference number of the other account | amount of the trans-action | date of the trans-action | name of the other account | page or reference number of the other account | amount of the trans-action |

Note the following points about the layout of this account:

- the name of the account is written at the top
- the account is divided into two identical halves, separated by a central double vertical line
- the left-hand side is called the 'debit' side ('debit' is abbreviated to 'Dr' – short for <u>DebtoR</u>)
- the right-hand side is called the 'credit' (or 'Cr') side
- the date, details and amount of the transaction are entered in the account
- the 'folio' column is used as a cross-referencing system to the other entry of the double-entry book-keeping transaction
- in the 'details' column is entered the name of the other account involved in the book-keeping transaction

In practice, each account would occupy a whole page in a handwritten book-keeping system but, to save space when doing exercises, it is usual to put several accounts on a page. In future, in this book, the account layout will be simplified to give more clarity as follows:

| Dr | **Wages Account** | | Cr |
|---|---|---|---|
| 20-1 | £ | 20-1 | £ |

This layout is often known in accounting jargon as a 'T' account; it will be used extensively in this book because it separates in a simple way the two sides – debit and credit – of the account. An alternative style of account has three money columns: debit, credit and balance. This type of account is commonly used for bank statements, building society passbooks and computer accounting statements. Because the balance of the account is calculated after every transaction, it is known as a running balance account (see page 26).

## DEBITS AND CREDITS

The principle of double-entry book-keeping is that for every business transaction:

- one account is debited, and
- one account is credited

Debit entries are on the left-hand side of the appropriate account, while credit entries are on the right. The rules for debits and credits are:

- **debit entry** – the account which gains value, or records an asset, or an expense
- **credit entry** – the account which gives value, or records a liability, or an income item

This is illustrated as follows:

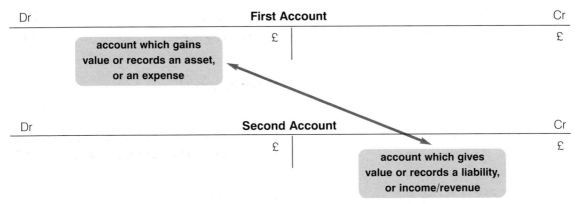

When one entry has been identified as a debit or credit, the other entry will be on the opposite side of the other account.

## EXAMPLE TRANSACTIONS

In order to put the theory of double-entry book-keeping into practice, we will look at some financial transactions undertaken by a new business which has just been set up by Jayne Hampson in 20-1:

| | |
|---|---|
| 1 September | Started in business with capital of £5,000, a cheque paid into the bank |
| 4 September | Bought office equipment £2,500, paying by cheque |
| 7 September | Paid rent of office £500, by cheque |
| 10 September | Received commission of £100, by cheque |
| 12 September | Withdrew £250 from the bank for own use (drawings) |
| 16 September | Received a loan of £1,000 from James Henderson by cheque |

All of these transactions involve the bank, and the business will enter them in its bank account. The bank account records money in the form of bank receipts and payments, ie cheques, standing orders, direct debits, BACS transfers, credit card transactions, and debit card transactions. (Most businesses also use a cash account to record transactions which involve money in the form of cash.)

With both bank account and cash account, the rules for debit and credit are:

* money in is recorded on the debit side
* money out is recorded on the credit side

Using these rules, the bank account of Jayne Hampson's business, after entering the transactions listed above, appears as:

| Dr | | **Bank Account** | | | Cr |
|---|---|---|---|---|---|
| 20-1 | | £ | 20-1 | | £ |
| 1 Sep | Capital | 5,000 | 4 Sep | Office equipment | 2,500 |
| 10 Sep | Commission | 100 | 7 Sep | Rent paid | 500 |
| 16 Sep | J Henderson: loan | 1,000 | 12 Sep | Drawings | 250 |
| | | Money in | | Money out | |

Note: the bank account shows the firm's record of how much has been paid into, and drawn out of, the bank - it is not exactly the same as the record of receipts and payments kept by the bank (we will compare the two in Chapter 10).

To complete the double-entry book-keeping transactions we need to:

* identify on which side of the bank account the transaction is recorded – debit (money in), or credit (money out)
* record the other double-entry transaction on the opposite side of the appropriate account
* note that business transactions involving cash will be entered in the cash account

The other accounts involved can now be recorded, and we shall look at the principles involved for each transaction.

# CAPITAL

Capital is the amount of money invested in the business by the owner (or owners). The amount is owed by the business back to the owner, although it is unlikely to be repaid immediately as the business would cease to exist. A capital account is used to record the amount(s) paid into the business; the book-keeping entries are:

● **capital introduced**

  – debit bank account, as in the case of Jayne Hampson, or cash account (or a fixed asset account where these form part of the capital)

  – credit capital account

---

**Example transaction**

1 Sep 20-1   Started in business with capital of £5,000, a cheque paid into the bank.

---

| Dr | | Capital Account | | Cr |
|---|---|---|---|---|
| 20-1 | £ | 20-1 | | £ |
| | | 1 Sep   Bank | | 5,000 |

Note: The dual aspect is that bank account has gained value and has been debited already (see account on page 21); capital account records a liability (to the owner) and is credited. Remember that the business is a separate entity, and this book-keeping entry looks at the transaction from the point of view of the business. The introduction of capital into a business is often the very first business transaction entered into the books of account.

# FIXED ASSETS

Fixed assets are items purchased by a business for use on a semi-permanent basis. Examples are premises, motor vehicles, machinery and office equipment. All of these are bought by a business with the intention that they will be used for some time in the business. Without fixed assets, it would be difficult to continue in business, eg without machinery it would prove difficult to run a factory; without delivery vans and lorries it would be difficult to transport the firm's products to its customers.

When a business buys fixed assets, the expenditure is referred to as capital expenditure. This means that items have been bought for use in the business for some years to come. By contrast, revenue expenditure (see next page) is where the items bought will be used by the business quite quickly. For example, the purchase of a car is capital expenditure, while the cost of fuel for the car is revenue expenditure. There is more on the difference between capital expenditure and revenue expenditure in Chapter 12.

## fixed assets and double-entry book-keeping

When fixed assets are bought, a separate account for each type of fixed asset is used, eg premises account, motor vehicles account, machinery account, etc. The book-keeping entries are:

● **purchase of a fixed asset**

  – debit fixed asset account (using the appropriate account)

  – credit bank account (or cash account)

**Example transaction**

4 Sep 20-1   Bought office equipment £2,500, paying by cheque.

| Dr | **Office Equipment Account** | | Cr |
|----|----|----|----|
| 20-1 | £ | 20-1 | £ |
| 4 Sep   Bank | 2,500 | | |

The other part of the dual aspect of this transaction is a credit to bank account: this has been entered already (see account on page 21).

# EXPENSES

Businesses pay various running expenses, such as rent paid, wages, electricity, telephone, vehicle running expenses, etc. These day-to-day expenses of running the business are termed revenue expenditure. A separate account is used in the accounting system for each main class of revenue expenditure, eg rent account, wages account, etc.

The book-keeping entries are:

● **payment of an expense**
   – debit expense account (using the appropriate account)
   – credit bank account (or cash account)

**Example transaction**

7 Sep 20-1   Paid rent of office £500, by cheque.

| Dr | **Rent Account** | | Cr |
|----|----|----|----|
| 20-1 | £ | 20-1 | £ |
| 7 Sep   Bank | 500 | | |

Note: The accounting rules followed are that we have debited the account which has gained value (rent paid – the business has had the use of the office for a certain time). The account which has given value (bank) has already been credited (see page 21).

## INCOME

From time-to-time a business may receive amounts of income, eg rent received, commission received, or fees received. These are recorded in separate accounts for each category of income, eg rent received account, commission received account. The book-keeping entries are:

● **receipt of income**
  - debit bank account (or cash account)
  - credit income account (using the appropriate account)

**Example transaction**

10 September 20-1   Received commission of £100, by cheque.

| Dr | | | **Commission Received Account** | | Cr |
|---|---|---|---|---|---|
| 20-1 | | £ | 20-1 | | £ |
| | | | 10 Sep   Bank | | 100 |

Note: We have already debited the account which has gained value (bank – see page 21) and credited the account which has given value (commission received).

## OWNER'S DRAWINGS

Drawings is the term used when the owner takes money, in cash or by cheque (or sometimes goods), from the business for personal use. A drawings account is used to record such amounts; the book-keeping entries for withdrawal of money are:

● **owner's drawings**
  - debit drawings account
  - credit bank account (or cash account)

**Example transaction**

12 Sep 20-1   Withdrew £250 from the bank for own use.

| Dr | | | **Drawings Account** | | Cr |
|---|---|---|---|---|---|
| 20-1 | | £ | 20-1 | | £ |
| 12 Sep   Bank | | 250 | | | |

The other part of the dual aspect of this transaction is a credit to bank account: this has been entered already (see page 21).

## LOANS

When a business receives a loan, eg from a relative or the bank, it is the cash account or bank account which gains value, while a loan account (in the name of the lender) records the liability.

- **loan received**
  - debit bank account (or cash account)
  - credit loan account (in name of the lender)

**Example transaction**

16 September 20-1   Received a loan of £1,000 from James Henderson by cheque

| Dr | | | James Henderson: Loan Account | | Cr |
|----|----|----|----|----|----|
| 20-1 | | £ | 20-1 | | £ |
| | | | 16 Sep    Bank | | 1,000 |

The debit entry has already been made in bank account (see page 21).

## FURTHER TRANSACTIONS

Using the accounts which we have seen already, here are some further transactions:

- **loan repayment**
  - debit loan account
  - credit bank account (or cash account)
- **sale of a fixed asset, or return of an unsuitable fixed asset**
  - debit bank account (or cash account)
  - credit fixed asset account

Note: sale of fixed assets is dealt with more fully in Chapter 14.

- **withdrawal of cash from the bank for use in the business**
  - debit cash account
  - credit bank account
- **payment of cash into the bank**
  - debit bank account
  - credit cash account

# RUNNING BALANCE ACCOUNTS

The layout of accounts that we have used has a debit side and a credit side. Whilst this layout is very useful when learning the principles of book-keeping, it is not particularly appropriate for practical business use. Most 'real-life' accounts have three money columns: debit transactions, credit transactions, and balance. A familiar example of this type of account is a bank statement and a building society passbook. With a three-column account, the balance is calculated after each transaction has been entered – hence the name running balance accounts. For handwritten accounts, it would be rather tedious to calculate the balance after each transaction (and a potential source of errors) but, using computer accounting, the calculation is carried out automatically.

The following is the bank account used earlier in this chapter (page 21), set out in 'traditional' format:

| Dr | | | | **Bank Account** | | Cr |
|---|---|---|---|---|---|---|
| 20-1 | | £ | 20-1 | | | £ |
| 1 Sep | Capital | 5,000 | 4 Sep | Office equipment | | 2,500 |
| 10 Sep | Commission | 100 | 7 Sep | Rent paid | | 500 |
| 16 Sep | J Henderson: loan | 1,000 | 12 Sep | Drawings | | 250 |

The account does not show the balance, and would need to be balanced (see Chapter 5).

In 'running balance' layout, the account appears as:

**Bank Account**

| 20-1 | | Debit | Credit | Balance |
|---|---|---|---|---|
| | | £ | £ | £ |
| 1 Sep | Capital | 5,000 | | 5,000 Dr |
| 4 Sep | Office equipment | | 2,500 | 2,500 Dr |
| 7 Sep | Rent paid | | 500 | 2,000 Dr |
| 10 Sep | Commission | 100 | | 2,100 Dr |
| 12 Sep | Drawings | | 250 | 1,850 Dr |
| 16 Sep | J Henderson: loan | 1,000 | | 2,850 Dr |

With a running balance account, it is necessary to state after each transaction whether the balance is debit (Dr) or credit (Cr). Note that the bank account in the books of this business has a debit balance, ie there is money in the bank – an asset.

# CHAPTER SUMMARY

- Every business transaction has a dual aspect.

- Business transactions are recorded in ledger accounts using double-entry book-keeping principles.

- Each double-entry book-keeping transaction involves a debit entry and a credit entry.

- Entries in the bank account and cash account are:
  - debit money in
  - credit money out

- Capital is the amount of money invested in the business by the owner. Capital introduced is recorded as:
  - debit bank account or cash account (or an asset account if an asset is introduced)
  - credit capital account

- Fixed assets are items purchased by a business for use on a permanent basis, eg premises, motor vehicles, machinery and office equipment. The purchase of such items is called capital expenditure.

- The purchase of fixed assets is recorded in the business accounts as:
  - debit fixed asset account
  - credit bank account (or cash account)

- Running expenses of a business, such as rent paid, wages, electricity, etc are called revenue expenditure.

- Expenses are recorded in the business accounts as:
  - debit expense account
  - credit bank account (or cash account)

- Receipt of income, eg rent received, commission received, fees received, is recorded as:
  - debit bank account (or cash account)
  - credit income account

- Drawings is where the owner takes money (or goods) from the business for personal use. The withdrawal of money is recorded as:
  - debit drawings account
  - credit bank account (or cash account)

- When a business receives a loan, it will be recorded as:
  - debit bank account (or cash account)
  - credit loan account in the name of the lender

In the next chapter we will continue with double-entry book-keeping and look at regular business transactions for purchases, sales and returns.

# QUESTIONS

NOTE: an asterisk (*) after the question number means that an answer to the question is given in Appendix 2.

**2.1** James Anderson has kept his bank account up-to-date, but has not got around to the other double-entry book-keeping entries. Rule up the other accounts for him, and make the appropriate entries.

| Dr | | | **Bank Account** | | | Cr |
|---|---|---|---|---|---|---|
| 20-1 | | £ | 20-1 | | | £ |
| 1 Feb | Capital | 7,500 | 6 Feb | Computer | | 2,000 |
| 14 Feb | Bank loan | 2,500 | 8 Feb | Rent paid | | 750 |
| 20 Feb | Commission received | 145 | 12 Feb | Wages | | 425 |
| | | | 23 Feb | Drawings | | 200 |
| | | | 25 Feb | Wages | | 380 |
| | | | 28 Feb | Van | | 6,000 |

**2.2*** The following are the business transactions of Tony Long for the month of May 20-2:

20-2

| | |
|---|---|
| 1 May | Started a business with capital of £6,000 in the bank |
| 4 May | Bought a machine for £3,500, paying by cheque |
| 6 May | Bought office equipment for £2,000, paying by cheque |
| 10 May | Paid rent £350, by cheque |
| 12 May | Obtained a loan of £1,000 from a friend, Lucy Warner, and paid her cheque into the bank |
| 15 May | Paid wages £250, by cheque |
| 17 May | Commission received £150, by cheque |
| 20 May | Drawings £85, by cheque |
| 25 May | Paid wages £135, by cheque |

You are to:

(a) Write up Tony Long's bank account

(b) Complete the double-entry book-keeping transactions

**2.3** Enter the following transactions into the double-entry book-keeping accounts of Jean Lacey:

20-5

| | |
|---|---|
| 1 Aug | Started in business with capital of £5,000 in the bank |
| 3 Aug | Bought a computer for £1,800, paying by cheque |
| 7 Aug | Paid rent £100, by cheque |
| 10 Aug | Received commission £200, in cash |

| 12 Aug | Bought office fittings £2,000, paying by cheque |
|---|---|
| 15 Aug | Received a loan, £1,000 by cheque, from a friend, Sally Orton |
| 17 Aug | Drawings £100, in cash |
| 20 Aug | Returned some of the office fittings (unsuitable) and received a refund cheque of £250 |
| 25 Aug | Received commission £150, by cheque |
| 27 Aug | Made a loan repayment to Sally Orton of £150, by cheque |

**2.4\***  Tom Griffiths has recently set up in business. He has made some errors in writing up his bank account. You are to set out the bank account as it should appear, rule up the other accounts for him, and make the appropriate entries.

| Dr | | | | Bank Account | | | Cr |
|---|---|---|---|---|---|---|---|
| 20-2 | | | £ | 20-2 | | | £ |
| 4 Mar | Office equipment | | 1,000 | 1 Mar | Capital | | 6,500 |
| 12 Mar | Drawings | | 175 | 5 Mar | Bank loan | | 2,500 |
| | | | | 7 Mar | Wages | | 250 |
| | | | | 8 Mar | Commission received | | 150 |
| | | | | 10 Mar | Rent paid | | 200 |
| | | | | 15 Mar | Van | | 6,000 |

**2.5**  Enter the following transactions into the double-entry book-keeping accounts of Caroline Yates:

20-7

| 1 Nov | Started in business with capital of £75,000 in the bank |
|---|---|
| 3 Nov | Bought a photocopier for £2,500, paying by cheque |
| 7 Nov | Received a bank loan of £70,000 |
| 10 Nov | Bought office premises £130,000, paying by cheque |
| 12 Nov | Paid rates of £3,000, by cheque |
| 14 Nov | Bought office fittings £1,500, paying by cheque |
| 15 Nov | Received commission of £300, in cash |
| 18 Nov | Drawings in cash £125 |
| 20 Nov | Paid wages £250, by cheque |
| 23 Nov | Paid £100 of cash into the bank |
| 25 Nov | Returned some of the office fittings (unsuitable) and received a refund cheque for £200 |
| 28 Nov | Received commission £200, by cheque |

**2.6**  Write up the bank account from question 2.5 in the form of a 'running balance' account.

# 3 DOUBLE-ENTRY BOOK-KEEPING: FURTHER TRANSACTIONS

This chapter continues with the principles of double-entry book-keeping and builds on the skills established in the previous chapter. We shall be looking at the dual aspect and the book-keeping required for the business transactions of:

- cash purchases
- cash sales
- credit purchases
- credit sales
- returns
- carriage

## PURCHASES AND SALES

Common business transactions are to buy and sell goods. These transactions are recorded in purchases account and sales account respectively. These two accounts are used to record the purchase and sale of the goods in which the business trades. For example, a shoe shop will buy shoes from the manufacturer and will record this in purchases account; as shoes are sold, the transactions will be recorded in sales account. Note that the book-keeping system does not use a 'goods account': instead, when buying goods, a purchases account is used; when selling goods, a sales account is used.

The normal entry on a purchases account is on the debit side – the account has gained value, ie the business has bought goods for resale. The normal entry on a sales account is on the credit side – the account has given value, ie the business has sold goods.

When a business buys an item for use in the business, eg a computer, this is debited to a separate account, because a fixed asset – see page 22 – has been purchased. Likewise, when a fixed asset is sold, it is not entered in the sales account.

## WORKED EXAMPLE: PURCHASES AND SALES

In order to put the theory of double-entry book-keeping for purchases and sales into practice, we will look at some financial transactions undertaken by Temeside Traders, a business which started trading on 1 October 20-1:

| | |
|---|---|
| 1 October | Started in business with capital of £7,000 paid into the bank |
| 2 October | Bought goods for £5,000, paying by cheque |
| 3 October | Sold some of the goods for £3,000, a cheque being received |
| 5 October | Bought computer for £700, paying by cheque |
| 10 October | Bought goods for £2,800, paying by cheque |
| 12 October | Sold some of the goods for £5,000, a cheque being received |
| 15 October | Paid rent £150, by cheque |

These transactions are entered into the book-keeping system as follows:

| Dr | | Bank Account | | | | Cr |
|---|---|---|---|---|---|---|
| 20-1 | | | £ | 20-1 | | £ |
| 1 Oct | Capital | | 7,000 | 2 Oct | Purchases | 5,000 |
| 3 Oct | Sales | | 3,000 | 5 Oct | Computer | 700 |
| 12 Oct | Sales | | 5,000 | 10 Oct | Purchases | 2,800 |
| | | | | 15 Oct | Rent paid | 150 |

| Dr | | Capital Account | | | | Cr |
|---|---|---|---|---|---|---|
| 20-1 | | | £ | 20-1 | | £ |
| | | | | 1 Oct | Bank | 7,000 |

| Dr | | Purchases Account | | | | Cr |
|---|---|---|---|---|---|---|
| 20-1 | | | £ | 20-1 | | £ |
| 2 Oct | Bank | | 5,000 | | | |
| 10 Oct | Bank | | 2,800 | | | |

| Dr | | Sales Account | | | | Cr |
|---|---|---|---|---|---|---|
| 20-1 | | | £ | 20-1 | | £ |
| | | | | 3 Oct | Bank | 3,000 |
| | | | | 12 Oct | Bank | 5,000 |

| Dr | | Computer Account | | | | Cr |
|---|---|---|---|---|---|---|
| 20-1 | | | £ | 20-1 | | £ |
| 5 Oct | Bank | | 700 | | | |

| Dr | | Rent Paid Account | | | | Cr |
|---|---|---|---|---|---|---|
| 20-1 | | | £ | 20-1 | | £ |
| 15 Oct | Bank | | 150 | | | |

**notes to worked example**

- Only one purchases account and one sales account is used to record the two different movements of the goods in which a business trades.

- The computer is a fixed asset, so its purchase is entered to a separate computer account.

- The purchases and sales made in the transactions above are called cash purchases and cash sales, because payment is immediate.

# CREDIT TRANSACTIONS

In the previous section, we looked at the book-keeping for cash purchases and cash sales, ie where payment is made immediately. However, in business, many transactions for purchases and sales are made on credit, ie the goods are bought or sold now, with payment (in cash, or by cheque) to be made at a later date. It is an important aspect of double-entry book-keeping to record the credit transaction as a purchase or a sale, and then record the second entry in an account in the name of the creditor or debtor, ie to record the amount owing by the firm to a creditor, or to the firm by a debtor.

Note that the term credit transactions does not refer to the side of an account. Instead, it means the type of transaction where money is not paid at the time of making the sale: payment will be made at a later date.

## credit purchases

Credit purchases are goods obtained from a supplier, with payment to take place at a later date. From the buyer's viewpoint, the supplier is a creditor.

The book-keeping entries are:

● **credit purchase**
  - debit purchases account
  - credit creditor's (supplier's) account

When payment is made to the creditor the book-keeping entries are:

● **payment made to creditor**
  - debit creditor's account
  - credit bank account or cash account

## credit sales

With credit sales, goods are sold to a customer who is allowed to settle the account at a later date. From the seller's viewpoint, the customer is a debtor.

The book-keeping entries are:

● **credit sale**

　– debit debtor's (customer's) account

　– credit sales account

When payment is received from the debtor the book-keeping entries are:

● **payment received from debtor**

　– debit bank account or cash account

　– credit debtor's account

## WORKED EXAMPLE: CREDIT TRANSACTIONS

A local business, Wyvern Wholesalers, has the following transactions in the year 20-1:

| 18 Sep | Bought goods, £250, on credit from Malvern Manufacturing Co, with payment to be made in 30 days' time |
| 20 Sep | Sold goods, £175, on credit to Strensham Stores, payment to be made in 30 days' time |
| 18 Oct | Paid £250 by cheque to Malvern Manufacturing Co |
| 20 Oct | Received a cheque for £175 from Strensham Stores |

These transactions will be recorded in the book-keeping system of Wyvern Wholesalers (previous transactions on accounts, if any, not shown) as follows:

| Dr | | | **Purchases Account** | | | Cr |
|----|----|----|----|----|----|----|
| 20-1 | | | £ | 20-1 | | £ |
| 18 Sep | Malvern Manufacturing Co | | 250 | | | |

| Dr | | | **Sales Account** | | | Cr |
|----|----|----|----|----|----|----|
| 20-1 | | | £ | 20-1 | | £ |
| | | | | 20 Sep | Strensham Stores | 175 |

| Dr | | | **Malvern Manufacturing Co** | | | Cr |
|----|----|----|----|----|----|----|
| 20-1 | | | £ | 20-1 | | £ |
| 18 Oct | Bank | | 250 | 18 Sep | Purchases | 250 |

| Dr | | Strensham Stores | | | Cr |
|---|---|---|---|---|---|
| 20-1 | | £ | 20-1 | | £ |
| 20 Sep | Sales | 175 | 20 Oct | Bank | 175 |

| Dr | | Bank Account | | | Cr |
|---|---|---|---|---|---|
| 20-1 | | £ | 20-1 | | £ |
| 20 Oct | Strensham Stores | 175 | 18 Oct | Malvern Manufacturing Co | 250 |

Note: the name of the other account involved has been used in the details column as a description.

## balancing off accounts

In the example above, after the transactions have been recorded in the books of Wyvern Wholesalers, the accounts of Malvern Manufacturing Co and Strensham Stores have the same amount entered on both debit and credit side. This means that nothing is owing to Wyvern Wholesalers, or is owed by it, ie the accounts have a 'nil' balance. In practice, as a business trades, there will be a number of entries on both sides of such accounts, and we shall see in Chapter 5 how accounts are 'balanced off' at regular intervals.

## fixed assets bought on credit

Fixed assets are often purchased on credit terms. As with the purchase of goods for resale, an account is opened in the name of the creditor, as follows:

- **purchase of a fixed asset on credit**
  - debit fixed asset account, eg computer account
  - credit creditor's (supplier's) account

When payment is made to the creditor the book-keeping entries are:

- **payment made to a creditor**
  - debit creditor's account
  - credit bank account or cash account

# PURCHASES RETURNS AND SALES RETURNS

From time-to-time goods bought or sold are returned, perhaps because the wrong items have been supplied (eg wrong type, size or colour), or because the goods are unsatisfactory. We will now see the book-keeping entries for returned goods.

- **Purchases returns** (or returns out) is where a business returns goods to a creditor (supplier). The book-keeping entries are:

  – debit creditor's (supplier's) account

  – credit purchases returns (or returns outwards) account

  Purchases returns are kept separate from purchases, ie they are entered in a separate purchases returns account rather than being credited to purchases account.

- **Sales returns** (or returns in) is where a debtor (customer) returns goods to the business. The book-keeping entries are:

  – debit sales returns (or returns in) account

  – credit debtor's (customer's) account

Sales returns are kept separate from sales, ie they are entered in a separate sales returns account rather than being debited to sales account.

## WORKED EXAMPLE: PURCHASES RETURNS AND SALES RETURNS

Wyvern Wholesalers has the following transactions during the year 20-1:

| | |
|---|---|
| 7 October | Bought goods, £280, on credit from B Lewis Ltd |
| 10 October | Returned unsatisfactory goods, £30, to B Lewis Ltd |
| 11 October | Sold goods, £125, on credit to A Holmes |
| 17 October | A Holmes returned goods, £25 |
| 26 October | Paid the amount owing to B Lewis Ltd by cheque |
| 29 October | A Holmes paid the amount owing in cash |

The transactions will be recorded in the book-keeping system of Wyvern Wholesalers (previous transactions on accounts, if any, not shown) as follows:

| Dr | | **Purchases Account** | | | Cr |
|---|---|---|---|---|---|
| 20-1 | | £ | 20-1 | | £ |
| 7 Oct | B Lewis Ltd | 280 | | | |

| Dr | | **B Lewis Ltd** | | | Cr |
|---|---|---|---|---|---|
| 20-1 | | £ | 20-1 | | £ |
| 10 Oct | Purchases Returns | 30 | 7 Oct | Purchases | 280 |
| 26 Oct | Bank | 250 | | | |

| Dr | Purchases Returns Account | | Cr |
|---|---|---|---|
| 20-1 | £ | 20-1 | £ |
| | | 10 Oct  B Lewis Ltd | 30 |

| Dr | Sales Account | | Cr |
|---|---|---|---|
| 20-1 | £ | 20-1 | £ |
| | | 11 Oct  A Holmes | 125 |

| Dr | A Holmes | | Cr |
|---|---|---|---|
| 20-1 | £ | 20-1 | £ |
| 11 Oct  Sales | 125 | 17 Oct  Sales Returns | 25 |
| | | 29 Oct  Cash | 100 |

| Dr | Sales Returns Account | | Cr |
|---|---|---|---|
| 20-1 | £ | 20-1 | £ |
| 17 Oct  A Holmes | 25 | | |

| Dr | Bank Account | | Cr |
|---|---|---|---|
| 20-1 | £ | 20-1 | £ |
| | | 26 Oct  B Lewis Ltd | 250 |

| Dr | Cash Account | | Cr |
|---|---|---|---|
| 20-1 | £ | 20-1 | £ |
| 29 Oct  A Holmes | 100 | | |

# CARRIAGE INWARDS AND CARRIAGE OUTWARDS

When goods are bought and sold, the cost of transporting the goods is referred to as 'carriage'.

Carriage inwards is where the buyer pays the carriage cost of purchases, eg an item is purchased by mail order, and the buyer has to pay the additional cost of delivery (and possibly packing also).

Carriage outwards is where the seller pays the carriage charge, eg an item is sold to the customer and described as 'delivery free'.

Both carriage inwards and carriage outwards are expenses and their cost should be debited to two separate accounts, carriage inwards account and carriage outwards account respectively.

# GENERAL PRINCIPLES OF DEBITS AND CREDITS

By now you should have a good idea of the principles of debits and credits. From the transactions we have considered in this and the previous chapter, the 'rules' can be summarised as follows:

**Debits** include

- purchases of goods for resale
- sales returns (or returns in) when goods previously sold are returned to the business
- purchase of fixed assets for use in the business
- expenses incurred by the business
- debtors where money is owed to the business
- money received through cash account or bank account
- drawings made by the owner of the business
- loan repayment, where a loan liability is reduced/repaid

**Credits** include

- sales of goods by the business
- purchases returns (or returns out) of goods previously bought by the business
- sale of fixed assets
- income received by the business
- creditors where money is owed by the business
- money paid out through cash account or bank account
- capital introduced into the business by the owner(s)
- loan received by the business

It is important to ensure, at an early stage, that you are clear about the principles of debits and credits. They are important for an understanding of book-keeping, and are essential for your later studies in business accounts.

To summarise the double-entry book-keeping 'rules':

- **debit entry** – the account which gains value, or records an asset, or an expense
- **credit entry** – the account which gives value, or records a liability, or an income item

## TYPES OF ACCOUNT

Within a book-keeping system there are different types of account: a distinction is made between personal and impersonal accounts. Personal accounts are in the names of people or businesses, eg the accounts for debtors and creditors. Impersonal accounts are the other accounts; these are usually divided between real accounts, which represent things such as cash, bank, computers, cars, machinery, etc, and nominal accounts, which record income and expenses such as sales, purchases, wages, etc.

These distinctions are shown in the diagram below.

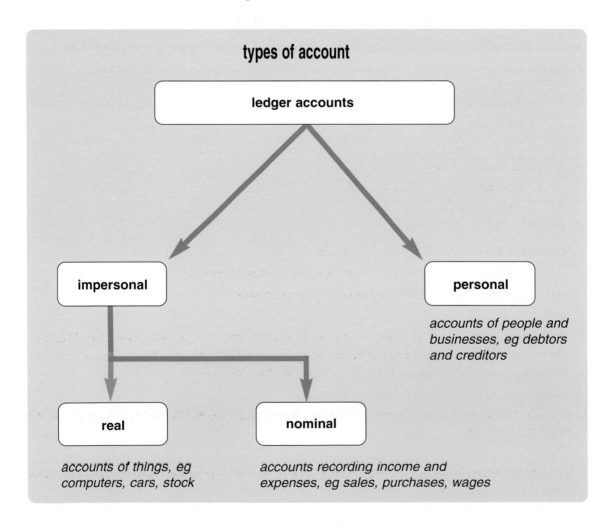

## CHAPTER SUMMARY

● Purchases account is used to record the purchase of goods in which the business trades: the normal entry is on the debit side.

● Sales account is used to record the sale of goods in which the business trades: the normal entry is on the credit side.

● The purchase of goods is recorded as:
  – debit purchases account
  – credit bank/cash account or, if bought on credit, creditor's account

● The sale of goods is recorded as:
  – debit bank/cash account or, if sold on credit, debtor's account
  – credit sales account

● Purchases returns (or returns out) are recorded as:
  – debit creditor's account
  – credit purchases returns account

● Sales returns (or returns in) are recorded as:
  – debit sales returns account
  – credit debtor's account

● 'Carriage' is the expense of transporting goods:
  – carriage inwards is the cost of carriage paid on purchases
  – carriage outwards is the cost of carriage paid on sales

● Accounts are divided between personal (the accounts of people, firms, eg debtors and creditors; also capital account), and impersonal accounts; impersonal accounts are sub-divided between real (the accounts of things), and nominal (the accounts of income and expenses).

Case Study 1 (page183) gives a fully worked example showing business transactions entered into the double-entry accounts.

In the next chapter we will look at the business documents used when goods are sold on credit to another business.

# QUESTIONS

NOTE: an asterisk (*) after the question number means that an answer to the question is given in Appendix 2.

3.1 The following are the business transactions of Evesham Enterprises for the month of October 20-2:

| | |
|---|---|
| 1 Oct | Started in business with capital of £2,500 in the bank |
| 2 Oct | Bought goods, £200, paying by cheque |
| 4 Oct | Sold goods, £150, a cheque being received |
| 6 Oct | Bought goods, £90, paying by cheque |
| 8 Oct | Sold goods, £125, a cheque being received |
| 12 Oct | Received a loan of £2,000 from J Smithson by cheque |
| 14 Oct | Bought goods, £250, paying by cheque |
| 18 Oct | Sold goods, £155, a cheque being received |
| 22 Oct | Bought a secondhand delivery van, £4,000, paying by cheque |
| 25 Oct | Paid wages, £375, by bank giro credit |
| 30 Oct | Sold goods, £110, a cheque being received |

You are to:

(a) Write up the firm's bank account

(b) Complete the double-entry book-keeping transactions

3.2* The following are the business transactions of Oxford Trading Company for the month of February 20-1:

| | |
|---|---|
| 1 Feb | Started in business with capital of £3,000 in the bank |
| 2 Feb | Sold goods, £250, a cheque being received |
| 3 Feb | Bought goods, £100, paying by cheque |
| 5 Feb | Paid wages, £150, by bank giro credit |
| 7 Feb | Sold goods, £300, a cheque being received |
| 12 Feb | Bought goods, £200, paying by cheque |
| 15 Feb | Received a loan of £1,000 from James Walters by cheque |
| 20 Feb | Bought a computer for £1,950, paying by cheque |
| 25 Feb | Sold goods, £150, a cheque being received |
| 27 Feb | Paid wages, £125, by bank giro credit |

You are to:

(a) Write up the firm's bank account

(b) Complete the double-entry book-keeping transactions

**3.3\*** Write up the bank account from question 3.2 in the form of a 'running balance' account.

**3.4\*** The following are the business transactions of Pershore Packaging for the month of January 20-1:

| | |
|---|---|
| 4 Jan | Bought goods, £250, on credit from AB Supplies Ltd |
| 5 Jan | Sold goods, £195, a cheque being received |
| 7 Jan | Sold goods, £150, cash being received |
| 10 Jan | Received a loan of £1,000 from J Johnson by cheque |
| 15 Jan | Paid £250 to AB Supplies Ltd by cheque |
| 17 Jan | Sold goods, £145, on credit to L Lewis |
| 20 Jan | Bought goods, £225, paying by cheque |
| 22 Jan | Paid wages, £125, in cash |
| 26 Jan | Bought office equipment, £160, on credit from Mercia Office Supplies Ltd |
| 29 Jan | Received a cheque for £145 from L Lewis |
| 31 Jan | Paid the amount owing to Mercia Office Supplies Ltd by cheque |

You are to record the transactions in the books of account.

**3.5** The following are the business transactions for April 20-2 of William King, who runs a food wholesaling business:

| | |
|---|---|
| 2 Apr | Bought goods, £200, on credit from Wyvern Producers Ltd |
| 4 Apr | Bought goods, £250, on credit from A Larsen |
| 5 Apr | Sold goods, £150, on credit to Pershore Patisserie |
| 7 Apr | Sold goods, £175, a cheque being received |
| 9 Apr | Returned goods, £50, to Wyvern Producers Ltd |
| 12 Apr | Sold goods, £110, a cheque being received |
| 15 Apr | Pershore Patisserie returned goods, £25 |
| 17 Apr | Bought a weighing machine for use in the business £250, on credit from Amery Scales Limited |
| 20 Apr | Paid Wyvern Producers Ltd £150, by cheque |
| 22 Apr | Pershore Patisserie paid the amount owing by cheque |
| 26 Apr | Returned goods, £45, to A Larsen |
| 28 Apr | Sold goods, £100, cash received |
| 29 Apr | Paid wages in cash, £90 |
| 30 Apr | Paid the amount owing to Amery Scales Ltd by cheque |

You are to record the transactions in the books of account.

**3.6**

The following are the business transactions for June 20-3 of Helen Smith who trades as 'Fashion Frocks':

| | |
|---|---|
| 2 Jun | Bought goods, £350, on credit from Designs Ltd |
| 4 Jun | Sold goods, £220, a cheque being received |
| 5 Jun | Sold goods, £115, cash received |
| 6 Jun | Returned goods, £100, to Designs Ltd |
| 7 Jun | Bought goods, £400, on credit from Mercia Knitwear Ltd |
| 10 Jun | Sold goods, £350, on credit to Wyvern Trade Supplies |
| 12 Jun | Sold goods, £175, a cheque being received |
| 15 Jun | Wyvern Trade Supplies returned goods, £50 |
| 17 Jun | Returned goods, £80, to Mercia Knitwear Ltd |
| 18 Jun | Paid the amount owing to Designs Ltd by cheque |
| 20 Jun | Sold goods, £180, cash received |
| 23 Jun | Bought goods, £285, on credit from Designs Ltd |
| 26 Jun | Paid rent in cash, £125 |
| 28 Jun | Received a cheque from Wyvern Trade Supplies for the amount owing |

You are to record the transactions in the books of account.

**3.7**

For each transaction below, complete the table on the next page to show the names of the accounts which will be debited and credited:

(a)     Bought goods, paying by cheque

(b)     Cheque received for sales

(c)     Bought goods on credit from Teme Traders

(d)     Sold goods on credit to L Harris

(e)     Returned unsatisfactory goods to Teme Traders

(f)     L Harris returns unsatisfactory goods

(g)     Received a loan from D Perkins, by cheque

(h)     Withdrew cash from the bank for use in the business

| Transaction | Account debited | Account credited |
|---|---|---|
| (a) | ..................................... | ..................................... |
| (b) | ..................................... | ..................................... |
| (c) | ..................................... | ..................................... |
| (d) | ..................................... | ..................................... |
| (e) | ..................................... | ..................................... |
| (f) | ..................................... | ..................................... |
| (g) | ..................................... | ..................................... |
| (h) | ..................................... | ..................................... |

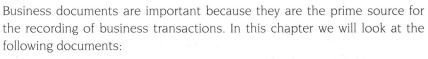

# 4 BUSINESS DOCUMENTS

Business documents are important because they are the prime source for the recording of business transactions. In this chapter we will look at the following documents:

- purchase order
- delivery note
- invoice
- credit note
- statement of account

We will also look at how cash discount – an allowance off the invoice price for quick settlement – is recorded in the book-keeping system.

## DOCUMENTS FOR A CREDIT TRANSACTION

You will see that the documents to be explained involve credit transactions, ie selling or buying with payment to be made at a later date. The normal stages in a credit transaction are:

**1** buyer prepares
- – purchase order

**2** seller prepares
- – delivery note
- – invoice
- – statement of account

**3** buyer sends payment by
- – cheque, or
- – bank transfer

If some or all of the goods are unsatisfactory and are returned, the seller prepares a credit note. The flow of these documents is shown in the diagram on the next page.

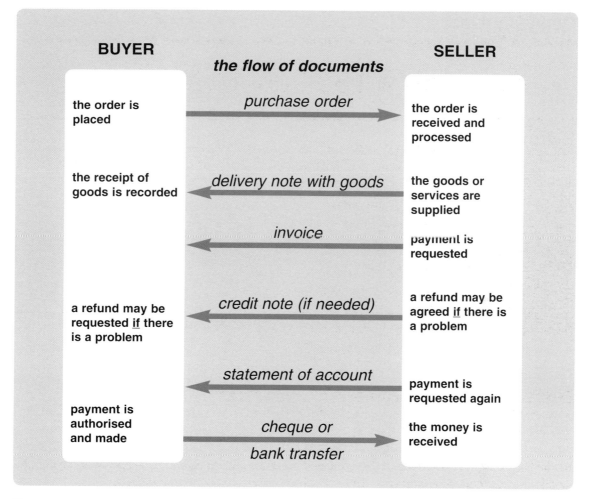

## PURCHASE ORDER

A purchase order is prepared by the buyer, and is sent to the seller. Details found on a purchase order include:

- number of purchase order
- name and address of buyer
- name and address of seller
- full description of the goods, reference numbers, quantity required and unit price
- date of issue
- signature of person authorised to issue the order

In order to keep control over purchases many businesses authorise certain people as buyers. In this way, purchases are controlled so that duplicate or unauthorised goods are not ordered.

# Delivery Note

When the business that is selling the goods despatches them to the buyer, a delivery note is prepared. This accompanies the goods and gives details of what is being delivered. When the goods are received by the buyer, a check can be made by the buyer to ensure that the correct goods have been delivered.

# Invoice

The invoice (see next page) is the most important document in a business transaction. It is prepared by the seller and is sent to the buyer. The invoice gives details of the goods supplied, and states the money amount to be paid by the buyer. The information to be found on an invoice includes:

- invoice number (serially numbered)
- name and address of seller
- name and address of buyer
- date of sale
- date that goods are supplied, including reference numbers, quantity supplied and unit price
- details of trade discount allowed (if any)
- total amount of money due
- terms of trade

## value added tax

Where the seller is registered for Value Added Tax (VAT), tax must be charged at the appropriate rate on all sales subject to VAT. The invoice will normally state:

- the seller's VAT Registration Number
- the date for tax purposes (the tax-point) on which the sale is made
- amount of VAT charged
- total amount of money due including VAT.

If the buyer of the goods is VAT-registered, then the buyer can claim back the amount of VAT on the invoice from the VAT authorities (HM Customs and Excise). The accounting implications of VAT are looked at in Chapter 7.

## terms of trade

The terms of trade are stated on an invoice to indicate the date by which the invoice amount is to be paid. The term 'net' on an invoice means that the invoice total is the amount to be paid; 'net 30 days' means that the amount is payable within 30 days of the invoice date.

Other terms include 'carriage paid' and 'E & OE'. This stands for 'errors and omissions excepted' which means that if there is a error or something left off the invoice by mistake, resulting in an incorrect final price, the supplier has the right to correct the mistake and demand the correct amount.

```
───────────────── INVOICE ─────────────────
```

# TREND FASHION DESIGNS LIMITED

Unit 45 Elgar Estate, Broadfield, BR7 4ER
Tel 01908 765314  Fax 01908 765951
VAT REG GB 0745 4672 76

invoice to

| **Zing Fashions** |
| **4 Friar Street** |
| **Broadfield** |
| **BR1 3RF** |

| invoice no | 787923 |
| account | 3993 |
| your reference | 47609 |

deliver to

**as above**

date/tax point    **01 10 05**

| product code | description | quantity | unit price | unit | total | trade discount % | net |
|---|---|---|---|---|---|---|---|
| 45B | **Trend tops (black)** | 40 | 12.50 | each | 500.00 | 10 | 450.00 |

| | |
|---|---|
| GOODS TOTAL | 450.00 |
| VAT | 78.75 |
| TOTAL | 528.75 |

**terms**
Net 30 days
Carriage paid
E & OE

## trade discount

Trade discount is the amount sometimes allowed as a reduction when goods are supplied to other businesses, but not when the sale is made to the general public. VAT is calculated on the net amount of the invoice, ie after deducting any trade discount allowed. In the invoice shown above, trade discount of 10% is allowed on clothes supplied to Zing Fashions, a shop. Note that trade discount is never shown in the accounts – only the amount after deduction of trade discount is recorded.

## cash discount

Cash discount is an allowance off the invoice amount for quick settlement, eg 2% cash discount for settlement within seven days. The buyer can choose whether to take up the cash discount by paying promptly, or whether to take longer to pay, perhaps thirty days from the invoice date, without cash discount. When cash discount is taken, it needs to be recorded in the accounts (see page 51).

It is important to note that where a cash discount is offered, VAT is calculated on the net amount of the invoice (ie value of goods supplied, less any trade discount allowed), less the amount of the cash discount, whether or not this discount is subsequently taken by the buyer. For example:

|  | net 30 days | 2% cash discount for settlement within 7 days, otherwise net 30 days |
|---|---|---|
|  | £ | £ |
| Net invoice amount | 100.00 | 100.00 |
| *add* VAT @ 17.5% | 17.50 | 17.15 |
| Invoice total | 117.50 | 117.15 |

In the first example (net 30 days), the amount of £117.50 is due within 30 days of the invoice date.

In the case of the 2% cash discount, the VAT amount is:

(£100.00 - £2.00 cash discount) x 17.5% = £17.15.

In this example, £117.15 is due within 30 days of the invoice date if no cash discount is taken. If the buyer settles within seven days and takes the cash discount, the amount to be paid will be:

(£100.00 - £2.00 cash discount) + VAT £17.15 = £115.15.

## format of invoices

Invoices (like other business documents) can be handwritten or typed on printed forms, or books of invoices can be bought in most stationers' shops. Invoicing is an ideal function for computerised accounting (see Chapter 11) and, for this purpose, pre-printed invoices are available in the form of continuous stationery. Also, increasingly nowadays, invoices are in electronic form (EDI – electronic data interchange) and the information needs to be 'captured' and put into the accounting system.

# CREDIT NOTE

If a buyer returns goods for some reason (eg faulty goods supplied), or requires a reduction in the amount owed (the buyer may have been overcharged) the seller prepares a credit note (see next page) to record the amount of the allowance made to the buyer.

```
━━━━━━━━━━━━━━━━━━━━━━ CREDIT NOTE ━━━━━━━━━━━━━━━━━━━━━
```

# TREND FASHION DESIGNS LIMITED

Unit 45 Elgar Estate, Broadfield, BR7 4ER
Tel 01908 765314  Fax 01908 765951
VAT REG GB 0745 4672 76

to

| Zing Fashions |
| 4 Friar Street |
| Broadfield |
| BR1 3RF |

| credit note no | 12157 |
| account | 3993 |
| your reference | 47609 |
| our invoice | 787923 |
| date/tax point | 10 10 05 |

| product code | description | quantity | unit price | unit | total | trade discount % | net |
|---|---|---|---|---|---|---|---|
| 45B | Trend tops (black) | 2 | 12.50 | each | 25.00 | 10 | 22.50 |

**Reason for credit**
**2 tops received damaged**
**(Your returns note no. R/N 2384)**

| | |
|---|---|
| GOODS TOTAL | 22.50 |
| VAT | 3.93 |
| TOTAL | 26.43 |

## STATEMENT OF ACCOUNT

At regular intervals, often at the end of each month, the seller sends a statement of account (see next page) to each debtor. This gives a summary of the transactions that have taken place since the previous statement and shows how much is currently owed. The details on a statement are:

- name and address of seller
- name and address of the debtor (buyer)
- date of the statement
- details of transactions, eg invoices, debit notes, credit notes, payments
- balance currently due

Most statements have three money columns: debit, credit and balance. The debit column is used to record the money amount of invoices and debit notes sent to the debtor; the credit column is for payments received and credit notes issued; the balance column shows the amount due, and is prepared on the 'running balance' (see page 26) basis, ie a new balance is shown after each transaction. The balance is usually a debit balance, which indicates that the buyer is a debtor in the seller's accounting records. Some statements of account also incorporate a remittance advice as a tear-off slip; this is returned to the seller together with the payment.

---

**——————— STATEMENT OF ACCOUNT ———————**

# TREND FASHION DESIGNS LIMITED

Unit 45 Elgar Estate, Broadfield, BR7 4ER
Tel 01908 765314  Fax 01908 765951
VAT REG GB 0745 4672 76

TO

**Zing Fashions
4 Friar Street
Broadfield
BR1 3RF**

account      **3993**

date      **31 10 02**

| date | details | debit £ | credit £ | balance £ |
|---|---|---|---|---|
| **01 10 02** | **Invoice 787923** | **528.75** | | **528.75** |
| **10 10 02** | **Credit note 12157** | | **26.43** | **502.32** |

| | | **AMOUNT NOW DUE** | **502.32** |
|---|---|---|---|

---

# PAYMENT

Before payment is made to the seller, the buyer must check that the goods have been received and are as ordered. The payment can then be authorised by an appointed employee and made by means of either a cheque (sent by post) or a bank credit transfer which passes the money from the buyer's bank account to the seller's account. Most bank credit transfers nowadays are made by BACS (Bankers Automated Clearing Services) computer transfer. If a cheque is posted to the seller, it is sent with a remittance advice, which shows the amount of the payment, and the transactions to which it relates. If a payment is sent through the bank a separate remittance advice will be mailed or faxed.

## RECORDING CASH DISCOUNT IN THE BOOK-KEEPING SYSTEM

We saw earlier in this chapter that cash discount is an allowance off the invoice amount for quick settlement, eg 2% cash discount for settlement within seven days. A business can be involved with cash discount in two ways:

* discount allowed to debtors
* discount received from creditors

Note that, although the terms 'discount allowed' and 'discount received' do not use the word 'cash', they do refer to cash discount.

### discount allowed

When cash discount is taken by a debtor it is entered into the accounts as shown by the following transactions:

| | |
|---|---|
| 10 October 20-2 | Sold goods, £100 (no VAT), on credit to P Henry, allowing her a cash discount of 2% for settlement within seven days |
| 15 October 20-2 | P Henry pays £98 by cheque |

| Dr | | | Sales Account | | Cr |
|---|---|---|---|---|---|
| 20-2 | | £ | 20-2 | | £ |
| | | | 10 Oct | P Henry | 100 |

| Dr | | | P Henry | | Cr |
|---|---|---|---|---|---|
| 20-2 | | £ | 20-2 | | £ |
| 10 Oct | Sales | 100 | 15 Oct | Bank | 98 |
| | | | 15 Oct | Discount allowed | 2 |
| | | 100 | | | 100 |

| Dr | | | Bank Account | | Cr |
|---|---|---|---|---|---|
| 20-2 | | £ | 20-2 | | £ |
| 15 Oct | P Henry | 98 | | | |

| Dr | | | Discount Allowed Account | | Cr |
|---|---|---|---|---|---|
| 20-2 | | £ | 20-2 | | £ |
| 15 Oct | P Henry | 2 | | | |

**Notes**

- The amount of the payment received from the debtor is entered in the bank account.
- The amount of discount allowed is entered in both the debtor's account and discount allowed account:
  - debit discount allowed account
  - credit debtor's account
- Discount allowed is an expense of the business, because it represents the cost of collecting payments more speedily from the debtors.
- The account of P Henry has been totalled to show that both the debit and credit money columns are the same – thus her account now has a nil balance (the method of balancing accounts is looked at in the next chapter).

## discount received

With cash discount received, a business is offered cash discount for quick settlement by its creditors. The following transactions give an example of this:

| 20 October 20-2 | Bought goods, £200 (no VAT), on credit from B Lewis Ltd; 2.5% cash discount is offered for settlement by the end of October |
| 30 October 20-2 | Paid B Lewis Ltd £195 by cheque |

| Dr | | Purchases Account | | | Cr |
|---|---|---|---|---|---|
| 20-2 | | £ | 20-2 | | £ |
| 20 Oct | B Lewis Ltd | 200 | | | |

| Dr | | B Lewis Ltd | | | Cr |
|---|---|---|---|---|---|
| 20-2 | | £ | 20-2 | | £ |
| 30 Oct | Bank | 195 | 20 Oct | Purchases | 200 |
| 30 Oct | Discount received | 5 | | | |
| | | 200 | | | 200 |

| Dr | | Bank Account | | | Cr |
|---|---|---|---|---|---|
| 20-2 | | £ | 20-2 | | £ |
| | | | 30 Oct | B Lewis Ltd | 195 |

| Dr | | Discount Received Account | | | Cr |
|---|---|---|---|---|---|
| 20-2 | | £ | 20-2 | | £ |
| | | | 30 Oct | B Lewis Ltd | 5 |

**Notes**

- The business is receiving cash discount from its creditor, and the amount is entered as:
  - debit creditor's account
  - credit discount received account
- Discount received account is an income account.
- The money columns of the account of B Lewis Ltd have been totalled to show that the account now has a nil balance.

## revision summary

- Cash discount – when taken – is recorded in the debtors' and creditors' accounts.
- Both discount allowed (an expenses account) and discount received (an income account) store up information until the end of the financial year, when it is used in the firm's profit and loss account – see Chapter 12.
- The cash book (see Chapter 8) is usually used for listing the amounts of discount received and allowed – transfers are then made at the end of each month to the respective discount accounts.
- Trade discount is never recorded in the double-entry accounts; only the net amount of an invoice is recorded after trade discount has been deducted.

# CHAPTER SUMMARY

- Correct documentation is important for businesses to be able to record accurately buying and selling transactions.
- There are a number of documents involved – the two most important are the purchase order and the invoice.
- A purchase order is a document which states the requirements of the buyer, and is sent to the seller.
- The invoice is prepared by the seller and states the value of goods sold and, hence, the amount to be paid by the buyer.
- Trade discount is often deducted when goods are sold to other businesses.
- Cash discount is an allowance off the invoice amount for quick settlement.
- Cash discount allowed is entered in the accounts as:
  - debit discount allowed account
  - credit debtor's account
- Cash discount received is entered as:
  - debit creditor's account
  - credit discount received account

- A credit note shows that the buyer is entitled to a reduction in the amount charged by the seller; it is used if:
  - some of the goods delivered were faulty, or incorrectly supplied
  - the price charged on the invoice was too high
- Statements of account are sent out regularly to each debtor of a business to show the amount currently due.

This chapter has looked at business documentation; the next chapter returns to double-entry book-keeping and looks at how accounts are balanced, and a trial balance is extracted.

# QUESTIONS

NOTE: an asterisk (*) after the question number means that an answer to the question is given in Appendix 2.

**4.1\*** Fill in the missing words from the following sentences:

(a) A ............................... ............................... is prepared by the buyer and sent to the seller and describes the goods to be supplied.

(b) The seller prepares the ..............................., which gives details of the goods supplied, and states the money amount to be paid by the buyer.

(c) ............................... ............................... is a deduction made in the price if the purchaser pays within a stated time.

(d) When the purchaser is in business, an amount of ...............................

............................... is sometimes allowed as a reduction in the price.

(e) The term ............................... on an invoice means that the invoice total is the amount to be paid.

(f) A government tax added to an invoice is called .............. .............. ..............

(g) If a buyer returns goods, the seller prepares a ............................... ...............................

(h) If a seller has undercharged on an invoice, a ............................... ............................... is issued which shows the extra amount to be charged to the buyer.

(i) At regular intervals the seller sends a summary of transactions to the buyer in the form of a ...............................

**4.2\***  Calculate the invoice price exclusive of VAT, the VAT chargeable (at 17.5 %), and the total due for the order below, assuming the three following apply (three separate amounts due are to be calculated):

(a)  Terms: net

(b)  Terms: 2.5% cash discount for settlement within 30 days

(c)  Terms: 5% cash discount for settlement within 30 days

Order details:  one office desk, price £175.00

**4.3**  You work for Jane Smith, a wholesaler of fashionwear, who trades from Unit 21, Eastern Industrial Estate, Wyvern, Wyvernshire, WY1 3XJ. A customer, Excel Fashions of 49 Highland Street, Longtown, Mercia, LT3 2XL, orders the following:

5 dresses at £30 each

3 suits at £45.50 each

4 coats at £51.50 each

Value Added Tax is to be charged at 17.5 per cent on all the items.

A  2.5 per cent cash discount is offered for full settlement within 14 days.

You are to prepare invoice number 2451, under today's date, to be sent to the customer.

**4.4**  You work for Deansway Trading Company, a wholesaler of office stationery, which trades from The Model Office, Deansway, Rowcester, RW1 2EJ. A customer, The Card Shop of 126 The Cornbow, Teamington Spa, Wyvernshire, WY33 0EG, orders the following:

5 boxes of assorted rubbers at £5 per box

100 shorthand notebooks at £4 for 10

250 ring binders at 50p each

Value Added Tax is to be charged at 17.5 per cent on all the items.

A  2.5 per cent cash discount is offered for full settlement within 14 days.

You are to prepare invoice number 8234, under today's date, to be sent to the customer.

**4.5** You have the following financial details about J Wilson, a customer of your organisation:

| | |
|---|---|
| 1 Mar | Balance due, £145 |
| 3 Mar | Goods sold to J Wilson, £210, invoice number 8119 |
| 10 Mar | Cheque received from J Wilson, £145 |
| 23 Mar | Goods returned by J Wilson, £50, credit note number CN 345 issued |
| 28 Mar | Goods sold to J Wilson, £180, invoice number 8245 |

You are to prepare the statement of account to be sent to the customer on 31 March. This should show clearly the balance due at the month-end.

**4.6** Enter the following transactions into the double-entry book-keeping accounts of Sonya Smith:

20-4

| | |
|---|---|
| 2 Feb | Bought goods £200, on credit from G Lewis |
| 4 Feb | Sold goods £150, on credit to L Jarvis |
| 7 Feb | Sold goods £240, on credit to G Patel |
| 10 Feb | Paid G Lewis the amount owing by cheque, after deducting a cash discount of 5% |
| 12 Feb | L Jarvis pays the amount owing by cheque, after deducting a cash discount of 2% |
| 16 Feb | Bought goods £160, on credit from G Lewis |
| 20 Feb | G Patel pays the amount owing by cheque, after deducting a cash discount of 2.5% |
| 24 Feb | Paid G Lewis the amount owing by cheque, after deducting a cash discount of 5% |

*Note: Ignore Value Added Tax*

**Chapters 1 - 4**

# MULTIPLE CHOICE QUESTIONS

Read each question carefully.
Choose the one answer you think is correct (calculators may be needed).
The answers are on page 568.

1    Which one of the following accounting personnel concerned with the accounts of a business is not an employee of that business?

A    external auditor
B    financial accountant
C    management accountant
D    internal auditor

2    The purchase of goods for resale on credit is recorded in the accounts as:

|   | Debit | Credit |
|---|-------|--------|
| A | supplier's account | purchases account |
| B | purchases account | cash account |
| C | purchases account | supplier's account |
| D | supplier's account | sales account |

3    The sale of goods to Williams for cash is recorded in the accounts as:

|   | Debit | Credit |
|---|-------|--------|
| A | Williams' account | sales account |
| B | sales account | Williams' account |
| C | sales account | cash account |
| D | cash account | sales account |

4    Unsatisfactory goods are returned to the supplier. This is recorded in the accounts as:

|   | Debit | Credit |
|---|-------|--------|
| A | sales returns account | supplier's account |
| B | purchases returns account | supplier's account |
| C | supplier's account | purchases returns account |
| D | supplier's account | purchases account |

**5** Which one of the following is a nominal account?

A      purchases

B      motor vehicles

C      J Smith, a debtor

D      bank

**6** A business buys a machine for use in the business on credit. This is recorded in the accounts as:

|  | Debit | Credit |
|---|---|---|
| A | machinery account | supplier's account |
| B | purchases account | supplier's account |
| C | machinery account | bank account |
| D | supplier's account | machinery account |

**7** The payment of wages in cash is recorded in the accounts as:

|  | Debit | Credit |
|---|---|---|
| A | wages account | drawings account |
| B | cash account | wages account |
| C | capital account | wages account |
| D | wages account | cash account |

**8** A loan is received from John Box. This is recorded in the accounts as:

|  | Debit | Credit |
|---|---|---|
| A | bank account | capital account |
| B | bank account | loan account: John Box |
| C | drawings account | loan account: John Box |
| D | loan account: John Box | bank account |

**9** The owner of the business transfers a computer to the business from personal assets. This is recorded in the accounts as:

|  | Debit | Credit |
|---|---|---|
| A | computer account | capital account |
| B | purchases account | computer account |
| C | capital account | computer account |
| D | computer account | sales account |

**10**    Which one of the following business documents is issued when goods are sold to another business?

A        invoice

B        credit note

C        purchase order

D        debit note

**11**    A business sells goods with a retail value of £500. The customer is allowed 20 per cent trade discount, and a cash discount of 2.5 per cent for settlement within seven days. If the invoice is settled within the seven-day period, and ignoring VAT, the business will receive a cheque for:

A        £487.50

B        £400.00

C        £390.00

D        £387.50

**12**    A business sells goods with a retail value of £1,000, plus VAT at 17.5 per cent. The customer is allowed 25 per cent trade discount, and a cash discount of 2.5 per cent for settlement within seven days. How much VAT will be charged on the invoice?

A        £175.00

B        £170.62

C        £131.25

D        £127.96

# 5 BALANCING ACCOUNTS – THE TRIAL BALANCE

With the 'traditional' form of account – a 'T' account – that we have used in Chapters 2 and 3, it is necessary to calculate the balance of each account from time-to-time, according to the needs of the business, and at the end of each financial year.

The balance of an account is the total of that account to date, eg the amount of wages paid, the amount of sales made. In this chapter we shall see how this balancing of accounts is carried out.

We shall then use the balances from each account in order to check the double-entry book-keeping by extracting a trial balance, which is a list of the balances of ledger accounts.

## BALANCING THE ACCOUNTS

At regular intervals, often at the end of each month, accounts are balanced in order to show the amounts, for example:

- owing to each creditor
- owing by each debtor
- of sales
- of purchases
- of sales returns (returns in)
- of purchases returns (returns out)
- of expenses incurred by the business
- of fixed assets, eg premises, machinery, etc owned by the business
- of capital and drawings of the owner of the business
- of other liabilities, eg loans

We have already noted earlier that, where running balance accounts (see page 26) are used, there is no need to balance each account, because the balance is already calculated – either manually or by computer – after each transaction.

## METHOD OF BALANCING ACCOUNTS

Set out below is an example of an account which has been balanced at the month-end:

| Dr | | | **Bank Account** | | Cr |
|---|---|---|---|---|---|
| 20-1 | | £ | 20-1 | | £ |
| 1 Sep | Capital | 5,000 | 2 Sep | Computer | 1,800 |
| 5 Sep | J Jackson: loan | 2,500 | 6 Sep | Purchases | 500 |
| 10 Sep | Sales | 750 | 12 Sep | Drawings | 100 |
| | | | 15 Sep | Wages | 200 |
| | | | 30 Sep | Balance c/d | 5,650 |
| | | 8,250 | | | 8,250 |
| 1 Oct | Balance b/d | 5,650 | | | |

The steps involved in balancing accounts are:

### Step 1

The entries in the debit and credit money columns are totalled; these totals are not recorded in ink on the account at this stage, but can be recorded either as sub-totals in pencil on the account, or noted on a separate piece of paper. In the example above, the debit side totals £8,250, while the credit side is £2,600.

### Step 2

The difference between the two totals is the balance of the account and this is entered on the account:

- on the side of the smaller total
- on the next available line
- with the date of balancing (often the last day of the month)
- with the description 'balance c/d', or 'balance carried down'

In the bank account above, the balance carried down is £8,250 – £2,600 = £5,650, entered in the credit column.

### Step 3

Both sides of the account are now totalled, including the balance which has just been entered, and the totals (the same on both sides) are entered on the same line in the appropriate column, and double underlined. The double underline indicates that the account has been balanced at this point using the figures above the total: the figures above the underline should not be added in to anything below the underline.

In the bank account above, the totals on each side of the account are £8,250.

**Step 4**

As we are using double-entry book-keeping, there must be an opposite entry to the 'balance c/d' calculated in Step 2. The same money amount is entered on the other side of the account below the double-underlined totals entered in Step 3. We have now completed both the debit and credit entry. The date is usually recorded as the next day after 'balance c/d', ie often the first day of the following month, and the description can be 'balance b/d' or 'balance brought down'.

In the example above, the balance brought down on the bank account on 1 October 20-1 is £5,650 debit; this means that, according to the firm's accounting records, there is £5,650 in the bank.

**a practical point**

When balancing accounts, use a pen and not a pencil. If any errors are made, cross them through neatly with a single line, and write the corrected version on the line below. Do not use correcting fluid: at best it conceals errors, at worst it conceals fraudulent transactions.

## FURTHER EXAMPLES OF BALANCING ACCOUNTS

| Dr | | | **Wages Account** | | | Cr |
|---|---|---|---|---|---|---|
| 20-1 | | £ | 20-1 | | | £ |
| 9 Apr | Bank | 750 | 30 Apr | Balance c/d | | 2,250 |
| 16 Apr | Bank | 800 | | | | |
| 23 Apr | Bank | 700 | | | | |
| | | 2,250 | | | | 2,250 |
| 1 May | Balance b/d | 2,250 | | | | |

The above wages account has transactions on one side only, but is still balanced in the same way. This account shows that the total amount paid for wages is £2,250.

| Dr | | | **B Lewis Ltd** | | | Cr |
|---|---|---|---|---|---|---|
| 20-1 | | £ | 20-1 | | | £ |
| 10 Apr | Purchases Returns | 30 | 7 Apr | Purchases | | 280 |
| 26 Apr | Bank | 250 | | | | |
| | | 280 | | | | 280 |

This account in the name of a creditor has a 'nil' balance after the transactions for April have taken place. The two sides of the account are totalled and, as both debit and credit side are the same amount, there is nothing further to do, apart from entering the double-underlined total.

| Dr | | | **A Holmes** | | | Cr |
|---|---|---|---|---|---|---|
| 20-1 | | £ | 20-1 | | | £ |
| 1 Apr | Balance b/d | 105 | 10 Apr | Bank | | 105 |
| 11 Apr | Sales | 125 | 11 Apr | Sales Returns | | 25 |
| | | | 30 Apr | Balance c/d | | 100 |
| | | 230 | | | | 230 |
| 1 May | Balance b/d | 100 | | | | |

This is the account of a debtor and, at the start of the month, there was a debit balance of £105 brought down from March. After the various transactions for April, there remains a debit balance of £100 owing at 1 May.

| Dr | | | **Office Equipment Account** | | Cr |
|---|---|---|---|---|---|
| 20-1 | | £ | 20-1 | | £ |
| 12 Apr | Bank | 2,000 | | | |

This account has just the one transaction and, in practice, there is no need to balance it. It should be clear that the account has a debit balance of £2,000, which is represented by the asset of office equipment.

| Dr | | | **Malvern Manufacturing Co** | | | Cr |
|---|---|---|---|---|---|---|
| 20-1 | | £ | 20-1 | | | £ |
| 29 Apr | Bank | 250 | 18 Apr | Purchases | | 250 |

This creditor's account has a 'nil' balance, with just one transaction on each side. All that is needed here is to double underline the amount on both sides.

# EXTRACTING A TRIAL BALANCE

The book-keeper extracts a trial balance from the accounting records in order to check the arithmetical accuracy of the double-entry book-keeping, ie that the debit entries equal the credit entries.

*A trial balance is a list of the balances of every account forming the ledger, distinguishing between those accounts which have debit balances and those which have credit balances.*

A trial balance is extracted at regular intervals – often at the end of each month.

## example of a trial balance

**Trial balance of A-Z Suppliers as at 31 January 20-1**

| Name of account | Dr £ | Cr £ |
|---|---:|---:|
| Purchases | 750 | |
| Sales | | 1,600 |
| Sales returns | 25 | |
| Purchases returns | | 50 |
| J Brown (debtor) | 155 | |
| T Sweet (creditor) | | 110 |
| Rent paid | 100 | |
| Wages | 150 | |
| Heating and lighting | 125 | |
| Office equipment | 500 | |
| Machinery | 1,000 | |
| Cash | 50 | |
| Bank | 455 | |
| J Williams – loan | | 800 |
| Capital | | 1,000 |
| Drawings | 250 | |
| | 3,560 | 3,560 |

**Notes**

- The debit and credit columns have been totalled and are the same amount. Thus the trial balance proves that the accounting records are arithmetically correct. (A trial balance does not prove the complete accuracy of the accounting records – see page 66.)

- The heading for a trial balance gives the name of the business whose accounts have been listed and the date it was extracted, ie the end of the accounting period.

- The balance for each account transferred to the trial balance is the figure brought down after the accounts have been balanced.

- As well as the name of each account, it is quite usual to show in the trial balance the account number. Most accounting systems give numbers to accounts – see Case Study 1 (page 183) – and these can be listed in a separate 'folio' or 'reference' column.

## DEBIT AND CREDIT BALANCES – GUIDELINES

Certain accounts always have a debit balance, while others always have a credit balance. You should already know these, but the lists set out below will act as a revision guide, and will also help in your understanding of trial balances.

**debit balances include:**
- cash account
- purchases account
- sales returns account (returns in)
- fixed asset accounts, eg premises, motor vehicles, machinery, office equipment, etc
- expenses accounts, eg wages, telephone, rent paid, carriage outwards, carriage inwards
- drawings account
- debtors' accounts (often, for the purposes of a trial balance, the balances of individual debtors' accounts are totalled, and the total is entered in the trial balance as 'debtors')

**credit balances include:**
- sales account
- purchases returns account (returns out)
- income accounts, eg rent received, commission received, fees received
- capital account
- loan account
- creditors' accounts (often a total is entered in the trial balance, rather than the individual balances of each account)

Note: bank account can be either debit or credit – it will be debit when the business has money in the bank, and credit when it is overdrawn.

## IF THE TRIAL BALANCE DOESN'T BALANCE . . .

If the trial balance fails to balance, ie the two totals are different, there is an error (or errors):
- either in the addition of the trial balance
- and/or in the double-entry book-keeping

The procedure for finding the error(s) is as follows:

- check the addition of the trial balance
- check that the balance of each account has been correctly entered in the trial balance, and under the correct heading, ie debit or credit
- check that the balance of every account in the ledger has been included in the trial balance
- check the calculation of the balance on each account
- calculate the amount that the trial balance is wrong, and then look in the accounts for a transaction for this amount: if one is found, check that the double-entry book-keeping has been carried out correctly
- halve the amount by which the trial balance is wrong, and look for a transaction for this amount: if it is found, check the double-entry book-keeping
- if the amount by which the trial balance is wrong is divisible by nine, then the error may be a reversal of figures, eg £65 entered as £56, or £45 entered as £54
- if the trial balance is wrong by a round amount, eg £10, £100, £1,000, the error is likely to be in the calculation of the account balances
- if the error(s) is still not found, it is necessary to check the book-keeping transactions since the date of the last trial balance, by going back to the original documents and primary accounting records

## ERRORS NOT SHOWN BY A TRIAL BALANCE

As mentioned earlier, a trial balance does not prove the complete accuracy of the accounting records. There are six types of errors that are not shown by a trial balance.

### error of omission

Here a business transaction has been completely omitted from the accounting records, ie both the debit and credit entries have not been made.

### reversal of entries

With this error, the debit and credit entries have been made in the accounts but on the wrong side of the two accounts concerned. For example, a cash sale has been entered wrongly as debit sales account, credit cash account – this should have been entered as a debit to cash account, and a credit to sales account.

### mispost/error of commission

Here, a transaction is entered to the wrong person's account. For example, a sale of goods on credit to A T Hughes has been entered as debit A J Hughes' account, credit sales account. Here, double-entry book-keeping has been completed but, when A J Hughes receives a statement of account, he or she will soon complain about being debited with goods not ordered or received.

## error of principle

This is when a transaction has been entered in the wrong type of account. For example, the cost of petrol for vehicles has been entered as debit motor vehicles account, credit bank account. The error is that motor vehicles account represents fixed assets, and the transaction should have been debited to the expense account for motor vehicle running expenses.

## error of original entry (or transcription)

Here, the correct accounts have been used, and the correct sides: what is wrong is that the amount has been entered incorrectly in both accounts. This could be caused by a 'bad figure' on an invoice or a cheque, or it could be caused by a 'reversal of figures', eg an amount of £45 being entered in both accounts as £54. Note that both debit and credit entries need to be made incorrectly for the trial balance still to balance; if one entry has been made incorrectly and the other is correct, then the error will be shown.

## compensating error

This is where two errors cancel each other out. For example, if the balance of purchases account is calculated wrongly at £10 too much, and a similar error has occurred in calculating the balance of sales account, then the two errors will compensate each other, and the trial balance will not show the errors.

Correction of errors is covered fully in Chapter 19.

## IMPORTANCE OF THE TRIAL BALANCE

A business will extract a trial balance on a regular basis to check the arithmetic accuracy of the book-keeping. However, the trial balance is also used as the starting point in the production of the final accounts of a business. These final accounts, which are produced once a year (often more frequently) comprise:

- **trading account**
- **profit and loss account**
- **balance sheet**

The final accounts show the owner(s) how profitable the business has been, what the business owns, and how the business is financed. The preparation of final accounts is an important aspect of Business Accounts and one which we shall be coming to in later chapters. For the moment, we can say that extraction of a trial balance is an important exercise in the business accounts process: it proves the book-keeper's accuracy, and also lists the account balances which form the basis for the final accounts of a business.

## CHAPTER SUMMARY

● The traditional 'T' account needs to be balanced at regular intervals – often at the month-end.

● When balancing accounts, the book-keeper must adhere strictly to the rules of double-entry book-keeping.

● When each account in the ledger has been balanced, a trial balance can be extracted.

● A trial balance is a list of the balances of every account forming the ledger, distinguishing between those accounts which have debit balances and those which have credit balances.

● A trial balance does not prove the complete accuracy of the accounting records; errors not shown by a trial balance are:

    – error of omission

    – reversal of entries

    – mispost/error of commission

    – error of principle

    – error of original entry

    – compensating error

● The trial balance is used as the starting point for the preparation of a business' final accounts.

Case Study 1 (page 183) gives a fully worked example showing business transactions entered into the double-entry accounts, which are then balanced and a trial balance extracted.

In the next chapter we will look at the division of the ledger into manageable sections, and we will see how an expanding accounting system uses primary accounting records to cope with large numbers of routine transactions.

## QUESTIONS

NOTE: an asterisk (*) after the question number means that an answer to the question is given in Appendix 2.

| 5.1 | The following are the business transactions of Andrew Johnstone, a retailer of computer software, for the months of January and February 20-9: |

**Transactions for January**

| 1 Jan | Started in business with £10,000 in the bank |
| 4 Jan | Paid rent on premises £500, by cheque |
| 5 Jan | Bought shop fittings £1,500, by cheque |
| 7 Jan | Bought stock of computer software £5,000, on credit from Comp Supplies Limited |
| 11 Jan | Software sales £1,000 paid into bank |

| 12 Jan | Software sales £1,250 paid into bank |
|---|---|
| 16 Jan | Software sales £850 on credit to Rowcester College |
| 20 Jan | Paid Comp Supplies Limited £5,000 by cheque |
| 22 Jan | Software sales £1,450 paid into bank |
| 25 Jan | Bought software £6,500 on credit from Comp Supplies Limited |
| 27 Jan | Rowcester College returns software £100 |

**Transactions for February**

| 2 Feb | Paid rent on premises £500 by cheque |
|---|---|
| 4 Feb | Software sales £1,550 paid into bank |
| 5 Feb | Returned faulty software, £150 to Comp Supplies Limited |
| 10 Feb | Software sales £1,300 paid into bank |
| 12 Feb | Rowcester College pays the amount owing by cheque |
| 15 Feb | Bought shop fittings £850 by cheque |
| 19 Feb | Software sales £1,600 paid into bank |
| 22 Feb | Paid Comp Supplies Limited the amount owing by cheque |
| 24 Feb | Bought software £5,500 on credit from Comp Supplies Limited |
| 25 Feb | Software sales £1,100 paid into bank |
| 26 Feb | Software sales £1,050 on credit to Rowcester College |

You are to:

(a) record the January transactions in the books of account, and balance each account at 31 January 20-9

(b) draw up a trial balance at 31 January 20-9

(c) record the February transactions in the books of account, and balance each account at 28 February 20-9

(d) draw up a trial balance at 28 February 20-9

**5.2**  Produce the trial balance of Jane Greenwell as at 28 February 20-1. She has omitted to open a capital account.

|  | £ |
|---|---|
| Bank overdraft | 1,250 |
| Purchases | 850 |
| Cash | 48 |
| Sales | 730 |
| Purchases returns | 144 |
| Creditors | 1,442 |
| Equipment | 2,704 |
| Van | 3,200 |
| Sales returns | 90 |
| Debtors | 1,174 |
| Wages | 1,500 |
| Capital | ? |

**5.3\***

The book-keeper of Lorna Fox has extracted the following list of balances as at 31 March 20-2:

| | £ |
|---|---|
| Purchases | 96,250 |
| Sales | 146,390 |
| Sales returns | 8,500 |
| Administration expenses | 10,240 |
| Wages | 28,980 |
| Telephone | 3,020 |
| Interest paid | 2,350 |
| Travel expenses | 1,045 |
| Premises | 125,000 |
| Machinery | 40,000 |
| Debtors | 10,390 |
| Bank overdraft | 1,050 |
| Cash | 150 |
| Creditors | 12,495 |
| Loan from bank | 20,000 |
| Drawings | 9,450 |
| Capital | 155,440 |

You are to:

(a) Produce the trial balance at 31 March 20-2.

(b) Take any three debit balances and any three credit balances and explain to someone who does not understand accounting why they are listed as such, and what this means to the business.

**5.4\***

Fill in the missing words from the following sentences:

(a) "You made an error of ...................................................... when you debited the cost of diesel fuel for the van to Vans Account."

(b)    "I've had the book-keeper from D Jones Limited on the 'phone concerning the statements of account that we sent out the other day. She says that there is a sales invoice charged that she knows nothing about. I wonder if we have done a ..................................... and it should be for T Jones' account?"

(c)    "There is a 'bad figure' on a purchases invoice – we have read it as £35 when it should be £55. It has gone through our accounts wrongly so we have an error of ......................... ......................... to put right."

(d)    "Although the trial balance balanced last week, I've since found an error of £100 in the calculation of the balance of sales account. We will need to check the other balances as I think we may have a ................................................. error."

(e)    "Who was in charge of that trainee last week? He has entered the payment for the electricity bill on the debit side of the bank and on the credit side of electricity – a ............................. of ..............................................."

(f)    "I found this purchase invoice from last week in amongst the copy letters. As we haven't put it through the accounts we have an error of ......................................................."

5.5    *"A trial balance does not prove the complete accuracy of the accounting records."*

You are to describe *four* types of error that are not shown by a trial balance.

Give an example of each type of error.

# 6 DIVISION OF THE LEDGER –
# PRIMARY ACCOUNTING RECORDS

As we saw in Chapter 1, the double-entry system involves the recording of transactions in accounts in the ledger. In this chapter we will see how, in order to cope with an expanding book-keeping system, the ledger is divided into separate sections. This is called the division of the ledger.

We will also examine how a business makes use of primary accounting records to summarise business transactions before they are entered into the double-entry system.

## DIVISION OF THE LEDGER

Double-entry book-keeping involves, as we have seen, making two entries in the ledger accounts for each business transaction. The traditional meaning of a ledger is a weighty leather-bound volume into which each account was entered on a separate page. With such a hand-written book-keeping system, as more and more accounts were opened, the point was reached where another ledger book was needed. Finally, in order to sort the accounts into a logical order, the accounting system was divided into four main sections, and this practice continues today:

- sales ledger, containing the accounts of debtors
- purchases ledger, containing the accounts of creditors
- cash books, containing the main cash book and the petty cash book
- general (or nominal) ledger, containing the nominal accounts (expenses, etc) and the real accounts (fixed assets, etc)

These four divisions comprise the ledger, and are illustrated in full on the opposite page. Most computer accounting programs (see Chapter 11) retain the four divisions of the ledger.

## USE OF THE DIVISIONS OF THE LEDGER

To see how the divisions of the ledger are used, we will look at a number of business transactions and see which ledgers are used and in which accounts the transactions are recorded:

**purchase of goods on credit**

- general ledger – debit purchases account
- purchases ledger – credit the account of the creditor (supplier)

# DIVISION OF THE LEDGER

## sales ledger

Sales ledger contains the accounts of debtors, and records:

* sales made on credit to customers of the business
* sales returns by customers
* payments received from debtors
* cash discount allowed for prompt settlement

Sales ledger does not record cash sales.

Sales ledger contains an account for each debtor and records the transactions with that debtor. A sales ledger control account (see Chapter 20) is often used to summarise the transactions on the accounts of debtors.

## purchases ledger

Purchases ledger contains the accounts of creditors, and records:

* purchases made on credit from suppliers of the business
* purchases returns made by the business
* payments made to creditors
* cash discount received for prompt settlement

Purchases ledger does not record cash purchases.

Purchases ledger contains an account for each creditor and records the transactions with that creditor. A purchases ledger control account (see Chapter 20) may be used to summarise the creditor account transactions.

## cash books

**Cash Book**

– records all transactions for bank account and cash account
– cash book is also often used for listing the amounts of cash discount received and allowed, and Value Added Tax, before transfer of the totals to the relevant accounts

**Petty Cash Book**

– records low-value cash payments – usually for expenses – that are too small to be entered in the main cash book

## general (nominal) ledger

The general (nominal) ledger contains the other accounts of the business:

**Nominal Accounts**

– sales account (cash and credit sales), sales returns
– purchases account (cash and credit purchases), purchases returns
– expenses and income, loans, capital, drawings
– Value Added Tax (where the business is VAT registered)
– profit and loss

**Real Accounts**

– fixed assets, eg computers, vehicles, machinery
– stock

**purchase of goods by cheque**
- general ledger – debit purchases account
- cash book – credit bank account

**sale of goods on credit**
- sales ledger – debit the account of the debtor (customer)
- general ledger – credit sales account

**sale of goods for cash**
- cash book – debit cash account
- general ledger – credit sales account

**purchase of a computer for use in the business, paying by cheque**
- general ledger – debit computer account (fixed asset)
- cash book – credit bank account

# PRIMARY ACCOUNTING RECORDS

The place where a business transaction is recorded for the first time, prior to entry in the ledger, is known as the primary accounting record or book of original entry. These comprise:

- sales day book (or sales journal)
- purchases day book (or purchases journal)
- sales returns day book (or sales returns journal)
- purchases returns day book (or purchases returns journal)
- cash book (see Chapter 8)
- petty cash book (see Chapter 9)
- general journal (see Chapter 18)

In the rest of this chapter we will see how the first four of these – the day books – fit into the accounting system. The other primary accounting records will be looked at in more detail in later chapters. We have already used cash account and bank account which, together, make up a business' cash book. In Chapter 8, we will see how the two accounts are brought together in one book. Cash book is the primary accounting record for receipts and payments in the forms of cash or cheque. Petty cash book is used mainly for small cash expenses and will be looked at in Chapter 9. General journal (often known more simply as the journal) is covered in Chapter 18.

# SALES DAY BOOK

The sales day book (which can also be called a sales journal, or sales book) is used by businesses that have a lot of separate sales transactions. The day book is simply a list of transactions, the total of which, at the end of the day, week, or month, is transferred to sales account. (When used as a weekly or monthly record, it is still called a day book.) Note that the day book is not part of double-entry book-keeping, but is used as a primary accounting record to give a total which is then entered into the accounts. By using a day book for a large number of transactions in this way, there are fewer transactions passing through the double-entry accounts. Also, the work of the accounts department can be divided up – one person can be given the task of maintaining the day book, while another can concentrate on keeping the ledger up-to-date.

The most common use of a sales day book is to record credit sales from invoices issued. We will see how it is used and will also incorporate Value Added Tax, at a rate of 17.5 per cent, into the transactions (VAT is looked at more fully in Chapter 7).

| example transactions | |
|---|---|
| 3 Jan 20-1 | Sold goods, £80 + VAT, on credit to E Doyle, invoice no 901 |
| 8 Jan 20-1 | Sold goods, £200 + VAT, on credit to A Sparkes, invoice no 902 |
| 12 Jan 20-1 | Sold goods, £80 + VAT, on credit to T Young, invoice no 903 |
| 18 Jan 20-1 | Sold goods, £120 + VAT, on credit to A Sparkes, invoice no 904 |

The sales day book is written up as follows:

| Sales Day Book | | | | | | |
|---|---|---|---|---|---|---|
| Date | Details | Invoice | Folio | Net | VAT | Gross |
| 20-1 | | | | £ | £ | £ |
| 3 Jan | E Doyle | 901 | SL 58 | 80 | 14 | 94 |
| 8 Jan | A Sparkes | 902 | SL 127 | 200 | 35 | 235 |
| 12 Jan | T Young | 903 | SL 179 | 80 | 14 | 94 |
| 18 Jan | A Sparkes | 904 | SL 127 | 120 | 21 | 141 |
| 31 Jan | Totals for month | | | 480 | 84 | 564 |

**Notes**
- Total net credit sales for the month are £480, and this amount is transferred to sales account in the general ledger.

- Total VAT charged on sales for the month has been totalled (£84), and is transferred to the credit side of VAT account in the general ledger. This is the amount of VAT charged by the business on sales made, and is due to the VAT authorities, HM Customs and Excise.
- The credit sales transactions are recorded in the personal accounts of the firm's debtors in the sales ledger, the amount debited to each account being the VAT-inclusive (gross) figure.
- The sales day book incorporates a folio column which cross-references each transaction to the personal account of each debtor. In this way, an audit trail is created so that a particular transaction can be traced from prime document (invoice), through the primary accounting record (sales day book), to the debtor's ledger account.
- The gross total (£564) is entered into the sales ledger control account (see Chapter 20).

The accounts to record the above transactions are:

## GENERAL LEDGER

| Dr | | | Sales Account | | Cr |
|---|---|---|---|---|---|
| 20-1 | | £ | 20-1 | | £ |
| | | | 31 Jan | Sales Day Book | 480 |

| Dr | | | Value Added Tax Account | | Cr |
|---|---|---|---|---|---|
| 20-1 | | £ | 20-1 | | £ |
| | | | 31 Jan | Sales Day Book | 84 |

## SALES LEDGER

| Dr | | E Doyle (account no 58) | | Cr |
|---|---|---|---|---|
| 20-1 | | £ | 20-1 | £ |
| 3 Jan | Sales | 94 | | |

| Dr | | A Sparkes (account no 127) | | Cr |
|---|---|---|---|---|
| 20-1 | | £ | 20-1 | £ |
| 8 Jan | Sales | 235 | | |
| 18 Jan | Sales | 141 | | |

| Dr | | T Young (account no 179) | | Cr |
|---|---|---|---|---|
| 20-1 | | £ | 20-1 | £ |
| 12 Jan | Sales | 94 | | |

## revision summary

Sales day book fits into the accounting system in the following way:

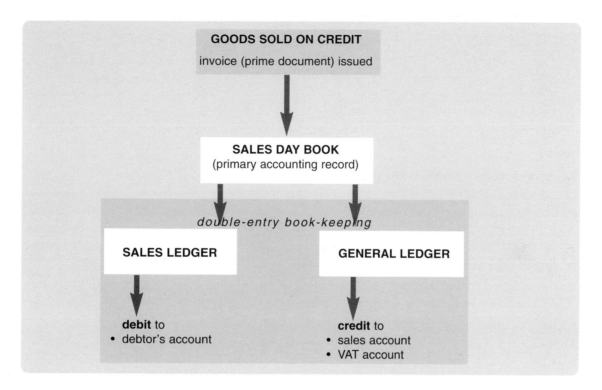

# PURCHASES DAY BOOK

This primary accounting record is used by businesses that have a lot of separate purchases transactions. The purchases day book lists the transactions for credit purchases from invoices received and, at the end of the day, week or month, the total is transferred to purchases account.

**example transactions**

| | |
|---|---|
| 2 Jan 20-1 | Bought goods, £80 + VAT, on credit from P Bond, his invoice no 1234 |
| 11 Jan 20-1 | Bought goods, £120 + VAT, on credit from D Webster, her invoice no A373 |
| 16 Jan 20-1 | Bought goods, £160 + VAT, on credit from P Bond, his invoice no 1247 |
| | *Note: VAT is to be charged at 17.5%* |

The purchases day book is written up as follows:

| Purchases Day Book | | | | | | |
|---|---|---|---|---|---|---|
| Date | Details | Invoice | Folio | Net | VAT | Gross |
| 20-1 | | | | £ | £ | £ |
| 2 Jan | P Bond | 1234 | PL 525 | 80 | 14 | 94 |
| 11 Jan | D Webster | A373 | PL 730 | 120 | 21 | 141 |
| 16 Jan | P Bond | 1247 | PL 525 | 160 | 28 | 188 |
| 31 Jan | Totals for month | | | 360 | 63 | 423 |

**Notes**

• Total net credit purchases for the month are £360, and this amount is transferred to purchases account in the general ledger.

• Total VAT payable on purchases for the month has been totalled (£63), and is transferred to the debit side of VAT account in the general ledger. This is the amount of VAT charged to the business by suppliers and can be claimed back by the business (provided it is registered for VAT), or offset against VAT due to the HM Customs and Excise (see also Chapter 7).

• The credit purchases transactions are recorded in the personal accounts of the firm's debtors in the purchases ledger, the amount credited to each account being the VAT-inclusive (gross) figure.

• The folio column gives a cross-reference to the creditors' accounts and provides an audit trail.

• The gross total (£423) is entered into the purchases ledger control account (see Chapter 20).

The accounts to record the above transactions (including a previous transaction on the VAT account) are:

## GENERAL LEDGER

| Dr | | Purchases Account | | | Cr |
|---|---|---|---|---|---|
| 20-1 | | £ | 20-1 | | £ |
| 31 Jan | Purchases Day Book | 360 | | | |

| Dr | | Value Added Tax Account | | | Cr |
|---|---|---|---|---|---|
| 20-1 | | £ | 20-1 | | £ |
| 31 Jan | Purchases Day Book | 63 | 31 Jan | Sales Day Book | 84 |

## PURCHASES LEDGER

| Dr | | P Bond (account no 525) | | | Cr |
|---|---|---|---|---|---|
| 20-1 | | £ | 20-1 | | £ |
| | | | 2 Jan | Purchases | 94 |
| | | | 16 Jan | Purchases | 188 |

| Dr | | D Webster (account no 730) | | Cr |
|---|---|---|---|---|
| 20-1 | £ | 20-1 | | £ |
| | | 11 Jan | Purchases | 141 |

## revision summary

Purchases day book fits into the accounting system in the following way:

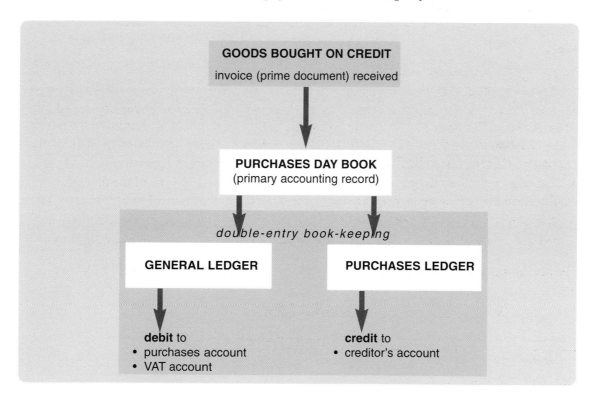

## RETURNS DAY BOOKS

Where a business has a sufficient number of sales returns and purchases returns each day, week or month, it will make use of the two returns books:

- **Sales Returns Day Book** – for goods previously sold on credit and now being returned to the business by its customers
- **Purchases Returns Day Book** – for goods purchased on credit by the business, and now being returned to the suppliers

The two returns day books operate in a similar way to the other day books: they are used to store information about returns until such time as it is transferred to the appropriate returns account. Note that, like all day books, the transactions are recorded from prime documents (credit notes issued for sales returns, and credit notes received for purchases returns). The returns day books are primary accounting records and do not form part of the double-entry book-keeping system: the information from the day book must be transferred to the appropriate account in the ledger.

**example transactions**

| 6 Jan 20-1 | Returned goods, £40 + VAT to P Bond, credit note no 406 received |
| 15 Jan 20-1 | T Young returns goods, £40 + VAT, credit note no CN702 issued |
| 20 Jan 20-1 | Returned goods, £40 + VAT to D Webster, credit note no 123 received |
| 25 Jan 20-1 | A Sparkes returns goods, £120 + VAT, credit note no CN703 issued |

*Note: VAT is to be charged at 17.5 per cent*

The sales returns day book and purchases returns day book are written up as follows:

| Sales Returns Day Book | | | | | | |
|---|---|---|---|---|---|---|
| Date | Details | Credit Note | Folio | Net | VAT | Gross |
| 20-1 | | | | £ | £ | £ |
| 15 Jan | T Young | CN702 | SL 179 | 40 | 7 | 47 |
| 25 Jan | A Sparkes | CN703 | SL 127 | 120 | 21 | 141 |
| 31 Jan | Totals for month | | | 160 | 28 | 188 |

| Purchases Returns Day Book | | | | | | |
|---|---|---|---|---|---|---|
| Date | Details | Credit Note | Folio | Net | VAT | Gross |
| 20-1 | | | | £ | £ | £ |
| 6 Jan | P Bond | 406 | PL 525 | 40 | 7 | 47 |
| 20 Jan | D Webster | 123 | PL 730 | 40 | 7 | 47 |
| 31 Jan | Totals for month | | | 80 | 14 | 94 |

**Notes**

- Total net sales returns and net purchases returns have been transferred to the sales returns account and purchases returns account respectively in the general ledger.
- Total VAT amounts are transferred to VAT account in the general ledger.
- The VAT-inclusive amounts of sales returns are credited to the debtors' personal accounts in the sales ledger; purchases returns are debited to the creditors' accounts in the purchases ledger.
- The gross totals will be entered into the sales ledger control account and purchases ledger control account (see Chapter 20).

The accounts to record the above transactions (including any other transactions already recorded on these accounts) are:

**GENERAL LEDGER**

| Dr | | | | Sales Returns Account | | | Cr |
|---|---|---|---|---|---|---|---|
| 20-1 | | | £ | 20-1 | | | £ |
| 31 Jan | Sales Returns Day Book | | 160 | | | | |

| Dr | | | | Purchases Returns Account | | | Cr |
|---|---|---|---|---|---|---|---|
| 20-1 | | | £ | 20-1 | | | £ |
| | | | | 31 Jan | Purchases Returns Day Book | | 80 |

| Dr | | | | Value Added Tax Account* | | | Cr |
|---|---|---|---|---|---|---|---|
| 20-1 | | | £ | 20-1 | | | £ |
| 31 Jan | Purchases Day Book | | 63 | 31 Jan | Sales Day Book | | 84 |
| 31 Jan | Sales Returns Day Book | | 28 | 31 Jan | Purchases Returns Day Book | | 14 |

* Chapter 7 on Value Added Tax will explain the significance of the balance on this account, and how it is dealt with.

**SALES LEDGER**

| Dr | | | | A Sparkes (account no 127) | | | Cr |
|---|---|---|---|---|---|---|---|
| 20-1 | | | £ | 20-1 | | | £ |
| 8 Jan | Sales | | 235 | 25 Jan | Sales Returns | | 141 |
| 18 Jan | Sales | | 141 | | | | |

| Dr. | | | T Young (account no 179) | | | Cr |
|---|---|---|---|---|---|---|
| 20-1 | | £ | 20-1 | | | £ |
| 12 Jan | Sales | 94 | 15 Jan | Sales Returns | | 47 |

## PURCHASES LEDGER

| Dr | | | P Bond (account no 525) | | | Cr |
|---|---|---|---|---|---|---|
| 20-1 | | £ | 20-1 | | | £ |
| 6 Jan | Purchases Returns | 47 | 2 Jan | Purchases | | 94 |
| | | | 16 Jan | Purchases | | 188 |

| Dr | | | D Webster (account no 730) | | | Cr |
|---|---|---|---|---|---|---|
| 20-1 | | £ | 20-1 | | | £ |
| 20 Jan | Purchases Returns | 47 | 11 Jan | Purchases | | 141 |

## revision summary

The two returns day books fit into the accounting system as follows:

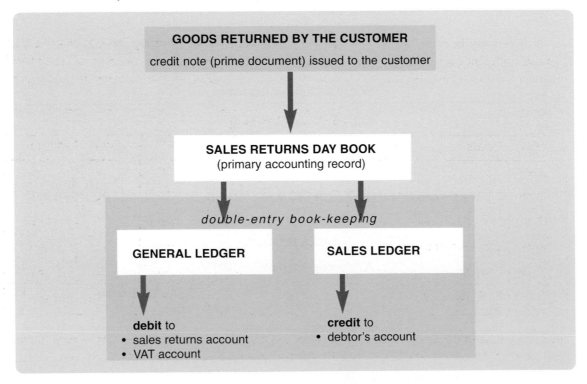

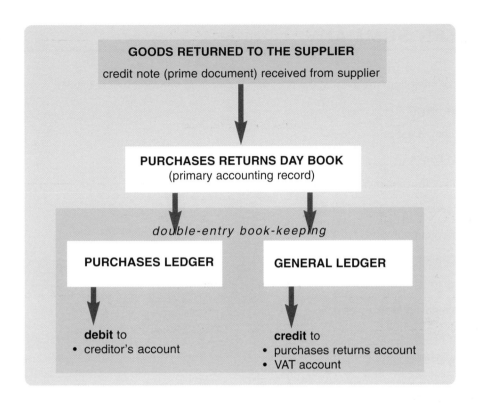

## ANALYSED DAY BOOKS

An analysed day book is used whenever a business needs to split its purchases, sales or returns between different categories of products, or between different departments. For example, a paint and wallpaper shop may decide to write up its purchases day book (invoice and folio columns not shown) as follows:

| Purchases Day Book | | | | | | |
|---|---|---|---|---|---|---|
| Date | Details | Paint | Wallpaper | Net | VAT | Gross |
| 20-1 | | £ | £ | £ | £ | £ |
| 8 Jan | DIY Wholesalers Ltd | 75 | 125 | 200 | 35 | 235 |
| 12 Jan | Luxor Paints Ltd | 120 | - | 120 | 21 | 141 |
| 16 Jan | Bond Supplies | 180 | 100 | 280 | 49 | 329 |
| 22 Jan | Southern Manufacturing Co | 60 | 100 | 160 | 28 | 188 |
| 31 Jan | Totals for month | 435 | 325 | 760 | 133 | 893 |

By using analysed day books, a business can keep track of the purchases, sales, etc of departments and assess their performance. See page 475 for an explanation of departmental accounts.

## CHAPTER SUMMARY

- Division of the ledger means that the accounts are divided between four sections:
  - sales ledger
  - purchases ledger
  - cash books
  - general (or nominal) ledger
- Primary accounting records include:
  - sales day book
  - purchases day book
  - sales returns day book
  - purchases returns day book
  - cash book
  - petty cash book
  - general journal
- A day book is a listing device which is used to take pressure off the main double-entry book-keeping system, and also allows the work of the accounts department to be split up amongst staff.
- Most businesses use day books for credit transactions only.
- An analysed day book is used when a business needs to know the purchases, sales, etc made by different departments or divisions of the business.

Having included Value Added Tax in the day books used in this chapter, and seen VAT applied to business documents in Chapter 4, in the next chapter we will look in more detail at this tax and how it affects businesses.

# QUESTIONS

NOTE: an asterisk (*) after the question number means that an answer to the question is given in Appendix 2.

**6.1***　Lucinda Lamille operates a clothes wholesaling business. All the goods she buys and sells are subject to Value Added Tax (at 17.5 per cent). The following transactions are to be entered in the purchases day book or sales day book, as appropriate.

20-6

| | |
|---|---|
| 1 Feb | Bought goods from Flair Clothing Co for £520 + VAT |
| 2 Feb | Sold goods to Wyvern Fashions for £200 + VAT |
| 4 Feb | Bought goods from Modernwear for £240 + VAT |
| 10 Feb | Sold goods to Zandra Smith for £160 + VAT |
| 15 Feb | Sold goods to Just Jean for £120 + VAT |
| 18 Feb | Bought goods from Quality Clothing for £800 + VAT |
| 23 Feb | Sold goods to Peter Sanders Menswear for £320 + VAT |
| 24 Feb | Sold goods to H Wilson for £80 + VAT |
| 26 Feb | Sold goods to Mercian Models for £320 + VAT |
| 28 Feb | Bought goods from Flair Clothing Co for £200 + VAT |

You are to:

(a)　write up the sales day book and the purchases day book

(b)　show how the VAT account will appear in her general ledger

**6.2**　James Scriven started in business as a furniture wholesaler on 1 February 20-2. He has registered for Value Added Tax. During the first month of business, the following credit transactions took place (VAT is charged at 17.5%):

| | |
|---|---|
| 1 Feb | Bought furniture for resale and received invoice no 961 from Softseat Ltd, £320 + VAT |
| 2 Feb | Bought furniture for resale and received invoice no 068 from PRK Ltd, £80 + VAT |
| 8 Feb | Sold furniture and issued invoice no 001 to High Street Stores, £440 + VAT |
| 14 Feb | Sold furniture and issued invoice no 002 to Peter Lounds Ltd, £120 + VAT |
| 15 Feb | Bought furniture for resale and received invoice no 529 from Quality Furnishings, £160 + VAT |
| 18 Feb | Sold furniture and issued invoice no 003 to Carpminster College, £320 + VAT |
| 19 Feb | Bought furniture for resale and received invoice no 984 from Softseat Ltd, £160 + VAT |
| 25 Feb | Sold furniture and issued invoice no 004 to High Street Stores, £200 + VAT |

You are to:

(a)  enter the above transactions in James Scriven's primary accounting records, and total the columns for the month

(b)  record the accounting entries in James Scriven's purchases ledger, sales ledger and general ledger

**6.3**

Anne Green owns a shop selling paint and decorating materials; she is registered for Value Added Tax. She has two suppliers, Wyper Ltd (account no 301) and M Roper & Sons (account no 302). During the month of May 20-2 Anne received the following business documents from her suppliers:

2 May     Invoice no 562 from M Roper & Sons for £190 + VAT

4 May     Invoice no 82 from Wyper Ltd for £200 + VAT

10 May    Invoice no 86 from Wyper Ltd for £210 + VAT

18 May    Invoice no 580 from M Roper & Sons for £180 + VAT

18 May    Credit note no 82 from M Roper & Sons for £30 + VAT

21 May    Invoice no 91 from Wyper Ltd for £240 + VAT

23 May    Credit note no 6 from Wyper Ltd for £40 + VAT

25 May    Invoice no 589 from M Roper & Sons for £98 + VAT

28 May    Credit note no 84 from M Roper & Sons for £38 + VAT

*Note*

VAT is charged at 17.5%. Ignore fractions of a penny, ie round *down* to a whole penny.

You are to:

(a)  enter the above transactions in the appropriate day books which are to be totalled at the end of May

(b)  enter the transactions in the appropriate accounts in Anne Green's ledgers. (The credit balances of Wyper Ltd and M Roper & Sons at the beginning of the month were £100 and £85 respectively.)

(c)  balance each account and bring down a balance on 1 June 20-2

**6.4\***

Lorna Pratt runs a computer software business, specialising in supplies to educational establishments. The business is registered for Value Added Tax. At the beginning of January 20-2 the balances in her ledgers were as follows:

| | | |
|---|---|---|
| Purchases ledger | Macstrad plc (account no 101) | £1,050.75 credit |
| | Amtosh plc (account no 102) | £2,750.83 credit |
| Sales ledger | Mereford College (account no 201) | £705.35 debit |
| | Carpminster College (account no 202) | £801.97 debit |

During the course of the month the following business documents are issued (all plus VAT at 17.5%):

| | | |
|---|---|---:|
| 2 Jan | Invoice from Macstrad plc, M1529 | £2,900.00 |
| 3 Jan | Invoice from Amtosh plc, A7095 | £7,500.00 |
| 5 Jan | Invoice to Mereford College, 1093 | £3,900.00 |
| 7 Jan | Invoice to Carpminster College, 1094 | £8,500.00 |
| 10 Jan | Credit note from Macstrad plc, MC105 | £319.75 |
| 12 Jan | Credit note from Amtosh plc, AC730 | £750.18 |
| 13 Jan | Credit note to Mereford College, CN109 | £850.73 |
| 14 Jan | Invoice to Carpminster College, 1095 | £1,800.50 |
| 14 Jan | Invoice to Mereford College, 1096 | £2,950.75 |
| 18 Jan | Invoice from Macstrad plc, M2070 | £1,750.00 |
| 19 Jan | Invoice from Amtosh plc, A7519 | £5,500.00 |
| 20 Jan | Invoice to Carpminster College, 1097 | £3,900.75 |
| 22 Jan | Invoice to Mereford College, 1098 | £1,597.85 |
| 23 Jan | Credit note from Macstrad plc, MC120 | £953.07 |
| 27 Jan | Credit note to Mereford College, CN110 | £593.81 |

Note: when calculating VAT amounts, ignore fractions of a penny, ie round down to a whole penny.

You are to:
(a)  enter the above transactions in the appropriate day books which are to be totalled at the end of January
(b)  record the accounting entries in Lorna Pratt's purchases ledger, sales ledger and general ledger

6.5*  For each transaction shown below, state
- the prime document
- the primary accounting record
- the account to be debited
- the account to be credited

(a)  bought goods on credit from A Cotton
(b)  sold goods on credit to D Law
(c)  cheque received for cash sales
(d)  returned damaged goods to A Cotton
(e)  paid gas bill by cheque
(f)  D Law returns damaged goods

# MULTIPLE CHOICE QUESTIONS

Read each question carefully.

Choose the one answer you think is correct (calculators may be needed).

The answers are on page 568.

**1**     A firm's cash account is as follows:

| Dr | | | **Cash Account** | | Cr |
|---|---|---|---|---|---|
| 20-1 | | £ | 20-1 | | £ |
| 1 Jan | Capital | 1,000 | 10 Jan | Computer | 500 |
| 19 Jan | Sales | 650 | 12 Jan | Purchases | 400 |
| | | | 27 Jan | Purchases | 350 |
| | | | 29 Jan | Electricity | 75 |

At 31 January 20-1, the balance of the account is:

A          credit £325

B          debit £1,650

C          debit £325

D          credit £1,325

**2**     A debit balance of £125 on the bank account in a firm's book-keeping
system means:

A          the firm has money in the bank of £125

B          the firm is overdrawn at the bank by £125

C          the owner's capital is £125

D          the balance of cash held by the firm is £125

**3**     A credit balance of £265 on T Smith's account in the books of J Wilson
means:

A          Smith owes Wilson £265

B          Wilson has paid Smith £265

C          Wilson owes Smith £265

D          Smith has bought goods from Wilson for £265

**Chapters 5 - 6**

**4**     Which one of the following always has a debit balance?
A          capital account
B          purchases account
C          sales account
D          purchases returns account

**5**     Which one of the following always has a credit balance?
A          cash account
B          premises account
C          capital account
D          drawings account

**6**     An amount has been entered into the book-keeping system as £65 instead of £56. The error is called:
A          compensating error
B          mispost
C          error of principle
D          error of original entry

**7**     The cost of fuel for vehicles has been debited in error to vehicles account. The error is called:
A          mispost
B          error of principle
C          error of original entry
D          error of omission

**8**     Which one of the following is not a division of the ledger?
A          general ledger
B          sales account
C          sales ledger
D          cash books

**9**     Sales ledger contains:
A          creditors' accounts
B          sales account
C          debtors' accounts
D          sales returns account

10   Which one of the following accounts is not contained in general ledger?
A       bank account
B       purchases returns account
C       vehicles account
D       loan account

11   Which one of the following is a primary accounting record?
A       sales ledger
B       trial balance
C       general ledger
D       petty cash book

12   The primary accounting record for a credit note received from a supplier is:
A       purchases returns day book
B       sales day book
C       sales returns day book
D       general journal

# 7 VALUE ADDED TAX

We have already seen in Chapter 4 how Value Added Tax (VAT) is added to invoices by businesses registered for VAT, and in Chapter 6 how the tax is dealt with in day books and in the book-keeping system. In this chapter we will explain:

● the nature of VAT

● the business account that needs to be kept for VAT

● how to complete a Value Added Tax Return

## REGISTERING FOR VAT

In the UK, most businesses with a significant amount of turnover (sales) must be registered for VAT. The turnover figure is normally increased annually as a part of the Chancellor of the Exchequer's budget proposals. Details of this and other aspects of VAT may be found on www.hmce.gov.uk

Once registered, a business is issued with a VAT registration number which is quoted on invoices and on other business documents. VAT is charged at the standard rate (quoted as 17.5 per cent in this chapter) on all taxable supplies, ie whenever the business sells goods, or supplies a service. From the supplier's viewpoint, the tax charged is known as output VAT. A number of items are zero-rated and no tax is charged when they are supplied: for example, food and children's clothing are zero rated. Certain items, such as domestic fuel, are charged at a reduced rate.

Most businesses registered for VAT pay to the VAT authorities (HM Customs and Excise):

• the amount of VAT collected on sales (output tax)

• less the amount of VAT charged to them (input tax) on all taxable supplies bought in, eg purchases, expenses, fixed assets

If the amount of input tax is larger than the output tax, the business claims a refund of the difference from HM Customs and Excise. A VAT return (see page 96) has to be completed every three months, although some businesses submit a return on an annual basis. Payment of VAT due (if the business is not claiming a refund) is made when the VAT return is submitted.

Small businesses may alternatively use a **flat rate scheme** which allows the calculation of VAT payable as a percentage of sales – so there is no need to calculate input and output VAT or even to identify the VAT element in individual transactions. It is a very simple scheme designed to cut down on the paperwork for small businesses.

# EXEMPT SUPPLIES

A few types of goods and services are neither standard-rated nor zero-rated for VAT: instead they are exempt. The effect of this is that the seller of such goods cannot charge VAT on outputs (as is the case with zero-rated goods). However, unlike the seller of zero-rated goods, the seller of exempt goods cannot claim back all the tax which has been paid on inputs. Examples of exempt supplies include postal services, loans of money, and certain types of education and health care.

# A TAX ON THE FINAL CONSUMER

VAT is a tax which is paid by the final consumer or user of the goods (except where the final user is registered for VAT). For example, a member of the public buying a computer at a total cost of £705 is paying VAT of £105 (ie 17.5 per cent of £600). This final consumer or user has to bear the cost of the VAT, but the tax is actually paid to HM Customs and Excise by all those involved in the manufacturing and selling process. This procedure is illustrated by the flow chart on the next page. The right-hand column shows the amount of VAT paid to HM Customs and Excise at each stage of the process. Note that, if the final consumer had been a business registered for VAT, it would be able to claim the £105 of VAT as an input tax, and would record the purchase in its books as:

– debit computer account                               £600
– debit Value Added Tax account                    £105
– credit bank account (or creditor's account)   £705

# VAT ACCOUNT

We have seen in the previous chapter how a VAT-registered business keeps a Value Added Tax Account as part of the book-keeping system in the general ledger. This records:

Debits (input tax)

- VAT on purchases
- VAT on fixed assets (except cars)
- VAT on expenses
- VAT on sales returns

Credits (output tax)

- VAT on sales and/or services
- VAT on purchases returns
- VAT on the sale of fixed assets

## collection of Value Added Tax

### manufacture and sale of a computer

**supplier of materials**

sells materials for £200 plus £35 VAT = £235

- keeps £200
- pays £35 to HM Customs & Excise

**manufacturer**

adds on margin and sells computer for £440 plus £77 VAT = £517

- keeps £440
- pays £42 to HM Customs & Excise (difference between £77 collected and £35 paid to supplier)

**shop**

adds on margin and sells computer for £600 plus £105 VAT = £705

- keeps £600
- pays £28 to HM Customs & Excise (difference between £105 collected and £77 paid to supplier)

**final consumer**

buys computer for £600 plus £105 VAT = £705

- pays nothing <u>directly</u> to HM Customs & Excise (the £105 has all been paid to the shop)

### VAT payments to HM Customs & Excise

£35

*plus*

£42

*plus*

£28

*plus*

£0

*equals*

£105

The VAT account shown in the previous chapter (page 81) for the month of January 20-1 is as follows:

| Dr | | | Value Added Tax Account | | | Cr |
|---|---|---|---|---|---|---|
| 20-1 | | £ | 20-1 | | | £ |
| 31 Jan | Purchases Day Book | 63 | 31 Jan | Sales Day Book | | 84 |
| 31 Jan | Sales Returns Day Book | 28 | 31 Jan | Purchases Returns Day Book | | 14 |
| 31 Jan | Balance c/d | 7 | | | | |
| | | 98 | | | | 98 |
| | | | 1 Feb | Balance b/d | | 7 |

At the end of January 20-1, the account has a credit balance of £7. This amount is owing to HM Customs and Excise and will be paid at the end of the three-month VAT period, along with the VAT due for the other two months of the VAT quarter. For example, if January is the first month of the VAT quarter, the account will be continued for a further two months until, at the end of March, the credit balance will be the amount owing to Customs and Excise. The amount will be paid in April (not later than the end of the month) by making the following book-keeping transaction:

– debit Value Added Tax account

– credit bank account (cheque or BACS payment)

If, at the end of the VAT quarter, there is a debit balance on the VAT account, this represents the amount due from Customs and Excise. A VAT return is completed and a payment is received (usually by bank giro credit) from Customs and Excise. This is recorded in the accounting records as:

– debit bank account
– credit Value Added Tax account

# VALUE ADDED TAX RETURN

For most businesses, a Value Added Tax Return (form VAT 100) must be completed every three months. The return is then sent to HM Customs and Excise, either with a payment for VAT due for the period, or a claim for repayment when input tax exceeds output tax.

**Example**

Wyvern Office Products Ltd has the following transactions, all of which are subject to VAT at 17.5%, for the three months ended 31 March 20-1:

| | Purchases | Expenses | Fixed assets | Sales |
|---|---|---|---|---|
| 20-1 | £ | £ | £ | £ |
| January | 5,000 | 1,000 | – | 10,000 |
| February | 6,000 | 1,400 | 3,000 | 12,000 |
| March | 7,000 | 1,800 | – | 14,000 |
| Total | 18,000 | 4,200 | 3,000 | 36,000 |

The VAT account will be written up as follows:

| Dr | | | Value Added Tax Account | | | Cr |
|---|---|---|---|---|---|---|
| 20-1 | | £ | | 20-1 | | £ |
| 31 Jan | Purchases Day Book | 875 | | 31 Jan | Sales Day Book | 1,750 |
| | Expenses | 175 | | 28 Feb | Sales Day Book | 2,100 |
| 28 Feb | Purchases Day Book | 1,050 | | 31 Mar | Sales Day Book | 2,450 |
| | Expenses | 245 | | | | |
| | Fixed assets | 525 | | | | |
| 31 Mar | Purchases Day Book | 1,225 | | | | |
| | Expenses | 315 | | | | |
| | | *4,410 | | | | |
| | Balance c/d | 1,890 | | | | |
| | | 6,300 | | | | 6,300 |
| 20 Apr | Bank | 1,890 | | 1 Apr | Balance b/d | 1,890 |

\* sub-totalled here for illustrative purposes (see below)

As can be seen from the account, the amount due to Customs and Excise on 1 April (£1,890) has been paid on 20 April. In this way the balance of the account is reduced to 'nil', and the account is ready to be used again in recording VAT transactions for the next VAT quarter. The payment will be sent to Customs and Excise, along with the firm's Value Added Tax Return (see the next page). This has been completed as follows (the notes refer to the box numbers on the VAT return):

**BOX 1**        This refers to the tax charged as output tax on sales invoices: here, it is £6,300.

**BOX 2**        This deals with VAT due to HM Customs and Excise in respect of goods bought from VAT-registered businesses in the other member states of the European Union: there is nothing to complete on this occasion.

**BOX 3**        This is the total of boxes 1 and 2.

**BOX 4**        This is the input tax on purchases, expenses and fixed assets: the total for the quarter is £4,410.

**BOX 5**        This is the difference between boxes 1 and 2, ie £6,300 − £4,410 = £1,890. As tax on outputs is greater than tax on inputs, this is the amount to be paid to Customs and Excise. If box 2 is greater than box 1, this indicates that a repayment is due from Customs and Excise.

**BOX 6**        This is the value of sales made during the period covered by the VAT return. In this example, the amount is £36,000. Note that this figure excludes any VAT.

**BOX 7**        This is the value of purchases, and other inputs such as expenses and fixed assets, for the period; here the amount is £18,000 + £4,200 + £3,000 = £25,200. Note that this figure excludes any VAT.

**BOXES 8 & 9**   These are completed with the total of any sales to, and any purchases from, other European Union member states.

The box on the left-hand lower section of the form is ticked to indicate that payment is enclosed. Finally, the declaration has to be signed and dated by an authorised person within the business.

---

**Value Added Tax Return**

**For the period**

01 01 -1 to 31 03 -1

For Official Use

SPECIMEN

HM Customs and Excise

WYVERN OFFICE PRODUCTS LIMITED
12 LOWER HYE STREET
MEREFORD
MR1 2JF

| Registration Number | Period |
|---|---|
| 841 1160 11 | 03 -1 |

**You could be liable to a financial penalty if your completed return and all the VAT payable are not received by the due date.**

Due date: 30 04 -1

For Official Use

Before you fill in this form please read the notes on the back and the VAT leaflet *"Filling in your VAT return"*. Fill in all boxes clearly in ink, and write 'none' where necessary. Don't put a dash or leave any box blank. If there are no pence write "**00**" in the pence column. **Do not** enter more than one amount in any box.

| For official use | | | £ | p |
|---|---|---|---|---|
| | VAT due in this period on **sales** and other outputs | 1 | 6,300 | 00 |
| | VAT due in this period on **acquisitions** from other **EC Member States** | 2 | NONE | |
| | Total VAT due (**the sum of boxes 1 and 2**) | 3 | 6,300 | 00 |
| | VAT reclaimed in this period on **purchases** and other inputs (including acquisitions from the EC) | 4 | 4,410 | 00 |
| | Net VAT to be paid to Customs or reclaimed by you **(Difference between boxes 3 and 4)** | 5 | 1,890 | 00 |
| | Total value of **sales** and all other outputs excluding any VAT. **Include your box 8 figure** | 6 | 36,000 | 00 |
| | Total value of **purchases** and all other inputs excluding any VAT. **Include your box 9 figure** | 7 | 25,200 | 00 |
| | Total value of all **supplies** of goods and related services, excluding any VAT, to other **EC Member States** | 8 | NONE | 00 |
| | Total value of all **acquisitions** of goods and related services, excluding any VAT, from other **EC Member States** | 9 | NONE | 00 |

**Retail schemes.** If you have used any of the schemes in the period covered by this return, enter the relevant letter(s) in this box.

DECLARATION: You, or someone on your behalf, must sign below.

If you are enclosing a payment please tick this box. ✓

I, ........ MATTHEW LLOYD ........ declare that the
(Full name of signatory in BLOCK LETTERS)

information given above is true and complete.

Signature .............. Date 20 APRIL 20 -1

**A false declaration can result in prosecution.**

L

**VAT 100**

## VAT CALCULATIONS

It is easy to calculate the VAT amount when the price of goods before the addition of VAT is known; eg using a rate of VAT of 17.5 per cent, goods costing £100 plus VAT of £17.50 gives a total cost of £117.50.

When the total cost including VAT is known, the amount of VAT is found by multiplying the amount by 17.5 and dividing by 117.5. For example:

| | | |
|---|---|---|
| Total cost | = | £117.50 |
| Amount of VAT is 17.5/117.5 of £117.50 | = | £ 17.50 |
| VAT-exclusive cost | = | £100.00 |

The VAT-exclusive price can be found by dividing the amount by 1.175. For example:

$$\frac{£117.50}{1.175} = \text{VAT-exclusive cost of } £100$$

Note that 1.175 (the figure you divide by) applies only with a rate of VAT of 17.5%. With a rate of 10%, for example, the figure you divide by is 1.1.

When calculating VAT amounts, fractions of a penny are ignored, ie the tax is rounded down to a whole penny.

## CHAPTER SUMMARY

- VAT-registered businesses charge VAT on all taxable supplies (sales).

- Most types of goods and services are taxable, but some are zero-rated, while others are exempt.

- A VAT account is used to record the amount of VAT charged on sales (output tax), and paid on purchases and expenses (input tax).

- A VAT-registered business must complete a Value Added Tax Return at certain intervals, commonly every three months, and either pay over to HM Customs and Excise the net amount of tax collected, or seek a refund where tax on inputs exceeds that on outputs.

In the next two chapters we will look at cash book and petty cash book – these are primary accounting records for cash and bank transactions.

# QUESTIONS

NOTE: an asterisk (*) after the question number means that an answer to the question is given in Appendix 2.

**7.1\***  The following is a summary of purchases and sales, excluding VAT, made by Wyvern Computers for the three months ended 30 June 20-4:

Purchases                    April £5,400,  May £4,800,  June £6,800

Sales                        April £8,200,  May £9,400,  June £10,800

All purchases and sales are subject to Value Added Tax at a rate of 17.5 per cent.

You are to:

(a)  calculate the VAT amounts for each month

(b)  show the VAT account for the quarter as it will appear in the general ledger, and balance the account at 30 June 20-4

(c)  explain the significance of the balance of the VAT account at 30 June 20-4 and how it will be dealt with

**7.2**  The following amounts include VAT at a rate of 17.5%:
- £11.75
- £10.34
- £0.94
- £14.10
- £6.50
- £2.21

You are to calculate for each amount:

(a)  the amount of VAT

(b)  the VAT-exclusive amount

**7.3**  Debbie Jones owns a fashion shop called 'Designer Labels'. She employs a book-keeper who uses a full set of double-entry accounts.

At the end of March 20-0, the book-keeper had not completed the VAT account for the month. The VAT totals from the four day books for March 20-0 were:

|                    | £     |
|--------------------|-------|
| purchases          | 735   |
| sales              | 1,120 |
| purchases returns  | 42    |
| sales returns      | 28    |

Note: the balance on VAT account on 1 March 20-0 was £805 credit; there were no other transactions on VAT account during the month.

You are to:

(a)  show the VAT account for March 20-0 in the books of Debbie Jones

(b)  balance the VAT account at 31 March 20-0

(c)  explain the meaning of the balance on the VAT account at 31 March 20-0

**7.4\*** Computer Supplies Ltd issued the following sales invoices (SI) and credit notes (CN) to customers during the week commencing 19 August 20-1. All sales are subject to Value Added Tax at 17.5% and the amounts shown are the gross values.

| Date | Number | Customer | Gross Amount |
|---|---|---|---|
| 20-1 | | | £ |
| 19 Aug | SI 1547 | E Newman | 183.30 |
| 20 Aug | SI 1548 | Wyvern Traders Ltd | 267.90 |
| 21 Aug | SI 1549 | Teme Supplies | 411.25 |
| 22 Aug | SI 1550 | Lugg Brothers & Co | 1,410.00 |
| 22 Aug | CN 121 | Wyvern Traders Ltd | 267.90 |
| 23 Aug | SI 1551 | E Newman | 470.00 |
| 23 Aug | CN 122 | E Newman | 91.65 |

Required:

(a) Prepare Computer Supplies Ltd's sales day book and sales returns day book for the week commencing 19 August 20-1, totalling the columns on 23 August 20-1.

(b) Explain how the totals from the day books will be recorded in the double-entry book-keeping system of Computer Supplies Ltd.

(c) The balance brought down on E Newman's account as at 1 August 20-1 was £440.00. Computer Supplies Ltd received a cheque on 7 August 20-1 for this amount. There were no other transactions with E Newman during the month of August other than those detailed above.

Show E Newman's personal account for August 20-1 as it would appear in Computer Supplies Ltd's ledger. Balance the account at the end of the month.

# 8 CASH BOOK

The cash book brings together the separate cash and bank transactions of a business into one 'book'.

The cash book is used to record the book-keeping transactions which involve the receipt and payment of money, for example cash, cheques and bank transfers.

The cash book forms part of the double-entry system.

Control of cash and money in the bank is very important for all businesses. A shortage of money may mean that wages and other day-to-day running expenses cannot be paid as they fall due. This could lead to the failure of the business.

## THE CASH BOOK IN THE ACCOUNTING SYSTEM

For most businesses, control of cash – including both bank and cash transactions – takes place in the cash books which comprise:

- cash book, for receipts and payments in cash and by cheque and bank transfer
- petty cash book (see next chapter), for low-value expense payments

The cash books combine the roles of primary accounting records and double-entry book-keeping. Cash books are:

- primary accounting records for cash and bank transactions
- double-entry accounts for cash and bank

## USES OF THE CASH BOOK

We have already used a separate cash account and bank account for double-entry book-keeping transactions. These two accounts are, in practice, brought together into one book under the title of cash book. This cash book is, therefore, used to record the money side of book-keeping transactions and is part of the double-entry system. The cash book is used for:

- **cash transactions**
  - all receipts in cash
  - most payments for cash, except for low-value expense payments (which are paid through petty cash book: see next chapter)
- **bank transactions**
  - all receipts by cheque and bank transfer (or payment of cash into the bank)
  - all payments by cheque or bank transfer (or withdrawal of cash from the bank)

The cash book is usually controlled by a **cashier** who:

- records receipts and payments by cheque and in cash
- makes cash payments, and prepares cheques and BACS payments for signature and authorisation
- pays cash and cheques received into the bank
- has control over the firm's cash, either in a cash till or cash box
- issues cash to the petty cashier who operates the firm's petty cash book (see next chapter)
- checks the accuracy of the cash and bank balances at regular intervals

It is important to note that transactions passing through the cash book must be supported by **documentary evidence**. In this way an audit trail is established which provides a link that can be checked and followed through the accounting system:

- prime document
- primary accounting record
- double-entry accounts

Such an audit trail is required both as a security feature within the business (to help to ensure that fraudulent transactions cannot be made), and also for taxation purposes – both for Value Added Tax and for the Inland Revenue.

The **cashier** has an important role to play within the accounting function of a business – most business activities will, at some point, involve cash or cheque transactions. Thus the cash book and the cashier are at the hub of the accounting system. In particular, the cashier is responsible for:

- issuing receipts for cash (and sometimes cheques) received
- making authorised payments in cash and by cheque against documents received (such as invoices and statements) showing the amounts due

At all times, payments can only be made by the cashier when authorised to do so by the appropriate person within the organisation, eg the accountant or the purchasing manager.

With so many transactions passing through the cash book, accounting procedures must include:

- security – of cash and cheque books, correct authorisation of payments
- confidentiality – that all cash/bank transactions, including cash and bank balances, are kept confidential

If the cashier has any queries about any transactions, he or she should refer them to the accounts supervisor.

## LAYOUT OF THE CASH BOOK

Although a cash book can be set out in many formats to suit the requirements of a particular business, a common format is the columnar cash book. This is set out like other double-entry accounts, with debit and credit sides, but there may be several money columns on each side. An example of a three column cash book (three money columns on each side) is shown below:

| Dr | | | | | | | | | | Cash Book | Cr | | | |
|---|---|---|---|---|---|---|---|---|---|---|---|---|
| Date | Details | Folio | Discount allowed | Cash | Bank | Date | Details | Folio | Discount received | Cash | Bank |
| | | | £ | £ | £ | | | | £ | £ | £ |
| | | | | | | | | | | | |

Note the following points:

- The debit side is used for receipts.
- The credit side is used for payments.
- On both the debit and credit sides there are separate money columns for cash receipts/payments and bank receipts/payments.
- A third money column on each side is used to record cash discount (that is, an allowance offered for quick settlement of the amount due, eg 2% cash discount for settlement within seven days).
- The discount column on the debit side is for discount allowed to customers.
- The discount column on the credit side is for discount received from suppliers.
- The discount columns are not part of the double-entry book-keeping system – they are used in the cash book as a listing device or memorandum column. As we will see in the worked example which follows, the columns are totalled at the end of the week or month, and the totals are then transferred into the double-entry system.

# WORKED EXAMPLE: TRANSACTIONS IN THE CASH BOOK

We will now look at some example transactions and then see how the three-column cash book is balanced at the month-end. The year is 20-7.

The transactions to be entered in the cash book are:

| 1 April | Balances at start of month: cash £300, bank £550 |
| 4 April | Received a cheque from S Wright for £98 – we have allowed her £2 cash discount |
| 7 April | Paid a cheque to S Crane for £145 – he has allowed £5 cash discount |
| 11 April | Paid wages in cash £275 |
| 14 April | Paid by cheque the account of T Lewis £120, deducting 2.5% cash discount |
| 17 April | J Jones settles in cash her account of £80, deducting 5% cash discount |
| 21 April | Withdrew £100 in cash from the bank for use in the business |
| 23 April | Received a cheque for £45 from D Whiteman in full settlement of her account of £48 |
| 28 April | Paid cash of £70 to S Ford in full settlement of our account of £75 |

All cheques are banked on the day of receipt.

The cash book records these transactions (as shown below) and, after they have been entered, is balanced on 30 April. (The other part of each double-entry book-keeping transaction is not shown here, but has to be carried out in order to record the transactions correctly.)

| Dr | | | | | | | | | | | | Cr |
|---|---|---|---|---|---|---|---|---|---|---|---|---|
| Date | Details | Folio | Discount allowed | Cash | Bank | Date | Details | Folio | Discount received | Cash | Bank | |
| | | | £ | £ | £ | | | | £ | £ | £ | |
| 20-7 | | | | | | 20-7 | | | | | | |
| 1 Apr | Balances b/d | | | 300 | 550 | 7 Apr | J Crane | | 5 | | 145 | |
| 4 Apr | S Wright | | 2 | | 98 | 11 Apr | Wages | | | 275 | | |
| 17 Apr | J Jones | | 4 | 76 | | 14 Apr | T Lewis | | 3 | | 117 | |
| 21 Apr | Bank | C | | 100 | | 21 Apr | Cash | C | | | 100 | |
| 23 Apr | D Whiteman | | 3 | | 45 | 28 Apr | S Ford | | 5 | 70 | | |
| | | | | | | 30 Apr | Balances c/d | | | 131 | 331 | |
| | | | 9 | 476 | 693 | | | | 13 | 476 | 693 | |
| 1 May | Balances b/d | | | 131 | 331 | | | | | | | |

Note that the transaction on 21 April – £100 withdrawn from the bank for use in the business – involves a transfer of money between cash and bank. As each transaction is both a receipt and a payment within the cash book, it is usual to indicate both of them in the folio column with a 'C' – this stands for 'contra' and shows that both parts of the transaction are in the same book.

## BALANCING THE CASH BOOK

We saw in Chapter 5 how accounts are balanced. The cash book is the ledger for cash account and bank account, and the procedure for balancing these accounts is exactly the same as for other ledger accounts.

The cash book in the worked example on the previous page is balanced in the following way:

- add the two cash columns and subtotal in pencil (ie £476 in the debit column, and £345 in the credit column); remember to erase the subtotals afterwards
- deduct the lower total from the higher (payments from receipts) to give the balance of cash remaining (£476 − £345 = £131)
- the higher total is recorded at the bottom of both cash columns in a totals 'box' (£476)
- the balance of cash remaining (£131) is entered as a balancing item above the totals box (on the credit side), and is brought down underneath the total on the debit side as the opening balance for next month (£131)
- the two bank columns are dealt with in the same way (£693 − £362 = £331)

Notice that, in the cash book shown above, the cash and bank balances have been brought down on the debit side. It may happen that the balance at bank is brought down on the credit side: this occurs when payments exceed receipts, and indicates a bank overdraft. It is very important to appreciate that the bank columns of the cash book represent the firm's own records of bank transactions and the balance at bank – the bank statement may well show different figures (see Chapter 10).

At the end of the month, each discount column is totalled separately – no attempt should be made to balance them. At this point, amounts recorded in the columns and the totals are not part of the double-entry system. However, the two totals are transferred to the double-entry system as follows:

- the total on the debit side (£9 in the example above) is debited to discount allowed account in the general (or nominal) ledger
- the total on the credit side (£13 in the example) is credited to discount received account, also in the general (or nominal) ledger

The opposite book-keeping entries will have already been entered in the debtors' and creditors' accounts respectively (see Chapter 4). The accounts appear as follows:

| Dr | | | **Discount Allowed Account** | | Cr |
|---|---|---|---|---|---|
| 20-7 | | £ | 20-7 | | £ |
| 30 Apr | Cash Book | 9 | | | |

| Dr | | | **Discount Received Account** | | Cr |
|---|---|---|---|---|---|
| 20-7 | | £ | 20-7 | | £ |
| | | | 30 Apr | Cash Book | 13 |

The two discount accounts represent an expense and income respectively and, at the end of the firm's financial year, the totals of the two accounts will be used in the calculation of profit. Where control accounts (see Chapter 20) are in use, the total of discount allowed is credited to the sales ledger control account, while the total of discount received is debited to the purchases ledger control account.

## THE CASH BOOK AS A PRIMARY ACCOUNTING RECORD

The cash book performs two functions within the accounting system:

- it is a primary accounting record for cash/bank transactions
- it forms part of the double-entry book-keeping system

The diagram below shows the flow involving:

- prime documents – cash and bank receipts and payments
- the cash book as a primary accounting record
- double-entry book-keeping, involving cash book and other ledgers

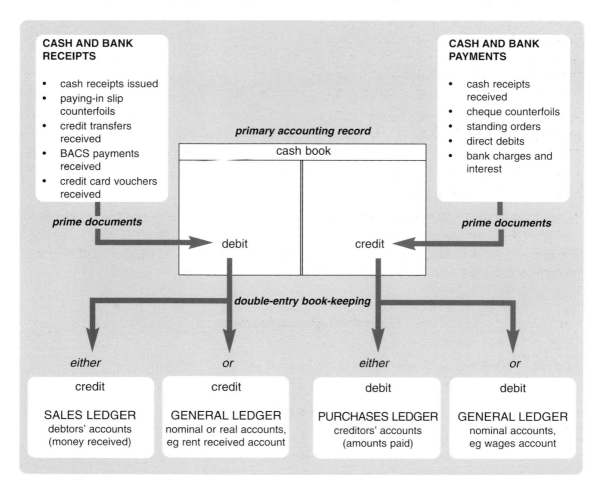

## CHECKING THE CASH BOOK

As the cash book forms such an integral part of a firm's book-keeping system, it is essential that transactions are recorded accurately and that balances are calculated correctly at regular intervals, eg weekly or monthly – depending on the needs of the business. How can the cash book be checked for accuracy?

### cash columns

To check the cash columns is easy. It is simply a matter of counting the cash in the cash till or box, and agreeing it with the balance shown by the cash book. In the example in the worked example on page 103, there should be £131 in the firm's cash till at 30 April 20-7. If the cash cannot be agreed in this way, the discrepancy needs to be investigated urgently.

### bank columns

How are these to be checked? We could, perhaps, enquire at the bank and ask for the balance at the month-end, or we could arrange for a bank statement to be sent to us at the end of each month. However, the balance of the account at the bank may well not agree with that shown by the bank columns of the cash book. There are several reasons why there may be a difference: for example, a cheque that has been written out recently to pay a bill may not yet have been recorded on the bank statement, ie it has been entered in the cash book, but is not yet on the bank statement. To agree the bank statement and the bank columns of the cash book, it is usually necessary to prepare a bank reconciliation statement, and this topic is dealt with fully in Chapter 10.

## WORKED EXAMPLE: CASH BOOK INCORPORATING VAT

A cash book can be adapted to suit the needs of a business – already we have seen how a three-column cash book uses a memorandum column for discounts allowed and received. Another common layout uses a fourth money column, for VAT, as shown in the worked example which follows. The VAT columns act as memorandum columns and, at the end of the week or month, are transferred to VAT account.

### question

On Monday, 2 June 20-7, the cash book of Eveshore Growers showed balances of £86 in cash and £248 in the bank. Transactions for the week were:

| | |
|---|---|
| 2 June | Paid insurance premium of £130 by cheque |
| 3 June | Cash sales of £282, including Value Added Tax |
| 3 June | Paid travel expenses in cash £47 (no Value Added Tax) |
| 3 June | Paid an invoice for £100 from A–Z Supplies by cheque after deducting £5 cash discount |
| 4 June | Received a cheque for £117 from a debtor, P Leech, who was settling his account balance of £120 after deducting £3 cash discount |

5 June    Cash sales of £423, including Value Added Tax
6 June    Cash purchase of £188, including Value Added Tax
6 June    Paid wages of £205, partly by cheque for £105 and partly in cash £100
6 June    Transferred £250 of cash into the bank

As cashier to Eveshore Growers, you are to:
* write up the cash book for the week commencing 2 June 20-7, using separate columns for discount, VAT, cash and bank
* balance the cash book at 6 June 20-7
* explain how the totals for the discount and VAT columns will be entered in the ledger of Eveshore Growers

The rate of Value Added Tax is 17.5%.  All cheques are banked on the day of receipt.

### answer

| Dr | | | | | | | **Cash Book** | | | | | | Cr |
|---|---|---|---|---|---|---|---|---|---|---|---|---|---|
| Date | Details | Folio | Disc't allowed | VAT | Cash | Bank | Date | Details | Folio | Disc't rec'd | VAT | Cash | Bank |
| 20-7 | | | £ | £ | £ | £ | 20-7 | | | £ | £ | £ | £ |
| 2 June | Balances b/d | | | | 86 | 248 | 2 June | Insurance | GL | | | | 130 |
| 3 June | Sales | GL | | 42 | 282 | | 3 June | Travel exp. | GL | | | 47 | |
| 4 June | P Leech | SL | 3 | | | 117 | 3 June | A-Z Supplies | PL | 5 | | | 95 |
| 5 June | Sales | GL | | 63 | 423 | | 6 June | Purchases | GL | | 28 | 188 | |
| 6 June | Cash | C | | | | 250 | 6 June | Wages | GL | | | 100 | 105 |
| | | | | | | | 6 June | Bank | C | | | 250 | |
| | | | | | | | 6 June | Balances c/d | | | | 206 | 285 |
| | | | 3 | 105 | 791 | 615 | | | | 5 | 28 | 791 | 615 |
| 7 June | Balances b/d | | | | 206 | 285 | | | | | | | |

* The folio columns have been completed as follows:
  GL  = general ledger (or NL for nominal ledger)
  SL  = sales ledger
  PL  = purchases ledger
  C   = contra (both parts of the transaction in the same book)
* With transactions involving sales ledger (ie P Leech) and purchases ledger (ie A–Z Supplies), no amount for VAT is shown in the VAT columns. This is because VAT has been charged on invoices issued and received and was recorded in the VAT account (via the day books) when the sale or purchase was made.
* VAT on cash sales and purchases, and other transactions, is recorded in the two VAT analysis columns.

The discount and VAT columns are dealt with as follows:
* discount allowed column – the total of £3 is debited to discount allowed account (general ledger)
* discount received column – the total of £5 is credited to discount received account (general ledger)
* VAT columns – the total of £105 is credited to VAT account in the general (or nominal) ledger, while the total of £28 is debited to VAT account

# ANALYSED CASH BOOK

Many businesses use an analysed cash book to provide more information. An analysed cash book divides receipts and payments between a number of categories.

Receipts could be divided between:

- the main sections of a business, such as (1) furniture, and (2) carpets, for a home furnishing shop
- (1) discount allowed, (2) Value Added Tax (where a business is registered for VAT), (3) sales paid for immediately in cash or by cheque, (4) sales ledger, ie receipts from debtors, (5) sundry items

Payments could be divided between:

- the main sections of a business, such as (1) compact discs, (2) audio tapes, and (3) video tapes, for an audio/video shop
- (1) discount received, (2) Value Added Tax, (3) purchases paid for immediately in cash or by cheque, (4) purchases ledger, ie payments to creditors, (5) sundry items

A business will use whatever analysis columns suit it best: the cash book should be adapted to meet the needs of the business in the best possible way.

## WORKED EXAMPLE: ANALYSED CASH BOOK

### question

Wyvern Auto Spares Limited buys car parts from manufacturers, and sells to local garages and to members of the public. The company is registered for VAT.

The business uses a cash book which analyses receipts and payments as follows:

| RECEIPTS | PAYMENTS |
|---|---|
| discount allowed | discount received |
| VAT | VAT |
| sales | purchases |
| sales ledger | purchases ledger |
| sundry receipts | sundry payments |

The following transactions are to be entered for the first week of December 20-7:

| | |
|---|---|
| 1 Dec | Balances from previous week: cash £255, bank £875 |
| 1 Dec | Sales for cash £240 + VAT |
| 1 Dec | A debtor, Main Street Garage, settles an invoice for £195, paying by cheque |
| 2 Dec | Paid rent on premises £325 (no VAT) by cheque |
| 2 Dec | Sales for cash £200 + VAT |
| 2 Dec | Paid an invoice for £250 from Boxhall Supplies Limited (a creditor) by cheque for £240, £10 being received for prompt settlement |
| 3 Dec | Transferred £500 of cash into the bank |

3 Dec    Paid for office stationery in cash, £40 + VAT

3 Dec    A debtor, A45 Service Station, settles an invoice for £143, paying £140 by cheque and
         receiving £3 discount for prompt settlement

4 Dec    Sales £320 + VAT, received half in cash, and half by cheque

4 Dec    Paid for urgently needed spares in cash, £80 + VAT

5 Dec    Paid an invoice for £155 from Vord Supplies (a creditor) by cheque for £150, £5 being
         received for prompt settlement

5 Dec    Sales for cash £200 + VAT

5 Dec    Paid wages £385 in cash

5 Dec    Balanced the cash book at the end of the week

As cashier to Wyvern Auto Spares Limited, you are to:
*   write up the analysed cash book for the week commencing 1 December 20-7
*   balance the cash book at 5 December 20-7

The rate of Value Added Tax is 17.5%. All cheques are banked on the day of receipt.

**answer** (see next page for notes)

**Dr (Receipts)**

| Date | Details | Folio | Cash | Bank | Discount allowed | VAT | Sales | Sales ledger | Sundry |
|------|---------|-------|------|------|------------------|-----|-------|--------------|--------|
| 20-7 | | | £ | £ | £ | £ | £ | £ | £ |
| 1 Dec | Balances b/d | | 255 | 875 | | | | | |
| 1 Dec | Sales | GL | 282 | | | 42 | 240 | | |
| 1 Dec | Main Street Garage | SL | | 195 | | | | 195 | |
| 2 Dec | Sales | GL | 235 | | | 35 | 200 | | |
| 3 Dec | Cash | C | | 500 | | | | | |
| 3 Dec | A45 Service Station | SL | | 140 | 3 | | | 140 | |
| 4 Dec | Sales | GL | 188 | 188 | | 56 | 320 | | |
| 5 Dec | Sales | GL | 235 | | | 35 | 200 | | |
| | | | 1,195 | 1,898 | 3 | 168 | 960 | 335 | |
| 6 Dec | Balances b/d | | 169 | 1,183 | | | | | |

**Cr (Payments)**

| Date | Details | Folio | Cash | Bank | Discount received | VAT | Purchases | Purchases ledger | Sundry |
|------|---------|-------|------|------|-------------------|-----|-----------|------------------|--------|
| 20-7 | | | £ | £ | £ | £ | £ | £ | £ |
| 2 Dec | Rent | GL | | 325 | | | | | 325 |
| 2 Dec | Boxhall Supplies Limited | PL | | 240 | 10 | | | 240 | |
| 3 Dec | Bank | C | 500 | | | | | | |
| 3 Dec | Office stationery | GL | 47 | | | 7 | | | 40 |
| 4 Dec | Purchases | GL | 94 | | | 14 | 80 | | |
| 5 Dec | Vord Supplies | PL | | 150 | 5 | | | 150 | |
| 5 Dec | Wages | GL | 385 | | | | | | 385 |
| 5 Dec | Balances c/d | | 169 | 1,183 | | | | | |
| | | | 1,195 | 1,898 | 15 | 21 | 80 | 390 | 750 |

## notes

- The analysed cash book analyses each receipt and payment between a number of headings. A business will adapt the cash book and use whatever analysis columns suit it best.

- For transactions involving sales ledger and purchases ledger, no amount for VAT is shown in the VAT columns. This is because VAT has been charged on invoices issued and received and was recorded in the VAT account (via the day books) when the sale or purchase was made.

- The cash and bank columns are balanced in the way described on page 104.

- The analysis columns are totalled at the end of the week and transferred to other accounts as follows:
  - discount allowed column total of £3 is debited to discount allowed account in the general (or nominal) ledger
  - discount received column total of £15 is credited to discount received account in the general (or nominal) ledger
  - Value Added Tax columns, the total of £168 is credited to VAT account in the general ledger, while the total of £21 is debited to the VAT account
  - sales column total of £960 is credited to sales account in the general ledger
  - purchases column total of £80 is debited to purchases account in the general ledger

- For a business which uses control accounts (see Chapter 20), the totals from the columns are also transferred directly to the control accounts as follows:
  - discount allowed, to the credit side of sales ledger control account
  - discount received, to the debit side of purchases ledger control account
  - sales ledger, to the credit side of sales ledger control account
  - purchases ledger, to the debit side of purchases ledger control account

## CHAPTER SUMMARY

- The cash book records receipts (debits) and payments (credits) both in cash (except for low-value expense payments) and by cheque.

- A basic layout for a cash book has money columns for cash transactions and bank transactions on both the debit and credit sides, together with a further column on each side for discounts.

- In the discount columns are recorded cash discounts: discounts allowed (to customers) on the debit side, and discounts received (from suppliers) on the payments side.

- Another common cash book layout incorporates columns for VAT.

- An analysed cash book is used to provide more information: it divides receipts and payments between a number of categories.

In the next chapter we will see how the petty cash book is used to record low-value expense payments.

# QUESTIONS

NOTE: an asterisk (*) after the question number means that an answer to the question is given in Appendix 2.

**8.1\*** You work as the cashier for Wyvern Publishing, a company which publishes a wide range of travel and historical books. As cashier, your main responsibility is for the firm's cash book. Explain to a friend what your job involves and the qualities required of a cashier.

**8.2\*** Walter Harrison is a sole trader who records his cash and bank transactions in a three-column cash book. The following are the transactions for June 20-2:

| | |
|---|---|
| 1 June | Balances: cash £280; bank overdraft £2,240 |
| 3 June | Received a cheque from G Wheaton for £195, in full settlement of a debt of £200 |
| 5 June | Received cash of £53 from T Francis, in full settlement of a debt of £55 |
| 8 June | Paid the amount owing to F Lloyd by cheque: the total amount due is £400 and Harrison takes advantage of a 2.5% per cent cash discount |
| 10 June | Paid wages in cash £165 |
| 12 June | Paid A Morris in cash, £100 less 3 per cent cash discount |
| 16 June | Withdrew £200 in cash from the bank for use in the business |
| 18 June | Received a cheque for £640 from H Watson in full settlement of a debt of £670 |
| 20 June | Paid R Marks £78 by cheque |
| 24 June | Paid D Farr £65 by cheque, in full settlement of a debt of £67 |
| 26 June | Paid telephone account £105 in cash |
| 28 June | Received a cheque from M Perry in settlement of his account of £240 – he has deducted 2.5% per cent cash discount |
| 30 June | Received cash £45 from K Willis |

You are to:

(a) enter the above transactions in Harrison's three column cash book, balance the cash and bank columns, and carry the balances down to 1 July

(b) total the two discount columns and transfer them to the appropriate accounts

**8.3** On 1 August 20-7, the balances in the cash book of Metro Trading Company were:

| | |
|---|---|
| Cash | £276 debit |
| Bank | £4,928 debit |

Transactions for the month were:

| | |
|---|---|
| 1 Aug | Received a cheque from Wild & Sons Limited, £398 |
| 5 Aug | Paid T Hall Limited a cheque for £541 in full settlement of a debt of £565 |

| 8 Aug | Paid wages in cash £254 |
|---|---|
| 11 Aug | Withdrew £500 in cash from the bank for use in the business |
| 12 Aug | Received a cheque for £1,755 from A Lewis Limited in full settlement of their account of £1,775 |
| 18 Aug | Paid F Jarvis £457 by cheque |
| 21 Aug | Received a cheque for £261 from Harvey & Sons Limited |
| 22 Aug | Paid wages in cash £436 |
| 25 Aug | Paid J Jones a cheque for £628 in full settlement of a debt of £661 |
| 27 Aug | Paid salaries by cheque £2,043 |
| 28 Aug | Paid telephone account by cheque £276 |
| 29 Aug | Received a cheque for £595 from Wild & Sons Limited in full settlement of their account of £610 |
| 29 Aug | Withdrew £275 in cash from the bank for use in the business |

All cheques are banked on the day of receipt.

You are to:
- Enter the above transactions in the three column cash book of Metro Trading Company.
- Balance the cash and bank columns at 31 August, and carry the balances down to September 1st.
- Total the two discount columns.

8.4 Thelma Cook keeps a 3-column Cash Book for her business. The following information referred to the month of March Year 6:

Year 6

| 1 March | Balances of Cash and Bank were £106 and £3,214 respectively |
|---|---|
| 2 March | Drew cheque no 10674 for rent of £250 |
| 3 March | Sales £1,050. Banked £950 of this on the same day |
| 5 March | Paid cleaning expenses of £35 from cash |
| 8 March | Sales banked £1,680 |
| 9 March | Drew cheque no 10675 for purchases costing £1,200 |
| 11 March | Drew cheque no 10676 for £150, to replenish cash in hand |
| 13 March | Sales banked £1,800 |
| 16 March | Paid postage of £50 from Cash |
| 18 March | Drew cheque no 10677 for £168, to pay a telephone bill |
| 20 March | Paid Stationery of £128 from Cash |
| 22 March | Drew cheque no 10678 for £150, to replenish cash in hand |
| 25 March | Sales banked £2,108 |

| 26 March | Paid miscellaneous expenses of £70 from Cash |
|---|---|
| 27 March | Drew cheque no 10679 for £2,000, to pay Wages |
| 29 March | Sales £2,200. Banked £2,000 of this on the same day |
| 30 March | Drew cheque no 10680 for £106, to pay an electricity bill |
| 31 March | Drew cheque no 10681 for £855 payable to D Coyne, in settlement of a debt of £900 |
| 31 March | Drew cheque no 10682 for £494 payable to F Cox, in settlement of a debt of £520 |
| 31 March | Received cheque for £720 from S Britton, in settlement of an amount of £750 |
| 31 March | Received cheque for £1,160 from D F Pratt, in settlement of an amount of £1,210 |

Required:
Write up the 3-column Cash Book, bringing down the balances at 1 April Year 6.

*LCCI Examinations Board*

**8.5\***  On 1 April 20-7, the balances in the cash book of Johnson Brothers were:

> Cash  £85 debit
>
> Bank  £718 credit (the business has a bank overdraft limit of £2,000)

Transactions for the month were:

| 3 Apr | Paid travelling expenses of £65 in cash |
|---|---|
| 4 Apr | Paid the telephone bill of £235 (including £35 of Value Added Tax) by cheque |
| 7 Apr | Jim Bowen, a debtor, settles an invoice for £90, paying £85 in cash and receiving £5 discount for prompt settlement |
| 10 Apr | Cash sales £470 (including Value Added Tax) received by cheque and paid into the bank |
| 14 Apr | Paid an invoice for £190 from M Hughes (a creditor) by cheque for £180, £10 being received for prompt settlement |
| 17 Apr | Cash purchases of £94 (including Value Added Tax) paid by cheque |
| 18 Apr | Received a cheque for £575 from J Burrows, a debtor, in full settlement of an invoice for £600 |
| 21 Apr | Cash sales of £188 (including Value Added Tax) received in cash |
| 22 Apr | Withdrew £200 in cash from the bank for use in the business |
| 24 Apr | Paid a cheque for £245 to Wilson Limited, a creditor, in full settlement of an invoice for £255 |
| 25 Apr | Paid wages in cash £350 |

You are to:
- Enter the above transactions in the cash book of Johnson Brothers, using columns for dates, details, discount, VAT, cash and bank.
- Balance the cash book at 30 April 20-7.
- Show how the totals for the discount and VAT columns will be entered in the accounts in the general ledger.

Calculate Value Added Tax at 17.5%.
All cheques are banked on the day of receipt.

**8.6**

David Lewis runs a shop selling carpets. He buys carpets from the manufacturers and sells to the public on cash terms and also to a few trade customers – such as carpet fitters – on credit terms. His business is registered for VAT.

He uses a cash book which analyses receipts between:
- discount allowed
- VAT
- sales
- sales ledger
- sundry

Payments are analysed between:
- discount received
- VAT
- purchases
- purchases ledger
- sundry

The following transactions take place during the week commencing 12 May 20-7 (all cheques are banked on the day of receipt):

| | |
|---|---|
| 12 May | Balances from previous week: cash £205.75, bank £825.30 |
| 12 May | Sales £534.62 (including VAT), cheque received |
| 12 May | Paid shop rent by cheque £255.50 (no VAT) |
| 13 May | Sales £164.50 (including VAT), cash received |
| 13 May | A debtor, T Jarvis, settles an invoice for £157.50, paying £155.00 by cheque, £2.50 discount being allowed for prompt settlement |
| 13 May | Paid an invoice for £368.20 from Terry Carpets Limited (a creditor) by cheque for £363.55 and receiving £4.65 discount for prompt settlement |
| 14 May | Sales £752.00 (including VAT), cheque received |

14 May Paid for stationery in cash, £28.20 (including VAT)

15 May Transferred £250 of cash into the bank

15 May Sales £264.37 (including VAT), cash received

15 May Paid an invoice for £295.80 from Longlife Carpets Limited (a creditor), paying £291.50 by cheque, £4.30 discount being received for prompt settlement

16 May Paid wages £314.20 in cash

16 May A debtor, Wyvern District Council, settles an invoice for £565.45, paying £560.45 by cheque and receiving £5.00 discount for prompt settlement

You are to:

- Enter the above transactions in the analysed cash book of David Lewis (VAT amounts should be rounded down to the nearest penny).

- Balance the cash book at 16 May 20-7.

- Explain how the totals for the columns will be entered in the accounts in the general ledger (David Lewis does not use control accounts).

Calculate Value Added Tax at 17.5%.

# 9 PETTY CASH BOOK

A petty cash book is used to record low-value cash payments for various small purchases and expenses incurred by a business or other organisation.

An amount of cash is handed by the main cashier to a member of staff, the petty cashier, who will be responsible for security of the money, and will make payments as appropriate against authorised petty cash vouchers.

In the context of the accounting system, the petty cash book is both

- a primary accounting record
- part of the double-entry system

## THE PETTY CASH PROCEDURE

The petty cash book is used to record low-value cash payments for purchases and expenses such as small items of stationery, postages, etc, items which it would not be appropriate to enter in the main cash book. Instead, an amount of cash is handed by the main cashier to a member of staff, the petty cashier, who is responsible for control of the petty cash, making cash payments when appropriate, keeping records of payments made and balancing the petty cash book at regular intervals.

In order to operate the petty cash system, the petty cashier needs the following:

- a petty cash book in which to record transactions
- a lockable cash box in which to keep the money
- a stock of blank petty cash vouchers (see page 120) for claims on petty cash to be made
- a lockable desk drawer in which to keep these items

### making a claim

An employee of a business is most likely to encounter the petty cash system when making claims for money for small purchases made. Before studying the form-filling procedures in detail, read the summary of a typical petty cash transaction set out below:

Your supervisor asks you to go and buy a box of computer disks from an office supplies shop.

You go to the shop and buy the computer disks. You pay for them in cash and keep the receipt (for £5.50) which you hand to the petty cashier on your return to the office.

The supervisor authorises a petty cash voucher which contains details of the purchase.

The petty cashier gives you £5.50 in cash.

The petty cashier attaches the receipt to the petty cash voucher and enters the details in the petty cash book.

## what items can be passed through petty cash book?

Petty cash is used to make small cash payments for purchases and expenses incurred by the business. Examples of the type of payments made from petty cash include:

- stationery items
- small items of office supplies
- casual wages
- window cleaning
- bus, rail and taxi fares (incurred on behalf of the business)
- meals and drinks (incurred on behalf of the business)
- postages
- tips and donations

Note that petty cash should not be used to pay for private expenses of employees, eg tea, coffee, and milk, unless the business has agreed these in advance. Usually the petty cashier will have a list of approved expenses which can be reimbursed.

A business will also decide on the maximum value of each transaction that can be paid out of petty cash; for example, £25 is a common figure.

## WORKED EXAMPLE: PETTY CASH EXPENSES

### question

You are working as an accounts clerk for Wyvern Engineering Limited. One of your duties is that of petty cashier.  Which of the following expenses would you allow to be paid out of petty cash?
*   envelopes for use in the office, £2.50
*   postage on an urgent parcel of engineering parts, £3.75
*   bus fare to work claimed by secretary £1.20
*   car mileage to work of office manager called in late at night when the burglar alarm went off (false alarm!), £5.50
*   tea and coffee for use in the office, £3.70
*   office window cleaning, £2.80
*   pot plant bought for reception area, £5.50
*   computer disks, £35.00
*   donation to local charity by the business, £5.00
*   meal allowance paid to a member of staff required to work during the lunch hour, £3.50

### answer

For most expenses it is clear whether or not they can be drawn from petty cash.  However, there are points to consider for some of the expenses.

| | |
|---|---|
| **Envelopes** | pay from petty cash |
| **Postage** | pay from petty cash |
| **Bus fare to work** | this is a personal expense and cannot be drawn from petty cash |
| **Car mileage** | travel to work is a personal expense, as seen with the previous item; however, as this expense was a special journey in the middle of the night in order to resolve a business problem, it can be paid from petty cash |
| **Tea and coffee** | this is a personal expense of employees and cannot normally be paid out of petty cash; however, if the ingredients were used to make drinks for official visitors and customers, it can be paid from petty cash |
| **Window cleaning** | pay from petty cash |
| **Pot plant** | pay from petty cash (but plants for the general office cannot be bought with the company's money) |
| **Computer disks** | this is a business expense but, in view of the amount (too large for petty cash), it should be paid by cheque from the cash book |
| **Donation** | pay from petty cash |
| **Meal allowance** | pay from petty cash, provided that it is company policy to make an allowance in these circumstances |

**notes**

- If the petty cashier is unable to resolve whether or not an expense can be paid from petty cash, the item should be referred to the accounts supervisor for a decision.

- Before payments can be made for petty cash expenses, they must be:
  - within the prescribed limit for petty cash expenses (for example, £25 maximum for any one expense item)
  - supported by documentary evidence, such as a receipt or a rail/bus ticket
  - authorised by the appropriate supervisor or manager

## THE IMPREST SYSTEM

Most petty cash books operate on the imprest system. With this method the petty cashier starts each week (or month) with a certain amount of money – the imprest amount. As payments are made during the week (or month) the amount of money will reduce and, at the end of the period, the cash will be made up by the main cashier to the imprest amount. For example:

| | |
|---|---|
| Started week with imprest amount | £100.00 |
| Total of petty cash amounts paid out during week | £80.50 |
| Cash held at end of week | £19.50 |
| Amount drawn from cashier to restore imprest amount | £80.50 |
| Cash at start of next week, ie imprest amount | £100.00 |

If, at any time, the imprest amount proves to be insufficient, further amounts of cash can be drawn from the cashier. Also, from time-to-time, it may be necessary to increase the imprest amount so that regular shortfalls are avoided.

## PETTY CASH VOUCHER

Payments out of petty cash are made only against correct documentation – usually a petty cash voucher (illustrated on the next page). Petty cash vouchers are completed as follows:

- details and amount of expenditure
- signature of the person making the claim and receiving the money
- signature of the person authorising the payment to be made
- additionally, most petty cash vouchers are numbered, so that they can be controlled, the number being entered in the petty cash book
- relevant documentation, eg receipt, should be attached to the petty cash voucher

Petty cash vouchers are the prime documents for the petty cash book.

```
petty cash voucher                          No.  807

                                date    12 May 20-7

description                                 amount (£)

C5 Envelopes                         │  1  │  50
10 Floppy disks                      │  6  │  50
                                     ├─────┼──────
                                     │  8  │  00
                         VAT         │  1  │  40
                                     │  9  │  40

signature     T Harris

authorised    R Singh
```

# LAYOUT OF A PETTY CASH BOOK

The petty cash book is both the primary accounting record and part of the double-entry system for petty cash transactions. Petty cash book can be set out as follows:

| Receipts | Date | Details | Voucher number | Total payment | ANALYSIS COLUMNS | | | | |
|---|---|---|---|---|---|---|---|---|---|
| | | | | | VAT | Postages | Stationery | Travel | Ledger |
| £ | | | | £ | £ | £ | £ | £ | £ |

The layout shows that:

- receipts from the main cashier are entered in the column on the extreme left
- there are columns for the date and details of all receipts and payments
- there is a column for the petty cash voucher number
- the total payment (ie the amount paid out on each petty cash voucher) is in the next column
- then follow the analysis columns which analyse each transaction entered in the 'total payment' column (note that VAT may need to be calculated – see below)

A business or organisation will use whatever analysis columns are most suitable for it and, indeed, there may be more columns than shown in the example. It is important that expenses are analysed to the correct columns so that the contents show a true picture of petty cash expenditure.

## PETTY CASH AND VAT

Value Added Tax is charged by VAT-registered businesses on their taxable supplies. Therefore, there will often be VAT included as part of the expense paid out of petty cash. However, not all expenses will have been subject to VAT. There are four possible circumstances:

* VAT has been charged at the standard rate
* VAT has not been charged because the supplier is not VAT-registered
* the zero rate of VAT applies, eg food and drink (but not meals which are standard-rated), books, newspapers, transport (but not taxis and hire cars)
* the supplies are exempt (eg financial services, postal services)

Often the indication of the supplier's VAT registration number on a receipt or invoice will tell you that VAT has been charged at the standard rate.

Where VAT has been charged, the amount of tax might be indicated separately on the receipt or invoice. However, for small money amounts it is quite usual for a total to be shown without indicating the amount of VAT. An example of a receipt which does not show the VAT content is illustrated below. The receipt is for a box of envelopes purchased from Wyvern Stationers. It shows:

* the name and address of the retailer
* the date and time of the transaction
* the VAT registration number of the retailer
* the price of the item – £4.70
* the amount of money given – a £10 note
* the amount of change given – £5.30

|  | Wyvern Stationers |
|---|---|
|  | 25 High St Mereford |
|  | 08 10 07  16.07 |
|  | VAT Reg 454 7106 34 |
| Salesperson | Rashid |
| Stationery | 4.70 |
| TOTAL | 4.70 |
| CASH | 10.00 |
| CHANGE | 5.30 |

What it does not show, however, is the VAT content of the purchase price – it only shows the price after the VAT has been added on.

How do you calculate purchase price before the VAT is added on?

The formula, with VAT at 17.5%, is:

price including VAT $\div$ 1.175 = price before VAT is added on

in this case ...

£4.70 $\div$ 1.175 = £4.00 = price before VAT is added on

The VAT content is therefore:

£4.70 less £4.00 = 70p

Here £0.70 will be entered in the VAT column in the petty cash book, £4.00 in the appropriate expense column, and the full £4.70 in the total payment column.

Remember when calculating VAT amounts that fractions of a penny are ignored, ie the tax is rounded down to a whole penny.

## WORKED EXAMPLE: PETTY CASH BOOK

A business keeps a petty cash book, which is operated on the imprest system. There are a number of authorised transactions (all of which, unless otherwise indicated, include VAT at 17.5%) to be entered for the week in the petty cash book:

|  |  |
|---|---|
| 20-7 | |
| 7 Apr | Started the week with an imprest amount of £50.00 |
| 7 Apr | Paid stationery £3.76 on voucher no. 47 |
| 7 Apr | Paid taxi fare £2.82 on voucher no. 48 |
| 8 Apr | Paid postages £0.75 (no VAT) on voucher no. 49 |
| 9 Apr | Paid taxi fare £4.70 on voucher no. 50 |
| 9 Apr | Paid J Jones, a creditor, £6.00 (no VAT shown in petty cash book – amount will be on VAT account already) on voucher no. 51 |
| 10 Apr | Paid stationery £3.76 on voucher no. 52 |
| 10 Apr | Paid postages £2.85 (no VAT) on voucher no. 53 |
| 11 Apr | Paid taxi fare £6.11 on voucher no. 54 |
| 11 Apr | Cash received to restore imprest amount, and petty cash book balanced at the end of the week |

The petty cash book is written up as follows:

| Receipts | Date | Details | Voucher number | Total payment | ANALYSIS COLUMNS | | | | |
|---|---|---|---|---|---|---|---|---|---|
| | | | | | VAT | Postages | Stationery | Travel | Ledger |
| £ | 20-7 | | | £ | £ | £ | £ | £ | £ |
| 50.00 | 7 April | Balance b/d | | | | | | | |
| | 7 April | Stationery | 47 | 3.76 | 0.56 | | 3.20 | | |
| | 7 April | Taxi fare | 48 | 2.82 | 0.42 | | | 2.40 | |
| | 8 April | Postages | 49 | 0.75 | | 0.75 | | | |
| | 9 April | Taxi fare | 50 | 4.70 | 0.70 | | | 4.00 | |
| | 9 April | J Jones | 51 | 6.00 | | | | | 6.00 |
| | 10 April | Stationery | 52 | 3.76 | 0.56 | | 3.20 | | |
| | 10 April | Postages | 53 | 2.85 | | 2.85 | | | |
| | 11 April | Taxi fare | 54 | 6.11 | 0.91 | | | 5.20 | |
| | | | | 30.75 | 3.15 | 3.60 | 6.40 | 11.60 | 6.00 |
| 30.75 | 11 April | Cash received | | | | | | | |
| | 11 April | Balance c/d | | 50.00 | | | | | |
| 80.75 | | | | 80.75 | | | | | |
| 50.00 | 11 April | Balance b/d | | | | | | | |

## PETTY CASH AND DOUBLE-ENTRY BOOK-KEEPING

When the petty cash book has been balanced, the petty cashier will prepare a summary which shows:

- debits to expenses accounts (and VAT account) in the general ledger in respect of each expenses column
- debits to creditors' accounts in the purchases ledger in respect of the ledger column (eg J Jones in the Worked Example)
- credit to cash book, being the amount drawn from the main cashier to restore the imprest amount of the petty cash book

For example, the postages in the worked example on the previous page will be debited as follows:

| Dr | | **Postages Account** | | Cr |
|----|----|----|----|----|
| 20-7 | | £ | 20-7 | £ |
| 11 Apr | Petty cash book | 3.60 | | |

From the petty cash book, debits are passed to the general ledger accounts as follows:

- VAT account, £3.15
- stationery account, £6.40
- postages account, £3.60
- travel expenses account, £11.60

The amount in the ledger column, £6.00, is debited to the account of J Jones in the purchases ledger.

Total debits in the Worked Example are £30.75 and this is the amount that has been drawn from the main cashier on 11 April. The petty cashier will complete a cheque requisition form either for the cash itself, or for a cheque made payable to cash. The petty cashier will take the cheque to the bank and obtain the cash. An example of a cheque requisition is shown on the next page.

The cheque is credited in the firm's cash book, so completing double-entry :

- debit petty cash book      £30.75
- credit cash book      £30.75

If a trial balance is extracted on 11 April (after the analysis columns have been debited to the respective accounts, and a credit entered in the cash book to restore the imprest amount) the balance of petty cash, £50.00, must be included as a debit balance in the trial balance – this is because petty cash book is part of the double-entry system.

```
┌─────────────────────────────────────────────┐
│                                               │
│   CHEQUE REQUISITION                          │
│                                               │
│   Amount          £30.75                      │
│                                               │
│   Payee           Cash                        │
│                                               │
│   Date            11 April 20-7               │
│                                               │
│   Details         Reimbursement of petty cash │
│                                               │
│   Signature       Jane Watkins, petty cashier │
│                                               │
│   Authorised by   Natalie Wilson, supervisor  │
│                                               │
│   Cheque no       017234                      │
│                                               │
└─────────────────────────────────────────────┘
```

*cheque requisition form*

# CONTROL OF PETTY CASH

In most businesses the petty cashier is responsible to the office manager for control of the petty cash and for correct recording of authorised petty cash transactions. Many businesses will set out in writing the procedures to be followed by the petty cashier. This is of benefit not only for the petty cashier to know the extent of his or her duties, but also to help the person who takes over at holiday or other times.

The main procedures for the operation and control of petty cash are:

- On taking over, the petty cashier should check that the petty cash book has been balanced and that the amount of cash held agrees with the balance shown in the book. If there is any discrepancy, this should be referred to the office manager immediately.
- Ensure that each week is started with the imprest amount of cash which has been agreed with the office manager.
- The petty cash is to be kept securely in a locked cash box, and control kept of the keys.
- Petty cash vouchers (in number order) are to be provided on request.
- Petty cash is paid out against correctly completed petty cash vouchers after checking that:
  - the voucher is signed by the person receiving the money
  - the voucher is signed by the person authorising payment (a list of authorised signatories will be provided)
  - a receipt (whenever possible) is attached to the petty cash voucher, and that receipt and petty cash voucher are for the same amount
- The petty cash book is written up (to include calculation of VAT amounts when appropriate), it is important that the petty cash book is accurate.

- Completed petty cash vouchers are stored safely – filed in numerical order. The vouchers will need to be kept for at least six years in the company's archives. They may be needed by the firm's auditors or in the event of other queries. Completed petty cash books will also need to be retained.
- A surprise check of petty cash will be made by the office manager – at any one time the cash held plus amounts of petty cash vouchers should equal the imprest amount.
- At the end of each week (or month) the petty cash book is to be balanced and an amount of cash drawn from the cashier equal to the amount of payments made, in order to restore the imprest amount.
- Details of the totals of each analysis column are to be given to the book-keeper so that the amount of each expense can be entered into the double-entry system.
- The petty cash book and cash in hand are to be presented to the office manager for checking.
- Any discrepancies are to be dealt with promptly; these may include:
  - a receipt and petty cash voucher total differing – the matter should be queried with the person who made the purchase
  - a difference between the totals of the analysis columns and the total payments column in the petty cash book – check the addition of the columns, the figures against the vouchers, the VAT calculations (does the VAT plus the analysis column amount equal the total payment amount?)
  - a difference between the cash in the petty cash box and the balance shown in the petty cash book – if this is not an arithmetic difference it may be a case of theft, and should be reported promptly to the office manager
  - where discrepancies and queries cannot be resolved, they should be referred to the office manager
- All aspects of petty cash are confidential and should not be discussed with others.

## CHAPTER SUMMARY

- The petty cash book records payments for a variety of low-value business expenses.

- The person responsible for maintaining the petty cash book is the petty cashier.

- Payment can only be made from the petty cash book against correct documentation – usually a petty cash voucher, which must be signed by the person authorising payment.

- Where a business is registered for Value Added Tax, it must record VAT amounts paid on petty cash purchases in a separate column in the petty cash book.

- At regular intervals – weekly or monthly – the petty cash book will be balanced; the main cashier will restore the imprest amount of cash and the total of each analysis column will be debited to the relevant account in the book-keeping system.

# QUESTIONS

NOTE: an asterisk (*) after the question number means that an answer to the question is given in Appendix 2.

**9.1\***  You work as an accounts clerk in the office of Temeside Printers Limited. One of your duties is that of petty cashier. Which of the following expenses will you allow to be paid out of petty cash?

(a)     postage on a parcel of printing sent to a customer, £3.85

(b)     a rubber date stamp bought for use in the office, £4.60

(c)     rail fare to work claimed by the office manager's secretary, £2.50

(d)     donation to charity, £5.00

(e)     tea and coffee for use by office staff, £5.50

(f)     mileage allowance claimed by works foreman who had to visit a customer, £4.80

(g)     meal allowance paid to assistant who had to work her lunch hour, £4.00

(h)     window cleaning, £3.50

(i)     purchase of shelving for the office, £55.00

(j)     taxi fare claimed for delivering an urgent parcel of printing to a customer, £6.25

Explain any expenses that you will refer to the accounts supervisor.

**9.2**  You are going on holiday and handing your job as petty cashier to a colleague who is not familiar with the security and confidentiality aspects of the job, although she can manage the paperwork. Prepare a checklist of the security and safety aspects of the job so that she can learn them more easily. Write them out as bullet points rather than as solid text – they will be more easily remembered in this format.

**9.3**  As petty cashier, prepare the petty cash vouchers shown on the next page under today's date for signature by the person making the claim.  You are authorised to approve payments up to £10.00.

Voucher no. 851:  £4.45 claimed by Jayne Smith for postage (no VAT) on an urgent parcel of spare parts sent to a customer, Evelode Supplies Limited.

Voucher no. 852:  £2.35 (including VAT) claimed by Tanya Howard for air mail envelopes bought for use in the office. Show on the petty cash voucher the amount of VAT.

What documentation will you require to be attached to each voucher?

**petty cash voucher**
No. 851

date

description
amount (£)

VAT

signature

authorised

**petty cash voucher**
No. 852

date

description
amount (£)

VAT

signature

authorised

**9.4**

S Rodger maintains her petty cash book on the imprest system; the imprest figure was set at £200. On 1 June Year 8 the balance of petty cash was £120. On that date she withdrew money from the bank to restore the balance to the imprest figure. During June Year 8 the following transactions took place:

| | |
|---|---|
| 2 June | Paid £5.20 for postage |
| 6 June | Paid £12.70 for rail fare |
| 9 June | Paid £8.50 for petrol |
| 14 June | Paid £10.00 for cleaning materials |
| 16 June | Paid £18.30 to S Lancaster, a creditor |

18 June     Paid £14.30 for petrol

20 June     Paid £6.70 for postage

24 June     Paid £12.40 for petrol

25 June     Paid £13.20 for rail fare

27 June     Paid £7.70 for postage

28 June     Paid £19.20 to W Rose, a creditor

30 June     Paid £14.80 for petrol

The analysis columns used by S Rodger are as follows: Postage, Travelling Expenses, Vehicle Expenses, Cleaning Expenses and Ledger Accounts

Required:

Enter the above transactions in S Rodger's Petty Cash Book for June Year 8 using the analysis columns mentioned above. Balance the Petty Cash Book at 30 June Year 8 and carry down the balance and then show the amount drawn from the bank to make up the imprest on 1 July Year 8.

*LCCI Examinations Board*

**9.5\*** The business for which you work is registered for VAT. The following petty cash amounts include VAT at 17.5% and you are required to calculate the amount that will be shown in the VAT column and the appropriate expense column (remember that VAT amounts should be rounded down to the nearest penny):

(a)     £9.40

(b)     £4.70

(c)     £2.35

(d)     £2.45

(e)     £5.60

(f)     £3.47

(g)     £8.75

(h)     94p

(i)     99p

(j)     £9.41

**9.6\*** On returning from holiday, you are told to take over the petty cash book. This is kept on the imprest system, the float being £75.00 at the beginning of each month. Analysis columns are used for VAT, travel, postages, stationery, meals, and miscellaneous.

Enter the following transactions for the month. The voucher amounts include VAT at 17.5% unless indicated.  You can assume that all payments have been authorised by the office manager:

20-7

| | |
|---|---|
| 1 Aug | Balance of cash £75.00 |
| 4 Aug | Voucher 39: taxi fare £3.80 |
| 6 Aug | Voucher 40: parcel postage £2.35 (no VAT) |
| 7 Aug | Voucher 41: pencils £1.26 |
| 11 Aug | Voucher 42: travel expenses £5.46 (no VAT) |
| 12 Aug | Voucher 43: window cleaner £8.50 (no VAT) |
| 14 Aug | Voucher 44: large envelopes £2.45 |
| 18 Aug | Voucher 45: donation to charity £5 (no VAT) |
| 19 Aug | Voucher 46: rail fare £5.60 (no VAT); meal allowance £5.00 (no VAT) |
| 20 Aug | Voucher 47: recorded delivery postage £0.75 (no VAT) |
| 22 Aug | Voucher 48: roll of packing tape £1.50 |
| 25 Aug | Voucher 49: excess postage paid £0.55 (no VAT) |
| 27 Aug | Voucher 50: taxi fare £5.40 |
| 29 Aug | Petty cash book balanced and cash received from cashier to restore imprest amount to £75.00 |

You are to show how the following will be recorded in the double-entry book-keeping system:

- the totals of the analysis columns
- the transfer of cash from the main cashier on 29 August

**9.7** Prepare a petty cash book with analysis columns for VAT, postages, travel, meals, and sundry office expenses.  Enter the following authorised transactions for the week. The voucher amounts include VAT at 17.5% unless indicated.

20-7

| | |
|---|---|
| 2 June | Balance of cash £100.00 |
| 2 June | Postages £6.35 (no VAT), voucher 123 |
| 3 June | Travel expenses £3.25 (no VAT), voucher 124 |
| 3 June | Postages £1.28 (no VAT), voucher 125 |
| 4 June | Envelopes £4.54, voucher 126 |
| 4 June | Window cleaning £5.50, voucher 127 |

5 June    Taxi fare £4.56, meals £10.85, voucher 128

5 June    Postages £8.56 (no VAT), packing materials £3.25, voucher 129

5 June    Taxi fare £4.50, meals £7.45, voucher 130

6 June    Marker pens £2.55, envelopes £3.80, voucher 131

6 June    Petty cash book balanced and cash received from cashier to restore imprest amount to £100.00

You are to show how the following will be recorded in the double-entry book-keeping system:

• the totals of the analysis columns

• the transfer of cash from the main cashier on 6 June

**9.8\***   Draw up a petty cash book with appropriate analysis columns and a VAT column, and enter the following transactions for the month. The voucher amounts include VAT at 17.5% unless indicated:

20-1

1 May    Balance of cash £150.00

1 May    Postages £7.00, voucher no 455, travel £2.85, voucher no 456 (no VAT on postages and travel)

2 May    Meal allowance £6.11, voucher no 457 (no VAT)

3 May    Taxi £4.70, voucher no 458

4 May    Stationery £3.76, voucher no 459

7 May    Postages £5.25, voucher no 460 (no VAT)

8 May    Travel £6.50, voucher no 461 (no VAT)

9 May    Meal allowance £6.11, voucher no 462 (no VAT)

10 May    Stationery £8.46, voucher no 463

14 May    Taxi £5.17, voucher no 464

17 May    Stationery £4.70, voucher no 465

21 May    Travel £3.50, voucher no 466, postages £4.50, voucher no 467 (no VAT on travel and postages)

23 May    Bus fares £3.80, voucher no 468 (no VAT)

26 May    Catering expenses £10.81, voucher no 469

27 May    Postages £3.50, voucher no 470 (no VAT), stationery £7.52, voucher no 471

28 May    Travel expenses £6.45, voucher no 472 (no VAT)

31 May    Cash received from cashier to restore imprest amount to £150.00

9.9

S Stevens runs a business where all receipts are paid into the firm's bank account at the end of each day. All payments are made by cheque except for those items costing less than £25 which are considered to be petty cash items.

The following transactions took place in February 20-8:

|  |  | £ |
|---|---|---:|
| 1 Feb | Balance at the bank (overdrawn) | 1,598.55 |
| | Petty cash balance | 30.40 |
| | Received an amount in cash from the bank to restore the imprest to £200 | |
| 5 Feb | Paid insurance | 120.50 |
| | Paid rent | 240.00 |
| | A cheque was received from S Kahn | 3,250.60 |
| | Paid for refreshments | 15.30 |
| | Bought postage stamps | 22.90 |
| 10 Feb | Paid sundry expenses | 12.45 |
| | Cash sales | 88.25 |
| 12 Feb | B Shean settled his account of £145 with a cheque for £140 | |
| | Received a cheque from H Shanks | 335.85 |
| | Paid cleaner's wages | 20.00 |
| 16 Feb | Paid motor expenses | 120.00 |
| | Paid a cheque for the purchase of goods for resale | 390.55 |
| | Paid for postage | 12.50 |
| | Received a cheque from S Groves in settlement of her account of £1,200 less 5% discount | |
| 19 Feb | S Stevens drew cheque for own use | 50.00 |
| | Paid for refreshments | 22.45 |
| | Sundry expenses | 10.00 |
| 26 Feb | Cash sales | 220.00 |
| | Received a cheque from C Bentley | 435.55 |
| | Paid a cheque for the purchase of goods for resale | 990.50 |

You are required to:

(a) Record the above entries in the petty cash book* and the bank cash book of S Stevens (the first available petty cash voucher is 34).

(b) Balance the accounts at the end of the month.

*Reproduced by kind permission of OCR Examinations*

Author's note: analysis columns for the petty cash book are sundry expenses, cleaning, postage and stationery, refreshments.

# 10 BANK RECONCILIATION STATEMENTS

Bank reconciliation statements form the link between the balance at bank shown in the cash book of a firm's book-keeping system and the balance shown on the bank statement received from the bank.

The reasons why the cash book and bank statement may differ are because:
- there are timing differences caused by:
  - unpresented cheques, ie the time delay between writing out (drawing) a cheque and recording it in the cash book, and the cheque being entered on the bank statement
  - outstanding lodgements, ie amounts paid into the bank, but not yet recorded on the bank statement
- the cash book has not been updated with items which appear on the bank statement and which should also appear in the cash book, eg bank charges

Assuming that there are no errors, both cash book and bank statement are correct, but need to be reconciled with each other, ie the closing balances need to be agreed.

## TIMING DIFFERENCES

The two main timing differences between the bank columns of the cash book and the bank statement are:

- **unpresented cheques**, ie cheques drawn, not yet recorded on the bank statement
- **outstanding lodgements**, ie amounts paid into the bank, not yet recorded on the bank statement

The first of these – unpresented cheques – is caused because, when a cheque is written out, it is immediately entered on the payments side of the cash book, even though it may be some days before the cheque passes through the bank clearing system and is recorded on the bank statement. Therefore, for a few days at least, the cash book shows a lower balance than the bank statement in respect of this cheque. When the cheque is recorded on the bank statement, the difference will disappear. We have looked at only one cheque here, but a business will often be issuing many cheques each day, and the difference between the cash book balance and the bank statement balance may be considerable.

With the second timing difference – outstanding lodgements – the firm's cashier will record a receipt in the cash book as he or she prepares the bank paying-in slip. However, the receipt may not be recorded by the bank on the bank statement for a day or so, particularly if it is paid in late in the day (when the bank will put it into the next day's work), or if it is paid in at a bank branch other than the one at which the account is maintained. Until the receipt is recorded by the bank the cash book will show a higher bank account balance than the bank statement. Once the receipt is entered on the bank statement, the difference will disappear.

These two timing differences are involved in the calculation known as the bank reconciliation statement. The business cash book must not be altered for these because, as we have seen, they will correct themselves on the bank statement as time goes by.

# UPDATING THE CASH BOOK

Besides the timing differences described above, there may be other differences between the bank columns of the cash book and the bank statement, and these do need to be entered in the cash book to bring it up-to-date. For example, the bank might make an automatic standing order payment on behalf of a business – such an item is correctly deducted by the bank, and it might be that the bank statement acts as a reminder to the business cashier of the payment: it should then be entered in the cash book.

Examples of items that show in the bank statement and need to be entered in the cash book include:

### receipts
- standing order and BACS (Bankers' Automated Clearing Services) receipts credited by the bank, eg payments from debtors (customers)
- bank giro credit (credit transfer) amounts received by the bank, eg payments from debtors (customers)
- dividend amounts received by the bank
- interest credited by the bank

### payments
- standing order and direct debit payments
- bank charges and interest
- unpaid cheques debited by the bank (ie cheques from debtors paid in by the business which have 'bounced' and are returned by the bank marked 'refer to drawer')

For each of these items, the cashier needs to check to see if they have been entered in the cash book; if not, they need to be recorded (provided that the bank has not made an error). If the bank has made an error, it must be notified as soon as possible and the incorrect transactions reversed by the bank in its own accounting records.

# THE BANK RECONCILIATION STATEMENT

This forms the link between the balances shown in the cash book and the bank statement.

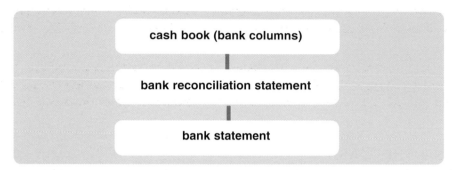

Upon receipt of a bank statement, reconciliation of the two balances is carried out in the following way:

- tick off the items that appear in both cash book and bank statement
- the unticked items on the bank statement are entered into the bank columns of the cash book to bring it up-to-date (provided none are errors made by the bank)
- the bank columns of the cash book are now balanced to find the revised figure
- the remaining unticked items from the cash book will be the timing differences
- the timing differences are used to prepare the bank reconciliation statement, which takes the following format (with example figures):

**XYZ TRADING LTD**
**Bank Reconciliation Statement as at 31 October 20-1**

|  |  |  | £ | £ |
|---|---|---|---:|---:|
| Balance at bank as per cash book |  |  |  | 525 |
|  |  |  |  |  |
| Add: unpresented cheques |  |  |  |  |
| J Lewis | cheque no. 0012378 | | 60 | |
| ABC Ltd | cheque no. 0012392 | | 100 | |
| Eastern Oil Company | cheque no. 0012407 | | 80 | |
|  |  |  |  | 240 |
|  |  |  |  | 765 |
|  |  |  |  |  |
| Less: outstanding lodgements |  |  | 220 | |
|  |  |  | 300 | |
|  |  |  |  | 520 |
| Balance at bank as per bank statement |  |  |  | 245 |

Notes:

- The layout shown on the opposite page starts from the cash book balance, and works towards the bank statement balance. A common variation of this layout is to start with the bank statement balance and to work towards the cash book balance (see page 138).

- If a bank overdraft is involved, brackets should be used around the numbers to indicate this for the cash book or bank statement balance. The timing differences are still added or deducted, as appropriate.

- Once the bank reconciliation statement agrees, it should be filed because it proves that the cash book (bank columns) and bank statement were reconciled at a particular date. If, next time it is prepared, it fails to agree, the previous statement is proof that reconciliation was reached at that time.

## WORKED EXAMPLE: BANK RECONCILIATION STATEMENT

The cashier of Severn Trading Co has written up the firm's cash book for the month of February 20-2, as follows (the cheque number is shown against payments):

| Dr | | | | | Cash Book | | | | | | Cr |
|---|---|---|---|---|---|---|---|---|---|---|---|
| Date | Details | | | Cash | Bank | Date | Details | | | Cash | Bank |
| 20-2 | | | | £ | £ | 20-2 | | | | £ | £ |
| 1 Feb | Balances b/d | | | 250.75 | 1,340.50 | 3 Feb | Appleton Ltd 123456 | | | | 675.25 |
| 7 Feb | A Abbott | | | | 208.50 | 5 Feb | Wages | | | 58.60 | |
| 10 Feb | Sales | | | 145.25 | | 12 Feb | Rent 123457 | | | | 125.00 |
| 13 Feb | Sales | | | 278.30 | | 14 Feb | Transfer to bank | C | | 500.00 | |
| 14 Feb | Transfer from cash | C | | | 500.00 | 17 Feb | D Smith & Co 123458 | | | | 421.80 |
| 20 Feb | Sales | | | 204.35 | | 24 Feb | Stationery | | | 75.50 | |
| 21 Feb | D Richards Limited | | | | 162.30 | 25 Feb | G Christie 123459 | | | | 797.55 |
| 26 Feb | Sales | | | 353.95 | | 27 Feb | Transfer to bank | C | | 500.00 | |
| 27 Feb | Transfer from cash | C | | | 500.00 | 28 Feb | Balances c/d | | | 98.50 | 954.00 |
| 28 Feb | P Paul Limited | | | | 262.30 | | | | | | |
| | | | | 1,232.60 | 2,973.60 | | | | | 1,232.60 | 2,973.60 |
| 1 Mar | Balances b/d | | | 98.50 | 954.00 | | | | | | |

The cash balance of £98.50 shown by the cash columns on 1 March has been agreed with the cash held in the firm's cash box.

The bank statement for February 20-2, which has just been received, is shown on the next page.

⊕ **National Bank plc**

**Branch** ..Bartown..............

TITLE OF ACCOUNT .. Severn Trading Company ................................

ACCOUNT NUMBER .. 67812318 ........................................    STATEMENT NUMBER 45

| DATE | PARTICULARS | PAYMENTS | RECEIPTS | BALANCE |
|---|---|---|---|---|
| 20-2 | | £ | £ | £ |
| 1 Feb | Balance brought forward | | | 1340.50 CR |
| 8 Feb | Credit | | 208.50 | 1549.00 CR |
| 10 Feb | Cheque no. 123456 | 675.25 | | 873.75 CR |
| 17 Feb | Credit | | 500.00 | 1373.75 CR |
| 17 Feb | Cheque no. 123457 | 125.00 | | 1248.75 CR |
| 24 Feb | Credit | | 162.30 | 1411.05 CR |
| 24 Feb | BACS credit: J Jarvis Ltd | | 100.00 | 1511.05 CR |
| 26 Feb | Cheque no. 123458 | 421.80 | | 1089.25 CR |
| 26 Feb | Direct debit: A-Z Finance | 150.00 | | 939.25 CR |
| 28 Feb | Credit | | 500.00 | 1439.25 CR |
| 28 Feb | Bank charges | 10.00 | | 1429.25 CR |

Note that the bank statement is prepared from the bank's viewpoint: thus a credit balance shows that the customer is a creditor of the bank, ie the bank owes the balance to the customer. In the customer's own cash book, the bank is shown as a debit balance, ie an asset.

As the month-end balance at bank shown by the cash book, £954.00, is not the same as that shown by the bank statement, £1,429.25, it is necessary to prepare a bank reconciliation statement. The steps are:

**1**  Tick off the items that appear in both cash book and bank statement.

**2**  The unticked items on the bank statement are entered into the bank columns of the cash book to bring it up-to-date. These are:

- receipt   24 Feb   BACS credit, J Jarvis Limited £100.00
- payments   26 Feb   Direct debit, A-Z Finance £150.00
-    28 Feb   Bank Charges, £10.00

In double-entry book-keeping, the other part of the transaction will need to be recorded in the accounts, eg in J Jarvis Ltd's account in the sales ledger, etc.

**3**  The cash book is now balanced to find the revised balance:

| Dr | | | **Cash Book (bank columns)** | | | Cr |
|---|---|---|---|---|---|---|
| 20-2 | | £ | 20-2 | | | |
| | Balance b/d | 954.00 | 26 Feb | A-Z Finance | | 150.00 |
| 24 Feb | J Jarvis Ltd | 100.00 | 28 Feb | Bank Charges | | 10.00 |
| | | | 28 Feb | Balance c/d | | 894.00 |
| | | 1,054.00 | | | | 1,054.00 |
| 1 Mar | Balance b/d | 894.00 | | | | |

**4** The remaining unticked items from the cash book are used in the bank reconciliation statement:

- receipt 28 Feb – P Paul Limited £262.30
- payment 25 Feb – G Christie (cheque no 123459) £797.55

These items are timing differences, which should appear on next month's bank statement.

**5** The bank reconciliation statement is now prepared, starting with the re-calculated cash book balance of £894.00.

---

**SEVERN TRADING CO.**
**Bank Reconciliation Statement as at 28 February 20-2**

|  | £ |
|---|---|
| Balance at bank as per cash book | 894.00 |
| *Add:* unpresented cheque, no. 123459 | 797.55 |
|  | 1,691.55 |
| *Less:* outstanding lodgement, P Paul Limited | 262.30 |
| Balance at bank as per bank statement | 1,429.25 |

---

With the above, a statement has been produced which starts with the amended balance from the cash book, and finishes with the bank statement balance, ie the two figures are reconciled.

Notes:

- The unpresented cheque is added back to the cash book balance because, until it is recorded by the bank, the cash book shows a lower balance than the bank statement.
- The outstanding lodgement is deducted from the cash book balance because, until it is recorded by the bank, the cash book shows a higher balance than the bank statement.

## PREPARING A BANK RECONCILIATION STATEMENT

In order to help you with the questions at the end of the chapter, here is a step-by-step summary of the procedure. Reconciliation of the cash book balance with that shown in the bank statement should be carried out in the following way:

**1** From the bank columns of the cash book tick off, in both cash book and bank statement, the receipts that appear in both.

**2** From the bank columns of the cash book tick off, in both cash book and bank statement, the payments that appear in both.

**3** Identify the items that are unticked on the bank statement and enter them in the cash book on the debit or credit side, as appropriate. If, however, the bank has made a mistake and debited or credited an amount in error, this should not be entered in the cash book, but should be notified to the bank for them to make the correction. The amount will need to be entered on the bank reconciliation statement – see section below, dealing with unusual items on bank statements: bank errors.

**4** The bank columns of the cash book are now balanced to find the up-to-date balance.

**5** Start the bank reconciliation statement with the balance brought down figure shown in the cash book.

**6** In the bank reconciliation statement add the unticked payments shown in the cash book – these will be unpresented cheques.

**7** In the bank reconciliation statement, deduct the unticked receipts shown in the cash book – these are outstanding lodgements.

**8** The resultant money amount on the bank reconciliation statement is the balance of the bank statement.

The layout which is often used for the bank reconciliation statement is that shown on page 137. The layout starts with the cash book balance and finishes with the bank statement balance. However, there is no reason why it should not commence with the bank statement balance and finish with the cash book balance: with this layout it is necessary to:

- deduct unpresented cheques

- add outstanding lodgements

The bank reconciliation statement of Severn Trading Company (see page 137) would then appear as:

---

**SEVERN TRADING COMPANY**
**Bank Reconciliation Statement as at 28 February 20-2**

|  | £ |
|---|---|
| Balance at bank as per bank statement | 1,429.25 |
| Less: unpresented cheque, no 123459 | 797.55 |
|  | 631.70 |
| Add: outstanding lodgement, P Paul Limited | 262.30 |
| Balance at bank as per cash book | 894.00 |

---

# DEALING WITH UNUSUAL ITEMS ON BANK STATEMENTS

The following are some of the unusual features that may occur on bank statements. As with other accounting discrepancies and queries, where they cannot be resolved they should be referred to a supervisor for guidance.

## out-of-date cheques

These are cheques that are more than six months' old. Where a business has a number of out-of-date – or 'stale' – cheques which have not been debited on the bank statement, they will continue to appear on the bank reconciliation statement. As the bank will not pay these cheques, they can be written back in the cash book, ie debit cash book (and credit the other double-entry account involved).

## returned cheques

A cheque received by a business is entered as a receipt in the cash book and then paid into the bank, but it may be returned by the drawer's (issuer's) bank  to the payee's bank because:

*   the drawer (the issuer) has stopped it
*   the drawer has no money (the cheque may be returned 'refer to drawer') – ie it has 'bounced'

A cheque returned in this way should be entered in the book-keeping system:

*   as a payment in the cash book on the credit side
*   as a debit to the account of the drawer of the cheque in the sales ledger (if it is a credit sale), or sales account if it is a cash sale

On the other hand, if the  business itself stops a cheque, the cheque drawn (issued) by the business will have been entered as a payment in the cash book (a credit). It should now be entered as:

*   a receipt on the debit side
*   a credit to the account of the payee, most probably in the purchases ledger (if it is a credit purchase)

## bank errors

Errors made by the bank can include:

*   A cheque deducted from the bank account which has not been drawn by the business – look for a cheque number on the bank statement that is different from the current cheque series: care, though, as it could be a cheque from an old cheque book.
*   A BACS payment (or other credit) shown on the bank statement for which the business is not the correct recipient. If in doubt, the bank will be able to give further details of the sender of the credit.
*   Standing orders and direct debits paid at the wrong time or for the wrong amounts. A copy of all standing order and direct debit mandates sent to the bank should be kept by the business for reference purposes.

When an error is found, it should be queried immediately with the bank. The item and amount should not be entered in the firm's cash book until the issue has been resolved. If, in the meantime, a bank reconciliation statement is to be prepared, the bank error should be shown separately:

*   if working from the cash book balance to the bank statement balance, deduct payments and add receipts that the bank has applied to the account incorrectly
*   if working from the bank statement balance to the cash book balance, add payments and deduct receipts that the bank has applied to the account incorrectly

## bank charges and interest

From time-to-time the bank will debit business customers' accounts with an amount for:

–   service charges, ie the cost of operating the bank account
–   interest, ie the borrowing cost when the business is overdrawn

Banks usually notify customers in writing before debiting the account.

## reconciliation of opening cash book and bank statement balances

If you look back to the example on page 135, you will see that both the cash book (bank columns) and the bank statement balance both started the month with the same balance: 1 February 20-2 £1,340.50.

In reality, it is unlikely that the opening cash book and bank statement balances will be the same. It will be necessary, in these circumstances, to prepare an opening bank reconciliation statement in order to prove that there are no errors between cash book and bank statement at the start of the month.

This is set out in the same format as the end-of-month bank reconciliation statement, and is best prepared immediately after ticking off the items that appear in both cash book and bank statement. The earliest unpresented cheques drawn and outstanding lodgements will comprise the opening bank reconciliation statement. Of course, where last month's bank reconciliation statement is available, such as in business, there is no need to prepare an opening reconciliation.

# IMPORTANCE OF BANK RECONCILIATION STATEMENTS

● A bank reconciliation statement is important because, in its preparation, the transactions in the bank columns of the cash book are compared with those recorded on the bank statement. In this way, any errors in the cash book or bank statement will be found and can be corrected (or advised to the bank, if the bank statement is wrong).

● The bank statement is an independent accounting record, therefore it will assist in deterring fraud by providing a means of verifying the cash book balance.

● By writing the cash book up-to-date, the organisation has an amended figure for the bank balance to be shown in the trial balance.

● Unpresented cheques over six months old – out-of-date cheques – can be identified and written back in the cash book (any cheque dated more than six months' ago will not be paid by the bank).

● It is good practice to prepare a bank reconciliation statement each time a bank statement is received. The reconciliation statement should be prepared as quickly as possible so that any queries – either with the bank statement or in the firm's cash book – can be resolved. Many firms will specify to their accounting staff the timescales for preparing bank reconciliation statements – as a guideline, if the bank statement is received weekly, then the reconciliation statement should be prepared within five working days.

# RECONCILIATION OF STATEMENTS FROM CREDITORS

Besides bank reconciliation statements, it is often necessary to reconcile the balance shown on a statement of account (see Chapter 4) received from a supplier with the supplier's (creditor's) account in the buyer's books:

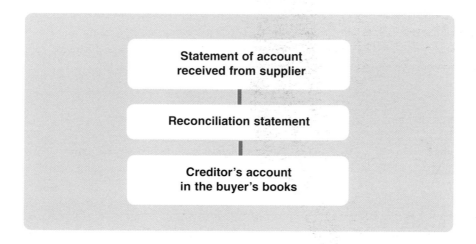

**Statement of account
received from supplier**

**Reconciliation statement**

**Creditor's account
in the buyer's books**

Assuming that there are no errors either on the statement of account or in the creditor's account, the discrepancies are caused by:

* items in transit, which have been invoiced by the supplier, but the invoice is not yet recorded by the buyer

* payments in the post or banking system, recorded by the buyer, but not yet received and recorded on the supplier's statement

* purchases returns, made by buyer but not yet recorded by the supplier

These three discrepancies are all caused by timing differences, ie the business document – invoice, payment, credit note – has not yet been recorded in the accounts of both buyer and seller. The reconciliation statement must take note of these.

## WORKED EXAMPLE: CREDITOR RECONCILIATION STATEMENT

### question

The following creditor's account appears in the purchases ledger of A Jarvis:

| Dr | | £ | 20-1 | | £ |
|---|---|---|---|---|---|
| **T Smith** | | | | | **Cr** |
| 10 Jan | Bank | 200 | 1 Jan | Balance b/d | 200 |
| 30 Jan | Bank | 150 | 12 Jan | Purchases | 150 |
| 31 Jan | Purchases returns | 25 | 25 Jan | Purchases | 125 |
| 31 Jan | Balance c/d | 100 | | | |
| | | 475 | | | 475 |
| | | | 1 Feb | Balance b/d | 100 |

The following statement of account is received from T Smith on 2 February:

| Statement of Account: A Jarvis | | Dr | Cr | Balance | |
|---|---|---|---|---|---|
| 20-1 | | £ | £ | £ | |
| 1 Jan | Balance b/d | 200 | | 200 | Dr |
| 9 Jan | Invoice no 374 | 150 | | 350 | Dr |
| 14 Jan | Payment received: thank you | | 200 | 150 | Dr |
| 20 Jan | Invoice no 382 | 125 | | 275 | Dr |
| 29 Jan | Invoice no 413 | 100 | | 375 | Dr |

You are to reconcile the creditor's account balance with that of the statement received by A Jarvis.

### answer

| Reconciliation of T Smith's statement of account as at 31 January 20-1 | | |
|---|---|---|
| | £ | |
| Balance of account at 31 January 20-1 | 100 | Cr |
| Add: payment sent on 30 January, not yet appearing on statement | 150 | |
| | 250 | Cr |
| Add: invoice no 413 sent by T Smith on 29 January, not yet received | 100 | |
| | 350 | |
| Add: purchases returns to T Smith on 31 January, not yet appearing on statement | 25 | |
| Balance of statement at 31 January 20-1 | 375 | |

As each of these items are timing differences, they will correct themselves within a few days as they are entered into the accounts of buyer and seller.

## CHAPTER SUMMARY

- A bank reconciliation statement is used to agree the balance shown by the bank columns of the cash book with that shown by the bank statement.

- Certain differences between the two are timing differences. The main timing differences are:
  - unpresented cheques
  - outstanding lodgements

  These differences will be corrected by time and, most probably, will be recorded on the next bank statement.

- Certain differences appearing on the bank statement need to be entered in the cash book to bring it up-to-date. These include:

  Receipts
  - standing order and BACS receipts credited by the bank
  - bank giro credit amounts received by the bank
  - dividend amounts received by the bank
  - interest credited by the bank

  Payments
  - standing order and direct debit payments
  - bank charges and interest
  - unpaid cheques debited by the bank

- The bank reconciliation statement makes use of the timing differences.

- Once prepared, a bank reconciliation statement is proof that the bank statement and the cash book (bank columns) were agreed at a particular date.

- Statements of account received from creditors may need to be reconciled with the creditor's account; discrepancies are caused by:
  - items in transit
  - payments in the post or banking system
  - purchases returns

The next chapter looks at the way in which computers are used to handle accounting records.

# QUESTIONS

10.1* The bank columns of Tom Reid's cash book for December 20-7 are as follows:

| 20-7 | Receipts | | £ | 20-7 | Payments | | £ |
|---|---|---|---|---|---|---|---|
| 1 Dec | Balance b/d | | 280 | 9 Dec | W Smith | 345123 | 40 |
| 12 Dec | P Jones | | 30 | 12 Dec | Rent | 345124 | 50 |
| 18 Dec | H Homer | | 72 | 18 Dec | Wages | 345125 | 85 |
| 29 Dec | J Hill | | 13 | 19 Dec | B Kay | 345126 | 20 |
| | | | | 31 Dec | Balance c/d | | 200 |
| | | | 395 | | | | 395 |

He then received his bank statement which showed the following transactions for December 20-7:

| | BANK STATEMENT | | | |
|---|---|---|---|---|
| | | Payments | Receipts | Balance |
| 20-7 | | £ | £ | £ |
| 1 Dec | Balance brought forward | | | 280 CR |
| 12 Dec | Credit | | 30 | 310 CR |
| 15 Dec | Cheque no. 345123 | 40 | | 270 CR |
| 17 Dec | Cheque no. 345124 | 50 | | 220 CR |
| 22 Dec | Credit | | 72 | 292 CR |
| 23 Dec | Cheque no. 345125 | 85 | | 207 CR |

You are to prepare a bank reconciliation statement which agrees with the bank statement balance.

10.2* The following is the Cash Book (bank columns only) for B Piper.

| B Piper Cash Book | | | | | |
|---|---|---|---|---|---|
| | | £ | | | £ |
| 22 November | Balance b/d | 1,300 | 23 November | K Ferris | 300 |
| 23 November | Sales | 700 | 25 November | M Burgon | 246 |
| 25 November | O Dyer | 375 | 26 November | J Moon | 183 |
| 27 November | C Hinds | 422 | 27 November | D Lusky | 96 |

The bank issued the following statement:

**BANK STATEMENT**

**Western Bank**
**Chesney Branch**

**In account with**: B Piper                    **Account No**: 1556

**All entries to:**  30 November inclusive and complete

| Date | Detail | Debit | Credit | Balance |
|---|---|---|---|---|
| | | £ | £ | £ |
| 22 Nov | BALANCE | | | 1,300 |
| 23 Nov | K Ferris | 300 | | 1,000 |
| 23 Nov | Sundries | | 700 | 1,700 |
| 25 Nov | M Burgon | 246 | | 1,454 |
| 25 Nov | O Dyer | | 375 | 1,829 |
| 30 Nov | Bank charges | 25 | | 1,804 |

DD = Direct Debit        SO = Standing Order

You are required to:

(a)   rewrite the Cash Book making any necessary adjustments. Balance the Cash Book at 30 November and bring down the balance.

(b)   prepare a Bank Reconciliation Statement as at 30 November.

*Pitman Qualifications*

The bank columns of P Gerrard's cash book for January 20-7 are as follows:

| 20-7 | Receipts | £ | 20-7 | Payments | | £ |
|---|---|---|---|---|---|---|
| 1 Jan | Balance b/d | 800.50 | 2 Jan | A Arthur Ltd | 001351 | 100.00 |
| 6 Jan | J Baker | 495.60 | 10 Jan | C Curtis | 001352 | 398.50 |
| 31 Jan | G Shotton Ltd | 335.75 | 13 Jan | Donald & Co | 001353 | 229.70 |
| | | | 14 Jan | Bryant & Sons | 001354 | 312.00 |
| | | | 23 Jan | P Reid | 001355 | 176.50 |
| | | | 31 Jan | Balance c/d | | 415.15 |
| | | 1,631.85 | | | | 1,631.85 |

He received his bank statement which showed the following transactions for January 20-7:

| | **BANK STATEMENT** | | | |
|---|---|---|---|---|
| | | Payments | Receipts | Balance |
| 20-7 | | £ | £ | £ |
| 1 Jan | Balance brought forward | | | 800.50 CR |
| 6 Jan | Cheque no. 001351 | 100.00 | | 700.50 CR |
| 6 Jan | Credit | | 495.60 | 1,196.10 CR |
| 13 Jan | BACS credit: T K Supplies | | 716.50 | 1,912.60 CR |
| 20 Jan | Cheque no. 001352 | 398.50 | | 1,514.10 CR |
| 23 Jan | Direct debit: Omni Finance | 207.95 | | 1,306.15 CR |
| 24 Jan | Cheque no. 001353 | 229.70 | | 1,076.45 CR |

You are to:

(a)   write the cash book up-to-date at 31 January 20-7

(b)   prepare a bank reconciliation statement at 31 January 20-7

The bank columns of Jane Doyle's cash book for May 20-7 are as follows:

| 20-7 | Receipts | £ | 20-7 | Payments | | £ |
|---|---|---|---|---|---|---|
| 1 May | Balance b/d | 300 | 2 May | P Stone | 867714 | 28 |
| 7 May | Cash | 162 | 14 May | Alpha Ltd | 867715 | 50 |
| 16 May | C Brewster | 89 | 29 May | E Deakin | 867716 | 110 |
| 23 May | Cash | 60 | | | | |
| 30 May | Cash | 40 | | | | |

She received her bank statement which showed the following transactions for May 20-7:

| BANK STATEMENT | | Payments | Receipts | Balance |
|---|---|---|---|---|
| 20-7 | | £ | £ | £ |
| 1 May | Balance brought forward | | | 326 CR |
| 1 May | Credit | | 54 | 380 CR |
| 5 May | Cheque no. 867714 | 28 | | 352 CR |
| 6 May | Cheque no. 867713 | 80 | | 272 CR |
| 7 May | Credit | | 162 | 434 CR |
| 16 May | Standing order: A-Z Insurance | 25 | | 409 CR |
| 19 May | Credit | | 89 | 498 CR |
| 20 May | Cheque no. 867715 | 50 | | 448 CR |
| 26 May | Credit | | 60 | 508 CR |
| 31 May | Bank Charges | 10 | | 498 CR |

You are to:

(a)    write the cash book up-to-date at 31 May 20-7

(b)    prepare an opening bank reconciliation statement at 1 May 20-7

(c)    prepare a bank reconciliation statement at 31 May 20-7

**10.5**  You work as an accounts clerk in the office of H James (Precision Engineering) Limited. One of your tasks at the end of each month is to reconcile the bank statement with the bank columns of the company's cash book. As you will be away on holiday over the next month-end, the office manager has asked you to write clear instructions in the form of a memorandum for the person who is to undertake this task when you are away.

**10.6\***  Vantage Products are one of your suppliers. Their account in your ledger is as follows:

| 20-8 | | £ | 20-8 | | £ |
|---|---|---|---|---|---|
| 12 Oct | Purchase returns | 75 | 1 Oct | Balance b/d | 1,625 |
| 28 Oct | Bank | 1,570 | 8 Oct | Purchases | 1,050 |
| 28 Oct | Discount | 55 | 19 Oct | Purchases | 1,675 |
| 30 Oct | Purchase returns | 105 | | | |
| 31 Oct | Balance c/d | 2,545 | | | |
| | | 4,350 | | | 4,350 |
| | | | 1 Nov | Balance b/d | 2,545 |

On 2 November, the following statement of account is received from Vantage Products.

|  |  | Debit | Credit | Balance |
|---|---|---|---|---|
| 20-8 |  | £ | £ | £ |
| 1 Oct | Balance |  |  | 3,175 |
| 3 Oct | Bank |  | 1,500 | 1,675 |
| 3 Oct | Discount |  | 50 | 1,625 |
| 8 Oct | Sales | 1,050 |  | 2,675 |
| 15 Oct | Returns inwards |  | 75 | 2,600 |
| 19 Oct | Sales | 1,675 |  | 4,275 |
| 28 Oct | Sales | 1,550 |  | 5,825 |

You are required to:

(a) Prepare a reconciliation statement, starting with the balance in your books of £2,545, to explain the difference between the balance in your ledger and the closing balance on the statement of account.

(b) If the outstanding balance in your ledger on 1 November was settled less 2.5% cash discount:
(i) state the amount of discount
(ii) state the amount of the cheque

*Reproduced by kind permission of OCR Examinations*

# MULTIPLE CHOICE QUESTIONS

Read each question carefully.

Choose the one answer you think is correct (calculators may be needed).

The answers are on page 568.

1    For a VAT-registered business, which of the following is output tax?

A    VAT on purchases

B    VAT on sales

C    VAT on expenses

D    VAT on fixed assets

2    A VAT-registered business buys a machine for £2000 excluding VAT, and pays by cheque. If VAT is at 17.5%, this transaction is recorded as:

|   | Debit | Credit |
|---|---|---|
| A | machinery account £2,350 | bank account £2,350 |
| B | machinery account £2,000 | bank account £1,650 |
|   |  | VAT account £350 |
| C | machinery account £2,000 | bank account £2,350 |
|   | VAT account £350 |  |
| D | machinery account £2,000 | bank account £2,000 |

3    A credit balance on a firm's VAT account means:

A    there is a book-keeping error – VAT account always has a debit balance

B    the firm owes VAT to HM Customs and Excise

C    the firm sells only zero-rated goods

D    the VAT authorities owe VAT to the firm

4    A pack of envelopes costs £5.17 including VAT at 17.5%. How much is the price excluding VAT?

A    £6.07

B    £4.80

C    £3.63

D    £4.40

**5** The cash book records:

A      receipts and payments in cash only

B      receipts and payments by cheque only

C      all receipts and payments both in cash and by cheque

D      receipts and payments both in cash (except for low-value expense payments) and by cheque

**6** The discount received column of the cash book is totalled at regular intervals and transferred to:

A      the credit side of discount received account

B      the debit side of discount received account

C      the debit side of general expenses account

D      the credit side of the trial balance

**7** Most petty cash books operate on the imprest system. This means that:

A      the petty cashier draws money from the main cashier as and when required

B      the main cashier has to authorise each petty cash payment

C      a copy has to be kept of each petty cash voucher

D      the petty cashier starts each week or month with a certain amount of money

**8** Which one of the following expenses is not normally allowed to be paid from petty cash?

A      casual wages

B      staff tea and coffee

C      window cleaning

D      small items of stationery

**9** A petty cash book is balanced at the end of each week and the cash float restored by the main cashier. At the start of a particular week the cash float is £50. Petty cash vouchers for the week total £34.56. How much will be received from the main cashier at the end of the week?

A      £50.00

B      £15.44

C      £34.56

D      £84.56

**10** When preparing a bank reconciliation statement, which one of the following is a timing difference?

A    unpresented cheques

B    bank charges and interest

C    bank giro credits received by the bank

D    standing order payments made by the bank

**11** A firm's cash book shows a balance at bank of £250; unpresented cheques total £350; outstanding lodgments total £200. What is the balance at bank as per the bank statement?

A    £100

B    £200

C    £250

D    £400

**12** Which one of the following will be entered in the cash book, but will not appear on the bank statement?

A    a dishonoured cheque

B    payment of cash to the petty cashier

C    wages cheque

D    bank charges and interest

# 11 AN INTRODUCTION TO COMPUTER ACCOUNTING

Although some businesses, particularly small ones, still use paper-based accounting systems, an increasing number are now operating computerised accounting systems. Small and medium-sized businesses can buy 'off-the-shelf' accounting programs from suppliers such as Sage while larger businesses often have custom-designed programs.

The accounting programs carry out functions such as invoicing, dealing with payments, paying wages and providing regular accounting reports such as trading and profit and loss accounts and balance sheets.

Businesses also make considerable use of computer spreadsheets, particularly for budgets. They can also be used for speeding up the processes in manual accounting systems, setting up a trial balance, for example.

The introduction of a computer accounting system can provide major advantages such as speed and accuracy of operation. There are also certain disadvantages, such as cost and training needs which the management of a business must appreciate before taking the decision to convert from a manual to a computerised accounting system. Full coverage of the implementation of a Sage Line 50 computer accounting system in a business is covered in Chapters 29 to 32 (pages 492 to 557).

## FEATURES OF COMPUTER ACCOUNTING

### facilities

A typical computer accounting program will offer a number of facilities:
- on-screen input and printout of sales invoices
- automatic updating of customer accounts in the sales ledger
- recording of suppliers' invoices
- automatic updating of supplier accounts in the purchases ledger
- recording of bank receipts
- making payments to suppliers and for expenses
- automatic updating of the general (nominal) ledger
- automatic adjustment of stock records

Payroll can also be computerised – often on a separate program.

## management reports

A computer accounting program can provide instant reports for management, for example:

- aged debtors' summary – a summary of customer accounts, showing overdue amounts
- trial balance, trading and profit and loss account and balance sheet
- stock valuation
- VAT Return
- payroll analysis

## computer accounting – ledger system

We have already have covered the 'Ledger' in Chapter 6. The 'Ledger' – which basically means 'the books of the business' is a term used to describe the way the accounts of the business are grouped into different sections:

- **sales ledger**, containing the accounts of debtors (customers)
- **purchases ledger**, containing the accounts of creditors (suppliers)
- **cash books**, containing the main cash book and the petty cash book
- **general ledger** (also called nominal ledger) containing the remaining accounts, eg expenses (including purchases), income (including sales), assets, loans, stock, VAT

The screens of a ledger computer accounting system are designed to be user-friendly. Look at the toolbar of the opening screen of a Sage™ accounting system shown below and then read the notes printed underneath.

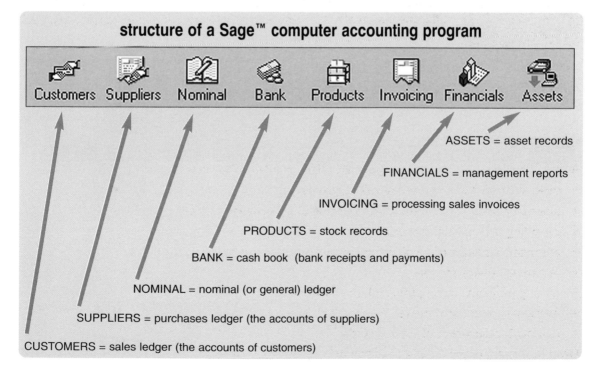

**structure of a Sage™ computer accounting program**

Customers   Suppliers   Nominal   Bank   Products   Invoicing   Financials   Assets

ASSETS = asset records

FINANCIALS = management reports

INVOICING = processing sales invoices

PRODUCTS = stock records

BANK = cash book  (bank receipts and payments)

NOMINAL = nominal (or general) ledger

SUPPLIERS = purchases ledger (the accounts of suppliers)

CUSTOMERS = sales ledger (the accounts of customers)

## using a computer accounting system

Computer input screens are designed to be easy to use. Their main advantage is that each transaction needs only to be input once, unlike in a manual double-entry system where two or three entries are required. In the example below, payment is made for copy paper costing £45.50. The input line includes the nominal account number of bank account (1200), the date of payment, the cheque number (234234), and the nominal account code for stationery expenses (7500). The net amount of £45.50 is entered and the computer automatically calculates the VAT. The appropriate amounts are then transferred by the computer to bank account, stationery expenses account and VAT account.

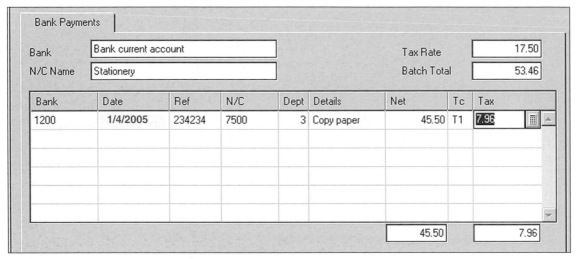

The screen below shows an invoice input screen. In this example 20 Enigma 35s are being invoiced to R Patel & Co in Salisbury. The computer will in due course print the invoice, which will contain the name of the seller as well as all the customer details held in the accounting program's database.

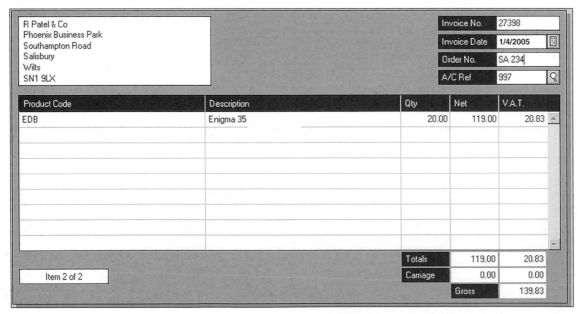

## computerised ledgers – an integrated system

A computerised ledger system is **fully integrated**. This means that when a business transaction is input on the computer it is recorded in a number of different accounting records at the same time. For example, when the sales invoice on the previous page is entered on the screen and the ledgers are 'updated' an integrated program will:

- record the amount of the invoice in the customer account R Patel & Co in the sales ledger
- record the amount of the invoice in the sales account and VAT account (if appropriate) in the general ledger
- reduce the stock of goods held (in this case Enigmas) in the stock records

At the centre of an integrated program is the nominal ledger which deals with all the accounts except customers' accounts and suppliers' accounts. It is affected one way or another by most transactions.

The diagram below shows how the three 'ledgers' can link with the nominal (general) ledger. You can see how an account in the nominal ledger is affected by each of these three transactions. This is the double-entry book-keeping system at work. The advantage of the computer system is that in each case only one entry has to be made. Life is made a great deal simpler by this.

Note that VAT account is omitted from this diagram for the sake of simplicity of illustration. VAT account will be maintained in the nominal (general) ledger and will be updated by all three of the transactions shown.

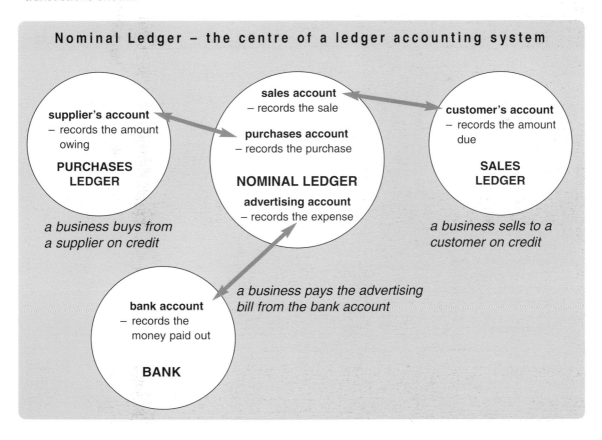

# COMPUTER SPREADSHEETS

A spreadsheet is a grid of boxes – 'cells' – set up on the computer, organised in rows and columns into which you can enter text and numbers. It enables you to make calculations with the figures. The computer program will work out the calculations automatically once you have entered an appropriate formula in the cell where the result of the calculations is required.

The major advantage of a spreadsheet is that if you change any of the figures the computer will automatically recalculate the total, saving you much time and effort.

Spreadsheets are used for a variety of functions in business:

- producing invoices – working out costs of products sold, calculating and adding on VAT and producing a sales total
- working out budgets for future expenditure
- working out sales figures for different products or areas

A commonly used spreadsheet program is Microsoft Excel.

Spreadsheets may be used in a wide variety of accounting functions. The first of the two examples illustrated here is very simple: it shows the two columns of a **trial balance**. The spreadsheet has been set up with columns for account names, debit balances, credit balances and totals for the columns. When the figures have been entered, they will automatically produce totals which should balance.

| | A | B | C | D | E | F | G |
|---|---|---|---|---|---|---|---|
| 1 | | Dr | Cr | | | | |
| 2 | | | | | | | |
| 3 | | | | | | | |
| 4 | Plant and machinery | 35000 | | | | | |
| 5 | Office equipment | 15000 | | | | | |
| 6 | Furniture and fixtures | 25000 | | | | | |
| 7 | Debtors control account | 45500 | | | | | |
| 8 | Bank current account | 12450 | | | | | |
| 9 | Creditors control account | | 32510 | | | | |
| 10 | Sales tax control account | | 17920 | | | | |
| 11 | Purchase tax control account | 26600 | | | | | |
| 12 | Loans | | 35000 | | | | |
| 13 | Ordinary Shares | | 75000 | | | | |
| 14 | Hardware sales | | 85000 | | | | |
| 15 | Software sales | | 15000 | | | | |
| 16 | Computer consultancy | | 2400 | | | | |
| 17 | Materials purchased | 69100 | | | | | |
| 18 | Advertising | 12400 | | | | | |
| 19 | Gross wages | 16230 | | | | | |
| 20 | Rent | 4500 | | | | | |
| 21 | General rates | 450 | | | | | |
| 22 | Electricity | 150 | | | | | |
| 23 | Telephone | 275 | | | | | |
| 24 | Stationery | 175 | | | | | |
| 25 | | | | | | | |
| 26 | | | | | | | |
| 27 | Total | 262830 | 262830 | | | | |

The second example of a computer spreadsheet used in the accounting process is a form of budget known as a **cash flow forecast**. This is a projection of the cash inflows and outflows of a business over a period of months. Each month the spreadsheet calculates the total inflow (row 11) and outflow (row 23) and uses them to calculate the net cash inflow/outflow (row 24). This figure is then used to calculate the projected bank balance of the business (row 26). This figure is useful as it will show if the business needs to borrow from the bank.

The advantage of the spreadsheet in this example is that if the business wishes to change any of the receipt or payment amounts – eg if the sales receipts increase – then the cashflow figures will automatically be recalculated, potentially saving hours of work.

| | A | B | C | D | E | F | G |
|---|---|---|---|---|---|---|---|
| 1 | **CORIANNE LIMITED** | | | | | | |
| 2 | **Cash flow forecast for the six months ending June 2004** | | | | | | |
| 3 | | JANUARY | FEBRUARY | MARCH | APRIL | MAY | JUNE |
| 4 | | £ | £ | £ | £ | £ | £ |
| 5 | Receipts | | | | | | |
| 6 | | | | | | | |
| 7 | | | | | | | |
| 8 | Sales Receipts | 3,000 | 3,000 | 4,000 | 4,000 | 4,000 | 4,000 |
| 9 | | | | | | | |
| 10 | Capital | 10,000 | | | | | |
| 11 | TOTAL RECEIPTS | 13,000 | 3,000 | 4,000 | 4,000 | 4,000 | 4,000 |
| 12 | Payments | | | | | | |
| 13 | Purchases | 5,000 | 1,750 | 1,750 | | 1,750 | 1,750 |
| 14 | Fixed Assets | 4,500 | 5,250 | | | | |
| 15 | Rent/Rates | 575 | 575 | 575 | 575 | 575 | 575 |
| 16 | Insurance | 50 | 50 | 50 | 50 | 50 | 50 |
| 17 | Electricity | 25 | 25 | 25 | 25 | 25 | 25 |
| 18 | Telephone | 150 | 15 | 15 | 15 | 15 | 15 |
| 19 | Stationery | 10 | 10 | 10 | 10 | 10 | 10 |
| 20 | Postage | 15 | 15 | 15 | 15 | 15 | 15 |
| 21 | Bank charges | 100 | | 75 | | | 75 |
| 22 | Advertising | 150 | 30 | 30 | 30 | 30 | 30 |
| 23 | TOTAL PAYMENTS | 10,575 | 7,720 | 2,545 | 720 | 2,470 | 2,545 |
| 24 | CASHFLOW FOR MONTH | 2,425 | - 4,720 | 1,455 | 3,280 | 1,530 | 1,455 |
| 25 | Bank Balance brought forward | - | 2,425 | - 2,295 | - 840 | 2,440 | 3,970 |
| 26 | Bank Balance carried forward | 2,425 | - 2,295 | - 840 | 2,440 | 3,970 | 5,425 |

# ADVANTAGES AND DISADVANTAGES OF COMPUTER ACCOUNTING

In this chapter so far we have stressed the advantages of the introduction of computers to carry out accounting functions in a business. There are, however, some disadvantages as well, and any business introducing computer accounting will need to weigh up carefully the 'pros and cons'. This is an area which has featured in past examinations.

The remainder of this chapter will deal with these advantages and disadvantages and provide an example in the form of a Worked Example based on the effect on employees of the introduction of a new computer accounting system.

## advantages of computer accounting

The main advantages of using a computer accounting program such as Sage include:

- **speed** – data entry on the computer with its formatted screens and built-in databases of customer and supplier details and stock records can be carried out far more quickly than any manual processing
- **automatic document production** – fast and accurate invoice and credit note printing, statement runs, payroll processing
- **accuracy** – there is less room for error as only one account entry is needed for each transaction rather than the two (or three) required in a manual double-entry system
- **up-to-date information** – the accounting records are automatically updated and so account balances (eg customer accounts) will always be up-to-date
- **availability of information** – the data can be made available to different users at the same time
- **management information** – reports can be produced which will help management monitor and control the business, for example the aged debtors analysis which shows which customer accounts are overdue, trial balance, trading and profit and loss account and balance sheet
- **VAT return** – the automatic production of figures for the regular VAT return
- **legibility** – the onscreen and printed data should always be legible and so will avoid errors caused by poor figures
- **efficiency** – better use is made of resources and time; cash flow should improve through better debt collection
- **staff motivation** – the system will require staff to be trained to use new skills, which can make them feel more valued

## disadvantages of computer accounting

The main disadvantages of using computer accounting programs include:

- **capital cost of installation** – the hardware and software will need to be budgeted for, not only as 'one-off' expenditure but also as recurrent costs because computers will need replacing and software updating
- **cost of training** – the staff will need to be trained in the use of the hardware and software
- **staff opposition** – motivation may suffer as some staff do not like computers, also there may be staff redundancies, all of which create bad feeling
- **disruption** – loss of work time and changes in the working environment when the computerised system is first introduced
- **system failure** – the danger of the system crashing and the subsequent loss of work when no back-ups have been made
- **back-up requirements** – the need to keep regular and secure back-ups in case of system failure
- **breaches of security** – the danger of people hacking into the system from outside, the danger of viruses, the incidence of staff fraud
- **health** dangers – the problems of bad backs, eyestrain and muscular complaints such as RSI

## WORKED EXAMPLE

### situation

Stitch-in-time Limited is an old-fashioned company which manufactures sewing machines. The Finance Director, Charles Cotton, is considering the introduction of a computer accounting system which will completely replace the existing manual double-entry system.

He is worried because he knows that the proposition will not go down very well with employees who have been with the company for a long time.

He asks you to prepare notes in which you are to set out:

(a)    the benefits to staff of the new scheme

(b)    the likely causes of staff dissatisfaction with the new scheme

### solution

(a)    **potential benefits to staff**

- the staff will be able to update their skills

- they will receive training

- they may get an increase in pay

- the training will increase their career prospects

- they will be motivated

- they will get job satisfaction

(b)    **causes of staff dissatisfaction**

- staff prefer doing the job in a way which is familiar to them

- they do not like computers

- they may see their jobs threatened as they worry that redundancies will occur

- they do not look forward to the disruption at the time of the changeover

- they worry about the possible bad effects to their health, having heard about RSI (Repetitive Strain Injury) and radiation and eye damage from computer screens

- they will be demotivated as they consider the new system 'mechanical' – they will have to sit in front of a computer for hours at a time and not be able to communicate so well with their colleagues as they have in the past

## CHAPTER SUMMARY

● Computer accounting systems save businesses time and money by automating many accounting processes, including the production of reports for management.

● Most computer accounting programs are based on the ledger system and integrate a number of different functions – one transaction will change accounting data in a number of different parts of the system.

● The different functions can include: sales ledger, purchases ledger, nominal (general) ledger, cash and bank payments, stock control, invoicing, report production

● It is common for a payroll processing program to be linked to the nominal ledger of a computer accounting program.

● Computer spreadsheets are often also used to carry out individual functions in an accounting system, for example the creation of budgets.

● A business must consider carefully all the advantages and disadvantages of computer accounting before installing a computerised system. The main advantages are speed, accuracy, availability of up-to-date information; the main disadvantages are cost, security implications and possible opposition from employees.

In the next chapter we look at how businesses present their final accounts at the end of each financial year.

## QUESTIONS

NOTE: an asterisk (*) after the question number means that an answer to the question is given in Appendix 2.

11.1* Explain **two** advantages to a business of using a computer accounting system to record financial transactions.

11.2* Describe **two** advantages of using a computer spreadsheet for a document such as a cash-flow forecast.

11.3* Explain how **three** different areas of the accounting system might benefit from the introduction of computer accounting.

11.4* A business is planning to introduce a computer accounting system and holds an employee meeting to explain the implications of the change. One employee asks 'I have heard that there are all sorts of risks to the computer data which could cause us to lose the lot.' Describe **two** of the main risks to the security of computer data.

**11.5**

Gerry Mann is the Finance Director of Colourways Limited, a design company. He wants to introduce a computer accounting system into the business, but is encountering opposition from Helen Baxill, an active trade union member who works in the Finance Department.

Describe:

(a)  the objections relating to staff working conditions and welfare that Helen is likely to raise to try and block the introduction of a computer system

(b)  the advantages to staff of a computer system that Gerry could use to persuade Helen to accept its introduction

---

### tutorial note

Chapters 29 to 32 of this text (pages 492 to 557) contain full coverage – including inputting exercises – of the operation of a Sage Line 50 computer accounting system.

# 12 FINAL ACCOUNTS

For most businesses, the final accounts, which are produced at the end of each financial year, comprise:

- trading account
- profit and loss account
- balance sheet

Final accounts can be presented in a vertical format, or a horizontal format. In this chapter we shall look at both. The vertical format, however, is more common nowadays and is used as the standard format in this book.

When preparing final accounts it is important to distinguish between capital expenditure and revenue expenditure.

## FINAL ACCOUNTS AND THE TRIAL BALANCE

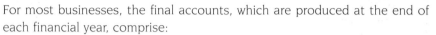

So far we have looked at the format of business accounts and the recording of different types of transactions. All that we have covered is usually carried out by the book-keeper. We will now see how the financial accountant takes to a further stage the information prepared by the book-keeper. The financial accountant will use the information from the accounting system, which is summarised in the trial balance (see Chapter 5), in order to produce the final accounts of a business.

The final accounts can be produced more often than once a year in order to give information to the owner(s) on how the business is progressing. However, it is customary to produce annual or final accounts for the benefit of the Inland Revenue, bank manager and other interested parties. Limited companies (see Chapter 25) have a legal responsibility to report to their shareholders each year, while non-trading organisations (such as clubs and societies – see Chapter 22) report financial results to the members annually.

The starting point for preparing final accounts is the trial balance prepared by the book-keeper. All the figures recorded on the trial balance are used in the final accounts. The trading account and the profit and loss account are both 'accounts' in terms of double-entry book-keeping. This means that amounts recorded in these accounts must also be recorded elsewhere in the book-keeping system. By contrast, the balance sheet is not an account, but is simply a statement of account balances remaining after the trading and profit and loss accounts have been prepared.

To help us with the preparation of final accounts we will use the trial balance, shown on the next page, which has been produced by the book-keeper at the end of the firm's financial year.

## TRIAL BALANCE OF WYVERN WHOLESALERS AS AT 31 DECEMBER 20-1

| | Dr £ | Cr £ |
|---|---|---|
| Sales | | 250,000 |
| Purchases | 156,000 | |
| Sales returns | 5,400 | |
| Purchases returns | | 7,200 |
| Discount received | | 2,500 |
| Discount allowed | 3,700 | |
| Stock at 1 January 20-1 | 12,350 | |
| Salaries | 46,000 | |
| Electricity and gas | 3,000 | |
| Rent and rates | 2,000 | |
| Sundry expenses | 4,700 | |
| Premises | 100,000 | |
| Equipment | 30,000 | |
| Vehicles | 21,500 | |
| Debtors | 23,850 | |
| Bank overdraft | | 851 |
| Cash | 125 | |
| Creditors | | 12,041 |
| Value Added Tax | | 3,475 |
| Capital | | 110,000 |
| Drawings | 10,442 | |
| Long-term loan | | 33,000 |
| | 419,067 | 419,067 |

Note: stock at 31 December 20-1 was valued at £16,300

You will see that the trial balance includes the stock value at the start of the year, while the end-of-year valuation is noted after the trial balance. For the purposes of financial accounting, the stock of goods for resale is valued by the business (and often verified by the auditor) at the end of each financial year, and the valuation is entered into the book-keeping system (see page 171). We will present the final accounts

- before adjustments for items such as accruals, prepayments, depreciation of fixed assets, bad debts written off, and provision for bad debts (each of which will be dealt with in Chapters 13 -15)
- in vertical format, ie in columnar form (the alternative layout – horizontal format – is looked at on page 174)

On page 171 we will look at the double-entry book-keeping for amounts entered in the trading and profit and loss accounts.

# TRADING ACCOUNT

The main activity of a trading business is to buy goods at one price and then to sell the same goods at a higher price. The difference between the two prices represents a profit known as *gross profit*. Instead of calculating the gross profit on each item bought and sold, we have seen how the book-keeping system stores up the totals of transactions for the year in either purchases account or sales account. Further, any goods returned are recorded in either purchases returns account or sales returns account.

At the end of the financial year (which can end at any date – it doesn't have to be the calendar year) the total of purchases and sales accounts, together with purchases returns and sales returns, are used to form the trading account. It is also necessary to take note of the value of stock of goods for resale held at the beginning and end of the financial year.

The trading account is set out as follows:

**TRADING ACCOUNT OF WYVERN WHOLESALERS**
**FOR THE YEAR ENDED 31 DECEMBER 20-1**

|  | £ | £ | £ |
|---|---|---|---|
| Sales |  |  | 250,000 |
| Less Sales returns |  |  | 5,400 |
| Net sales (or turnover) |  |  | 244,600 |
| Opening stock (1 January 20-1) |  | 12,350 |  |
| Purchases | 156,000 |  |  |
| Carriage in | – |  |  |
| Less Purchases returns | 7,200 |  |  |
| Net purchases |  | 148,800 |  |
|  |  | 161,150 |  |
| Less Closing stock (31 December 20-1) |  | 16,300 |  |
| Cost of Goods Sold |  |  | 144,850 |
| **Gross profit** |  |  | 99,750 |

## notes on trading account

● **Sales and purchases** only include items in which the business trades – items to be kept for use in the business, such as machinery, are not included in sales and purchases but are classified as fixed assets.

● **Adjustments** are made for the value of stock in the store or warehouse at the beginning and end of the financial year. The opening stock is added to the purchases because it has been sold during the year. The closing stock is deducted from purchases because it has not been sold; it will form the opening stock for the next financial year, when it will be added to next year's figure for purchases.

- The figure for **cost of goods sold** (often written as 'cost of sales') represents the cost to the business of the goods which have been sold in this financial year. Cost of goods sold is:

    opening stock
    + purchases
    + carriage in (see below)
    − purchases returns
    − closing stock
    = cost of goods sold

- **Gross profit** is calculated as:

    sales
    − sales returns
    = net sales
    − cost of goods sold
    = gross profit

    If cost of goods sold is greater than net sales, the business has made a *gross loss*.

- **Carriage in** is the expense to the business of having purchases delivered (eg if you buy from a mail order company, you often have to pay the post and packing – this is the 'carriage in' cost). The cost of carriage in is added to purchases.

- **Net sales** (often described as turnover) is:

    sales
    − sales returns
    = net sales

- **Net purchases** is:

    purchases
    + carriage in
    − purchases returns
    = net purchases

## PROFIT AND LOSS ACCOUNT

In the profit and loss account are listed the various running expenses (or revenue expenditure) of the business. The total of running expenses is deducted from gross profit to give net profit for the year. Net profit is an important figure: it shows the profitability of the business after all expenses, and how much has been earned by the business for the owner(s). It is on this profit, after certain adjustments, that the tax liability will be based.

The profit and loss account follows on from the trading account and is set out as follows:

**PROFIT AND LOSS ACCOUNT OF WYVERN WHOLESALERS**
**FOR THE YEAR ENDED 31 DECEMBER 20-1**

|  | £ | £ | £ |
|---|---|---|---|
| **Gross profit** | | | 99,750 |
| Add  Discount received | | | 2,500 |
| | | | 102,250 |
| Less expenses: | | | |
| Discount allowed | | 3,700 | |
| Salaries | | 46,000 | |
| Electricity and gas | | 3,000 | |
| Rent and rates | | 2,000 | |
| Sundry expenses | | 4,700 | |
| | | | 59,400 |
| **Net profit** | | | 42,850 |

Notes:

- The various running expenses shown in the profit and loss account can be listed to suit the needs of a particular business: the headings used here are for illustrative purposes only.
- Amounts of income are also included in profit and loss account, eg discount received in the example; these are added to gross profit.
- The net profit is the amount the business earned for the owner(s) during the year; it is important to note that this is not the amount by which the cash/bank balance has increased during the year.
- If the total of expenses exceeds gross profit (and other income), the business has made a net loss.
- Drawings by the owner(s) are not listed as an expense in profit and loss account – instead, they are deducted from capital (see balance sheet below).
- If the owner of the business has taken goods for his or her own use, the amount should be deducted from purchases and added to drawings (see also page 207).

The trading account and the profit and loss account are usually combined together, rather than being shown as separate accounts, as shown in the 'vertical format' at the top of the next page.

The trading and profit and loss account forms part of the double-entry book-keeping system and can also be set out in 'horizontal' format (see page 174).

## service sector businesses

You should note that when preparing the final accounts of a service sector business – such as a secretarial agency, solicitors, estate agents, doctor – a trading account will not be prepared because, instead of trading in goods, the business supplies services. Thus the final accounts will consist of a profit and loss account and balance sheet. The profit and loss account, instead of starting with gross profit, will commence with the income from the business activity, such as 'fees', 'income from clients', 'charges', 'work done'. Other items of income, such as discount received, are added, and the expenses are then listed and deducted to give the net profit, or net loss, for the accounting period.  An example is shown at the bottom of the next page.

## TRADING AND PROFIT AND LOSS ACCOUNT OF WYVERN WHOLESALERS
## FOR THE YEAR ENDED 31 DECEMBER 20-1

| | £ | £ | £ |
|---|---|---|---|
| Sales | | | 250,000 |
| Less Sales returns | | | 5,400 |
| Net sales | | | 244,600 |
| Opening stock (1 January 20-1) | | 12,350 | |
| Purchases | 156,000 | | |
| Carriage in | – | | |
| Less Purchases returns | 7,200 | | |
| Net purchases | | 148,800 | |
| | | 161,150 | |
| Less Closing stock (31 December 20-1) | | 16,300 | |
| Cost of Goods Sold | | | 144,850 |
| **Gross profit** | | | 99,750 |
| Add Discount received | | | 2,500 |
| | | | 102,250 |
| Less expenses: | | | |
| Discount allowed | | 3,700 | |
| Salaries | | 46,000 | |
| Electricity and gas | | 3,000 | |
| Rent and rates | | 2,000 | |
| Sundry expenses | | 4,700 | |
| | | | 59,400 |
| **Net profit** | | | 42,850 |

## PROFIT AND LOSS ACCOUNT OF WYVERN SECRETARIAL AGENCY
## FOR THE YEAR ENDED 31 DECEMBER 20-1

| | £ | £ |
|---|---|---|
| Income from clients | | 110,000 |
| Less expenses: | | |
| Salaries | 64,000 | |
| Heating and Lighting | 2.000 | |
| Telephone | 2.000 | |
| Rent and Rates | 6,000 | |
| Sundry Expenses | 3,000 | |
| | | 77,000 |
| **Net profit** | | 33,000 |

# BALANCE SHEET

The trading and profit and loss account shows two types of profit – gross profit and net profit, respectively – for the financial year (or such other time period as may be chosen by the business). A balance sheet, by contrast, shows the state of the business at one moment in time. It lists the assets and the liabilities at a particular date, but is not part of the double-entry book-keeping system.

The balance sheet of Wyvern Wholesalers, using the figures from the trial balance on page 163, is as follows:

| | £ | £ | £ |
|---|---|---|---|
| **BALANCE SHEET OF WYVERN WHOLESALERS** | | | |
| **AS AT 31 DECEMBER 20-1** | | | |
| **Fixed Assets** | | | |
| Premises | | | 100,000 |
| Equipment | | | 30,000 |
| Vehicles | | | 21,500 |
| | | | 151,500 |
| **Current Assets** | | | |
| Stock | | 16,300 | |
| Debtors | | 23,850 | |
| Cash | | 125 | |
| | | 40,275 | |
| **Less Current Liabilities** | | | |
| Creditors | 12,041 | | |
| Value Added Tax | 3.475 | | |
| Bank overdraft | 851 | | |
| | | 16,367 | |
| **Working Capital** | | | 23,908 |
| | | | 175,408 |
| **Less Long-term Liabilities** | | | |
| Loan | | | 33,000 |
| **NET ASSETS** | | | 142,408 |
| | | | |
| **FINANCED BY:** | | | |
| **Capital** | | | |
| Opening capital | | | 110,000 |
| Add net profit | | | 42,850 |
| | | | 152,850 |
| Less drawings | | | 10,442 |
| | | | 142,408 |

## notes on the balance sheet

● **assets**

Assets are items or amounts owned or owed to the business, and are normally listed in increasing order of liquidity, ie the most permanent assets are listed first.

Fixed assets are long-term assets, and are divided between tangible fixed assets, which have material substance such as premises, equipment, vehicles, and intangible fixed assets, such as goodwill (see below).

Current assets are short-term assets which continually change from day-to-day, such as stock, debtors, bank (if not overdrawn) and cash.

● **intangible fixed assets**

Intangible fixed assets (not shown in the balance sheet above) will appear on some balance sheets, and are listed before the tangible fixed assets. An intangible asset does not have material substance, but belongs to the business and has value. A common example of an intangible fixed asset is goodwill, which is where a business has bought another business and paid an agreed amount for the existing reputation and customer connections (the goodwill).

● **liabilities**

Liabilities are items or amounts owed by the business.

Current liabilities are amounts owing at the balance sheet date and due for repayment within 12 months or less (eg creditors, Value Added Tax, bank overdraft).

Long-term liabilities are borrowings where repayment is due in more than 12 months (eg loans, bank loans).

● **capital and working capital**

Capital is money owed by the business to the owner. It is usual practice to show on the balance sheet the owner's investment at the start of the year plus net profit for the year less drawings for the year; this equals the owner's investment at the end of the year, ie at the balance sheet date.

Working capital is the excess of current assets over current liabilities. Without working capital, a business cannot continue to operate.

## significance of the balance sheet

The balance sheet shows the assets used by the business and how they have been financed. The concept may be expressed as a formula:

|  | Fixed assets |
|---|---|
| *plus* | Working capital |
| *minus* | Long-term liabilities |
| *equals* | Net assets |
| *equals* | Capital |

The vertical presentation balance sheet agrees the figure for net assets (£142,408), with capital.

# PREPARATION OF FINAL ACCOUNTS FROM A TRIAL BALANCE

The trial balance contains the basic figures necessary to prepare the final accounts but, as we shall see in the next section, the figures are transferred from the double-entry accounts of the business. Nevertheless, the trial balance is a suitable summary from which to prepare the final accounts. The information needed for the preparation of each of the final accounts needs to be picked out from the trial balance in the following way:

- go through the trial balance and write against the items the final account in which each appears
- 'tick' each figure as it is used – each item from the trial balance appears in the final accounts once only
- the year-end (closing) stock figure is not listed in the trial balance, but is shown as a note; the closing stock appears twice in the final accounts – firstly in the trading account, and secondly in the balance sheet (as a current asset).

If this routine is followed with the trial balance of Wyvern Wholesalers, it then appears as follows.

| TRIAL BALANCE OF WYVERN WHOLESALERS AS AT 31 DECEMBER 20-1 | | | | |
|---|---|---|---|---|
| | Dr £ | Cr £ | | |
| Sales | | 250,000 | T | ✔ |
| Purchases | 156,000 | | T | ✔ |
| Sales returns | 5,400 | | T | ✔ |
| Purchases returns | | 7,200 | T | ✔ |
| Discount received | | 2,500 | P & L *(income)* | ✔ |
| Discount allowed | 3,700 | | P & L *(expense)* | ✔ |
| Stock 1 January 20-1 | 12,350 | | T | ✔ |
| Salaries | 46,000 | | P & L *(expense)* | ✔ |
| Electricity and gas | 3,000 | | P & L *(expense)* | ✔ |
| Rent and rates | 2,000 | | P & L *(expense)* | ✔ |
| Sundry expenses | 4,700 | | P & L *(expense)* | ✔ |
| Premises | 100,000 | | BS *(fixed asset)* | ✔ |
| Equipment | 30,000 | | BS *(fixed asset)* | ✔ |
| Vehicles | 21,500 | | BS *(fixed asset)* | ✔ |
| Debtors | 23,850 | | BS *(current asset)* | ✔ |
| Bank overdraft | | 851 | BS *(current liability)* | ✔ |
| Cash | 125 | | BS *(current asset)* | ✔ |
| Creditors | | 12,041 | BS *(current liability)* | ✔ |
| Value Added Tax | | 3,475 | BS *(current liability)* | ✔ |
| Capital | | 110,000 | BS *(capital)* | ✔ |
| Drawings | 10,442 | | BS *(capital)* | ✔ |
| Long-term loan | | 33,000 | BS *(long-term liability)* | ✔ |
| | 419,067 | 419,067 | | |
| Stock at 31 December 20-1 was valued at £16,300 | | | T | ✔ |
| | | | BS *(current asset)* | ✔ |

Note: T = trading account; P & L = profit and loss account; BS = balance sheet

# DOUBLE-ENTRY BOOK-KEEPING AND THE FINAL ACCOUNTS

We have already noted earlier in this chapter that the trading and profit and loss account forms part of the double-entry book-keeping system. Therefore, each amount recorded in this account must have an opposite entry elsewhere in the accounting system. In preparing the trading and profit and loss account we are, in effect, emptying each account that has been storing up a record of the transactions of the business during the course of the financial year and transferring it to the trading and profit and loss account.

## trading account

In the trading account of Wyvern Wholesalers the balance of purchases account is transferred as follows (debit trading account; credit purchases account):

| Dr | | | **Purchases Account** | | | Cr |
|---|---|---|---|---|---|---|
| 20-1 | | £ | 20-1 | | | £ |
| 31 Dec | Balance b/d (ie total for year) | 156,000 | 31 Dec | Trading account | | 156,000 |

The account now has a nil balance and is ready to receive the transactions for next year.

The balances of sales, sales returns, and purchases returns accounts are cleared to nil in a similar way and the amounts transferred to trading account, as debits or credits as appropriate.

Stock account, however, is dealt with differently. Stock is valued for financial accounting purposes at the end of each year (it is also likely to be valued more regularly in order to provide management information). Only the annual stock valuation is recorded in stock account, and the account is not used at any other time. After the book-keeper has extracted the trial balance, but before preparation of the trading account, the stock account appears as follows:

| Dr | | **Stock Account** | | | Cr |
|---|---|---|---|---|---|
| 20-1 | | £ | 20-1 | | £ |
| 31 Dec | Balance b/d | 12,350 | | | |

This balance, which is the opening stock valuation for the year, is transferred to the trading account to leave a nil balance, as follows (debit trading account; credit stock account):

| Dr | | **Stock Account** | | | Cr |
|---|---|---|---|---|---|
| 20-1 | | £ | 20-1 | | £ |
| 31 Dec | Balance b/d | 12,350 | 31 Dec | Trading account | 12,350 |

The closing stock valuation for the year is now recorded on the account as an asset (debit stock account; credit trading account):

| Dr | | Stock Account | | | Cr |
|---|---|---|---|---|---|
| 20-1 | | £ | 20-1 | | £ |
| 31 Dec | Balance b/d | 12,350 | 31 Dec | Trading account | 12,350 |
| 31 Dec | Trading account | 16,300 | 31 Dec | Balance c/d | 16,300 |
| 20-2 | | | | | |
| 1 Jan | Balance b/d | 16,300 | | | |

The closing stock figure is shown on the balance sheet as a current asset, and will be the opening stock in next year's trading account.

## profit and loss account

Expenses and income items are transferred from the double-entry accounts to the profit and loss account. For example, the salaries account of Wyvern Wholesalers has been storing up information during the year and, at the end of the year, the total is transferred to profit and loss account (debit profit and loss account; credit salaries account):

| Dr | | Salaries Account | | | Cr |
|---|---|---|---|---|---|
| 20-1 | | £ | 20-1 | | £ |
| 31 Dec | Balance b/d | 46,000 | 31 Dec | Profit and loss account | 46,000 |
| | (ie total for year) | | | | |

The salaries account now has a nil balance and is ready to receive transactions for 20-2, the next financial year.

## net profit

After the profit and loss account has been completed, the amount of net profit (or net loss) is transferred to the owner's capital account. The book-keeping entries are:

- **net profit**
  - debit profit and loss account
  - credit capital account

● **net loss**

    – debit capital account

    – credit profit and loss account

A net profit increases the owner's stake in the business by adding to capital account, while a net loss decreases the owner's stake.

## drawings

At the same time the account for drawings, which has been storing up the amount of drawings during the year is also transferred to capital account:

    – debit capital account

    – credit drawings account

Thus the total of drawings for the year is debited to capital account.

## capital account

When these transactions are completed, the capital account for Wyvern Wholesalers appears as:

| Dr | | | **Capital Account** | | Cr |
|---|---|---|---|---|---|
| 20-1 | | £ | 20-1 | | £ |
| 31 Dec | Drawings for year | 10,442 | 31 Dec | Balance b/d | 110,000 |
| 31 Dec | Balance c/d | 142,408 | 31 Dec | Profit and loss account | |
| | | | | (net profit for year) | 42,850 |
| | | 152,850 | | | 152,850 |
| 20-2 | | | 20-2 | | |
| | | | 1 Jan | Balance b/d | 142,408 |

Note: It is the balance of capital account at the end of the year, ie £142,408, which forms the total for the capital section of the balance sheet. Whilst this figure could be shown on the balance sheet by itself, it is usual to show capital at the start of the year, with net profit for the year added, and drawings for the year deducted. In this way, the capital account is summarised on the balance sheet.

## balance sheet

Unlike the trading and profit and loss account, the balance sheet is not part of the double-entry accounts. The balance sheet is made up of those accounts which remain with balances after the trading and profit and loss account transfers have been made. Thus it consists of asset and liability accounts, including capital.

# HORIZONTAL PRESENTATION OF FINAL ACCOUNTS

So far in this chapter we have used the vertical presentation for setting out the final accounts of a business, ie we have started at the top of the page and worked downwards in columnar or narrative style. An alternative method is the horizontal presentation, where each of the financial statements is presented in the format of a two-sided account. The set of final accounts presented earlier would appear, in horizontal style, as follows:

**TRADING ACCOUNT OF WYVERN WHOLESALERS**
**FOR THE YEAR ENDED 31 DECEMBER 20-1**

| | £ | £ | | £ |
|---|---|---|---|---|
| Opening stock | | 12,350 | Sales | 250,000 |
| Purchases | 156,000 | | Less Sales returns | 5,400 |
| Carriage in | - | | Net sales | 244,600 |
| Less Purchases returns | 7,200 | | | |
| Net purchases | | 148,800 | | |
| | | 161,150 | | |
| Less Closing stock | | 16,300 | | |
| Cost of Goods Sold | | 144,850 | | |
| Gross profit c/d | | 99,750 | | |
| | | 244,600 | | 244,600 |

**PROFIT AND LOSS ACCOUNT OF WYVERN WHOLESALERS**
**FOR THE YEAR ENDED 31 DECEMBER 20-1**

| | £ | | £ |
|---|---|---|---|
| Discount allowed | 3,700 | Gross profit b/d | 99,750 |
| Salaries | 46,000 | Discount received | 2,500 |
| Electricity and gas | 3,000 | | |
| Rent and rates | 2,000 | | |
| Sundry expenses | 4,700 | | |
| Net profit | 42,850 | | |
| | 102,250 | | 102,250 |

### BALANCE SHEET OF WYVERN WHOLESALERS
### AS AT 31 DECEMBER 20-1

| | £ | £ | | £ | £ |
|---|---|---|---|---|---|
| **Fixed Assets** | | | **Capital** | | |
| Premises | | 100,000 | Opening capital | | 110,000 |
| Equipment | | 30,000 | Add net profit | | 42,850 |
| Vehicles | | 21,500 | | | 152,850 |
| | | 151,500 | Less drawings | | 10,442 |
| **Current Assets** | | | | | 142,408 |
| Stock | 16,300 | | **Long-term Liabilities** | | |
| Debtors | 23,850 | | Loan | | 33,000 |
| Cash | 125 | | | | 175,408 |
| | | 40,275 | **Current Liabilities** | | |
| | | | Creditors | 12,041 | |
| | | | Value Added Tax | 3,475 | |
| | | | Bank overdraft | 851 | |
| | | | | | 16,367 |
| | | 191,775 | | | 191,775 |

## a choice of formats

In your study of Business Accounts you will see both forms of presentation from time-to-time in the accounts of different businesses and organisations. The vertical format is more common nowadays and is used as the standard format in this book. As you will appreciate, both forms of presentation use the same information and, after a while, you will soon be able to 'read' either version.

## a 'pro-forma' vertical presentation of final accounts

Many students studying final accounts for the first time find it helpful to be able to follow a set layout, or pro-forma – certainly in the early stages. A sample layout for final accounts is included in Appendix 1 (page 559). There are some items included that will be covered in later chapters, and the layout will need to be amended to fit the needs of partnership (Chapter 23) and limited company final accounts (Chapter 25).

# CAPITAL EXPENDITURE AND REVENUE EXPENDITURE

When preparing final accounts it is important to distinguish between capital expenditure and revenue expenditure.

## capital expenditure

Capital expenditure can be defined as expenditure incurred on the purchase, alteration or improvement of fixed assets. For example, the purchase of a car for use in the business is capital expenditure. Included in capital expenditure are such costs as:

- delivery of fixed assets
- installation of fixed assets
- improvement (but not repair) of fixed assets
- legal costs of buying property

## revenue expenditure

Revenue expenditure is expenditure incurred on running expenses. For example, the cost of petrol or diesel for the car (above) is revenue expenditure. Included in revenue expenditure are the costs of:

- maintenance and repair of fixed assets
- administration of the business
- selling and distributing the goods or products in which the business trades

## capital expenditure and revenue expenditure – the differences

Capital expenditure is shown on the balance sheet, while revenue expenditure is an expense in the profit and loss account. It is important to classify these types of expenditure correctly in the accounting system. For example, if the cost of the car was shown as an expense in profit and loss account, then net profit would be reduced considerably, or a net loss recorded; meanwhile, the balance sheet would not show the car as a fixed asset – clearly this is incorrect as the business owns the asset.

Study the following examples and the table on the next page; they both show the differences between capital expenditure and revenue expenditure.

- **cost of building an extension to the factory £30,000, which includes £1,000 for repairs to the existing factory**
  - capital expenditure, £29,000
  - revenue expenditure, £1,000 (because it is for repairs to an existing fixed asset)

- **a plot of land has been bought for £20,000, the legal costs are £750**
  - capital expenditure £20,750 (the legal costs are included in the capital expenditure, because they are the cost of acquiring the fixed asset, ie the legal costs are capitalised)

- **the business' own employees are used to install a new air conditioning system: wages £1,000, materials £1,500**
  - capital expenditure £2,500 (an addition to the property); note that, in cases such as this, revenue expenditure, ie wages and materials purchases, will need to be reduced to allow for the transfer to capital expenditure

- **own employees used to repair and redecorate the premises: wages £500, materials £750**
  - revenue expenditure £1,250 (repairs and redecoration are running expenses)

- **purchase of a new machine £10,000, payment for installation and setting up £250**
  - capital expenditure £10,250 (costs of installation of a fixed asset are capitalised)

Only by allocating capital expenditure and revenue expenditure correctly between the balance sheet and the profit and loss account can the final accounts reflect accurately the financial state of the business. The chart below shows the main items of capital expenditure and revenue expenditure associated with three major fixed assets – buildings, vehicles and computers.

|  | **capital expenditure** | **revenue expenditure** |
|---|---|---|
| *BUILDINGS* | • cost of building<br>• cost of extension<br>• carriage on raw materials used<br>• legal fees<br>• labour cost of own employees used supervising the building<br>• installation of utilities, eg gas, water, electricity | • general maintenance<br>• repairs<br>• redecoration |
| *VEHICLES* | • net cost, including any optional extras<br>• delivery costs<br>• number plates<br>• changes to the vehicle | • fuel<br>• road fund licence<br>• extended warranty<br>• painting company logo<br>• insurance<br>• servicing and repairs |
| *COMPUTERS* | • net cost<br>• installation and testing<br>• modifications, including memory upgrades, to meet specific needs of business<br>• installation of special wiring<br>• cost of air conditioning to computer room<br>• staff training (where directly related to new equipment)<br>• computer programs (but can be classified as revenue expenditure if cost is low and will have little impact on final accounts) | • data storage discs<br>• printer paper and other consumables<br>• insurance<br>• computer programs (or can be classified as capital expenditure if cost is high and will have a large impact on final accounts) |

## CHAPTER SUMMARY

● The final accounts of a business comprise:

  • trading account, which shows gross profit

  • profit and loss account, which shows net profit

  • balance sheet, which shows the assets and liabilities of the business at the year-end

  Appendix 1 (page 559) gives a specimen layout for final accounts.

● The starting point for the preparation of final accounts is the summary of the information from the accounting records contained in the book-keeper's trial balance.

● Each item from the trial balance is entered into the final accounts once only.

● Any notes to the trial balance, such as the closing stock, affect the final accounts in two places.

● The trading account and profit and loss account form part of the double-entry book-keeping system – amounts entered must be recorded elsewhere in the accounts.

● The balance sheet is not part of the double-entry system; it lists the assets and liabilities at a particular date.

● Final accounts can be presented in either a vertical or a horizontal format.

● Capital expenditure is expenditure incurred on the purchase, alteration or improvement of fixed assets.

● Revenue expenditure is expenditure incurred on running expenses.

There is more material to cover in connection with final accounts, and the next few chapters deal with accruals and prepayments, depreciation of fixed assets, bad debts and provision for bad debts, and accounting concepts and stock valuation. In addition the more specialist final accounts of partnerships (Chapter 23), limited companies (Chapter 25), and manufacturing businesses (Chapter 26), will be studied. Final accounts can also be analysed and interpreted (Chapter 28) to give the user of the accounts information about the financial state of the business.

Case Study 1 follows after the questions at the end of this chapter; it looks at a fully worked example of a handwritten book-keeping system.

# QUESTIONS

12.1* The following information has been extracted from the business accounts of Matthew Lloyd for his first year of trading which ended on 31 December 20-8:

| | £ |
|---|---|
| Purchases | 94,350 |
| Sales | 125,890 |
| Stock at 31 December 20-8 | 5,950 |
| Rates | 4,850 |
| Heating and lighting | 2,120 |
| Wages and salaries | 10,350 |
| Office equipment | 8,500 |
| Vehicles | 10,750 |
| Debtors | 3,950 |
| Bank balance | 4,225 |
| Cash | 95 |
| Creditors | 1,750 |
| Value Added Tax | 450 |
| Capital at start of year | 20,000 |
| Drawings for year | 8,900 |

You are to prepare the trading and profit and loss account of Matthew Lloyd for the year ended 31 December 20-8, together with his balance sheet at that date.

12.2 Complete the table below for each item (a) to (g) indicating with a tick:

• whether the item would normally appear in the debit or credit column of the trial balance

• in which final account the item would appear at the end of the accounting period and whether as a debit or credit

| | TRIAL BALANCE | | FINAL ACCOUNTS | | | |
|---|---|---|---|---|---|---|
| | | | TRADING & P& L | | BALANCE SHEET | |
| | Debit | Credit | Debit | Credit | Debit | Credit |
| (a) Salaries | | | | | | |
| (b) Purchases | | | | | | |
| (c) Debtors | | | | | | |
| (d) Sales returns | | | | | | |
| (e) Discount received | | | | | | |
| (f) Vehicle | | | | | | |
| (g) Capital | | | | | | |

**12.3*** You are to fill in the missing figures for the following businesses:

| | Sales | Opening Stock | Purchases | Closing Stock | Gross Profit | Expenses | Net Profit/ (Loss)* |
|---|---|---|---|---|---|---|---|
| | £ | £ | £ | £ | £ | £ | £ |
| Business A | 20 000 | 5 000 | 10 000 | 3 000 | ........ | 4 000 | ........ |
| Business B | 35 000 | 8 000 | 15 000 | 5 000 | ........ | ......... | 10 000 |
| Business C | ......... | 6 500 | 18 750 | 7 250 | 18 500 | 11 750 | ........ |
| Business D | 45 250 | 9 500 | ......... | 10 500 | 20 750 | ......... | 10 950 |
| Business E | 71 250 | ........ | 49 250 | 9 100 | 22 750 | 24 450 | ........ |
| Business F | 25 650 | 4 950 | 13 750 | ........ | 11 550 | ......... | (3 450) |

* Note: a net loss is indicated in brackets

**12.4*** The following trial balance has been extracted by the book-keeper of John Adams at 31 December 20-7:

| | Dr £ | Cr £ |
|---|---|---|
| Stock at 1 January 20-7 | 14,350 | |
| Purchases | 114,472 | |
| Sales | | 259,688 |
| Rates | 13,718 | |
| Heating and lighting | 12,540 | |
| Wages and salaries | 42,614 | |
| Vehicle expenses | 5,817 | |
| Advertising | 6,341 | |
| Premises | 75,000 | |
| Office equipment | 33,000 | |
| Vehicles | 21,500 | |
| Debtors | 23,854 | |
| Bank | 1,235 | |
| Cash | 125 | |
| Capital at 1 January 20-7 | | 62,500 |
| Drawings | 12,358 | |
| Loan from bank | | 35,000 |
| Creditors | | 17,281 |
| Value Added Tax | | 2,455 |
| | 376,924 | 376,924 |

Stock at 31 December 20-7 was valued at £16,280.

You are to prepare the trading and profit and loss account of John Adams for the year ended 31 December 20-7, together with his balance sheet at that date.

**12.5** The following trial balance has been extracted by the book-keeper of Clare Lewis at 31 December 20-4:

| | Dr £ | Cr £ |
|---|---|---|
| Debtors | 18,600 | |
| Creditors | | 12,140 |
| Valus Added Tax | | 1,210 |
| Bank overdraft | | 4,610 |
| Capital at 1 January 20-4 | | 25,250 |
| Sales | | 144,810 |
| Purchases | 96,318 | |
| Stock at 1 January 20-4 | 16,010 | |
| Salaries | 18,465 | |
| Heating and lighting | 1,820 | |
| Rent and rates | 5,647 | |
| Vehicles | 9,820 | |
| Office equipment | 5,500 | |
| Sundry expenses | 845 | |
| Vehicle expenses | 1,684 | |
| Drawings | 13,311 | |
| | 188,020 | 188,020 |

Stock at 31 December 20-4 was valued at £13,735.

You are to prepare the trading and profit and loss account of Clare Lewis for the year ended 31 December 20-4, together with her balance sheet at that date.

**12.6** Classify the following costs as either capital expenditure or as revenue expenditure

(a)     purchase of vehicles

(b)     rent paid on premises

(c)     wages and salaries

(d)     legal fees relating to the purchase of property

(e)     redecoration of the office

(f)     installation of air-conditioning in the office

(g)     wages of own employees used to build extension to the stockroom

(h)     installation and setting up of a new machine

**12.7** The following transactions relate to AB Stores, a small retail business which separates direct selling expenses from other overhead expenses:

Purchase of new weighing equipment for use within the business.

Rent received from sub-letting office space over the business.

Payment of business rate to the local authority.

Cost of extension to the rear of the business.

Wages of sales assistants.

Legal fees paid in connection with the extension.

You are required to:

(a)   Enter each item under one of the three headings:

   (i)    Capital expenditure

   (ii)   Revenue expenditure

   (iii)  Revenue receipt

(b)   State which items would appear in:

   (i)    The trading account

   (ii)   The profit and loss account

   (iii)  The balance sheet

Note: your answer should be in table form.

*Reproduced by kind permission of OCR Examinations*

# WYVERN METAL SUPPLIES HANDWRITTEN BOOK-KEEPING

This Case Study is a fully worked example of a handwritten book-keeping system. It looks at the routine transactions of a sole trader business, Wyvern Metal Supplies, which is a supplier of specialist steel and other metals to local businesses. Wyvern Metal Supplies is registered for Value Added Tax, and all its purchases and sales are subject to VAT.

## THE BOOK-KEEPING SYSTEM

Wyvern Metal Supplies operates a handwritten book-keeping system which is divided into: sales ledger, purchases ledger, general ledger and cash book.

Day books are used for sales, purchases, and returns. A journal (see Chapter 18) is used for the year-end transfers to the trading and profit and loss account. Note: control accounts (see Chapter 20) are not used.

The business transactions are for the month of December 20-1. They include:

- credit sales
- credit purchases
- receipts and payments, including cash discount allowed and received
- expenses and drawings

All transactions are cross-referenced in the accounts to show the use of the folio column. The abbreviations used are:

| | |
|---|---|
| SL = sales ledger | SDB = sales day book |
| PL = purchases ledger | PDB = purchases day book |
| GL = general ledger | SRDB = sales returns day book |
| CB = cash book | PRDB = purchases returns day book |
| C = contra, ie both transactions are in the same book | |

The firm's financial year ends on 31 December 20-1, at which date the final accounts are prepared. As this Case Study is intended to show routine transactions, no adjustments are shown in the final accounts for:

- accruals and prepayments (see Chapter 13)
- provision for depreciation of fixed assets (see Chapter 14)
- bad debts written off, and provision for bad debts (see Chapter 15)

These adjustments are brought together in Case Study 2 on page 296.

# TRIAL BALANCE

The trial balance of the business at 30 November 20-1, after eleven months' trading in the financial year, is as follows:

| TRIAL BALANCE OF WYVERN METAL SUPPLIES AS AT 30 NOVEMBER 20-1 | | Folio | Dr £ | Cr £ |
|---|---|---|---|---|
| Sales | | GL101 | | 180,500 |
| Purchases | | GL102 | 81,300 | |
| Sales returns | | GL103 | 850 | |
| Purchases returns | | GL104 | | 430 |
| Wages and salaries | | GL105 | 45,800 | |
| Vehicle running expenses | | GL106 | 2,700 | |
| Office expenses | | GL107 | 7,810 | |
| Rates | | GL108 | 4,030 | |
| Rent paid | | GL109 | 13,200 | |
| Discount allowed | | GL110 | 2,100 | |
| Discount received | | GL111 | | 980 |
| Delivery van | | GL112 | 12,000 | |
| Office equipment | | GL113 | 5,000 | |
| Stock at 1 January 20-1 | | GL114 | 16,170 | |
| Value Added Tax | | GL115 | | 2,750 |
| Capital | | GL116 | | 30,000 |
| Drawings | | GL117 | 18,700 | |
| Cash | | CB | 255 | |
| Bank | | CB | 5,785 | |
| Debtors: | Eveshore Engineering Ltd | SL201 | 4,000 | |
| | Wyvern Wiring Co Ltd | SL202 | 4,400 | |
| | Speciality Forgings | SL203 | 6,720 | |
| Creditors: | Axis Supplies Ltd | PL301 | | 7,830 |
| | Quality Alloys Ltd | PL302 | | 5,330 |
| | Midlands Steel Co Ltd | PL303 | | 3,000 |
| | | | 230,820 | 230,820 |

# TRANSACTIONS FOR DECEMBER 20-1

| | |
|---|---|
| 1 Dec | Bought goods, £2,000 + VAT, on credit from Quality Alloys Ltd; received invoice no 7651 |
| 2 Dec | Sold goods, £1,000 + VAT, on credit to Wyvern Wiring Co Ltd; issued invoice no 5310 |
| 3 Dec | Received a cheque from Eveshore Engineering Ltd in full settlement of the amount owing, less 2.5% cash discount |
| 4 Dec | Paid office expenses, £200 + VAT, by cheque |
| 4 Dec | Paid the amount owing to Midlands Steel Co Ltd by cheque, after deducting 2.5% cash discount |
| 5 Dec | Bought goods, £1,000 + VAT, on credit from Axis Supplies Ltd; received invoice no AS791 |
| 5 Dec | Owner's drawings, £250, in cash |
| 8 Dec | Returned goods, £40 + VAT, to Quality Alloys Ltd; received credit note no 0278 |
| 8 Dec | Withdrew £500 of cash from the bank for business use |
| 9 Dec | Sold goods, £1,440 + VAT, on credit to Speciality Forgings; issued invoice no 5311 |
| 10 Dec | Bought office equipment, £320 + VAT, paying by cheque no 365129 |
| 10 Dec | Wyvern Wiring Co Ltd returns goods, £80 + VAT; credit note no 159 issued |
| 11 Dec | Paid the amount owing to Quality Alloys Ltd by cheque |
| 12 Dec | Paid vehicle running expenses, £120 + VAT, in cash |
| 12 Dec | Sold goods, £800 + VAT, on credit to Eveshore Engineering Ltd; issued invoice no 5312 |
| 15 Dec | Received a cheque from Wyvern Wiring Co Ltd for the amount owing on 1 December, less 2.5% cash discount |
| 16 Dec | Sold goods £2,200 + VAT, on credit to Speciality Forgings; issued invoice no 5313 |
| 16 Dec | Paid wages and salaries £5,500 by cheque |
| 17 Dec | Bought goods, £1,520 + VAT, on credit from Midlands Steel Co Ltd; received invoice no 9432 |
| 17 Dec | Eveshore Engineering Ltd returns goods, £200 + VAT, credit note no 160 issued |
| 18 Dec | Paid office expenses, £94 including VAT, by cheque |
| 18 Dec | Received a cheque from Speciality Forgings for £6,720 |
| 19 Dec | Returned goods, £120 + VAT, to Midlands Steel Co Ltd; received credit note no CN732 |
| 19 Dec | Paid rent, £1,200 + VAT, by cheque |
| 22 Dec | Sold goods, £1,600 + VAT, on credit to Wyvern Wiring Co Ltd; issued invoice no 5314 |
| 22 Dec | Bought goods, £1,800 + VAT, on credit from Quality Alloys Ltd; received invoice no 7943 |
| 23 Dec | Sold goods, £1,320 + VAT, on credit to Eveshore Engineering Ltd; issued invoice no 5315 |
| 24 Dec | Owner's drawings, £450, by cheque |
| 29 Dec | Received a cheque from Speciality Forgings for £4,000 |

- At 31 December 20-1, the closing stock is valued at £20,200.
- VAT is charged at 17.5 per cent.
- For simplicity, calculate the amounts of the cash discount allowed and received on the gross amounts due, ie including VAT.

# DAY BOOKS

## SALES DAY BOOK

| Date | Details | Invoice No | Folio | Net | VAT | Gross |
|------|---------|-----------|-------|-----|-----|-------|
| 20-1 | | | | £ | £ | £ |
| 2 Dec | Wyvern Wiring Co Ltd | 5310 | SL202 | 1,000 | 175 | 1,175 |
| 9 Dec | Speciality Forgings | 5311 | SL203 | 1,440 | 252 | 1,692 |
| 12 Dec | Eveshore Engineering Ltd | 5312 | SL201 | 800 | 140 | 940 |
| 16 Dec | Speciality Forgings | 5313 | SL203 | 2,200 | 385 | 2,585 |
| 22 Dec | Wyvern Wiring Co Ltd | 5314 | SL202 | 1,600 | 280 | 1,880 |
| 23 Dec | Eveshore Engineering Ltd | 5315 | SL201 | 1,320 | 231 | 1,551 |
| 31 Dec | Totals for month | | | 8,360 | 1,463 | 9,823 |
| | | | | GL101 | GL115 | |

## PURCHASES DAY BOOK

| Date | Details | Invoice No | Folio | Net | VAT | Gross |
|------|---------|-----------|-------|-----|-----|-------|
| 20-1 | | | | £ | £ | £ |
| 1 Dec | Quality Alloys Ltd | 7651 | PL302 | 2,000 | 350 | 2,350 |
| 5 Dec | Axis Supplies Ltd | AS791 | PL301 | 1,000 | 175 | 1,175 |
| 17 Dec | Midlands Steel Co Ltd | 9432 | PL303 | 1,520 | 266 | 1,786 |
| 22 Dec | Quality Alloys Ltd | 7943 | PL302 | 1,800 | 315 | 2,115 |
| 31 Dec | Totals for month | | | 6,320 | 1,106 | 7,426 |
| | | | | GL102 | GL115 | |

## SALES RETURNS DAY BOOK

| Date | Details | Credit Note no. | Folio | Net | VAT | Gross |
|------|---------|-----------------|-------|-----|-----|-------|
| 20-1 | | | | £ | £ | £ |
| 10 Dec | Wyvern Wiring Co Ltd | 159 | SL202 | 80 | 14 | 94 |
| 17 Dec | Eveshore Engineering Ltd | 160 | SL201 | 200 | 35 | 235 |
| 31 Dec | Totals for month | | | 280 | 49 | 329 |
| | | | | GL103 | GL115 | |

| PURCHASES RETURNS DAY BOOK | | | | | | |
|---|---|---|---|---|---|---|
| Date | Details | Credit Note No | Folio | Net | VAT | Gross |
| 20-1 | | | | £ | £ | £ |
| 8 Dec | Quality Alloys Ltd | 0278 | PL302 | 40 | 7 | 47 |
| 19 Dec | Midlands Steel Co Ltd | CN732 | PL303 | 120 | 21 | 141 |
| 31 Dec | Totals for month | | | 160 | 28 | 188 |
| | | | | GL104 | GL115 | |

## THE LEDGER ACCOUNTS

The ledger accounts include year-end transfers, where appropriate, to the trading and profit and loss account (these are set out on page 196). An asterisk (*) shows a monthly total taken from a day book.

**GENERAL LEDGER**

| Dr | | | Sales  (account no 101) | | | Cr |
|---|---|---|---|---|---|---|
| 20-1 | | £ | 20-1 | | | £ |
| 31 Dec | Trading account | 188,860 | 1 Dec | Balance b/d | | 180,500 |
| | | | 31 Dec | Sales Day Book* | SDB | 8,360 |
| | | 188,860 | | | | 188,860 |

| Dr | | | Purchases  (account no 102) | | | Cr |
|---|---|---|---|---|---|---|
| 20-1 | | £ | 20-1 | | | £ |
| 1 Dec | Balance b/d | 81,300 | 31 Dec | Trading account | | 87,620 |
| 31 Dec | Purchases Day Book*  PDB | 6,320 | | | | |
| | | 87,620 | | | | 87,620 |

| Dr | | | Sales returns  (account no 103) | | | Cr |
|---|---|---|---|---|---|---|
| 20-1 | | £ | 20-1 | | | £ |
| 1 Dec | Balance b/d | 850 | 31 Dec | Trading account | | 1,130 |
| 31 Dec | Sales Returns Day Book* SRDB | 280 | | | | |
| | | 1,130 | | | | 1,130 |

Dr                         **Purchases returns  (account no 104)**                         Cr

| 20-1 | | £ | 20-1 | | £ |
|---|---|---|---|---|---|
| 31 Dec | Trading account | 590 | 1 Dec | Balance b/d | 430 |
| | | | 31 Dec | Purchases Returns Day Book* | |
| | | | | PRDB | 160 |
| | | 590 | | | 590 |

Dr                         **Wages and salaries  (account no 105)**                         Cr

| 20-1 | | | £ | 20-1 | | £ |
|---|---|---|---|---|---|---|
| 1 Dec | Balance b/d | | 45,800 | 31 Dec | Profit and loss account | 51,300 |
| 16 Dec | Bank | CB | 5,500 | | | |
| | | | 51,300 | | | 51,300 |

Dr                         **Vehicle running expenses  (account no 106)**                         Cr

| 20-1 | | | £ | 20-1 | | £ |
|---|---|---|---|---|---|---|
| 1 Dec | Balance b/d | | 2,700 | 31 Dec | Profit and loss account | 2,820 |
| 12 Dec | Cash | CB | 120 | | | |
| | | | 2,820 | | | 2,820 |

Dr                         **Office expenses  (account no 107)**                         Cr

| 20-1 | | | £ | 20-1 | | £ |
|---|---|---|---|---|---|---|
| 1 Dec | Balance b/d | | 7,810 | 31 Dec | Profit and loss account | 8,090 |
| 4 Dec | Bank | CB | 200 | | | |
| 18 Dec | Bank | CB | 80 | | | |
| | | | 8,090 | | | 8,090 |

Dr                         **Rates  (account no 108)**                         Cr

| 20-1 | | £ | 20-1 | | £ |
|---|---|---|---|---|---|
| 1 Dec | Balance b/d | 4,030 | 31 Dec | Profit and loss account | 4,030 |

Dr                         **Rent paid  (account no 109)**                         Cr

| 20-1 | | | £ | 20-1 | | £ |
|---|---|---|---|---|---|---|
| 1 Dec | Balance b/d | | 13,200 | 31 Dec | Profit and loss account | 14,400 |
| 19 Dec | Bank | CB | 1,200 | | | |
| | | | 14,400 | | | 14,400 |

| Dr | **Discount allowed  (account no 110)** | | Cr |
|---|---|---|---|
| 20-1 | | £ | 20-1 | | £ |

| Dr | | | | | | Cr |
|---|---|---|---|---|---|---|
| 20-1 | | | £ | 20-1 | | £ |
| 1 Dec | Balance b/d | | 2,100 | 31 Dec | Profit and loss account | 2,310 |
| 31 Dec | Cash Book* | CB | 210 | | | |
| | | | 2,310 | | | 2,310 |

\* Total for the month taken from the appropriate column in the cash book (see page 191)

| Dr | | **Discount received  (account no 111)** | | | | Cr |
|---|---|---|---|---|---|---|
| 20-1 | | | £ | 20-1 | | £ |
| 31 Dec | Profit and loss account | | 1,055 | 1 Dec | Balance b/d | 980 |
| | | | | 31 Dec | Cash Book* | CB | 75 |
| | | | 1,055 | | | 1,055 |

\* Total for the month taken from the appropriate column in the cash book (see page 191)

| Dr | | **Delivery van  (account no 112)** | | | Cr |
|---|---|---|---|---|---|
| 20-1 | | £ | 20-1 | | £ |
| 1 Dec | Balance b/d | 12,000 | 31 Dec | Balance c/d | 12,000 |
| 20-2 | | | 20-2 | | |
| 1 Jan | Balance b/d | 12,000 | | | |

| Dr | | **Office equipment  (account no 113)** | | | | Cr |
|---|---|---|---|---|---|---|
| 20-1 | | | £ | 20-1 | | £ |
| 1 Dec | Balance b/d | | 5,000 | 31 Dec | Balance c/d | 5,320 |
| 10 Dec | Bank | CB | 320 | | | |
| | | | 5,320 | | | 5,320 |
| 20-2 | | | | 20-2 | | |
| 1 Jan | Balance b/d | | 5,320 | | | |

| Dr | **Stock  (account no 114)** | | | Cr |
|---|---|---|---|---|
| 20-1 | | £ | 20-1 | | £ |
| 1 Dec | Balance b/d | 16,170 | 31 Dec | Trading account | 16,170 |
| 31 Dec | Trading account | 20,200 | 31 Dec | Balance c/d | 20,200 |
| 20-2 | | | 20-2 | | |
| 1 Jan | Balance b/d | 20,200 | | | |

Dr             **Value Added Tax (account no 115)**             Cr

| 20-1 | | | £ | 20-1 | | | £ |
|---|---|---|---|---|---|---|---|
| 31 Dec | Purchases Day Book* | PDB | 1,106 | 1 Dec | Balance b/d | | 2,750 |
| 31 Dec | Sales Returns Day Book* | SRDB | 49 | 31 Dec | Sales Day Book* | SDB | 1,463 |
| 31 Dec | Cash Book† | CB | 336 | 31 Dec | Purchases Returns Day Book* | | |
| 31 Dec | Balance c/d | | 2,750 | | | PRDB | 28 |
| | | | 4,241 | | | | 4,241 |
| | | | | 20-2 | | | |
| | | | | 1 Jan. | Balance b/d | | 2,750 |

\*   monthly total taken from the appropriate day book

†   monthly total taken from the VAT column in the cash book

Dr             **Capital (account no 116)**             Cr

| 20-1 | | | £ | 20-1 | | | £ |
|---|---|---|---|---|---|---|---|
| 31 Dec | Drawings | GL117 | 19,400 | 1 Dec | Balance b/d | | 30,000 |
| 31 Dec | Balance c/d | | 33,435 | 31 Dec | Profit and loss account§ | | 22,835 |
| | | | 52,835 | | | | 52,835 |
| 20-2 | | | | 20-2 | | | |
| | | | | 1 Jan. | Balance b/d | | 33,435 |

§   net profit for the year, calculated in the profit and loss account (page 197)

Dr             **Drawings (account no 117)**             Cr

| 20-1 | | | £ | 20-1 | | | £ |
|---|---|---|---|---|---|---|---|
| 1 Dec | Balance b/d | | 18,700 | 31 Dec | Capital | GL116 | 19,400 |
| 5 Dec | Cash | CB | 250 | | | | |
| 24 Dec | Bank | CB | 450 | | | | |
| | | | 19,400 | | | | 19,400 |

## CASH BOOK

### Debit side

| Date | Details | | VAT £ | Discount allowed £ | Cash £ | Bank £ |
|---|---|---|---|---|---|---|
| 20-1 | | | | | | |
| 1 Dec | Balances b/d | | | | 255 | 5,785 |
| 3 Dec | Eveshore Engineering Ltd SL201 | | | 100 | | 3,900 |
| 8 Dec | Bank | C | | | 500 | |
| 15 Dec | Wyvern Wiring Co Ltd | SL202 | | 110 | | 4,290 |
| 18 Dec | Speciality Forgings | SL203 | | | | 6,720 |
| 29 Dec | Speciality Forgings | SL203 | | | | 4,000 |
| | | | GL 115 | 210 GL 110 | 755 | 24,695 |
| 20-2 | | | | | | |
| 1 Jan | Balances b/d | | | | 364 | 5,572 |

### Credit side

| Date | Details | | VAT £ | Discount received £ | Cash £ | Bank £ |
|---|---|---|---|---|---|---|
| 20-1 | | | | | | |
| 4 Dec | Office expenses | GL107 | 35 | | | 235 |
| 4 Dec | Midlands Steel Co Ltd | PL303 | | 75 | | 2,925 |
| 5 Dec | Drawings | GL117 | | | | 500 |
| 8 Dec | Cash | C | | | 250 | |
| 10 Dec | Office equipment | GL113 | 56 | | | 376 |
| 11 Dec | Quality Alloys Ltd | PL302 | | | | 7,633 |
| 12 Dec | Vehicle running expenses | GL106 | 21 | | 141 | |
| 16 Dec | Wages and salaries | GL105 | | | | 5,500 |
| 18 Dec | Office expenses | GL107 | 14 | | | 94 |
| 19 Dec | Rent | GL109 | 210 | | | 1,410 |
| 24 Dec | Drawings | GL117 | | | | 450 |
| 31 Dec | Balances c/d | | | | 364 | 5,572 |
| | | | 336 GL 115 | 75 GL 111 | 755 | 24,695 |
| 20-2 | | | | | | |

- In the VAT columns of the cash book, no VAT is shown for transactions involving the sales ledger (eg Eveshore Engineering Ltd) and purchases ledger (eg Midlands Steel Co Ltd). This is because VAT has been charged on invoices issued and received and was recorded in the VAT account (via the appropriate day book) when the sale or purchase was made. However, VAT on cash sales and purchases, and other transactions, is recorded in the VAT columns of the cash book.

- For simplicity, the amounts of cash discount allowed and received have been calculated on the gross amounts due, ie including VAT

## SALES LEDGER

| Dr | **Eveshore Engineering Ltd  (account no 201)** | | | | Cr |
|---|---|---|---|---|---|
| 20-1 | | | £ | 20-1 | | | £ |

| Dr | | | | **Eveshore Engineering Ltd  (account no 201)** | | | Cr |
|---|---|---|---|---|---|---|---|
| 20-1 | | | £ | 20-1 | | | £ |
| 1 Dec | Balance b/d | | 4,000 | 3 Dec | Bank | CB | 3,900 |
| 12 Dec | Sales | SDB | 940 | 3 Dec | Discount allowed | CB | 100 |
| 23 Dec | Sales | SDB | 1,551 | 17 Dec | Sales returns | SRDB | 235 |
| | | | | 31 Dec | Balance c/d | | 2,256 |
| | | | 6,491 | | | | 6,491 |
| 20-2 | | | | 20-2 | | | |
| 1 Jan | Balance b/d | | 2,256 | | | | |

| Dr | | | | **Wyvern Wiring Co Ltd  (account no 202)** | | | Cr |
|---|---|---|---|---|---|---|---|
| 20-1 | | | £ | 20-1 | | | £ |
| 1 Dec | Balance b/d | | 4,400 | 8 Dec | Sales returns | SRDB | 94 |
| 2 Dec | Sales | SDB | 1,175 | 15 Dec | Bank | CB | 4,290 |
| 22 Dec | Sales | SDB | 1,880 | 15 Dec | Discount allowed | CB | 110 |
| | | | | 31 Dec | Balance c/d | | 2,961 |
| | | | 7,455 | | | | 7,455 |
| 20-2 | | | | 20-2 | | | |
| 1 Jan | Balance b/d | | 2,961 | | | | |

| Dr | | | | **Speciality Forgings  (account no 203)** | | | Cr |
|---|---|---|---|---|---|---|---|
| 20-1 | | | £ | 20-1 | | | £ |
| 1 Dec | Balance b/d | | 6,720 | 18 Dec | Bank | CB | 6,720 |
| 9 Dec | Sales | SDB | 1,692 | 29 Dec | Bank | CB | 4,000 |
| 16 Dec | Sales | SDB | 2,585 | 31 Dec | Balance c/d | | 277 |
| | | | 10,997 | | | | 10,997 |
| 20-2 | | | | 20-2 | | | |
| 1 Jan | Balance b/d | | 277 | | | | |

**PURCHASES LEDGER**

| Dr | | **Axis Supplies Ltd  (account no 301)** | | Cr |
|---|---|---|---|---|
| 20-1 | | £ | 20-1 | | | £ |
| 31 Dec | Balance c/d | 9,005 | 1 Dec | Balance b/d | | 7,830 |
| | | | 5 Dec | Purchases | PDB | 1,175 |
| | | 9,005 | | | | 9,005 |
| 20-2 | | | 20-2 | | | |
| | | | 1 Jan | Balance b/d | | 9,005 |

| Dr | | **Quality Alloys Ltd  (account no 302)** | | Cr |
|---|---|---|---|---|
| 20-1 | | | £ | 20-1 | | | £ |
| 8 Dec | Purchases returns | PRDB | 47 | 1 Dec | Balance b/d | | 5,330 |
| 11 Dec | Bank | CB | 7,633 | 1 Dec | Purchases | PDB | 2,350 |
| 31 Dec | Balance c/d | | 2,115 | 22 Dec | Purchases | PDB | 2,115 |
| | | | 9,795 | | | | 9,795 |
| 20-2 | | | | 20-2 | | | |
| | | | | 1 Jan | Balance b/d | | 2,115 |

| Dr | | **Midlands Steel Co Ltd  (account no 303)** | | Cr |
|---|---|---|---|---|
| 20-1 | | | £ | 20-1 | | | £ |
| 4 Dec | Bank | CB | 2,925 | 1 Dec | Balance b/d | | 3,000 |
| 4 Dec | Discount received | CB | 75 | 17 Dec | Purchases | PDB | 1,786 |
| 19 Dec | Purchases returns | PRDB | 141 | | | | |
| 31 Dec | Balance c/d | | 1,645 | | | | |
| | | | 4,786 | | | | 4,786 |
| 20-2 | | | | 20-2 | | | |
| | | | | 1 Jan | Balance b/d | | 1,645 |

# Trial Balance at the Month-End

| TRIAL BALANCE OF WYVERN METAL SUPPLIES AS AT 31 DECEMBER 20-1 | | | |
|---|---|---|---|
| (before preparation of the final accounts) | | | |
| | Folio | Dr | Cr |
| | | £ | £ |
| Sales | GL101 | | 188,860 |
| Purchases | GL102 | 87,620 | |
| Sales returns | GL103 | 1,130 | |
| Purchases returns | GL104 | | 590 |
| Wages and salaries | GL105 | 51,300 | |
| Vehicle running expenses | GL106 | 2,820 | |
| Office expenses | GL107 | 8,090 | |
| Rates | GL108 | 4,030 | |
| Rent paid | GL109 | 14,400 | |
| Discount allowed | GL110 | 2,310 | |
| Discount received | GL111 | | 1,055 |
| Delivery van | GL112 | 12,000 | |
| Office equipment | GL113 | 5,320 | |
| Stock at 1 January 20-1 | GL114 | 16,170 | |
| Value Added Tax | GL115 | | 2,750 |
| Capital | GL116 | | 30,000 |
| Drawings | GL117 | 19,400 | |
| Cash | CB | 364 | |
| Bank | CB | 5,572 | |
| *Debtors:   Eveshore Engineering Ltd | SL201 | 2,256 | |
| Wyvern Wiring Co Ltd | SL202 | 2,961 | |
| Speciality Forgings | SL203 | 277 | |
| *Creditors:  Axis Supplies Ltd | PL301 | | 9,005 |
| Quality Alloys Ltd | PL302 | | 2,115 |
| Midlands Steel Co Ltd | PL303 | | 1,645 |
| | | 236,020 | 236,020 |

\*   Instead of showing the balance of individual debtors and creditors accounts, the total of each ledger section could be recorded: see also control accounts (Chapter 20).

## notes to the trial balance

In the trial balance on the previous page:

- the stock account balance of £16,170 is before the year-end transfers in respect of the closing stock – valued at £20,200 – are entered into the accounts (see the next section)

- the capital account balance of £30,000, and drawings account balance of £19,400, are before the year-end transfers are made to capital account in respect of net profit from the profit and loss account – see page 197 – and drawings (see the next section)

# YEAR-END JOURNAL ENTRIES

At the end of the financial year a number of transfers are made to transfer the balances of certain accounts to the trading and profit and loss account, and also in connection with capital account and drawings account. We have already seen in Chapter 12 the double-entry book-keeping for these transfers. In order to keep an accurate record, an entry is made in the journal for each of these non-regular transactions. We shall look at journal entries in more detail in Chapter 18.

The journal entries to be made in respect of the year-end transfers of Wyvern Metal Supplies are shown on the next page.

You should note that the trading and profit and loss account is located in the general ledger; however, because of its importance within the general ledger it is not normally allocated an account number.

| JOURNAL | | | | |
|---|---|---|---|---|

| Date | Details | Folio | Dr | Cr |
|---|---|---|---|---|
| 20-1 | | | £ | £ |
| 31 Dec | Trading account | GL | 87,620 | |
| | Purchases | GL102 | | 87,620 |
| | Sales | GL101 | 188,860 | |
| | Trading account | GL | | 188,860 |
| | Purchases returns | GL104 | 590 | |
| | Trading account | GL | | 590 |
| | Trading account | GL | 1,130 | |
| | Sales returns | GL103 | | 1,130 |
| | Trading account (opening stock) | GL | 16,170 | |
| | Stock (opening stock) | GL114 | | 16,170 |
| | Stock (closing stock) | GL114 | 20,200 | |
| | Trading account (closing stock) | GL | | 20,200 |

*Transfer of purchases, sales, purchases returns, sales returns, and stock balance to the trading account in order to calculate gross profit for the year-ended 31 December 20-1*

| 31 Dec | Discount received | GL111 | 1,055 | |
|---|---|---|---|---|
| | Profit and loss account | GL | | 1,055 |
| | Profit and loss account | GL | 51,300 | |
| | Wages and salaries | GL105 | | 51,300 |
| | Profit and loss account | GL | 2,820 | |
| | Vehicle running expenses | GL106 | | 2,820 |
| | Profit and loss account | GL | 8,090 | |
| | Office expenses | GL107 | | 8,090 |
| | Profit and loss account | GL | 4,030 | |
| | Rates | GL108 | | 4,030 |
| | Profit and loss account | GL | 14,400 | |
| | Rent paid | GL109 | | 14,400 |
| | Profit and loss account | GL | 2,310 | |
| | Discount allowed | GL110 | | 2,310 |

*Transfer of income and expenditure to the profit and loss account in order to calculate net profit for the year-ended 31 December 20-1*

| 31 Dec | Profit and loss account | GL | 22,835 | |
|---|---|---|---|---|
| | Capital | GL116 | | 22,835 |
| | Capital | GL116 | 19,400 | |
| | Drawings | GL117 | | 19,400 |

*Transfer of net profit and drawings to capital account at the end of the financial year*

# FINAL ACCOUNTS

**WYVERN METAL SUPPLIES**

**TRADING AND PROFIT AND LOSS ACCOUNT FOR THE YEAR ENDED 31 DECEMBER 20-1**

|  | £ | £ | £ |
|---|---|---|---|
| Sales |  |  | 188,860 |
| Less Sales returns |  |  | 1,130 |
| Net sales |  |  | 187,730 |
| Openlng stock |  | 16,170 |  |
| Purchases | 87,620 |  |  |
| Less Purchases returns | 590 |  |  |
| Net purchases |  | 87,030 |  |
|  |  | 103,200 |  |
| Less Closing stock |  | 20,200 |  |
| Cost of Goods Sold |  |  | 83,000 |
| **Gross profit** |  |  | 104,730 |
| Add: Discount received |  |  | 1,055 |
|  |  |  | 105,785 |
| Less expenses: |  |  |  |
| Wages and salaries |  | 51,300 |  |
| Vehicle running expenses |  | 2,820 |  |
| Office expenses |  | 8,090 |  |
| Rates |  | 4,030 |  |
| Rent paid |  | 14,400 |  |
| Discount allowed |  | 2,310 |  |
|  |  |  | 82,950 |
| **Net profit** |  |  | 22,835 |

**WYVERN METAL SUPPLIES**

**BALANCE SHEET AS AT 31 DECEMBER 20-1**

|  | £ | £ | £ |
|---|---|---|---|
| **Fixed Assets** | | | |
| Delivery van | | | 12,000 |
| Office equipment | | | 5,320 |
| | | | 17,320 |
| **Current Assets** | | | |
| Stock | | 20,200 | |
| Debtors* | | 5,494 | |
| Bank | | 5,572 | |
| Cash | | 364 | |
| | | 31,630 | |
| **Less Current Liabilities** | | | |
| Creditors** | 12,765 | | |
| Value Added Tax† | 2,750 | | |
| | | 15,515 | |
| **Working Capital** | | | 16,115 |
| **NET ASSETS** | | | 33,435 |
| | | | |
| **FINANCED BY:** | | | |
| **Capital** | | | |
| Opening capital | | | 30,000 |
| Add Net profit | | | 22,835 |
| | | | 52,835 |
| Less Drawings | | | 19,400 |
| | | | 33,435 |

**Notes**

\* The debtors figure is the total of the Sales Ledger balances.

\*\* The creditors figure is the total of the Purchases Ledger balances.

† In this balance sheet VAT is a liability and, assuming 31 December 20-1 is the end of the VAT quarter, the amount due to HM Customs and Excise will be paid by 31 January 20-2.

## CASE STUDY SUMMARY

●      In this Case Study we have looked at the routine business transactions passing through the handwritten book-keeping system of a sole trader.

●      The primary accounting records used are:

- sales day book
- purchases day book
- sales returns day book
- purchases returns day book
- journal (see Chapter 18)

●      The business transactions are then entered into the ledger. This is split into:

- sales ledger
- purchases ledger
- general ledger
- cash book

●      A trial balance is extracted at the end of the month.

●      Final accounts are prepared comprising:

- trading and profit and loss account
- balance sheet

Transfers are recorded in the journal and made from the ledger to the trading and profit and loss account.

Case Study 2 (on page 296) uses the information from the trial balance at 31 December 20-1 in this Case Study, and makes adjustments in the final accounts for:

- accruals and prepayments (see Chapter 13)
- provision for depreciation (see Chapter 14)
- bad debts written off, and provision for bad debts (see Chapter 15)

# 13 ACCRUALS AND PREPAYMENTS

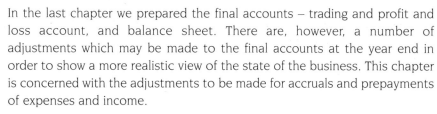

In the last chapter we prepared the final accounts – trading and profit and loss account, and balance sheet. There are, however, a number of adjustments which may be made to the final accounts at the year end in order to show a more realistic view of the state of the business. This chapter is concerned with the adjustments to be made for accruals and prepayments of expenses and income.

To illustrate the effect of adjustments for accruals and prepayments on final accounts we will be referring to the set of accounts of Wyvern Wholesalers – see Chapter 12, pages 167 and 168.

## ACCRUAL OF EXPENSES

*An accrual is an amount due in an accounting period which is unpaid at the end of that period.*

In the final accounts, accrued expenses are:

- added to the expense from the trial balance before listing it in the profit and loss account
- shown as a current liability in the year end balance sheet

The reason for dealing with accruals in this way is to ensure that the profit and loss account records the cost that has been incurred for the year, instead of simply the amount that has been paid. In other words, the expense is adjusted to relate to the time period covered by the profit and loss account. The year end balance sheet shows a liability for the amount that is due, but unpaid.

In this book, and generally in accounting exercises, details of accruals (and prepayments – see below) will usually appear as a note to the trial balance.

### example of an accrual expense

The trial balance of Wyvern Wholesalers (see page 163) shows a debit balance for electricity and gas of £3,000. Before preparing the final accounts, an electricity bill for £250 is received on 1 January 20-2, ie on the first day of the new financial year. As this bill is clearly for electricity used in 20-1, an adjustment needs to be made in the final accounts for 20-1 to record this accrued expense.

In the profit and loss account, the total cost of £3,250 (ie £3,000 from the trial balance, plus £250 accrued) will be recorded as an expense. In the balance sheet, £250 will be shown as a separate current liability of 'accruals'.

## accruals – the book-keeping records

In the double-entry records, accruals must be shown as an amount owing at the end of the financial year. Thus the account for electricity and gas in the records of Wyvern Wholesalers will appear as follows:

| Dr | | | Electricity and Gas Account | | | Cr |
|---|---|---|---|---|---|---|
| 20-1 | | £ | 20-1 | | | £ |
| 31 Dec | Balance b/d (trial balance total) | 3,000 | 31 Dec | Profit and loss account | | 3,250 |
| 31 Dec | Balance c/d | 250 | | | | |
| | | 3,250 | | | | 3,250 |
| 20-2 | | | 20-2 | | | |
| | | | 1 Jan | Balance b/d | | 250 |

Notes:

- The book-keeper's trial balance showed the debit side balance brought down of £3,000

- As £250 is owing for electricity at the end of the year, the transfer to profit and loss account is the cost that has been incurred for the year – this amounts to £3,250

- The balance remaining on the account – a credit balance of £250 – is the amount of the accrual, which is listed on the balance sheet at 31 December 20-1 as a current liability

- Later on, for example on 5 January, the electricity bill is paid by cheque and the account for 20-2 now appears as:

| Dr | | | Electricity and Gas Account | | | Cr |
|---|---|---|---|---|---|---|
| 20-2 | | £ | 20-2 | | | £ |
| 5 Jan | Bank | 250 | 1 Jan | Balance b/d | | 250 |

The effect of the payment on 5 January is that the account now has a 'nil' balance and the bill received on 1 January will not be recorded as an expense in the profit and loss account drawn up at the end of 20-2.

## effect on profit

Taking note of the accrual of an expense has the effect of reducing a previously reported net profit. As the expenses have been increased, net profit is less (but there is no effect on gross profit). Thus, the net profit of Wyvern Wholesalers reduces by £250 from £42,850 to £42,600.

# PREPAYMENT OF EXPENSES

*A prepayment is a payment made in advance of the accounting period to which it relates.*

A prepayment is, therefore, the opposite of an accrual: with a prepayment of expenses, some part of the expense has been paid in advance.

In the final accounts, prepaid expenses are:

- deducted from the expense amount of the trial balance before listing it in the profit and loss account
- shown as a current asset in the year end balance sheet

As with accruals, the reason for dealing with prepaid expenses in this way is to ensure that the profit and loss account records the cost incurred for the year, and not the amount that has been paid – the profit and loss account expense relates to the time period covered by the profit and loss account. The year end balance sheet shows an asset for the amount that has been prepaid.

## example of a prepaid expense

The owner of Wyvern Wholesalers tells you that the trial balance (see page 163) figure for rent and rates of £2,000, includes £100 of rent paid in advance for January 20-2. An adjustment needs to be made in the final accounts for 20-1 to record this prepaid expense.

In the profit and loss account, the cost of £1,900 (ie £2,000 from the trial balance, less £100 prepaid) will be recorded as an expense. In the balance sheet, £100 will be shown as a separate current asset of 'prepayments'.

## prepayments – the book-keeping records

In the double-entry records, prepayments must be shown as an asset at the end of the financial year. Thus the account for rent and rates in the records of Wyvern Wholesalers will appear as follows:

| Dr | | | Rent and Rates Account | | | Cr |
|---|---|---|---|---|---|---|
| 20-1 | | £ | 20-1 | | | £ |
| 31 Dec | Balance b/d (trial balance total) | 2,000 | 31 Dec | Profit and loss account | | 1,900 |
| | | | 31 Dec | Balance c/d | | 100 |
| | | 2,000 | | | | 2,000 |
| 20-2 | | | | | | |
| 1 Jan | Balance b/d | 100 | | | | |

Notes:

- The trial balance total for rent and rates is £2,000
- As £100 is prepaid at the end of the year, the transfer to profit and loss account is the cost that has been incurred for the year of £1,900
- The balance remaining on the account – a debit balance of £100 – is the amount of the prepayment, which is listed on the balance sheet at 31 December 20-1 as a current asset
- The debit balance of £100 on 1 January 20-2 will be included in the expenses for rent and rates for the year and will be transferred to profit and loss account on 31 December 20-2

## effect on profit

Taking note of the prepayment of an expense has the effect of increasing a previously reported net profit – expenses have been reduced, so net profit is greater.

## stocks of office supplies

At the end of a financial year most businesses have stocks of office supplies which have been recorded as expenses during the year, such as stationery, postage stamps (or a balance held in a franking machine). Technically, at the end of each year, these items should be valued and treated as a prepayment for next year, so reducing the expense in the current year's profit and loss account. However, in practice, this is done only when the stock of such items is substantial enough to affect the accounts in a material way. The firm's accountant will decide at what level the prepayment will apply.

To give an example of office stocks, the trial balance total for postages of a business at the year-end is £1,050; stocks of postage stamps at the same date are £150. The business will record an expense of £900 (£1,050, less £150) in the profit and loss account, while £150 is listed on the balance sheet as a current asset 'stocks of postage stamps'.

## ACCRUALS AND PREPAYMENTS IN FINAL ACCOUNTS

We have looked at the separate effect of dealing with accruals and prepayments. Let us now see how they are presented in the final accounts of Wyvern Wholesalers (see pages 167 and 168). Remember that we are taking note of the following items at 31 December 20-1:

- electricity accrued £250
- rent prepaid £100

## trading and profit and loss account

As there is no effect on gross profit, the details of the trading account are not shown here. The profit and loss section appears as shown below. Note that the calculations for accruals and prepayments do not appear in the final accounts; they are presented here for illustrative purposes only.

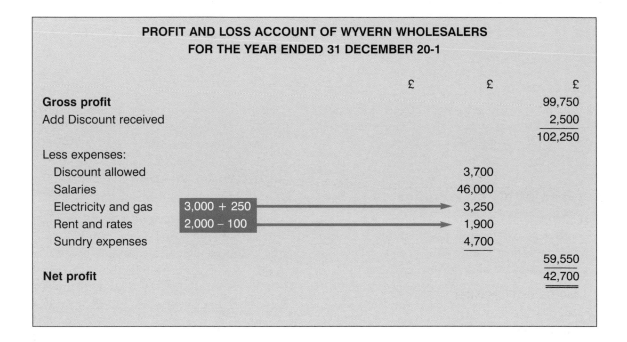

**PROFIT AND LOSS ACCOUNT OF WYVERN WHOLESALERS**
**FOR THE YEAR ENDED 31 DECEMBER 20-1**

|  | £ | £ | £ |
|---|---|---|---|
| **Gross profit** |  |  | 99,750 |
| Add Discount received |  |  | 2,500 |
|  |  |  | 102,250 |
| Less expenses: |  |  |  |
| Discount allowed |  | 3,700 |  |
| Salaries |  | 46,000 |  |
| Electricity and gas   3,000 + 250 |  | 3,250 |  |
| Rent and rates   2,000 − 100 |  | 1,900 |  |
| Sundry expenses |  | 4,700 |  |
|  |  |  | 59,550 |
| **Net profit** |  |  | 42,700 |

The effect of taking note of accruals and prepayments is to alter net profit:

|  | £ |
|---|---|
| Net profit (before adjustments) | 42,850 |
| Add rent prepaid | 100 |
|  | 42,950 |
| Less electricity accrued | 250 |
| Net profit (after adjustments) | 42,700 |

## balance sheet

The balance sheet is shown below with the accruals and prepayments shaded and arrowed. These items do appear in the final accounts, (but not the shading and arrows).

### BALANCE SHEET OF WYVERN WHOLESALERS
### AS AT 31 DECEMBER 20-1

|  | £ | £ | £ |
|---|---|---|---|
| **Fixed Assets** | | | |
| Premises | | | 100,000 |
| Equipment | | | 30,000 |
| Vehicles | | | 21,500 |
| | | | 151,500 |
| **Current Assets** | | | |
| Stock | | 16,300 | |
| Debtors | | 23,850 | |
| Prepayments | | 100 | |
| Cash | | 125 | |
| | | 40,375 | |
| **Less Current Liabilities** | | | |
| Creditors | 12,041 | | |
| Value Added Tax | 3,475 | | |
| Accruals | 250 | | |
| Bank | 851 | | |
| | | 16,617 | |
| **Working Capital** | | | 23,758 |
| | | | 175,258 |
| Less Long-term Liabilities | | | |
| Loan | | | 33,000 |
| **NET ASSETS** | | | 142,258 |
| **FINANCED BY** | | | |
| **Capital** | | | |
| Opening capital | | | 110,000 |
| Add net profit | | | 42,700 |
| | | | 152,700 |
| Less drawings | | | 10,442 |
| | | | 142,258 |

## ACCRUALS AND PREPAYMENTS OF INCOME

Just as expenses can be accrued or prepaid at the end of a financial year, income amounts can also be accrued or prepaid also.

### accrual of income

Here, income of a business is due but unpaid at the end of the financial year. For example, commission receivable might have been earned, but the payment is received after the end of the financial year to which it relates. In the final accounts, accrual of income is:

- added to the income amount from the trial balance before listing it in the profit and loss account
- shown as a current asset (eg commission receivable) in the year end balance sheet

### prepayment of income

Here, the income of a business has been paid in advance by the payer. For example, the rent receivable account for the financial year could include an advance payment received from a tenant in respect of the next financial year.

In the final accounts, prepayment of income is:

- deducted from the income amount from the trial balance before listing it in the profit and loss account
- shown as a current liability (eg rent receivable prepaid) in the year end balance sheet

As with expenses, the objective of taking note of accruals and prepayments of income is to ensure that the amount stated in the profit and loss account relates to the period covered by that account.

## OPENING BALANCES ON EXPENSE OR INCOME ACCOUNTS

So far in this chapter, we have looked at adjustments which take place at the end of a financial year. We have seen, though, that these cause the account to have an opening balance at the beginning of the next financial year. With such an account there are likely to be four separate figures making up the expense or income account:

- amount owing or prepaid at the beginning of the year (opening balance)
- amount paid (or received, if an income account) during the course of the year
- amount to be transferred to profit and loss account at the end of the financial year
- amount owing or prepaid at the end of the year (closing balance)

For the purposes of examination questions, if any three of these are known, the fourth – or 'missing' figure – can be calculated. For example, we are given the following information about the vehicle expenses account for 20-1:

- owing at beginning of year £35
- amount paid in year £350
- owing at end of year £55

The 'missing' figure here, is the amount to be transferred to profit and loss account at the year-end. It is calculated (in account form) as follows:

| Dr | | Vehicle Expenses Account | | | Cr |
|---|---|---|---|---|---|
| 20-1 | | £ | 20-1 | | £ |
| | Bank | 350 | 1 Jan | Balance b/d | 35 |
| 31 Dec | Balance c/d | 55 | 31 Dec | Profit and loss account (missing figure) | 370 |
| | | 405 | | | 405 |
| 20-2 | | | 20-2 | | |
| | | | 1 Jan | Balance b/d | 55 |

Applying the above principles will help you to solve quite complex expenses and income problems set as part of an examination question. For example, where an expense account deals with two expenses, such as electricity and gas account, and one expense is prepaid at the start of the year while the other is accrued!

# PRIVATE EXPENSES AND GOODS FOR OWN USE

Adjustments also have to be made in the final accounts for the amount of any business facilities that are used by the owner for private purposes. These adjustments are for private expenses and goods for own use.

## private expenses

Sometimes the owner of a business uses business facilities for private purposes, eg telephone, or car. The owner will agree that part of the expense shall be charged to him or her as drawings, while the other part represents a business expense.

For example, the balance of the telephone account is £600 at the year-end, and the owner agrees that this should be split as one-quarter private use, and three-quarters to the business. The book-keeping entries to record such adjustments are:

- debit drawings account
- credit telephone account    with the amount of private use

- debit profit and loss account
- credit telephone account    with the amount of business use

The telephone account will be completed at the end of the year as follows:

| Dr | | Telephone Account | | Cr |
|---|---|---|---|---|
| 20-1 | £ | 20-1 | | £ |
| 31 Dec   Balance b/d | 600 | 31 Dec   Drawings | | 150 |
| | | 31 Dec   Profit and loss account | | 450 |
| | 600 | | | 600 |

## goods for own use

When the owner of a business takes some of the goods in which the business trades for his or her own use, the double-entry book-keeping is:

– debit drawings account

– credit purchases account

When working from a trial balance to produce the final accounts, goods for own use should be deducted from purchases and added to drawings.

# INCOME AND EXPENDITURE ACCOUNTING

In this chapter we have made adjustments for accruals and prepayments to ensure that the profit and loss account shows the correct amount of income and expenses for the financial year, ie what should have been paid, instead of what has actually been paid. In doing this we are adopting the principle of income and expenditure accounting. If we simply used the trial balance figures, we would be following the principle of receipts and payments accounting, ie comparing money coming in, with money going out: this would usually give a false view of the net profit for the year.

The principle of income and expenditure accounting is applied in the same way to purchases and sales, although no adjustments are needed because of the way in which these two are handled in the accounting records. For purchases, the amount is entered into the accounts when the supplier's invoice is received, although the agreement to buy will be contained in the legal contract which exists between buyer and seller. From the accounting viewpoint, it is receipt of the supplier's invoice that causes an accounting entry to be made; the subsequent payment is handled as a different accounting transaction. A business could have bought goods, not paid for them yet, but will have a purchases figure to enter into the trading account. Doubtless the creditors will soon be wanting payment!

Sales are recorded in a similar way – when the invoice for the goods is sent, rather than when payment is made. This applies the principle of income and expenditure accounting. In this way, a business could have made a large amount of sales, which will be entered in the trading account, but may not yet have received any payments.

The way in which accounts are adjusted to take note of accruals and prepayments is formally recognised in the accruals (or matching) concept, which is discussed in more detail on page 270.

# CHAPTER SUMMARY

● Final accounts are prepared on the income and expenditure basis, rather than the receipts and payments basis.

● An adjustment should be made at the end of the financial year in respect of accruals and prepayments.

● In the final accounts, accrued expenses are:
  • added to the expense from the trial balance
  • shown as a current liability in the balance shoot

● Prepaid expenses are:
  • deducted from the expense from the trial balance
  • shown as a current asset in the balance sheet

● An accrual of income is:
  • added to the income amount from the trial balance
  • shown as a current asset in the balance sheet

● A prepayment of income is:
  • deducted from the income amount from the trial balance
  • shown as a current liability in the balance sheet

● Adjustments also need to be made in the business accounts for:
  • private expenses
  • goods for own use

Accruals and prepayments are just one type of adjustment made at the end of a financial year in order to present the financial statements more accurately. The next chapter continues the theme by considering depreciation of fixed assets.

## QUESTIONS

NOTE:
An asterisk (*) after the question number means that an answer to the question is given in Appendix 2.
When preparing final accounts you may wish to refer to the specimen layout given in Appendix 1 (see pages 560-561).

**13.1** Explain how the following would be dealt with in the profit and loss account, and balance sheet of a business with a financial year end of 31 December 20-2:

(a) Wages and salaries paid to 31 December 20-2 amount to £55,640. However, at that date, £1,120 is owing: this amount is paid on 4 January 20-3.

(b) Rates totalling £3,565 have been paid to cover the period 1 January 20-2 to 31 March 20-3.

(c) A computer is rented at a cost of £150 per month. The rental for January 20-3 was paid in December 20-2 and is included in the total payments during 20-2 which amount to £1,950.

**13.2** The following information has been extracted from the accounts of Southtown Supplies, a wholesaling business, for the year ended 31 December 20-9:

|  | £ |
|---|---|
| Sales | 420,000 |
| Purchases | 280,000 |
| Stock at 1 January 20-9 | 70,000 |
| Stock at 31 December 20-9 | 60,000 |
| Rent and rates | 10,250 |
| Electricity | 3,100 |
| Telephone | 1,820 |
| Salaries | 35,600 |
| Vehicle expenses | 13,750 |

Note: at 31 December 20-9:
• rent prepaid is £550
• salaries owing are £450

You are to prepare the trading and profit and loss account of Southtown Supplies for the year ended 31 December 20-9.

**13.3\*** After completion of the trading account the following balances remain in the ledgers of A Brown at 30 April 20-8:

|  | £ |
|---|---|
| Gross profit | 24,560 |
| Rent paid | 2,500 |
| Rent received | 1,675 |
| Motor expenses | 3,250 |
| Insurance paid | 750 |
| Wages paid | 3,750 |
| Office expenses (stationery, postage, etc) | 1,000 |
| Telephone paid | 860 |
| Drawings | 3,000 |
| Capital | 10,000 |
| Motor vehicles | 15,000 |
| Office equipment | 1,000 |
| Stock | 5,000 |
| Cash | 125 |

The following information needs to be taken into consideration:

(i)     Rent owed to us of £325
(ii)    There was an unpaid invoice for motoring expenses £150
(iii)   Of the insurance paid, £140 refers to the year commencing 1 May 20-8
(iv)    Wages due but unpaid £190
(v)     There was a stock of stationery and postage stamps valued at £50

You are required to:

(a)   Prepare the rent received, motor expenses, insurance, wages and office expenses accounts to record the balances shown, the amounts to be transferred to the profit and loss account and the balances to be brought forward to the next year.

(b)   Prepare a profit and loss account for the year ended 30 April 20-8.

A balance sheet is not required.

*Reproduced by kind permission of OCR Examinations*

13.4   H Eggleton has just completed preparation of her profit and loss account for the year ended 28 February 20-8. The following balances remain on her books:

|  | £ |
|---|---|
| Freehold property | 50,000 |
| Motor vehicles | 12,600 |
| Machinery | 2,500 |
| Fixtures and fittings | 1,250 |
| Stock of goods at 28 February 20-8 | 4,760 |
| Debtors | 540 |
| Bank overdraft | 3,250 |
| Cash in hand | 390 |
| Creditors | 550 |
| Mortgage | 10,000 |
| Wages (credit balance) | 900 |
| Insurance (debit balance) | 380 |
| Cash taken from bank for own use | 2,000 |
| Net profit for the year ended 28 February 20-8 | 13,970 |
| Capital (balance at 1 March 20-7) | ? |

(a)   You are required to prepare the balance sheet as at 28 February 20-8 clearly showing all the items under appropriate headings.

(b)   H Eggleton has taken drawings in 4 equal instalments on 2 June 20-7, 28 August 20-7, 1 December 20-7 and 10 February 20-8. Write up the drawings account and capital account as they would appear in H Eggleton's ledger at 28 February 20-8.

*Reproduced by kind permission of OCR Examinations*

**13.5\*** The following trial balance has been extracted by the book-keeper of Don Smith, who runs a wholesale stationery business, at 31 December 20-8:

|  | Dr | Cr |
|---|---|---|
|  | £ | £ |
| Debtors | 24,325 |  |
| Creditors |  | 15,408 |
| Value Added Tax |  | 4,276 |
| Capital |  | 30,000 |
| Bank |  | 1,083 |
| Rent and rates | 10,862 |  |
| Electricity | 2,054 |  |
| Telephone | 1,695 |  |
| Salaries | 55,891 |  |
| Vehicles | 22,250 |  |
| Office equipment | 7,500 |  |
| Vehicle expenses | 10,855 |  |
| Drawings | 15,275 |  |
| Discount allowed | 478 |  |
| Discount received |  | 591 |
| Purchases | 138,960 |  |
| Sales |  | 257,258 |
| Stock at 1 January 20-8 | 18,471 |  |
|  | 308,616 | 308,616 |

Notes at 31 December 20-8:

• stock was valued at £14,075

• rates are prepaid £250

• electricity owing £110

• salaries are owing £365

You are to prepare the trading and profit and loss account of Don Smith for the year ended 31 December 20-8, together with his balance sheet at that date.

**13.6** The following trial balance has been extracted by the book-keeper of John Barclay at 30 June 20-9:

|  | Dr | Cr |
|---|---|---|
|  | £ | £ |
| Sales |  | 864,321 |
| Purchases | 600,128 |  |
| Sales returns | 2,746 |  |
| Purchases returns |  | 3,894 |
| Office expenses | 33,947 |  |
| Salaries | 122,611 |  |
| Vehicle expenses | 36,894 |  |
| Discounts allowed | 3,187 |  |
| Discounts received |  | 4,951 |
| Debtors and creditors | 74,328 | 52,919 |
| Value Added Tax |  | 10,497 |
| Stock at 1 July 20-8 | 63,084 |  |
| Vehicles | 83,500 |  |
| Office equipment | 23,250 |  |
| Land and buildings | 100,000 |  |
| Bank loan |  | 75,000 |
| Bank | 1,197 |  |
| Capital |  | 155,000 |
| Drawings | 21,710 |  |
|  | 1,166,582 | 1,166,582 |

Notes at 30 June 20-9:

• stock was valued at £66,941

• motor vehicle expenses owing £1,250

• office expenses prepaid £346

• goods costing £250 were taken by John Barclay for his own use

You are to prepare the trading and profit and loss account of John Barclay for the year ended 30 June 20-9, together with his balance sheet at that date.

# MULTIPLE CHOICE QUESTIONS

Read each question carefully.
Choose the one answer you think is correct (calculators may be needed).
The answers are on page 568.

**1**    Gross profit is:

A       sales less sales returns, minus cost of goods sold

B       sales less sales returns, minus purchases, less purchases returns

C       sales, minus expenses

D       sales, less sales returns, minus closing stock

**2**    At the end of a financial year the cost of carriage in is:

A       debited to the profit and loss account

B       debited to carriage out account

C       debited to the trading account

D       debited to sales account

**3**    Net profit is:

A       gross profit, plus other income, minus expenses

B       increase in the bank balance

C       sales minus expenses

D       capital account minus expenses

**4**    Which one of the following does not appear in profit and loss account?

A       salaries

B       machinery

C       rent received

D       salespersons' commission

Questions 5 to 9 relate to the following account:

| Dr | | | Rent and Rates Account | | Cr |
|---|---|---|---|---|---|
| 20-1 | | £ | 20-1 | | £ |
| 1 Jan | Balance (rates) b/d | 450 | 31 Dec | Profit and loss account | 4,350 |
| 31 Mar | Bank (rent) | 500 | 31 Dec | Balance (rates) c/d | 600 |
| 15 May | Bank (rates) | 1,200 | | | |
| 1 Jul | Bank (rent) | 500 | | | |
| 3 Oct | Bank (rent) | 550 | | | |
| 20 Nov | Bank (rates) | 1,200 | | | |
| 31 Dec | Balance (rent) c/d | 550 | | | |
| | | 4,950 | | | 4,950 |
| | | | | | |
| 20-2 | | | 20-2 | | |
| 1 Jan | Balance (rates) b/d | 600 | 1 Jan | Balance (rent) b/d | 550 |

5    The balance on 1 January 20-1 is:

A        rates prepaid

B        rates for the year ended 31 December 20-0

C        rates accrued

D        a refund due

6    The transfer to profit and loss account for rates in respect of the year ended 31 December 20-1 is:

A        £600

B        £2,100

C        £2,250

D        £4,350

7    The transfer to profit and loss account for rent in respect of the year ended 31 December 20-1 is:

A        £550

B        £2,100

C        £2,250

D        £4,950

**8**   The amount paid in respect of rates in the year ended 31 December 20-1 is:

A    £1,550

B    £2,400

C    £4,350

D    £4,950

*(Please refer to the Rent and Rates Account on the previous page for the data for this question.)*


**9**   The amount of rent accrued at 31 December 20-1 is:

A    Nil

B    £550

C    £600

D    £4,950

*(Please refer to the Rent and Rates Account on the previous page for the data for this question.)*


**10**   Wages accrued are shown as a:

A    current asset in the balance sheet

B    debit balance in wages account

C    fixed asset in the balance sheet

D    credit balance in wages account


**11**   Net assets are:

A    fixed assets + working capital – long-term liabilities

B    capital + working capital – long-term liabilities

C    fixed assets – working capital + long-term liabilities

D    fixed assets + capital + long-term liabilities


**12**   An example of an intangible fixed asset is:

A    premises

B    debtors

C    goodwill

D    bank loan

# 14 DEPRECIATION OF FIXED ASSETS

Fixed assets, for example machinery and vehicles, fall in value as time goes by, largely as a result of wear and tear. This reduction in value is measured by what is known as depreciation. In business accounts it is necessary to record an estimate of depreciation in the accounting records.

In this chapter we will:

● define depreciation

● consider the methods of calculating depreciation

● look at the book-keeping entries for depreciation

● apply depreciation to the final accounts

● investigate the book-keeping entries when a fixed asset is sold

● see how a revaluation of assets is recorded in the accounting system

## WHAT IS DEPRECIATION?

*Depreciation is a way of measuring the amount of the fall in value of fixed assets over a period of time.*

Most fixed assets fall in value over time and, in business accounts, it is necessary, in order to present a realistic view of the business, to measure the amount of the fall in value. This is done by showing an expense – called 'provision for depreciation of fixed assets' – in the profit and loss account, and recording the asset at a lower value than cost price in the balance sheet. The profit and loss expense is called a provision for depreciation because it is an estimate of both the fall in value and the time period; the estimate is linked to the cost price of the asset. Depreciation is a further application of the accruals concept, because we are recognising the timing difference between payment for the fixed asset and the asset's fall in value.

The main factors which cause fixed assets to depreciate are:

• wear and tear through use, eg vehicles, machinery, etc

• passage of time, eg the lease on a building

• depletion, eg extraction of stone from a quarry

• economic reasons

– obsolescence, eg a new design of machine which does the job better and faster makes the old machine obsolete

– inadequacy, eg a machine no longer has the volume capacity to meet the needs of the business

Fixed assets – even buildings – are depreciated over their useful economic life. The only exception is land, which does not normally depreciate (unless it is a quarry or a mine, when it will have a limited useful economic life). Land and buildings are sometimes increased in value from time-to-time, ie a revaluation takes place, and this is recorded in the accounts (see page 231).

## METHODS OF CALCULATING DEPRECIATION

There are several different ways in which we can allow for the fall in value of fixed assets. All of these are estimates, and it is only when the asset is sold or scrapped that we will know the accuracy of the estimate (see page 227). The two most common methods of calculating depreciation are:

- straight-line method
- reducing balance method

Other methods used include:

- units of output (or service)
- sum of the digits

For the calculations of depreciation amounts we will use the following data:

**MACHINE**

| | |
|---|---|
| Cost price on 1 January 20-1 | £2,000 (net of VAT) |
| Estimated life | 4 years |
| Estimated production: | |
| year 1 | 60,000 units |
| year 2 | 50,000 units |
| year 3 | 25,000 units |
| year 4 | 25,000 units |
| total | 160,000 units |
| Estimated scrap value at end of four years | £400 |

### straight-line method

With this method, a fixed percentage is written off the original cost of the asset each year. For this example, twenty-five per cent will be written off each year by the straight-line method. The depreciation amount (ignoring for the moment any residual or scrap value) for each year is:

$$£2,000 \times 25\% = £500 \text{ per year}$$

The depreciation percentage will be decided by a business on the basis of what it considers to be the useful economic life of the asset. Thus, twenty-five per cent each year gives a useful economic life of four years (assuming a nil residual value at the end of its life).

Different classes of fixed assets are often depreciated at different rates, eg motor vehicles may be depreciated at a different rate to office equipment. It is important that, once a particular method and rate of depreciation has been selected, depreciation should be applied consistently, ie methods and rates are not changed from year-to-year without good reason.

The method of calculating straight-line depreciation, taking into account the asset's estimated sale proceeds at the end of its useful economic life, is:

$$\frac{\text{cost of asset} - \text{estimated residual (scrap or salvage) sale proceeds}}{\text{number of years' expected use of asset}}$$

For example, the machine is expected to have a residual (scrap or salvage) value of £400, so the depreciation amount will be:

$$\frac{£2,000 - £400}{4 \text{ years}} = £400 \text{ per year (ie 20\% per annum on cost)}$$

## reducing balance method

With this method, a fixed percentage is written off the reduced balance each year. The reduced balance is cost of the asset less depreciation to date. For example, the machine is to be depreciated by 33.3% (one-third) each year, using the reducing balance method. The depreciation amounts for the four years of ownership are:

| | |
|---|---:|
| Original cost | £2,000 |
| Year 1 depreciation: 33.3% of £2,000 | £667 |
| Value at end of year 1 | £1,333 |
| Year 2 depreciation: 33.3% of £1,333 | £444 |
| Value at end of year 2 | £889 |
| Year 3 depreciation: 33.3% of £889 | £296 |
| Value at end of year 3 | £593 |
| Year 4 depreciation: 33.3% of £593 | £193 |
| Value at end of year 4 | £400 |

Note that the figures have been rounded to the nearest £, and year 4 depreciation has been adjusted by £5 to leave a residual value of £400.

The formula to calculate the percentage of reducing balance depreciation is:

$$r = 1 - \sqrt[n]{\frac{s}{c}}$$

In this formula:

r  =  percentage rate of depreciation

n  =  number of years

s  =  salvage (residual) value

c  =  cost of asset

In the example above the 33.3% is calculated as:

$$r = 1 - \sqrt[4]{\frac{400}{2,000}}$$

$$r = 1 - \sqrt[4]{0.2}$$   (to find the fourth root press the square root key on the calculator twice)

$$r = 1 - 0.669$$

$$r = 0.331 \text{ or } 33.1\% \text{ (which is close to the 33.3\% used above)}$$

## straight-line and reducing balance methods compared

The following tables use the depreciation amounts calculated above.

| | | straight-line depreciation | | |
|---|---|---|---|---|
| Year | 1<br>Original<br>cost | 2<br>Depreciation<br>for year | 3<br>Depreciation<br>to date | 4<br>Net book value<br>(ie column 1-3) |
| | £ | £ | £ | £ |
| 1 | 2,000 | 400 | 400 | 1,600 |
| 2 | 2,000 | 400 | 800 | 1,200 |
| 3 | 2,000 | 400 | 1,200 | 800 |
| 4 | 2,000 | 400 | 1,600 | 400 |

Note: Net book value is cost, less depreciation to date, ie column 1, less column 3.

These calculations will be used in the final accounts (see page 225) as follows: taking year 2 as an example, the profit and loss account will be charged with £400 (column 2) as an expense, while the balance sheet will record £1,200 (column 4) as the net book value.

| reducing balance depreciation | | | | |
|---|---|---|---|---|
| | *1* | *2* | *3* | *4* |
| Year | Original cost | Depreciation for year | Depreciation to date | Net book value (ie column 1-3) |
| | £ | £ | £ | £ |
| 1 | 2,000 | 667 | 667 | 1,333 |
| 2 | 2,000 | 444 | 1,111 | 889 |
| 3 | 2,000 | 296 | 1,407 | 593 |
| 4 | 2,000 | 193 | 1,600 | 400 |

In the final accounts, using year 3 as an example, £296 (column 2) will be charged as an expense in profit and loss account, while £593 (column 4) is the net book value that will be shown in the balance sheet. Depreciation in the final accounts is covered in more detail on page 225.

Using these tables, we will now see how the two methods compare:

| | straight-line method | reducing balance method |
|---|---|---|
| **depreciation amount** | Same money amount each year – see chart below | Different money amounts each year: more than straight-line in early years, less in later years – see chart below |
| **depreciation percentage** | Lower depreciation percentage required to achieve same residual value | Higher depreciation percentage required to achieve same residual value – but can never reach a nil value |
| **suitability** | Best used for fixed assets likely to be kept for the whole of their expected lives, eg machinery, office equipment, fixtures and fittings | Best used for fixed assets which depreciate more in early years and which are not kept for the whole of expected lives, eg vehicles |

The year-by-year depreciation amounts of the machine in the example are shown on the following bar chart:

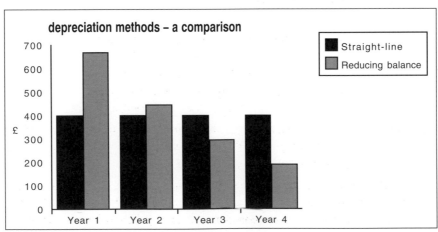

## other methods of calculating depreciation

● **Units of output (or service) method**

This method estimates:

－ the number of units to be produced by a machine, or

－ the number of hours of operation of a machine, or

－ the number of miles expected from a vehicle

over its expected life. Depreciation for a given year is calculated by reference to the number of units/hours/miles for that year.

For example, the machine referred to earlier is to be depreciated by £1,600 (ie £2,000 – £400 residual value). As the total number of units to be produced by the machine is expected to be 160,000, then each year's depreciation will be calculated at £100 for every 10,000 units produced (£1,600 ÷ 160,000 units).

Depreciation amounts will be:

| | | |
|---|---|---|
| Year 1 | £600 | depreciation for year |
| Year 2 | £500 | depreciation for year |
| Year 3 | £250 | depreciation for year |
| Year 4 | £250 | depreciation for year |
| | £1,600 | total depreciation |

This method has the benefit of linking usage (ie units/hours/miles) to the depreciation amount. In years of high usage, depreciation is higher than in years of low usage. As the asset gets older, so the usage may be lower, but repair costs may be increasing: in this way the total expense (depreciation + repair costs) will probably be a similar amount from year-to-year.

● **Sum of the digits method**

With this method, the depreciation amount each year is calculated on the sum of the number of years of useful life. For example, the machine is expected to last for four years: the sum of the digits is 1 + 2 + 3 + 4 = 10. Depreciation is now applied to the amount to be written off, £1,600 (ie £2,000 – £400 residual value) as follows:

| | | | |
|---|---|---|---|
| Year 1 | 4/10 x £1,600 | = £640 | depreciation for year |
| Year 2 | 3/10 x £1,600 | = £480 | depreciation for year |
| Year 3 | 2/10 x £1,600 | = £320 | depreciation for year |
| Year 4 | 1/10 x £1,600 | = £160 | depreciation for year |
| | | £1,600 | total depreciation |

In using this method, note that the digits count down from the number of years of estimated life, ie the depreciation for year 1 is higher than that for year 2, etc. In this way, sum of the digits depreciation is similar to the reducing balance method.

Note that whichever depreciation method is used, the total net profits of the business over the life of the asset are the same. The various depreciation methods will cause the net profit for individual years to be different but, overall, the same total depreciation is charged to the profit and loss account.

# BOOK-KEEPING ENTRIES FOR DEPRECIATION

Once the amounts of depreciation have been calculated using the methods described in the previous section, they can be recorded in the book-keeping system. The procedure is to use two accounts for each class of fixed assets:

- fixed asset account, which records the cost price of the asset (remember that the value of the asset can include certain other capital costs, eg installation costs – see page 176)

- provision for depreciation account, which records the amount of depreciation for the asset

## example book-keeping entries

A machine is purchased for £2,000 net of VAT on 1 January 20-1. It is decided to depreciate it at twenty per cent each year, using the straight-line method. The firm's financial year runs from 1 January to 31 December. The accounting records for the first four years will be:

| Dr | | Machinery Account | | | Cr |
|---|---|---|---|---|---|
| 20-1 | | £ | 20-1 | | £ |
| 1 Jan | Bank | 2,000 | | | |

This account remains with the balance of £2,000, which is the cost price of the machine. The other transactions on 1 January 20-1 are to bank account and VAT account – these have not been shown.

| Dr | | Provision for Depreciation Account – Machinery | | | Cr |
|---|---|---|---|---|---|
| 20-1 | | £ | 20-1 | | £ |
| 31 Dec | Balance c/d | 400 | 31 Dec | Profit and loss account | 400 |
| 20-2 | | | 20-2 | | |
| 31 Dec | Balance c/d | 800 | 1 Jan | Balance b/d | 400 |
| | | | 31 Dec | Profit and loss account | 400 |
| | | 800 | | | 800 |
| 20-3 | | | 20-3 | | |
| 31 Dec | Balance c/d | 1,200 | 1 Jan | Balance b/d | 800 |
| | | | 31 Dec | Profit and loss account | 400 |
| | | 1,200 | | | 1,200 |
| 20-4 | | | 20-4 | | |
| 31 Dec | Balance c/d | 1,600 | 1 Jan | Balance b/d | 1,200 |
| | | | 31 Dec | Profit and loss account | 400 |
| | | 1,600 | | | 1,600 |
| 20-5 | | | 20-5 | | |
| | | | 1 Jan | Balance b/d | 1,600 |

The provision for depreciation account stores up the amounts of depreciation year by year. Notice that, while the asset account of machinery has a debit balance, provision for depreciation has a credit balance. The difference between the two balances at any time will tell us the book value of the asset, ie what it is worth according to our accounting records. For example, at 31 December 20-3, the book value of the machine is £800 (£2,000 cost, less £1,200 depreciation to date).

When a business owns several fixed assets of the same class, eg several machines, it is usual practice to maintain only one asset account and one provision for depreciation account for that class. This does mean that the calculation of amounts of depreciation can become quite complex – particularly when assets are bought and sold during the year. It may be helpful, in an examination question, to calculate the separate depreciation amount for each machine, or asset, before amalgamating the figures as the year's depreciation charge.

We will look at how to deal with the sale of an asset on page 227.

# DEPRECIATION AND FINAL ACCOUNTS

## profit and loss account

The depreciation amount calculated for each class of asset is listed amongst the other expenses as a provision for depreciation for that particular class of asset. For example, to consider the machine depreciated on the previous page, the profit and loss account will show 'provision for depreciation: machinery £400' amongst the other expenses. You will, by now, appreciate that the double-entry book-keeping for depreciation is:

– debit profit and loss account

– credit provision for depreciation account

## balance sheet

Each class of fixed asset should be shown at cost price (or revaluation – see page 231), less total depreciation to date (ie this year's depreciation, plus depreciation from previous years if any). The resulting figure is the net book value of the fixed asset.

The usual way of setting these out in a balance sheet (using figures for the machine on page 224) is:

**Balance sheet (extract) ................. as at 31 December 20-1**

|  | £ | £ | £ |
|---|---|---|---|
|  | Cost | Dep'n to date | Net |
| **Fixed Assets** |  |  |  |
| Machinery | 2,000 | 400 | 1,600 |
| Vehicles, etc | x | x | x |
|  | x | x | x |

**Balance sheet (extract)** ................. **as at 31 December 20-2**

|  | £ | £ | £ |
|---|---|---|---|
|  | Cost | Dep'n to date | Net |
| **Fixed Assets** |  |  |  |
| Machinery | 2,000 | 800 | 1,200 |
| Vehicles, etc | X | X | X |
|  | X | X | X |

Notice, from the above, how depreciation to date increases with the addition of each further year's depreciation. At the same time, the net figure reduces – it is this net figure which is added to the other fixed assets to give a sub-total for this section of the balance sheet.

## trial balance figures

When preparing final accounts from a trial balance, the trial balance often gives separate figures for the cost of an asset and its depreciation to date at the start of the year. For example:

**Trial Balance of** ................. **as at 31 December 20-3**

|  | Dr | Cr |
|---|---|---|
|  | £ | £ |
| Machinery at cost | 2,000 |  |
| Provision for depreciation: machinery |  | 800 |

If a note to the trial balance then says, for example, to "provide for depreciation on machinery for the year at twenty per cent on cost", this indicates that the trial balance figure is at the start of the year. Accordingly, depreciation of £400 for 20-3 must be calculated and shown as an expense in profit and loss account.

The balance sheet will then show:

**Balance sheet (extract)** ................. **as at 31 December 20-3**

|  | £ | £ | £ |
|---|---|---|---|
|  | Cost | Dep'n to date | Net |
| **Fixed Assets** |  |  |  |
| Machinery | 2,000 | 1,200 | 800 |
| Vehicles, etc | X | X | X |
|  | X | X | X |

## depreciation policies of a business

In examination questions and assessments, information will be given – where it is needed – on the depreciation policies of the business whose accounts you are preparing. In particular, the information will be given on what to do when a fixed asset is bought part of the way through a firm's financial year. The choices here will be to allocate depreciation for the part of the year that it is owned; alternatively the firm may choose to provide for depreciation for the whole year on assets held at the end of the year.

# DEPRECIATION: A NON-CASH EXPENSE

It is very important to realise that depreciation is a non-cash expense: unlike most of the other expenses in the profit and loss account, no cheque is written out, or cash paid, for depreciation. In cash terms, depreciation causes no outflow of money. Nevertheless, it is correct, in the final accounts of a business, to show an allowance for depreciation in the profit and loss account, and to reduce the value of the fixed asset in the balance sheet. This is because the business has had the use of the asset, and needs to record the fall in value as an expense in order to present a true picture of its financial state. Thus we are led back to the definition of depreciation as 'a way of measuring the amount of the fall in value of fixed assets over a period of time', ie it is an accounting adjustment.

As depreciation is a non-cash expense, it should be noted that depreciation is not a method of providing a fund of cash which can be used to replace the asset at the end of its life. In order to do this, it is necessary to create a separate fund into which cash is transferred at regular intervals. This technique is often known as a sinking fund, and it needs to be represented by a separate bank account, eg a deposit account, which can be drawn against when the new fixed asset is to be purchased. This, however, is not a common practice.

# SALE OF FIXED ASSETS

When a fixed asset is sold or disposed, it is necessary to bring together:

- the original cost of the asset
- depreciation provided over the life of the asset
- sale proceeds

These figures are transferred from the appropriate accounts in the double-entry book-keeping system to a disposals account (also known as a sale of assets account). The disposals account will enable us to calculate the 'profit' or 'loss' on sale of the asset (more correctly the terms are 'over-provision' and 'under-provision' of depreciation, respectively). The book-keeping transactions are:

- **original cost of the asset**
  - debit disposals account
  - credit fixed asset account

  with the cost price of the fixed asset now sold

- **depreciation provided to date**
  - debit provision for depreciation account
  - credit disposals account

  with depreciation provided over the life of the asset

  Note that the amount of depreciation provided to date may need to be calculated for the correct period, eg if disposal takes place part of the way through a financial year and the firm's policy is to charge part-years.

- **sale proceeds**
  - debit bank/cash account
  - credit disposals account

  with the sale proceeds of the asset

- **loss on sale**
  - debit profit and loss account
  - credit disposals account

  with the amount of under-provision of depreciation

- **profit on sale**
  - debit disposals account
  - credit profit and loss account

  with the amount of over-provision of depreciation

Small adjustments for under- or over-provision of depreciation will usually be needed because it is impossible, at the start of an asset's life, to predict exactly what it will sell for in a number of years' time.

## WORKED EXAMPLE – SALE OF ASSET: BOOK-KEEPING ENTRIES

To illustrate the transactions described above, we will use the machine purchased for £2,000 (net of VAT) on 1 January 20-1, which is depreciated at twenty per cent each year, using the straight-line depreciation method. On 31 December 20-3, the machine is sold for £600 (net of VAT); the company's accounting policy is to depreciate assets in the year of sale. The calculations are:

| | |
|---|---:|
| cost price of machine (net of VAT) | £2,000 |
| less provision for depreciation to date | £1,200 |
| net book value at date of sale | £800 |
| selling price (net of VAT) | £600 |
| LOSS ON SALE | £200 |

The book-keeping entries (excluding bank account and VAT account) are:

| Dr | | Machinery Account | | | Cr |
|---|---|---|---|---|---|
| 20-1 | | £ | 20-3 | | £ |
| 1 Jan | Bank | 2,000 | 31 Dec | Disposals account | 2,000 |

| Dr | | Provision for Depreciation Account – Machinery | | | Cr |
|---|---|---|---|---|---|
| 20-1 | | £ | 20-1 | | £ |
| 31 Dec | Balance c/d | 400 | 31 Dec | Profit and loss account | 400 |
| 20-2 | | | 20-2 | | |
| 31 Dec | Balance c/d | 800 | 1 Jan | Balance b/d | 400 |
| | | | 31 Dec | Profit and loss account | 400 |
| | | 800 | | | 800 |
| 20-3 | | | 20-3 | | |
| 31 Dec | Disposals account | 1,200 | 1 Jan | Balance b/d | 800 |
| | | | 31 Dec | Profit and loss account | 400 |
| | | 1,200 | | | 1,200 |

| Dr | | Disposals Account – Machinery | | | Cr |
|---|---|---|---|---|---|
| 20-3 | | £ | 20-3 | | £ |
| 31 Dec | Machinery account | 2,000 | 31 Dec | Provision for dep'n account | 1,200 |
| | | | 31 Dec | Bank | 600 |
| | | | 31 Dec | Profit and loss account (loss on sale) | 200 |
| | | 2,000 | | | 2,000 |

---

**Profit and loss account (extract) ......... for the year ended 31 December 20-3**

| | £ | £ |
|---|---|---|
| Gross profit | | x |
| Less: | | |
| Provision for depreciation: machinery | 400 | |
| Loss on sale of machinery | 200 | |

---

Please see the next page for notes on these entries.

- In the machinery account, which is always kept 'at cost', the original price of the asset is transferred at the date of sale to disposals account. In this example, a nil balance remains on machinery account; however it is quite likely that the machinery account includes several machines, only one of which is being sold – in this case, there would be a balance on machinery account comprising the cost prices of the remaining machines.

- In provision for depreciation account, the amount of depreciation relating to the machine sold is transferred to disposals account. In this example, as only one machine is owned, the whole balance is transferred. However, if there were machines remaining, only part of the balance would be transferred – the amount remaining on the account relates to the remaining machines.

- Disposals account would balance without the need for a profit and loss account transfer if the depreciation rate used reflected exactly the fall in value of the machine. In practice, this is unlikely to happen, so a transfer to profit and loss account must be made. In this example, it is an under-provision of depreciation (loss on sale), and the profit and loss account lists an extra expense. If there had been an over-provision of depreciation (profit on sale), an item of additional income would be shown in profit and loss account.

## part-exchange of an asset

Instead of selling an old fixed asset for cash, it is quite common to part-exchange it for a new asset. This is exactly the same as if a person trades in an old car for a new (or newer) one. Once the part-exchange allowance has been agreed, the book-keeping entries for disposal are as detailed earlier except that, instead of sale proceeds, there will be entries for the part-exchange amount:

– debit fixed asset account

– credit disposals account

The remainder of the purchase cost of the new fixed asset paid by cheque is debited to fixed asset account and credited to bank account in the usual way. For a VAT-registered business there will be amounts to record in the VAT account.

For example, the machine referred to earlier in this section is part-exchanged on 31 December 20-3 at an agreed value of £600 (excluding VAT) for a new machine costing £2,500 (excluding VAT). The balance is paid by cheque. Machinery account will now be shown as:

| Dr | | | **Machinery Account** | | | Cr |
|---|---|---|---|---|---|---|
| 20-1 | | £ | 20-3 | | | £ |
| 1 Jan | Bank | 2,000 | 31 Dec | Disposals account | | 2,000 |
| 20-3 | | | | | | |
| 31 Dec | Disposals account (part-exchange allowance) | 600 | 31 Dec | Balance c/d | | 2,500 |
| 31 Dec | Bank (balance paid by cheque) | 1,900 | | | | |
| | | 2,500 | | | | 2,500 |
| 20-4 | | | | | | |
| 1 Jan | Balance b/d | 2,500 | | | | |

Notes:

- This gives two debits (£600 and £1,900) in machinery account for a single machine.
- Disposals account will be unchanged, except that the description for the credit transaction of £600 will be machinery account, instead of bank.

## REVALUATION OF A FIXED ASSET

From time-to-time fixed assets are revalued at a higher value. In practice, the most likely asset to be revalued is property. After an asset has been revalued, depreciation is calculated on the revalued amount. When a fixed asset is revalued, a reserve is created which adds to the value of the owner's capital. The book-keeping procedure is:

- debit fixed asset account
- credit capital account

### WORKED EXAMPLE: REVALUATION OF A FIXED ASSET

A business owns premises which is shown in the accounts on 1 January 20-1 at the original cost of £100,000. The premises have been revalued on 31 December 20-1 at £150,000 and it has been decided to record this value in the accounting system. The balance on the owner's capital account on 31 December 20-1 is £200,000 before the revaluation is recorded.

| Dr | | Premises Account | | | Cr |
|---|---|---|---|---|---|
| 20-1 | | £ | 20-1 | | £ |
| 1 Jan | Balance b/d | 100,000 | | | |
| 31 Dec | Capital account | 50,000 | | | |

| Dr | | Capital Account | | | Cr |
|---|---|---|---|---|---|
| 20-1 | | £ | 20-1 | | £ |
| | | | 1 Jan | Balance b/d | 200,000 |
| | | | 31 Dec | Premises account (revaluation) | 50,000 |

### notes

- Both premises account and the owner's capital account have been increased by the amount of the revaluation. The owner's stake in the business is now £250,000.
- There is no new cash in the business – a non-cash book-keeping entry has recorded the increase in value. If the premises were sold for the revalued amount, cash would be received.
- The revaluation transaction has not been recorded in profit and loss account because it is a capital transaction rather than a revenue transaction. (When we come to deal with company final accounts in Chapter 25 – we shall see that a revaluation amount is placed in a separate account which is grouped under the general heading of 'capital reserves'.)

# FRS 15: TANGIBLE FIXED ASSETS

Financial Reporting Standard (FRS) no. 15, entitled Tangible Fixed Assets, is the accounting standard (see Chapter 17) which sets out the rules for dealing with depreciation in financial accounts. FRS 15 states that:

- fixed assets having a known useful economic life must be depreciated
- any acceptable depreciation method can be used to spread the cost of the fixed asset consistently over its useful economic life
- depreciation amounts are normally based on the cost of the fixed assets

# CHAPTER SUMMARY

- Depreciation is a measure of the amount of the fall in value of fixed assets over a time period.

- Two common methods of calculating depreciation are the straight-line method and the reducing balance method. Other methods include units of output (or service), and sum of the digits methods.

- In terms of book-keeping, two accounts are used for each class of fixed asset:
  - fixed asset account
  - provision for depreciation account

  The depreciation amount for each class of fixed asset is included amongst the expenses in profit and loss account, while the value of the asset, as shown in the balance sheet, is reduced by the same amount.

- Depreciation is a non-cash expense.

- When a fixed asset is sold, it is necessary to make an adjustment in respect of any under-provision (loss on sale) or over-provision (profit on sale) of depreciation during the life of the asset. The amount is calculated by means of a disposals account, and is then transferred to profit and loss account.

- When assets are revalued at a higher value, the owner's stake in the business is increased. This is a capital transaction (rather than revenue) and does not pass through profit and loss account.

- FRS 15, 'Tangible Fixed Assets', sets out the accounting standard for depreciation

In the next chapter we look at another expense to be shown in profit and loss account: bad debts, and provision for bad debts.

# QUESTIONS

NOTE: an asterisk (*) after the question number means that an answer to the question is given in Appendix 2.

**14.1\*** Martin Hough, sole owner of Juicyburger, a fast food shop, operating from leased premises in the town, is suspicious of his accountant, Mr S Harris, whom he claims doesn't really understand the food business. On the telephone he asks Mr Harris why depreciation is charged on a rigid formula, as surely no-one really knows how much his equipment is worth, and in fact he might not get anything for it. Draft a reply to Mr Hough from Mr Harris explaining the importance of depreciation and its application to final accounts.

**14.2\*** On 1 January 20-1, Martin Jackson bought a car for £12,000. In his final accounts, which have a year-end of 31 December, he has been depreciating it at 25 per cent per annum using the reducing balance method. On 31 December 20-3 he sells the car for £5,500 (cheque received). His accounting policy is to depreciate assets in the year of sale.

You are to show:

(a)   The provision for depreciation account for 20-1, 20-2 and 20-3.

(b)   The balance sheet extract at 31 December 20-1 and 20-2.

(c)   The asset disposal account.

Round your answer down to whole £s where appropriate.

**14.3** Rachael Hall's financial year runs to 31 December. On 1 January 20-8 her accounts show that she owns a car with an original cost of £12,000 and depreciation to date of £7,200.

On 1 October 20-8, Rachael bought a new car at a cost of £15,000. She traded in the old car at a part-exchange value of £5,500 and paid the balance by cheque.

Rachael depreciates vehicles at 20 per cent per year using the straight-line method. Her accounting policy is to charge a full year's depreciation in the year of purchase, but none in the year of sale.

You are to show the following for the year 20-8:

(a)      vehicles account

(b)      provision for depreciation account – vehicles

(c)      disposals account – vehicles

(d)      balance sheet extract at 31 December 20-8

14.4 The following list of balances has been extracted from the books of John Henson at 31 December 20-8:

| | £ |
|---|---|
| Purchases | 71,600 |
| Sales | 122,000 |
| Stock at 1 January 20-8 | 6,250 |
| Vehicle running expenses | 1,480 |
| Rent and rates | 5,650 |
| Office expenses | 2,220 |
| Discount received | 285 |
| Wages and salaries | 18,950 |
| Office equipment | 10,000 |
| Vehicle | 12,000 |
| Debtors | 5,225 |
| Creditors | 3,190 |
| Value Added Tax | 1,720 |
| Capital | 20,000 |
| Drawings for the year | 13,095 |
| Cash at bank | 725 |

You are to prepare the trading and profit and loss account of John Henson for the year ended 31 December 20-8, together with his balance sheet at that date, taking into account:

- closing stock of £8,500
- depreciation of office equipment for the year £1,000
- depreciation of vehicle for the year £3,000

**14.5**   Simon Ado is a plumber. His trial balance as at 31 October is as follows:

|  | Dr £ | Cr £ |
|---|---|---|
| Van | 8,000 | |
| Tools and equipment | 3,000 | |
| Bank | | 90 |
| Cash | 320 | |
| Creditors | | 85 |
| Sales (work done) | | 19,480 |
| Purchases of materials | 3,415 | |
| Advertising | 210 | |
| Telephone | 710 | |
| Motor expenses | 580 | |
| Drawings | 6,400 | |
| Capital | | 2,960 |
| Discount received | | 200 |
| Opening stock | 180 | |
| | 22,815 | 22,815 |

The following additional information is available:

(1)   Stock at 31 October amounted to £190.

(2)   The van was purchased during the year and should be depreciated at 25% on cost.

(3)   The tools and equipment purchased during the year should be depreciated 10% per annum of book value.

(4)   During the year an amount of £120 was paid in advance for an advertising campaign to be carried out the following year.

You are required to:

(a)   prepare Simon Ado's trading, profit and loss account for the year ended 31 October.

(b)   prepare Simon Ado's balance sheet as at 31 October.

*Pitman Qualifications*

**14.6\*** The following trial balance has been extracted by the book-keeper of Hazel Harris at 31 December 20-4:

|  | Dr £ | Cr £ |
|---|---|---|
| Bank loan |  | 75,000 |
| Capital |  | 125,000 |
| Purchases and sales | 465,000 | 614,000 |
| Building repairs | 8,480 |  |
| Vehicles at cost | 12,000 |  |
| Provision for depreciation on vehicles |  | 2,400 |
| Vehicle expenses | 2,680 |  |
| Land and buildings at cost | 100,000 |  |
| Bank overdraft |  | 2,000 |
| Furniture and fittings at cost | 25,000 |  |
| Provision for depreciation on furniture and fittings |  | 2,500 |
| Wages and salaries | 86,060 |  |
| Discounts | 10,610 | 8,140 |
| Drawings | 24,000 |  |
| Rates and insurance | 6,070 |  |
| Debtors and creditors | 52,130 | 38,730 |
| Value Added Tax |  | 3,120 |
| General expenses | 15,860 |  |
| Stock at 1 January 20-4 | 63,000 |  |
|  | 870,890 | 870,890 |

Notes at 31 December 20-4:

- Stock was valued at £88,000

- Wages and salaries outstanding: £3,180

- Rates and insurance paid in advance: £450

- Depreciate vehicles at 20 per cent using the straight-line method

- Depreciate furniture and fittings at 10 per cent using the straight-line method

- Buildings are not to be depreciated

You are to prepare her trading and profit and loss accounts for the year ended 31 December 20-4, together with her balance sheet at that date.

**14.7\***

Gee Ltd is a manufacturer of screws. Its financial year ends on 31 March.

It maintains a total machines account, and a separate total provision for depreciation account.

Gee Ltd provides depreciation on its machines at a rate of 10% per annum on the straight line basis. This is calculated on the machines in the total machine account at the end of the financial year, regardless of when they were purchased. Depreciation is not provided on machines disposed of during the financial year.

Analysis of the opening balances at 1 April Year 5 showed:

|  | Machines Account | Provision for Depreciation Account |
|---|---|---|
|  | £ | £ |
| Machine C | 10,500 | 4,200 |
| Machine D | 18,200 | 3,640 |
| Total | 28,700 | 7,840 |

The following transactions relate to subsequent years:

| Year ended 31 March | Purchases | Sales proceeds from disposal |
|---|---|---|
| Year 6 | Machine E  £16,100 |  |
| Year 7 | Machine F  £25,300 | Machine C  £7,200 |
| Year 8 | Machine G  £5,400 | Machine D  £9,000 |

REQUIRED:

Prepare, in the books of Gee Ltd:

(a)     the total Machines Account for the years ended 31 March Years 6, 7 and 8.

(b)     the total Provision for Depreciation Account for the years ended 31 March Years 6, 7 and 8.

(c)     the Machines Disposal Account for the years ended 31 March Years 7 and 8.

(d)     a Balance Sheet extract showing the entries for machines at 31 March Year 8.

*LCCI Examinations Board*

# 15 BAD DEBTS AND PROVISION FOR BAD DEBTS

Most businesses selling their goods and services to other businesses do not receive payment immediately. Instead, they often have to allow a period of credit and, until the payment is received, they have a current asset of debtors. Unfortunately, it is likely that not all debtors will eventually settle the amount they owe, ie the amounts are bad debts which have to be written off. At the same time a business needs to make a provision for bad debts, which allows for debtors who may not pay.

In this chapter we will:

● distinguish between bad debts and provision for bad debts

● prepare the accounting entries for bad debts, and consider the effect on the final accounts

● prepare the accounting entries to make a provision for bad debts, and consider the effect on the final accounts

● look at the procedures a business may use in order to minimise the risk of bad debts

## BAD DEBTS AND PROVISION FOR BAD DEBTS

*A bad debt is a debt owing to a business which it considers will never be paid.*

Let us consider a business with debtors of £10,000. This total will, most probably, be made up of a number of debtors' accounts. At any one time, a few of these accounts will be bad, and therefore the amount is uncollectable: these are bad debts, and they need to be written off, ie the business will give up trying to collect the debt and will accept the loss.

*Provision for bad debts is the estimate by a business of the likely percentage of its debtors which may go bad during any one accounting period.*

There are likely to be some debtors' accounts which, although they are not yet bad, may be giving some concern as to their ability to pay: a provision for bad debts (or doubtful debts) needs to be made in respect of these. The one thing the business with debtors of £10,000 cannot do is to show this debtors' amount as a current asset in the balance sheet: to do so would be to imply to the user of the balance sheet that the full £10,000 is collectable. Instead, this gross debtors' figure might be reduced in two stages, for example:

• debtors' accounts with balances totalling £200 are to be written off as bad

• a general provision for bad debts is to be made amounting, in this case, to two per cent of remaining debtors

Thus the debtors' figure becomes:

| | |
|---|---:|
| Gross debtors | £10,000 |
| Less: bad debts written off | £200 |
| | £9,800 |
| Less: provision for bad debts at 2% | £196 |
| Net debtors (recorded in balance sheet) | £9,604 |

The amount of the provision for bad debts (here 2%) will vary from business to business, depending on the past experience of receiving payment, the nature of the business and the current economic climate.

Bad debts and provision for bad debts is an application of the accounting concept of prudence (see Chapter 17). By reducing the debtors' figure, through the profit and loss account and balance sheet, a more realistic view is shown of the amount that the business can expect to receive.

## TREATMENT OF BAD DEBTS

Bad debts are written off when they become uncollectable. This means that all reasonable efforts to recover the amount owing have been exhausted, ie statements and letters have been sent to the debtor requesting payment, and legal action, where appropriate, or the threat of legal action has failed to obtain payment.

In writing off a debtor's account as bad, the business is bearing the cost of the amount due. The debtor's account is closed and the amount (or amounts, where a number of accounts are dealt with in this way) is debited to bad debts written off account. This account stores up the amounts of account balances written off during the year (in much the same way as an expense account). At the end of the financial year, the balance of the account is transferred to profit and loss account, where it is described as bad debts written off.

In terms of book-keeping, the transactions are:

– debit bad debts written off account

– credit debtor's account

with the amount of the bad debt.

At the end of the financial year, bad debts written off account is transferred to profit and loss account:

– debit profit and loss account

– credit bad debts written off account

with the total of bad debts written off for the year.

## WORKED EXAMPLE: TREATMENT OF BAD DEBTS

The following debtor's account is in the sales ledger:

| Dr | | | T Hughes | | | Cr |
|---|---|---|---|---|---|---|
| 20-1 | | £ | | 20-1 | | £ |
| 5 Jan | Sales | 55 | | 8 May | Bank | 25 |
| | | | | 6 Jul | Cash | 5 |

It is now 15 December 20-1 and you are reviewing the debtors' accounts before the end of the financial year on 31 December. Your business has sent statements and 'chaser' letters to T Hughes – the last letter was dated 30 September, and was returned marked 'gone away, not known at this address'. Nothing further has been heard from T Hughes. You take the decision to write off this account as a bad debt; the account will be closed off as follows:

| Dr | | | T Hughes | | | Cr |
|---|---|---|---|---|---|---|
| 20-1 | | £ | | 20-1 | | £ |
| 5 Jan | Sales | 55 | | 8 May | Bank | 25 |
| | | | | 6 Jul | Cash | 5 |
| | | | | 15 Dec | Bad debts written off | 25 |
| | | 55 | | | | 55 |

The balance is transferred to the 'holding' account, bad debts written off, together with other accounts written off. At the end of the financial year, the total of this account is transferred to profit and loss account:

| Dr | | | Bad Debts Written Off Account | | | Cr |
|---|---|---|---|---|---|---|
| 20-1 | | £ | | 20-1 | | £ |
| 15 Dec | T Hughes | 25 | | 31 Dec | Profit and loss account | 200 |
| 15 Dec | A Lane | 85 | | | | |
| 15 Dec | A Harvey | 90 | | | | |
| | | 200 | | | | 200 |

In final accounts, the effect of writing off debts as bad is to reduce the previously reported profit – in the example above, by £200. Note that:

- If you are preparing final accounts and the figure for bad debts is shown in the trial balance (debit side), simply record the amount as an expense in profit and loss account – the debtors' figure has been reduced already.

- If the bad debts figure is not already shown in the trial balance, and a note tells you to write off a certain debt as bad, you need to list the amount as an expense in profit and loss account and reduce the debtors' figure for the balance sheet.

## VAT relief on bad debts

A VAT-registered business can reclaim VAT originally charged on debts which are now being written off. However, in order to claim relief, the debt must be more than six months overdue, ie more than six months from the date the payment was originally due. Thus a sale made on 30-day terms on 1 January would be due for payment on 31 January; if this sale is written off as a bad debt, VAT relief would be available after 31 July.

## bad debts recovered

If, by chance, a former debtor whose account has been written off as bad, should make a payment, the book-keeping entries are:

- debit cash/bank account
- credit debtor's account
- debit debtor's account
- credit either, bad debts written off account, or, bad debts recovered account

The latter account, bad debts recovered, is used where a business has substantial debtors and is successful in chasing its bad debts. If a recovery is a rare event – perhaps once a year – the practical accounting solution is to credit bad debts written off account. Having recovered payment from the former debtor, if the customer now wishes to buy goods or services, it is prudent to insist on cash payment for some time to come!

# TREATMENT OF PROVISION FOR BAD DEBTS

Provision for bad debts is different from writing off a bad debt because there is the possibility – not the certainty – of future bad debts. The debtors' figure (after writing off bad debts) is reduced either by totalling the balances of the accounts that may not pay or, more likely, by applying a percentage to the total figure for debtors. The percentage chosen will be based on past experience and will vary from business to business – for example, a hire purchase company may well use a higher percentage than a bank.

## initial creation of a provision for bad debts

The procedure for the provision for bad debts – also known as a provision for doubtful debts – comes after writing off bad debts (if any). The steps are:

1   A business, at the end of the financial year, estimates the percentage of its debtors which may go bad, say two per cent
2   The provision is calculated (eg £9,800 x 2% = £196)
3   The provision is recorded in the book-keeping system:
    - debit profit and loss account
    - credit provision for bad debts account

**4** In the final accounts, the amount of the provision is:

- listed in the profit and loss account as an expense called provision for bad debts
- deducted from the debtors' figure in the current assets section of the balance sheet, eg:

|  | £ | £ | £ |
|---|---|---|---|
| **Current Assets** | | | |
| Stock | | X | |
| Debtors | 9,800 | | |
| Less provision for bad debts | 196 | | |
| | | 9,604 | |
| Prepayments | | X | |
| Bank | | X | |
| Cash | | X | |
| | | X | |

Note that the business, in creating a provision for bad debts, is presenting a realistic and prudent estimate of its debtor position.

## ADJUSTMENTS TO PROVISION FOR BAD DEBTS

Once a provision for bad debts has been created, the only adjustments that need to be made to the provision for bad debts are as a result of:

- a policy change in the provision, eg an increase in the fixed percentage from 2% to 5%
- an arithmetic adjustment in the provision as a result of a change in the total of debtors, eg increase in debtors of £5,000 will require a higher provision

When either of these two situations arises, the adjustment to the existing position will be:

- either upwards (increase in provision percentage, or increase in debtor figure)
- or downwards (decrease in provision percentage, or decrease in debtor figure)

An **increase in the provision** is recorded in the book-keeping system as follows:

- debit profit and loss account*
- credit provision for bad debts account

with the amount of the increase

* described as 'increase in provision for bad debts', and listed in the expenses section.

For the purposes of the balance sheet, the amount of the increase is added to the existing provision to give the new figure for provision for bad debts (which is deducted from the debtors' figure), ie the balance at the end of the year is used.

A **decrease in the provision** is recorded as:

- – debit provision for bad debts account
- – credit profit and loss account*

with the amount of the decrease

\* described as 'reduction in provision for bad debts', and listed in the income section

For the balance sheet, the amount of the new provision is shown, ie the lower amount (existing provision less amount of decrease).

Note that provision for bad debts and bad debts written off are completely separate adjustments: the two should not be confused. It is quite usual to see in a profit and loss account entries for both bad debts (written off) and provision for bad debts (the creation or adjustment of provision for bad debts).

## WORKED EXAMPLE: PROVISION FOR BAD DEBTS

A business decides to create a provision for bad debts of five per cent of its debtors. After writing off bad debts, the debtors figures at the end of each of three years are:

| | |
|---|---|
| 20-1 | £10,000 |
| 20-2 | £15,000 |
| 20-3 | £12,000 |

### book-keeping entries

Creating the provision (20-1)

- – debit profit and loss account
- – credit provision for bad debts account

with £10,000 x 5% = £500

Increasing the provision (20-2)

- – debit profit and loss account
- – credit provision for bad debts account

with £5,000 (increase in debtors) x 5% = £250

Decreasing the provision (20-3)

- – debit provision for bad debts account
- – credit profit and loss account

with £3,000 (decrease in debtors) x 5% = £150

The provision for bad debts account is as follows:

| Dr | | | Provision for Bad Debts Account | | | Cr |
|---|---|---|---|---|---|---|
| 20-1 | | £ | 20-1 | | | £ |
| 31 Dec | Balance c/d | 500 | 31 Dec | Profit and loss account | | 500 |
| 20-2 | | | 20-2 | | | |
| 31 Dec | Balance c/d | 750 | 1 Jan | Balance b/d | | 500 |
| | | | 31 Dec | Profit and loss account | | 250 |
| | | | | (increase in provision) | | |
| | | 750 | | | | 750 |
| 20-3 | | | 20-3 | | | |
| 31 Dec | Profit and loss account | 150 | 1 Jan | Balance b/d | | 750 |
| | (decrease in provision) | | | | | |
| 31 Dec | Balance c/d | 600 | | | | |
| | | 750 | | | | 750 |
| 20-4 | | | 20-4 | | | |
| | | | 1 Jan | Balance b/d | | 600 |

## the final accounts

The effect of the above transactions on the final accounts is shown in the following table:

| Year | Profit and loss account | | Balance sheet | | |
|---|---|---|---|---|---|
| | Expense | Income | Debtors | Less provision for bad debts | Net debtors |
| | £ | £ | £ | £ | £ |
| 20-1 | 500 | - | 10,000 | 500 | 9,500 |
| 20-2 | 250 | - | 15,000 | 750 | 14,250 |
| 20-3 | - | 150 | 12,000 | 600 | 11,400 |

The profit and loss account and balance sheet extracts for each year are as follows:

**20-1**    **Profit and loss account (extract) for the year ended 31 December 20-1**

| | £ | £ |
|---|---|---|
| **Gross profit** | | x |
| Less expenses: | | |
| Provision for bad debts | 500 | |

**Balance sheet (extract) as at 31 December 20-1**

| | £ | £ | £ |
|---|---|---|---|
| **Current Assets** | | | |
| Stock | | x | |
| Debtors | 10,000 | | |
| Less provision for bad debts | 500 | | |
| | | 9,500 | |

**20-2**  **Profit and loss account (extract) for the year ended 31 December 20-2**

| | £ | £ |
|---|---|---|
| **Gross profit** | | x |
| Less expenses: | | |
| Increase in provision for bad debts | 250 | |

**Balance sheet (extract) as at 31 December 20-2**

| | £ | £ | £ |
|---|---|---|---|
| **Current Assets** | | | |
| Stock | | x | |
| Debtors | 15,000 | | |
| Less provision for bad debts | 750 | | |
| | | 14,250 | |

**20-3**  **Profit and loss account (extract) for the year ended 31 December 20-3**

| | £ | £ |
|---|---|---|
| **Gross profit** | | x |
| Add income: | | |
| Reduction in provision for bad debts | | 150 |

**Balance sheet (extract) as at 31 December 20-3**

| | £ | £ | £ |
|---|---|---|---|
| **Current Assets** | | | |
| Stock | | x | |
| Debtors | 12,000 | | |
| Less provision for bad debts | 600 | | |
| | | 11,400 | |

**Note:**

When preparing final accounts in an examination question or assessment, there will be a note to the trial balance telling you to make an adjustment to the provision for bad debts. Sometimes you will be told a percentage figure, eg 'provision for bad debts is to be maintained at five per cent of debtors'; alternatively, you may be told the new provision figure (be careful of the wording – distinguish between 'increase the provision **to** £750' and 'increase the provision **by** £750').

# MINIMISING THE RISK OF BAD DEBTS

Having studied the technicalities of accounting for bad debts, and creating a provision for bad debts, it is appropriate to look at ways in which businesses selling on credit can minimise the risks. The following are some of the procedures that can be followed:

- When first approached by an unknown business wishing to buy goods on credit, the seller should ask for references. One of these should be the buyer's bank, and the others (normally two) should be from traders with whom the buyer has previously done business.

- The seller, before supplying goods on credit, should take up both references and obtain satisfactory replies.

- Once satisfactory replies have been received, a credit limit for the customer should be established, and an account opened in the sales ledger. The amount of the credit limit will depend very much on the expected amount of future business – for example, £1,000 might be appropriate. The credit limit should not normally be exceeded – the firm's credit controller or financial accountant will approve any transactions above the limit.

- Invoices and month-end statements of account should be sent out promptly; invoices should state the terms of trade (see page 46), and statements should analyse the balance to show how long it has been outstanding, eg 'over 30 days, over 60 days, over 90 days' – computer-produced statements can show this automatically.

- If a customer does not pay within a reasonable time, the firm should follow established procedures in order to chase up the debt promptly. These procedures are likely to include 'chaser' letters, the first of which points out that the account is overdue, with a later letter threatening legal action. Whether or not legal action is taken will depend on the size of the debt – for a small amount the costs and time involved in taking legal action may outweigh the benefits of recovering the money.

## the use of an aged schedule of debtors

To help with credit control, many firms produce an aged schedule of debtors at the end of each month. This analyses individual debtor balances into the time that the amount has been owing. Thus it shows the long outstanding debts that are, potentially, bad debtors, against whom early action is necessary. An aged schedule is easily produced using a computer accounting system (see Chapter 11).

An aged schedule of debtors can also be used to calculate the provision for bad debts. For example, a business has the following schedule of debtors at the end of its financial year:

| Days outstanding | Debtors |
|---|---|
| | £ |
| Current (up to 30 days) | 50,000 |
| 31 to 60 | 26,000 |
| 61 to 90 | 10,000 |
| 91 and over | 4,000 |
| | 90,000 |

Provision for bad debts is to be calculated by providing for 25% on debts which have been outstanding for 91 days and over, 10% on debts outstanding for 61-90 days, and 2% on debts outstanding for 31-60 days. No provision is to be made on current debts.

Provision for bad debts is calculated as:

|  |  |  | £ |
|---|---|---|---:|
| Current | £50,000 (no provision) | = | nil |
| 31-60 days | £26,000 x 2% | = | 520 |
| 61-90 days | £10,000 x 10% | = | 1,000 |
| 91 days and over | £4,000 x 25% | = | 1,000 |
| Provision for bad debts to be created (or adjusted) to | | | 2,520 |

# CHAPTER SUMMARY

- A bad debt is a debt owing to a business which it considers will never be paid.

- A provision for bad debts is the estimate by a business of the likely percentage of its debtors which may go bad during any one accounting period.

- The specific order for dealing with bad debts and provisions should be followed:
  - write off bad debts (if any)
  - create (or adjust) provision for bad debts

- To write off a bad debt:
  - debit bad debts written off account
  - credit debtor's account
  At the end of the financial year the bad debts written off account is transferred as an expense, to profit and loss account.

- To create a provision for bad debts:
  - debit profit and loss account
  - credit provision for bad debts account

- In the balance sheet, provision for bad debts is deducted from debtors.

- Having created a provision for bad debts, it will usually be adjusted either upwards or downwards in later years in line with the change in the level of debtors.

- A business should follow set procedures when opening new accounts in order to minimise the risk of bad debts.

The next chapter looks at how the various adjustments considered in the last three chapters can be shown formally on the trial balance. This technique is known as the extended trial balance.

# QUESTIONS

NOTE: an asterisk (*) after the question number means that an answer to the question is given in Appendix 2.

**15.1**

You are the book-keeper at Waterston Plant Hire. At 31 December 20-8, the end of the financial year, the business has gross debtors of £20,210. The owner decides to:

(a)    write off, as bad debts, the accounts of:

|  |  |
|---|---|
| P Ross | £55 |
| J Ball | £105 |
| L Jones | £50 |

(b)    make a provision for bad debts of 2.5% of debtors (after writing off the above bad debts)

You are to explain how these transactions will be recorded in the final accounts at the end of the financial year.

**15.2***

Ross Engineering has an existing provision for bad debts of £300, based on 5 per cent of debtors. After writing off bad debts, the amounts of debtors at the end of the next two financial years are found to be:

|  |  |
|---|---|
| 30 June 20-1 | £8,000 |
| 30 June 20-2 | £7,000 |

The business continues to keep the provision for bad debts equal to 5 per cent of debtors.

As an accounts assistant at Ross Engineering, you are to show how the provision for bad debts will be adjusted at the end of the financial years ended 30 June 20-1 and 30 June 20-2, and how it will be recorded in the appropriate final accounts.

**15.3**

Wong Pau Yen provides you with the following information

TRIAL BALANCE AS AT 31 AUGUST

|  | Dr £ | Cr £ |
|---|---|---|
| Capital | | 24,230 |
| Plant and machinery (cost £20,000) | 16,000 | |
| Vehicles (cost £10,000) | 6,400 | |
| Opening stock | 1,200 | |
| Cash | 100 | |
| Bank | | 1,690 |
| Purchases and returns | 51,000 | 900 |
| Sales and returns | 1,300 | 94,600 |
| Creditors | | 1,660 |
| Debtors | 8,500 | |
| Heat and light | 1,400 | |
| Wages and salaries | 18,600 | |
| Rent and rates | 6,240 | |
| Motor expenses | 1,340 | |
| Sundry expenses | 6,400 | |
| Drawings | 7,600 | |
| | 126,080 | 126,080 |

You should take the following into consideration:

(1)     closing stock at 31 August was £1,300

(2)     depreciation is to be provided as follows:

　　–     plant and machinery – 10% on cost (straight line basis)

　　–     vehicles – 20% on reducing (diminishing) balance basis

(3)     a provision for bad debts is to be created of 4% of debtors

(4)     you should provide for:

　　–     wages and salaries in arrears – £1,060

　　–     rent and rates accrued due at the end of year – £130

　　–     prepaid sundry expenses – £360

YOU ARE REQUIRED TO:

(a)     prepare a trading, profit and loss account for the year ended 31 August

(b)     prepare a balance sheet as at that date

*Pitman Qualifications*

15.4* The following trial balance has been extracted by the book-keeper of James Jenkins, who owns a patisserie and coffee lounge, as at 30 June 20-9:

|  | Dr £ | Cr £ |
|---|---:|---:|
| Capital | | 36,175 |
| Drawings | 19,050 | |
| Purchases and sales | 105,240 | 168,432 |
| Stock at 1 July 20-8 | 9,427 | |
| Debtors and creditors | 3,840 | 5,294 |
| Value Added Tax | | 1,492 |
| Returns | 975 | 1,237 |
| Discounts | 127 | 243 |
| Wages and salaries | 30,841 | |
| Vehicle expenses | 1,021 | |
| Rent and rates | 8,796 | |
| Heating and lighting | 1,840 | |
| Telephone | 355 | |
| General expenses | 1,752 | |
| Bad debts written off | 85 | |
| Vehicle at cost | 8,000 | |
| Provision for depreciation on vehicle | | 3,500 |
| Shop fittings at cost | 6,000 | |
| Provision for depreciation on shop fittings | | 2,400 |
| Provision for bad debts | | 150 |
| Cash | 155 | |
| Bank | 21,419 | |
| | 218,923 | 218,923 |

Notes at 30 June 20-9:
- stock was valued at £11,517
- vehicle expenses owing £55
- rent prepaid £275
- depreciate the vehicle at 25 per cent per annum, using the reducing balance method
- depreciate shop fittings at 10 per cent per annum, using the straight-line method
- the provision for bad debts is to be equal to 2.5 per cent of debtors

You are to prepare the trading and profit and loss account of James Jenkins for the year ended 30 June 20-9, together with his balance sheet at that date.

15.5  The following Trial Balance was extracted from the books of D Martin, a sole trader, on 31 December Year 6:

|  | £ | £ |
|---|---|---|
| Capital at 1 January Year 6 |  | 184,460 |
| Drawings | 40,000 |  |
| Freehold premises at cost | 160,000 |  |
| Motor vehicles at cost | 30,000 |  |
| Office furniture at cost | 10,000 |  |
| Stock at 1 January Year 6 | 21,480 |  |
| Provision for depreciation, 1 January Year 6 |  |  |
| Motor vehicles |  | 8,000 |
| Office furniture |  | 2,500 |
| Rent | 18,000 |  |
| Electricity | 3,800 |  |
| Salaries | 50,100 |  |
| Purchases and Sales | 191,200 | 337,200 |
| Carriage outwards | 6,000 |  |
| Insurance | 4,200 |  |
| Carriage inwards | 1,200 |  |
| Debtors and Creditors | 31,400 | 7,880 |
| Bad debts | 2,400 |  |
| Provision for Doubtful Debts 1 January Year 6 |  | 1,970 |
| Bank interest | 720 |  |
| Bank overdraft |  | 7,000 |
| Cash in hand | 600 |  |
| Telephone | 3,200 |  |
| Returns Inwards and Outwards | 4,950 | 3,600 |
| Discounts | 2,700 | 2,090 |
| Loan from D Samson repayable Year 12 |  | 26,000 |
| Sale of motor vehicle |  | 1,250 |
|  | 581,950 | 581,950 |

*this question is continued on the next page . . .*

Additional information at 31 December Year 6:

(1)    Stock was valued at £24,900

(2)    Prepayments were:

      Insurance     £780

      Rent          £4,000

(3)    Accrued charges were:

      Electricity     £360

      Salaries      £3,200

      Loan interest   £2,600

(4)    Depreciation to be provided on cost price at the following rates per annum:

      Motor vehicles  20%

      Office furniture  10%

(5)    The item 'sale of motor vehicle' shown in the trial balance represents cash received from the sale of a motor vehicle on 1 January Year 6. The motor vehicle was purchased on 1 January Year 3 at a cost of £5,000. Depreciation rates have remained the same since 1 January Year 1. No entries have been made in respect of this sale except for the trial balance item.

(6)    The provision for bad debts is to be adjusted to 5% of debtors.

REQUIRED:

Prepare for D Martin:

(a)    a trading and profit and loss account for the year ended 31 December Year 6

(b)    a balance sheet as at 31 December Year 6

*LCCI Examinations Board*

**Chapters 14 - 15**

# MULTIPLE CHOICE QUESTIONS

Read each question carefully.
Choose the one answer you think is correct (calculators may be needed).
The answers are on page 568.

1    A machine costs £5,000 and is expected to last for five years. At the
     end of this time, it is estimated it will have a residual (scrap) value of
     £500. The annual amount of depreciation, using the straight-line
     method will be:

     A    £900

     B    £1,000

     C    £1,100

     D    £1,250

2    A car costs £12,000 and is expected to be kept for four years. At the
     end of this time, it is estimated that it will be sold for £4,000. Using the
     reducing balance method of depreciation, what percentage (to the
     nearest whole number) will be used each year?

     A    20%

     B    24%

     C    25%

     D    26%

3    A car is being depreciated using the reducing balance method. The
     original cost of the car was £15,000. At the end of year three it has a
     net book value of £5,145. What percentage of reducing balance is
     being used?

     A    20%

     B    25%

     C    30%

     D    35%

4    A computer is being depreciated over five years using the sum of the
     digits method. The original cost was £8,000 and the estimated
     residual (scrap) value is £500. How much will be the depreciation
     amount for year 4?

A    £2,000

B    £1,600

C    £1,500

D    £1,000

**5**    A bus costs £85,000 and is expected to last for five years during which time it will cover 250,000 miles. It is then expected to be sold for £10,000. Depreciation is on the units of output method. How much will be the depreciation amount for this year, during which it has covered 60,000 miles?

A    £17,000

B    £15,000

C    £18,000

D    £20,000

**6**    The depreciation charge in profit and loss account will reduce:

A    gross profit

B    net profit

C    bank balance

D    current assets

**7**    The book-keeping entries to record a profit on sale of fixed assets are:

|   | Debit | Credit |
|---|---|---|
| A | fixed asset account | profit and loss account |
| B | disposals account | profit and loss account |
| C | profit and loss account | disposals account |
| D | bank account | profit and loss account |

**8**    A machine, which originally cost £1,000, is sold for £350. The provision for depreciation account relevant to this machine shows a balance of £620. This means that there is:

A    a loss on sale of £380

B    a profit on sale of £350

C    a loss on sale of £30

D    a profit on sale of £30

**9**   The book-keeping entries to record a decrease in provision for bad debts are:

|   | Debit | Credit |
|---|-------|--------|
| A | profit and loss | provision for bad debts |
| B | bad debts written off | profit and loss |
| C | provision for bad debts | profit and loss |
| D | bank | provision for bad debts |

**10**   An increase in provision for bad debts will:

A    decrease net profit for the year

B    increase gross profit for the year

C    decrease the cash/bank balance

D    increase net profit for the year

**11**   A trial balance shows debtors of £48,000 and a provision for bad debts of £2,200. It is decided to make the provision for bad debts equal to five per cent of debtors. What book-keeping entry will be made on the provision for bad debts account?

A    debit £200

B    debit £2,400

C    credit £200

D    credit £2,200

**12**   The profit and loss account of a business has been prepared showing a net loss of £2,350. A reduction of £150 in the provision of bad debts should have been made, and bad debts of £70 should have been written off. Net loss will now be:

A    £2,130

B    £2,270

C    £2,430

D    £2,570

# 16  THE EXTENDED TRIAL BALANCE

In the previous four chapters we have looked at the preparation of year-end accounts from a two-column trial balance, and have dealt with adjustments for accruals and prepayments, depreciation of fixed assets, bad debts written off, and provision for bad debts. In this chapter we shall see how the final accounts, together with adjustments, can be produced from a more elaborate form of trial balance known as the extended trial balance. This sets out debit and credit columns for:

● the ledger balances

● adjustments to the figures

● the year-end accounts where the figures are used: ie trading and profit and loss account (combined together), and balance sheet

## FINAL ACCOUNTS AND THE TRIAL BALANCE

The trial balance, as we have seen in earlier chapters, provides the starting point for the preparation of final accounts. There are two trial balance formats:

• the two-column trial balance (which we have used previously)

• the trial balance extended into a number of columns (see worked examples which follow)

The extended trial balance (ETB) gives an understanding of the principles of final accounts by showing

• the profit (or loss) made by the business during the accounting period

• the assets, liabilities and capital of the business at the end of the accounting period

The extended trial balance format is often used by accountancy firms as a first step towards preparing year-end accounts for their clients. When the adjustments (closing stock, accruals, prepayments, depreciation, bad debts) have been completed, it provides a posting sheet for making transfers between accounts within the general ledger.

We will see the use of the extended trial balance through two worked examples based on the year-end accounts of Tara Smith, who owns a designer fashion shop in town:

• the first example incorporates only the adjustment for closing stock

• the second example incorporates adjustments for accruals and prepayments, depreciation of fixed assets, bad debts written off, and provision for bad debts

## EXTENDED TRIAL BALANCE: WORKED EXAMPLE 1

The trial balance of Tara Smith, in two-column format, is shown below:

**TARA SMITH, TRADING AS "THE FASHION SHOP"**
**Trial balance as at 31 December 20-8**

| Name of account | Dr £ | Cr £ |
|---|---:|---:|
| Stock at 1 January 20-8 | 12,500 | |
| Purchases | 105,000 | |
| Sales | | 155,000 |
| Administration expenses | 6,200 | |
| Wages | 23,500 | |
| Rent paid | 750 | |
| Telephone | 500 | |
| Interest paid | 4,500 | |
| Travel expenses | 550 | |
| Premises | 100,000 | |
| Shop fittings | 20,000 | |
| Debtors | 10,500 | |
| Bank | 5,450 | |
| Cash | 50 | |
| Capital | | 75,000 |
| Drawings | 7,000 | |
| Loan from bank | | 50,000 |
| Creditors | | 14,500 |
| Value Added Tax | | 2,000 |
| | 296,500 | 296,500 |

Note: stock at 31 December 20-8 was valued at £10,500

The layout on the next page shows how an extended trial balance uses columns and rows to prepare the final accounts of Tara Smith. Note that the profit and loss account column incorporates the trading account (the layout of the extended trial balance can be amended to suit the needs of the user and could include columns for a separate trading account if required).

The steps to complete the extended trial balance are as follows:

## step 1

Enter the trial balance details into the description and ledger balances columns. Total the debit and credit columns of ledger balances to show that the trial balance proves the arithmetical accuracy of the book-keeping. Note that the blank lines after premises and shop fittings will be used for depreciation amounts – see Worked Example 2 (page 261).

**EXTENDED TRIAL BALANCE**   TARA SMITH TRADING AS "THE FASHION SHOP"   31 DECEMBER 20-8

| Description | Ledger balances Dr £ | Ledger balances Cr £ | Adjustments Dr £ | Adjustments Cr £ | Profit and loss Dr £ | Profit and loss Cr £ | Balance sheet Dr £ | Balance sheet Cr £ |
|---|---|---|---|---|---|---|---|---|
| Stocks at 1 Jan 20-8 | 12,500 | | | | 12,500 | | | |
| Purchases | 105,000 | | | | 105,000 | | | |
| Sales | | 155,000 | | | | 155,000 | | |
| Administration expenses | 6,200 | | | | 6,200 | | | |
| Wages | 23,500 | | | | 23,500 | | | |
| Rent paid | 750 | | | | 750 | | | |
| Telephone | 500 | | | | 500 | | | |
| Interest paid | 4,500 | | | | 4,500 | | | |
| Travel expenses | 550 | | | | 550 | | | |
| Premises | 100,000 | | | | | | 100,000 | |
| Shop fittings | 20,000 | | | | | | 20,000 | |
| Debtors | 10,500 | | | | | | 10,500 | |
| Bank | 5,450 | | | | | | 5,450 | |
| Cash | 50 | | | | | | 50 | |
| Capital | | 75,000 | | | | | | 75,000 |
| Drawings | 7,000 | | | | | | 7,000 | |
| Loan from bank | | 50,000 | | | | | | 50,000 |
| Creditors | | 14,500 | | | | | | 14,500 |
| Value Added Tax | | 2,000 | | | | | | 2,000 |
| | | | | | | | | |
| Closing stock: Profit and loss | | | | 10,500 | | 10,500 | | |
| Closing stock: Balance sheet | | | 10,500 | | | | 10,500 | |
| Accruals | | | | | | | | |
| Prepayments | | | | | | | | |
| Depreciation | | | | | | | | |
| Bad debts | | | | | | | | |
| Provision for bad debts:adjustment | | | | | | | | |
| | | | | | | | | |
| Net profit/loss | | | | | 12,000 | | | 12,000 |
| | 296,500 | 296,500 | 10,500 | 10,500 | 165,500 | 165,500 | 153,500 | 153,500 |

## step 2

Transfer to the profit and loss columns (which incorporate the trading account) the rows for

- opening stock

- purchases made by the business

- sales made by the business (together with any small amounts of income)

- revenue expenditure of the business

Ensure that debit balances from the trial balance rows are entered in the debit column of profit and loss account; credit balances are entered in the credit column.

## step 3

Transfer to the balance sheet columns the remaining rows from the trial balance. These represent:

- assets

- liabilities

- capital

- drawings

## step 4

Deal with adjustments – in this example, the only adjustment is for the valuation of closing stock at 31 December 20-8. In the adjustments columns the amount of closing stock is credited to the profit and loss account and debited to the balance sheet (see page 172 for the book-keeping entries for closing stock). Transfer the adjustment for closing stock to:

- profit and loss – credit column

- balance sheet – debit column

Now total the debit and credit adjustment columns; note that totals are the same, ie they balance. We shall be using the other adjustment items in Worked Example 2 (page 261).

In the profit and loss columns, total the money amounts and then, just like balancing an account, enter the amount required to make both debit and credit sides equal: here it is £12,000. If the amount is entered on the debit side, it represents the net profit of the business for the accounting period; if on the credit side, it is a loss. For Tara Smith, it is a profit of £12,000 for the financial year.

## step 5

Enter the net profit or loss in the balance sheet column, but on the opposite side to that in profit and loss. For example, with Tara Smith's business, the amount of the net profit row is £12,000, which is:

- entered in the debit column of profit and loss

- entered in the credit column of the balance sheet

Now total the debit and credit balance sheet columns. They balance with the same total – here £153,500 – which proves that the balance sheet balances.

# THE DUAL ASPECT OF ADJUSTMENTS

Worked Example 1 (on the last three pages) incorporated only the adjustment for closing stock. As we have seen in previous chapters, other adjustments may be made for accruals and prepayments, depreciation of fixed assets, bad debts written off, and provision for bad debts.

When preparing final accounts in the previous chapters, we have seen how each adjustment needs to be reflected in two aspects of the year-end accounts. The following are examples of how we have dealt with the main adjustments:

**Accrual of expenses**

- – increase expense in profit and loss account
- – current liability in balance sheet

**Prepayment of expenses**

- – decrease expense in profit and loss account
- – current asset in balance sheet

**Provision for depreciation of fixed assets**

- – expense in profit and loss account
- – fixed asset value reduced in balance sheet

**Bad debts written off**

- – expense in profit and loss account
- – debtors' figure reduced in balance sheet

**Creation of, or increase in, provision for bad debts**

- – expense in profit and loss account
- – debtors' figure reduced in balance sheet by total amount of provision

**Decrease in provision for bad debts**

- – income in profit and loss account
- – debtors' figure reduced in balance sheet by total amount of provision

Using the extended trial balance format, we start with the trial balance from the book-keeping records and then use the adjustments columns to record accruals and prepayments, depreciation, bad debts and provision for bad debts. The adjusted figures are then recorded under the appropriate headings of profit and loss account and balance sheet. The adjustments are illustrated in the worked example which follows.

## EXTENDED TRIAL BALANCE: WORKED EXAMPLE 2

Using the trial balance of Tara Smith at 31 December 20-8, shown in Worked Example 1, we will make the following adjustments at that date:

- stock was valued at £10,500
- telephone expenses accrued £100
- rent prepaid £75
- depreciate the premises at 2 per cent per annum, using the straight-line method
- depreciate the shop fittings at 25 per cent per annum, using the reducing balance method
- write off bad debts of £100
- create a provision for bad debts of £250

The layout on the next page shows how these adjustments are incorporated into the extended trial balance; we have already dealt with closing stock in Worked Example 1.

### accrual of expenses

- in the adjustments columns:
  - record £100 on the debit side of the telephone row
  - record £100 on the credit side of the accruals row
- on the debit side of the profit and loss account columns the total cost of the telephone row is now £600 (ie £500 from the trial balance, plus £100 accrual)
- on the credit side of the balance sheet columns £100 from the accruals row is shown as a liability of the business

### prepayment of expenses

- in the adjustments columns:
  - record £75 on the credit side of the rent paid row
  - record £75 on the debit side of the prepayments row
- on the credit side of the profit and loss columns the total cost of rent paid is now £675 (ie £750 from the trial balance, less £75 prepaid)
- on the debit side of the balance sheet columns £75 from the prepayments row is shown as an asset of the business

### depreciation of fixed assets

The depreciation amounts are:

- premises: 2 per cent per annum straight-line, ie £2,000
- shop fittings: 25 per cent per annum reducing balance, ie £5,000

The depreciation is shown in the extended trial balance as follows:

- in the description columns:
  - on the blank line below premises write in 'provision for depreciation: premises'
  - on the blank line below shop fittings write in 'provision for depreciation: shop fittings'

- in the adjustment columns:
  - record £7,000 (ie £2,000 + £5,000) on the debit side of the 'depreciation for year' row
  - record £2,000 on the credit side of the 'provision for depreciation: premises' row
  - record £5,000 on the credit side of the 'provision for depreciation: shop fittings' row
- on the debit side of the profit and loss columns record the depreciation for year of £7,000
- on the credit side of the balance sheet columns record the £2,000 and £5,000 provision for depreciation on the two classes of assets

As this is the first year that Tara Smith has recorded depreciation, both depreciation for year and provision for depreciation amounts are the same.

## bad debts written off

The adjustment to write off bad debts is shown in the extended trial balance as follows:
- in the adjustments columns:
  - record £100 on the debit side of the bad debts row
  - record £100 on the credit side of the debtors row
- on the debit side of the profit and loss account columns record the bad debts written off of £100
- on the debit side of the balance sheet columns show debtors as a net figure of £10,400 (ie £10,500 less £100 written off)

## provision for bad debts

Here Tara Smith is creating a new provision for bad debts of £250; it is shown in the extended trial balance as follows:
- in the adjustments columns:
  - record £250 on the debit side of the 'provision for bad debts: adjustment' row
  - record £250 on the credit side of the provision for bad debts row
- in the profit and loss account columns record the £250 amount of the 'provision for bad debts: adjustment' as an expense in the debit column
- in the balance sheet columns show provision for bad debts £250 on the credit side

Note that, where an existing provision for bad debts is to be increased, the above principles are followed, with the balance sheet columns showing the total amount, ie existing provision plus increase. To reduce an existing provision, then the reverse entries will be made.

In the extended trial balance:
- 'provision for bad debts: adjustment' is shown in the profit and loss account and records the amount to create, increase or decrease the provision each year
- 'provision for bad debts' is shown in the credit column of the balance sheet and is the accumulated total of the provision

## extended trial balance

The extended trial balance of Tara Smith, incorporating the above adjustments is shown on the next page. The altered figures have been shaded for illustrative purposes. Note that net profit will be different from that shown in Worked Example 1 because of the effect of the adjustments.

**EXTENDED TRIAL BALANCE    TARA SMITH TRADING AS "THE FASHION SHOP"    31 DECEMBER 20-8**

| Description | Ledger balances | | Adjustments | | Profit and loss | | Balance sheet | |
|---|---|---|---|---|---|---|---|---|
| | Dr £ | Cr £ | Dr £ | Cr £ | Dr £ | Cr £ | Dr £ | Cr £ |
| Stocks at 1 Jan 20-8 | 12,500 | | | | 12,500 | | | |
| Purchases | 105,000 | | | | 105,000 | | | |
| Sales | | 155,000 | | | | 155,000 | | |
| Administration expenses | 6,200 | | | | 6,200 | | | |
| Wages | 23,500 | | | | 23,500 | | | |
| Rent paid | 750 | | | 75 | 675 | | | |
| Telephone | 500 | | 100 | | 600 | | | |
| Interest paid | 4,500 | | | | 4,500 | | | |
| Travel expenses | 550 | | | | 550 | | | |
| Premises | 100,000 | | | | | | 100,000 | |
| Provision for depreciation: premises | | | | 2,000 | | | | 2,000 |
| Shop fittings | 20,000 | | | | | | 20,000 | |
| Provision for depreciation: shop fittings | | | | 5,000 | | | | 5,000 |
| Debtors | 10,500 | | | 100 | | | 10,400 | |
| Bank | 5,450 | | | | | | 5,450 | |
| Cash | 50 | | | | | | 50 | |
| Capital | | 75,000 | | | | | | 75,000 |
| Drawings | 7,000 | | | | | | 7,000 | |
| Loan from bank | | 50,000 | | | | | | 50,000 |
| Creditors | | 14,500 | | | | | | 14,500 |
| Value Added Tax | | 2,000 | | | | | | 2,000 |
| Provision for bad debts | | | | 250 | | | | 250 |
| Closing stock: Profit & loss | | | 10,500 | | | 10,500 | | |
| Closing stock: Balance sheet | | | | 10,500 | | | 10,500 | |
| Accruals | | | | 100 | | | | 100 |
| Prepayments | | | 75 | | | | 75 | |
| Depreciation | | | 7,000 | | 7,000 | | | |
| Bad debts | | | 100 | | 100 | | | |
| Provision for bad debts:adjustment | | | 250 | | 250 | | | |
| | | | | | | | | |
| Net profit/loss | | | | | 4,625 | | | 4,625 |
| | 296,500 | 296,500 | 18,025 | 18,025 | 165 500 | 165,500 | 153,475 | 153,475 |

# ETBs and Conventional Accounts

The extended trial balance does not present final accounts in the conventional format used by accountants, but it does ensure that the dual aspect of each adjustment is dealt with correctly, and that no item from the trial balance is overlooked. As a consequence, ETBs are frequently used by accountancy firms in the preparation of year-end accounts for their clients.

Using the 'conventional' format, the year-end accounts of Tara Smith will be presented as shown below and on the next page.

**TRADING AND PROFIT AND LOSS ACCOUNT OF TARA SMITH
FOR THE YEAR ENDED 31 DECEMBER 20-8**

|  | £ | £ |
|---|---|---|
| Sales |  | 155,000 |
| Opening stock | 12,500 |  |
| Purchases | 105,000 |  |
|  | 117,500 |  |
| Less Closing Stock | 10,500 |  |
| Cost of Goods Sold |  | 107,000 |
| **Gross profit** |  | 48,000 |
|  |  |  |
| Less expenses: |  |  |
| Administration expenses | 6,200 |  |
| Wages | 23,500 |  |
| Rent paid | 675 |  |
| Telephone | 600 |  |
| Interest paid | 4,500 |  |
| Travel expenses | 550 |  |
| Provision for Depreciation: premises | 2,000 |  |
| shop fittings | 5,000 |  |
| Bad debts written off | 100 |  |
| Provision for bad debts | 250 |  |
|  |  | 43,375 |
| **Net profit** |  | 4,625 |

### BALANCE SHEET OF TARA SMITH AS AT 31 DECEMBER 20-8

| | £ | £ | £ |
|---|---|---|---|
| **Fixed Assets** | Cost | Dep'n to date | Net |
| | | | |
| Premises | 100,000 | 2,000 | 98,000 |
| Shop fittings | 20,000 | 5,000 | 15,000 |
| | 120,000 | 7,000 | 113,000 |
| | | | |
| **Current Assets** | | | |
| Stock | | 10,500 | |
| Debtors | 10,400 | | |
| Less provision for bad debts | 250 | | |
| | | 10,150 | |
| Prepayment | | 75 | |
| Bank | | 5,450 | |
| Cash | | 50 | |
| | | 26,225 | |
| **Less Current Liabilities** | | | |
| Creditors | 14,500 | | |
| Accrual | 100 | | |
| Value Added Tax | 2,000 | | |
| | | 16,600 | |
| **Working Capital** | | | 9,625 |
| | | | 122,625 |
| **Less Long-term Liabilities** | | | |
| Loan from bank | | | 50,000 |
| **NET ASSETS** | | | 72,625 |
| | | | |
| | | | |
| **FINANCED BY** | | | |
| **Capital** | | | |
| Opening capital | | | 75,000 |
| Add net profit | | | 4,625 |
| | | | 79,625 |
| Less drawings | | | 7,000 |
| | | | 72,625 |

# CHAPTER SUMMARY

● The extended trial balance records adjustments for accruals and prepayments, depreciation of fixed assets, bad debts written off, and provision for bad debts.

● Once adjusted, the various figures from the trial balance are allocated to the profit and loss account (which incorporates the trading account) and the balance sheet.

● The extended trial balance is often used by accountancy firms in preparing year-end accounts on behalf of their clients.

Having looked, in the last few chapters, at some specific methods of adjusting accounts to take note of accruals and prepayments, depreciation, bad debts and provision for bad debts, the next chapter considers the basic framework – or concepts – within which financial statements are prepared, and looks at stock valuation.

# QUESTIONS

NOTE: an asterisk (*) after the question number means that an answer to the question is given in Appendix 2.

16.1    The following trial balance has been extracted by the book-keeper of Alan Harris at 30 June 20-2:

|  | Dr £ | Cr £ |
|---|---|---|
| Stock at 1 July 20-1 | 13,250 | |
| Capital | | 70,000 |
| Premises | 65,000 | |
| Vehicle | 5,250 | |
| Purchases | 55,000 | |
| Sales | | 85,500 |
| Administration expenses | 850 | |
| Wages | 9,220 | |
| Rent paid | 1,200 | |
| Telephone | 680 | |
| Interest paid | 120 | |
| Travel expenses | 330 | |
| Debtors | 1,350 | |
| Creditors | | 6,400 |
| Value Added Tax | | 1,150 |
| Bank | 2,100 | |
| Cash | 600 | |
| Drawings | 8,100 | |
| | 163,050 | 163,050 |

Note: stock at 30 June 20-2 was valued at £18,100

You are to prepare the figures for the final accounts of Alan Harris for the year ended 30 June 20-2, using the extended trial balance method.

**16.2*** The following trial balance has been extracted by the book-keeper of Paul Sanders, who runs an office supplies business, at 31 December 20-3:

|  | Dr | Cr |
|---|---|---|
|  | £ | £ |
| Purchases and sales | 51,225 | 81,762 |
| Returns | 186 | 254 |
| Stock at 1 January 20-3 | 6,031 | |
| Discounts | 324 | 438 |
| Motor expenses | 1,086 | |
| Wages and salaries | 20,379 | |
| Electricity | 876 | |
| Telephone | 1,241 | |
| Rent and rates | 4,565 | |
| Sundry expenses | 732 | |
| Bad debts written off | 219 | |
| Debtors and creditors | 1,040 | 7,671 |
| Value Added Tax | | 1,301 |
| Bank | 3,501 | |
| Cash | 21 | |
| Vehicles at cost | 15,000 | |
| Provision for depreciation on vehicles | | 3,000 |
| Office equipment at cost | 10,000 | |
| Provision for depreciation on office equipment | | 5,000 |
| Capital | | 25,000 |
| Drawings | 8,000 | |
|  | 124,426 | 124,426 |

Notes at 31 December 20-3:

- stock was valued at £8,210

- electricity owing  £102

- rent prepaid  £251

- depreciate vehicles at 20 per cent and office equipment at 10 per cent per annum, using the straight-line method

- create a provision for bad debts of 5 per cent of debtors

You are to prepare the figures for the final accounts of Paul Sanders for the year ended 31 December 20-3, using the extended trial balance method.

# 17 THE REGULATORY FRAMEWORK OF ACCOUNTING

In this chapter we will explain how the regulatory framework of accounting provides the 'rules' to be followed when preparing final accounts. These rules take the form of:

● accounting concepts

● accounting standards

If the same rules have been followed, then broad comparisons can be made between the final accounts of different businesses.

Later in the chapter we will see how the accounting 'rules' relating to the valuation of stock are applied. We will also look in more detail at stock valuation.

## ACCOUNTING CONCEPTS

There are several basic accounting concepts that are followed when preparing accounts:

- business entity - see also Chapter 1, page 10
- money measurement - see also Chapter 1, page 10
- historical cost
- duality
- materiality
- going concern
- accruals
- consistency
- prudence

### business entity concept

This refers to the fact that final accounts record and report on the activities of one particular business. They do not include the assets and liabilities of those who play a part in owning or running the business. Thus the owner's personal assets and liabilities are kept separate from those of the business: the main links between the business and the owner's personal funds are capital and drawings.

## money measurement concept

This means that, in the final accounts, all items are expressed in the common denominator of money. Only by using money can items be added together to give, for example, net profit, or a balance sheet total. The disadvantage of money measurement is that it is unable to record items which cannot be expressed in money terms. For example, a business with an efficient management, and good labour relations, will appear to have the same value as one that is overstaffed and has poor labour relations: only in the longer term, with different levels of profit and balance sheet structure, will the differences between the two become apparent.

## historical cost concept

This concept, which is an extension of money measurement, follows the principle that assets and liabilities are recorded in the accounts at historical cost, ie the actual amount of the transaction. Thus a stock of goods for resale which cost £5,000 is recorded at that historical cost; a bank loan for £10,000 is recorded at that amount; a vehicle costing £12,500 is recorded at that amount.

The main advantages of the historical cost concept are that it is:

- verifiable – there is a prime document (eg an invoice) that confirms the amount recorded in the accounts
- objective – there are no valuations to apply, which are subjective and may vary depending on the circumstances (eg the value of a car will be different when offered for sale to a garage for cash, when offered as part-exchange for a new car, or when advertised as a private sale in the local paper)

The main disadvantages of the historical cost concept are that it cannot record:

- the change in value – upwards or downwards – of assets over time
- the effects of inflation

Falls in the value of fixed assets are dealt with by using depreciation methods in the accounts; from time-to-time, fixed assets such as land may be revalued upwards to reflect increases in market values. Both of these are subjective techniques, but are well-recognised in accounting. Inflation is rather more difficult, as there is no definitive way for dealing with it in the accounts.

## duality concept

This concept means that each financial transaction is recorded by means of two opposite accounting entries (debit and credit), but of equal values. Thus double-entry book-keeping is an example of the duality concept in practice.

## materiality concept

Some items in accounts have such a low monetary value that it is not worthwhile recording them separately, ie they are not 'material'. Examples of this include:

- Small expense items, such as donations to charities, the purchase of plants for the office, window cleaning, etc, do not justify their own separate expense account; instead they are grouped together in a sundry expenses account.

- End-of-year stocks of office stationery, eg paper clips, staples, photocopying paper, etc, are often not valued for the purpose of final accounts, because the amount is not material and does not justify the time and effort involved. This does mean, however, that the cost of all stationery purchased during the year is charged as an expense to profit and loss account – technically wrong, but not material enough to affect the final accounts.

- Low-cost fixed assets are often charged as an expense in profit and loss account, instead of being classed as capital expenditure, eg a stapler, waste-paper basket, etc. Strictly, these should be treated as fixed assets and depreciated each year over their estimated life; in practice, because the amounts involved are not material, they are treated as profit and loss account expenses.

Materiality depends very much on the size of the business. A large company may consider that items of less than £1,000 are not material; a small company will usually use a much lower figure. What is material, and what is not becomes a matter of judgement.

## going concern concept

This presumes that the business to which the final accounts relate will continue to trade in the foreseeable future. The trading and profit and loss account and balance sheet are prepared on the basis that there is no intention to reduce significantly the size of the business or to liquidate the business. If the business was not a going concern, assets would have very different values, and the balance sheet would be affected considerably. For example, a large, purpose-built factory has considerable value to a going concern business but, if the factory had to be sold, it is likely to have a limited use for other industries, and therefore will have a lower market value. The latter case is the opposite of the going concern concept and would be described as a *gone concern*. Also, in a gone concern situation, extra depreciation would need to be charged as an expense to profit and loss account to allow for the reduced value of fixed assets.

## accruals (or matching) concept

This means that expenses and revenues must be matched so that they concern the same goods or services and the same time period. We have already put this concept into practice in Chapter 13, where expenses and revenues were adjusted to take note of prepayments and accruals. The trading and profit and loss account should always show the amount of the expense that should have been incurred, ie the expenditure for the year, whether or not it has been paid. This is the principle of income and expenditure accounting, rather than using receipts and payments as and when they fall due.

Further examples of the accruals concept are:

- debtors
- creditors
- depreciation
- bad debts
- provision for bad debts
- opening and closing stock adjustments in profit and loss account

## consistency concept

This requires that, when a business adopts particular accounting methods, it should continue to use such methods consistently. For example, a business that decides to make a provision for depreciation on machinery at ten per cent per annum, using the straight-line method, should continue to use that percentage and method for future final accounts for this asset. Of course, having once chosen a particular method, a business is entitled to make changes provided there are good reasons for so doing, and a note to the final accounts would explain what has happened. By applying the consistency concept, direct comparison between the final accounts of different years can be made. Further examples of the use of the consistency concept are:

- stock valuation (seepage 273 in this chapter)
- the application of the materiality concept

## prudence concept

This concept, also known as conservatism in accounting, requires that final accounts should always, where there is any doubt, report a conservative figure for profit or the valuation of assets. To this end, profits are not to be anticipated and should only be recognised when it is reasonably certain that they will be realised; at the same time all known liabilities should be provided for. A good example of the prudence concept is where a provision is made for bad debts (see Chapter 15) – the debtors have not yet gone bad, but it is expected, from experience, that a certain percentage will eventually need to be written off as bad debts. The valuation of stock (see later in this chapter) also follows the prudence concept. 'Anticipate no profit, but anticipate all losses' is a summary of the concept which, in its application, prevents an over-optimistic presentation of a business through the final accounts.

Note: The concepts apply equally to the final accounts of sole traders, partnerships and limited companies. In the case of limited companies the concepts of going concern, accruals, consistency and prudence are given legal force in the Companies Act 1985, and a company which does not apply them will receive a qualified audit report from its auditors.

# ACCOUNTING POLICIES

Accounting policies are the methods used by an individual business to show the effect of transactions, and to record assets and liabilities, in its accounts. For example, straight-line and reducing balance are two ways of recording depreciation in the accounts – a business will select, as its accounting policy, a particular method for each class of fixed asset to be depreciated.

A business selects its accounting policies to fit in with the objectives of:

- relevance – the financial information is useful to users of accounts
- reliability – the financial information can be depended upon by users
- comparability – financial information can be compared with that from previous accounting periods

- understandability – users can understand the financial information provided

An accounting standard (see next section), Financial Reporting Standard No 18, entitled *Accounting policies*, sets out how businesses are to select and report their accounting policies.

## ACCOUNTING STANDARDS

Over the last thirty years, accounting standards have been developed to provide the rules, or framework, of accounting. The intention has been to reduce the variety of alternative accounting treatments. This framework for accounting is represented by **Statements of Standard Accounting Practice** and **Financial Reporting Standards**.

Statements of Standard Accounting Practice (SSAPs) are no longer issued, but those still current come under the control of the Accounting Standards Board. This Board requires accountants to observe the applicable accounting standards, and to disclose and explain significant departures from the standards. A number of SSAPs have been replaced with Financial Reporting Standards (FRSs) as part of an attempt to reduce the number of permissible accounting treatments.

The main accounting standards relevant to topics covered in this book are set out below:

### SSAP 5 Accounting for Value Added Tax

VAT is a tax on the supply of goods and services, which is borne by the final consumer but is collected at each stage of the production and distribution chain. VAT is covered in detail in Chapter 7.

Most businesses with a turnover (sales) above a certain figure must be registered for VAT.

At regular intervals, businesses pay the VAT Authorities (HM Customs and Excise Department):

- the amount of output tax collected on sales made
- less the amount of input tax on goods and services purchased

If the amount of input tax is greater than output tax, the business claims a refund of the difference from HM Customs and Excise.

A VAT-registered business does not normally include VAT in the income and expenditure of the business – whether for capital or revenue items. For example, the purchase of goods for £100 plus VAT is recorded in purchases account as £100 (the VAT is debited to VAT account). By contrast, a business not registered for VAT records the cost as £117.50 (current VAT rate of 17.5%).

Some goods and services (such as postal services, loans of money, sales or lettings of land) are exempt from VAT – the effect of this is that the supplier cannot charge output tax, and can claim back only a proportion of input tax as agreed with the VAT authorities.

Irrecoverable VAT is where a business registered for VAT cannot reclaim input tax (for example on cars, other than for resale); thus the total cost, including VAT, is entered into the accounts as the expenditure.

A VAT-registered business does not normally include VAT in the financial statements – whether for capital or revenue items. A business not registered for VAT will include input VAT as a cost in the financial statements.

## SSAP 9 Stocks and long-term contracts

This sets out the broad rule that stock should be valued at cost or, where lower, selling price – see the Section that follows at the bottom of this page.

## FRS 15 Tangible fixed assets

This requires that fixed assets having a known useful economic life are to be depreciated (note that land is not depreciated – unless it is a mine or a quarry). See Chapter 14.

Any acceptable depreciation method can be used to spread the cost of the fixed asset consistently over its useful economic life.

Depreciation amounts are normally based on the cost of the fixed assets.

## FRS 18 Accounting policies

The objective of this standard is to ensure that for all material items:

- a business selects the accounting policies most appropriate to its particular circumstances for the purpose of giving a true and fair view
- the accounting policies are reviewed regularly to ensure that they remain appropriate, and are changed when necessary
- sufficient information is disclosed in the financial statements to enable users to understand the accounting policies adopted and how they have been implemented

See also page 271, above.

# VALUATION OF STOCK

The control and valuation of stock is an important aspect in the efficient management of a business. Manual or computer records are used to show the amount of stock held and its value at any time during the year. However, at the end of the financial year it is essential for a business to make a physical stock-take for use in the final accounts. This involves stock control personnel going into the stores, the shop, or the warehouse and counting each item. The counted stock for each type of stock held is then valued as follows:

*number of items held x stock valuation per item = stock value*

The auditors of a business may make random checks to ensure that the stock value is correct.

The value of stock at the beginning and end of the financial year is used to calculate the figure for cost of sales. Therefore, the stock value has an effect on profit for the year.

Stock is valued at:

- either what it cost the business to buy the stock (including additional costs to bring the product or service to its present location and condition, such as delivery charges)
- or the net realisable value – the actual or estimated selling price (less any further costs, such as selling and distribution)

The stock valuation is often described as being at the lower of cost and net realisable value. This valuation is taken from SSAP 9 and applies the prudence concept (see page 271 above). It is illustrated as follows:

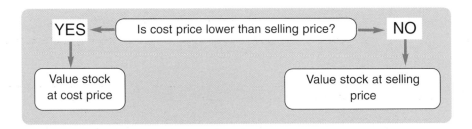

Thus two different stock values are compared:

- cost, including additional costs such as delivery charges
- net realisable value (the amount the stock will sell for), less any further costs such as selling and distribution

The difficulty in stock valuation is in finding out the cost price of stock – this is not easy when quantities of a particular stock item are continually being bought in – often at different prices – and then sold. Some businesses will have stock in a number of different forms, eg a manufacturing business (see Chapter 26) will have stocks of raw materials, work-in-progress and finished goods.

## Different Methods Used in Stock Valuation

Firms use different methods to calculate the cost price of stock. Three commonly used methods are:

- **FIFO** (first in, first out)  This method assumes that the first stocks acquired are the first to be sold or used, so that the valuation of stock on hand at any time consists of the most recently acquired stock.
- **LIFO** (last in, first out)  Here it is assumed that the last stocks acquired are the first to be sold or used, so that the stock on hand is made up of earlier purchases.
- **AVCO** (average cost)  Here the average cost of items held at the beginning of the year is calculated; as new stocks are bought a new average cost is calculated (based on a weighted average, using the number of units bought as the weighting).

The use of a particular method does not necessarily correspond with the method of physical distribution adopted in a firm's stores. For example, in a car factory one starter motor of type X is the same as another, and no-one will be concerned if the storekeeper issues one from the last batch received, even if the FIFO system has been adopted. However, perishable goods are always physically handled on the basis of first in, first out, even if the accounting stock records use another method.

Having chosen a suitable stock valuation method, a business will continue to use that method unless there are good reasons for making the change. This is in line with the consistency concept of accounting.

## STOCK VALUATION RECORDS

In order to be able to calculate accurately the price at which stocks of materials are issued to production, and to ascertain quickly a valuation of closing stock, the following method of recording stock data is suggested:

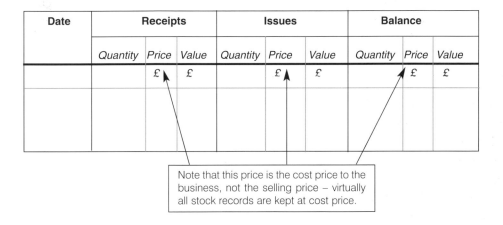

| Date | Receipts | | | Issues | | | Balance | | |
|---|---|---|---|---|---|---|---|---|---|
| | Quantity | Price | Value | Quantity | Price | Value | Quantity | Price | Value |
| | | £ | £ | | £ | £ | | £ | £ |
| | | | | | | | | | |

Note that this price is the cost price to the business, not the selling price – virtually all stock records are kept at cost price.

## WORKED EXAMPLE: STOCK RECORDS

In order to show how the stock records would appear under FIFO, LIFO and AVCO, we will use the data set out below to calculate the stock values using all three methods in turn.

| | |
|---|---|
| January | Opening stock of 40 units at a cost of £3.00 each |
| February | Bought 20 units at a cost of £3.60 each |
| March | Sold 36 units for £6 each |
| April | Bought 20 units at a cost of £3.75 each |
| May | Sold 25 units for £6 each |

# FIFO

## STORES LEDGER RECORD

| Date | Receipts | | | Issues | | | Balance | | |
|------|----------|------|-------|----------|------|-------|----------|------|--------|
| | Quantity | Price | Value | Quantity | Price | Value | Quantity | Price | Value |
| | | £ | £ | | £ | £ | | £ | £ |
| Jan | Balance | | | | | | 40 | 3.00 | 120.00 |
| Feb | 20 | 3.60 | 72.00 | | | | 40 | 3.00 | 120.00 |
| | | | | | | | 20 | 3.60 | 72.00 |
| | | | | | | | 60 | | 192.00 |
| March | | | | 36 | 3.00 | 108.00 | 4 | 3.00 | 12.00 |
| | | | | | | | 20 | 3.60 | 72.00 |
| | | | | | | | 24 | | 84.00 |
| April | 20 | 3.75 | 75.00 | | | | 4 | 3.00 | 12.00 |
| | | | | | | | 20 | 3.60 | 72.00 |
| | | | | | | | 20 | 3.75 | 75.00 |
| | | | | | | | 44 | | 159.00 |
| May | | | | 4 | 3.00 | 12.00 | | | |
| | | | | 20 | 3.60 | 72.00 | | | |
| | | | | 1 | 3.75 | 3.75 | 19 | 3.75 | 71.25 |

# LIFO

## STORES LEDGER RECORD

| Date | Receipts | | | Issues | | | Balance | | |
|------|----------|------|-------|----------|------|-------|----------|------|--------|
| | Quantity | Price | Value | Quantity | Price | Value | Quantity | Price | Value |
| | | £ | £ | | £ | £ | | £ | £ |
| Jan | Balance | | | | | | 40 | 3.00 | 120.00 |
| Feb | 20 | 3.60 | 72.00 | | | | 40 | 3.00 | 120.00 |
| | | | | | | | 20 | 3.60 | 72.00 |
| | | | | | | | 60 | | 192.00 |
| March | | | | 20 | 3.60 | 72.00 | | | |
| | | | | 16 | 3.00 | 48.00 | 24 | 3.00 | 72.00 |
| April | 20 | 3.75 | 75.00 | | | | 24 | 3.00 | 72.00 |
| | | | | | | | 20 | 3.75 | 75.00 |
| | | | | | | | 44 | | 147.00 |
| May | | | | 20 | 3.75 | 75.00 | | | |
| | | | | 5 | 3.00 | 15.00 | 19 | 3.00 | 57.00 |

## AVCO

### STORES LEDGER RECORD

| Date | Receipts | | | Issues | | | Balance | | |
|------|----------|---|---|--------|---|---|---------|---|---|
| | Quantity | Price | Value | Quantity | Price | Value | Quantity | Price | Value |
| | | £ | £ | | £ | £ | | £ | £ |
| Jan | Balance | | | | | | 40 | 3.00 | 120.00 |
| Feb | 20 | 3.60 | 72.00 | | | | 40 | 3.00 | 120.00 |
| | | | | | | | 20 | 3.60 | 72.00 |
| | | | | | | | 60 | 3.20 | 192.00 |
| March | | | | 36 | 3.20 | 115.20 | 24 | 3.20 | 76.80 |
| April | 20 | 3.75 | 75.00 | | | | 24 | 3.20 | 76.80 |
| | | | | | | | 20 | 3.75 | 75.00 |
| | | | | | | | 44 | 3.45 | 151.80 |
| May | | | | 25 | 3.45 | 86.25 | 19 | 3.45 | 65.55 |

Note: Average cost is calculated by dividing the quantity held in stock into the value of the stock. For example, at the end of February, the average cost is £192 ÷ 60 units = £3.20.

The closing stock valuations at the end of May under each method show cost prices of:

> FIFO    £71.25
> LIFO    £57.00
> AVCO    £65.55

There is quite a difference, and this has come about because different stock methods have been used.

## effect on profit

In the example above, the selling price was £6 per unit. The effect on gross profit of using different stock valuations is shown in the following trading accounts:

| | FIFO | LIFO | AVCO |
|---|------|------|------|
| | £ | £ | £ |
| Sales: 61 units at £6 | 366.00 | 366.00 | 366.00 |
| Opening stock: 40 units at £3 | 120.00 | 120.00 | 120.00 |
| Purchases:    20 units at £3.60 | | | |
|            20 Units at £3.75 | 147.00 | 147.00 | 147.00 |
| | 267.00 | 267.00 | 267.00 |
| Less Closing stock:  19 units | 71.25 | 57.00 | 65.55 |
| Cost of Goods Sold | 195.75 | 210.00 | 201.45 |
| Gross profit | 170.25 | 156.00 | 164.55 |
| | 366.00 | 366.00 | 366.00 |

In times of rising prices, FIFO produces the highest profit, LIFO the lowest, and AVCO between the other two. However, over the life of a business, total profit is the same in total, whichever method is chosen: the profit is allocated to different years depending on which method is used.

## COMPARISON OF FIFO, LIFO AND AVCO

### FIFO (first in, first out)

**Advantages:**

* realistic, ie it assumes that goods are issued in order of receipt
* it is easy to calculate
* stock valuation comprises actual prices at which items have been bought
* the closing stock valuation is close to the most recent prices

**Disadvantages:**

* prices at which goods are issued are not necessarily the latest prices
* in times of rising prices, profits will be higher than with other methods (resulting in more tax to pay)

### LIFO (last in, first out)

**Advantages:**

* goods are issued at the latest prices
* it is easy to calculate

**Disadvantages:**

* illogical, ie it assumes goods are issued in reverse order from that in which they are received
* the closing stock valuation is not usually at most recent prices
* when stocks are being run down, issues will 'dip into' old stock at out-of-date prices

### AVCO (average cost)

**Advantages:**

* over a number of accounting periods reported profits are smoothed, ie both high and low profits are avoided
* fluctuations in purchase price are evened out so that issues do not vary greatly
* logical, ie it assumes that identical units, even when purchased at different times, have the same value
* closing stock valuation is close to current market values (in times of rising prices, it will be below current market values)

**Disadvantages:**

* difficult to calculate, and calculations may be to several decimal places
* issues and stock valuation are usually at prices which never existed
* issues may not be at current prices and, in times of rising prices, will be below current prices

The important point to remember is that a business must adopt a consistent stock valuation policy, ie it should choose one method of finding the cost price, and not change it without good reason. FIFO and AVCO are more commonly used than LIFO; in particular, LIFO usually results in a stock valuation for the final accounts which bears little relationship to recent costs.

## CATEGORIES OF STOCK

Statement of Standard Accounting Practice No 9 requires that, in calculating the lower of cost and net realisable value, note should be taken of:

- separate items of stock, or
- groups of similar items

This means that the stock valuation 'rule' must be applied to each separate item of stock, or each group or category of similar stocks. The total cost cannot be compared with the total net realisable value. For example, a decorator's shop has two main categories of stock, paints and wallpapers; they are valued as follows:

|  | Cost | Net realisable value |
|---|---|---|
|  | £ | £ |
| Paints | 2,500 | 2,300 |
| Wallpapers | 5,000 | 7,500 |
|  | 7,500 | 9,800 |

The correct stock valuation is £7,300, which takes the lower of cost and net realisable value for each group of stock, ie

|  | £ |
|---|---|
| Paints (at net realisable value) | 2,300 |
| Wallpapers (at cost) | 5,000 |
|  | 7,300 |

Note that this valuation is the lowest possible choice, so indicating that stock valuation follows the prudence concept of accounting.

## STOCK LOSSES

From time-to-time an event such as a fire, a flood, or a theft may cause stock losses. After such an event it is necessary to calculate the amount of stock losses for insurance purposes; this topic is explained in Chapter 21.

## CHAPTER SUMMARY

- The accounting concepts followed when preparing accounts are: business entity, money measurement, historical cost, duality, going concern, accruals (matching), consistency and prudence.
  Accounting standards comprise SSAPs and FRSs.

- The usual valuation for stock is at the lower of cost and net realisable value (SSAP 9).

- Common methods of accounting for stock include:
  - FIFO (first in, first out)
  - LIFO (last in, first out)
  - AVCO (average cost, based on a weighted average)

- Having chosen one stock valuation method, a business should apply it consistently.

In the last five chapters we have looked at the preparation of final accounts, and a number of adjustments, in some detail. Case Study 2 (page 296) puts these adjustments into context by bringing them all together in a set of final accounts.

So far in our studies of business accounts, we have concerned ourselves with the accounts of a sole trader business – later in the book we will consider the more specialist final accounts of partnerships (Chapter 23), limited companies (Chapter 25) and manufacturing businesses (Chapter 26).

For the next chapter we will see how the journal is used to record adjustments to final accounts, and other transactions.

## QUESTIONS

NOTE: an asterisk (*) after the question number means that an answer to the question is given in Appendix 2.

17.1    The accounting concepts applied when preparing accounts include:

- the going concern concept
- the accruals concept
- the consistency concept
- the prudence concept

You are to explain each of these concepts, giving in each case an example to illustrate an application of the concept.

**17.2\***  A discussion is taking place between Jane Smith, a sole trader, who owns a furniture shop, and her husband, John, who solely owns an engineering business. The following points are made:

(a)  John says that, having depreciated his firm's machinery last year on the reducing balance method, for this year he intends to use the straight-line method. By doing this he says that he will deduct less depreciation from profit and loss account, so his net profit will be higher and his bank manager will be impressed. He says he might revert back to reducing balance method next year.

(b)  At the end of her financial year, Jane comments that the stock of her shop had cost £10,000. She says that, as she normally adds 50 per cent to cost price to give the selling price, she intends to put a value of £15,000 for closing stock in the final accounts.

(c)  John's car is owned by his business but he keeps referring to it as my car. Jane reminds him that it does not belong to him, but to the firm. He replies that of course it belongs to him and, furthermore, if the firm went bankrupt, he would be able to keep the car.

(d)  John's business has debtors of £30,000. He knows that, included in this figure is a bad debt of £2,500. He wants to show £30,000 as debtors in the year-end balance sheet in order to have a high figure for current assets.

(e)  On the last day of her financial year, Jane sold a large order of furniture, totalling £3,000, to a local hotel. The furniture was invoiced and delivered from stock that day, before year-end stocktaking commenced. The payment was received early in the new financial year and Jane now asks John if she will be able to put this sale through the accounts for the new year, instead of the old, but without altering the figures for purchases and closing stock for the old year.

(f)  John says that his accountant talks of preparing his accounts on a going concern basis. John asks Jane if she knows of any other basis that can be used, and which it is usual to follow.

You are to take each of the points and state the correct accounting treatment, referring to appropriate accounting concepts.

**17.3\***  A furniture shop sells coffee tables amongst the lines that it sells. The stock movements for coffee tables in February 20-8 were:

| | |
|---|---|
| 1 February | Stock of 10 tables brought forward at a cost of £30 each |
| 4 February | Sold 2 tables |
| 7 February | Sold 5 tables |
| 10 February | Bought 12 tables at £32 each |
| 12 February | Sold 6 tables |
| 17 February | Sold 4 tables |
| 20 February | Bought 8 tables at £31 each |

| 24 February | Sold 4 tables |
| 27 February | Sold 3 tables |

Each table sells at £50. Stock is valued on the FIFO (first in, first out) basis.

You are to calculate the value of:

(a)    sales for February

(b)    closing stock at 28 February

(c)    cost of sales for February

**17.4**  The following balances were extracted from the ledger of a business on 31 March Year 7:

| Sales | £107,800 |
| Purchases | £54,200 |
| Stocks (1 January Year 7) | £17,300 |

The stocks held on 31 March Year 7 have been valued at £16,200. The stocks held on 1 January and 31 March were valued at cost after a physical stock take had been undertaken on both of these dates.

However, prior to the preparation of the trading account for the first quarter of Year 7, the following items relating to the stocks were discovered:

(1)    Stocks at 1 January Year 7:

(1.1)    12 items in stock which had cost £15 each had been shown at a total cost value of £80 in the stock valuation calculation.

(1.2)    Some items with a cost valuation of £250 had been overlooked in the physical stock take.

All of the items mentioned in (1.1) and (1.2) above had been sold in the quarter ended 31 March Year 7.

(2)    Stocks at 31 March Year 7:

(2.1)    Items valued at their cost price of £1,750 had a combined total sales value of £1,250.

(2.2)    One of the stock sheets used to determine the stock valuation had been undercast by £3,000.

(2.3)    An items which had cost £190 had its selling price of £300 reduced by 50% on 31 March Year 7.

REQUIRED:

(a)    Prepare statements to show the revised stock valuations for:

(1)  Opening stocks at 1 January Year 7

(2)  Closing stocks at 31 March Year 7

(b)    Prepare a trading account for the quarter ended 31 March Year 7.

*LCCI Examinations Board*

**17.5\*** A business buys twenty units of a product in January at a cost of £3.00 each; it buys ten more in February at £3.50 each, and ten in April at £4.00 each. Eight units are sold in March, and sixteen are sold in May.

You are to calculate the value of closing stock at the end of May using:

(a) FIFO (first in, first out)

(b) LIFO (last in, first out)

(c) AVCO (average cost)

Note: where appropriate, work to the nearest penny.

**17.6** (a) Vee Limited has only one stock item. The balance at 1 September Year 3 was 30 units valued at £300. During September, there were the following stock movements:

| Date Year 3 | Purchase Price £ | In Units | Out Units |
|---|---|---|---|
| 3 September | 11.00 | 40 | |
| 6 September | 12.00 | 100 | |
| 7 September | | | 50 |
| 8 September | 14.00 | 70 | |
| 10 September | | | 80 |
| 15 September | 11.50 | 150 | |
| 17 September | | | 60 |
| 18 September | | | 40 |
| 24 September | | | 90 |
| 28 September | 12.00 | 200 | |
| 30 September | | | 70 |

Vee Limited values stock on a weighted average cost basis, calculating a new average cost each time units are purchased. The units already in stock and those received are used to work out the weighted average cost.

REQUIRED:

Calculate, for Vee Limited, the balance of the stock in hand and its value on each of the days in September Year 3 listed above.

Note: Calculations should be made to three decimal places for unit prices and to the nearest £ for stock valuations.

(b) Units issued were sold at £14 each until and including 10 September. From 11 September onwards, the price was increased to £16 per unit.

REQUIRED:

Prepare a trading account for September Year 3.

*LCCI Examinations Board*

# 18 THE JOURNAL

The journal is the primary accounting record for non-regular transactions, eg purchase and sale of fixed assets on credit, correction of errors, end-of-year transfers (such as depreciation and provision for bad debts), and other transfers.

As a primary accounting record, the journal is not part of double-entry book-keeping; instead the journal is used to list transactions before they are entered into the accounts.

## USES OF THE JOURNAL

The journal completes the accounting system by providing the primary accounting record for non-regular transactions, which are not recorded in any other primary accounting record. The categories of such non-regular transactions include:

- opening entries
- purchase and sale of fixed assets on credit
- correction of errors
- other non-regular transactions or adjustments

We shall look at each of these uses in this chapter, except for correction of errors, which is covered in Chapter 19.

The reasons for using a journal are:

- to provide a primary accounting record for non-regular transactions
- to eliminate the need for remembering why non-regular transactions were put through the accounts – the journal acts as a notebook
- to reduce the risk of fraud, by making it difficult for unauthorised transactions to be entered in the accounting system
- to reduce the risk of errors, by listing the transactions that are to be put into the double-entry accounts
- to ensure that entries can be traced back to a prime document, thus providing an audit trail for non-regular transactions

# THE JOURNAL – A PRIMARY ACCOUNTING RECORD

The journal is a primary accounting record; it is not, therefore, part of the double-entry book-keeping system. The journal is used to list the transactions that are then to be put through the accounts. The accounting system for non-regular transactions is as follows:

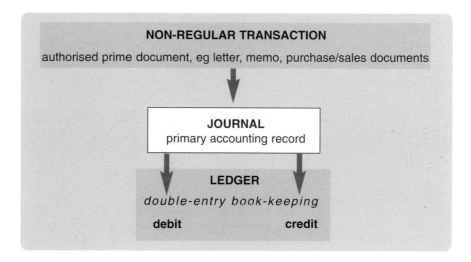

Look at the way the journal is set out with a sample transaction, and then read the notes that follow.

| Date | Details | Folio | Dr | Cr |
|------|---------|-------|-----|-----|
| 20-1 | | | £ | £ |
| 1Jan | Bank | CB | 10,000 | |
| | Capital | GL | | 10,000 |
| | *Opening capital introduced* | | | |

- the names of the accounts to be debited and credited in the book-keeping system are written in the details column; it is customary to show the debit transaction first
- the money amount of each debit and credit is stated in the appropriate columns
- the folio column cross-references to the division of the ledger where each account will be found (it can also include an account number)
- a journal entry always balances, ie debit and credit entries are for the same amount or total
- it is usual to include a brief narrative explaining why the transaction is being carried out, and making reference to the prime document whenever possible (when answering questions you should always include a narrative unless specifically told otherwise)
- each journal entry is complete in itself and is ruled off to separate it from the next entry

## OPENING ENTRIES

These are the transactions which open the accounts of a new business. For example, a first business transaction is:

*1 Jan 20-1        Started in business with £10,000 in the bank*

This non-regular transaction is entered in the journal as follows:

| Date | Details | Folio | Dr | Cr |
|---|---|---|---|---|
| 20-1 | | | £ | £ |
| 1 Jan | Bank | CB | 10,000 | |
| | Capital | GL | | 10,000 |
| | *Opening capital introduced* | | | |

After the journal entry has been made, the transaction can be recorded in the double-entry accounts.

Here is another opening entries transaction to be recorded in the journal:

*1 Feb 20-2        Started in business with cash £100, bank £5,000, stock £1,000, machinery £2,500, creditors £850*

The journal entry is:

| Date | Details | Folio | Dr | Cr |
|---|---|---|---|---|
| 20-2 | | | £ | £ |
| 1 Feb | Cash | CB | 100 | |
| | Bank | CB | 5,000 | |
| | Stock account | GL | 1,000 | |
| | Machinery | GL | 2,500 | |
| | Creditors' accounts | PL | | 850 |
| | Capital | GL | | 7,750 |
| | | | 8,600 | 8,600 |
| | *Assets and liabilities* | | | |
| | *at the start of business* | | | |

Notes:

• Capital is in this example the balancing figure, ie assets minus liabilities.

• The journal is the primary accounting record for all opening entries, including cash and bank; however the normal primary accounting record for other cash/bank transactions is the cash book.

• The amounts from the journal entry will now need to be recorded in the double-entry accounts.

# PURCHASE AND SALE OF FIXED ASSETS ON CREDIT

The purchase and sale of fixed assets are non-regular business transactions which are recorded in the journal as the primary accounting record. Only credit transactions are entered in the journal (because cash/bank transactions are recorded in the cash book as the primary accounting record). However, a business (or an examination question) may choose to journalise cash entries: strictly, though, this is incorrect as two primary accounting records are being used.

*15 Apr 20-3*  *Bought a machine for £1,000 plus VAT (at 17.5%) on credit from Machinery Supplies Limited, purchase order no 2341.*

| Date | Details | Folio | Dr | Cr |
|---|---|---|---|---|
| 20-3 | | | £ | £ |
| 15 Apr | Machinery | GL | 1,000 | |
| | VAT | GL | 175 | |
| | Machinery Supplies Limited* | PL | | 1,175 |
| | | | 1,175 | 1,175 |
| | *Purchase of machine,* | | | |
| | *purchase order 2341* | | | |

*20 May 20-4*  *Car sold for £2,500 on credit to Wyvern Motors Limited (no VAT chargeable).*

| Date | Details | Folio | Dr | Cr |
|---|---|---|---|---|
| 20-4 | | | £ | £ |
| 20 May | Wyvern Motors Limited* | SL | 2,500 | |
| | Disposals | GL | | 2,500 |
| | | | | |
| | *Sale of car, registration no 201 HAB* | | | |

Note that disposal of the car will require calculation of any profit or loss on sale. The journal entries for a disposal are shown in the next Section.

* Instead of entering these transactions in the purchases ledger and sales ledger, an alternative treatment would be to open general ledger accounts for the creditor (Machinery Supplies Limited) and the debtor (Wyvern Motors Limited). This would avoid confusion with trade creditors (in the purchases ledger) and trade debtors (in the sales ledger).

# OTHER TRANSACTIONS

All other non-regular transactions or adjustments need to be recorded in the journal. Many of these take place at the end of a firm's financial year and are concerned with:

- transfers to the trading and profit and loss account
- accruals and prepayments
- expenses charged to the owner's drawings
- goods for the owner's use
- provision for depreciation
- disposal of fixed assets
- bad debts written off
- provision for bad debts

## transfers to trading and profit and loss account

As we have seen earlier (Chapter 12), the trading and profit and loss account forms part of double-entry book-keeping. Therefore, each amount recorded in trading and profit and loss account must have an opposite entry in another account: such transfers are recorded in the journal as the primary accounting record.

*31 Dec 20-1     Balance of salaries account, £23,500, transferred to profit and loss account (debit profit and loss account; credit salaries account)*

| Date | Details | Folio | Dr | Cr |
|---|---|---|---|---|
| 20-1 | | | £ | £ |
| 31 Dec | Profit and loss | GL | 23,500 | |
| | Salaries | GL | | 23,500 |
| | *Transfer to profit and loss of* | | | |
| | *expenditure for the year* | | | |

*31 Dec 20-1     Closing stock has been valued at £12,500 and is to be entered into the accounts*

| Date | Details | Folio | Dr | Cr |
|---|---|---|---|---|
| 20-1 | | | £ | £ |
| 31 Dec | Stock | GL | 12,500 | |
| | Trading | GL | | 12,500 |
| | *Stock valuation at 31 December 20-1* | | | |
| | *transferred to trading account* | | | |

Remember that the closing stock valuation for the year is recorded in stock account as an asset (debit stock account; credit trading account).

## accruals and prepayments

The amounts of accruals and prepayments (see Chapter 13) are recorded in the accounts: such transfers are recorded in the journal as the primary accounting record.

*31 Dec 20-1*    *The balance of electricity account is £500. An electricity bill for £100 is received on 4 January 20-2 and relates to costs incurred in 20-1.*

| Date | Details | Folio | Dr | Cr |
|------|---------|-------|-----|-----|
| 20-1 | | | £ | £ |
| 31 Dec | Profit and loss | GL | 600 | |
| | Electricity | GL | | 600 |
| | *Transfer to profit and loss account* | | | |
| | *of expenditure for the year* | | | |

The above transaction leaves a credit balance on electricity account, being the amount due at 31 December 20-1.

*31 Dec 20-1*    *The balance of rent paid account is £750. Of this, £675 relates to 20-1, while £75 is a prepayment for 20-2*

| Date | Details | Folio | Dr | Cr |
|------|---------|-------|-----|-----|
| 20-1 | | | £ | £ |
| 31 Dec | Profit and loss | GL | 675 | |
| | Rent paid | GL | | 675 |
| | *Transfer to profit and loss account* | | | |
| | *of expenditure for the year* | | | |

The above transaction leaves a debit balance on rent paid account, being the amount prepaid at 31 December 20-1.

## expenses charged to owner's drawings

Sometimes the owner of a business uses business facilities for private use, eg telephone, or car. The owner will agree that part of the expense shall be charged to him or her as drawings, while the other part represents a business expense. The book-keeping entry to record the adjustment is:

– debit drawings account

– credit expense account, eg telephone

*31 Dec 20-1*    *The balance of telephone account is £600; of this, one-quarter is the estimated cost of the owner's private usage*

The journal entry is:

| Date | Details | Folio | Dr | Cr |
|---|---|---|---|---|
| 20-1 | | | £ | £ |
| 31 Dec | Drawings | GL | 150 | |
| | Telephone | GL | | 150 |
| | *Transfer of private use to* | | | |
| | *drawings account* | | | |

## goods for the owner's use

When the owner of a business takes some of the goods in which the business trades for his or her own use, the double-entry book-keeping is:

– debit drawings account

– credit purchases account

*15 Oct 20-1     Owner of the business takes goods for own use, £105 (no VAT)*

The journal entry is:

| Date | Details | Folio | Dr | Cr |
|---|---|---|---|---|
| 20-1 | | | £ | £ |
| 15 Oct | Drawings | GL | 105 | |
| | Purchases | GL | | 105 |
| | *Goods taken for own use* | | | |
| | *by the owner* | | | |

Note that where a business is VAT-registered, VAT must be accounted for on goods taken by the owner

## provision for depreciation

As we have seen in Chapter 14, the amount of provision for depreciation on fixed assets is recorded in the profit and loss account:

– debit profit and loss account

– credit provision for depreciation account

*31 Dec 20-1     Provision for depreciation on a machine is calculated at £400 for the year*

The journal entry is:

| Date | Details | Folio | Dr | Cr |
|---|---|---|---|---|
| 20-1 | | | £ | £ |
| 31 Dec | Profit and loss | GL | 400 | |
| | Provision for depreciation – machinery | GL | | 400 |
| | *Depreciation charge for year* | | | |
| | *on machine* | | | |

## disposal of fixed assets

When a fixed asset is sold or disposed, the book-keeping entries (see page 228) bring together:

- the original cost of the asset
- depreciation provided over the life of the asset
- sale proceeds

31 Dec 20-3    *A machine had been bought on 1 January 20-1 (ie three years ago) for £2,000 (net of VAT). Provision for depreciation (including the current year) totals £1,200. On 31 December 20-3 the machine is sold for £600 plus VAT (cheque received)*

The journal entry is:

| Date | Details | Folio | Dr | Cr |
|------|---------|-------|-----|-----|
| 20-3 | | | £ | £ |
| 31 Dec | Disposals | GL | 2,000 | |
| | Machinery | GL | | 2,000 |
| | Provision for depreciation account | | | |
| | – machinery | GL | 1,200 | |
| | Disposals | GL | | 1,200 |
| | Bank | CB | 705 | |
| | Disposals | GL | | 600 |
| | VAT | GL | | 105 |
| | Profit and loss | GL | 200 | |
| | Disposals | GL | | 200 |
| | | | 4,105 | 4,105 |
| | *Sale of machine no. 123456; loss on sale £200 transferred to profit and loss account* | | | |

(If you wish to check the book-keeping entries for this transaction, they are set out on page 229.)

## bad debts written off

We have already seen, in Chapter 15, the double-entry book-keeping entries to write off a debtor's account as bad:

- debit bad debts written off account
- credit debtor's account

15 Dec 20-1    *Write off the account of T Hughes, which has a balance of £25, as a bad debt*

The journal entry is:

| Date | Details | Folio | Dr | Cr |
|------|---------|-------|-----|-----|
| 20-1 | | | £ | £ |
| 15 Dec | Bad debts written off | GL | 25 | |
| | T Hughes | SL | | 25 |
| | *Account written off as a* | | | |
| | *bad debt – see memo dated* | | | |
| | *14 December 20-1* | | | |

## provision for bad debts

In Chapter 15 we saw that the creation of a provision for bad debts is recorded in the profit and loss account:

– debit profit and loss account

– credit provision for bad debts account

*31 Dec 20-1      A provision for bad debts of £500 is to be created*

The journal entry is:

| Date | Details | Folio | Dr | Cr |
|------|---------|-------|-----|-----|
| 20-1 | | | £ | £ |
| 31 Dec | Profit and loss | GL | 500 | |
| | Provision for bad debts | GL | | 500 |
| | *Creation of a provision for bad debts* | | | |

An existing provision for bad debts will usually be increased or decreased as the level of debtors changes. The book-keeping entries (see Chapter 15) are:

**increasing the provision**

– debit profit and loss account

– credit provision for bad debts account

**decreasing the provision**

– debit provision for bad debts account

– credit profit and loss account

*31 Dec 20-2      The existing provision for bad debts is to be increased by £250*

The journal entry is shown on the next page:

| Date | Details | Folio | Dr | Cr |
|------|---------|-------|-----|-----|
| 20-2 | | | £ | £ |
| 31 Dec | Profit and loss | GL | 250 | |
| | Provision for bad debts | GL | | 250 |
| | | | | |
| | *Increase in provision for bad debts* | | | |

## CHAPTER SUMMARY

● The journal is used to list non-regular transactions.

● The journal is a primary accounting record – it is not a double-entry account.

● The journal is used for:
   – opening entries
   – purchase and sale of fixed assets on credit
   – correction of errors
   – other non-regular transactions or adjustments

Case Study 2 which follows the questions at the end of this chapter shows how the adjustments for accruals and prepayments, depreciation, bad debts, and provision for bad debts are made in a set of accounts, together with the journal entries.

In the next chapter we will look at correction of errors, and the use of the journal for listing such non-regular transactions.

## QUESTIONS

NOTE: an asterisk (*) after the question number means that an answer to the question is given in Appendix 2.

**18.1***  Lucy Wallis started in business on 1 May 20-8 with the following assets and liabilities:

|  | £ |
|--|--|
| Vehicle | 6,500 |
| Fixtures and fittings | 2,800 |
| Opening stock | 4,100 |
| Cash | 150 |
| Loan from husband | 5,000 |

You are to prepare Lucy's opening journal entry, showing clearly her capital at 1 May 20-8.

**18.2** Show the journal entries for the following transfers which relate to Trish Hall's business for the year ended 31 December 20-8:

(a) Closing stock is to be recorded in the accounts at a valuation of £22,600.

(b) Telephone expenses for the year, amounting to £890, are to be transferred to profit and loss account.

(c) Salaries account shows a balance of £22,950, but £980 is owing; the amount due for the year is to be transferred to profit and loss account.

(d) Photocopying expenses account shows a balance of £1,240, but this includes copier rental of £80 in respect of January and February 20-9; the amount due for the year is to be transferred to profit and loss account.

(e) Motoring expenses account shows a balance of £800; one-quarter of this is for Trish Hall's private motoring; three-quarters is to be transferred to profit and loss account.

(f) Trish has taken goods for her own use of £175 (no VAT).

(g) Depreciation on fixtures and fittings for the year is calculated at £500.

(h) A machine had been bought on 1 January 20-6 for £5,000 (net of VAT). Provision for depreciation (including the current year) totals £3,750. On 31 December 20-8 the machine is sold for £2,000 plus VAT, a cheque being received.

(i) The sales ledger account of N Marshall, which has a debit balance of £125, is to be written off as a bad debt (VAT relief on bad debts is not available).

This is the only bad debt written off during the year; the amount is to be transferred to profit and loss account.

(j) The provision for bad debts is £550; the amount is to be reduced to £450.

**18.3*** Henry Lewis is setting up the book-keeping system for his new business, which sells office stationery. He decides to use the following primary accounting records:

- Journal
- Sales Day Book
- Purchases Day Book
- Sales Returns Day Book
- Purchases Returns Day Book
- Cash Book

The following business transactions take place:

(a)    He receives an invoice from Temeside Traders for £956 for goods supplied on credit

(b)    He issues an invoice to Malvern Models for £176 of goods

(c)    He buys a computer for use in his business for £2,000 on credit from A-Z Computers Limited

(d)    He issues a credit note to Johnson Brothers for £55 of goods

(e)    A debtor, Melanie Fisher, settles the balance of her account, £107, by cheque

(f)    He makes cash sales of £25

(g)    Henry Lewis withdraws cash £100 for his own use

(h)    He pays a creditor, Stationery Supplies Limited, the balance of the account, £298, by cheque

(i)    A debtor, Jim Bowen, with an account balance of £35 is to be written off as a bad debt

(j)    A credit note for £80 is received from a creditor, Ian Johnson

You are to take each business transaction in turn and state:

* the name of the primary accounting record

* the name of the account to be debited

* the name of the account to be credited

Note: VAT is to be ignored.

# WYVERN METAL SUPPLIES: YEAR-END ADJUSTMENTS TO THE FINAL ACCOUNTS

This Case Study uses the trial balance, from Case Study 1, of Wyvern Metal Supplies at 31 December 20-1 and makes adjustments to the final accounts. The adjustments are for:

- accruals
- prepayments
- provision for depreciation
- bad debts written off
- provision for bad debts

Appropriate journal entries (see Chapter 18) are made in order to keep a record of these non-regular transactions.

## ADJUSTMENTS TO BE MADE

This Case Study starts with the trial balance extracted by the book-keeper of Wyvern Metal Supplies at 31 December 20-1 (see page 194) in Case Study 1.

The owner of Wyvern Metal Supplies, in conjunction with the firm's accountant, has decided to make the following year-end adjustments at 31 December 20-1:

- Wages and salaries of £1,100 are owing
- Business rates are prepaid by £600
- Depreciation for the year, using the straight-line method, is to be provided for on the delivery van at twenty per cent per annum and on the office equipment at ten per cent per annum. The provision for depreciation is to apply to assets held at the end of the financial year.
- A debtor, Speciality Forgings, has gone out of business and it is decided to write this account off as a bad debt (VAT relief on the bad debt is not available)
- A 5% provision for bad debts (to nearest £) is to be made against the remaining debtors

### journal entries

Journal entries in respect of these adjustments are shown on the next page (other journal entries are not shown). The previous chapter explained journal entries, where similar types of transaction were seen.

| JOURNAL | | | | |
|---|---|---|---|---|
| **Date** | **Details** | **Folio** | **Dr** | **Cr** |
| 20-1<br>31 Dec | Profit and loss<br>Wages and salaries<br><br>*Transfer to profit and loss account of expenditure<br>for the year:*<br>amount paid in year          £51,300<br>add amount owing          £1,100<br>transfer to profit and loss    £52,400 | GL<br>GL105 | £<br>52,400 | £<br><br>52,400 |
| 31 Dec | Profit and loss<br>Rates<br><br>*Transfer to profit and loss account of expenditure<br>for the year:*<br>amount paid in year          £4,030<br>less prepayment          £600<br>transfer to profit and loss    £3,430 | GL<br>GL108 | 3,430 | <br>3,430 |
| 31 Dec | Profit and loss<br>Provision for depreciation – delivery van<br><br>*Annual depreciation, using the straight-line method<br>at 20% p.a. on delivery van* | GL<br>GL118 | 2,400 | <br>2,400 |
| 31 Dec | Profit and loss<br>Provision for depreciation – office equipment<br><br>*Annual depreciation, using the straight-line method<br>at 10% p.a. on office equipment* | GL<br>GL119 | 532 | <br>532 |
| 31 Dec | Bad debts written off<br>Speciality Forgings<br><br>*Bad debt written off on written instruction<br>of credit controller (memo dated 15 December)* | GL120<br>SL203 | 277 | <br>277 |
| 31 Dec | Profit and loss<br>Bad debts written off<br><br>*Transfer to profit and loss account at the year-end* | GL<br>GL120 | 277 | <br>277 |
| 31 Dec | Profit and loss<br>Provision for bad debts<br><br>*Creation of provision for bad debts at<br>5% of debtors (5% x £5,217)* | GL<br>GL121 | 261 | <br>261 |

## THE LEDGER ACCOUNTS

Shown below are the ledger accounts which are:

- either existing accounts affected by the adjustments to the final accounts
- or new accounts

The accounts, as originally prepared by the book-keeper, ie before adjustment, are shown in Case Study 1 (pages 183-199). Accounts which are not affected by the adjustments to the final accounts have not been reprinted here.

**GENERAL LEDGER**

| Dr | | | | **Wages and salaries  (account no 105)** | | | Cr |
|---|---|---|---|---|---|---|---|
| 20-1 | | | £ | 20-1 | | | £ |
| 1 Dec | Balance b/d | | 45,800 | 31 Dec | Profit and loss account | | 52,400 |
| 16 Dec | Bank | CB | 5,500 | | | | |
| 31 Dec | Balance c/d | | 1,100 | | | | |
| | | | 52,400 | | | | 52,400 |
| 20-2 | | | | 20-2 | | | |
| | | | | 1 Jan | Balance b/d | | 1,100 |

*Note: The credit balance of £1,100 on the account at the end of the year is recorded on the balance sheet as an accrual.*

| Dr | | | **Rates  (account no 108)** | | | Cr |
|---|---|---|---|---|---|---|
| 20-1 | | £ | 20-1 | | | £ |
| 1 Dec | Balance b/d | 4,030 | 31 Dec | Profit and loss account | | 3,430 |
| 31 Dec | Balance c/d | 600 | | | | |
| | | 4,030 | | | | 4,030 |
| 20-2 | | | 20-2 | | | |
| 1 Jan | Balance b/d | 600 | | | | |

*Note: The debit balance of £600 on the account at the end of the year is recorded on the balance sheet as a prepayment.*

| Dr | | **Provision for depreciation: delivery van  (account no 118)** | | | Cr |
|---|---|---|---|---|---|
| 20-1 | | £ | 20-1 | | £ |
| 31 Dec | Balance c/d | 2,400 | 31 Dec | Profit and loss account | 2,400 |
| 20-2 | | | 20-2 | | |
| | | | 1 Jan | Balance b/d | 2,400 |

| Dr | **Provision for depreciation: office equipment  (account no 119)** | | Cr |
|---|---|---|---|
| 20-1 | £ | 20-1 | £ |
| 31 Dec   Balance c/d | 532 | 31 Dec   Profit and loss account | 532 |
| 20-2 | | 20-2 | |
| | | 1 Jan   Balance b/d | 532 |

*Note: The credit balances on the two provision for depreciation accounts are shown on the balance sheet as deductions from their respective fixed asset accounts: this gives the net book value figure for each asset. In subsequent years further provisions for depreciation will be made to these accounts.*

| Dr | **Bad debts written off  (account no 120)** | | | Cr |
|---|---|---|---|---|
| 20-1 | | £ | 20-1 | £ |
| 31 Dec   Speciality Forgings | SL203 | 277 | 31 Dec   Profit and loss account | 277 |

*Note: See also the account of the debtor, Speciality Forgings, below. Bad debts written off account stores up amounts written off during the year. At the year-end, the total of the account is transferred to profit and loss account as an expense.*

| Dr | **Provision for bad debts  (account no 121)** | | Cr |
|---|---|---|---|
| 20-1 | £ | 20-1 | £ |
| 31 Dec   Balance c/d | 261 | 31 Dec   Profit and loss account | 261 |
| 20-2 | | 20-2 | |
| | | 1 Jan   Balance b/d | 261 |

*Note: The credit balance on this account is shown on the balance sheet as a deduction from debtors to give the net debtors figures which represents the estimate of debtors which are collectable. In subsequent years the balance of this account will need to be adjusted for changes in the level of debtors, or changes in the percentage of the provision.*

**SALES LEDGER**

| Dr | **Speciality Forgings  (account no 203)** | | | Cr |
|---|---|---|---|---|
| 20-1 | | £ | 20-1 | £ |
| 1 Dec   Balance b/d | | 6,720 | 18 Dec   Bank | CB | 6,720 |
| 9 Dec   Sales | SDB | 1,692 | 29 Dec   Bank | CB | 4,000 |
| 16 Dec   Sales | SDB | 2,585 | 31 Dec   Bad debts written off GL120 | 277 |
| | | 10,997 | | 10,997 |

## ADJUSTED FINAL ACCOUNTS

After incorporating the year-end adjustments the final accounts appear as follows (there is no change to gross profit):

**WYVERN METAL SUPPLIES**

**TRADING AND PROFIT AND LOSS ACCOUNT FOR THE YEAR ENDED 31 DECEMBER 20-1**

| | £ | £ | £ |
|---|---|---|---|
| Sales | | | 188,860 |
| Less Sales returns | | | 1,130 |
| Net sales | | | 187,730 |
| Opening stock | | 16,170 | |
| Purchases | 87,620 | | |
| Less Purchases returns | 590 | | |
| Net purchases | | 87,030 | |
| | | 103,200 | |
| Less Closing stock | | 20,200 | |
| Cost of Goods Sold | | | 83,000 |
| **Gross Profit** | | | 104,730 |
| Add: Discount received | | | 1,055 |
| | | | 105,785 |
| Less expenses: | | | |
| Wages and salaries | | 52,400 | |
| Vehicle running expenses | | 2,820 | |
| Office expenses | | 8,090 | |
| Rates | | 3,430 | |
| Rent paid | | 14,400 | |
| Discount allowed | | 2,310 | |
| Bad debt written off | | 277 | |
| Provision for bad debts | | 261 | |
| Provision for depreciation: | | | |
| delivery van | | 2,400 | |
| office equipment | | 532 | |
| | | | 86,920 |
| **Net Profit** | | | 18,865 |

*Note: As the net profit is different from that calculated in Case Study 1, the transfer from profit and loss account to capital account will be £18,865.*

**WYVERN METAL SUPPLIES**
**BALANCE SHEET AS AT 31 DECEMBER 20-1**

| | £ | £ | £ |
|---|---|---|---|
| **Fixed Assets** | Cost | Dep'n to date | Net |
| Delivery van | 12,000 | 2,400 | 9,600 |
| Office equipment | 5,320 | 532 | 4,788 |
| | 17,320 | 2,932 | 14,388 |
| **Current Assets** | | | |
| Stock | | 20,200 | |
| Debtors | 5,217 | | |
| Less provision for bad debts | 261 | | |
| | | 4,956 | |
| Prepayment | | 600 | |
| Bank | | 5,572 | |
| Cash | | 364 | |
| | | 31,692 | |
| **Less Current Liabilities** | | | |
| Creditors | 12,765 | | |
| Value Added Tax | 2,750 | | |
| Accrual | 1,100 | | |
| | | 16,615 | |
| **Working Capital** | | | 15,077 |
| **NET ASSETS** | | | 29,465 |
| | | | |
| **FINANCED BY:** | | | |
| **Capital** | | | |
| Opening capital | | | 30,000 |
| Add Net profit | | | 18,865 |
| | | | 48,865 |
| Less Drawings | | | 19,400 |
| | | | 29,465 |

# CASE STUDY SUMMARY

The adjustments in this Case Study are made to enable the final accounts to show a more realistic view of the state of the business. They are examples of the application of the accounting concepts set out in Statement of Standard Accounting Practice No. 2, 'Disclosure of accounting policies' (see pp. 270-271):

- accruals concept – accruals and prepayments, provision for depreciation, stock valuation
- consistency concept – provision for depreciation, provision for bad debts, stock valuation
- prudence concept – provision for depreciation, provision for bad debts, stock valuation
- going concern – stock valuation, asset values

# 19 CORRECTION OF ERRORS

In any book-keeping system there is always the possibility of an error. Ways to avoid errors, or ways to reveal them sooner, include:
- division of the accounting function between a number of people
- regular circulation of statements to debtors, who will check the transactions on their accounts and advise any discrepancies
- checking statements received from creditors
- extraction of a trial balance at regular intervals
- the preparation of bank reconciliation statements
- checking cash and petty cash balances against cash held
- the use of control accounts (see Chapter 20)
- the use of a computer accounting program

Despite all of these, errors will still occur from time-to-time and, in this chapter, we shall look at:
- correction of errors not shown by a trial balance
- correction of errors shown by a trial balance, using a suspense account
- the effect of correcting errors on profit and the balance sheet

## ERRORS NOT SHOWN BY A TRIAL BALANCE

In Chapter 5 we have already seen that some types of errors in a book-keeping system are not revealed by a trial balance. These are:

- error of omission
- reversal of entries
- mispost/error of commission
- error of principle
- error of original entry (or transcription)
- compensating error

Although these errors are not shown by a trial balance, they are likely to come to light if the procedures suggested in the introduction, above, are followed. For example, a debtor will soon let you know if their account has been debited with goods they did not buy. When an error is found, it needs to be corrected by means of a journal entry which shows the book-keeping entries that have been passed.

We will now look at an example of each of the errors not shown by a trial balance, and will see how it is corrected by means of a journal entry. (A practical hint which may help in correcting errors is to write out the 'T' accounts as they appear with the error; then write in the correcting entries and see if the result has achieved what was intended.) Note that the journal narrative includes document details.

## error of omission

*Credit sale of goods, £200 plus VAT (at 17.5%) on invoice 4967 to H Jarvis completely omitted from the accounting system; the error is corrected on 12 May 20-8*

| Date | Details | Folio | Dr | Cr |
|---|---|---|---|---|
| 20-8 | | | £ | £ |
| 12 May | H Jarvis | SL | 235 | |
| | Sales | GL | | 200 |
| | VAT | GL | | 35 |
| | | | 235 | 235 |
| | Invoice 4967 omitted from the accounts. | | | |

This type of error can happen in a very small business – often where the book-keeping is done by one person. For example, an invoice, when typed out, is 'lost' down the back of a filing cabinet. In a large business, particularly one using a computer accounting system, it should be impossible for this error to occur. Also, if documents are numbered serially, then none should be mislaid.

## reversal of entries

*A payment, on 3 May 20-8 by cheque of £50 to a creditor, S Wright, has been debited in the cash book and credited to Wright's account; this is corrected on 12 May 20-8*

| Date | Details | Folio | Dr | Cr |
|---|---|---|---|---|
| 20-8 | | | £ | £ |
| 12 May | S Wright | PL | 50 | |
| | Bank | CB | | 50 |
| | S Wright | PL | 50 | |
| | Bank | CB | | 50 |
| | | | 100 | 100 |
| | Correction of £50 reversal of entries: receipt no. 93459 | | | |

To correct this type of error it is best to reverse the entries that have been made incorrectly (the first two journal entries), and then to put through the correct entries. Although it will correct the error, it is wrong to debit Wright £100 and credit bank £100. This is because there was never a transaction for this amount – the original transaction was for £50.

As noted earlier, it is often an idea to write out the 'T' accounts, complete with the error, and then to write in the correcting entries. As an example, the two accounts involved in this last error are shown with the error made on 3 May, and the corrections made on 12 May indicated by the shading (the opening credit balance of S Wright's account is shown as £50):

| Dr | | | **S Wright** | | | Cr |
|----|----|----|----|----|----|----|
| 20-8 | | £ | 20-8 | | | £ |
| 12 May | Bank | 50 | 1 May | Balance b/d | | 50 |
| 12 May | Bank | 50 | 3 May | Bank | | 50 |
| | | 100 | | | | 100 |

| Dr | | | **Cash Book (bank columns)** | | | Cr |
|----|----|----|----|----|----|----|
| 20-8 | | £ | 20-8 | | | £ |
| 3 May | S Wright | 50 | 12 May | S Wright | | 50 |
| | | | 12 May | S Wright | | 50 |

The accounts now show a net debit transaction of £50 on S Wright's account, and a net credit transaction of £50 on bank account, which is how this payment to a creditor should have been recorded in order to clear the balance on the account.

## mispost/error of commission

*Credit sales of £47 including VAT (at 17.5%) have been debited to the account of J Adams, instead of the account of J Adams Ltd; the error is corrected on 15 May 20-8*

| Date | Details | Folio | Dr | Cr |
|------|---------|-------|----|----|
| 20-8 | | | £ | £ |
| 15 May | J Adams Ltd | SL | 47 | |
| | J Adams | SL | | 47 |
| | *Correction of mispost of invoice 327* | | | |

This type of error can be avoided, to some extent, by the use of account numbers, and by persuading the customer to quote the account number or reference on each transaction. All computer accounting systems use numbers/references to identify accounts, but it is still possible to post a transaction to the wrong account.

## error of principle

*The cost of diesel fuel, £30 (excluding VAT), has been debited to vehicles account; the error is corrected on 20 May 20-8*

| Date | Details | Folio | Dr | Cr |
|------|---------|-------|-----|-----|
| 20-8 | | | £ | £ |
| 20 May | Vehicle running expenses account | GL | 30 | |
| | Vehicles account | GL | | 30 |
| | *Correction of error: voucher no. 647* | | | |

This type of error is similar to a mispost except that, instead of the wrong person's account being used, it is the wrong class of account. In the above example, the vehicle running costs must be kept separate from the cost of the asset – vehicles. Correcting this error will have an effect on both profit and loss account and balance sheet (if already prepared) – see page 308.

## error of original entry (or transcription)

*Postages of £45 paid by cheque entered in the accounts as £54; the error is corrected on 27 May 20-8*

| Date | Details | Folio | Dr | Cr |
|------|---------|-------|-----|-----|
| 20-8 | | | £ | £ |
| 27 May | Bank | CB | 54 | |
| | Postages | GL | | 54 |
| | Postages | GL | 45 | |
| | Bank | CB | | 45 |
| | | | 99 | 99 |
| | *Correction of error: postages of £45* | | | |
| | *entered into the accounts as £54* | | | |

This error could have been corrected by debiting bank and crediting postages with £9, being the difference between the two amounts. However, there was no original transaction for this amount, and it is better to reverse the wrong transaction and put through the correct one. A reversal of figures either has a difference of nine (as above), or an amount divisible by nine. An error of original entry can also be a 'bad' figure on a cheque or an invoice, entered wrongly into both accounts.

## compensating error

*Rates account is overcast (overadded) by £100; sales account is also overcast by the same amount; the error is corrected on 31 May 20-8*

| Date | Details | Folio | Dr | Cr |
|------|---------|-------|-----|-----|
| 20-8 | | | £ | £ |
| 31 May | Sales account | GL | 100 | |
| | Rates account | GL | | 100 |
| | *Correction of overcast on rates account* | | | |
| | *and sales account* | | | |

Here, an account with a debit balance – rates – has been overcast; this is compensated by an overcast on an account with a credit balance – sales. There are several permutations on this theme, eg two debit balances, one overcast, one undercast; a debit balance undercast, a credit balance undercast.

## important notes to remember

We have just looked at several journal entries in connection with the correction of errors. Remember that:

- The journal is the primary accounting record for non-regular transactions. The journal entries must then be recorded in the book-keeping system.

- When a business uses control accounts (see Chapter 20) which are incorporated into the double-entry book-keeping system, the transactions from the journal must be recorded in the sales ledger or purchase ledger control accounts and in the memorandum accounts for debtors or creditors.

## TRIAL BALANCE ERRORS: USE OF SUSPENSE ACCOUNT

There are many types of errors revealed by a trial balance. Included amongst these are:

- omission of one part of the double-entry transaction
- recording two debits or two credits for a transaction
- recording a different amount for a transaction on the debit side from the credit side
- errors in the calculation of balances (not compensated by other errors)
- error in transferring the balance of an account to the trial balance
- error of addition in the trial balance

When errors are shown, the trial balance is 'balanced' by recording the difference in a suspense account. For example, on 31 December 20-1 the trial balance totals are:

|  | Dr | Cr |
|---|---|---|
|  | £ | £ |
| Trial balance totals | 100,000 | 99,850 |
| Suspense account |  | 150 |
|  | 100,000 | 100,000 |

A suspense account is opened in the general ledger with, in this case, a credit balance of £150:

| Dr | | Suspense Account | | Cr |
|---|---|---|---|---|
| 20-1 | | £ | 20-1 | £ |
|  |  |  | 31 Dec Trial balance difference | 150 |

A detailed examination of the book-keeping system is now made in order to find the errors. As errors are found, they are corrected by means of a journal entry. The journal entries will balance, with one part of the entry being either a debit or credit to suspense account. In this way, the balance on suspense account is eliminated by book-keeping transactions. Using the above suspense account, the following errors are found and corrected on 15 January 20-2:

- sales account is undercast by £100
- a payment to a creditor, A Wilson, for £65, has been recorded in the bank as £56
- telephone expenses of £55 have not been entered in the expenses account
- stationery expenses £48 have been debited to both the stationery account and the bank account

These errors are corrected by journal entries shown below. Note that the journal narrative includes details of dates and cheque numbers.

| Date | Details | Folio | Dr | Cr |
|---|---|---|---|---|
| 20-2 | | | £ | £ |
| 15 Jan | Suspense account | GL | 100 | |
| | Sales account | GL | | 100 |
| | *Undercast on 23 December 20-1 now corrected* | | | |
| 15 Jan | Bank account | CB | 56 | |
| | Suspense account | GL | | 56 |
| | Suspense account | GL | 65 | |
| | Bank account | CB | | 65 |
| | | | 121 | 121 |
| | *Payment to A Wilson for £65 (cheque no. 783726) on* | | | |
| | *30 December 20-1 entered in bank as £56 in error* | | | |
| 15 Jan | Telephone expenses account | GL | 55 | |
| | Suspense account | GL | | 55 |
| | *Omission of entry in expenses account:* | | | |
| | *paid by cheque no 783734* | | | |
| 15 Jan | Suspense account | GL | 48 | |
| | Bank account | CB | | 48 |
| | Suspense account | GL | 48 | |
| | Bank account | CB | | 48 |
| | | | 96 | 96 |
| | *Correction of error: payment by cheque no 783736* | | | |
| | *debited in error to bank account* | | | |

After these journal entries have been recorded in the accounts, suspense account appears as:

| Dr | | | Suspense Account | | | Cr |
|---|---|---|---|---|---|---|
| 20-2 | | £ | 20-1 | | | £ |
| 15 Jan | Sales | 100 | 31 Dec | Trial balance difference | | 150 |
| 15 Jan | Bank | 65 | 20-2 | | | |
| 15 Jan | Bank | 48 | 15 Jan | Bank | | 56 |
| 15 Jan | Bank | 48 | 15 Jan | Telephone expenses | | 55 |
| | | 261 | | | | 261 |

Thus all the errors have now been found, and suspense account has a nil balance.

Note that if final accounts have to be prepared after creating a suspense account but before the errors are found, the balance of suspense account is shown, depending on the balance, as either a current asset (debit balance) or a current liability (credit balance). Nevertheless, the error must be found at a later date and suspense account eliminated.

# EFFECT ON PROFIT AND BALANCE SHEET

The correction of errors, whether shown by a trial balance or not, often has an effect on the profit figure calculated before the errors were found. For example, an undercast of sales account, when corrected, will increase gross and net profits and, of course, the profit figure shown in the balance sheet. Some errors, however, only affect the balance sheet, eg an error involving a creditor's account. The diagram that follows shows the effect of errors when corrected on gross profit, net profit and the balance sheet.

**TRADING ACCOUNT**

| Correction of error | Gross profit | Net profit | Balance sheet |
|---|---|---|---|
| sales undercast/understated | increase | increase | net profit increase |
| sales overcast/overstated | decrease | decrease | net profit decrease |
| purchases undercast/understated | decrease | decrease | net profit decrease |
| purchases overcast/overstated | increase | increase | net profit increase |
| opening stock undervalued | decrease | decrease | net profit decrease |
| opening stock overvalued | increase | increase | net profit increase |
| closing stock undervalued | increase | increase | net profit increase<br>stock increase |
| closing stock overvalued | decrease | decrease | net profit decrease<br>stock decrease |

### PROFIT AND LOSS ACCOUNT

| Correction of error | Gross profit | Net profit | Balance sheet |
|---|---|---|---|
| expense undercast/understated | - | decrease | decrease in net profit |
| expense overcast/overstated | - | increase | increase in net profit |
| income undercast/understated | - | increase | increase in net profit |
| income overcast/overstated | - | decrease | decrease in net profit |

### BALANCE SHEET

| Correction of error | Gross profit | Net profit | Balance sheet |
|---|---|---|---|
| asset undercast/understated | - | - | increase asset |
| asset overcast/overstated | - | - | decrease asset |
| liability undercast/understated | - | - | increase liability |
| liability overcast/overstated | - | - | decrease liability |

Some questions and assessments on correction of errors require the preparation of a statement showing the amended profit after errors have been corrected. We will look at the errors shown on page 307 and see how their correction affects the net profit (assume the net profit before adjustments is £10,000).

### Statement of corrected net profit for the year ended 31 December 20-1

|  | £ |
|---|---|
| Net profit (unadjusted) | 10,000 |
| Add sales undercast | 100 |
|  | 10,100 |
| Less additional telephone expenses | 55 |
| Adjusted net profit | 10,045 |

Note: the other two errors do not affect net profit.

The effect on the balance sheet of correcting the errors is:

• net profit increases £45

• bank balance reduces £105 (+£56, −£65, −£48, −£48)

• the credit balance of £150 in suspense account (shown as a current liability) is eliminated

The balance sheet will now balance without the need for a suspense account – the errors have been found and corrected.

# CHAPTER SUMMARY

- Correction of errors is always a difficult topic to put into practice: it tests knowledge of book-keeping procedures and it is all too easy to make the error worse than it was in the first place! The secret of dealing with this topic well is to write down – in account format – what has gone wrong. It should then be relatively easy to see what has to be done to put the error right.

- Errors not shown by a trial balance: error of omission, reversal of entries, mispost/error of commission, error of principle, error of original entry (or transcription), compensating error.

- Errors shown by a trial balance include: omission of one part of the book-keeping transaction, recording two debits/credits for a transaction, recording different amounts in the two accounts, calculating balances, transferring balances to the trial balance.

- All errors are non-regular transactions and need to be corrected by means of a journal entry: the book-keeper then needs to record the correcting transactions in the accounts.

- When error(s) are shown by a trial balance, the amount is placed into a suspense account. As the errors are found, journal entries are made which 'clear out' the suspense account.

- Correction of errors may have an effect on gross profit and net profit, and on the figures in the balance sheet. It may be necessary to restate net profit and to adjust the balance sheet.

In the next chapter we shall look at the use of control accounts which are used as a checking device for a section of the ledgers.

# QUESTIONS

NOTE: an asterisk (*) after the question number means that an answer to the question is given in Appendix 2.

19.1*  Elaine Rowe extracted the following balances from her books on 31 May 20-8:

|  | £ |
|---|---|
| Equipment | 9,750 |
| General expenses | 1,394 |
| Sales | 15,863 |
| Purchases | 7,590 |
| Sales returns | 426 |
| Purchases returns | 674 |
| Creditors | 2,095 |
| Drawings | 1,420 |
| Debtors | 3,738 |
| Bank overdraft | 372 |
| Capital | 5,314 |

A short time later the following errors and omissions were discovered:

(i)     a sales invoice for £392 had not been entered in the sales day book

(ii)    a cheque of £545 received from a customer had not been recorded in the books

(iii)   an invoice for £196 received from a supplier had been entered in the accounts twice

(iv)    Elaine Rowe had taken £150 by cheque for her own use but no entries had been made in the accounts

You are required to prepare a trial balance as at 31 May 20-8 after considering the above information.

*Reproduced by kind permission of OCR Examinations*

**19.2**   The trial balance of Thomas Wilson balanced. However, a number of errors have been found in the book-keeping system:

(a)     Credit sale of £150 to J Rigby has not been entered in the accounts.

(b)     A payment by cheque for £125 to H Price Limited, a creditor, has been recorded in the account of H Prince.

(c)     The cost of a new delivery van, £10,000, has been entered to vehicle expenses account.

(d)     Postages of £55, paid by cheque, have been entered on the wrong sides of both accounts.

(e)     The totals of the purchases day book and the purchases returns day book have been undercast by £100.

(f)     A payment for £89 from L Johnson, a debtor, has been entered in the accounts as £98.

You are to take each error in turn and:
*       state the type of error
*       show the correcting journal entry
Note: VAT is to be ignored

**19.3\***   In reviewing the books of Ellen Summers, the following errors were found:

(1)     A payment of £60, from office cash, for the purchase of stationery, had not been recorded in the books of account.

(2)     A bill for repairs to premises, £715, had been debited to Premises Account.

(3)     Some office equipment for use in the firm's own office, had been purchased on credit £420 from Doogan Ltd. This had been entered in the accounts of Doogan Ltd and Office Equipment as £470.

(4)     Ellen Summers had withdrawn £200 from the firm's bank account for personal use. This had not been recorded in the books of account.

(5)     An invoice for £630 for the purchase of equipment for use in the firm's own office was entered in the Purchases Account.

(6)     The account of J Hailes was credited in error in respect of goods purchased on credit from J Hales, £320.

REQUIRED:

(a)     Classify each of the above types of error.

(b)     Prepare a statement as follows to show the effect that each of the errors would have, if uncorrected, upon the net profit for the year of Ellen Summers.

Your answer should be set out as follows:

**Effect of errors on net profit**

|     | Over-stated | No effect | Under-stated |
| --- | --- | --- | --- |
| (1) |     |     |     |
| (2) |     |     |     |
| (3) |     |     |     |
| (4) |     |     |     |
| (5) |     |     |     |
| (6) |     |     |     |

In each case place a tick (✓) in the appropriate column.

(c)     Prepare journal entries to correct these errors.
        Note: Narrations are not required.

*LCCI Examinations Board*

**19.4\***
Jeremy Johnson extracts a trial balance from his book-keeping records on 30 September 20-8. Unfortunately the trial balance fails to balance and the difference, £19 debit, is placed to a suspense account pending further investigation.

The following errors are later found:

(a)    A cheque payment of £85 for office expenses has been entered in the cash book but no entry has been made in the office expenses account.

(b)    A payment for photocopying of £87 by cheque has been correctly entered in the cash book, but is shown as £78 in the photocopying account.

(c)    The sales returns day book has been overcast by £100.

(d)    Commission received of £25 has been entered twice in the account.

You are to:

*    make journal entries to correct the errors

*    show the suspense account after the errors have been corrected

**19.5**
The draft final accounts of Joan Boddy Ltd for the year to 31 January 20-8 showed a net profit for the year of £34,765. There was a difference on the trial balance, and this had been posted to a suspense account with the balance being included in the profit and loss account. During the audit the following errors and omissions were discovered.

(i)    Trade debtors had been shown as £27,153. However, bad debts of £303 had not been written-off, and the provision for doubtful debtors shown as £650 should have been adjusted to 2% of debtors.

(ii)    On the insurance account the prepayment of £243 at 31 January 20-7 had not been brought down as an opening balance.

(iii)    A payment for rent correctly shown in the cash book at £870 had been posted to the rent account as £780.

(iv)    The stock of finished goods had been undervalued by £1,300.

(v)    The wages account had been incorrectly totalled at £26,222 and should have been £1,000 less than this.

(vi)    A payment in the petty cash book of £12 had been posted to motor expenses but should have been printing and stationery.

You are required to:

(a)   Prepare the journal entries necessary to correct the errors and state whether the error would have caused the trial balance to disagree.

(b)   Prepare a statement to show what the correct net profit is after rectifying the above errors and omissions.

(c)   Write up the suspense account.

*Reproduced by kind permission of OCR Examinations*

# MULTIPLE CHOICE QUESTIONS

Read each question carefully.
Choose the one answer you think is correct (calculators may be needed).
The answers are on page 568.

**1**   A business should not, without good reason, change its method of depreciation. This follows the concept of:

A   money measurement

B   going concern

C   prudence

D   consistency

**2**   'Anticipate no profit, but anticipate all losses' is a summary of the concept of:

A   accruals

B   prudence

C   consistency

D   business entity

**3**   Stock is valued at:

A   cost price

B   net realisable value

C   lower of cost and net realisable value

D   replacement price

**4**   One of the main advantages of FIFO as a stock valuation method is that:

A   it is realistic and assumes that goods are issued in order of receipt

B   goods are issued at the latest prices

C   fluctuations in purchase price are evened out

D   in times of rising prices, profits will be higher

**5** Which one of the following transactions will not be recorded in the general journal?

A      credit purchase of a fixed asset

B      credit sale of goods to a customer

C      write off of a bad debt

D      transfer of expenses at the year-end to profit and loss account

**6** The payment for business rates has been debited to the premises account. This is:

A      an error of original entry

B      an error of principle

C      an error of commission

D      a reversal of entries

**7** A credit purchase of £63 from T Billington has been entered in the accounts as £36. This is:

A      a reversal of entries

B      an error of original entry

C      a compensating error

D      an error of omission

**8** A receipt of £20 by cheque from L Jarvis, a customer, has been debited to Jarvis' account and credited to bank account in error. Which entry will correct the error?

|  | Debit | Credit |
|---|---|---|
| A | Bank account £20 | L Jarvis £20 |
|  | Bank account £20 | L Jarvis £20 |
| B | Bank account £20 | L Jarvis £20 |
| C | L Jarvis £40 | Bank account £20 |
| D | L Jarvis £20 | Bank account £20 |
|  | L Jarvis £20 | Bank account £20 |

**9**     A trial balance fails to agree by £75 and the difference is placed to a suspense account. Later it is found that a credit sale for this amount has not been entered in the sales account. Which entry will correct the error?

|   | *Debit* | *Credit* |
|---|---------|----------|
| A | Suspense account  £75 | Sales account  £75 |
| B | Suspense account  £150 | Sales account  £150 |
| C | Sales account  £75 | Suspense account  £75 |
| D | – | Sales account  £75 |

**10**    The book-keeper has entered a receipt of £100 from a customer on the wrong side of the debtor's account. Assuming that there are no other errors, the trial balance will show:

A     debit side £100 more than credit side

B     debit side £200 more than credit side

C     credit side £100 more than debit side

D     credit side £200 more than debit side

**11**    Sales account has been undercast by £100. When this is corrected:

A     gross and net profits will decrease by £100

B     gross and net profits will not change

C     the balance sheet will not be affected

D     gross and net profits will increase by £100

**12**    Closing stock is found to be overvalued by £250. When this is corrected:

A     gross and net profits will decrease by £250

B     gross and net profits will increase by £250

C     the balance sheet will not be affected

D     gross and net profits will not change

# 20 CONTROL ACCOUNTS

Control accounts are used as 'master' accounts which control a number of subsidiary ledger accounts (see the diagram below).

A control account (also known as a totals account) is used to record the totals of transactions passing through the subsidiary accounts.

In this way, the balance of the control account will always be equal (unless an error has occurred) to the total balances of the subsidiary accounts.

Two commonly-used control accounts are:

- sales ledger control account – the total of the debtors
- purchases ledger control account – the total of the creditors

In this chapter we shall look at:

- the concept of control accounts
- the layout of sales ledger and purchases ledger control accounts
- the use of control accounts as an aid to the management of a business

## THE CONCEPT OF CONTROL ACCOUNTS

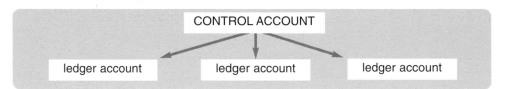

The illustration above shows how a control account acts as a master account for a number of subsidiary accounts. The principle is that, if the total of the opening balances for subsidiary accounts is known, together with the total of amounts increasing these balances, and the total of amounts decreasing these balances, then the total of the closing balances for the subsidiary accounts can be calculated.

For example:

|  | £ |
|---|---|
| Total of opening balances | 50,000 |
| Add increases | 10,000 |
|  | 60,000 |
| Less decreases | 12,000 |
| Total of closing balances | 48,000 |

The total of the closing balances can now be checked against a separate listing of the subsidiary accounts to ensure that the two figures agree. If so, it proves that the ledgers within the section are correct (subject to any errors such as misposts and compensating errors). Let us now apply this concept to one of the divisions of the ledger – sales ledger.

The diagram on page 320 shows the personal accounts which form the entire sales ledger of a particular business (in practice there would, of course, be more than four accounts involved). The sales ledger control account acts as a totals account, which records totals of the transactions passing through the individual accounts which it controls. Notice that transactions appear in the control account on the same side as they appear in the individual accounts. It follows that the control account acts as a checking device for the individual accounts which it controls. Thus, control accounts act as an aid to locating errors: if the control account and subsidiary accounts agree, then the error is likely to lie elsewhere. In this way the control account acts as an intermediate checking device – proving the arithmetical accuracy of the ledger section.

Normally the whole of a ledger section is controlled by one control account, eg sales ledger control account and purchases ledger control account. However, it is also possible to have a number of separate control accounts for subdivisions of the sales ledger and purchases ledger, eg sales ledger control account A-K, purchases ledger control account S-Z, etc. It is for a business – the user of the accounting system – to decide what is most suitable, taking into account the number of accounts in the sales and purchases ledger, together with the type of book-keeping system – manual or computerised.

In the diagram on page 320 the sales ledger control account and subsidiary accounts are agreed at the beginning and end of the month, as follows:

| **Reconciliation of sales ledger control account with debtor balances** | | |
|---|---|---|
| | 1 January 20-1 | 31 January 20-1 |
| | £ | £ |
| A Ackroyd | 100 | 150 |
| B Barnes | 200 | 200 |
| C Cox | 50 | 180 |
| D Douglas | 150 | 150 |
| **Sales ledger control account** | 500 | 680 |

Note: The business will decide how often to reconcile the control account with the subsidiary accounts – weekly, monthly, quarterly or annually.

| Dr | | | SALES LEDGER CONTROL ACCOUNT | | Cr |
|---|---|---|---|---|---|
| 20-1 | | £ | 20-1 | | £ |
| 1 Jan | Balances b/d | 500 | 31 Jan | Bank | 443 |
| 31 Jan | Sales | 700 | 31 Jan | Discount allowed | 7 |
| | | | 31 Jan | Sales returns | 70 |
| | | | 31 Jan | Balances c/d | 680 |
| | | 1,200 | | | 1,200 |
| 1 Feb | Balances b/d | 680 | | | |

| Dr | | | A Ackroyd | | Cr |
|---|---|---|---|---|---|
| 20-1 | | £ | 20-1 | | £ |
| 1 Jan | Balance b/d | 100 | 10 Jan | Bank | 98 |
| 6 Jan | Sales | 150 | 10 Jan | Discount allowed | 2 |
| | | | 31 Jan | Balance c/d | 150 |
| | | 250 | | | 250 |
| 1 Feb | Balance b/d | 150 | | | |

| Dr | | | B Barnes | | Cr |
|---|---|---|---|---|---|
| 20-1 | | £ | 20-1 | | £ |
| 1 Jan | Balance b/d | 200 | 13 Jan | Bank | 195 |
| 6 Jan | Sales | 250 | 13 Jan | Discount allowed | 5 |
| | | | 27 Jan | Sales returns | 50 |
| | | | 31 Jan | Balance c/d | 200 |
| | | 450 | | | 450 |
| 1 Feb | Balance b/d | 200 | | | |

| Dr | | | C Cox | | Cr |
|---|---|---|---|---|---|
| 20-1 | | £ | 20-1 | | £ |
| 1 Jan | Balance b/d | 50 | 20 Jan | Bank | 50 |
| 15 Jan | Sales | 200 | 29 Jan | Sales returns | 20 |
| | | | 31 Jan | Balance c/d | 180 |
| | | 250 | | | 250 |
| 1 Feb | Balance b/d | 180 | | | |

| Dr | | | D Douglas | | Cr |
|---|---|---|---|---|---|
| 20-1 | | £ | 20-1 | | £ |
| 1 Jan | Balance b/d | 150 | 30 Jan | Bank | 100 |
| 20 Jan | Sales | 100 | 31 Jan | Balance c/d | 150 |
| | | 250 | | | 250 |
| 1 Feb | Balance b/d | 150 | | | |

# Sales Ledger Control Account

The layout of a sales ledger control account (or debtors' control account) is shown below. Study the layout carefully and then read the text which explains the additional items.

| Dr | Sales Ledger Control Account | Cr |
|---|---|---|
| | £ | £ |
| Balances b/d (large amount) | | Balances b/d (small amount) |
| Credit sales | | Cash/cheques received from debtors |
| Returned cheques | | Cash discount allowed |
| Interest charged to debtors | | Sales returns |
| Balances c/d (small amount) | | Bad debts written off |
| | | Set-off/contra entries |
| | | Balances c/d (large amount) |
| | ———— | ———— |
| | ════ | ════ |
| Balances b/d (large amount) | | Balances b/d (small amount) |

● **Balances b/d**

In the layout above there is a figure for balances b/d on both the debit side and the credit side of the control account. The usual balance on a debtor's account is debit and so this will form the large balance on the debit side. However, from time-to-time, it is possible for some debtors to have a credit balance on their accounts. This may come about, for example, because they have paid for goods, and then returned them, or because they have overpaid in error: the business owes them the amount due, ie they have a credit balance for the time being. Such credit balances are always going to be in the minority and so they will be for the smaller amount. Clearly, if there are small credit balances at the beginning of the month, there are likely to be credit balances at the month-end, and these need to be recorded separately as balances carried down – do not 'net off' the two types of balances. In a balance sheet, the small credit balances should be included with creditors.

● **Credit sales**

Only credit sales – and not cash sales – are entered in the control account because it is this transaction that is recorded in the debtors' accounts. The total sales of the business will comprise both credit and cash sales.

● **Returned cheques**

If a debtor's cheque is returned unpaid by the bank, ie the cheque has 'bounced', then entries have to be made in the book-keeping system to record this. These entries are:

– debit debtor's account

– credit cash book (bank columns)

As a transaction has been made in a debtor's account, then the amount must also be recorded in the sales ledger control account – on the debit side.

● **Interest charged to debtors**

Sometimes a business will charge a debtor for slow payment of an account. The entries are:

- debit debtor's account

- credit interest received account

As a debit transaction has been made in the debtor's account, so a debit entry must be recorded in the control account.

● **Bad debts written off**

The book-keeping entries for writing off a bad debt (see Chapter 15) are:

- debit bad debts written off account

- credit debtor's account

As you can see, a credit transaction is entered in a debtor's account. The control account 'masters' the sales ledger and so the transaction must also be recorded as a credit transaction in the control account.

Note, however, that provision for bad debts (see Chapter 15) is not entered in the control account. The book-keeping entries to create a provision are:

- debit profit and loss account

- credit provision for bad debts account

As neither of these transactions involves a debtor's personal account, there is no entry in the control account. (Watch out for this 'trap' in questions!)

● **Set-off/contra entries**

See page 325.

## PURCHASES LEDGER CONTROL ACCOUNT

The specimen layout for the purchases ledger control account (or creditors' control account) is shown below. Study the format and read the notes which follow.

| Dr | | Purchases Ledger Control Account | Cr |
|---|---|---|---|
| | £ | | £ |
| Balances b/d (small amount) | | Balances b/d (large amount) | |
| Cash/cheques paid to creditors | | Credit purchases | |
| Cash discount received | | Interest charged by creditors | |
| Purchases returns | | Balances c/d (small amount) | |
| Set-off/contra entries | | | |
| Balances c/d (large amount) | —— | | —— |
| | ══ | | ══ |
| Balances b/d (small amount) | | Balances b/d (large amount) | |

● **Balances b/d**

As with sales ledger control account, it is possible to have balances on both sides of the account. For purchases ledger, containing the accounts of creditors, the large balance b/d is always on the credit side. However, if a creditor has been overpaid, the result may be a small debit balance b/d. It may also be that there are closing balances on both sides of the account at the end of the period. In the balance sheet, any small debit balances should be included with debtors.

● **Credit purchases**

Only credit purchases – and not cash purchases – are entered in the control account. However, the total purchases of the business will comprise both credit and cash purchases.

● **Interest charged by creditors**

If creditors charge interest because of slow payment, this must be recorded on both the creditor's account and the control account.

● **Set-off/contra entries**

See page 325.

## reconciliation of purchases ledger control account

The diagram on the next page shows how a purchases ledger control account acts as a totals account for the creditors of a business.

Reconciliation of the balances on the purchases ledger control account and subsidiary accounts is made as follows:

**Reconciliation of purchases ledger control account with creditor balances**

|  | 1 January 20-1 £ | 31 January 20-1 £ |
|---|---|---|
| F Francis | 100 | 200 |
| G Gold | 200 | 350 |
| H Harris | 300 | 500 |
| I Ingram | 400 | 900 |
| **Purchases ledger control account** | 1,000 | 1,950 |

| Dr | | | **PURCHASES LEDGER CONTROL ACCOUNT** | | | Cr |
|---|---|---|---|---|---|---|
| 20-1 | | £ | 20-1 | | | £ |
| 31 Jan | Purchases returns | 150 | 1 Jan | Balances b/d | | 1,000 |
| 31 Jan | Bank | 594 | 31 Jan | Purchases | | 1,700 |
| 31 Jan | Discount received | 6 | | | | |
| 31 Jan | Balances c/d | 1,950 | | | | |
| | | 2,700 | | | | 2,700 |
| | | | 1 Feb | Balances b/d | | 1,950 |

| Dr | | | **F Francis** | | Cr |
|---|---|---|---|---|---|
| 20-1 | | £ | 20-1 | | £ |
| 17 Jan | Bank | 98 | 1Jan | Balance b/d | 100 |
| 17 Jan | Discount received | 2 | 3 Jan | Purchases | 200 |
| 31 Jan | Balance c/d | 200 | | | |
| | | 300 | | | 300 |
| | | | 1 Feb | Balance b/d | 200 |

| Dr | | | **G Gold** | | Cr |
|---|---|---|---|---|---|
| 20-1 | | £ | 20-1 | | £ |
| 15 Jan | Purchases returns | 50 | 1 Jan | Balance b/d | 200 |
| 28 Jan | Bank | 100 | 9 Jan | Purchases | 300 |
| 31 Jan | Balance c/d | 350 | | | |
| | | 500 | | | 500 |
| | | | 1 Feb | Balance b/d | 350 |

| Dr | | | **H Harris** | | Cr |
|---|---|---|---|---|---|
| 20-1 | | £ | 20-1 | | £ |
| 28 Jan | Purchases returns | 100 | 1 Jan | Balance b/d | 300 |
| 30 Jan | Bank | 200 | 17 Jan | Purchases | 500 |
| 31 Jan | Balance c/d | 500 | | | |
| | | 800 | | | 800 |
| | | | 1 Feb | Balance b/d | 500 |

| Dr | | | **I Ingram** | | Cr |
|---|---|---|---|---|---|
| 20-1 | | £ | 20-1 | | £ |
| 22 Jan | Bank | 196 | 1 Jan | Balance b/d | 400 |
| 22 Jan | Discount received | 4 | 27 Jan | Purchases | 700 |
| 31 Jan | Balance c/d | 900 | | | |
| | | 1,100 | | | 1,100 |
| | | | 1 Feb | Balance b/d | 900 |

# SET-OFF/CONTRA ENTRIES

These entries occur when the same person or business has an account in both sales ledger and purchases ledger, ie they are both buying from, and selling to, the business whose accounts we are preparing. For example, M Patel Ltd has the following accounts in the sales and purchases ledgers:

### SALES LEDGER

| Dr | | A Smith | | Cr |
|---|---|---|---|---|
| | | £ | | £ |
| Balance b/d | | 200 | | |

### PURCHASES LEDGER

| Dr | | A Smith | | Cr |
|---|---|---|---|---|
| | | £ | | £ |
| | | | Balance b/d | 300 |

From these accounts we can see that:

- A Smith owes M Patel Ltd £200 (sales ledger)

- M Patel Ltd owes A Smith £300 (purchases ledger)

To save each having to write out a cheque to send to the other, it is possible (with A Smith's agreement) to set-off one account against the other, so that they can settle their net indebtedness with one cheque. The book-keeping entries in M Patel's books will be:

– debit A Smith (purchases ledger) £200

– credit A Smith (sales ledger) £200

The accounts will now appear as:

### SALES LEDGER

| Dr | | A Smith | | Cr |
|---|---|---|---|---|
| | | £ | | £ |
| Balance b/d | | 200 | Set-off: purchases ledger | 200 |

### PURCHASES LEDGER

| Dr | | A Smith | | Cr |
|---|---|---|---|---|
| | | £ | | £ |
| Set-off: sales ledger | | 200 | Balance b/d | 300 |

The net result is that M Patel Ltd owes A Smith £100. The important point to note is that, because transactions have been recorded in the personal accounts, an entry needs to be made in the two control accounts:

– debit purchases ledger control account with the amount set-off

– credit sales ledger control account with the amount set-off

The set-off adjustment is invariably recorded in the control accounts in this way.

# Sources of Information for Control Accounts

Control accounts use totals (remember that their other name is totals accounts) for the week, month, quarter or year – depending on what time period is decided upon by the business. The totals come from a number of sources in the accounting system:

## sales ledger control account

• total credit sales (including VAT) – from the 'gross' column of the sales day book

• total sales returns (including VAT) – from the 'gross' column of the sales returns day book

• total cash/cheques received from debtors – from the cash book

• total discount allowed – from the discount allowed column of the cash book, or from discount allowed account

• bad debts – from the journal, or bad debts written off account

## purchases ledger control account

• total credit purchases (including VAT) – from the 'gross' column of the purchases day book

• total purchases returns (including VAT) – from the 'gross' column of the purchases returns day book

• total cash/cheques paid to creditors – from the cash book

• total discount received – from the discount received column of the cash book, or from discount received account

Note that when using a computer accounting system, relevant transactions are automatically recorded on the control account

# CONTROL ACCOUNTS AS AN AID TO MANAGEMENT

● **instant information**

When the manager of a business needs to know the figure for debtors or creditors – important information for the manager – the balance of the appropriate control account will give the information immediately. There is no need to add up the balances of all the debtors' or creditors' accounts. With a computer accounting system, the control accounts can be printed at any time.

● **prevention of fraud**

The use of a control account makes fraud more difficult – particularly in a manual accounting system. If a fraudulent transaction is to be recorded on a personal account, the transaction must also be entered in the control account. As the control account will be either maintained by a supervisor, and/or checked regularly by the manager, the control account adds another level of security within the accounting system.

● **location of errors**

We have already seen in this chapter how control accounts can help in locating errors. Remember, though, that a control account only proves the arithmetical accuracy of the accounts which it controls – there could still be errors, such as misposts and compensating errors, within the ledger section.

● **construction of final accounts**

A further use of control accounts is to help with the construction of final accounts when a business has not kept double-entry accounts and a trial balance cannot be extracted - see Chapter 21, which deals with incomplete records.

# CONTROL ACCOUNTS AND BOOK-KEEPING

A business must decide how to use control accounts in its book-keeping system. The commonest way of doing this is to incorporate the control accounts into double-entry book-keeping.

The control accounts therefore form part of the double-entry system: the balances of the sales ledger control account and the purchases ledger control account are recorded in the trial balance as the figures for debtors and creditors respectively. This means that the personal accounts of debtors and creditors are not part of double-entry, but are separate memorandum accounts which record how much each debtor owes, and how much is owed to each creditor. From time-to-time, the balances of the memorandum accounts are agreed with the balance of the appropriate control account.

The diagrams on the next two pages show how the sales ledger control account and the purchases ledger control account are incorporated into the double-entry book-keeping system (general ledger), with the individual debtors' and creditors' accounts kept in the form of memorandum accounts.

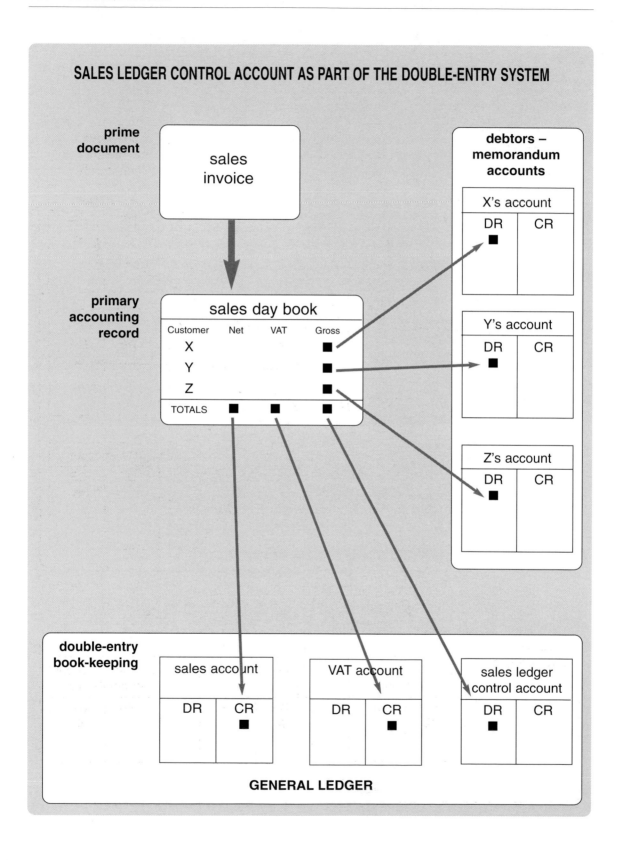

**SALES LEDGER CONTROL ACCOUNT AS PART OF THE DOUBLE-ENTRY SYSTEM**

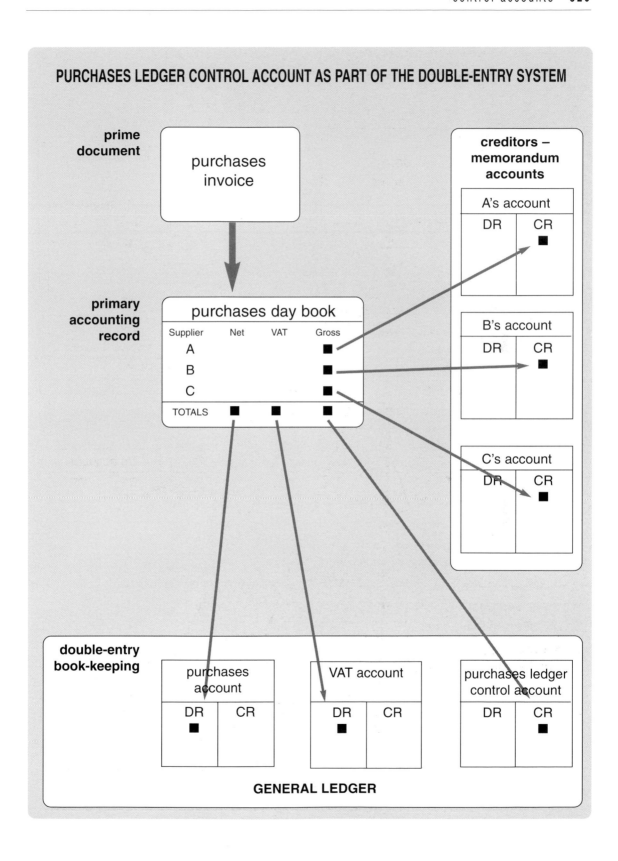

**PURCHASES LEDGER CONTROL ACCOUNT AS PART OF THE DOUBLE-ENTRY SYSTEM**

prime document

purchases invoice

creditors – memorandum accounts

A's account

| DR | CR |
|----|----|
|    | ■  |

primary accounting record

purchases day book

| Supplier | Net | VAT | Gross |
|----------|-----|-----|-------|
| A        |     |     | ■     |
| B        |     |     | ■     |
| C        |     |     | ■     |
| TOTALS   | ■   | ■   | ■     |

B's account

| DR | CR |
|----|----|
|    | ■  |

C's account

| DR | CR |
|----|----|
|    | ■  |

double-entry book-keeping

purchases account

| DR | CR |
|----|----|
| ■  |    |

VAT account

| DR | CR |
|----|----|
| ■  |    |

purchases ledger control account

| DR | CR |
|----|----|
|    | ■  |

**GENERAL LEDGER**

When sales ledger and purchases ledger control accounts are in use and journal entries are made (eg for correction of errors – see Chapter 19), transactions involving debtors' and creditors' accounts must be recorded in:

- the appropriate control account
- memorandum accounts for debtors or creditors

## CHAPTER SUMMARY

- Control accounts (or totals accounts) are 'master' accounts, which control a number of subsidiary accounts.

- Two commonly used control accounts are:
  - sales ledger control account
  - purchases ledger control account

- Transactions are recorded on the same side of the control account as on the subsidiary accounts.

- Set-off/contra entries occur when one person has an account in both sales and purchases ledger, and it is agreed to set-off one balance against the other to leave a net balance. This usually results in the following control account entries:
  - debit purchases ledger control account
  - credit sales ledger control account

- Control accounts are an aid to management:
  - in giving immediate, up-to-date information on the total of debtors or creditors
  - by making fraud more difficult
  - in helping to locate errors
  - in assisting with the preparation of accounts from incomplete records

- Control accounts are normally incorporated into the double-entry book-keeping system. The subsidiary accounts are set up as separate memorandum accounts.

In the next chapter we shall use control accounts in the preparation of accounts from incomplete records – where the owner of the business has not followed double-entry book-keeping principles. Control accounts will be used to help us find missing figures.

# QUESTIONS

NOTE: an asterisk (*) after the question number means that an answer to the question is given in Appendix 2.

**20.1\***  Prepare a sales ledger control account for the month of June 20-1 from the following information:

| 20-1 | | £ |
|---|---|---|
| 1 Jun | Sales ledger balances | 17,491 |
| 30 Jun | Credit sales for month | 42,591 |
| | Sales returns | 1,045 |
| | Payments received from debtors | 39,024 |
| | Cash discount allowed | 593 |
| | Bad debts written off | 296 |

The debtors figure at 30 June is to be entered as the balancing figure.

**20.2\***  Prepare a purchases ledger control account for the month of April 20-2 from the following information:

| 20-2 | | £ |
|---|---|---|
| 1 Apr | Purchases ledger balances | 14,275 |
| 30 Apr | Credit purchases for month | 36,592 |
| | Purchases returns | 653 |
| | Payments made to creditors | 31,074 |
| | Cash discount received | 1,048 |
| | Transfer of credit balances to sales ledger | 597 |

The creditors figure at 30 April is to be entered as the balancing figure.

**20.3\***  The following accounts appear in the Sales ledger of Desmond Ainsley:

| Dr | | **S Day** | | Cr | |
|---|---|---|---|---|---|
| | | £ | | | £ |
| 1 Sep | Balance b/d | 6,000 | 4 Sep | Cash Book | 3,000 |
| 20 Sep | Sales Day Book | 1,400 | | | |

| Dr | | **E Tait** | | Cr | |
|---|---|---|---|---|---|
| | | £ | | | £ |
| 15 Sep | Sales Day Book | 720 | | | |

| Dr | | N Mack | | Cr |
|---|---|---|---|---|
| | £ | | | £ |
| 1 Sep   Balance b/d | 3,750 | 15 Sep | Cash Book | 1,750 |
| 30 Sep   Sales Day Book | 1,000 | | | |

On 30 September, Desmond Ainsley discovered the following:

(1)    A payment of £200 from E Tait on 25 September had been omitted from her account.

(2)    S Day returned goods costing £140 to Desmond Ainsley on 23 September.

(3)    N Mack was entitled to £250 cash discount, which had been omitted.

You are required to:

(a)    redraft the three ledger accounts, adjusting for the above items.

(b)    prepare the Sales Ledger Control Account for September.

(c)    list the balances on the individual ledger accounts and agree the total to the total on the Control Account.

*Pitman Qualifications*

**20.4**   The sales ledger of Rowcester Traders contains the following accounts on 1 February 20-8:

| | |
|---|---|
| Arrow Valley Retailers | balance £826.40 debit |
| B Brick (Builders) Limited | balance £59.28 debit |
| Mereford Manufacturing Company | balance £293.49 debit |
| Redgrove Restorations | balance £724.86 debit |
| Wyvern Warehouse Limited | balance £108.40 debit |

The following transactions took place during February:

3 Feb    Sold goods on credit to Arrow Valley Retailers £338.59, and to Mereford Manufacturing Company £127.48

7 Feb    Redgrove Restorations returned goods £165.38

15 Feb    Received a cheque from Wyvern Warehouse Limited for the balance of the account after deduction of 2.5% cash discount

17 Feb    Sold goods on credit to Redgrove Restorations £394.78, and to Wyvern Warehouse Limited £427.91

20 Feb    Arrow Valley Retailers settled an invoice for £826.40 by cheque after deducting 2.5% cash discount

24 Feb    Mereford Manufacturing Company returned goods £56.29

28 Feb    Transferred the balance of Mereford Manufacturing Company's account to the company's account in the purchases ledger

28 Feb    Wrote off the account of B Brick (Builders) Limited as a bad debt

You are to:

(a) write up the personal accounts in the sales ledger of Rowcester Traders for February 20-8, balancing them at the end of the month

(b) prepare a sales ledger control account for February 20-8, balancing it at the end of the month

(c) reconcile the control account balance with the debtors' accounts at 1 February and 28 February 20-8.

Note: VAT is to be ignored on all transactions and day books are not required.

**20.5** The following information has been extracted from the books of Miss Bluebell, as at 30 September 20-7:

| | £ |
|---|---|
| Sales ledger debit balances 1.9.07 | 12,000 |
| Sales ledger credit balances 1.9.07 | 800 |
| Sales ledger credit balances 30.9.07 | 120 |

Transactions during the month:

| Sales to customers: | £ |
|---|---|
| Miss Primrose | 15,500 |
| Mrs Kaur | 3,200 |
| Mr Green | 4,450 |

| | £ |
|---|---|
| Returns from customers | 738 |
| Discount allowed to customers | 1,000 |
| Bad debts written off | 1,377 |
| Cash refund made to Mr Green | 111 |
| A cheque from Mrs Kaur dishonoured | 130 |
| Receipts from customers  – cash | 700 |
| – bank | 25,000 |

(a) You are required to prepare a sales ledger control account for the month of September 20-7.

(b) The total of debit balances in the sales ledger on 30 September 20-7 was £6,007. Compare this with the control account balance you have calculated and suggest reasons for the difference.

*Reproduced by kind permission of OCR Examinations*

# 21 INCOMPLETE RECORDS

So far our studies of financial accounting have concentrated on the double-entry system and, from this, we have extracted a trial balance and prepared final accounts. However, many smaller businesses do not use the double-entry system, and no trial balance is available. Such businesses keep some records – incomplete records – and, at the end of the year, it is the task of the accountant to construct the final accounts from these.

This chapter looks at:

- the information available when constructing final accounts from incomplete records
- how information that is required can be calculated
- the use of gross profit mark-up and margin in incomplete records accounting
- how stock losses – goods 'lost' as a result of fire, flood or theft – are calculated for insurance purposes

## WHAT ARE INCOMPLETE RECORDS?

'Incomplete records' is the term used where the book-keeping system does not use double-entry principles and no trial balance is available. Some records are kept and the accountant will construct final accounts by:

- using the information available (see below)
- seeing what information may not be available, and how 'missing' figures can be calculated

### information available to the accountant

The basic financial record kept by most businesses is a cash book, often operated as a single-entry system. In practice, even if a cash book has not been kept, it is usually possible to reconstruct it from banking records, although this task can prove to be time-consuming. Other financial information will be available so that, in all, the accountant has the following to work from:

- cash book – the basic record for any single entry system
- banking details – statements, paying-in books, cheque counterfoils
- invoices – both received (for purchases) and sent (for sales) during the year
- expenses – during the year

- records of assets and liabilities – fixed and current assets, long-term and current liabilities, both at the beginning and end of the year
- details of fixed assets – bought or sold during the year

Information which may not be available, and will need to be calculated includes:

- capital at the beginning of the financial year
- purchases and sales for the year
- cash book summary
- profit for the year

## the tools of accounting

In the two Worked Examples which follow (below and on page 341) we shall see how to take the financial information that is available and, using the tools of accounting, construct the accounts that are required. The tools of accounting that may be needed are:

- the use of an opening trial balance, or statement of assets and liabilities
- the construction of a cash account and/or bank account
- the use of control accounts – sales ledger control account and purchases ledger control account

In addition, the following may be of use:

- the accounting equation (assets – liabilities = capital)
- gross profit mark-up and margin (see page 346)
- the format of the trading and profit and loss account and balance sheet

The two Worked Examples make use of these tools of accounting, although it should be emphasised that no two incomplete records situations are the same; however practice will help to develop your skills in this aspect of business accounts.

## WORKED EXAMPLE 1: JAYNE PERRY – STATIONERY SUPPLIES

The following information has been taken from the incomplete records of Jayne Perry, who runs a small stationery supplies business.

### LIST OF ASSETS AND LIABILITIES

|  | 1 Jan 20-8 | 31 Dec 20-8 |
|---|---|---|
|  | £ | £ |
| Shop fittings | 8,000 | 8,000 |
| Stock | 25,600 | 29,800 |
| Debtors | 29,200 | 20,400 |
| Bank balance | 5,000 | not known |
| Creditors | 20,800 | 16,000 |
| Expenses owing | 200 | 300 |

**BANK SUMMARY FOR 20-8**

|  | £ |
|---|---|
| Receipts from debtors | 127,800 |
| Payments to creditors | 82,600 |
| Drawings | 12,500 |
| Business expenses | 30,600 |

In the text which follows we shall see how Jayne Perry's accountant will construct the final accounts for 20-8 from incomplete records. The information to be calculated is:

- opening capital, at the beginning of the financial year
- cash book summary for the year
- purchases and sales for the year
- profit for the year, and a year-end balance sheet

Note: VAT is to be ignored in all these transactions

# OPENING CAPITAL

Opening capital is needed in Jayne Perry's case because a year-end balance sheet is to be prepared. In other situations with incomplete records, opening capital may be stated, being the difference between assets and liabilities. To calculate the capital at the beginning of the financial year, we use the formula:  *assets – liabilities = capital.*

This is presented as a statement of assets and liabilities as follows:

**JAYNE PERRY**
**STATEMENT OF ASSETS AND LIABILITIES**
**as at 1 January 20-8**

|  | £ | £ |
|---|---|---|
| **Assets** | | |
| Shop fittings | | 8,000 |
| Stock | | 25,600 |
| Debtors | | 29,200 |
| Bank balance | | 5,000 |
| | | 67,800 |
| **Less Liabilities** | | |
| Creditors | 20,800 | |
| Expenses owing | 200 | |
| | | 21,000 |
| **Capital at 1 January 20-8** | | 46,800 |

Notes:

- Here, the bank balance is an asset, ie money in the bank; if it was marked as an overdraft, it would be included amongst the liabilities.

- Look out for the opening bank balance or overdraft being stated elsewhere in the information; for example, a bank summary may be given which starts with the bank figure at the beginning of the year – this figure must be included in the statement of assets and liabilities, which is used to calculate opening capital.

## CASH BOOK SUMMARY

A cash book summary enables us to find out the cash and bank balances at the year-end. (Sometimes this is not necessary, as a cash book may have been prepared already by the owner of the business.) In practice, the entries on the firm's bank statement can be used to produce a summary of receipts and payments for the year. In the case of Jayne Perry's business, the cash book (bank columns) are:

| Dr | | | **Cash Book  (bank columns)** | | | Cr |
|---|---|---|---|---|---|---|
| 20-8 | | £ | 20-8 | | | £ |
| 1 Jan | Balance b/d | 5,000 | | Payments to creditors | | 82,600 |
| | Receipts from debtors | 127,800 | | Drawings | | 12,500 |
| | | | | Expenses | | 30,600 |
| | | | 31 Dec | Balance c/d | | 7,100 |
| | | 132,800 | | | missing figure | 132,800 |
| 20-9 | | | 20-9 | | | |
| 1 Jan | Balance b/d | 7,100 | | | | |

The bank balance of £7,100 on 31 December 20-8 is calculated by filling in the missing figure.

Notes:
- When preparing a cash book summary, look out for an opening bank balance that is overdrawn; this is entered on the credit side.
- At the end of the cash book summary, a credit balance brought down is an overdraft.

## PURCHASES AND SALES

In calculating purchases and sales, we need to take note of the creditors and debtors at both the beginning and the end of the year. The important point to note is that payments to creditors are not the same as purchases for the year (because of the change in the level of creditors). Likewise, receipts from debtors are not the same as sales (because of the change in debtors). Only in a business which trades solely on cash terms and has no debtors/creditors would the receipts and payments be the figures for sales and purchases.

## calculating purchases and sales

The method of calculating the purchases and sales figures is:

- **purchases for year** = payments to creditors in the year, less creditors at the beginning of the year, plus creditors at the end of the year

- **sales for year** = receipts from debtors in the year, less debtors at the beginning of the year, plus debtors at the end of the year

When calculating purchases and sales, also take note of any cash discounts received and allowed and, for sales, bad debts written off.

The figures from Jayne Perry's business are:

**purchases** = £82,600 − £20,800 + £16,000 = £77,800

**sales** = £127,800 − £29,200 + £20,400 = £119,000

## use of control accounts

The use of control accounts (or totals accounts) is recommended for calculating purchases and sales in incomplete records questions. The information for purchases comes from the Worked Example :

| Dr | | **Purchases Ledger Control Account** | | | Cr |
|---|---|---|---|---|---|
| 20-8 | | £ | 20-8 | | £ |
| | Payments to creditors | 82,600 | 1 Jan | Balances b/d | 20,800 |
| 31 Dec | Balances c/d | 16,000 | | Purchases (missing figure) | ? |
| | | 98,600 | | | 98,600 |
| 20-9 | | | 20-9 | | |
| | | | 1 Jan | Balances b/d | 16,000 |

The missing figure of purchases for the year is calculated as:

£98,600 − £20,800 = £77,800

In a similar way, the sales figure can be calculated:

| Dr | | **Sales Ledger Control Account** | | | Cr |
|---|---|---|---|---|---|
| 20-8 | | £ | 20-8 | | £ |
| 1 Jan | Balances b/d | 29,200 | | Receipts from debtors | 127,800 |
| | Sales (missing figure) | ? | 31 Dec | Balances c/d | 20,400 |
| | | 148,200 | | | 148,200 |
| 20-9 | | | 20-9 | | |
| 1 Jan | Balances b/d | 20,400 | | | |

The missing figure of sales for the year is £148,200 − £29,200 = £119,000

The control account method, although its use is not essential in incomplete records questions, does bring a discipline to calculating the two important figures of purchases and sales. Do not forget that the control accounts give the figures for credit purchases and sales: cash purchases and sales need to be added, where applicable, to obtain total purchases and sales for the year.

## purchases and sales – summary

Whichever method of calculating purchases or sales is used – calculation, or a control account – four pieces of information are usually required:

* opening balance
* closing balance
* payments or receipts for the year
* purchases or sales for the year

Provided that any three are known, the fourth can be calculated – the figure for purchases and sales was the missing figure in the examples above. However if, for example, we know the opening and closing debtors totals, together with sales for the year, then it is a simple matter to calculate the missing figure for receipts from debtors.

Remember that, if they are applicable, cash discounts allowed and received and, for sales, bad debts written off, should also be incorporated into the control accounts.

# PREPARATION OF THE FINAL ACCOUNTS

## trading and profit and loss account

Having calculated the figures for purchases and sales, we can now begin to prepare the trading and profit and loss account. The section as far as gross profit is:

**JAYNE PERRY**
**TRADING AND PROFIT AND LOSS ACCOUNT**
**for the year ended 31 December 20-8**

|  | £ | £ |
|---|---|---|
| Sales |  | 119,000 |
| Opening stock | 25,600 |  |
| Purchases | 77,800 |  |
|  | 103,400 |  |
| Less Closing stock | 29,800 |  |
|  |  |  |
| Cost of Goods Sold |  | 73,600 |
| **Gross profit** |  | 45,400 |

The profit and loss account follows but, before we are able to complete this, we need to know the figure for expenses for the year. The relevant information from the Worked Example is:

* bank payments for expenses during year, £30,600
* expenses owing at 1 January 20-8, £200
* expenses owing at 31 December 20-8, £300

Like the calculation of purchases and sales, we cannot simply use the bank payments figure for expenses; we must take note of cash payments, together with accruals (and prepayments). The calculation is:

**expenses for year** = bank and cash payments less accruals at the beginning of the year (or plus prepayments), plus accruals at the end of the year (or less prepayments)

Thus the figure for Jayne Perry's business expenses is:

£30,600 – £200 + £300 = £30,700.

Alternatively, expenses can be calculated by means of a control account:

| Dr | | | **Expenses Control Account** | | | Cr |
|---|---|---|---|---|---|---|
| 20-8 | | £ | 20-8 | | | £ |
| | Cash/bank | 30,600 | 1 Jan | Balance b/d | | 200 |
| 31 Dec | Balance c/d | 300 | 31 Dec | Profit and loss account | | |
| | | | | (missing figure) | | ? |
| | | 30,900 | | | | 30,900 |
| 20-9 | | | 20-9 | | | |
| | | | 1 Jan | Balance b/d | | 300 |

The missing figure is £30,900 - £200 = £30,700.

Jayne Perry's profit and loss account concludes as follows:

| | £ |
|---|---|
| **Gross profit** | 45,400 |
| Less: | |
| Expenses | 30,700 |
| **Net profit** | 14,700 |

## balance sheet

The balance sheet can now be prepared using the assets and liabilities from the Worked Example.

**JAYNE PERRY**
**BALANCE SHEET**
**as at 31 December 20-8**

|  | £ | £ | £ |
|---|---|---|---|
| **Fixed Assets** | | | |
| Shop fittings | | | 8,000 |
| **Current Assets** | | | |
| Stock | | 29,800 | |
| Debtors | | 20,400 | |
| Bank | | 7,100 | |
| | | 57,300 | |
| **Less Current Liabilities** | | | |
| Creditors | 16,000 | | |
| Accruals | 300 | | |
| | | 16,300 | |
| **Working Capital** | | | 41,000 |
| **NET ASSETS** | | | 49,000 |
| | | | |
| **FINANCED BY:** | | | |
| **Capital** | | | |
| Opening capital | | | 46,800 |
| Add net profit | | | 14,700 |
| | | | 61,500 |
| Less drawings | | | 12,500 |
| | | | 49,000 |

## WORKED EXAMPLE 2: ELECTROPARTS

*We will now look at a more comprehensive example of incomplete records accounting. This incorporates points on depreciation and the sale of a fixed asset. You may like to work through the Worked Example before comparing your solution with the one shown.*

John Anstey owns a small business, Electroparts, which supplies spare parts for a wide range of electrical goods – cookers, fridges, freezers, kettles, dishwashers, etc. Most of his customers are self-employed repairers who buy parts for specific jobs from his trade counter – John allows them credit terms; some sales are made to members of the public carrying out 'do-it-yourself' repairs – these customers pay in cash at the time of sale. All purchases from suppliers are made on credit.

John does not keep a full set of accounting records; however, the following information has been produced for the year ended 31 December 20-4:

## ASSETS AND LIABILITIES OF ELECTROPARTS AT 1 JANUARY 20-4

| | | £ | £ |
|---|---|---:|---:|
| ASSETS | Buildings at cost | 100,000 | |
| | Less provision for depreciation | 10,000 | |
| | | | 90,000 |
| | Fixtures and fittings at cost | 15,000 | |
| | Less provision for depreciation | 7,500 | |
| | | | 7,500 |
| | | | 97,500 |
| | Stock | 24,400 | |
| | Debtors | 21,650 | |
| | Prepayment: general expenses | 140 | |
| | Cash | 250 | |
| | | | 46,440 |
| | Total Assets | | 143,940 |
| LIABILITIES | Creditors | 15,950 | |
| | Bank overdraft | 12,850 | |
| | Total Liabilities | | 28,800 |
| CAPITAL | | | 115,140 |

## SUMMARY OF THE BANK ACCOUNT (YEAR ENDED 31 DECEMBER 20-4)

| | £ | | £ |
|---|---:|---|---:|
| Cash sales | 45,280 | Balance b/d | 12,850 |
| Receipts from debtors | 177,410 | Payments to creditors | 149,620 |
| Sale proceeds of fixtures | | General expenses | 17,340 |
| and fittings | 1,950 | Wages | 18,280 |
| | | Drawings | 25,390 |
| | | Balance c/d | 1,160 |
| | 224,640 | | 224,640 |

## OTHER INFORMATION

- On 31 December 20-4, stock was valued at £28,400
- Depreciation is calculated at the rate of 2% on the cost of buildings and 10% on the cost of fixtures and fittings held at the end of the financial year. No depreciation is calculated in the year of sale/disposal
- Fixtures and fittings purchased on 1 January 20-2 for £2,500 were sold on 30 September 20-4, the purchaser paying by cheque
- The proceeds from cash sales are placed in the till and paid into the bank account at the end of the day, apart from a cash float which is retained in the till; the amount of the cash float was £250 until October, when it was increased to £500
- On 31 December 20-4, creditors were £18,210, debtors were £23,840 and £210 was owing for general expenses
- During the year, bad debts of £870 have been written off

John Anstey asks you to:

1 Calculate the amount of credit sales during the year
2 Calculate the total sales during the year
3 Calculate the amount of purchases during the year
4 Calculate the profit or loss on the sale of fixtures and fittings
5 Calculate the figure for general expenses to be shown in the profit and loss account for the year ended 31 December 20-4
6 Prepare the trading and profit and loss account for the year ended 31 December 20-4
7 Prepare the balance sheet at 31 December 20-4
  Note: VAT is to be ignored on all the above transactions

## ANSWER

**1** Dr                          **Sales Ledger Control Account**              Cr

| 20-4 | | £ | 20-4 | | £ |
|---|---|---|---|---|---|
| 1 Jan | Balances b/d | 21,650 | | Receipts from debtors | 177,410 |
| | Credit sales | | | Bad debts written off | 870 |
| | (missing figure) | 180,470 | 31 Dec | Balances c/d | 23,840 |
| | | 202,120 | | | 202,120 |

**2** Dr                          **Sales Account**              Cr

| 20-4 | | £ | 20-4 | | £ |
|---|---|---|---|---|---|
| | Trading account | | | Credit sales (see above) | 180,470 |
| | (sales for year) | 226,000 | | Cash sales | 45,280 |
| | | | | Increase in cash float | 250 |
| | | 226,000 | | | 226,000 |

**3** Dr                          **Purchases Ledger Control Account**              Cr

| 20-4 | | £ | 20-4 | | £ |
|---|---|---|---|---|---|
| | Payments to creditors | 149,620 | 1 Jan | Balances b/d | 15,950 |
| 31 Dec | Balance c/d | 18,210 | | Purchases | |
| | | | | (missing figure) | 151,880 |
| | | 167,830 | | | 167,830 |

**4** **Profit or loss on disposal of fixtures and fittings**

| | | |
|---|---|---|
| Depreciation per year | £250 | |
| Number of years' depreciation | 2 | (20-2, 20-3; no depreciation in year of sale) |
| Provision for depreciation | £500 | |

| Dr | | | | **Disposals Account** | | Cr |
|---|---|---|---|---|---|---|
| 20-4 | | £ | 20-4 | | | £ |
| 30 Sep | Fixtures and fittings | 2,500 | 30 Sep | Provision for depreciation | | 500 |
| | | | 30 Sep | Bank (sale proceeds) | | 1,950 |
| | | | 31 Dec | Profit and loss account | | |
| | | | | (loss on sale) | | 50 |
| | | 2,500 | | | | 2,500 |

**5**

| Dr | | | **General Expenses Control Account** | | Cr |
|---|---|---|---|---|---|
| 20-4 | | £ | 20-4 | | £ |
| 1 Jan | Balance b/d | 140 | 31 Dec Profit and loss account | | |
| | Bank | 17,340 | (missing figure) | | 17,690 |
| 31 Dec | Balance c/d | 210 | | | |
| | | 17,690 | | | 17,690 |

**6**

**JOHN ANSTEY, TRADING AS 'ELECTROPARTS'**
**TRADING AND PROFIT AND LOSS ACCOUNT**
**for the year ended 31 December 20-4**

| | £ | £ |
|---|---|---|
| Sales | | 226,000 |
| Opening stock | 24,400 | |
| Purchases | 151,880 | |
| | 176,280 | |
| Less Closing stock | 28,400 | |
| Cost of Goods Sold | | 147,880 |
| **Gross profit** | | 78,120 |
| | | |
| Less expenses: | | |
| General expenses | 17,690 | |
| Loss on sale of fixtures and fittings | 50 | |
| Provision for depreciation: buildings | 2,000 | |
| fixtures and fittings | *1,250 | |
| Bad debts written off | 870 | |
| Wages | 18,280 | |
| | | 40,140 |
| **Net profit** | | 37,980 |

*Note

| | |
|---|---|
| Fixtures and fittings at cost on 1 January 20-4 | £15,000 |
| Less cost price of fixtures and fittings sold 30 September 20-4 | £2,500 |
| Fixtures and fittings at cost on 31 December 20-4 | £12,500 |
| Depreciation at 10% | £1,250 |

**7**

**JOHN ANSTEY, TRADING AS 'ELECTROPARTS'**
**BALANCE SHEET**
**as at 31 December 20-4**

| | £ | £ | £ |
|---|---|---|---|
| **Fixed Assets** | Cost | Dep'n to date | Net |
| | | | |
| Buildings | 100,000 | 12,000 | 88,000 |
| Fixtures and fittings | 12,500 | *8,250 | 4,250 |
| | 112,500 | 20,250 | 92,250 |
| | | | |
| **Current Assets** | | | |
| Stock | | 28,400 | |
| Debtors | | 23,840 | |
| Bank | | 1,160 | |
| Cash | | 500 | |
| | | 53,900 | |
| | | | |
| **Less Current Liabilities** | | | |
| Creditors | 18,210 | | |
| Accrual: general expenses | 210 | | |
| | | 18,420 | |
| **Working Capital** | | | 35,480 |
| **NET ASSETS** | | | 127,730 |
| | | | |
| **FINANCED BY:** | | | |
| **Capital** | | | |
| Opening capital (from assets and liabilities at 1 January 20-4) | | | 115,140 |
| Add net profit | | | 37,980 |
| | | | 153,120 |
| Less drawings | | | 25,390 |
| Closing capital | | | 127,730 |

*Note

| | |
|---|---|
| Provision for depreciation of fixtures and fittings at 1 January 20-4 | 7,500 |
| Less provision for depreciation on asset sold | 500 |
| | 7,000 |
| Depreciation for year (see profit and loss account) | 1,250 |
| Provision for depreciation of fixtures and fittings at 31 December 20-4 | 8,250 |

# The Use of Gross Profit Mark-up and Margin

It is often necessary to use accounting ratios and percentages in the preparation of final accounts from incomplete records. The topic of ratios and percentages is covered fully in Chapter 28.

The two main percentages used for incomplete records accounting are:

- gross profit mark-up
- gross profit margin

It is quite common for a business to establish its selling price by reference to either a mark-up or a margin. The difference between the two is that:

- mark-up is a profit percentage added to buying or cost price
- margin is a percentage profit based on the selling price

For example, a product is bought by a retailer at a cost of £100; the retailer sells it for £125, ie

| cost price | + | gross profit | = | selling price |
|---|---|---|---|---|
| £100 | + | £25 | = | £125 |

The **mark-up** is:

$$\frac{\text{gross profit}}{\text{cost price}} \times \frac{100}{1} = \frac{£25}{£100} \times \frac{100}{1} = \mathbf{25\%}$$

The **margin** is:

$$\frac{\text{gross profit}}{\text{selling price}} \times \frac{100}{1} = \frac{£25}{£125} \times \frac{100}{1} = \mathbf{20\%}$$

In incomplete records accounting, mark-up or the margin percentages can be used to calculate either cost of goods sold (which, if opening stock and closing stock are known, will enable the calculation of purchases) or sales. We will now look at two examples.

## example 1

- Cost of goods sold is £150,000
- Mark-up is 40%
- What are sales?

$$\text{Gross profit} = £150,000 \times \frac{40}{100} = £60,000$$

**Sales** = cost of goods sold + gross profit, ie £150,000 + £60,000 = **£210,000**

## example 2

- Sales are £450,000
- Margin is 20%
- Opening stock is £40,000; closing stock is £50,000
- What are purchases?

Gross profit $= £450,000 \times \dfrac{20}{100} = £90,000$

Cost of goods sold $=$ sales $-$ gross profit, ie £450,000 $-$ £90,000 $=$ £360,000

The purchases calculation is:

| | | |
|---|---|---|
| Opening stock | | £40,000 |
| + | Purchases (missing figure) | ? |
| − | Closing stock | £50,000 |
| = | Cost of goods sold | £360,000 |
| **Purchases** | | **= £370,000** |

# Stock Losses

A loss of stock may occur as a result of an event such as a fire, a flood or a theft. When such a loss occurs, an estimate of the value of the stock lost needs to be made in order for the business to make an insurance claim (always assuming that the stock was adequately insured). The value is calculated by preparing an accounting summary to the date of the event, and often making use of margins and mark-ups. The calculations are best carried out in three steps:

| | | |
|---|---|---|
| **1** | | Opening stock |
| | + | Purchases |
| | = | Cost of stock available for sale |
| | | |
| **2** | | Sales |
| | − | Gross profit (using normal gross profit margin) |
| | = | Cost of goods sold |
| | | |
| **3** | | Cost of stock available for sale (from 1, above) |
| | − | Cost of goods sold (2, above) |
| | = | Estimated closing stock |
| | − | Value of stock remaining or salvaged |
| | = | Value of stock lost through fire, flood or theft |

## WORKED EXAMPLE: THEFT OF STOCK

### question

Peter Kamara runs Clothing Supplies, a small clothing wholesalers. Peter is convinced that various items of clothing have been stolen during the year and he asks you to calculate, from the accounting details, the value of stock stolen. The following information is available:

- sales for the year, £500,000
- purchases for the year, £310,000
- the gross profit margin achieved on all sales is 40 per cent
- opening stock at the beginning of the year, £15,000
- closing stock at the end of the year, £22,000

### answer

**CALCULATION OF STOCK LOSS FOR THE YEAR**

|  | £ | £ |
|---|---|---|
| Opening stock | | 15,000 |
| Purchases | | 310,000 |
| **Cost of stock available for sale** | | 325,000 |
| Sales | 500,000 | |
| Less Normal gross profit margin (40%) | 200,000 | |
| **Cost of Goods Sold** | | 300,000 |
| Estimated closing stock | | 25,000 |
| Less Actual closing stock | | 22,000 |
| **Value of stock loss** | | 3,000 |

# CHAPTER SUMMARY

- Incomplete records is the term used where the book-keeping system does not use double-entry principles.

- In order to prepare final accounts, the accountant may well have to calculate:
  - capital at the beginning of the financial year
  - cash book summary
  - purchases and sales for the year
  - profit for the year

- On the basis of these calculations, the accountant can then construct the final accounts without recourse to a trial balance.

- Two ratios and percentages used in incomplete records accounting are:
  - gross profit mark-up
  - gross profit margin

- The value of stock losses caused by fire, flood or theft is calculated using margins and mark-ups.

In the next chapter we will look at a specialised type of account for clubs and societies – income and expenditure accounts. Normally such accounts are not prepared on the double-entry system and you will need to apply your incomplete records skills!

# QUESTIONS

**21.1*** Jane Price owns a fashion shop called 'Trendsetters'. She has been in business for one year and, although she does not keep a full set of accounting records, the following information has been produced for the first year of trading, which ended on 31 December 20-8:

Summary of the business bank account for the year ended 31 December 20-8:

|  | £ |
| --- | --- |
| Capital introduced | 60,000 |
| Receipts from sales | 153,500 |
| Payments to suppliers | 95,000 |
| Advertising | 4,830 |
| Wages | 15,000 |
| Rent and rates | 8,750 |
| General expenses | 5,000 |
| Shop fittings | 50,000 |
| Drawings | 15,020 |

Summary of assets and liabilities as at 31 December 20-8:

|  | £ |
| --- | --- |
| Shop fittings at cost | 50,000 |
| Stock | 73,900 |
| Debtors | 2,500 |
| Creditors | 65,000 |

Other information:
- Jane wishes to depreciate the shop fittings at 20% per year using the straight-line method
- At 31 December 20-8, rent is prepaid by £250, and wages of £550 are owing

You are to:

(a) Calculate the amount of sales during the year.

(b) Calculate the amount of purchases during the year.

(c) Calculate the figures for
- rent and rates
- wages
to be shown in the profit and loss account for the year ended 31 December 20-8

(d) Prepare Jane Price's profit and loss account for the year ended 31 December 20-8.

(e) Draw up Jane Price's balance sheet as at 31 December 20-8.

Note: VAT is to be ignored on all the above transactions.

**21.2**

Bill Thomas ran a small retail business – all of his sales were for cash which was immediately banked, and he carried no stock of materials or of finished goods. All payments were made by cheque. The opening balance on the bank account was £4,690.

Listed below are details of the prepayments and accruals as shown in his balance sheets as at 31 December 20-6 and 31 December 20-7, together with details of all the debit entries shown in the profit and loss account for the year to 31 December 20-7. His sales for the year amounted to £85,998.

| Prepayments as at 31 December | 20-6 | 20-7 |
| --- | --- | --- |
| | £ | £ |
| Rent | 450 | 400 |
| Insurance | 40 | 25 |

| Creditors and Accruals as at 31 December | 20-6 | 20-7 |
| --- | --- | --- |
| | £ | £ |
| Telephone | 350 | 250 |
| Purchases | 1,345 | 2,456 |
| Motor expenses | 50 | 25 |
| Wages | 345 | 567 |
| Professional fees | 0 | 50 |
| Subscriptions | 35 | 0 |

Debit entries in the profit and loss account for the year ended 31 December 20-7

| | £ |
| --- | --- |
| Telephone | 1,000 |
| Rent | 1,500 |
| Insurance | 750 |
| Purchases | 42,845 |
| Motor expenses | 1,254 |
| Wages | 25,641 |
| Professional fees | 275 |
| Subscriptions | 35 |

You are required to:

(a)     Prepare the bank account for the year to 31 December 20-7.

(b)     State the amount of net profit made by the business for the year ended 31 December 20-7.

*Reproduced by kind permission of OCR Examinations*

21.3

Mr Sidhu runs a small wholesale business but has found that he has very little time spare to keep full accounting records.

Knowing that you have recently completed a finance course he has come to you requesting assistance with the preparation of this year's final accounts.

From the information supplied you have been able to extract the following data:

| | Balance at 1.10.20-6 | Balance at 30.9.20-7 |
|---|---|---|
| | £ | £ |
| Premises | 20,000 | 20,000 |
| Fixtures | 4,000 | ? |
| Stock | 9,000 | 11,000 |
| Trade debtors | 1,400 | 1,800 |
| Balance at bank | 1,300 | ? |
| Trade creditors | 2,700 | 3,300 |
| Capital | 32,400 | ? |
| Rates (accrued) | 1,000 | 400 |
| Electricity (prepaid) | 400 | 600 |

The summary of his bank account is as follows:

| RECEIPTS: | £ |
|---|---|
| Cheques from debtors | 20,600 |

| PAYMENTS: | £ |
|---|---|
| Cheques to suppliers | 18,400 |
| Sundry expenses | 1,000 |
| Fixtures | 800 |
| Drawings | 3,200 |
| Electricity | 1,000 |
| Rates | 1,500 |
| Rent | 1,800 |

Other information:
During the year Mr Sidhu took stock worth £100 for his own use.

You are required to prepare for Mr Sidhu a trading and profit and loss account for the year ended 30 September 20-7 and a balance sheet as on that date.

Ignore depreciation.

*Reproduced by kind permission of OCR Examinations*

# 22    CLUB AND SOCIETY ACCOUNTS

Up until now, we have been dealing with the financial accounting records of businesses. We have seen how profit – the primary objective of a business – is calculated in the profit and loss account. We now turn to the accounts of non-profit making organisations – such as clubs and societies – where the primary objective is to provide facilities and services to members. In this chapter we will look at:

● the differences in accounting terminology between business and non-profit making organisations
● the preparation of club/society year-end accounts
● the different accounting treatments for aspects of club/society accounts

It is for the treasurer of the club/society to maintain proper accounting records, and these will be audited either by another member, or by an outside accountant. The important point is that the highest standards of financial recording should still be maintained, and often those who work in accounting find themselves elected to the job of treasurer of a club or society.

## ACCOUNTING TERMINOLOGY

Businesses and non-profit making organisations – such as clubs and societies – differ in their aims and accounting terminology, as shown in the table below.

|  | Business | Non-profit making organisation |
|---|---|---|
| PRIMARY OBJECTIVE | To make a profit | To provide facilities and services to members |
| MAIN ACCOUNTING STATEMENTS | Trading and profit and loss account | Income and expenditure account |
|  | Balance sheet | Balance sheet |
| FINANCIAL PERFORMANCE | Profit | Surplus of income over expenditure |
|  | Loss | Deficit |
| FUNDING | Capital | Accumulated fund |

# ACCOUNTING RECORDS OF A CLUB OR SOCIETY

Few clubs and societies keep accounting records in double-entry form. For most clubs, the treasurer keeps a cash book, which is a simple version of the cash book used by businesses. It records receipts paid into the bank and payments made from the bank, together with cash receipts and payments. The cash book is ruled off and balanced at the end of the financial year.

Often a summary of the cash book is presented to members in the form of a receipts and payments account (see example on page 356); for a very small club, this information forms the 'year-end accounts'. However, there are two accounting problems in using a receipts and payments account:

- accruals and prepayments cannot be made
- the distinction between capital and revenue expenditure cannot be made

Thus, whilst a receipt and payments account may be suitable for a small club which meets infrequently or deals in small amounts of money, a larger club needs to produce final accounts in the form of:

- income and expenditure account
- balance sheet

# INCOME AND EXPENDITURE ACCOUNT

The income and expenditure account of a club or society lists the income and deducts the expenditure using a layout similar to a profit and loss account. The account will then show:

- either a surplus of income over expenditure
- or a deficit of expenditure over income

The income and expenditure account is prepared from the receipts and payments account, taking note of:

- accruals
- prepayments
- provision for depreciation of fixed assets

Capital expenditure, eg the purchase of a new lawnmower for a cricket club, is not recorded in the income and expenditure account, although depreciation of the lawnmower will be shown.

A major source of income for a club is members' subscriptions. Some members will prepay subscriptions for the next financial year, while others will be late in paying, or may never pay at all, ceasing to be members. Unless the club has a different policy, the treasurer calculates the subscriptions that should have been received, as shown in the formula on the next page:

|  | subscriptions received in year | 1 |
|---|---|---|
| add | subscriptions prepaid at start of year | 2 |
| less | subscriptions owing at start of year | 3 |
| less | subscriptions paid in advance at end of the year | 4 |
| add | subscriptions due but unpaid at end of the year | 5 |
| equals | subscription income for year to be shown in income and expenditure account | 6 |

The subscriptions are best calculated by means of a control account, the format of which is shown below. The numbers in the grey boxes refer to the parts of the formula set out above.

| Dr | | Subscriptions Control Account | | Cr |
|---|---|---|---|---|
| | £ | | | £ |
| Balance at start of year (subscriptions owing) | 3 | Balance at start of year (subscriptions prepaid) | | 2 |
| Income and expenditure account (subscription income for year) | 6 | Subscriptions received in year | | 1 |
| Balance at end of year (subscriptions prepaid) | 4 | Balance at end of year (subscriptions owing) | | 5 |

In the balance sheet of the club, subscriptions in advance are recorded as a current liability, while subscriptions due but unpaid are a current asset – debtors for subscriptions. This method of handling subscriptions takes note of prepayments and accruals and is the way in which we would deal with such items in the accounts of a business. However, in practice, the treasurer of a club may decide not to record subscriptions due but unpaid as debtors because, unlike a business, the club will not sue for unpaid amounts. The most realistic approach is to ignore such subscriptions – if they are subsequently paid, they can be brought into that year's income.

Other sources of income for clubs/societies include:

- trading activities, eg a bar, catering facilities
- donations received
- room lettings to other organisations
- special activities, eg jumble sale, dinner dance

# BALANCE SHEET

The balance sheet of a club/society is presented in a very similar way to that of a business. The major difference is that, instead of capital, a club has an accumulated fund. If the accumulated fund is not known at the start of the financial year, it is calculated as:

*assets  –  liabilities  =  accumulated fund*

In the balance sheet a surplus from the income and expenditure account is added to the accumulated fund, while a deficit is deducted.

# TRADING ACTIVITIES

Although the primary objective of clubs and societies and other non-profit making organisations is to provide facilities and services to members, many organisations carry out an activity on a regular basis with the intention of making a profit. Examples of such trading activities include:

- a bar for the use of members
- provision of catering facilities for members
- the purchase of goods to sell to members on favourable terms, eg seeds and fertilisers by a gardening society

In the year-end accounts, the treasurer should prepare a separate account for such activities so as to show the profit or loss. The layout of this account is exactly the same as that for a trading business, with opening stock, closing stock, purchases and sales. Any direct costs associated with the trading activity – such as the wages of bar staff – will be included. The profit or loss on trading activities is then taken to the income and expenditure account.

# FUND-RAISING EVENTS

Most clubs and societies organise fund-raising events from time-to-time, eg jumble sales, raffles, coffee mornings, etc. It is usual to show the separate profit or loss on such events within the income and expenditure account. This is done by linking the income and the expenses together, for example:

|  | £ | £ |
|---|---|---|
| **Income** | | |
| Christmas Fayre | | |
| takings | 550 | |
| less expenses | 210 | |
| profit | | 340 |

# WORKED EXAMPLE: SOUTH DEMPSEY TENNIS CUB

## situation

At the beginning of the financial year, on 1 January 20-2, the assets and liabilities of the South Dempsey Tennis Club were:

- bank balance, £431
- furniture and fittings, £1,000
- sports equipment, £1,250
- bar stock, £210

For the year ended 31 December 20-2, the following receipts and payments account was prepared by the treasurer:

**RECEIPTS AND PAYMENTS ACCOUNT**
**for the year ended 31 December 20-2**

| RECEIPTS | £ | PAYMENTS | £ |
|---|---|---|---|
| Balance b/d | 431 | Rent paid | 2,500 |
| Subscriptions | 1,875 | Electricity | 295 |
| Bar takings | 3,700 | Bar purchases | 1,210 |
| Donation | 100 | Bar wages | 790 |
| Sale of raffle tickets | 310 | Raffle prizes | 120 |
|  |  | Sports equipment | 500 |
|  |  | Secretary's expenses | 730 |
|  |  | Sundry expenses | 220 |
|  |  | Balance c/d | 51 |
|  | 6,416 |  | 6,416 |

The shortcomings of the receipts and payments account are that:

- It ignores the fact that subscriptions of £1,875 include £175 paid by members in advance for next year.
- There is bar stock of £320 at the end of the year.
- Rent of £500 has been paid for the first quarter of next year (a prepayment)
- The acquisition of sports equipment of £500 is shown along with other payments; it needs to be identified and listed on the balance sheet as a fixed asset.
- At the end of the year, furniture is valued at £800, and sports equipment is valued at £1,500.

As the receipts and payments account does not show an entirely true picture of the club's affairs for the year, it is decided to use the information in the preparation of the:

- income and expenditure account
- balance sheet

## workings

The steps to prepare the year-end accounts of the club are:

- an opening trial balance – to calculate the accumulated fund at the start of the year
- a closing trial balance – incorporating amounts from the receipts and payments account (or summary of the club's cash book)
- year-end accounts, ie income and expenditure account and balance sheet

The opening trial balance is as follows:

---

**SOUTH DEMPSEY TENNIS CLUB**
**Opening trial balance as at 1 January 20-2**

|  | Dr £ | Cr £ |
|---|---|---|
| Bank balance | 431 | |
| Furniture and fittings | 1,000 | |
| Sports equipment | 1,250 | |
| Bar stock at 1 Jan 20-2 | 210 | |
| Accumulated fund | | *2,891 |
| | 2,891 | 2,891 |

\* calculated as the 'missing figure'

---

The year-end trial balance incorporates the figures from the opening trial balance and the amounts from the receipts and payments account. Note that sports equipment is shown as £1,750 (ie £1,250 from the opening trial balance, plus additions of £500 shown in the receipts and payments account). The trial balance is as follows:

---

**SOUTH DEMPSEY TENNIS CLUB**
**Trial balance as at 31 December 20-2**

|  | Dr £ | Cr £ |
|---|---|---|
| Bank balance | 51 | |
| Furniture and fittings | 1,000 | |
| Sports equipment (£1,250 + £500) | 1,750 | |
| Bar stock at 1 Jan 20-2 | 210 | |
| Accumulated fund | | 2,891 |
| Subscriptions | | 1,875 |
| Bar takings | | 3,700 |
| Donations | | 100 |
| Sale of raffle tickets | | 310 |
| Rent paid | 2,500 | |
| Electricity | 295 | |
| Bar purchases | 1,210 | |
| Bar wages | 790 | |
| Raffle prizes | 120 | |
| Secretary's expenses | 730 | |
| Sundry expenses | 220 | |
| | 8,876 | 8,876 |

---

In preparing the income and expenditure account, note is taken of the following adjustments:
- Provision for depreciation of fixed assets
  furniture, £1,000 – £800 = £200 depreciation
  sports equipment, £1,750 – £1,500 = £250 depreciation
- Subscriptions in advance of £175; thus the amount recorded in the income and expenditure account is £1,875 – £175 = £1,700. Note that subscriptions which are due but unpaid are often, in practice, ignored for the year's accounts – they are often paid late, if indeed they are paid at all.
- Rent prepaid £500; thus the amount recorded in the income and expenditure account is £2,500 – £500 = £2,000.
- Bar closing stock of £320, which is dealt with in the same way as the closing stock of a business.

The income and expenditure account and balance sheet are presented in conventional format as shown on the next page. Note the following points:

- The profit on the bar has been calculated separately in a 'bar trading account' and then brought into the income and expenditure account. It is usual for clubs and societies to show the figures relating to main trading activities in a separate account.
- The donation received has been shown as income; as it is a relatively small amount this would seem to be the correct treatment (see also page 361). Had it been a much larger amount, it would have been taken directly to the balance sheet.
- The profit on the raffle has been disclosed within the income and expenditure account; an alternative treatment would be to show the cost of raffle prizes as expenditure.
- A surplus of income over expenditure (as here) is the equivalent of a business making a net profit, while a deficit is the equivalent of a net loss. The surplus is added to the accumulated fund – the equivalent of a business' capital – in the balance sheet (a deficit would be deducted).

---

**SOUTH DEMPSEY TENNIS CLUB**
**BAR TRADING ACCOUNT**
**for the year ended 31 December 20-2**

|  | £ | £ |
|---|---|---|
| Bar takings |  | 3,700 |
| Opening stock | 210 |  |
| Purchases | 1,210 |  |
|  | 1,420 |  |
| Less Closing stock | 320 |  |
|  | 1,100 |  |
| Bar wages | 790 |  |
|  |  | 1,890 |
| **Profit on bar** |  | 1,810 |

## SOUTH DEMPSEY TENNIS CLUB
### INCOME AND EXPENDITURE ACCOUNT
### for the year ended 31 December 20-2

|  | £ | £ |
|---|---:|---:|
| **Income** | | |
| Profit on bar | | 1,810 |
| Subscriptions | | 1,700 |
| Donation | | 100 |
| Sale of raffle tickets | 310 | |
| Less raffle prizes | 120 | |
| Profit on raffle | | 190 |
| | | 3,800 |
| | | |
| **Less Expenditure** | | |
| Rent | 2,000 | |
| Electricity | 295 | |
| Secretary's expenses | 730 | |
| Sundry expenses | 220 | |
| Provision for depreciation: | | |
| furniture | 200 | |
| sports equipment | 250 | |
| | | 3,695 |
| **Surplus of income over expenditure** | | 105 |

## SOUTH DEMPSEY TENNIS CLUB
### BALANCE SHEET
### as at 31 December 20-2

|  | £ | £ |
|---|---:|---:|
| **Fixed Assets** | | |
| Furniture and fittings (at valuation) | | 800 |
| Sports equipment (at valuation) | | 1,500 |
| | | 2,300 |
| | | |
| **Current Assets** | | |
| Bar stock | 320 | |
| Prepayment (rent) | 500 | |
| Bank | 51 | |
| | 871 | |
| | | |
| **Less Current Liabilities** | | |
| Subscriptions in advance | 175 | |
| **Working Capital** | | 696 |
| **NET ASSETS** | | 2,996 |
| | | |
| **REPRESENTED BY** | | |
| Accumulated fund | | 2,891 |
| Surplus of income over expenditure | | 105 |
| | | 2,996 |

# CLUB ACCOUNTS: PROBLEM AREAS

There are a number of possible areas that need to be clarified by a newly appointed treasurer of a club or society. These are the club's policy on:

* overdue subscriptions
* life membership
* entrance/joining fees
* donations received
* depreciation

The club's rules should state how these are to be handled in the accounts; if not, a new treasurer will have to see how they were dealt with in previous years, or ask the committee for a decision.

## overdue subscriptions

We have seen earlier (page 353) that the practical policy adopted by most treasurers is to ignore overdue subscriptions (but an adjustment is made for prepaid subscriptions). However, in questions and assessments, unless instructed otherwise, overdue subscriptions should be treated as accruals, and subscriptions in advance as prepayments.

## life membership

Some clubs and societies offer life membership in exchange for a one-off payment. The problem for the treasurer is whether to record this payment as income for the year in which it is received, or to credit it to a reserve account (eg Life Subscriptions Account), the balance of which is then transferred bit-by-bit over a number of years to the income and expenditure account. The time period for this will depend on the nature of the club: for example, the 'Over-eighties Gentleman's Dining Club' is likely to transfer its life subscriptions account to income rather more quickly than will a stamp collecting club.

An example of an accounting policy of a club is:

"Three per cent of the life subscriptions account is released to income each year."

The policy for accounting for life membership will always be stated clearly in questions.

## entrance or joining fees

Often a one-off charge is made in the year of joining a club as an entrance fee. It is possible to justify making such a charge by arguing that it covers the cost of processing new members' applications; on the other hand it gives extra income to the club and, once a person is a member, it acts as an incentive for them to remain a member (because, if their membership lapsed, the joining fee would be payable again upon rejoining).

The treasurer needs to know how to account for the joining fee:

* either, it is treated as income for the year of joining (but this could distort income if a membership 'drive' was held in one particular year)
* or, it is credited to an entrance fees account which is transferred to income over a number of years

## donations received

There are two alternative accounting treatments which can be used for donations received:

- record the amount as income in the income and expenditure account, or
- record the amount as an addition to the accumulated fund in the balance sheet

The first method treats the donation as income for the year, while the second capitalises the amount (ie records it on the balance sheet). As to which is to be used depends very much on the amount of the donation in relation to the size of the club's activities – the accounting concept of materiality applies. For example, a £10 donation would normally be recorded as income; however, a legacy of several thousands of pounds from a deceased club member ought to be capitalised and added to the accumulated fund. If the club rules do not state how donations received are to be dealt with in the accounts, the treasurer must use his or her own judgement and will probably apply the materiality concept.

Remember that, in practice, donations will not always be cash amounts, other assets could be donated, eg a plot of land, a work of art. Here the asset will need to be valued and recorded in the accounts. In the case of assets other than cash, it is likely that they will need to be capitalised and recorded on the balance sheet.

## depreciation

As in the final accounts of a business, fixed assets should be depreciated in club accounts; the same principles will apply (see Chapter 14). Provision for depreciation for the year is charged as an expense in the income and expenditure account, while the asset is shown in the balance sheet at cost less depreciation to date, to give the net book value.

Often clubs simply value fixed assets at the end of each financial year. The fall in value, subject to any acquisitions or sales, is the provision for depreciation for the year which is charged as an expense in the income and expenditure account. The fixed asset will then be shown at the reduced value in the year end balance sheet.

# PRACTICAL POINTS FOR TREASURERS

As noted in the introduction to this chapter, the treasurer of a club/society is responsible for maintaining proper accounting records. The same high standards of financial recording as would be applied to the accounts of a business should be used by the club treasurer. Two areas are of particular importance:

## authority to spend

Before making payments, the treasurer must ensure that he or she has the authority to spend the club's money. For 'one-off' transactions, eg the purchase of a new lawnmower by a cricket club, the minutes of the relevant committee meeting will show that the purchase was agreed. For regular activities, eg small expenses such as printing, electricity, the club's rules will authorise the treasurer to make payment against invoices received.

### documentary evidence

The treasurer should ensure that there is documentary evidence for every transaction passing through the accounts of the club. For example, payments should only be made against invoices received in the name of the club, while a receipt should be given for all money received. In this way, an audit trail is created. All documents should be retained for the use of the club's auditor, who will check the accounting records after the end of each financial year. The documents should then be stored for at least six years in case there are subsequent queries.

## CHAPTER SUMMARY

- Unlike a business, a non-profit making organisation – such as a club or society – does not base its activities on profit, but operates for the benefit of its members.

- Many clubs and societies have large sums of money passing through their hands and, like businesses, need tight accounting controls.

- The year-end accounts of a club consist of:
  - income and expenditure account
  - balance sheet

- Where a club carries out a trading activity with the intention of making a profit, a separate account is often prepared for the activity.

- Accounting policies on which the treasurer needs guidance from the club's committee are:
  - overdue subscriptions
  - life membership
  - entrance/joining fees
  - donations received
  - depreciation

In the next chapter we return to business accounts and look at the year-end accounts of a partnership.

# QUESTIONS

NOTE: an asterisk (*) after the question number means that an answer to the question is given in Appendix 2.

**22.1*** Westside Sports Club was set up on 1 July 20-8. At the end of the first year, the treasurer prepares a receipts and payments account as follows:

### RECEIPTS AND PAYMENTS ACCOUNT
#### for the year ended 30 June 20-9

| RECEIPTS | £ | PAYMENTS | £ |
|---|---|---|---|
| Subscriptions | 1,540 | Equipment | 1,500 |
| Competition entry fees | 498 | Postage and stationery | 197 |
| Sale of snacks | 1,108 | Rent paid | 550 |
| | | Competition expenses | 320 |
| | | Purchase of snacks | 520 |
| | | Balance c/d | 59 |
| | 3,146 | | 3,146 |

Additional information at 30 June 20-9:
- subscriptions paid in advance for next year, £80
- rent owing, £100
- stock of snacks is valued at £70
- equipment is to be depreciated at 20%

You are to prepare the income and expenditure account and balance sheet of Westside Sports Club for the year ended 30 June 20-9.

**22.2** The assets and liabilities of the Southwick Social Club as at 1 July 20-3 were:
- bank balance, £580
- bar stock, £540
- furniture and equipment, £2,500
- rent owing, £120

For the year ended 30 June 20-4, the treasurer prepared the following receipts and payments account:

### RECEIPTS AND PAYMENTS ACCOUNT
#### for the year ended 30 June 20-4

| RECEIPTS | £ | PAYMENTS | £ |
|---|---|---|---|
| Balance b/d | 580 | Bar purchases | 3,975 |
| Subscriptions | 2,790 | Dinner dance expenses | 1,280 |
| Bar takings | 6,380 | Secretary's expenses | 890 |
| Dinner dance ticket sales | 790 | Bar wages | 1,530 |
| | | Rent paid | 940 |
| | | Furniture and equipment | 1,710 |
| | | Balance c/d | 215 |
| | 10,540 | | 10,540 |

Additional information at 30 June 20-4:

• bar stocks are valued at £630

• furniture and equipment is valued at £3,500

• subscriptions prepaid for next year, £210

• rent owing, £190

You are to prepare the income and expenditure account and balance sheet of Southwick Social Club for the year ended 30 June 20-4.

**22.3\*** Yesteryear Vintage Car Club is concerned with the history and running of vintage cars. It owns a range of cars which are available for hire by members. The financial year of the club ends on 31 December.

At 1 January Year 46, the club's assets and liabilities were:

|  | £ |
|---|---|
| Subscriptions owing from Year 45 | 640 |
| Vintage cars | 124,000 |
| Bank balance | 7,266 |
| General expenses owing | 540 |

The following Receipts and payments account was prepared for the year ended 31 December Year 46:

| Year 46 | RECEIPTS | £ | Year 46 | PAYMENTS | £ |
|---|---|---|---|---|---|
| 1 Jan | Balance b/d | 7,266 | 31 Dec | Heating and lighting | 2,976 |
| 31 Dec | Subscriptions | 21,700 | | Expenses of social activities | 11,740 |
| | Social activities | 18,460 | | Hire of films | 620 |
| | Amount received from | | | Administration and general | |
| | insurance company | 7,900 | | expenses | 6,040 |
| | Hire of cars | 8,600 | | Maintenance and servicing | |
| | | | | of cars | 9,165 |
| | | | | Repairs to cars | 3,856 |
| | | | | Purchase of car | 12,100 |
| | | | | Promotional costs | 1,350 |
| | | | | Rent | 7,200 |
| | | | | Balance c/d | 8,879 |
| | | 63,926 | | | 63,926 |

Additional information at 31 December Year 46 was available as follows:

(1) The amount received from the insurance company was for a car destroyed by fire. The book value of this asset at 1 January Year 46 was £9,800

(2) Subscriptions in arrears, £780

Subscriptions in advance, £700

(3) Prepaid administration expenses, £420

(4) Accrued due: Heating and lighting, £630

Rent, £440

REQUIRED:

Prepare for the Yesteryear Vintage Car Club:

(a) a statement calculating the accumulated fund at 1 January Year 46

(b) an income and expenditure account for the year ended 31 December Year 46

(c) a balance sheet at 31 December Year 46

*LCCI Examinations Board*

**22.4**   The Blandford Railway Social Club compiles its income and expenditure accounts and balance sheet to 31 October in each year. On 1 November 20-5 the club's assets and liabilities were as follows:

|  | £ | £ |
|---|---|---|
| Club house at cost | | 62,000 |
| Fixtures and fittings | 15,000 | |
| Accumulated depreciation | (3,000) | 12,000 |
| Office equipment | 1,200 | |
| Accumulated depreciation | (120) | 1,080 |
| Balance at bank | | 3,142 |
| Cash in hand | | 60 |
| Subscriptions prepaid | | 194 |
| Subscriptions in arrears | | 68 |
| Stock (bar) | | 342 |
| Creditor (bar stock) | | 189 |
| Ground rent prepaid | | 200 |

A summary of the cash book for the year ended 31 October 20-6 was as follows:

| Date | | Cash | Bank | Date | | Cash | Bank |
|---|---|---|---|---|---|---|---|
| | | £ | £ | | | £ | £ |
| 31 Oct | Balance b/d | 60 | 3,142 | 31 Oct | Purchases (bar) | | 5,210 |
| 31 Oct | Subscriptions rec'd | 80 | 10,140 | 31 Oct | Wages (bar) | | 2,175 |
| 31 Oct | Donations | | 3,000 | 31 Oct | Stationery | 15 | 106 |
| 31 Oct | Sale of fittings | | 1,000 | 31 Oct | New fixtures | | 13,000 |
| 31 Oct | Bar sales | | 8,121 | 31 Oct | Ground rent | | 600 |
| | | | | 31 Oct | Sundries | 40 | 212 |
| | | | | 31 Oct | Balance c/d | 85 | 4,100 |
| | | 140 | 25,403 | | | 140 | 25,403 |
| 1 Nov | Balance b/d | 85 | 4,100 | | | | |

The following additional information is given at 31 October 20-6:

| | £ |
|---|---|
| Subscriptions in arrears | 121 |
| Subscriptions prepaid | 110 |
| Creditor (bar stock) | 294 |
| Stock (bar) | 312 |

- Ground rent was £100 per month, part of which is in arrears at 31 October 20-6.

- Depreciation is to be calculated at 20% of net book value annually on fittings and office equipment.

- The cost of the fittings sold was £1,642 with a net book value at date of sale £1,100.

You are required to prepare an income and expenditure account for the year ended 31 October 20-6, showing clearly the profit or loss on the bar, and a balance sheet on that date.

NOTE: Workings must be shown.

*Reproduced by kind permission of OCR Examinations*

# MULTIPLE CHOICE QUESTIONS

Read each question carefully.
Choose the one answer you think is correct (calculators may be needed).
The answers are on page 568.

1       Which one of the following does not appear in purchases ledger control account?

    A       cash discount allowed

    B       set-off/contra entry

    C       cash/cheques paid to creditors

    D       purchases returns

2       Which one of the following does not appear in sales ledger control account?

    A       cash discount allowed

    B       returned cheques

    C       bad debts written off

    D       provision for bad debts

3       You have the following information:

* opening creditor balances at the start of the month       £18,600
* cash/cheques paid to creditors during month       £9,400
* purchases returns       £800
* creditor balances at the month-end       £17,500

What is the amount of credit purchases for the month?

    A       £9,100

    B       £9,700

    C       £10,000

    D       £11,300

**4** You have the following information:
- opening debtor balances at the start of the month £12,500
- cash/cheques received from debtors during month £7,300
- credit sales during month £6,600
- sales returns during month £500

What is the amount of the debtor balances at the month-end?
A £11,300
B £12,300
C £12,700
D £13,200

**5** You are to set-off a sales ledger debit balance of £100 against a purchases ledger credit balance of £150. The entries in the control accounts will be:

A debit purchases ledger control account £150 and credit sales ledger control account £150

B debit sales ledger control account £100 and credit purchases ledger control account £100

C debit purchases ledger control account £100 and credit sales ledger control account £100

D debit sales ledger control account £150 and credit purchases ledger control account £150

**6** You are preparing a trading account from incomplete records. Debtors at the start of the year were £2,500, and at the end were £3,250. Cheques received from debtors total £17,850; cash sales total £2,500. What is the sales figure for the year?
A £17,850
B £19,600
C £20,350
D £21,100

**7** Cost of goods sold for the year is £200,000.
Mark-up is 30%.
What are sales for the year?
A £60,000
B £140,000
C £200,000
D £260,000

**8**    Sales for the year are £100,000.

Gross profit margin is 25%.

Opening stock is £10,000; closing stock is £12,000.

What are purchases for the year?

A    £25,000

B    £73,000

C    £77,000

D    £125,000

**9**    A club's receipts and payments account is:

A    similar to a balance sheet

B    a summarised cash and bank account

C    similar to a profit and loss account

D    a deposit account at the bank

**10**    The loss made by a club is recorded in its accounts as:

A    drawings

B    deficit

C    surplus

D    depreciation

**11**    In a club balance sheet, subscriptions paid in advance are recorded as:

A    a current asset

B    a current liability

C    an addition to the accumulated fund

D    a fixed asset

**12**    Members' subscriptions of £30 were overdue at the beginning of the year. £2,020 was received during the year, including the overdue amount, and £18 for subscriptions in advance for the following year. What amount will be shown for subscriptions in the income and expenditure account for the year?

A    £1,972

B    £2,008

C    £2,038

D    £2,068

# 23 PARTNERSHIP ACCOUNTS

So far, when discussing financial accounts, we have considered the accounts of a sole trader, ie one person in business. However, a partnership is a common form of business unit, and can be found in the form of:

- sole traders who have joined together with others in order to raise finance and expand the business
- family businesses, such as builders, car repairers, gardeners
- professional firms such as solicitors, accountants, doctors, dentists

In this chapter we look at

- the definition of a partnership
- the accounting requirements of the Partnership Act 1890
- the accounting requirements which may be incorporated into a partnership agreement
- the use of capital accounts and current accounts
- the appropriation of profits
- the layout of the capital section of the balance sheet

## DEFINITION OF A PARTNERSHIP

The Partnership Act of 1890 defines a partnership as:

*the relation which subsists between persons carrying on a business in common with a view of profit*

Normally, partnerships consist of between two and twenty partners (exceptions being large professional firms, eg solicitors and accountants). Partnerships are cheap and easy to set up, but the main disadvantages are the frequency of internal disputes and the liability in law of each partner for the dealings and business debts of the whole firm.

### accounting requirements of a partnership

The accounting requirements of a partnership are:

- either to follow the rules set out in the Partnership Act 1890
- or – and more likely – for the partners to agree amongst themselves, by means of a partnership agreement (see page 372), to follow different accounting rules

Unless the partners agree otherwise, the Partnership Act 1890 states the following accounting rules:

- profits and losses are to be shared equally between the partners
- no partner is entitled to a salary
- partners are not entitled to receive interest on their capital
- interest is not to be charged on partners' drawings
- when a partner contributes more capital than agreed, he or she is entitled to receive interest at five per cent per annum on the excess

As noted above, the partners may well decide to follow different accounting rules – these will be set out in a partnership agreement (see the next page).

## YEAR END ACCOUNTS OF A PARTNERSHIP

A partnership prepares the same type of year end accounts as a sole trader business:

- trading and profit and loss account
- balance sheet

The main difference is that, immediately after the profit and loss account, follows an appropriation section (often described as an appropriation account). This shows how the net profit from profit and loss account is shared amongst the partners.

### example of sharing profits

Exe, Wye and Zed are partners sharing profits and losses equally; their profit and loss account for the current year shows a net profit of £60,000. The appropriation of profits appears as:

**EXE, WYE AND ZED**
**PROFIT AND LOSS APPROPRIATION ACCOUNT**
**for the year ended ..............**

|  | £ |
|---|---|
| Net profit | 60,000 |
| Share of profits: | |
|     Exe | 20,000 |
|     Wye | 20,000 |
|     Zed | 20,000 |
| | 60,000 |

The above is a simple appropriation of profits. A more complex appropriation account (see pages 375 to 376) deals with other accounting points from the partnership agreement (see next section).

# PARTNERSHIP AGREEMENT

The accounting rules from the Partnership Act are often varied with the agreement of all partners, by means of a partnership agreement. In particular, a partnership agreement will usually cover the following:

- division of profits and losses between partners
- partners' salaries/commission
- whether interest is to be allowed on capital and at what rate
- whether interest is to be charged on partners' drawings, and at what rate

The money amounts involved for each of these points (where allowed by the partnership agreement) are shown in the partnership appropriation account (see page 375).

## division of profits and losses between partners

The Partnership Act states that, in the absence of an agreement to the contrary, profits and losses are to be shared equally. A partner's share of the profits is normally taken out of the business in the form of drawings. Clearly, if one partner has contributed much more capital than the other partner(s), it would be unfair to apply this clause from the Act. Consequently, many partnerships agree to share profits and losses on a different basis – often in the same proportions as they have contributed capital. The important point, though, is that if the partnership agreement (or an examination question) is silent on this matter, then the Partnership Act applies and profits and losses are shared equally.

## partners' salaries/commission

Although the Act says that no partner is entitled to a salary, it is quite usual in the partnership agreement for one or more partners to be paid a salary. The reason for doing this is that often in a partnership, one of the partners spends more time working in the partnership than the other(s). The agreement to pay a salary is in recognition of the work done. Note that partners' salaries are not shown as an expense in profit and loss account; instead, they appear in the partnership appropriation account (see page 375).

Many professional partnerships, such as solicitors and accountants, have junior partners who receive a partnership salary because they work full-time in the business. Most junior partners have not contributed any capital, but they are liable for business debts. (In a partnership, there may not be a requirement to contribute capital – unless the partnership agreement states otherwise – however, most partners will do so.)

As an alternative to a salary, a partner might be paid a commission on sales. As with a salary, this is not shown as an expense in the profit and loss account, but appears in the partnership appropriation account.

## interest allowed on capital

Many partnerships include a clause in their partnership agreement which allows interest to be paid on capital; the rate of interest will be stated also. This clause is used to compensate partners for the loss of use of their capital, ie it is not available to invest elsewhere. Often, interest is allowed on capital in partnerships where profits and losses are shared equally – it is one way of partly adjusting for different capital balances. As noted earlier, the Partnership Act does not permit interest to be paid on capital, so reference to it must be made in the partnership agreement.

When calculating interest on capital, it may be necessary to allow for part years. For example:

| | |
|---|---|
| 1 January 20-1 capital balance | £20,000 |
| 1 July 20-1 additional capital contributed | £4,000 |
| the rate of interest allowed on capital | 10 per cent per annum |
| the partnership's financial year-end | 31 December |

Interest allowed on capital is calculated as:

| | |
|---|---|
| 1 January - 30 June  £20,000 x 10% (for 6 months) | £1,000 |
| 1 July - 31 December  £24,000 x 10% (for 6 months) | £1,200 |
| Interest allowed on capital for year | £2,200 |


## interest charged on partners' drawings

In order to discourage partners from drawing out too much money from the business early in the financial year, the partnership agreement may stipulate that interest is to be charged on partners' drawings, and at what rate. This acts as a penalty against early withdrawal when the business may be short of cash. For example:

| | |
|---|---|
| a partner's drawings for the year | £24,000 |
| withdrawal at the end of each quarter (31 March, 30 June, 30 September, 31  December) | £6,000 |
| the rate of interest charged on partners' drawings | 10 per cent per annum |
| the partnership's financial year-end | 31 December |

Interest charged is calculated as:

| | |
|---|---|
| 31 March: £6,000 x 10% x 9 months | £450 |
| 30 June: £6,000 x 10% x 6 months | £300 |
| 30 September: £6,000 x 10% x 3 months | £150 |
| Interest charged on partner's drawings for year | £900 |

No interest is charged on the withdrawal on 31 December, because it is at the end of the financial year. The amount of interest charged on drawings for the year is shown in the partnership appropriation account (see page 375), where it increases the profit to be shared amongst the partners.

## other points

● **interest on loans**

If a partner makes a loan to the partnership, the rate of interest to be paid needs to be agreed, otherwise the rate specified in the Partnership Act 1890 applies – five per cent per annum.

Interest on loans is charged as an expense in the profit and loss account, and is not shown in the appropriation account.

● **interest on current accounts**

The partnership agreement may state that interest is to be allowed at a specified rate on the credit balance of partners' current accounts (see below), and is to be charged on debit balances.

# CAPITAL ACCOUNTS AND CURRENT ACCOUNTS

The important book-keeping difference between a sole trader and a partnership is that each partner usually has a capital account and a current account. The capital account is normally fixed, and only alters if a permanent increase or decrease in capital contributed by the partner takes place. The current account is fluctuating and it is to this account that:

- share of profits is credited
- share of loss is debited
- salary (if any), or commissions, are credited
- interest allowed on partners' capital is credited
- drawings are debited
- interest charged on partners' drawings is debited

Thus, the current account is treated as a working account, while capital account remains fixed, except for capital introduced or withdrawn.

A partner's current account will have the following layout:

| Dr | | **Partner A: Current Account** | | Cr |
|---|---|---|---|---|
| | £ | | | £ |
| Drawings | | Balance b/d | | |
| Interest charged on | | Share of net profit | | |
| drawings* | | Salary (or commissions)* | | |
| Balance c/d | | Interest allowed on capital* | | |

\*  if these items are allowed by the partnership agreement

Note that whilst the normal balance on a partner's current account is credit, when the partner has drawn out more than his or her share of the profits, then the balance will be debit.

# APPROPRIATION OF PROFITS

As we have seen earlier in this chapter, the appropriation section (often described as the appropriation account) follows the profit and loss account and shows how net profit has been divided amongst the partners. The example which follows shows a partnership salary (not to be shown in profit and loss account), interest allowed on partners' capital, and interest charged on partners' drawings.

## example

Aye and Bee are in partnership sharing profits and losses 60 per cent and 40 per cent respectively. Net profit for the year ended 31 March 20-5 is £42,000.

At 1 April 20-4 (the start of the year), the partners have the following balances:

|  | Capital account £ | Current account £ |
|---|---|---|
| Aye | 40,000 | 2,000 Cr |
| Bee | 30,000 | 400 Cr |

There have been no changes to the capital accounts during the year; interest is allowed on partners' capitals at the rate of eight per cent per year.

Bee is entitled to a salary of £16,000 per year.

On 30 September 20-4 (half-way through the financial year), partners' drawings were made: Aye £18,000, Bee £24,000; there were no other drawings. Interest is charged on partners' drawings at the rate of ten per cent per year.

The appropriation of profits will be made as follows:

**AYE AND BEE**
**PROFIT AND LOSS APPROPRIATION ACCOUNT FOR THE YEAR ENDED 31 MARCH 20-5**

|  | £ | £ |
|---|---|---|
| **Net profit** |  | 42,000 |
| Add interest charged on partners' drawings: |  |  |
| Aye (£18,000 ÷ 2 x 10%) | 900 |  |
| Bee (£24,000 ÷ 2 x 10%) | 1200 |  |
|  |  | 2,100 |
|  |  | 44,100 |

*(continued on next page)*

|  |  | (from previous page) | 44,100 |
|---|---|---|---|

**Less appropriation of profits:**

Salary: Bee · · · 16,000

Interest allowed on partners' capitals:

| | | | |
|---|---|---|---|
| Aye | | 3,200 | |
| Bee | | 2,400 | |
| | | | 5,600 |
| | | | 22,500 |

**Share of remaining profits:**

| | | | |
|---|---|---|---|
| Aye (60%) | | 13,500 | |
| Bee (40%) | | 9,000 | |
| | | | 22,500 |

Note that all of the available profit, after allowing for any salary, and interest charged and allowed, is shared amongst the partners, in the ratio in which they share profits and losses.

The partners' current accounts for the year appear as:

| Dr | | Aye | Bee | | **Partners' Current Accounts** | Aye | Bee | Cr |
|---|---|---|---|---|---|---|---|---|
| 20-4/-5 | | £ | £ | 20-4/-5 | | £ | £ | |
| 31 Mar | Drawings for year | 18,000 | 24,000 | 1 Apr | Balances b/d | 2,000 | 400 | |
| 31 Mar | Interest on drawings | 900 | 1,200 | | Salary | – | 16,000 | |
| 31 Mar | Balance c/d | – | 2,600 | 31 Mar | Interest on capital | 3,200 | 2,400 | |
| | | | | 31 Mar | Share of profits | 13,500 | 9,000 | |
| | | | | 31 Mar | Balance c/d | 200 | – | |
| | | 18,900 | 27,800 | | | 18,900 | 27,800 | |
| 20-5/-6 | | | | 20-5/-6 | | | | |
| 1 Apr | Balance b/d | 200 | – | 1 Apr | Balance b/d | – | 2,600 | |

Note that Aye has drawn more out of the current account than the balance of the account; accordingly, at the end of the year, Aye has a debit balance on the account with the partnership. By contrast, Bee has a credit balance of £2,600 on current account.

# BALANCE SHEET

Within the balance sheet of a partnership must be shown the year end balances on each partner's capital and current account. However, it is usual to show the transactions that have taken place on each account in summary form, in the same way that, in a sole trader's balance sheet, net profit for the year is added and drawings for the year are deducted.

The other sections of the balance sheet – fixed assets, current assets and current liabilities – are presented in the same way as for a sole trader.

The following is an example balance sheet layout for the 'Financed by' section (the other sections of the balance sheet are not shown). It details the capital and current accounts of the partnership of Aye and Bee.

**BALANCE SHEET (EXTRACT) OF AYE AND BEE AS AT 31 MARCH 20-5**

| | £ | £ | £ |
|---|---|---|---|
| **FINANCED BY** | | | |
| **Capital Accounts** | | | |
| Aye | | 40,000 | |
| Bee | | 30,000 | |
| | | | 70,000 |
| | | | |
| **Current Accounts** | AYE | BEE | |
| Opening balance | 2,000 | 400 | |
| Add: salary | - | 16,000 | |
| interest on capital | 3,200 | 2,400 | |
| share of profit | 13,500 | 9,000 | |
| | 18,700 | 27,800 | |
| Less: drawings | 18,000 | 24,000 | |
| interest on drawings | 900 | 1,200 | |
| | (200) | 2,600 | |
| | | | 2,400 |
| | | | 72,400 |

Note that an examination question or assessment will call either for the preparation of the partners' current accounts, as shown on the previous page, or for the detailed balance sheet extract, as shown here.

# CHAPTER SUMMARY

● A partnership is formed when two or more (usually up to a maximum of twenty) people set up in business.

● The Partnership Act 1890 states certain accounting rules, principally that profits and losses must be shared equally.

● Many partnerships over-ride the accounting rules of the Act by creating a partnership agreement which covers:

  • division of profits and losses between partners

  • partners' salaries/commissions

  • whether interest is to be allowed on capital, and at what rate

  • whether interest is to be charged on partners' drawings, and at what rate

● The usual way to account for partners' capital is to maintain a fixed capital account for each partner. This is complemented by a fluctuating current account which is used as a working account for share of profits, drawings, etc.

● The final accounts of partnerships are similar to those of sole traders, but incorporate

  • an appropriation account as a continuation of the profit and loss account

  • individual capital and current accounts for each partner shown in the balance sheet

In the next chapter we continue the theme of partnerships and look at changes in partnerships, such as the admission of a new partner, retirement of a partner.

# QUESTIONS

NOTE: an asterisk (*) after the question number means that an answer to the question is given in Appendix 2.

**23.1\*** Lysa and Mark are in partnership and own a shop, 'Trends', which sells fashionable teenage clothes. The following figures are extracted from their accounts for the year ended 31 December 20-8:

| | £ | |
|---|---|---|
| Capital accounts at 1 January 20-8: | | |
| Lysa | 50,000 | Cr |
| Mark | 40,000 | Cr |
| | | |
| Current accounts at 1 January 20-8: | | |
| Lysa | 420 | Cr |
| Mark | 1,780 | Cr |
| | | |
| Drawings for the year: | | |
| Lysa | 13,000 | |
| Mark | 12,250 | |

Interest on capital for the year:

| | |
|---|---|
| Lysa | 2,500 |
| Mark | 2,000 |

Share of profits for the year:

| | |
|---|---|
| Lysa | 9,300 |
| Mark | 9,300 |

Notes:

- no partner is entitled to a salary
- there is no interest charged on drawings

You are to show the partners' capital and current accounts for the year ended 31 December 20-8.

**23.2\*** John James and Steven Hill are in partnership and own a wine shop called 'Grapes'. The following trial balance has been taken from their accounts for the year ended 31 December 20-1, after the calculation of gross profit.

| | Dr | Cr |
|---|---|---|
| | £ | £ |
| Capital accounts: | | |
| James | | 38,000 |
| Hill | | 32,000 |
| Current accounts: | | |
| James | 3,000 | |
| Hill | | 1,000 |
| Drawings: | | |
| James | 14,000 | |
| Hill | 18,000 | |
| Gross profit | | 89,000 |
| Rent and rates | 7,500 | |
| Advertising | 12,000 | |
| Heat and light | 3,500 | |
| Wages and salaries | 18,000 | |
| Sundry expenses | 4,000 | |
| Shop fittings at cost | 20,000 | |
| *Stock at 31 December 20-1 | 35,000 | |
| Bank | 29,000 | |
| Debtors | 6,000 | |
| Creditors | | 8,000 |
| Value Added Tax | | 2,000 |
| | 170,000 | 170,000 |

* Closing stock is included in the trial balance because gross profit for the year has already been calculated.

Notes at 31 December 20-1:

- profits and losses are to be shared equally
- depreciation is to be charged on the shop fittings at 10% per year

You are to

(a) prepare the partnership profit and loss account (incorporating the appropriation account) for the year ended 31 December 20-1, together with the partnership balance sheet at that date

(b) show the partners' capital and current accounts for the year ended 31 December 20-1

**23.3** Perch and Trout are in partnership sharing profits and losses in the ratio 60:40.

The partnership agreement provides that interest on partners' capital accounts should be allowed at the rate of 10% per annum. Interest should be charged on drawings.

The following information has been made available for the year ended 30 September 1997.

Net profit for the year £30,500.

|  | Perch | | Trout | |
| --- | --- | --- | --- | --- |
|  | £ | | £ | |
| Capital accounts 1 October 1996 | 20,000 | | 15,000 | |
| Current accounts 1 October 1996 | 1,800 | (Cr) | 3,400 | (Dr) |
| Drawings for the year | 12,785 | | 18,275 | |
| Salary to be credited | – | | 6,000 | |
| Interest on drawings | 640 | | 910 | |

You are required to:

(a) prepare the partnership appropriation account for the year ended 30 September 1997

(b) prepare each of the partners' current accounts for the same period

*Reproduced by kind permission of OCR Examinations*

**23.4** Tuigamala and Tatupu are in partnership, sharing profits and losses in the ratio 3:1. The following trial balance was extracted after the preparation of their trading account for the year ended 31 December.

|  |  | Dr £ | Cr £ |
|---|---|---:|---:|
| Provision for depreciation: | Equipment | | 2,000 |
| Provision for depreciation: | Fixtures | | 1,800 |
| Bank balance | | | 830 |
| Drawings: | Tuigamala | 1,600 | |
| | Tatupu | 900 | |
| Equipment at cost | | 20,000 | |
| Fixtures at cost | | 9,000 | |
| Premises at cost | | 40,000 | |
| Commission received | | | 200 |
| Debtors and creditors | | 16,000 | 7,500 |
| Current accounts: | Tuigamala | 200 | |
| | Tatupu | nil | nil |
| Provision for doubtful debts | | | 320 |
| Gross profit | | | 24,000 |
| Insurances | | 950 | |
| Wages and salaries | | 2,550 | |
| Cash | | 450 | |
| Capital accounts: | Tuigamala | | 40,000 |
| | Tatupu | | 15,000 |
| | | 91,650 | 91,650 |

At 31 December the following information needs to be taken into consideration:

(1)     The provision for doubtful debts is to be maintained at 2% of debtors

(2)     Commission received of £300 is still owed

(3)     An insurance invoice of £50 has yet to be paid

(4)     £150 of wages have been prepaid

(5)     Depreciation needs to be provided for on the following basis:

     (i)     Equipment at 10% straight line method

     (ii)     Fixtures at 15% reducing (diminishing) balance method

(6)     The partnership agreement provides for the following:

     (i)     Interest on drawings is charged at 5% per annum

     (ii)     Interest on capital is allowed at 8% per annum

     (iii)     Tatupu is to receive a salary of £3,745

You are required to:

(a)     prepare the partnership profit and loss account for the year ended 31 December

(b)     prepare the partnership appropriation account for the year ended 31 December

(c)     prepare each partner's current account at 31 December

(d)     prepare the partners' balance sheet as at 31 December

*Pitman Qualifications*

# 24 CHANGES IN PARTNERSHIPS

In this chapter we will continue our study of partnerships by describing the principles involved, and the accounting entries, for:
- admission of a new partner
- retirement of a partner
- death of a partner
- changes in profit-sharing ratios
- revaluation of assets
- dissolution of a partnership

Before we look at each of these, we need to consider the goodwill of the business, which will feature in each of the changes listed above.

## GOODWILL

The balance sheet of a partnership, like that of many businesses, rarely indicates the true 'going concern' value of the business: usually the recorded figures under-estimate the worth of a business. There are two main reasons for this:

- Prudence concept. If there is any doubt about the value of assets, they are stated at the lowest possible figure.

- Goodwill. A going concern business will often have a value of goodwill, because of various factors, eg the trade that has been built up, the reputation of the business, the location of the business – leading to increased trade, the skill of the workforce, and the success at developing new products.

### definition of goodwill

Goodwill can formally be defined in accounting terms as:

*the difference between the value of a business as a whole, and the aggregate (total) of the value of its separate assets, less liabilities.*

For example, an existing business is bought for £500,000, with the separate assets and liabilities being worth £450,000 net; goodwill is, therefore, £50,000.

Thus goodwill has a value as an intangible asset to the owner or owners of a going concern business, whether or not it is recorded on the balance sheet. As you will see in the sections which follow, a valuation has to be placed on goodwill whenever a change takes place in a partnership.

## valuation of goodwill

The valuation of goodwill is always subject to negotiation between the people concerned if, for instance, a partnership business is to be sold. Two commonly-used methods of valuing goodwill are:

- average profits
- super profits

With the average profits method, goodwill is valued at the average net profit over the last, say, three years multiplied by an agreed figure, perhaps five times. For example:

- net profit 20-1 £10,000, 20-2 £14,000, 20-3 £12,000
- goodwill is to be valued at five times the average profit of the last three years

Goodwill, therefore, is valued at £12,000 x 5 = £60,000

For the super profits method, goodwill is based on the extra profit generated by the business above the amount that would be earned if the capital of the business was invested elsewhere with similar risks.

For example:

- the capital of a partnership is £100,000
- profits after payment of a salary to each partner are £15,000 per year
- the general level of interest for savers is ten per cent per year, gross of tax
- goodwill is to be valued at five times the super profits

The profits of this partnership are £5,000 per year higher than would be earned if the capital was invested in a bank or building society account: this is the amount of the super profits. Goodwill, therefore, is valued at £5,000 x 5 = £25,000.

In a balance sheet, goodwill is shown as an intangible fixed asset. It is only recorded on the balance sheet when it has been purchased, eg a sole trader or a partnership purchasing goodwill when taking over another business. It should then:

- either, be depreciated (or amortised) to profit and loss account over its estimated economic life (generally up to a maximum of twenty years)

- or, if the estimated economic life is deemed to be indefinite, the goodwill need not be amortised, provided that its continuing existence can be justified (by means of an annual 'impairment review')

We will now see how goodwill is used whenever changes are made to partnerships, eg the admission of a new partner, retirement of a partner, etc. For each of these changes, a value for goodwill is agreed and this amount is temporarily debited to goodwill account, and credited to the partners' capital accounts in their profit-sharing ratio; after the change in the partnership, as you will see, the partners' capital accounts are debited and goodwill account is credited. Thus a 'nil' balance remains on goodwill account and, therefore, it is not recorded on the partnership balance sheet. This follows the prudence concept, and is the method commonly followed when changes are made to partnerships.

## ADMISSION OF A NEW PARTNER

A new partner – who can only be admitted with the consent of all existing partners – is normally charged a premium for goodwill. This is because the new partner will start to share in the profits of the business immediately and will benefit from the goodwill established by the existing partners. If the business was to be sold shortly after the admission of a new partner, a price will be agreed for goodwill and this will be shared amongst all the partners (including the new partner). To make allowance for this benefit it is necessary to make book-keeping adjustments in the partners' capital accounts. The most common way of doing this is to use a goodwill account which is opened by the old partners with the agreed valuation of goodwill and, immediately after the admission of the new partner, is closed by transfer to the partners' capital accounts, including that of the new partner.

The procedures on admission of a new parter are:

- agree a valuation for goodwill
- old partners
  - debit goodwill with the amount of goodwill
  - credit partners' capital accounts (in their old profit-sharing ratio) with the amount of goodwill
- old partners + new partner
  - debit partners' capital accounts (in their new profit-sharing ratio) with the amount of goodwill
  - credit goodwill with the amount of goodwill

The effect of this is to charge the new partner with a premium for goodwill.

## WORKED EXAMPLE: ADMISSION OF A NEW PARTNER

### question

Al and Ben are in partnership sharing profits and losses equally. Their balance sheet as at 31 December 20-1 is as follows:

| BALANCE SHEET OF AL AND BEN AS AT 31 DECEMBER 20-1 | |
| --- | --- |
| | £ |
| Net assets | 80,000 |
| Capital accounts: | |
| Al | 45,000 |
| Ben | 35,000 |
| | 80,000 |

On 1 January 20-2 the partners agree to admit Col into the partnership, with a new profit-sharing ratio of 2:2:1. Goodwill has been agreed at a valuation of £25,000. Col will bring £20,000 of cash into the business as his capital and premium for goodwill.

Show the procedures on the admission of Col into the partnership.

## answer

- goodwill has been valued at £25,000
- old partners:
  - -- debit goodwill      £25,000
  - – credit capital accounts (in their old profit-sharing ratio)
    - Al                      £12,500
    - Ben                    £12,500
- old partners + new partner
  - – debit capital accounts (in their new profit-sharing ratio)
    - Al                      £10,000
    - Ben                    £10,000
    - Col                    £5,000
  - – credit goodwill      £25,000

The capital accounts of the partners, after the above transactions have been recorded, appear as:

| Dr | | | | **Partners' Capital Accounts** | | | Cr |
|---|---|---|---|---|---|---|---|
| | Al | Ben | Col | | Al | Ben | Col |
| | £ | £ | £ | | £ | £ | £ |
| Goodwill written off | 10,000 | 10,000 | 5,000 | Balances b/d | 45,000 | 35,000 | - |
| Balances c/d | 47,500 | 37,500 | 15,000 | Goodwill created | 12,500 | 12,500 | - |
| | | | | Bank | - | - | 20,000 |
| | 57,500 | 47,500 | 20,000 | | 57,500 | 47,500 | 20,000 |
| | | | | Balances b/d | 47,500 | 37,500 | 15,000 |

The balance sheet, following the admission of Col, appears as:

---

**BALANCE SHEET OF AL, BEN AND COL AS AT 1 JANUARY 20-2**

| | | £ |
|---|---|---|
| Net assets | | 100,000 |
| Capital accounts: | | |
| Al | (£45,000 + £12,500 - £10,000) | 47,500 |
| Ben | (£35,000 + £12,500 - £10,000) | 37,500 |
| Col | (£20,000 - £5,000) | 15,000 |
| | | 100,000 |

---

In this way, the new partner has paid the existing partners a premium of £5,000 for a one-fifth share of the profits of a business with a goodwill value of £25,000. Note that, although a goodwill account has been used, it has been fully utilised and, therefore, does not appear on the balance sheet.

# RETIREMENT OF A PARTNER

When a partner retires it is necessary to calculate how much is due to the partner in respect of capital and profits. The partnership deed normally includes provision for retirement. The most common procedure requires goodwill to be valued and operates in a similar way to the admission of a new partner, as follows:

- agree a valuation for goodwill
- old partners
  - debit goodwill with the amount of goodwill
  - credit partners' capital accounts (in their old profit-sharing ratio) with the amount of goodwill
- remaining partners
  - debit partners' capital accounts (in their new profit-sharing ratio) with the amount of goodwill
  - credit goodwill with the amount of goodwill

The effect of this is to credit the retiring partner with the amount of the goodwill built up whilst he or she was a partner. This amount, plus the retiring partner's capital and current account balances can then be paid out of the partnership bank account. (If there is insufficient money for this, it is quite usual for a retiring partner to leave some of the capital in the business as a loan, which is repaid over a period.)

## WORKED EXAMPLE: RETIREMENT OF A PARTNER

### question

Jan, Kay and Lil are in partnership sharing profit and losses in the ratio of 2:2:1 respectively. Partner Jan decides to retire on 31 December 20-1 when the partnership balance sheet is as follows:

| BALANCE SHEET OF JAN, KAY AND LIL AS AT 31 DECEMBER 20-1 | |
|---|---:|
| | £ |
| Net assets | 100,000 |
| Capital accounts: | |
| Jan | 35,000 |
| Kay | 45,000 |
| Lil | 20,000 |
| | 100,000 |

Goodwill is agreed at a valuation of £30,000. Kay and Lil are to continue in partnership and will share profits and losses in the ratio of 2:1 respectively. Jan agrees to leave £20,000 of the amount due to her as a loan to the new partnership.

Show the procedures on the retirement of Jan from the partnership.

**answer**
- goodwill has been valued at £30,000
- old partners:
  - debit goodwill    £30,000
  - credit capital accounts (in their old profit-sharing ratio of 2:2:1)
    - Jan        £12,000
    - Kay        £12,000
    - Lil        £6,000
- remaining partners
  - debit capital accounts (in their new profit-sharing ratio of 2:1)
    - Kay        £20,000
    - Lil        £10,000
  - credit goodwill    £30,000

The balance of Jan's capital account is now £47,000 (ie £35,000 + goodwill of £12,000). Of this, £20,000 will be retained in the business as a loan, and £27,000 will be paid from the partnership bank account.

The balance sheet, after the retirement of Jan, appears as:

---

**BALANCE SHEET OF KAY AND LIL AS AT 1 JANUARY 20-2**

|  | £ |
|---|---|
| Net assets (£100,000 - £27,000 paid to Jan) | 73,000 |
| Less Loan account of Jan | 20,000 |
|  | 53,000 |
|  |  |
| Capital accounts: |  |
| Kay (£45,000 + £12,000 - £20,000) | 37,000 |
| Lil  (£20,000 + £6,000 - £10,000) | 16,000 |
|  | 53,000 |

---

The effect of this is that the remaining partners have bought out Jan's £12,000 share of the goodwill of the business, ie it has cost Kay £8,000, and Lil £4,000. If the business was to be sold later, Kay and Lil would share the goodwill obtained from the sale in their new profit-sharing ratio.


# DEATH OF A PARTNER

The accounting procedures on the death of a partner are very similar to those for a partner's retirement. The only difference is that the amount due to the deceased partner is placed in an account called 'Executors (or Administrators) of X deceased' pending payment.

# CHANGES IN PROFIT-SHARING RATIOS

It may be necessary, from time-to-time, to change the profit-sharing ratios of partners. A partner's share of profits might be increased because of an increase in capital in relation to the other partners, or because of a more active role in running the business. Equally, a share of profits may be decreased if a partner withdraws capital or spends less time in the business. Clearly the agreement of all partners is needed to make changes, and the guidance of the partnership agreement should be followed.

Generally, a change in profit-sharing ratios involves establishing a figure for goodwill, even if the partnership is to continue with the same partners; this is to establish how much goodwill was built up while they shared profits in their old ratios. Each partner will, therefore, receive a value for the goodwill based on the old profit-sharing ratio.

## WORKED EXAMPLE: CHANGES IN PROFIT-SHARING RATIOS

### question

Col and Des are in partnership sharing profits and losses equally. The balance sheet at 31 December 20-1 is as follows:

| BALANCE SHEET OF COL AND DES AS AT 31 DECEMBER 20-1 | |
|---|---|
| | £ |
| Net assets | 60,000 |
| | |
| Capital accounts: | |
| Col | 35,000 |
| Des | 25,000 |
| | 60,000 |

The partners agree that, as from 1 January 20-2, Col will take a two-thirds share of the profits and losses, with Des taking one-third. It is agreed that goodwill shall be valued at £30,000.
Show the procedures on the change in the profit-sharing ratio.

### answer
- goodwill has been valued at £30,000
- old profit-sharing ratio:
  - debit goodwill      £30,000
  - credit capital accounts (in their old profit-sharing ratio of 1:1)
    - Col      £15,000
    - Des      £15,000
- new profit-sharing ratio:
  - debit capital accounts (in their new profit-sharing ratio of 2:1)
    - Col      £20,000
    - Des      £10,000
  - credit goodwill      £30,000

The balance sheet at 1 January 20-2 appears as:

---

**BALANCE SHEET OF COL AND DES AS AT 1 JANUARY 20-2**

| | £ |
|---|---|
| Net assets | 60,000 |
| Capital accounts: | |
| Col   (£35,000 + £15,000 – £20,000) | 30,000 |
| Des   (£25,000 + £15,000 – £10,000) | 30,000 |
| | 60,000 |

---

The effect is that Col has 'paid' Des £5,000 to increase his share of the profits from half to two-thirds. This may seem inequitable but neither partner is worse off in the event of the business being sold, assuming that the business is sold for £90,000 (£60,000 assets + £30,000 goodwill). Before the change in the profit-sharing ratio they would have received:

Col  £35,000 capital + £15,000 half-share of goodwill  =  £50,000
Des  £25,000 capital + £15,000 half-share of goodwill  =  £40,000

After the change, they will receive:

Col  £30,000 capital + £20,000 two-thirds share of goodwill  =  £50,000
Des  £30,000 capital + £10,000 one-third share of goodwill  =  £40,000

Thus, as far as the capital positions are concerned, the partners remain unchanged: it is only the profit-sharing ratios that will be different as from 1 January 20-2. Also, any increase in goodwill above the £30,000 figure will be shared in the new ratio.

# REVALUATION OF ASSETS

So far in this chapter we have looked at the adjustments made for goodwill in various changes made to partnerships. Goodwill, however, reflects only one aspect of a partner's interest in the business. For example, some of the assets may have appreciated in value, but adjustments may not have been made in the accounts; other assets may have fallen in value, while provisions for depreciation and/or bad debts may have been too much or too little. With a change in the personnel of a partnership, a revaluation account may be needed to correct any discrepancies in values. The accounting procedure is:

- **increase in the value of an asset**
  - debit asset account with the amount of the increase
  - credit revaluation account with the amount of the increase
- **reduction in the value of an asset**
  - debit revaluation account the amount of the reduction
  - credit asset account the amount of the reduction
- **increase in provision for depreciation/bad debts**
  - debit revaluation account with the amount of the increase
  - credit provision account with the amount of the increase

- **reduction in provision for depreciation/bad debts**
  - debit provision account with the amount of the reduction
  - credit revaluation account the amount of the reduction

After these adjustments have been recorded in the books of account, the balance of the revaluation account is divided among the partners in their profit-sharing ratios.

## WORKED EXAMPLE: REVALUATION OF ASSETS

### question

Matt, Nia and Olly are in partnership sharing profits and losses equally. On 31 December 20-1 their balance sheet is as follows:

### BALANCE SHEET OF MATT, NIA AND OLLY AS AT 31 DECEMBER 20-1

|                           | £       | £            | £       |
|---------------------------|---------|--------------|---------|
| **Fixed Assets**          | Cost    | Dep'n to date | Net     |
| Premises                  | 100,000 | -            | 100,000 |
| Machinery                 | 50,000  | 10,000       | 40,000  |
|                           | 150,000 | 10,000       | 140,000 |
|                           |         |              |         |
| **Current Assets**        |         |              |         |
| Stock                     |         | 30,000       |         |
| Debtors                   |         | 20,000       |         |
| Bank                      |         | 5,000        |         |
|                           |         | 55,000       |         |
| **Less Current Liabilities** |      |              |         |
| Creditors                 |         | 25,000       |         |
| **Working Capital**       |         |              | 30,000  |
| **NET ASSETS**            |         |              | 170,000 |
|                           |         |              |         |
| **FINANCED BY**:          |         |              |         |
| **Capital accounts**      |         |              |         |
| Matt                      |         |              | 60,000  |
| Nia                       |         |              | 60,000  |
| Olly                      |         |              | 50,000  |
|                           |         |              | 170,000 |

Olly decides to retire at 31 December 20-1; Matt and Nia are to continue the partnership and will share profits and losses equally. The following valuations are agreed:

| Goodwill  | £30,000  |
|-----------|----------|
| Premises  | £150,000 |
| Machinery | £30,000  |
| Stock     | £21,000  |

A provision for bad debts equal to five per cent of debtors is to be made.

Olly agrees that the moneys owing on retirement are to be retained in the business as a long-term loan. Show the revaluation account, and adjusted balance sheet at 1 January 20-2.

## answer

| Dr | Revaluation Account | | | Cr |
|---|---|---|---|---|
| **20-1** | £ | **20-1** | | £ |
| 31 Dec Provision for depreciation: | | 31 Dec Goodwill | | 30,000 |
| Machinery | 10,000 | Premises | | 50,000 |
| Stock | 9,000 | | | |
| Provision for bad debts | 1,000 | | | |
| Capital accounts: | | | | |
| Matt (one-third) | 20,000 | | | |
| Nia (one-third) | 20,000 | | | |
| Olly (one-third) | 20,000 | | | |
| | 80,000 | | | 80,000 |

Note that the amount of goodwill has been credited to revaluation account (and thus to the capital accounts); it will, later, be debited to the capital accounts of the two remaining partners - in this way it will not feature on the balance sheet.

**BALANCE SHEET OF MATT AND NIA AS AT 1 JANUARY 20-2**

| | Cost £ | Dep'n to date £ | Net £ |
|---|---|---|---|
| **Fixed Assets** | | | |
| Premises | 150,000 | - | 150,000 |
| Machinery | 50,000 | 20,000 | 30,000 |
| | 200,000 | 20,000 | 180,000 |
| **Current Assets** | | | |
| Stock | | 21,000 | |
| Debtors | 20,000 | | |
| Less provision for bad debts | 1,000 | | |
| | | 19,000 | |
| Bank | | 5,000 | |
| | | 45,000 | |
| **Less Current Liabilities** | | | |
| Creditors | | 25,000 | |
| **Working Capital** | | | 20,000 |
| | | | 200,000 |
| **Less Long-term Liabilities** | | | |
| Loan account of Olly (£50,000 + £20,000) | | | 70,000 |
| **NET ASSETS** | | | 130,000 |
| **FINANCED BY** | | | |
| **Capital accounts** | | | |
| Matt (£60,000 + £20,000 – £15,000 goodwill debited) | | | 65,000 |
| Nia (£60,000 + £20,000 – £15,000 goodwill debited) | | | 65,000 |
| | | | 130,000 |

# PARTNERSHIP CHANGES: SPLIT YEARS

Any of the changes in partnerships that we have looked at so far in this chapter may occur during the course of an accounting year, rather than at the end of it. For example, part-way through the year:

- the partners may decide to admit a new partner
- a partner might retire, or die
- the partners may decide to change their profit-sharing ratios

To avoid having to prepare final accounts at the date of the change, it is usual to continue the accounts until the normal year-end. Then, when profit for the year has been calculated, it is necessary to apportion the profit between the two parts of the financial year, ie to split the year into the period before the change, and the period after the change. This is often done by assuming that the profit for the year has been earned at an equal rate throughout the year. The apportionment is done by dividing the appropriation account between the two time periods.

## WORKED EXAMPLE: SPLIT YEARS

### question

Raj and Sam are in partnership; their partnership agreement states:
- interest is allowed on partners' capital accounts at the rate of ten per cent per annum
- Sam receives a partnership salary of £18,000 per annum
- the balance of partnership profits and losses are shared between Raj and Sam in the ratio 2:1 respectively

At the beginning of the financial year, on 1 January 20-1, the balances of the partners' capital accounts were:

|       |          |
|-------|----------|
| Raj   | £70,000  |
| Sam   | £50,000  |

During the year ended 31 December 20-1, the net profit of the partnership was £50,500 before appropriations. The profit arose uniformly throughout the year.

On 1 October 20-1, Raj and Sam admitted Tom as a partner. Tom introduced £40,000 in capital on this date.

The partnership agreement was amended on 1 October 20-1 as follows:
- interest is allowed on partners' capital accounts at the rate of ten per cent per annum
- Sam and Tom are each to receive a partnership salary of £12,000 per annum
- the balance of partnership profits and losses are to be shared between Raj, Sam and Tom in the ratio of 2:2:1 respectively

Prepare the appropriation account of the partnership for the year.

**answer**

### PROFIT AND LOSS APPROPRIATION ACCOUNT OF RAJ, SAM AND TOM
### FOR THE YEAR ENDED 31 DECEMBER 20-1

| | 9 months to 30 September £ | 3 months to 31 December £ | Total for year £ |
|---|---|---|---|
| Net profit | 37,875 | 12,625 | 50,500 |
| | | | |
| Less appropriation of profits: | | | |
| | | | |
| Salaries: | | | |
| Sam  £18,000 pa x 9 months | 13,500 | – | |
| £12,000 pa x 3 months | | 3,000 | 16,500 |
| | | | |
| Tom  £12,000 pa x 3 months | | 3,000 | 3,000 |
| | | | |
| Interest on partners' capitals: | | | |
| Raj  £70,000 @ 10% pa x 9 months | 5,250 | – | |
| £70,000 @ 10% pa x 3 months | – | 1,750 | 7,000 |
| | | | |
| Sam  £50,000 @ 10% pa x 9 months | 3,750 | – | |
| £50,000 @ 10% pa x 3 months | – | 1,250 | 5,000 |
| | | | |
| Tom  £40,000 @ 10% pa x 3 months | – | 1,000 | 1,000 |
| | 15,375 * | 2,625 ** | 18,000 |
| | | | |
| | | | |
| Share of remaining profits: | | | |
| Raj | (2/3) 10,250 | (2/5) 1,050 | 11,300 |
| | | | |
| Sam | (1/3)  5,125 | (2/5) 1,050 | 6,175 |
| | | | |
| Tom | – | (1/5)   525 | 525 |
| | 15,375 | 2,625 | 18,000 |

*    Raj and Sam shared profits 2:1 respectively
**   Raj, Sam and Tom shared profits 2:2:1 respectively

# DISSOLUTION OF A PARTNERSHIP

There are various reasons why a partnership may come to an end:

- a partnership may be formed for a fixed term or for a specific purpose and, at the end of that term or when that purpose has been achieved, it is dissolved
- a partnership might be dissolved as a result of bankruptcy, or because a partner retires or dies and no new partners can be found to keep the firm going
- sales may fall due to changes in technology and product obsolescence, with the partners not feeling it is worthwhile to seek out and develop new products
- at the other end of the scale, the business might expand to such an extent that, in order to acquire extra capital needed for growth, the partnership may be dissolved and a limited company formed to take over its assets and liabilities.

Whatever the reason for dissolving the partnership, the accounts have to be closed. A realisation (or dissolution) account is used to record the closing transactions, and this account shows the net gain or loss that is available for distribution among the partners. The Partnership Act 1890 requires that moneys realised from the sale of assets are to be applied in the following order:

- in settlement of the firm's debts, other than those to partners
- in repayment of partners' loans
- in settlement of partners' capital and current accounts

## steps to close the books of a partnership

- Asset accounts (except for cash and bank) are closed by transfer to realisation account:
  - debit realisation (or dissolution) account
  - credit asset accounts
- Provisions accounts, eg depreciation, bad debts, are transferred to realisation account:
  - debit provision account
  - credit realisation account
- As assets are sold, the proceeds are placed to cash/bank account, and the sum recorded in realisation account:
  - debit cash/bank account
  - credit realisation account
- If a partner takes over any assets, the value is agreed and the amount is deducted from the partner's capital account and transferred to realisation account:
  - debit partner's capital account
  - credit realisation account
- As expenses of realisation are incurred, they are paid from cash/bank account and entered in realisation account:
  - debit realisation account
  - credit cash/bank account

- Creditors are paid off:
  - debit creditors' accounts
  - credit cash/bank account
- The balance of realisation account, after all assets have been sold and all creditors have been paid, represents the profit or loss on realisation, and is transferred to the partners' capital accounts in the proportion in which profits and losses are shared. If a profit has been made, the transactions are:
  - debit realisation account
  - credit partners' capital accounts

  Where a loss has been made, the entries are reversed
- Partners' loans (if any) are repaid:
  - debit partners' loan accounts
  - credit cash/bank account
- Partners' current accounts are transferred to capital accounts:
  - debit partners' current accounts
  - credit partners' capital accounts

  If a partner has a debit balance on current account, the entries will be reversed
- If any partner now has a debit balance on capital account, he or she must introduce cash to clear the balance:
  - debit cash/bank account
  - credit partner's capital account
- The remaining cash and bank balances are used to repay the credit balances on partners' capital accounts:
  - debit partners' capital accounts
  - credit cash/bank account

## WORKED EXAMPLE: DISSOLUTION OF A PARTNERSHIP

### question

Dan, Eve and Fay are in partnership, sharing profits and losses equally. As a result of falling sales they decide to dissolve the partnership as from 31 December 20-2. The balance sheet at that date is shown on the next page:

BALANCE SHEET OF DAN, EVE AND FAY AS AT 31 DECEMBER 20-2

|  | £ | £ | £ |
|---|---|---|---|
| **Fixed Assets** | Cost | Dep'n to date | Net |
| Machinery | 25,000 | 10,000 | 15,000 |
| Delivery van | 10,000 | 5,000 | 5,000 |
|  | 35,000 | 15,000 | 20,000 |
| **Current Assets** |  |  |  |
| Stock |  | 12,000 |  |
| Debtors |  | 10,000 |  |
| Bank |  | 3,000 |  |
|  |  | 25,000 |  |
| **Less Current Liabilities** |  |  |  |
| Creditors |  | 8,000 |  |
| **Working Capital** |  |  | 17,000 |
| **NET ASSETS** |  |  | 37,000 |
| **FINANCED BY** |  |  |  |
| **Capital accounts** |  |  |  |
| Dan |  |  | 13,000 |
| Eve |  |  | 12,000 |
| Fay |  |  | 12,000 |
|  |  |  | 37,000 |

The sale proceeds of the assets are machinery £12,000, stock £8,000, debtors £9,000. Dan is to take over the delivery van at an agreed valuation of £3,000. The expenses of realisation amount to £2,000. Show the realisation account, partners' capital accounts and bank account to record the dissolution of the partnership.

**answer**

| Dr | | **Realisation Account** | Cr |
|---|---|---|---|
|  | £ |  | £ |
| Machinery | 25,000 | Provisions for depreciation: | |
| Delivery van | 10,000 | machinery | 10,000 |
| Stock | 12,000 | delivery van | 5,000 |
| Debtors | 10,000 | Bank: machinery | 12,000 |
| Bank: realisation expenses | 2,000 | Bank: stock | 8,000 |
|  |  | Bank: debtors | 9,000 |
|  |  | Dan's capital account: van | 3,000 |
|  |  | Loss on realisation: | |
|  |  | Dan (one-third) | 4,000 |
|  |  | Eve (one-third) | 4,000 |
|  |  | Fay (one-third) | 4,000 |
|  | 59,000 |  | 59,000 |

| Dr | | | | **Partners' Capital Accounts** | | | | Cr |
|---|---|---|---|---|---|---|---|---|
| | Dan | Eve | Fay | | Dan | Eve | Fay |
| | £ | £ | £ | | £ | £ | £ |
| Realisation account: | | | | Balances b/d | 13,000 | 12,000 | 12,000 |
| delivery van | 3,000 | - | - | | | | |
| Realisation account: | | | | | | | |
| loss | 4,000 | 4,000 | 4,000 | | | | |
| Bank | 6,000 | 8,000 | 8,000 | | | | |
| | 13,000 | 12,000 | 12,000 | | 13,000 | 12,000 | 12,000 |

| Dr | | **Bank Account** | | Cr |
|---|---|---|---|---|
| | £ | | | £ |
| Balance b/d | 3,000 | Realisation account: expenses | | 2,000 |
| Machinery | 12,000 | Creditors | | 8,000 |
| Stock | 8,000 | Capital accounts: | | |
| Debtors | 9,000 | Dan | | 6,000 |
| | | Eve | | 8,000 |
| | | Fay | | 8,000 |
| | 32,000 | | | 32,000 |

As can be seen from the above accounts, the assets have been realised, the liabilities paid, and the balances due to the partners have been settled; the partnership has been dissolved.

# CHAPTER SUMMARY

- Goodwill is an intangible fixed asset.

- There are several methods of valuing goodwill; two commonly-used methods are:
  - average profits
  - super profits

- Goodwill should only be shown in the balance sheet when it has been purchased; it should then be:
  - either, amortised to profit and loss account over its estimated economic life
  - or, if the estimated economic life is deemed to be indefinite, the goodwill need not be amortised, provided that its continuing existence can be justified

- With partnerships, goodwill is normally calculated for transactions involving changes in the structure of the business to cover:
  - admission of a new partner
  - retirement of a partner

- death of partner
- changes in profit-sharing ratios

In accordance with the prudence concept, a goodwill account is normally created just before the change, and then deleted immediately after the change, ie it does not appear on the partnership balance sheet.

When changes take place part-way through the financial year, it is necessary to apportion the profit between the two parts of the financial year, usually by assuming that the profit has been earned at a uniform rate throughout the year.

- A revaluation account is used whenever assets are revalued prior to making changes to the personnel of the partnership.

- When a partnership is dissolved, a realisation account is used to record the sale proceeds of assets, and to calculate any profit or loss on realisation due to the partners.

In the next chapter we shall look at another form of business entity: the limited liability company. This is different from sole traders and partnerships in that it has its own corporate identity in law, and more stringent accounting requirements.

## QUESTIONS

NOTE: an asterisk (*) after the question number means that an answer to the question is given in Appendix 2.

**24.1\*** Jim and Maisie are in partnership sharing profits and losses in the ratio 3:2. At 31 December 20-1 the balances of their capital accounts are £60,000 and £40,000 respectively. Current accounts are not used by the partnership.

On 1 January 20-2, Matt is admitted into the partnership, with a new profit-sharing ratio of 3:2:1. Goodwill has been agreed at a valuation of £48,000. Matt will bring £28,000 of cash into the business as his capital and premium for goodwill.

For the year ended 31 December 20-2, the partnership profits amount to £60,000, and the partners' drawings were:

|  | £ |
|---|---|
| Jim | 12,000 |
| Maisie | 12,000 |
| Matt | 8,000 |

Jim retired on 1 January 20-3 and the firm's goodwill was then agreed to be worth £72,000. His capital and his share of the goodwill were left as a loan to the firm. Maisie and Matt agreed to share future profits and losses in the ratio 2:1.

You are to show the partners' capital accounts for the period from 31 December 20-1 to 1 January 20-3.

24.2 Northwood and Varley are in partnership sharing profits and losses in a 3:2 ratio. Their partnership balance sheet at 31 December Year 8, the end of the financial year, is as follows:

| Fixed Assets | £ | £ |
|---|---|---|
| Goodwill | 18,000 | |
| Buildings | 72,200 | |
| Fixtures and fittings | 21,800 | |
| | | 112,000 |
| **Current Assets** | | |
| Stock | 12,720 | |
| Debtors | 15,300 | |
| Cash at bank | 8,080 | |
| | 36,100 | |
| **Amounts due within 1 year** | | |
| **(Current Liabilities)** | | |
| Creditors | 7,400 | |
| | | 28,700 |
| | | 140,700 |
| **Capital Accounts** | | |
| Northwood | 82,000 | |
| Varley | 52,000 | |
| | | 134,000 |
| **Current Accounts** | | |
| Northwood | 4,360 | |
| Varley | 2,340 | |
| | | 6,700 |
| | | 140,700 |

On 31 December Year 8, Northwood decided to retire. On that date:

(1)    Goodwill was valued at £23,000.

(2)    The buildings were valued at £80,000.

(3)    An amount of £1,200, owed by a debtor, was considered to be irrecoverable, and this balance was written off.

(4)    The stock valuation of £12,720 included 100 items at their cost price of £12 each. Their selling price on 31 December Year 8 was £9 each.

On 1 January Year 9 Varley admitted Rodger to the partnership. The new partnership agreement was that profits and losses should be shared in a 4:1 ratio. At the commencement of the new partnership, Rodger introduced the following assets:

|  | £ |
|---|---|
| Car | 12,000 |
| Cash banked | 40,000 |
| Goodwill | 8,000 |

On the day he retired, Northwood agreed to provide a loan of £50,000 to the new partnership, repayable in 3 years. This was provided from the amount owing to him from the partnership with Varley. Any balance due to him from the partnership, after making the loan, was immediately paid by cheque.

From the commencement of their partnership, Varley and Rodger agreed not to show any goodwill in their partnership books.

You are required to prepare the following:

(a)     the revaluation account for the Northwood and Varley partnership

(b)     the partnership bank account

(c)     the partnership goodwill account

(d)     the balance sheet at 1 January Year 9 for the Varley and Rodger partnership

*LCCI Examinations Board*

24.3*   Cedar, Elm and Pine were in partnership, sharing profits and losses equally. The balance sheet of the business at 31 December Year 13 is shown below:

| Fixed Assets | £ | £ | £ |
|---|---|---|---|
| Land and buildings |  |  | 901,080 |
| Equipment |  |  | 154,790 |
| Vehicles |  |  | 36,130 |
|  |  |  | 1,092,000 |
| Current Assets |  |  |  |
| Stock |  | 74,000 |  |
| Debtors |  | 102,000 |  |
|  |  | 176,000 |  |
| Less Current Liabilities |  |  |  |
| Trade creditors | 182,800 |  |  |
| Bank overdraft | 613,300 |  |  |
|  |  | 796,100 |  |
|  |  |  | (620,100) |
|  |  |  | 471,900 |

|  |  |  |
|---|---:|---:|
| Capital Accounts | | |
| Cedar | | 140,000 |
| Elm | | 70,000 |
| Pine | | 42,000 |
| | | 252,000 |
| | | |
| Current Accounts | | |
| Cedar | 10,000 | |
| Elm | 16,000 | |
| Pine | (6,100) | 19,900 |
| Loan account – Cedar | | 200,000 |
| | | 471,900 |

Following trading losses, the partners dissolved the partnership and entered into an arrangement with Meredew Limited.

The terms of the arrangement were:

(1)  Meredew Ltd purchased the land and buildings, the equipment, three of the vehicles and the stock for a total of £1,030,000.

(2)  Meredew Ltd paid £908,000 into the partnership bank account. The balance of the purchase consideration was settled in ordinary shares in Meredew Ltd.

The partnership paid the amounts due to creditors and repaid the loan from Cedar.

The partnership collected all the amounts due from debtors, with the exception of £12,400 which was written off as bad debts. Partnership dissolution expenses amounted to £1,500.

The remaining vehicle was taken over by Elm at an agreed valuation of £8,000.

Pine was unable to contribute any funds to the dissolution. Any debit balance on capital account which a partner could not make good was to be borne by the other partners in proportion to their capital balances at 31 December Year 13.

You are required to prepare the following accounts to close the books of the partnership at 31 December Year 13:

(a)  dissolution account

(b)  capital accounts in columnar form

(c)  Meredew Ltd

(d)  bank

*LCCI Examinations Board*

# 25 LIMITED COMPANY ACCOUNTS

In the last two chapters we looked at the accounting requirements of partnerships. In this chapter we turn our attention to the limited company and look at:

- the advantages of forming a limited company
- the differences between a private limited company, a public limited company, and a company limited by guarantee
- the information contained in a company's Memorandum of Association and its Articles of Association
- the differences between ordinary shares and preference shares
- the concept of reserves, and the difference between capital reserves and revenue reserves
- the appropriation section of a company's profit and loss account
- the layout of a company's balance sheet

## ADVANTAGES OF FORMING A LIMITED COMPANY

A limited company is a separate legal entity, owned by shareholders and run by directors.

The limited company is often chosen as the legal status of a business for a number of reasons:

### limited liability

The shareholders (members) of a company can only lose the amount of their investment, being the money paid already, together with any money unpaid on their shares (unpaid instalments on new share issues, for example). Thus, if the company became insolvent (went 'bust'), shareholders would have to pay any unpaid instalments to help repay the creditors. As this is an unlikely occurance, shareholders are in a very safe position: their personal assets, unless pledged as security to a lender, are not available to the company's creditors.

### separate legal entity

A limited company is a separate legal entity from its owners. Anyone taking legal action proceeds against the company and not the individual shareholders.

### ability to raise finance

A limited company can raise substantial funds from outside sources by the issue of shares:

- for the larger public company – from the public on the Stock Exchange or the Alternative Investment Market

- for the smaller company privately from Venture Capital companies, relatives and friends

Companies can also raise finance by means of debentures (see page 406).

## membership

A member of a limited company is a person who owns at least one share in that company. The minimum number of members is two, but there is no upper limit. A member of a company is the same as a shareholder.

## other factors

A limited company is usually a much larger business unit than a sole trader or partnership. This gives the company a higher standing and status in the business community, allows it to benefit from economies of scale, and makes it of sufficient size to employ specialists for functions such as production, marketing, finance and personnel.

# THE COMPANIES ACT

Limited companies are regulated by the Companies Act 1985, as amended by the Companies Act 1989. Under the terms of the 1985 Act there are two main types of limited company: the larger public limited company (abbreviated to 'Plc'), which is defined in the Act, and the smaller company, traditionally known as a private limited company (abbreviated to 'Ltd'), which is any other limited company. A further type of company is limited by guarantee.

## public limited company (Plc)

A company may become a public limited company if it has:

- issued share capital of over £50,000
- at least two members (shareholders) and at least two directors

A public limited company may raise capital from the public on the Stock Exchange or the Alternative Investment Market, and the new issues and privatisations of recent years are examples of this.
A public limited company does not have to issue shares on the stock markets, and not all do so.

## private limited company (Ltd)

The private limited company is the most common form of limited company. The term private is not set out in the Companies Act 1985, but it is a traditional description, and well describes the smaller company, often in family ownership. A private limited company has:

- no minimum requirement for issued share capital
- at least two members (shareholders) and at least one director

The shares are not traded publicly, but are transferable between individuals, although valuation will be more difficult for shares not quoted on the stock markets.

## company limited by guarantee

A company limited by guarantee is not formed with share capital, but relies on the guarantee of its members to pay a stated amount in the event of the company's insolvency. Examples of such companies include charities and artistic organisations.

# GOVERNING DOCUMENTS OF COMPANIES

There are a number of documents required by the Companies Act in the setting-up of a company. Two essential governing documents are the Memorandum of Association and the Articles of Association.

The Memorandum of Association, the constitution of the company, regulates the affairs of the company to the outside world and contains five main clauses:

1. name of the company (together with the words 'public limited company' or 'limited', as appropriate)
2. capital of the company (the amount that can be issued in shares: the authorised share capital)
3. 'objects' of the company, ie what activities the company can engage in; under the Companies Act the objects can be stated as being those of 'a general commercial company', ie the company can engage in any commercial activity
4. registered office of the company (not the address, but whether it is registered in England and Wales, or in Scotland)
5. a statement that the liability of the members is limited

Articles of Association, regulate the internal administration of the company, including the powers of directors and the holding of company meetings.

# ACCOUNTING REQUIREMENTS OF THE COMPANIES ACT

The Companies Act 1985 (as amended by the Companies Act 1989) not only requires the production of accounts, but also states the detailed information that must be disclosed. For larger companies the accounts are audited by external auditors – this is a costly and time-consuming exercise (smaller and medium-sized companies are often exempt from audit). The accounts must be submitted within nine months of the financial year-end to Companies House, where they are available for public inspection. A copy of the accounts is available to all shareholders, together with a report on the company's activities during the year.

In this chapter we will study the 'internal use' accounts, rather than being concerned with the detailed accounting requirements of the Companies Act. It might be that, as part of your future accounting studies, you will study the preparation of such 'published accounts', as they are often known.

Before we examine the financial statements in detail we will look first at the principal ways in which a company raises finance: shares. There are different types of shares which appear in a company's balance sheet as the company's share capital.

# TYPES OF SHARES ISSUED BY LIMITED COMPANIES

The authorised share capital is stated in the Memorandum of Association and is the maximum share capital that the company is allowed to issue. The authorised share capital may not be the same as the issued share capital; under company law the issued capital cannot exceed the amount authorised. If a company which has issued the full extent of its authorised share capital wishes to make an increase, it must first pass the appropriate resolution at a general meeting of the shareholders.

The authorised and issued share capital may be divided into a number of classes or types of share; the main types are ordinary shares and, less commonly, preference shares. These shares usually carry voting rights – thus shareholders have a say at the annual general meeting and at any other shareholders' meetings.

## ordinary (equity) shares

These are the most commonly issued class of share which carry the main 'risks and rewards' of the business: the risks are of losing part or all of the value of the shares if the business loses money or becomes insolvent; the rewards are that they take a share of the profits – in the form of dividends – after allowance has been made for all expenses of the business, including loan interest, taxation, and after preference dividends (if any). When a company makes large profits, it will have the ability to pay higher dividends to the ordinary shareholders; when losses are made, the ordinary shareholders may receive no dividend.

Companies rarely pay out all of their profits in the form of dividends; most retain some profits as reserves. These can always be used to enable a dividend to be paid in a year when the company makes little or no profit, always assuming that the company has sufficient cash in the bank to make the payment. Ordinary shareholders, in the event of the company becoming insolvent, will be the last to receive any repayment of their investment: other creditors will be paid off first.

## preference shares

Preference shares usually carry a fixed percentage rate of dividend – for example, ten per cent of nominal value. Their dividends are paid in preference to those of ordinary shareholders; but they are only paid if the company makes profits. In the event of the company ceasing to trade, the 'preference' will also extend to repayment of capital before the ordinary shareholders.

## nominal and market values of shares

Each share has a nominal value – or face value – which is entered in the accounts. Shares may be issued with nominal values of 5p, 10p, 25p, 50p or £1, or indeed for any amount. Thus a company with an authorised share capital of £100,000 might state in its Memorandum of Association that this is divided up into:

| | |
|---|---:|
| 100,000 ordinary shares of 50p each | £50,000 |
| 50,000 ten per cent preference shares of £1 each | £50,000 |
| | £100,000 |

The nominal value usually bears little relationship to the market value . This is the price at which issued – or 'secondhand' – shares are traded. Share prices of a quoted public limited company may be listed in the Financial Times.

## issue price

This is the price at which shares are issued to shareholders by the company – either when the company is being set up, or at a later date when it needs to raise more funds. The issue price is either at par (ie the nominal value), or above nominal value. In the latter case, the amount of the difference between issue price and nominal value is known as a share premium: for example – nominal value £1.00; issue price £1.50; therefore share premium is 50p per share.

## LOANS AND DEBENTURES

In addition to money provided by shareholders, who are the owners of the company, further funds can be obtained by borrowing in the form of loans or debentures. Both loans and debentures usually carry a fixed rate of interest that must be paid, just like other business expenses, whether a company makes profits or not. As loan and debenture interest is a business expense, this is shown in the profit and loss account along with all other expenses. In the event of the company ceasing to trade, loan and debenture-holders would be repaid before any shareholders.

## TRADING AND PROFIT AND LOSS ACCOUNT

A limited company uses the same form of financial statements as a sole trader or partnership. However there are two expense items commonly found in the profit and loss account of a limited company that are not found in those of other business types:

- directors' remuneration – ie amounts paid to directors; as directors are employed by the company, their pay appears amongst the expenses of the company
- debenture interest – as already noted, when debentures are issued by companies, the interest is shown as an expense in the profit and loss account

A limited company follows the profit and loss account with an appropriation section to show how the net profit has been distributed. The diagram on pages 408 and 409 shows an example of a limited company's trading and profit and loss account. (See also Appendix 1 for a specimen format.)

## BALANCE SHEET

Balance sheets of limited companies follow the same layout as those we have seen earlier, but the capital section is more complex because of the different classes of shares that may be issued, and the various reserves. The diagram on pages 410 and 411 shows the balance sheet of Orion Limited as an example.

# RESERVES

A limited company rarely distributes all its profits to its shareholders. Instead, it will often keep part of the profits earned each year in the form of reserves. As the balance sheet of Orion Limited shows (page 411), there are two types of reserves:

- capital reserves, which are created as a result of a non-trading profit
- revenue reserves, which are retained profits from profit and loss account

## capital reserves

Examples of capital reserves (which cannot be used to fund dividend payments) include:

- **Revaluation reserve**. This occurs when a fixed asset, most probably property, is revalued in the balance sheet. The amount of the revaluation is placed in a revaluation reserve where it increases the value of the shareholders' investment in the company. Note, however, that this is purely a 'book' adjustment – no cash has changed hands.

  For example, the following company revalues its property from £500,000 to £750,000.

### Balance sheet (extracts)

| | £ |
|---|---|
| Before revaluation | |
| Fixed asset: property at cost | 500,000 |
| Share capital: ordinary shares of £1 each | 500,000 |
| After revaluation | |
| Fixed asset: property at revaluation | 750,000 |
| Share capital: ordinary shares of £1 each | 500,000 |
| Capital reserve: revaluation reserve | 250,000 |
| | 750,000 |

- **Share premium account**. An established company may issue additional shares to the public at a higher amount than the nominal value. For example, Orion Ltd (page 411) seeks finance for further expansion by issuing additional ordinary shares. Although the shares have a nominal value of £1 each, because Orion is a well-established company, the shares are issued at £1.50 each. Of this amount, £1 is recorded in the issued share capital section, and the extra 50p is the share premium.

## revenue reserves

These are often left as the balance of the appropriation section of the profit and loss account: this balance is commonly described as 'profit and loss account balance' or 'balance of retained profits'. Alternatively, they may be transferred from the appropriation section to a named revenue reserve account, such as general reserve, or a revenue reserve for a specific purpose, such as reserve for the replacement of machinery. Transfers to or from these named revenue reserve accounts are made in the appropriation section of the profit and loss account.

## reserves: profits not cash

It should be noted that reserves – both capital and revenue – are not a cash fund to be used whenever the company needs money, but are in fact represented by assets shown on the balance sheet. The reserves record the fact that the assets belong to the shareholders via their ownership of the company.

## EXAMPLE ACCOUNTS

On the next four pages are set out the trading and profit and loss account and balance sheet for Orion Limited, a private limited company. Explanations of the financial statements are set out on the left- hand page.

The **expenses** of a limited company include directors' remuneration and interest paid on debentures (if debentures have been issued).

The company has recorded a **net profit** of £43,000 in its profit and loss account – this is brought into the appropriation section.

**Corporation tax**, the tax that a company has to pay, based on its profits, is shown in the appropriation section. We shall not be studying the calculations for corporation tax in this book. It is, however, important to see how the tax is recorded in the financial statements.

The company has already paid **interim dividends** on the two classes of shares it has in issue (ordinary shares and preference shares); these would, most probably, have been paid just over half-way through the company's financial year. The company also proposes to pay a **final dividend** to its shareholders: these will be paid in the early part of the next financial year. Note that a dividend is often expressed as an amount per share, based on the nominal value, eg 5p per £1 nominal value share (which is the same as a five per cent dividend).

Added to **net profit** is a **balance** of £41,000. This represents profits of the company from previous years that have not been distributed as dividends. Note that the appropriation section shows a balance of retained profits at the year-end of £50,000. Such retained profits form a revenue reserve (see page 407) of the company.

**ORION LIMITED**
# TRADING AND PROFIT AND LOSS ACCOUNT
## for the year ended 31 December 20-7

|  | £ | £ |
|---|---:|---:|
| Sales | | 725,000 |
| Opening stock | 45,000 | |
| Purchases | <u>381,000</u> | |
| | 426,000 | |
| Less closing stock | <u>50,000</u> | |
| Cost of Goods Sold | | <u>376,000</u> |
| **Gross Profit** | | 349,000 |
| | | |
| Less expenses: | | |
|     Directors' remuneration | 75,000 | |
|     Debenture interest | 6,000 | |
|     Other overheads | <u>225,000</u> | |
| | | <u>306,000</u> |
| **Net profit for year before taxation** | | 43,000 |
| Less corporation tax | | <u>15,000</u> |
| Profit for year after taxation | | 28,000 |
| | | |
| Less  interim dividends paid | | |
|     ordinary shares | 5,000 | |
|     preference shares | 2,000 | |
|     final dividends proposed | | |
|     ordinary shares | 10,000 | |
|     preference shares | <u>2,000</u> | |
| | | <u>19,000</u> |
| Retained profit for year | | 9,000 |
| Add balance of retained profits at beginning of year | | <u>41,000</u> |
| Balance of retained profits at end of year | | <u>50,000</u> |

Limited company balance sheets usually distinguish between:

**intangible fixed assets**, which do not have material substance but belong to the company and have value, eg goodwill (the amount paid for the reputation and connections of a business that has been taken over), patents and trademarks; intangible fixed assets are depreciated (or amortised, in the case of goodwill) in the same way as tangible fixed assets.

**tangible fixed assets**, which have material substance, such as premises, equipment, vehicles.

As well as the usual **current liabilities**, for limited companies, this section also contains the amount of proposed dividends (but not dividends that have been paid in the year) and the amount of corporation tax to be paid within the next twelve months. The amounts for both of these items are also included in the appropriation section of the profit and loss account.

**Long-term liabilities** are those that are due to be repaid more than twelve months from the date of the balance sheet, eg loans and debentures.

**Authorised share capital** is included on the balance sheet 'for information', but is not added into the balance sheet total, as it may not be the same amount as the issued share capital.

**Issued share capital** shows the classes and number of shares that have been issued. In this balance sheet, the shares are described as being fully paid, meaning that the company has received the full amount of the value of each share from the shareholders. Sometimes shares will be partly paid, eg ordinary shares of £1, but 75p paid. This means that the company can make a call on the shareholders to pay the extra 25p to make the shares fully paid.

**Capital reserves** are created as a result of non-trading profit.

**Revenue reserves** are retained profits from profit and loss account.

The total for **shareholders' funds** represents the stake of the shareholders in the company. It comprises share capital (ordinary and preference shares), plus reserves (capital and revenue reserves).

## ORION LIMITED
### Balance sheet as at 31 December 20-7

| Fixed Assets | Cost £ | Dep'n to date £ | Net £ |
|---|---|---|---|
| *Intangible* | | | |
| Goodwill | 50,000 | 20,000 | 30,000 |
| *Tangible* | | | |
| Freehold land and buildings | 180,000 | 20,000 | 160,000 |
| Machinery | 230,000 | 90,000 | 140,000 |
| Fixtures and fittings | 100,000 | 25,000 | 75,000 |
| | 560,000 | 155,000 | 405,000 |

| Current Assets | | | |
|---|---|---|---|
| Stock | | 50,000 | |
| Debtors | | 38,000 | |
| Bank | | 22,000 | |
| Cash | | 2,000 | |
| | | 112,000 | |

| Less Current Liabilities | | | |
|---|---|---|---|
| Creditors | 30,000 | | |
| Proposed dividends | 12,000 | | |
| Corporation tax | 15,000 | | |
| | | 57,000 | |
| **Working Capital** | | | 55,000 |
| | | | 460,000 |

| Less Long-term Liabilities | | | |
|---|---|---|---|
| 10% debentures | | | 60,000 |
| **NET ASSETS** | | | 400,000 |

| FINANCED BY: | | |
|---|---|---|
| **Authorised Share Capital** | | |
| 100,000 10% preference shares of £1 each | | 100,000 |
| 600,000 ordinary shares of £1 each | | 600,000 |
| | | 700,000 |

| **Issued Share Capital** | | |
|---|---|---|
| 40,000 10% preference shares of £1 each, fully paid | | 40,000 |
| 300,000 ordinary shares of £1 each, fully paid | | 300,000 |
| | | 340,000 |

| **Capital Reserve** | | |
|---|---|---|
| Share premium account | | 10,000 |

| **Revenue Reserve** | | |
|---|---|---|
| Profit and loss account | | 50,000 |
| **SHAREHOLDERS' FUNDS** | | 400,000 |

# CHAPTER SUMMARY

● A limited company has a separate legal entity from its owners.

● A company is regulated by the Companies Act 1985 (as amended by the Companies Act 1989), and is owned by shareholders and managed by directors.

● A limited company may be either a public limited company or a private limited company.

● The liability of shareholders is limited to any money unpaid on their shares.

● The main types of shares that may be issued by companies are ordinary shares and preference shares.

● Borrowings in the form of loans and debentures are a further source of finance.

● The final accounts of a company include an appropriation section, which follows the profit and loss account.

● The balance sheet of a limited company is similar to that of sole traders and partnerships but the capital and reserves section reflects the ownership of the company by its shareholders:
  – a statement of the authorised and issued share capital
  – details of capital reserves and revenue reserves

In the next chapter we continue with the year-end accounts of businesses and look at the layout used when firms buy in raw materials and manufacture products which are then sold as finished goods.

# QUESTIONS

NOTE: an asterisk (*) after the question number means that an answer to the question is given in Appendix 2.

**25.1**  Mason Motors Limited is a second-hand car business. The following information is available for the year ended 31 December 20-1:

- balance of retained profits from previous years stands at £100,000

- net profit for the year was £75,000

- it has been agreed that a transfer to a general reserve of £20,000 is to be made

- corporation tax of £20,050 is to be paid on the year's profit

- it has been agreed that a dividend of 10% is to be paid on the issued share capital of £100,000

You are to:

(a)  Set out the appropriation section of the profit and loss account for Mason Motors Limited for the year ended 31 December 20-1.

(b)  One of the directors of the company asks if the £20,000 being transferred to general reserve could be used to rebuild the garage forecourt. How would you reply?

**25.2\***  The following figures are taken from the accounting records of Jobseekers Limited, a recruitment agency, at the end of the financial year on 31 December 20-6:

|  | £ |
|---|---|
| Issued share capital (£1 ordinary shares) | 100,000 |
| Premises at cost | 175,000 |
| Depreciation of premises to date | 10,500 |
| Office equipment at cost | 25,000 |
| Depreciation of office equipment to date | 5,000 |
| Goodwill at cost | 20,000 |
| Amortisation of goodwill to date | 6,000 |
| Stock at 31 December 20-6 | 750 |
| Debtors | 42,500 |
| Creditors | 7,250 |
| Bank overdraft | 13,950 |
| Bank loan | 55,000 |
| Net profit for year before taxation | 68,200 |
| Corporation tax for the year | 14,850 |
| Interim ordinary dividend paid | 10,000 |
| Final ordinary dividend proposed | 40,000 |
| Retained profit at 1 January 20-6 | 7,350 |

You are to prepare the appropriation section of the profit and loss account (starting with net profit) for the year ended 31 December 20-6, together with a balance sheet at that date.

**25.3\***  BRT Limited has an authorised capital of 500,000 ordinary shares of £1 each, of which 300,000 are issued and 50,000 6% preference shares of £1 each, of which 30,000 are issued.

The net profit for the year ended 30 June 20-7 was £132,880 and the balance on the appropriation account at 1 July 20-6 was £72,730.

The directors resolved:
- (i) to put £95,500 into a new General Reserve
- (ii) to pay the preference dividend
- (iii) to recommend an ordinary dividend of 5p per share

In addition to the liabilities arising from the appropriation account, there were general creditors of £55,800. Fixed assets totalled £447,000 and current assets were £144,410.
You are required to prepare the appropriation account and balance sheet of the company as at 30 June 20-7.

*Reproduced by kind permission of OCR Examinations*

**25.4\*** The following trial balance was extracted from the books of Sidbury Trading Co. Ltd., a local stationery supplies firm, as at 31 December 20-2:

|  | £ | £ |
|---|---|---|
| Share capital | | 240,000 |
| Freehold land and buildings at cost | 142,000 | |
| Vans at cost | 55,000 | |
| Provision for depreciation on vans at 1 January 20 2 | | 21,800 |
| Purchases and sales | 189,273 | 297,462 |
| Rent and rates | 4,000 | |
| General expenses | 9,741 | |
| Wages and salaries | 34,689 | |
| Bad debts written off | 948 | |
| Provision for doubtful debts at 1 January 20-2 | | 1,076 |
| Directors' salaries | 25,000 | |
| Debtors and creditors | 26,482 | 14,555 |
| Value Added Tax | | 2,419 |
| Retained profit at 1 January 20-2 | | 18,397 |
| Stock at 1 January 20-2 | 42,618 | |
| Bank | 65,958 | |
| | 595,709 | 595,709 |

You are given the following additional information:

- The authorised share capital is 300,000 ordinary shares of £1 each; all the shares which have been issued are fully paid
- Wages and salaries outstanding at 31 December 20-2 amounted to £354
- The provision for doubtful debts is to be increased by £124
- Stock at 31 December 20-2 is valued at £47,288
- Rent and rates amounting to £400 were paid in advance at 31 December 20-2
- It is proposed to pay a dividend of £8,000 for 20-2
- Depreciation on vans is to be charged at the rate of 20 per cent per annum on cost
- Corporation tax of £12,000 is to be provided for

You are to prepare appropriate final accounts for the year 20-2, together with a balance sheet at 31 December 20-2.

**25.5** Playfair Ltd has an authorised share capital of 50,000 ordinary shares of £1 each and 10,000 8% preference shares of £1 each. At 31 December 20-3, the following trial balance was extracted:

|  | £ | £ |
|---|---:|---:|
| Ordinary share capital |  | 50,000 |
| 8% preference share capital |  | 8,000 |
| Plant and machinery at cost | 34,000 |  |
| Motor vehicles at cost | 16,000 |  |
| Debtors and creditors | 34,980 | 15,900 |
| Value Added Tax |  | 1,970 |
| Bank | 14,505 |  |
| 10% debentures |  | 9,000 |
| Stock (1 January 20-3) | 25,200 |  |
| General expenses | 11,020 |  |
| Purchases and sales | 164,764 | 233,384 |
| Bad debts written off | 2,400 |  |
| Debenture interest | 900 |  |
| Discounts | 325 | 640 |
| Salaries | 24,210 |  |
| Insurance | 300 |  |
| Provision for depreciation: |  |  |
| plant and machinery |  | 16,000 |
| motor vehicles |  | 7,200 |
| Directors' fees | 17,000 |  |
| Interim preference dividend paid | 320 |  |
| Profit and loss account  (1 January 20-3) |  | 3,300 |
| Provision for bad debts (1 January 20-3) |  | 530 |
|  | 345,924 | 345,924 |

Additional information:

- Stock at 31 December 20-3 is valued at £28,247
- Depreciation on plant and machinery is to be provided for at the rate of 10 per cent per annum calculated on cost
- Depreciation on motor vehicles is to be provided for at the rate of 20 per cent per annum using the reducing balance method
- Insurance prepaid at 31 December 20-3 amounted to £60
- General expenses owing at 31 December 20-3 amounted to £110
- The provision for bad debts is to be increased to £750

- The directors propose to pay an ordinary dividend of 6 per cent to the ordinary shareholders and to pay the remaining dividend due to the preference shareholders • £2,000 is to be transferred to General Reserve
- Corporation tax of £4,000 is to be provided for

You are to prepare appropriate final accounts for the year ended 31 December 20-3, together with a balance sheet at that date.

25.6   A list of balances extracted from the ledgers of Albermane Ltd were as follows as at 31 December 20-6:

|  | £ |
|---|---|
| Profit and loss account to 31 December 20-6 | 151,000 |
| General reserve to 31 December 20-5 | 31,000 |
| Undistributed profits to 31 December 20-5 | 48,000 |
| Balance at bank (Dr) | 23,000 |
| Cash in hand | 6,000 |
| Deposit account at bank | 4,000 |
| Fixtures at cost | 141,000 |
| Provision for depreciation on fixtures | 30,500 |
| Vehicles at cost | 20,000 |
| Provision for depreciation on vehicles | 5,000 |
| Debtors' control account | 101,000 |
| Creditors' control account | 94,000 |
| Prepayments | 4,500 |
| Stock | 360,000 |
| Ordinary shares at £1 | 180,000 |
| 6% Preference shares | 100,000 |
| 6% Debentures | 20,000 |

The directors have declared a full dividend on the preference shares and a full and final ordinary share dividend of 5% of the net profit for the year ended 31 December 20-6, and have proposed a further £15,000 be transferred to general reserve. Debenture interest of £1,200 was also paid in the year.

You are required to:

(a)   prepare the profit and loss appropriation account of Albermane Ltd to 31  December 20-6

(b)   prepare a balance sheet as at 31 December 20-6

(c)   explain briefly why the 'reserves' of the company are greater than the cash and bank totals.

*Reproduced by kind permission of OCR Examinations*

**Chapters 23 - 25**

# MULTIPLE CHOICE QUESTIONS

Read each question carefully.
Choose the one answer you think is correct (calculators may be needed).
The answers are on page 568.

1     In the absence of a partnership agreement, which one of the following contravenes the provisions of the Partnership Act 1890?

A     no partner is entitled to a salary
B     profits and losses are to be shared in proportion to capital
C     partners are not entitled to receive interest on their capital
D     interest is not to be charged on partners' drawings

2     A partnership may choose to over-ride some or all of the accounting rules in the Partnership Act 1890 by the partners entering into a separate:

A     appropriation account
B     memorandum of association
C     partnership agreement
D     articles of association

3     Profits of a two-person partnership are £32,800 before the following are taken into account:

• interest on partners' capital accounts, £1,800
• interest on partners' drawings, £200
• salary of one partner, £10,000

If the remaining profits are shared equally, how much will each partner receive?

A     £10,600
B     £11,400
C     £12,200
D     £16,400

**4** Where changes in partnerships take place, a goodwill account is opened, usually temporarily. After the change has taken place, goodwill account is usually written off. This follows the accounting concept of:

A     prudence

B     accruals

C     going concern

D     consistency

**5** A final debit balance on a partnership realisation account means that there is:

A     an error in the book-keeping records

B     a profit on realisation

C     goodwill

D     a loss on realisation

**6** On dissolution of a partnership, the Partnership Act 1890 requires that moneys realised from the sale of assets are to be applied first to:

A     settlement of partners' current accounts

B     repayments of partners' loans

C     settlement of partners' capital accounts

D     settlement of the firm's debts

**7** Which one of the following does not appear in the appropriation section of the profit and loss account of a limited company?

A     corporation tax

B     proposed dividends

C     directors' remuneration

D     balance of retained profits

**8** In the final accounts of a limited company debenture interest is:

A     debited in the trading account

B     debited in the profit and loss account

C     debited in the appropriation section of the profit and loss account

D     shown as a long-term liability in the balance sheet

**9**     Reserves in a company belong to the:

A     ordinary shareholders

B     directors

C     debenture holders

D     creditors

**10**    Revenue reserves in a limited company balance sheet are:

A     the difference between the cost and book value of fixed assets

B     amount of proposed dividends

C     the total of provisions for depreciation and bad debts

D     profit retained in the business

**11**    Which one of the following is not a revenue reserve?

A     general reserve

B     revaluation reserve

C     reserve for the replacement of machinery

D     profit and loss account

**12**    Which one of the following is not included in shareholders' funds?

A     ordinary share capital

B     debentures

C     preference share capital

D     capital reserves

# 26 MANUFACTURING ACCOUNTS

In previous chapters we have concerned ourselves with the accounts of businesses that trade, ie buy and sell goods without carrying out a manufacturing process. However, many firms buy raw materials and manufacture products which are then sold as finished goods. The final accounts for a manufacturer include a manufacturing account which brings together all the elements of cost making up the production cost. In this chapter we will:

- consider the manufacturing process
- study the elements of cost
- prepare a manufacturing account

## THE MANUFACTURING PROCESS AND ELEMENTS OF COST

The diagram below shows, in outline, the manufacturing process and the costs incurred at each stage.

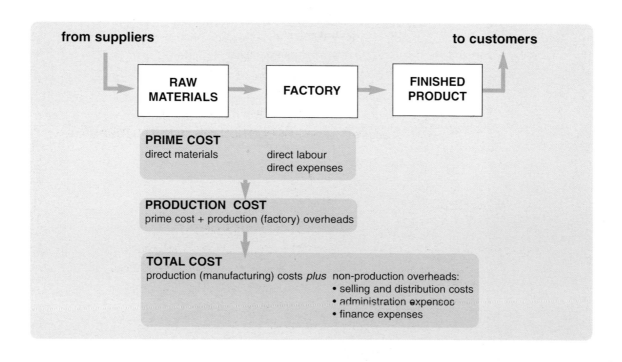

Note that there are four main elements of cost which make up the manufacturing (or production) cost:

1  **direct materials** – the raw materials that are required in manufacturing the finished product
2  **direct labour** – this is the cost of the workforce engaged in production, eg machine operators (note that the wages of factory supervisors are a production overhead and are usually described as 'indirect labour')
3  **direct expenses** – these include any special costs that can be identified with each unit produced, eg a royalty payable to the designer of the product for each unit made, or the hire of specialist machinery to carry out a particular manufacturing task
4  **production (factory) overheads** – all the other costs of manufacture, eg wages of supervisors, rent of factory, depreciation of factory machinery, heating and lighting of factory

Prime cost is the basic cost of manufacturing a product before the addition of production overheads. It consists of the first three costs, ie

*direct materials + direct labour + direct expenses = prime cost*

Production cost is the factory cost of making the product after the addition of production overheads, and is:

*prime cost + production (factory) overheads = production (or manufacturing) cost*

## Manufacturing Account

The final accounts of a manufacturer are structured as follows:

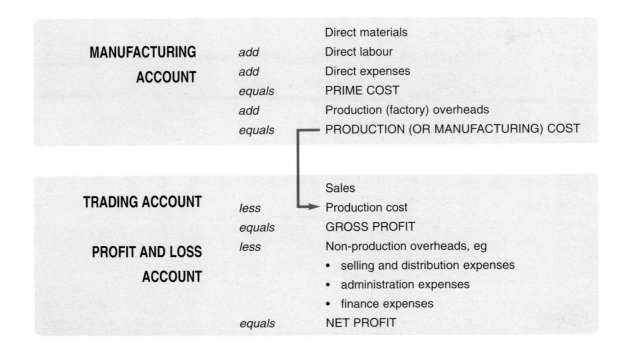

The layout of a manufacturing, trading and profit and loss account (with figures) is shown below. Study the format and read the notes that follow.

---

**ALPHA MANUFACTURING COMPANY**
**MANUFACTURING, TRADING AND PROFIT AND LOSS ACCOUNT**
**for the year ended 31 December 20-2**

| | £ | £ |
|---|---|---|
| Opening stock of raw materials | | 5,000 |
| Add Purchases of raw materials | | 50,000 |
| | | 55,000 |
| Less Closing stock of raw materials | | 6,000 |
| COST OF RAW MATERIALS USED | | 49,000 |
| Direct labour | | 26,000 |
| Direct expenses | | 2,500 |
| PRIME COST | | 77,500 |
| Add     Production (factory) overheads: | | |
| Indirect materials | 2,000 | |
| Indirect labour | 16,000 | |
| Rent of factory | 5,000 | |
| Depreciation of factory machinery | 10,000 | |
| Factory light and heat | 4,000 | |
| | | 37,000 |
| | | 114,500 |
| Add Opening stock of work-in-progress | | 4,000 |
| | | 118,500 |
| Less Closing stock of work-in-progress | | 3,000 |
| PRODUCTION (OR MANUFACTURING) COST OF GOODS COMPLETED | | 115,500 |
| | | |
| Sales | | 195,500 |
| Opening stock of finished goods | 6,500 | |
| Production (or manufacturing) cost of goods completed | 115,500 | |
| | 122,000 | |
| Less Closing stock of finished goods | 7,500 | |
| COST OF GOODS SOLD | | 114,500 |
| **Gross profit** | | 81,000 |
| Less Non-production overheads: | | |
| Selling and distribution expenses | 38,500 | |
| Administration expenses | 32,000 | |
| Finance expenses | 3,500 | |
| | | 74,000 |
| **Net profit** | | 7,000 |

## notes

- Production cost (or manufacturing cost) is the final figure of the manufacturing account.
- A manufacturing account forms one part of the year-end accounts for a manufacturing business, and precedes the trading account. The latter is prepared in the usual way except that production cost takes the place of purchases. However, some businesses both manufacture goods and buy in finished goods, in which case the figures will be shown for both production cost and purchases of goods for resale.
- In the trading account, the opening and closing stocks are the finished goods held by a business.
- Manufacturing businesses usually hold stocks of goods in three different forms:
  - raw materials: commodities and components purchased from suppliers required in manufacturing the finished product
  - work-in-progress: products in course of manufacture at a particular moment in time
  - finished goods: products on which the manufacturing process has been completed and which are ready for sale

Note that, with raw materials, there may be the cost of carriage in to be added, and an amount for purchases returns to be deducted.

The first two stocks appear in the manufacturing account, while finished goods stock is in the trading account.

- Certain expenses might be apportioned between the manufacturing account and the profit and loss account – for example, rates might be apportioned two-thirds to the factory (production overhead) and one-third to the office (non-production overhead).
- The balance sheet follows on from the manufacturing and profit and loss account and includes the closing stock valuation of all three forms of stock.

## unit cost of goods manufactured

When the production cost has been ascertained, the unit cost can be calculated as follows:

$$\textit{Unit cost} \quad = \quad \frac{\textit{Production cost of goods completed}}{\textit{Number of units completed}}$$

For example, if the manufacturing account on page 422 represented production of 200,000 units, the unit cost for the year was:

$$\textit{Unit cost} \quad = \quad \frac{\textit{£115,500}}{\textit{200,000}} \quad = \quad \textit{£0.58 per unit}$$

# TRANSFER PRICES AND FACTORY PROFIT

Some manufacturing businesses transfer completed goods from the factory to the warehouse at, for example, 'factory cost plus ten per cent' (the transfer price). The objective in doing this is for the factory to make a notional profit which is added into net profit at a later stage. This might enable the unit cost of goods manufactured to be compared with the cost of buying in completed goods from an outside source. Also, by showing a factory profit, the profit (or loss) from trading activities (as distinct from manufacturing) can be identified separately.

Referring back to the manufacturing account on page 422 and amending the figures to allow for a factory 'profit' of ten per cent, the final part of the manufacturing account, and the trading and profit and loss account appear as follows:

|  | £ | £ |
|---|---|---|
| PRODUCTION COST | | 115,500 |
| Factory profit of ten per cent | | 11,550 |
| PRODUCTION COST OF GOODS COMPLETED (including profit) | | 127,050 |
| | | |
| Sales | | 195,500 |
| Opening stock of finished goods | 6,500 | |
| Production (or manufacturing) cost of goods completed | 127,050 | |
| | 133,550 | |
| Less Closing stock of finished goods | 7,500 | |
| COST OF GOODS SOLD | | 126,050 |
| **Gross profit** | | 69,450 |
| Less Non-production overheads: | | |
|     Selling and distribution expenses | 38,500 | |
|     Administration expenses | 32,000 | |
|     Finance expenses | 3,500 | |
| | | 74,000 |
| Loss from trading | | (4,550) |
| Add Factory profit | | 11,550 |
| **Net profit** | | 7,000 |

Note that the final net profit is unchanged, but the manufacturing cost is higher, and gross profit is lower. The factory profit is added back in the profit and loss account, after showing separately the profit or loss from trading. The reason for doing this is to make the factory and the warehouse into separate profit centres.

## provision for unrealised profit on finished goods stocks

A business using the 'factory profit' method may choose to value stocks of finished goods at manufacturing cost plus manufacturing profit. For example, the business whose manufacturing account is shown above, might value finished goods stocks as:

**Opening stock** (1 January 20-2)

manufacturing cost (£6,500) + manufacturing profit of 10 per cent (£650) = £7,150

**Closing stock** (31 December 20-2)

manufacturing cost (£7,500) + manufacturing profit of 10 per cent (£750) = £8,250

The logic behind valuing finished goods stocks in this way is to show more clearly the profit from the separate sections of the business, ie manufacturing and trading. It will apply particularly where goods are both manufactured and bought in as finished goods from outside manufacturers. The trading account now compares 'like with like', ie own-manufactured goods are priced to include a profit, while the bought-in goods include the supplier's profit. At the end of the financial year the closing stock of own-manufactured goods includes an element of unrealised profit.

Statement of Standard Accounting Practice No 9 (Stocks and long-term contracts) – see Chapter 17 – requires that stocks should be shown in the balance sheet at cost price if purchased, or cost of production if manufactured. (Note that if realisable value is lower than cost, then this will be used instead.) In order to comply with SSAP 9, it is necessary to account for the element of unrealised profit included in the finished goods stock valuation. This is done through an account called provision for unrealised profit, which is used to adjust downwards the closing stock figure in the balance sheet to cost price.

For example, using the adjusted finished goods opening and closing stock figures of £7,150 (above) and £8,250 (which include manufacturing profits of £650 and £750 respectively), the provision for unrealised profit account appears as:

| Dr | | | **Provision for Unrealised Profit Account** | | Cr |
|---|---|---|---|---|---|
| 20-2 | | £ | 20-2 | | £ |
| 31 Dec | Balance c/d | 750 | 1 Jan | Balance b/d | 650 |
| | (adjustment in respect | | | (adjustment in respect | |
| | of closing stock) | | | of opening stock) | |
| | | | 31 Dec | Profit and loss account | 100 |
| | | 750 | | | 750 |
| 20-3 | | | 20-3 | | |
| | | | 1 Jan | Balance b/d | 750 |

Note that the increase in provision for unrealised profit of £100 is shown as an expense in profit and loss account. It is recorded as a deduction from factory profit shown in the profit and loss account, eg

| | £ | £ |
|---|---|---|
| Factory profit | 11,550 | |
| Less increase in provision for unrealised profit | 100 | |
| | | 11,450 |

If there is a fall in the value of finished goods stock during the year, then there will be a decrease in the provision for unrealised profit, and this will be added to the factory profit shown in the profit and loss account.

Stock account uses the finished goods stock valuations which include the manufacturing profit, as follows:

| Dr | | **Stock Account** | | | Cr |
|---|---|---|---|---|---|
| 20-2 | | £ | 20-2 | | £ |
| 1 Jan | Balance b/d (opening stock) | 7,150 | 31 Dec | Trading account | 7,150 |
| 31 Dec | Trading account (closing stock) | 8,250 | 31 Dec | Balance c/d | 8,250 |
| 20-3 | | | 20-3 | | |
| 1 Jan | Balance b/d | 8,250 | | | |

The balance sheet figure at 31 December 20-2 for finished goods stocks shows the net value, ie:

| | £ |
|---|---|
| Finished goods stock | 8,250 |
| Less Provision for unrealised profit | 750 |
| Net value | 7,500 |

As can be seen this reduces the closing stock value of finished goods to cost price, and enables the balance sheet valuation to comply with SSAP 9.

# CHAPTER SUMMARY

● A manufacturing account brings together all the elements of cost which make up production (or manufacturing) cost.

● A manufacturing account shows prime cost and the production (or manufacturing) cost.

● A manufacturer usually holds stock in three different forms:

   – raw materials, used in the calculation of cost of raw materials used

   – work-in-progress, used in the calculation of manufacturing (or production) cost

   – finished goods, used in the calculation of cost of goods sold

● Profit and loss account shows the non-production overheads.

● A transfer price is sometimes used to enable a factory to earn a notional profit.

In the next chapter we turn to cash flow statements. These focus on the money flowing in and out of a business during the accounting period.

# QUESTIONS

NOTE: an asterisk (*) after the question number means that an answer to the question is given in Appendix 2.

**26.1\***  Allocate the following costs to

- manufacturing account
- profit and loss account

(a)   factory rent

(b)   production supervisors' wages

(c)   insurance of factory buildings

(d)   depreciation of office photocopier

(e)   sales commission

(f)   raw materials purchased

(g)   advertising

**26.2\***  The following figures relate to the accounts of Barbara Francis, who operates a furniture manufacturing business, for the year ended 31 December 20-8:

| | £ |
|---|---|
| Stocks of raw materials, 1 January 20-8 | 31,860 |
| Stocks of raw materials, 31 December 20-8 | 44,790 |
| Stocks of finished goods, 1 January 20-8 | 42,640 |
| Stocks of finished goods, 31 December 20-8 | 96,510 |
| Purchases of raw materials | 237,660 |
| Sale of finished goods | 796,950 |
| Rent and rates | 32,920 |
| Manufacturing wages | 234,630 |
| Manufacturing power | 7,650 |
| Manufacturing heat and light | 2,370 |
| Manufacturing sundry expenses and maintenance | 8,190 |
| Salaries | 138,700 |
| Advertising | 22,170 |
| Office expenses | 7,860 |
| Depreciation of manufacturing plant and machinery | 7,450 |

Rent and rates are to be apportioned 75% to manufacturing and 25% to administration.

You are to prepare manufacturing and profit and loss accounts for the year-ended 31 December 20-8, to show clearly:

- cost of raw materials used

- prime cost

- cost of production (factory) overheads

- production cost of goods completed

- cost of goods sold

- gross profit for the year

- net profit for the year

Explain, by memorandum, to Miss Francis why you have presented the accounts in such a form, and what they show.

**26.3\*** A manufacturer values the closing stock of finished goods at factory cost plus 20 per cent. For 20-9 the opening and closing stocks (including profit of 20 per cent) were £12,000 and £18,000 respectively. Show the transactions on provision for unrealised profit account for the year ended 31 December 20-9.

**26.4** The following balances have been extracted from the books of Yeoh Siew Wyin as at 31 August 20-6:

|  | £ |
|---|---|
| Stock at 1 September 20-5: | |
| Raw materials | 28,600 |
| Work in progress | 51,200 |
| Finished goods | 92,000 |
| Provision for doubtful debts at 1 September 20-5 | 1,220 |
| Purchases of raw materials | 96,300 |
| Returns of raw materials | 500 |
| Sales | 274,200 |
| Discount allowed | 750 |
| Discount received | 800 |
| Production wages | 28,900 |
| Office salaries | 12,200 |
| Production equipment (cost £80,000) | 45,000 |
| Office equipment at cost | 6,200 |

|                            | £     |
|----------------------------|-------|
| Carriage on raw materials  | 1,010 |
| Rent and rates             | 9,000 |
| Heat and light             | 1,400 |
| Insurance                  | 600   |

The following information is also relevant at 31 August 20-6:

(i)     Closing stocks are:

| Raw materials    | £26,300 |
|------------------|---------|
| Work in progress | £46,900 |
| Finished goods   | £76,500 |

(ii)    The following amounts remain outstanding:

| Rent and rates   | £1,500 |
|------------------|--------|
| Heat and light   | £700   |
| Production wages  | £2,900 |

(iii)   £50 insurance has been prepaid

(iv)    Three-fifths of insurance relates to the factory and the remainder to the office

(v)     Five-sevenths of heat and light relates to the factory and the remainder to the office

(vi)    Two-thirds of rent and rates relates to the factory and the remainder to the office

(vii)   The provision for doubtful debts is to be reduced to £1,060

(viii)  Depreciation is to be provided:
        – on production equipment at 25% reducing (diminishing) balance basis
        – on office equipment at 50% on cost, straight line method

You are required to:

(a)     prepare a manufacturing account for the year ended 31 August 20-6

(b)     prepare a trading and profit and loss account for the year ended 31 August 20-6

*Pitman Qualifications*

26.5    The following balances were extracted from the books of Jason Manufacturing Company
        Limited at 31 December Year 10:

|  | £ |
|---|---|
| Stock of raw materials at 1 January Year 10 | 15,000 |
| Selling and distribution expenses | 28,250 |
| Purchases of raw materials | 284,050 |
| Sales of finished goods | 904,294 |
| Administrative expenses | 173,900 |
| Factory direct wages | 176,380 |
| Stock of finished goods at 1 January Year 10 | 45,765 |
| Interim preference dividend paid | 12,000 |
| Factory indirect wages | 37,628 |
| Profit and loss account at 1 January Year 10 | 392,286 |
| Factory indirect expenses | 23,285 |
| Work-in-progress at 1 January Year 10 (factory cost) | 10,070 |
| Financial expenses | 24,125 |
| Interim ordinary share dividend paid | 20,000 |
| Investment | 300,000 |
| 8% preference shares of £1 each, fully paid | 300,000 |
| Ordinary shares of £1 each, fully paid | 1,000,000 |
| Freehold premises at cost | 850,000 |
| Plant and machinery at cost | 236,100 |
| Motor vehicles at cost | 45,000 |
| Fixtures and fittings at cost | 62,000 |
| Debtors | 49,150 |
| Creditors | 21,706 |
| Provision for depreciation at 1 January Year 10: |  |
| Plant and machinery | 80,000 |
| Motor vehicles | 17,000 |
| Fixtures and fittings | 28,000 |
| Bank balance (Dr) | 350,583 |

Additional information:

(1)    Depreciation to be charged on cost:
       Plant and machinery at 20% per annum (factory expense)
       Motor vehicles at 20% per annum (selling expense)
       Fixtures and fittings at 15% per annum (administrative expenses)

|     |                                                  |         |
| --- | ------------------------------------------------ | ------- |
| (2) | Stocks at 31 December Year 10:                   | £       |
|     | Raw materials                                    | 18,420  |
|     | Finished goods                                   | 50,240  |
|     | Work-in-progress (factory cost)                  | 8,950   |

|     |                                                  |         |
| --- | ------------------------------------------------ | ------- |
| (3) | At 31 December Year 10:                          |         |
|     | Accrued selling and distribution expenses        | 1,795   |
|     | Prepaid administrative expenses                  | 3,200   |

(4) The directors agreed to recommend the following dividends:
Preference share final
Ordinary share final of £0.03 per share

(5) The investments are all due for repayment before 30 June Year 11

(6) Authorised capital:
   500,000 8% Preference shares of £1 each
   1,250,000 Ordinary shares of £1 each

You are required to prepare, for Jason Manufacturing Company Limited, in vertical form:

(a) (i) Manufacturing account for the year ended 31 December Year 10

(ii) Trading and profit and loss and appropriation account for the year ended 31 December Year 10

(b) Balance sheet at 31 December Year 10

*LCCI Examinations Board*

# 27 CASH FLOW STATEMENTS

In this chapter we study the cash flow statement, which links profit from the profit and loss account with changes in assets and liabilities in the balance sheet, and the effect on the cash of the business.

We will cover:

- an appreciation of the need for a cash flow statement
- the cash flows for the main sections of the statement
- how the cash flows relate to the main areas of business activity
- the interpretation of cash flow statements

## INTRODUCTION

The profit and loss account shows profitability, and the balance sheet shows asset strength. While these two financial statements give us a great deal of information on the progress of a business during an accounting period, profit does not equal cash, and strength in assets does not necessarily mean a large bank balance. The cash flow statement links profit with changes in assets and liabilities, and the effect on the cash of the business.

*A cash flow statement uses information from the accounting records (including profit and loss account and balance sheet), and shows an overall view of money flowing in and out of a business during an accounting period.*

Such a statement explains to the owner or shareholders why, after a year of good profits for example, there is a reduced balance at the bank or a larger bank overdraft at the year-end than there was at the beginning of the year. The cash flow statement concentrates on the liquidity of the business: it is a lack of cash (a lack of liquidity) that causes most businesses to fail and not poor products or services. The importance of the cash flow statement is such that all but smaller limited companies must include the statement as a part of their accounts. For sole traders and partnerships, the information that the statement contains is of considerable interest to the owner(s) and to a lender, such as a bank.

In this chapter we will look at two Worked Examples – one for a sole trader and one for a limited company. The format used in this chapter for the cash flow statement is that which is set out in Financial Reporting Standard No.1.

# FORMAT OF THE CASH FLOW STATEMENT

Cash flow statements are divided into eight sections:

1    Operating activities

2    Returns on investments and servicing of finance

3    Taxation

4    Capital expenditure and financial investment

5    Acquisitions and disposals

6    Equity dividends paid

7    Management of liquid resources

8    Financing

The cash flows for the year affecting each of these main areas of business activity are shown in the statement, although not every business will have cash flows under each of the eight sections.

The diagram on the next page shows the main cash inflows and outflows under each heading, and indicates the content of the cash flow statement. The first section – operating activities – needs a word of further explanation, particularly as it is the main source of cash flow for most businesses.

## operating activities

The net cash inflow from operating activities is calculated by using figures from the profit and loss account and balance sheet as follows:

• operating profit (ie net profit, before deduction of interest)

• add depreciation for the year

• add decrease in debtors, or deduct increase in debtors

• add increase in creditors, or deduct decrease in creditors

• add decrease in stock, or deduct increase in stock

Note that depreciation is added to profit because depreciation is a non-cash expense, that is, no money is paid out by the business in respect of depreciation charged to profit and loss account.

# LAYOUT OF A CASH FLOW STATEMENT

A cash flow statement uses a common layout which can be amended to suit the particular needs of the business for which it is being prepared. The example layout shown on page 435 – with specimen figures included – is commonly used. A specimen format is included in Appendix 1.

## CASH FLOW STATEMENT

**Operating activities**
- Operating profit (ie net profit, before deduction of interest)
- Depreciation charge for the year (see page 441 for treatment of a profit or a loss on sale of fixed assets)
- Changes in debtors, creditors and stock

**Returns on investments and servicing of finance**
- Inflows: interest received, dividends received
- Outflows: interest paid, dividends paid on preference shares (but not ordinary shares – see below)

**Taxation**
- Outflow: corporation tax paid by limited companies during the year

**Capital expenditure and financial investment**
- Inflows: sale proceeds from fixed assets and investments
- Outflows: purchase cost of fixed assets and investments

**Acquisitions and disposals**
- Inflows: sale proceeds from investments and interests in
  - subsidiary companies (where more than 50 per cent of the shares in another company is owned)
  - associated companies (where between 20 per cent and 50 per cent of the shares in another company is owned)
  - joint ventures (where a project is undertaken jointly with another company)
- Outflows: purchase cost of investments in subsidiary companies, associated companies, and of interests in joint ventures

**Equity dividends paid**
- Outflow: the amount of dividends paid to equity (ordinary) shareholders during the year (where the cash flow statement is for a sole trader or partnership, the amount of drawings will be shown here)

**Management of liquid resources**
- Inflows: sale proceeds from short-term investments that are almost as good as cash – such as treasury bills (a form of government debt), and term deposits of up to a year with a bank
- Outflows: purchase of short-term liquid investments

**Financing**
- Inflows: receipts from increase in capital /share capital, raising/increase of loans
- Outflows: repayment of capital/share capital/loans

*Contents of a Cash Flow Statement*

**ABC LIMITED**
**CASH FLOW STATEMENT FOR THE YEAR ENDED 31 DECEMBER 20-1**

| | £ | £ |
|---|---:|---:|
| **Operating activities:** | | |
| Operating profit (note: before tax and interest) | 75,000 | |
| Depreciation for year | 10,000 | |
| Decrease in stock | 2,000 | |
| Increase in debtors | (5,000) | |
| Increase in creditors | 7,000 | |
| *Net cash inflow from operating activities* | | 89,000 |
| | | |
| **Returns on investments and servicing of finance:** | | |
| Interest received | 10,000 | |
| Interest paid | (5,000) | |
| | | 5,000 |
| **Taxation:** | | |
| Corporation tax paid (note: amount paid during year) | | (6,000) |
| | | |
| **Capital expenditure and financial investment:** | | |
| Payments to acquire fixed assets | (125,000) | |
| Receipts from sales of fixed assets | 15,000 | |
| | | (110,000) |
| **Acquisitions and disposals:** | | |
| Purchase of subsidiary undertakings | ( – ) | |
| Sale of a business | – | – |
| | | |
| **Equity dividends paid:** (note: amount paid during year) | | (22,000) |
| *Cash outflow before use of liquid resources and financing* | | (44,000) |
| | | |
| **Management of liquid resources:** | | |
| Purchase of treasury bills | (250,000) | |
| Sale of treasury bills | 200,000 | |
| | | (50,000) |
| **Financing:** | | |
| Issue of share capital | 275,000 | |
| Repayment of capital/share capital | ( – ) | |
| Increase in loans | – | |
| Repayment of loans | (90,000) | |
| | | 185,000 |
| **Increase in cash** | | 91,000 |

*Example of a Cash Flow Statement – see notes on the next page*

Notes:

- The separate amounts shown for each section can, if preferred, be detailed in a note to the cash flow statement.

- Money amounts shown in brackets indicate a deduction or, where the figure is a sub-total, a negative figure.

- The changes in the main working capital items of stock, debtors and creditors have an effect on cash balances. For example, a decrease in stock increases cash, while an increase in debtors reduces cash.

- The cash flow statement concludes with a figure for the increase or decrease in cash. This is calculated from the subtotals of each of eight sections of the statement.

## WORKED EXAMPLE: A SOLE TRADER CASH FLOW STATEMENT

### question

Samantha Smith runs a children's clothes shop in rented premises in a small market town. Her balance sheets for the last two years are as follows:

**BALANCE SHEETS AS AT 31 DECEMBER**

|  | 20-1 | | | 20-2 | | |
|---|---|---|---|---|---|---|
|  | £ | £ | £ | £ | £ | £ |
|  | Cost | Dep'n | Net | Cost | Dep'n | Net |
| **Fixed Assets** | | | | | | |
| Shop fittings | 1,500 | 500 | 1,000 | 2,000 | 750 | 1,250 |
| **Current Assets** | | | | | | |
| Stock | | 3,750 | | | 4,850 | |
| Debtors | | 625 | | | 1,040 | |
| Bank | | 220 | | | – | |
| | | 4,595 | | | 5,890 | |
| **Less Current Liabilities** | | | | | | |
| Creditors | 2,020 | | | 4,360 | | |
| Bank | – | | | 725 | | |
| | | 2,020 | | | 5,085 | |
| **Working Capital** | | | 2,575 | | | 805 |
| | | | 3,575 | | | 2,055 |
| **Less Long-term Liabilities** | | | | | | |
| Loan from husband | | | – | | | 1,000 |
| **NET ASSETS** | | | 3,575 | | | 1,055 |

continued on next page

| FINANCED BY | | |
|---|---|---|
| **Capital** | £ | £ |
| Opening capital | 3,300 | 3,575 |
| Add net profit for year | 5,450 | 4,080 |
| | 8,750 | 7,655 |
| Less drawings | 5,175 | 6,600 |
| | 3,575 | 1,055 |

Note: Interest paid on the loan and bank overdraft in 20-2 was £450.

Samantha Smith says to you: "I cannot understand why I am overdrawn at the bank by £725 on 31 December 20-2 when I made a profit of £4,080 during the year". She asks you to help her by explaining why this is.

### answer

A cash flow statement will give Samantha Smith the answer:

**CASH FLOW STATEMENT FOR THE YEAR ENDED 31 DECEMBER 20-2**

| | £ | £ |
|---|---|---|
| **Operating activities:** | | |
| Operating profit (before interest) | 4,530 | |
| Depreciation for year | 250 | |
| Increase in stock | (1,100) | |
| Increase in debtors | (415) | |
| Increase in creditors | 2,340 | |
| *Net cash inflow from operating activities* | | 5,605 |
| **Returns on investments and servicing of finance:** | | |
| Interest paid | | (450) |
| **Taxation:** | | |
| Corporation tax paid | | not applicable |
| **Capital expenditure and financial investment:** | | |
| Payments to acquire fixed assets | | (500) |
| **Equity dividends paid:** (drawings) | | (6,600) |
| *Cash outflow before use of liquid resources and financing* | | (1,945) |
| **Financing:** | | |
| Loan from husband | | 1,000 |
| **Decrease in cash** | | (945) |

**Points to note from the Cash Flow Statement**

- Net profit for the year (before interest) is calculated as:

  | | |
  |---|---|
  | net profit for 20-2 | £4,080 |
  | interest for 20-2 | £ 450 |
  | | £4,530 |

- Depreciation for the year of £250 is the amount of the increase in depreciation to date shown on the balance sheets, that is, £750 minus £500.

- An increase in stock and debtors reduces the cash available to the business (because stock is being bought, debtors are being allowed more time to pay). In contrast, an increase in creditors gives an increase in cash (because creditors are allowing Samantha Smith more time to pay).

- In this example there is no tax paid (because Samantha Smith is a sole trader who will be taxed as an individual, unlike a company which pays tax on its profits); however, the place where tax would appear is indicated on the cash flow statement.

- As this is a sole trader busines, drawings are shown on the cash flow statement in place of equity dividends.

- The change in the bank balance is summarised as follows: from a balance of £220 in the bank to an overdraft of £725 is a 'swing' in the bank of minus £945, which is the amount of the decrease in cash shown by the cash flow statement.

**Your explanation to Samantha Smith**

In this example, the statement highlights the following points for the owner of the business:

- net cash inflow from operating activities is £5,605, whereas owner's drawings are £6,600; this state of affairs cannot continue for long

- fixed assets costing £500 have been purchased

- a long-term loan of £1,000 has been raised from her husband

- over the year there has been a decrease in cash of £945, this trend cannot be continued for long

- by the end of 20-2 the business has an overdraft of £725, caused mainly by the excessive drawings of the owner

- in conclusion, the liquidity position of this business has deteriorated over the two years, and corrective action will be necessary

## WORKED EXAMPLE: LIMITED COMPANY CASH FLOW STATEMENT

### question

The balance sheets of Newtown Trading Company Limited for 20-6 and 20-7 are as follows:

| | | 20-6 | | | 20-7 | |
|---|---|---|---|---|---|---|
| | £ | £ | £ | £ | £ | £ |
| | Cost | Dep'n | Net | Cost | Dep'n | Net |
| **BALANCE SHEETS AS AT 31 DECEMBER** | | | | | | |
| Fixed Assets | 47,200 | 6,200 | 41,000 | 64,000 | 8,900 | 55,100 |
| **Current Assets** | | | | | | |
| Stock | | 7,000 | | | 11,000 | |
| Debtors | | 5,000 | | | 3,700 | |
| Bank | | 1,000 | | | 500 | |
| | | 13,000 | | | 15,200 | |
| **Less Current Liabilities** | | | | | | |
| Creditors | 3,500 | | | 4,800 | | |
| Proposed dividends | 2,000 | | | 2,500 | | |
| Corporation tax | 1,000 | | | 1,500 | | |
| | | 6,500 | | | 8,800 | |
| **Working Capital** | | | 6,500 | | | 6,400 |
| | | | 47,500 | | | 61,500 |
| **Less Long-term Liabilities** | | | | | | |
| Debentures | | | 5,000 | | | 3,000 |
| **NET ASSETS** | | | 42,500 | | | 58,500 |
| **FINANCED BY** | | | | | | |
| Ordinary share capital | | | 30,000 | | | 40,000 |
| Share premium account | | | 1,500 | | | 2,500 |
| Retained profits | | | 11,000 | | | 16,000 |
| **SHAREHOLDERS' FUNDS** | | | 42,500 | | | 58,500 |

Note: Interest paid on the loan in 20-7 was £400.

Prepare a cash flow statement for the year ended 31 December 20-7 and comment on the main points highlighted by the statement.

**answer**

### NEWTOWN TRADING COMPANY LIMITED
### CASH FLOW STATEMENT FOR THE YEAR ENDED 31 DECEMBER 20-7

| | £ | £ |
|---|---|---|
| **Operating activities:** | | |
| Operating profit (before interest)* | 9,400 | |
| Depreciation for year** | 2,700 | |
| Increase in stock | (4,000) | |
| Decrease in debtors | 1,300 | |
| Increase in creditors | 1,300 | |
| *Net cash inflow from operating activities* | | 10,700 |
| | | |
| **Returns on investments and servicing of finance:** | | |
| Interest paid | | (400) |
| | | |
| **Taxation:** | | |
| Corporation tax paid | | (1,000) |
| | | |
| **Capital expenditure and financial investment:** | | |
| Payments to acquire fixed assets | | (16,800) |
| | | |
| **Equity dividends paid:** | | (2,000) |
| *Cash outflow before use of liquid resources and financing* | | (9,500) |
| | | |
| **Financing:** | | |
| Issue of ordinary shares at a premium | | |
| ie £10,000 + £1,000 = | 11,000 | |
| Repayment of debentures | (2,000) | |
| | | 9,000 |
| **Decrease in cash** | | (500) |

**Notes**

* Calculation of the operating profit for 20-7 before interest, tax and dividends:

| | £ |
|---|---|
| increase in retained profits | 5,000 |
| interest paid in 20-7 | 400 |
| proposed dividends, 20-7 | 2,500 |
| corporation tax, 20-7 | 1,500 |
| operating profit before interest, tax and dividends | 9,400 |

** Depreciation charged: £8,900 – £6,200  = £2,700

Both proposed dividends and corporation tax – which are current liabilities at 31 December 20-6 – are paid in 20-7. Likewise, the current liabilities for dividends and tax at 31 December 20-7 will be paid in 20-8 (and will appear on that year's cash flow statement).

how useful is the cash flow statement?

The following points are highlighted by the statement on the previous page:

- net cash inflow from operating activities is £10,700
- a purchase of fixed assets of £16,800 has been made, financed partly by operating activities, and partly by an issue of shares at a premium
- the bank balance during the year has fallen by £500, ie from £1,000 to £500
- in conclusion, the picture shown by the cash flow statement is that of a business which is generating cash from its operating activities and using them to build for the future

# PROFIT OR LOSS ON SALE OF FIXED ASSETS

When a business sells fixed assets it is most unlikely that the resultant sale proceeds will equal the net book value (cost price, less depreciation to date). The accounting solution, as we have already seen in Chapter 14, is to transfer any small profit or loss on sale – non-cash items – to profit and loss account. However, such a profit or loss on sale must be handled with care when preparing a cash flow statement because, in such a statement we have to adjust for non-cash items when calculating the net cash inflow from operating activities; at the same time we must separately identify the amount of the sale proceeds of fixed assets in the capital expenditure section.

## example of profit or loss on sale of fixed assets in a cash flow statement

H & J Wells are electrical contractors. For the year ended 30 June 20-2 their profit and loss account is as follows:

|  |  | £ | £ |
|---|---|---:|---:|
| Gross profit |  |  | 37,500 |
| Less expenses: |  |  |  |
| General expenses |  | 23,000 |  |
| Provision for depreciation: | machinery | 2,000 |  |
|  | vehicles | 3,000 |  |
|  |  |  | 28,000 |
| Net profit |  |  | 9,500 |

## profit on sale

During the course of the year they have sold the following fixed asset; it has not yet been recorded in their profit and loss account:

|  |  | £ |
|---|---|---:|
| Machine | cost price | 1,000 |
|  | depreciation to date | 750 |
|  | net book value | 250 |
|  | sale proceeds | 350 |

As the machine has been sold for £100 more than book value, this sum is shown in profit and loss account, as follows:

|  |  | £ | £ |
|---|---|---|---|
| Gross profit |  |  | 37,500 |
| Profit on sale of fixed assets |  |  | 100 |
|  |  |  | 37,600 |
| Less expenses: |  |  |  |
| General expenses |  | 23,000 |  |
| Provision for depreciation: machinery | | 2,000 | |
| vehicles | | 3,000 | |
|  |  |  | 28,000 |
| Net profit |  |  | 9,600 |

The cash flow statement, based on the amended profit and loss account, will include the following figures:

---

**CASHFLOW STATEMENT (EXTRACT) OF H & J WELLS**
**FOR THE YEAR ENDED 30 JUNE 20-2**

|  | £ | £ |
|---|---|---|
| **Operating activities:** |  |  |
| Operating profit (before interest) | 9,600 |  |
| Depreciation | 5,000 |  |
| Profit on sale of fixed assets | (100) |  |
| (Increase)/decrease in stock | . . . |  |
| (Increase)/decrease in debtors | . . . |  |
| Increase/(decrease) in creditors | . . . |  |
| Net cash inflow from operating activities |  | 14,500 |
|  |  |  |
| **Capital expenditure and financial investment:** |  |  |
| Payments to acquire fixed assets | (. . .) |  |
| Receipts from sales of fixed assets | 350 |  |
|  |  | 350 |

---

Note that profit on sale of fixed assets is deducted in the operating activities section because it is non-cash income. (Only the sections of the cash flow statement affected by the sale are shown above.)

## loss on sale

If the machine had been sold for £150, this would have given a 'loss on sale' of £100. This amount would be debited to profit and loss account, to give an amended net profit of £9,400.

The effect on the cash flow statement would be twofold:

- In the operating activities section, loss on sale of fixed assets of £100 would be added; the net cash inflow from operating activities remains at £14,500 (which proves that both profit and loss on sale of fixed assets are non-cash items)

- In the capital expenditure section, receipts from sales of fixed assets would be £150

### conclusion: profit or a loss on sale of fixed assets

The rule for dealing with a profit or a loss on sale of fixed assets in cash flow statements is:

- add the amount of the loss on sale, or deduct the amount of the profit on sale, to or from the net profit when calculating the net cash flow from operating activities

- show the total sale proceeds, ie the amount of the cheque received, as receipts from sales of fixed assets in the capital expenditure section

# USING THE CASH FLOW STATEMENT

The cash flow statement is important because it identifies the sources of cash flowing into the business and shows how they have been used. We need to read the statement in conjunction with the other two financial statements – trading and profit and loss account and balance sheet – and also in the context of the previous year's statements. The following points should also be borne in mind:

- Like the other financial statements, the cash flow statement uses the money measurement concept (page 10). This means that only items which can be recorded in money terms can be included; also we must be aware of the effect of inflation when comparing one year with the next.

- We are looking for a reasonable cash flow from operating activities each year – this is the cash from the trading activities of the business.

- Changes in the working items of stock, debtors and creditors need to be put into context. For example, it would be a warning sign if there were large increases in these items in a business with a falling operating profit, and such a trend would put a strain on the liquidity of the business.

- The statement will show the amount of investment made during the year (eg the purchase of fixed assets). In general there should be a link between the cost of the investment and an increase in loans and/or capital – it isn't usual to finance fixed assets from short-term sources, such as a bank overdraft.

- Where there has been an increase in loans and/or capital, look to see how the cash has been used. Was it to buy fixed assets or other investments, or to finance stocks and debtors, or other purposes?

- The statement, as a whole, links profit with changes in cash. Both of these are important: without profits the business cannot generate cash (unless it sells fixed assets), and without cash it cannot pay bills as they fall due.

## CHAPTER SUMMARY

● The objective of a cash flow statement is to show an overall view of money flowing in and out of a business during an accounting period.

● A cashflow statement is divided into eight sections:

1   operating activities

2   returns on investments and servicing of finance

3   taxation

4   capital expenditure and financial investment

5   acquisitions and disposals

6   equity dividends paid

7   management of liquid resources

8   financing

● The Financial Reporting Standard No. 1 on cash flow statements provides a specimen layout.

● Larger limited companies are required to include a cash flow statement as a part of their published accounts. They are also useful statements for sole traders, partnerships and smaller limited companies.

In the next chapter we look at the important area of interpreting and understanding what the accounting statements tell us about the strengths and weaknesses of a business. To help us in this we shall be calculating ratios, percentages and other performance indicators.

# QUESTIONS

NOTE: an asterisk (*) after the question number means that an answer to the question is given in Appendix 2.

**27.1***  John Smith has been in business for two years. He is puzzled by his balance sheets because, although they show a profit for each year, his bank balance has fallen and is now an overdraft. He asks for your assistance to explain what has happened. The balance sheets are as follows:

### BALANCE SHEET AS AT 31 DECEMBER

| | | 20-1 | | | 20-2 | |
|---|---|---|---|---|---|---|
| | £ | £ | £ | £ | £ | £ |
| | Cost | Dep'n | Net | Cost | Dep'n | Net |
| **Fixed Assets** | | | | | | |
| Fixtures and fittings | 3,000 | 600 | 2,400 | 5,000 | 1,600 | 3,400 |
| **Current Assets** | | | | | | |
| Stock | | 5,500 | | | 9,000 | |
| Debtors | | 750 | | | 1,550 | |
| Bank | | 850 | | | – | |
| | | 7,100 | | | 10,550 | |
| **Current Liabilities** | | | | | | |
| Creditors | 2,500 | | | 2,750 | | |
| Bank overdraft | – | | | 2,200 | | |
| | | 2,500 | | | 4,950 | |
| **Working Capital** | | | 4,600 | | | 5,600 |
| **NET ASSETS** | | | 7,000 | | | 9,000 |
| **FINANCED BY** | | | | | | |
| **Capital** | | | 5,000 | | | 7,000 |
| Add  Net profit for year | | | 8,750 | | | 11,000 |
| | | | 13,750 | | | 18,000 |
| Less Drawings | | | 6,750 | | | 9,000 |
| | | | 7,000 | | | 9,000 |

Note: Interest paid on the bank overdraft in 20-2 was £250.

You are to prepare a cash flow statement for the year-ended 31 December 20-2.

27.2 Richard Williams runs a stationery supplies shop; his balance sheets for the last two years are:

**BALANCE SHEET AS AT 30 SEPTEMBER**

| | 20-5 | | | 20-6 | | |
|---|---|---|---|---|---|---|
| | £ | £ | £ | £ | £ | £ |
| | Cost | Dep'n | Net | Cost | Dep'n | Net |
| **Fixed Assets** | 60,000 | 12,000 | 48,000 | 70,000 | 23,600 | 46,400 |
| **Current Assets** | | | | | | |
| Stock | | 9,800 | | | 13,600 | |
| Debtors | | 10,800 | | | 15,000 | |
| | | 20,600 | | | 28,600 | |
| **Less Current Liabilities** | | | | | | |
| Creditors | 7,200 | | | 14,600 | | |
| Bank overdraft | 1,000 | | | 4,700 | | |
| | | 8,200 | | | 19,300 | |
| **Working Capital** | | | 12,400 | | | 9,300 |
| | | | 60,400 | | | 55,700 |
| **Less Long-term Liabilities** | | | | | | |
| Bank loan | | | 10,000 | | | 15,000 |
| **NET ASSETS** | | | 50,400 | | | 40,700 |
| **FINANCED BY** | | | | | | |
| **Capital** | | | 50,000 | | | 50,400 |
| Add Net profit/(loss) | | | 10,800 | | | (1,500) |
| | | | 60,800 | | | 48,900 |
| Less Drawings | | | 10,400 | | | 8,200 |
| | | | 50,400 | | | 40,700 |

Note: Loan and overdraft interest paid in 20-6 was £2,200.

You are to prepare a cash flow statement for the year-ended 30 September 20-6.

**27.3** Using the balance sheets of Richard Williams in question 27.2, prepare revised cash flow statements for the year to 30 September 20-6, to take note of the following:

*Situation 1*

A fixed asset with a cost price of £5,000 and depreciation to date of £3,000 was sold for £2,500.

*Situation 2*

A fixed asset with a cost price of £5,000 and depreciation to date of £3,000 was sold for £1,500.

Notes:

- two separate cash flow statements for the year ended 30 September 20-6 are required
- assume that the balance sheet for 20-6 already includes the sale transactions, ie do not adjust the net loss by the amount of the profit or loss on sale, or the bank account by the sale proceeds

**27.4** Martin Jackson is a shareholder in Retail News Limited, a company that operates a chain of newsagents throughout the West Midlands. Martin comments that, whilst the company is making reasonable profits, the bank balance has fallen quite considerably. He provides you with the following information for Retail News Limited:

**BALANCE SHEET AS AT 31 DECEMBER**

|  | 20-4 | | 20-5 | | 20-6 | |
| --- | --- | --- | --- | --- | --- | --- |
|  | £000 | £000 | £000 | £000 | £000 | £000 |
| **Fixed Assets** at cost |  | 252 |  | 274 |  | 298 |
| Add Additions during year |  | 22 |  | 24 |  | 26 |
|  |  | 274 |  | 298 |  | 324 |
| Less Depreciation to date |  | 74 |  | 98 |  | 118 |
|  |  | 200 |  | 200 |  | 206 |
| **Current Assets** |  |  |  |  |  |  |
| Stock | 50 |  | 64 |  | 70 |  |
| Debtors | 80 |  | 120 |  | 160 |  |
| Bank | 10 |  | – |  | – |  |
|  | 140 |  | 184 |  | 230 |  |
| **Less Current Liabilities** |  |  |  |  |  |  |
| Creditors | 56 |  | 72 |  | 78 |  |
| Bank | – |  | 10 |  | 46 |  |
| Proposed dividends | 16 |  | 20 |  | 16 |  |
| Corporation tax | 4 |  | 5 |  | 8 |  |
|  | 76 |  | 107 |  | 148 |  |
| **Working Capital** |  | 64 |  | 77 |  | 82 |
| **NET ASSETS** |  | 264 |  | 277 |  | 288 |
| **FINANCED BY** |  |  |  |  |  |  |
| **Share Capital** |  | 200 |  | 210 |  | 210 |
| Retained profits |  | 64 |  | 67 |  | 78 |
|  |  | 264 |  | 277 |  | 288 |

Note: Interest paid on the bank overdraft was: £3,000 in 20-5, and £15,000 in 20-6.
You are to prepare a cash flow statement for the years ended for 20-5 and 20-6.

**27.5*** The balance sheets of Lallan Limited for the two years to 31 August were as follows:

| | 20-5 | | 20-6 | |
|---|---|---|---|---|
| | £000 | £000 | £000 | £000 |
| **Fixed Assets** | | 1,660 | | 1,960 |
| Less depreciation | | 420 | | 860 |
| | | 1,240 | | 1,100 |
| **Current Assets** | | | | |
| Stock | 540 | | 590 | |
| Debtors | 220 | | 350 | |
| Bank | nil | | 10 | |
| Cash | 20 | | 50 | |
| | 780 | | 1,000 | |
| **Creditors:** | | | | |
| **Amounts falling due within one year** | | | | |
| Bank overdraft | 20 | | nil | |
| Trade creditors | 240 | | 350 | |
| Current taxation | 20 | | 30 | |
| Proposed dividends | 60 | | 80 | |
| | 340 | | 460 | |
| **Net Current Assets** | | 440 | | 540 |
| **Total Assets less Current Liabilities** | | 1,680 | | 1,640 |
| **Creditors:** | | | | |
| **Amounts falling due after more than one year** | | | | |
| Debenture loan | | 400 | | 250 |
| | | 1,280 | | 1,390 |
| **Financed by:** | | | | |
| Ordinary share capital | | 800 | | 900 |
| Profit and loss account | | 480 | | 490 |
| | | 1,280 | | 1,390 |

Note: Ignore interest on the debenture loan.

You are to prepare a cash flow statement in accordance with FRS 1: Cash Flow Statements for the year ended 31 August 20-6.

*Pitman Qualifications*

# MULTIPLE CHOICE QUESTIONS

Read each question carefully.
Choose the one answer you think is correct (calculators may be needed).
The answers are on page 568.

**1**     The manufacturing account calculates

A     production cost of goods completed

B     gross profit on goods sold

C     cost of goods sold

D     non-production overheads

**2**     In manufacturing, direct materials + direct labour + direct expenses
equals:

A     production overheads

B     prime cost

C     production cost

D     non-production overheads

**3**     Which of the following numbered items will be included in the prime
cost of Diglis Manufacturing Limited?

1     purchases of raw materials

2     rent of factory

3     wages paid to production line employees

4     royalties payable to the designer of the product

A     1,2,3

B     1,2,4

C     1,3,4

D     2,3,4

**4**     Which one of the following does not appear in a manufacturing
account?

A     depreciation of factory machinery

B     supervisors' wages

C     depreciation of office equipment

D     factory heating and lighting

5     In a manufacturing business, royalties are included under the heading of:

A     selling and distribution costs

B     production overheads

C     raw materials

D     direct expenses

6     For a manufacturing business, which type of stock is recorded in the trading account?

A     raw materials

B     work-in-progress

C     partly manufactured goods

D     finished goods

7     Which of the following will be charged to profit and loss account in the year-end accounts of Martley Manufacturing Company Limited?

A     royalties payable to the designer of the product

B     depreciation of factory machinery

C     carriage in costs of raw materials

D     salaries of administrative staff

8     A cash flow statement shows:

A     net profit for the year

B     change in working capital for the year

C     the cash flowing in and out of the business during the year

D     a reconciliation with the bank statement balance

9     Which one of the following items, in a cash flow statement, would not be shown in the operating activities section?

A     dividends paid

B     depreciation for year

C     change in debtors

D     change in stock

**10**     Which one of the following items, in a cash flow statement, would not be shown in the returns on investments and servicing of finance section?

A     interest paid

B     repayment of long-term loan

C     dividends received

D     interest received

**11**     In a cash flow statement, which one of the following items would be shown in the capital expenditure and financial investment section?

A     interest received

B     sale of fixed assets

C     change in debtors

D     long-term loan raised

**12**     In a cash flow statement, which one of the following items would be shown in the financing section?

A     dividends paid

B     decrease in cash

C     repayment of a long-term loan

D     corporation tax paid

# 28 INTERPRETATION OF ACCOUNTS

The final accounts of businesses are often interpreted for decision-making, planning and control purposes in order to assess strengths and weaknesses. A business needs to be performing well in areas of profitability, solvency/liquidity, and asset utilisation.

In this chapter we examine:

- the importance of interpretation of financial statements
- the main accounting ratios and performance indicators
- a commentary on trends shown by the main accounting ratios
- how to report on the overall financial situation of a business
- limitations in the interpretation of accounts

## INTERESTED PARTIES

Interpretation of accounts is not always made by an accountant; interested parties include:

- general management of the business, who need to make financial decisions affecting the future development of the business
- bank manager, who is being asked to lend money to finance the business
- creditors, who wish to assess the likelihood of receiving payment
- customers, who wish to be assured of continuity of supplies in the future
- shareholders of a limited company, who wish to be assured that their investment is sound
- prospective investors in a limited company, who wish to compare comparative strengths and weaknesses
- employees and trade unions, who wish to check on the financial prospects of the business
- government departments, eg Inland Revenue, HM Customs and Excise, that wish to check they are receiving the amount due to them

In all of these cases, the interested party will be able to calculate the main ratios, percentages and performance indicators. By doing this, the strengths and weaknesses of the business will be highlighted and appropriate conclusions can be drawn.

# TYPES OF ACCOUNTING RATIOS & PERFORMANCE INDICATORS

The general term 'accounting ratios' is usually used to describe the calculations aspect of interpretation of accounts. The term ratio is, in fact, partly misleading because the performance indicators include percentages, time periods, as well as ratios in the strict sense of the word.

Most ratios are applicable to sole traders, partnerships and limited companies; however, as we will see, there are a number which relate specifically to the share capital and reserves of limited companies.

The main themes covered by the interpretation of accounts are:

* profitability, the relationship between profit and sales turnover, assets and capital employed

* solvency/liquidity, which considers the stability of the business on both a short-term and long-term basis

* asset utilisation, the effective and efficient use of assets

* investment ratios, which examine the returns to shareholders in companies

# MAKING USE OF ACCOUNTING RATIOS

It is important when examining a set of financial statements and calculating accounting ratios to relate them to reference points or standards. These points of reference might be to:

* establish trends from past years, to provide a standard of comparison

* benchmark against other businesses in the same industry

* compare with standards assumed to be satisfactory by the interested party, eg a bank

Above all, it is important to understand the relationships between ratios: one ratio may give an indication of the state of the business, but this needs to be supported by other ratios. Ratios can indicate symptoms, but the cause will then need to be investigated.

Another use of ratios is to estimate forward the likely profit or balance sheet of a business. For example, it might be assumed that the same gross profit percentage as last year will also apply next year; thus, given an estimated increase in sales, it is a simple matter to estimate gross profit. In a similar way, by making use of ratios, net profit and the balance sheet can be forecast.

Whilst all of the ratios calculated in this chapter use figures from the profit and loss account and balance sheet, the cash flow statement is important too. It assists in confirming the views shown by the accounting ratios and provides further evidence of the position.

Look first at the diagram on the next two pages. It shows the ways in which the profitability of a business is assessed. Then read the section 'Profitability' which follows.

**Gross profit/sales percentage** $=$ $\dfrac{\text{Gross profit}}{\text{Sales}} \times \dfrac{100}{1}$

**Expense/sales percentage** $=$ $\dfrac{\text{Specified selling expenses}}{\text{Sales}} \times \dfrac{100}{1}$

**Operating profit/sales percentage** $=$ $\dfrac{\text{Operating profit*}}{\text{Sales}} \times \dfrac{100}{1}$

\* profit before interest and tax

**Net profit/sales percentage** $=$ $\dfrac{\text{Net profit}}{\text{Sales}} \times \dfrac{100}{1}$

**Return on capital employed** $=$ $\dfrac{\text{Operating profit}}{\text{Capital employed*}} \times \dfrac{100}{1}$

\* share capital + reserves + long-term liabilities

**Return on net assets employed** $=$ $\dfrac{\text{Net profit}}{\text{Net assets*}} \times \dfrac{100}{1}$

\* defined (for ratio analysis) as:
fixed assets + current assets − current liabilities

OTHER PROFITABILITY RATIOS (explained in the text):
- return on equity
- return on net assets employed
- primary ratio

**Wyvern Trading Company Limited**
# TRADING AND PROFIT AND LOSS ACCOUNT
**for the year ended 31 December 20-7**

|  | £000s | £000s |
|---|---|---|
| **Sales** |  | 1,430 |
| Opening stock | 200 |  |
| Purchases | 1,000 |  |
|  | 1,200 |  |
| Less Closing stock | 240 |  |
| Cost of Goods Sold |  | 960 |
| **Gross profit** |  | 470 |
| Less expenses: |  |  |
| **Selling expenses** | 150 |  |
| Administration expenses | 140 |  |
|  |  | 290 |
| **Operating profit** |  | 180 |
| Less: Debenture interest |  | 10 |
| **Net profit for year before taxation** |  | 170 |
| Less: Corporation tax |  | 50 |
| Profit for year after taxation |  | 120 |
| Less: |  |  |
| preference dividend paid | 25 |  |
| ordinary dividend proposed | 75 |  |
|  |  | 100 |
| Retained profit for the year |  | 20 |
| Add balance of retained profits at beginning of year |  | 180 |
| Balance of retained profits at end of year |  | 200 |

# BALANCE SHEET (extract)

| | |
|---|---|
| **Net assets employed** (fixed assets + current assets − current liabilities) | 1,550 |
| **Capital employed** (share capital + reserves + long-term liabilities) | 1,550 |

*Notes:*
- *For ratio analysis, capital employed and net assets employed are the same amount*
- *Items used in the ratios on the opposite page are shown in bold type on a grey background*

# PROFITABILITY

One of the main objectives of a business is to make a profit. Profitability ratios examine the relationship between profit and sales turnover, assets and capital employed. Before calculating the profitability ratios, it is important to read the profit and loss account in order to review the figures.

The key profitability ratios are illustrated on the previous two pages. We will be calculating the accounting ratios from these figures in the Worked Example (pages 467 - 473).

## gross profit percentage

This expresses, as a percentage, the gross profit (sales minus cost of sales) in relation to sales. For example, a gross profit percentage of 20 per cent means that for every £100 of sales made, the gross profit is £20.

The gross profit percentage should be similar from year-to-year for the same business. It will vary between organisations in different areas of business, eg the gross profit percentage on jewellery is considerably higher than that on food. A significant change from one year to the next, particularly a fall in the percentage, requires investigation into the buying and selling prices.

Gross profit percentage, and also net profit percentage (see next page), needs to be considered in context. For example, a supermarket may well have a lower gross profit percentage than a small corner shop but, because of the supermarket's much higher turnover, the amount of profit will be much higher. Whatever the type of business, gross profit – both as an amount and a percentage – needs to be sufficient to cover the overheads (expenses),  and then to give an acceptable return on capital.

## expense/sales percentage

A large expense item can be expressed as a percentage of sales: for example, the relationship between advertising and sales might be found to be 10 per cent in one year, but 20 per cent the next year. This could indicate that an increase in advertising had failed to produce a proportionate increase in sales.

Note that each expense falls into one of three categories of cost:

- fixed costs, or
- variable costs, or
- semi-variable costs

Fixed costs remain constant despite other changes. Variable costs alter with changed circumstances, such as increased output or sales. Semi-variable costs combine both a fixed and a variable element, eg hire of a car at a basic (fixed) cost, with a variable cost per mile. It is important to appreciate the nature of costs when interpreting accounts: for example, if sales this year are twice last year's figure, not all expenses will have doubled.

## operating profit percentage

Net profit percentage is calculated after loan and bank interest has been charged to profit and loss account. Thus it may be distorted when comparisons are made between two different businesses where one is heavily financed by means of loans, and the other is financed by owner's capital. The solution is to calculate the operating profit percentage which uses profit before interest and tax.

## net profit percentage

As with gross profit percentage, the net profit percentage should be similar from year-to-year for the same business, and should also be comparable with other firms in the same line of business. Net profit percentage should, ideally, increase from year-to-year, which indicates that the profit and loss account costs are being kept under control. Any significant fall should be investigated to see if it has been caused by

- a fall in gross profit percentage
- and/or an increase in one particular expense, eg wages and salaries, advertising, etc

## return on capital employed (ROCE)

This expresses the profit of a business in relation to the owner's capital. For this calculation, the capital at the start of the year should, ideally, be used; if this is not known, the year-end capital figure can be used. The percentage return is best thought of in relation to other investments, eg a building society might offer a return of five per cent, or a bank might offer three per cent on a deposit account. A person running a business is investing a sum of money in that business, and the profit is the return that is achieved on that investment. However, it should be noted that the risks in running a business are considerably greater than depositing the money with a building society or bank, and an additional return to allow for the extra risk is needed.

For limited companies, the calculation of return on capital employed must take note of their different methods of financing. It is necessary to distinguish between the ordinary shareholders' investment (the equity) and the capital employed by the company, which includes preference shares and debentures/long-term loans:

|        | *Ordinary share capital*         |
|--------|----------------------------------|
|        | *Ordinary share capital*         |
| *add*    | *Reserves (capital and revenue)* |
| *equals* | *Equity*                         |
| *add*    | *Preference share capital*       |
| *add*    | *Debentures/long-term loans*     |
| *equals* | *Capital Employed*               |

The reason for including preference shares and debentures/long-term loans in the capital employed is that the company has the use of the money from these contributors for the foreseeable future, or certainly for a fixed time period. These different definitions of capital employed give further accounting ratios:

**return on equity**

Percentage return on equity (also known as return on owners' equity) =

$$\frac{\textit{Profit after tax - preference dividend (if any)}}{\textit{Ordinary share capital + reserves}} \quad x \quad \frac{100}{1}$$

Note that we use the profit after tax and preference dividends (if any), ie it is the profit available for the ordinary shareholders after all other parties (corporation tax, preference share dividend) have been deducted.

**return on capital employed**

Percentage return on capital employed =

$$\frac{\textit{Net profit for year + interest on debentures/long-term loans}}{\textit{Ordinary share capital + reserves + preference share capital}} \quad x \quad \frac{100}{1}$$
$$\textit{+ debentures/long-term loans}$$

Note that, here, the profit is before interest on debentures/long-term loans, ie it is the profit available to the providers of capital (shown as the divisor in the calculation), and before deduction of corporation tax.

**primary ratio**

Return on capital employed is perhaps the most effective ratio used in financial analysis. It is often known as the primary ratio, since it can be broken down into the two secondary factors of:

- net (or operating) profit percentage (see page 457)
- asset turnover ratio (see page 463)

The relationship between the three is:

| *Net profit percentage* | | *Asset turnover ratio* | | *Return on capital employed* |
|:---:|:---:|:---:|:---:|:---:|
| $\dfrac{\text{Net profit}^{\dagger}}{\text{Sales}}$ | X | $\dfrac{\text{Sales}}{\substack{\text{Net assets}^{*}\text{(or}\\ \text{capital employed}^{**})}}$ | = | $\dfrac{\text{Net profit}^{\dagger}}{\text{Capital employed}^{**}}$ |

[†] net profit *or* operating profit

[*] Net assets: defined (for ratio analysis) as fixed assets + current assets – current liabilities

[**] Capital employed: defined as capital/share capital + reserves + long-term liabilities

For example, if a business has a net profit of £50,000, sales of £500,000 and net assets and capital employed of £250,000, the three figures are:

$$\frac{£50,000}{£500,000} \quad \times \quad \frac{£500,000}{£250,000} \quad = \quad \frac{£50,000}{£250,000}$$

$$10\% \quad \times \quad 2 \text{ times} \quad = \quad 20\%$$

The primary ratio is used to help us appreciate that the same return on capital employed can be achieved in different ways, depending on the type of business. Thus, one business may have a net profit percentage of 10 per cent, but an asset turnover of 2 times, while for a different business the respective values might be 2 per cent and 10 times: for both the return on capital employed is 20 per cent. These examples illustrate why, for example, an engineering firm and a supermarket could be equally profitable.

## return on net assets employed

Percentage return on net assets =

$$\frac{\textit{Net profit for year}}{\textit{Net assets*}} \quad x \quad \frac{\textit{100}}{\textit{1}}$$

*fixed assets + current assets − current liabilities

This is an important ratio as it relates the profitability of the business to the value of the net assets in use. It is another way of expressing return on capital employed, but relating profit to assets.

# SOLVENCY/LIQUIDITY

Solvency/liquidity ratios measure the financial stability of the business, ie the ability of the business to pay its way – both on a short-term and long-term basis. For the short-term we focus our attention on the current assets and current liabilities sections of the balance sheet; for the long-term we look at long-term liabilities and the 'financed by' sections.

The key solvency/liquidity ratios are shown on pages 464 and 465, which are linked to the balance sheet of Wyvern Trading Company Limited. The ratios are calculated in the Worked Example (pages 467 - 473).

## working capital

*Working capital  =  Current assets – Current liabilities*

Working capital is needed by all businesses in order to finance day-to-day trading activities. Sufficient working capital enables a business to hold adequate stocks, allow a measure of credit to its customers (debtors), and to pay its suppliers (creditors) as payments fall due.

## working capital ratio (or current ratio)

*Working capital ratio  =  Current assets :  Current liabilities*

Working capital ratio uses figures from the balance sheet and measures the relationship between current assets and current liabilities. Although there is no ideal working capital ratio, an acceptable ratio is about 2:1, ie £2 of current assets to every £1 of current liabilities. However, a business in the retail trade may be able to work with a lower ratio, eg 1.5:1 or even less, because it deals mainly in sales for cash and so does not have a large figure for debtors. A working capital ratio can be too high: if it is above 3:1 an investigation of the make-up of current assets and current liabilities is needed: eg the business may have too much stock, too many debtors, or too much cash at the bank, or even too few creditors.

## liquid ratio (or quick ratio, or acid test)

$$Liquid\ ratio\ =\ \frac{Current\ assets\ -\ \ stock}{Current\ liabilities}$$

The liquid ratio uses the current assets and current liabilities from the balance sheet, but stock is omitted. This is because stock is the most illiquid current asset: it has to be sold, turned into debtors, and then the cash has to be collected from the debtors. Also, some of the stock included in the balance sheet figure may be unsaleable or obsolete. Thus the liquid ratio provides a direct comparison between debtors/cash/bank and short-term liabilities. The balance between liquid assets, that is debtors and cash/bank, and current liabilities should, ideally, be about 1:1, ie £1 of liquid assets to each £1 of current liabilities. At this ratio a business is expected to be able to pay its current liabilities from its liquid assets; a figure below 1:1, eg 0.75:1, indicates that the firm would have difficulty in meeting pressing demands from creditors. However, as with the working capital ratio, some businesses are able to operate with a lower liquid ratio than others.

## capital gearing

Capital gearing percentage  =

$$\frac{\text{Long-term loans (including any preference shares)}}{\text{Capital (ordinary shares + reserves)}} \quad x \quad \frac{100}{1}$$

Whilst the working capital and liquid ratios focus on whether the business can pay its way in the short-term, capital gearing is concerned with long-term financial stability. Here we measure how much of the business is financed by debt (including preference shares) against capital (ordinary shares plus reserves). The higher the gearing percentage, the less secure will be the equity capital of the business and, therefore, the future of the business. This is because debt is costly in terms of interest payments (particularly if interest rates are variable). It is difficult to set a standard for an acceptable gearing ratio: in general terms most investors (or lenders) would not wish to see debt exceeding equity, ie a gearing percentage of greater than 100% is undesirable.

Capital gearing can also be expressed as a ratio, ie debt:equity. Thus a gearing percentage of 100% is a ratio of 1:1.

## interest cover

$$\frac{\text{Net profit + interest (ie operating profit)}}{\text{Interest}} \quad = \quad \text{Interest cover}$$

The interest cover ratio, linked closely to gearing, considers the safety margin (or cover) of profit over the interest payable by a business. For example, if the operating profit of a business was £10,000, and interest payable was £5,000, this would give interest cover of 2, which is a low figure. If the interest was £1,000, this would give interest cover of 10 which is a higher and much more acceptable figure. Thus, the conclusion to draw is that the higher the interest cover, the better (although there is an argument for having some debt).

## ASSET UTILISATION

Asset utilisation measures how effectively management controls the current  aspects of the business – principally stock, debtors and creditors. Like all accounting ratios, comparison needs to be made either with figures for the previous year, or with a similar firm.

## stock turnover

$$\frac{\text{Average stock}}{\text{Cost of goods sold}} \quad x \quad \text{365 days}$$

Stock turnover is the number of days' stock held on average. This figure will depend on the type of goods sold by the business. For example, a market trader selling fresh flowers, who finishes each day when sold out, will have a stock turnover of one day. By contrast, a jewellery shop – because it may hold large stocks of jewellery – will have a much slower stock turnover, perhaps sixty or ninety days, or longer. Nevertheless, stock turnover must not be too long, bearing in mind the type of business, and a business which is improving in efficiency will have a quicker stock turnover comparing one year with the previous one, or with the stock turnover of similar businesses.

Stock turnover can also be expressed as number of times per year:

$$\text{Stock turnover (times per year)} = \frac{\text{Cost of good sold}}{\text{Average stock}}$$

A stock turnover of, say, twelve times a year means that about thirty days' stock is held. Note that stock turnover can only be calculated where a business buys and sells goods; it cannot be used for a business that provides a service.

## debtors' collection period

$$\frac{\text{Debtors}}{\text{Credit sales}} \quad x \quad 365 \ days$$

This calculation shows how many days, on average, debtors take to pay for goods sold to them by the business. The figure of credit sales for the year may not be  disclosed in the trading account, in which case the sales figure should be used. Some businesses make the majority of their sales on credit but others, such as shops, will have a considerably lower proportion of credit sales.

The debt collection time can be compared with that for the previous year, or with that of a similar business. In Britain, most debtors should make payment within about 30 days; however, sales made abroad will take longer for the proceeds to be received. A comparison from year-to-year of the collection period is a measure of the firm's efficiency at collecting the money that is due to it.

## creditors' payment period

$$\frac{\text{Trade creditors}}{\text{Credit purchases}} \quad x \quad 365 \ days$$

This calculation is the opposite aspect to that of debtors: here we are measuring the speed it takes to pay creditors. While creditors can be a useful temporary source of finance, delaying payment too long may cause problems. This ratio is most appropriate for businesses that buy and sell goods; it cannot be used for a business that provides a service; it is also difficult to interpret when a business buys in some goods and, at the same time, provides a service, eg an hotel. Generally, though, we would expect to see the creditor days period longer than the debtor days, ie money is being received from debtors before it is paid out to creditors.

Note that there is invariably an inconsistency in calculating both debtors' collection and creditors' payment periods: the figures for debtors and creditors on the balance sheet include VAT, while sales and purchases from the trading account exclude VAT. Strictly, therefore, we are not comparing like with like; however, the comparison should be made with reference to the previous year, or a similar company, calculated on the same basis from year-to-year.

## asset turnover ratio

$$\frac{Sales}{Net\ assets}$$

This ratio measures the efficiency of the use of net assets in generating sales. An increasing ratio from one year to the next indicates greater efficiency. A fall in the ratio may be caused either by a decrease in sales, or an increase in net assets – perhaps caused by the purchase or revaluation of fixed assets, or increased stockholding, or increased debtors as a result of poor credit control.

Different types of businesses will have very different asset turnover ratios. For example a supermarket, with high sales and relatively few assets, will have a very high figure; by contrast, an engineering business, with lower sales and a substantial investment in fixed and current assets, will have a much lower figure. As we have seen in the primary ratio (page 458), asset turnover and net profit percentage are the two factors which go to making up return on capital employed; therefore, although different types of businesses will have differing asset turnover ratios, they could have the same return on capital employed.

## proprietary ratio

The proprietary ratio, which may also be expressed as a percentage, indicates the proportion of owners' funds to the tangible assets (tangible fixed assets + current assets) of the business. It is calculated as follows:

$$\frac{Ordinary\ shareholders'\ (or\ owners')\ funds}{Tangible\ assets*}$$

\* Tangible assets: assets which have material substance, unlike intangible assets, such as goodwill

As a guideline a ratio of around 0.5:1, or 50 per cent, should be considered as the minimum desirable figure. This shows that half of the tangible assets are owned by the ordinary shareholders or owners, and half by contributors of other types of share and loan capital and by creditors. Intangible assets, such as goodwill, are excluded from this calculation because they would, most probably, be worthless in the event of the forced sale of the business.

Now study the diagram on the next two pages; it sets out and summarises the accounting ratios and performance indicators which illustrate solvency and the levels of asset utilisation.

# SOLVENCY/LIQUIDITY RATIOS

**Working capital ratio** =

$$\frac{\text{Current assets}}{\text{Current liabilities}}$$

**Liquid ratio** =

$$\frac{\text{Current assets} - \text{stock}}{\text{Current liabilities}}$$

**Capital gearing percentage** =

$$\frac{\text{Long-term loans (including preference shares)}}{\text{Capital (ordinary shares + reserves)}} \times \frac{100}{1}$$

# ASSET UTILISATION RATIOS

**Stock turnover (days)** =

$$\frac{\text{Average stock*}}{\text{Cost of goods sold}} \times 365 \text{ days}$$

\* usually taken as: (opening stock + closing stock) ÷ 2;
alternatively, if opening stock figure not available, use closing
stock in calculation

**Debtors' collection period (days)** =

$$\frac{\text{Debtors}}{\text{Credit sales}} \times 365 \text{ days}$$

**Creditors' payment period (days)** =

$$\frac{\text{Trade creditors}}{\text{Credit purchases}} \times 365 \text{ days}$$

**Asset turnover ratio** =

$$\frac{\text{Sales}}{\text{Net assets*}}$$

\* defined (for ratio analysis) as:
fixed assets + current assets – current liabilities

## other ratios

| | |
|---|---|
| *solvency/liquidity* – | interest cover ratio* |
| *asset utilisation* – | proprietary ratio* |

\*explained in the text

**Wyvern Trading Company Limited**
# BALANCE SHEET
**as at 31 December 20-7**

| Fixed Assets | Cost £000s | Dep'n to date £000s | Net £000s |
|---|---|---|---|
| Premises | 850 | – | 850 |
| Fixtures and fittings | 300 | 120 | 180 |
| Vehicles | 350 | 100 | 250 |
| | 1,500 | 220 | 1,280 |

| Current Assets | | | |
|---|---|---|---|
| Stock | | 240 | |
| Debtors | | 150 | |
| Bank/cash | | 135 | |
| | | 525 | |

| Less Current Liabilities | | | |
|---|---|---|---|
| Creditors | 130 | | |
| Proposed ordinary dividend | 75 | | |
| Corporation tax | 50 | | |
| | | 255 | |

| Working Capital | | | 270 |
|---|---|---|---|
| | | | 1,550 |

| Less Long-term Liabilities | | | |
|---|---|---|---|
| 10% Debentures | | | 100 |
| NET ASSETS | | | 1,450 |

**FINANCED BY**
**Authorised and Issued Share Capital**

| | | |
|---|---|---|
| 1,000,000 ordinary shares of £1 each, fully paid | | 1,000 |
| 250,000 10% preference shares of £1 each, fully paid | | 250 |
| | | 1,250 |

**Revenue Reserve**

| | | |
|---|---|---|
| Profit and loss account | | 200 |
| SHAREHOLDERS' FUNDS | | 1,450 |

## PROFIT AND LOSS ACCOUNT  (extract)

| | |
|---|---|
| **Cost of goods sold** | 960 |
| **Credit sales** | 1,430 |
| **Credit purchases** | 1,000 |

*Note: Items used in ratios are shown in bold type with a grey background.*

*Key accounting ratios for solvency/liquidity and asset utilisation*

# INVESTMENT RATIOS

Investment ratios are used by business people and investors who intend to buy either a whole business, or holdings of shares in limited companies. The ratios will help to assess the performance of the company in which they wish to invest.

## dividend yield

$$\frac{\text{Ordinary share dividend (in pence)}}{\text{Market price of ordinary share (in pence)}} \quad x \quad \frac{100}{1}$$

Investors in companies which are quoted on the stock market can obtain this information from the share price pages of the financial press. The dividend yield gives the investor the annual percentage return paid on a quoted share. However, dividend yield is an inadequate measure because it ignores the overall profits – or 'earnings' – available for the ordinary shareholders; retained profits (ie that part of profits not paid as dividends) should help to boost the share price, so giving investors capital growth rather than income.

## earnings per share

$$\frac{\text{Net profit, after corporation tax and preference dividends}}{\text{Number of issued ordinary shares}}$$

Earnings per share (or EPS) measures the amount of profit earned by each share, after corporation tax and preference dividends. Comparisons can be made with previous years to provide a basis for assessing the company's performance.

## earnings yield

$$\frac{\text{Earnings per ordinary share (in pence)}}{\text{Market price of ordinary share (in pence)}} \quad x \quad \frac{100}{1}$$

This compares, in percentage terms, the earnings per ordinary share (after corporation tax and preference dividends) with the market price per share. It is an important calculation for investors because it shows the return earned by the company on each ordinary share. Some part of the earnings will, most likely, have been paid to investors, while the rest will have been retained in the company and should help to increase the capital value of the shares.

## price/earnings ratio

$$\frac{\text{Market price of ordinary share (in pence)}}{\text{Earnings per ordinary share (in pence)}} \quad = \quad \text{Price/earnings ratio}$$

The price/earnings ratio (or P/E ratio, as it is often abbreviated) compares the current market price of a share with the earnings (after corporation tax) of that share. For example, if a particular share has a market price of £3, and the earnings per share in the current year are 30p, then the P/E ratio is 10. This simply means that a person buying the share for £3 is paying ten times the last reported earnings of that share.

Investors use the P/E ratio to help them make decisions as to the 'expensiveness' of a share. In general, high P/E ratios (ie a higher number) indicate that the stock market price has been pushed up in anticipation of an expected improvement in earnings: therefore, the share is now expensive. The reason for a low P/E ratio is usually that investors do not expect much (if any) growth in the company's earnings in the foreseeable future.

P/E ratio is simply a reciprocal of the earnings yield (see above). Thus a P/E ratio of 10 is the same as an earnings yield of 10 per cent; a P/E ratio of 20 is the same as an earnings yield of 5 per cent.

## dividend cover

$$\frac{\textit{Net profit, after corporation tax and preference dividends}}{\textit{Ordinary dividends}}$$

This figure shows the margin of safety between the amount of profit a company makes and the amount paid out in dividends. The figure must be greater than 1 if the company is not to use past retained profits to fund the current dividend. A figure of 5 as dividend cover indicates that profit exceeds dividend by five times – a healthy sign. The share price pages in the financial press quote the figure under the column headed 'cover' or 'cvr'.

## WORKED EXAMPLE: WYVERN TRADING COMPANY

Interpretation of accounts is much more than the mechanical process of calculating a number of ratios; instead, it involves the analysis of the relationships between the figures in the accounts and the presentation of the information gathered in a meaningful way to interested parties.

In the example which follows, we will look at the set of accounts of a limited company. For clarity, one year's accounts are given although, in practice, more than one year's accounts should be used. The comments given indicate what should be looked for when analysing and interpreting a set of accounts.

### question

The following are the accounts of Wyvern Trading Company Limited. The business trades in office supplies and sells to the public through its three retail shops in the Wyvern area; it also delivers direct to businesses in the area from its modern warehouse on a local business park.

**Wyvern Trading Company Limited**
**TRADING AND PROFIT AND LOSS ACCOUNT**
**for the year ended 31 December 20-7**

|  | £000s | £000s |
|---|---:|---:|
| Sales | | 1,430 |
| Opening stock | 200 | |
| Purchases | 1,000 | |
| | 1,200 | |
| Less Closing stock | 240 | |
| Cost of Goods Sold | | 960 |
| **Gross profit** | | 470 |
| Less expenses: | | |
| Selling expenses | 150 | |
| Administration expenses | 140 | |
| | | 290 |
| **Operating profit** | | 180 |
| Less: Debenture interest | | 10 |
| **Net profit for year before taxation** | | 170 |
| Less: Corporation tax | | 50 |
| Profit for year after taxation | | 120 |
| Less: | | |
| preference dividend paid | 25 | |
| ordinary dividend proposed | 75 | |
| | | 100 |
| Retained profit for the year | | 20 |
| Add balance of retained profits at beginning of year | | 180 |
| Balance of retained profits at end of year | | 200 |

### Wyvern Trading Company Limited
### BALANCE SHEET
### as at 31 December 20-7

| Fixed Assets | Cost £000s | Dep'n to date £000s | Net £000s |
|---|---|---|---|
| Premises | 850 | – | 850 |
| Fixtures and fittings | 300 | 120 | 180 |
| Vehicles | 350 | 100 | 250 |
| | 1,500 | 220 | 1,280 |

**Current Assets**

| | | | |
|---|---|---|---|
| Stock | | 240 | |
| Debtors | | 150 | |
| Bank/cash | | 135 | |
| | | 525 | |

**Less Current Liabilities**

| | | | |
|---|---|---|---|
| Creditors | 130 | | |
| Proposed ordinary dividend | 75 | | |
| Corporation tax | 50 | | |
| | | 255 | |

| **Working Capital** | 270 |
|---|---|
| | 1,550 |

| **Less Long-term Liabilities** | |
|---|---|
| 10% debentures | 100 |
| **NET ASSETS** | 1,450 |

**FINANCED BY:**
**Authorised and Issued Share Capital**

| | |
|---|---|
| 1,000,000 ordinary shares of £1 each, fully paid | 1,000 |
| 250,000 10% preference shares of £1 each, fully paid | 250 |
| | 1,250 |

**Revenue Reserve**

| | |
|---|---|
| Profit and loss account | 200 |
| **SHAREHOLDERS' FUNDS** | 1,450 |

Note: the current market price of the ordinary shares is £1.25.

## answer

We will now analyse the accounts from the point of view of a potential investor. All figures shown are in £000s.

PROFITABILITY
**Gross profit/sales percentage**

$$\frac{£470}{£1,430} \quad x \quad \frac{100}{1} \qquad\qquad = \quad 32.87\%$$

**Specified expense: selling expenses to sales**

$$\frac{£150}{£1,430} \quad x \quad \frac{100}{1} \qquad\qquad = \quad 10.49\%$$

**Operating profit/sales percentage**

$$\frac{£180}{£1,430} \quad x \quad \frac{100}{1} \qquad\qquad = \quad 12.59\%$$

**Net profit/sales percentage**

$$\frac{£170}{£1,430} \quad x \quad \frac{100}{1} \qquad\qquad = \quad 11.89\%$$

**Return on capital employed**

$$\frac{£170 + £10}{£1,000 + £250 + £200 + £100} \quad x \quad \frac{100}{1} \qquad = \quad 11.61\%$$

**Return on equity**

$$\frac{£120 - £25}{£1,000 + £200} \quad x \quad \frac{100}{1} \qquad\qquad = \quad 7.92\%$$

**Return on net assets\* employed**

$$\frac{£170}{£1,550} \quad x \quad \frac{100}{1} \qquad\qquad = \quad 10.97\%$$

\* fixed assets + current assets – current liabilities

**Primary ratio**
12.59% (operating profit %) x 0.922 (asset turnover ratio) $\qquad = \quad 11.61\%$

The gross and net profit percentages seem to be acceptable figures for the type of business, although comparisons should be made with those of the previous accounting period. A business should always aim at least to hold its percentages and, ideally, to make a small improvement. A significant fall in the percentages may indicate a poor buying policy, poor pricing (perhaps caused by competition), and the causes should be investigated.

Selling expenses seem to be quite a high percentage of sales. As these are likely to be a relatively fixed cost, it would seem that the business could increase sales turnover without a corresponding increase in sales expenses.

The small difference between net profit percentage and operating profit percentage indicates that finance costs are relatively low.

Return on capital employed is satisfactory, but could be better. The primary ratio shows how return on capital employed has been held back by a sluggish asset turnover ratio (see page 463). At 11.61% return on capital employed is less than two percentage points above the ten per cent cost of the preference shares and debentures (ignoring the taxation advantages of issuing debentures). Return on equity is 7.92% and needs to be compared with the returns available elsewhere. This is not to suggest that the directors (who may well own the majority of the shares) should sell up: the business is likely to provide them (and others) with employment – directors' remuneration having been deducted before arriving at the profit figure used in the calculations. The figure for return on net assets employed confirms the mediocre performance of the company in this area.

## SOLVENCY/LIQUIDITY

**Working capital ratio**

$$\frac{£525}{£255} \qquad = \qquad 2.06:1$$

**Liquid ratio**

$$\frac{(£525 - £240)}{£255} \qquad = \qquad 1.12:1$$

**Capital gearing**

$$\frac{£250 + £100}{£1,000 + £200} \quad \times \quad \frac{100}{1} \qquad = \qquad 29\% \text{ or } 0.29:1$$

**Interest cover**

$$\frac{£170 + £10}{£10} \qquad = \qquad 18 \text{ times}$$

The working capital and liquid ratios are excellent: they are slightly higher than the expected 'norms' of 2:1 and 1:1 respectively (although many companies operate successfully with lower ratios); however, they are not too high which would be an indication of inefficient use of assets.

The capital gearing percentage is low: anything up to 100% (1:1) could be seen. With a low figure of 29% this indicates that the company could borrow more money if it wished to finance, say, expansion plans (there are plenty of fixed assets for a lender – such as a bank – to take as security for a loan). The interest cover figure of 18 is very high and shows that the company has no problems in paying interest.

All-in-all, the company is very solvent, with no solvency or liquidity problems.

## ASSET UTILISATION

**Stock turnover**

$$\frac{(£200 + £240) \div 2 \ \times \ 365}{£960} \qquad\qquad = \text{83.6 days (or 4.36 times per year)}$$

**Debtors' collection period**

$$\frac{£150 \ \times \ 365}{£1,430} \qquad\qquad = \text{38.3 days}$$

**Creditors' payment period**

$$\frac{£130 \ \times \ 365}{£1,000} \qquad\qquad = \text{47.4 days}$$

**Asset turnover ratio**

$$\frac{£1,430}{£1,550*} \qquad\qquad = \ 0.92{:}1$$

\* fixed assets + current assets – current liabilities

**Proprietory ratio**

$$\frac{£1,000 + £200}{£1,280 + £525} \qquad\qquad = \ 0.66{:}1$$

This group of ratios shows the main weakness of the company: not enough business is passing through for the size of the company. Stock turnover is very low for an office supplies business: the stock is turning over only every 83 days – surely it should be faster than this. Debtors' collection period is acceptable on the face of it – 30 days would be better – but quite a volume of the sales will be made through the retail outlets in cash. This amount should, if known, be deducted from the sales turnover before calculating the debtors' collection period: thus the collection period is, in reality, longer than that calculated. Creditors' payment period is quite leisurely for this type of business – long delays could cause problems with suppliers in the future. The asset turnover ratio says it all: this type of business should be able to obtain a much better figure:

- either, sales need to be increased using the same net assets

- or, sales need to be maintained, but net assets reduced

The proprietory ratio is good: above the suggested minimum figure of 50 per cent, indicating that the ordinary shareholders are financing 66% of the tangible assets.

## INVESTMENT RATIOS

**Dividend yield\***

$$\frac{£75}{(1,000 \times £1.25)} \ \times \ \frac{100}{1} \qquad\qquad = \ 6\%$$

\* like a number of investment ratios, this can be calculated either per share, or on the total shares in issue (as above).

**Earnings per share**

$$\frac{(£170 - £50 - £25)}{1,000}$$ = 9.5 pence per share

**Earnings yield**

$$\frac{9.5p}{125p} \times \frac{100}{1}$$ = 7.6%

**Price/earnings ratio**

$$\frac{125p}{9.5p}$$ = 13.16 times

**Dividend cover**

$$\frac{(£170 - £50 - £25)}{£75}$$ = 1.27 times

These ratios indicate that the company is not highly profitable for its shareholders (although shares are often bought for potential capital gains rather than income). The dividend yield is only 6 per cent, and the dividend is covered just 1.27 times: if profits were to fall, it is unlikely that the current level of dividend could be sustained. The lower price/earnings ratio seems appropriate for this company.

## CASH FLOW STATEMENT

As well as the profit and loss account and balance sheet, we would need to see the company's cash flow statement to assist in confirming the views shown by the accounting ratios. In particular, we would be looking at:

- the cash inflow from operating activities
- the purchase of fixed assets, and how these have been financed
- the amount of dividends paid during the year
- the change in the bank and cash balances over the year

## CONCLUSION

This appears to be a profitable business, although there may be some scope for cutting down somewhat on the profit and loss account selling expenses (administration expenses could be looked at too). The business offers a reasonable return on capital, although things could be improved.

The company is solvent and has good working capital and liquid capital ratios. Gearing is low – a good sign during times of variable interest rates.

The main area of weakness is in asset utilisation. It appears that the company could do much to reduce the days for stock turnover and the debtors' collection period; at the same time creditors could be paid faster. Asset turnover is very low for this type of business and it does seem that there is much scope for expansion within the structure of the existing company. As the benefits of expansion flow through to the final accounts, the investment ratios will show an improvement from their present leisurely performance.

# Limitations in the Interpretation of Accounts

Although accounting ratios can usefully highlight strengths and weaknesses, they should always be considered as a part of the overall assessment of a business, rather than as a whole. We have already seen the need to place ratios in context and relate them to a reference point or standard. The limitations of ratio analysis should always be borne in mind.

## retrospective nature of accounting ratios

Accounting ratios are usually retrospective, based on previous performance and conditions prevailing in the past. They may not necessarily be valid for making forward projections: for example, a large customer may become insolvent, so threatening the business with a bad debt, and also reducing sales in the future.

## differences in accounting policies

When the accounts of a business are compared, either with previous years' figures, or with figures from a similar business, there is a danger that the comparative accounts are not drawn up on the same basis as those currently being worked on. Different accounting policies, in respect of depreciation and stock valuation for instance, may well result in distortion and invalid comparisons.

## inflation

Inflation may prove a problem, as most financial statements are prepared on an historic cost basis, that is, assets and liabilities are recorded at their original cost. As a result, comparison of figures from one year to the next may be difficult. In countries where inflation is running at high levels any form of comparison becomes practically meaningless.

## reliance on standards

We have already mentioned guideline standards for some accounting ratios, for instance 2:1 for the working capital ratio. There is a danger of relying too heavily on such suggested standards, and ignoring other factors in the balance sheet. An example of this would be to criticise a business for having a low current ratio when the business sells the majority of its goods for cash and consequently has a very low debtors figure: this would in fact be the case with many well-known and successful retail companies. Large manufacturing businesses are able to operate with lower working capital ratios because of their good reputation and creditworthiness.

## other considerations

**Economic**: The general economic climate and the effect this may have on the nature of the business, eg in an economic downturn retailers are usually the first to suffer, whereas manufacturers feel the effects later.

**State of the business**: The chairman's report for a limited company should be read in conjunction with the final accounts and cash flow statements to ascertain an overall view of the state of the business. Of great importance are the products of the company and their stage in the product life cycle, eg is a car manufacturer relying on old models, or is there an up-to-date product range which appeals to buyers?

**Comparing like with like**: Before making comparisons between 'similar' businesses (or, indeed, departments or divisions – see below – within the same business), we need to ensure that we are comparing 'like with like'. Differences, such as the acquisition of assets – renting premises compared with ownership, leasing vehicles compared with ownership – will affect the profitability of the business and the structure of the balance sheet; likewise, the long-term financing of a business – the balance between share capital/owner's capital and loans – will also have an effect.

# THE USE OF DEPARTMENTAL ACCOUNTS

As well as calculating accounting ratios for a business as a whole, where a business is split into a number of different departments or divisions, departmental accounts can be used to identify the gross and net profits of the separate sections. For example, consider a large store which is divided into several different departments such as furniture, clothes, kitchenware, electrical goods, etc; which of the following statements of profit do you think the management of the business will find more useful?

(a)    Gross profit for store           £150,000

(b)    Gross profit:

| | | |
|---|---|---|
| furniture | £20,000 | profit |
| clothes | £80,000 | profit |
| kitchenware | (£10,000) | loss |
| electrical | £60,000 | profit |
| Total | £150,000 | |

Clearly the profit analysed between departments enables the management to identify and then investigate the poor performance of a particular department.

While a department usually forms a physical part of the rest of the business, its manager may have considerable autonomy with regard to purchasing goods, staffing levels and selling prices. The manager may well be set targets by the management and then left to decide how to achieve these targets. A departmental accounting system will show if the targets have been achieved.

# DEPARTMENTAL TRADING ACCOUNTS

In order to prepare a departmental trading account, an analysis of purchases and sales between departments has to be made in the accounting system, together with a departmental stock-take at the end of the accounting period.

## WORKED EXAMPLE: DEPARTMENTAL TRADING ACCOUNTS

### question

Wyvern Superstore Ltd has the following information about its three departments – carpets, clothes and furniture, for the year ended 31 December 20-1:

|  |  | £ |
|---|---|---|
| Sales: |  |  |
|  | Carpets | 220,000 |
|  | Clothes | 350,000 |
|  | Furniture | 150,000 |
| Purchases: |  |  |
|  | Carpets | 130,000 |
|  | Clothes | 180,000 |
|  | Furniture | 100,000 |

| Stock: |  | 1 Jan 20-1 | 31 Dec 20-1 |
|---|---|---|---|
|  |  | £ | £ |
|  | Carpets | 50,000 | 55,000 |
|  | Clothes | 60,000 | 70,000 |
|  | Furniture | 35,000 | 30,000 |

Prepare the departmental trading account for the year and calculate the gross profit percentage for each department and the business as a whole.

## answer

| | Carpet department | | Clothes department | | Furniture department | | Total | |
|---|---|---|---|---|---|---|---|---|
| **WYVERN SUPERSTORE LTD** DEPARTMENTAL TRADING ACCOUNT FOR THE YEAR ENDED 31 DECEMBER 20-1 | | | | | | | | |
| | £ | £ | £ | £ | £ | £ | £ | £ |
| Sales | | 220,000 | | 350,000 | | 150,000 | | 720,000 |
| Opening stock | 50,000 | | 60,000 | | 35,000 | | 145,000 | |
| Purchases | 130,000 | | 180,000 | | 100,000 | | 410,000 | |
| | 180,000 | | 240,000 | | 135,000 | | 555,000 | |
| Less Closing stock | 55,000 | | 70,000 | | 30,000 | | 155,000 | |
| Cost of Goods Sold | | 125,000 | | 170,000 | | 105,000 | | 400,000 |
| Gross profit | | 95,000 | | 180,000 | | 45,000 | | 320,000 |
| | | | | | | | | |
| Gross profit percentage | | 43% | | 51% | | 30% | | 44% |

The gross profit figures and their relative gross profit percentages for each department will lead to an investigation into the reasons for the poor performance of a particular department. For example, the 30 per cent gross profit percentage achieved by the Furniture Department is well below that of the other two departments and of the store as a whole; the reasons for this need to be investigated.

## departmental profit and loss accounts

The departmental analysis can be carried further than the trading account by analysing the profit and loss account items. Each department must be charged with its share of the various expense items, using the following guidelines:

- Expenses directly attributable to a particular department should be allocated to that department.

- Selling expenses, for example advertising, should be apportioned to departments in the same proportions as their net sales.

- Administration expenses and general expenses are often apportioned on the basis of net sales.

- For other expenses, a suitable basis of apportionment should be used. For example, expenses of running the building, eg heating, lighting, rent, business rates, buildings insurance – might be apportioned on the basis of the floor area occupied by each department. Insurance premiums on the stock might be charged to departments on the basis of the average stock value.

- Interest may be charged to departments based on the estimated amount of capital employed by each department.

## WORKED EXAMPLE: DEPARTMENTAL PROFIT & LOSS ACCOUNTS

### question

Wyvern Superstore Ltd (see above) has the following expenses for the year ended 31 December 20-1:

|  |  | £ |
|---|---|---|
| Salaries: | Carpet department | 25,000 |
|  | Clothes department | 40,000 |
|  | Furniture department | 20,000 |
|  |  |  |
| Advertising |  | 36,000 |
| Administration |  | 72,000 |
| Rent and rates |  | 60,000 |
| Heating and lighting |  | 10,000 |

The expenses are to be apportioned as follows:
* advertising and administration – on the basis of sales
* rent and rates, and heating and lighting – on the basis of floor area, which is carpets one-quarter, clothes one-quarter, and furniture one-half

Prepare the departmental profit and loss account for the year, commencing with the departmental gross profits from the example above, and calculate the net profit percentage for each department and the business as a whole.

### answer

**WYVERN SUPERSTORE LTD**
**DEPARTMENTAL PROFIT & LOSS ACCOUNT FOR THE YEAR ENDED 31 DECEMBER 20-1**

|  | Carpet department | | Clothes department | | Furniture department | | Total | |
|---|---|---|---|---|---|---|---|---|
|  | £ | £ | £ | £ | £ | £ | £ | £ |
| Gross profit |  | 95,000 |  | 180,000 |  | 45,000 |  | 320,000 |
| Salaries | 25,000 |  | 40,000 |  | 20,000 |  | 85,000 |  |
| Advertising | 11,000 |  | 17,500 |  | 7,500 |  | 36,000 |  |
| Administration | 22,000 |  | 35,000 |  | 15,000 |  | 72,000 |  |
| Rent and rates | 15,000 |  | 15,000 |  | 30,000 |  | 60,000 |  |
| Heating and lighting | 2,500 |  | 2,500 |  | 5,000 |  | 10,000 |  |
|  |  | 75,500 |  | 110,000 |  | 77,500 |  | 263,000 |
| Net profit/(loss) |  | 19,500 |  | 70,000 |  | (32,500) |  | 57,000 |
|  |  |  |  |  |  |  |  |  |
| Net Profit Percentages |  | 9% |  | 20% |  | (22%) |  | 8% |

## loss-making departments

When a departmental profit and loss account identifies a loss-making department, thoughts will inevitably turn towards closing that department in order to 'save' costs. However, the management needs to remember that, if the department is closed, there is unlikely to be a large reduction in profit and loss account expenses (or 'overheads') – rent and rates, heating and lighting, and administration costs will continue to be paid and will have to be shared out amongst the remaining departments. Moreover, closing one department may well affect the sales of others: eg closing the furniture department of a store may result in reduced sales in the carpet department.

Faced with a loss-making department, the management should consider one of the following actions:

- keep the department open, identifying the reasons for the loss and correcting them
- close the department and expand other departments into its floor area
- look for a more profitable use of the floor area occupied by the poor-performing department
- lease the floor area to another business

# CHAPTER SUMMARY

*The key accounting ratios are summarised in this chapter on pages 454 and 464.*
*A 'help sheet' to assist with the key accounting ratios is given in Appendix 1.*

- Accounting ratios are numerical values – percentages, time periods, ratios – extracted from the financial statements of businesses.

- Accounting ratios can be used to measure:
  - profitability
  - solvency/liquidity
  - asset utilisation
  - investment potential

- Comparisons need to be made with previous financial statements, or those of similar companies.

- There are a number of limitations to be borne in mind when drawing conclusions from accounting ratios:
  - retrospective nature, based on past performance
  - differences in accounting policies
  - effects of inflation when comparing year-to-year
  - reliance on standards
  - economic and other factors

- Departmental accounts are used to identify the gross and net profits of different departments or divisions within a business.

- Separate departmental trading and profit and loss accounts are prepared, although guidelines need to be established for charging expenses to each department.

# QUESTIONS

**28.1***  The following information is taken from the profit and loss accounts of two plcs:

|  | A plc | B plc |
|---|---|---|
|  | £m | £m |
| Sales | 55.7 | 22.3 |
| Cost of Goods Sold | (49.1) | (10.2) |
| GROSS PROFIT | 6.6 | 12.1 |
| Expenses | (4.4) | (6.3) |
|  |  |  |
| Interest paid | (0.6) | (1.1) |
| NET PROFIT BEFORE TAX | 1.6 | 4.7 |
|  |  |  |
| Note: Capital employed | £8.8m | £34.3m |

You are to calculate, for each company:
- gross profit percentage
- net profit percentage
- operating profit percentage
- return on capital employed

**28.2***  The following is taken from the balance sheets of two plcs:

|  | C plc | D plc |
|---|---|---|
|  | £m | £m |
| Stock | 3.8 | 4.1 |
| Debtors | 4.5 | 0.7 |
| Bank/(bank overdraft) | (0.4) | 6.3 |
| Creditors | 5.1 | 10.7 |
| Long-term loans | 3.2 | 2.1 |
| Ordinary share capital | 4.5 | 8.4 |
| Reserves | 1.4 | 4.7 |
|  |  |  |
| Notes: |  |  |
| Sales for year | 43.9 | 96.3 |
| Purchases for year | 32.4 | 85.1 |
| Cost of goods sold for year | 33.6 | 84.7 |

You are to calculate, for each company:
- working capital ratio
- liquid ratio

- debtors' collection period
- creditors' payment period
- stock turnover
- gearing ratio

One company runs department stores, the other is a chemical manufacturer. Which is which? Why is this?

**28.3\*** The following is taken from the balance sheets of two plcs:

|  | ABC plc | XYZ plc |
|---|---|---|
| Ordinary dividend for year | £750,000 | £1,250,000 |
| Number of issued ordinary shares of £1 each | 5,000,000 | 15,000,000 |
| Current market price per share | £1.50 | £6.00 |
| Net profit after corporation tax and preference dividends | £1,500,000 | £5,500,000 |

Note: both companies are in the same industry.
For each business, calculate:

- dividend yield

- earnings per share

- earnings yield

- price/earnings ratio

- dividend cover

You are to state in which company would you invest for (a) capital growth, (b) income.

**28.4** The following information relates to two businesses, A and B:

|  | business A £000s | business B £000s |
|---|---|---|
| **PROFIT AND LOSS ACCOUNT (EXTRACTS)** | | |
| Sales | 3,057 | 1,628 |
| Cost of Goods Sold | 2,647 | 911 |
| **Gross Profit** | 410 | 717 |
| Overheads | 366 | 648 |
| **Net Profit** | 44 | 69 |

|  | business A | | business B | |
|---|---|---|---|---|
|  | £000s | £000s | £000s | £000s |
| **SUMMARISED BALANCE SHEETS** | | | | |
| **Fixed Assets** | | 344 | | 555 |
| **Current Assets** | | | | |
| Stock | 242 | | 237 | |
| Debtors | 6 | | 269 | |
| Bank | 3 | | 1 | |
|  | 251 | | 507 | |
| **Less Current Liabllities** | 195 | | 212 | |
| **Working Capital** | | 56 | | 295 |
| **NET ASSETS** | | 400 | | 850 |
| **FINANCED BY:** | | | | |
| **Capital** | | 400 | | 850 |

One business operates a chain of grocery supermarkets; the other is a heavy engineering company. You are to calculate the following accounting ratios for both businesses:

(a) gross profit percentage

(b) net profit percentage

(c) stock turnover (use balance sheet figure as average stock)

(d) working capital ratio

(e) liquid ratio

(f) debtors' collection period

(g) return on capital employed

Indicate which company you believe to be the grocery supermarket chain and which the heavy engineering business. Briefly explain the reasons for your choice based on the ratios calculated and the accounting information.

28.5 The following summarised information is available to you:

**J D ROWLES: TRADING AND PROFIT AND LOSS ACCOUNT (extracts)**
**for the years ended 30 April 20-5 and 30 April 20-6**

|  | 20-5 | 20-6 |
|---|---|---|
|  | £ | £ |
| Sales (all on credit) | 120,000 | 200,000 |
| Cost of Goods Sold | 80,000 | 150,000 |
| **Gross profit** | 40,000 | 50,000 |
| Expenses | 10,000 | 15,000 |
| **Net profit** | 30,000 | 35,000 |

## BALANCE SHEET (EXTRACTS) AS AT 30 APRIL 20-5 AND 30 APRIL 20-6

|  | 20-5 | | | 20-6 | | |
|---|---|---|---|---|---|---|
|  | £ | £ | £ | £ | £ | £ |
| **Fixed Assets** |  |  | 15,000 |  |  | 12,000 |
| **Current Assets** |  |  |  |  |  |  |
| Stock |  | 7,000 |  |  | 18,000 |  |
| Debtors |  | 12,000 |  |  | 36,000 |  |
| Bank |  | 1,000 |  |  | – |  |
|  |  | 20,000 |  |  | 54,000 |  |
| **Less Current Liabilities** |  |  |  |  |  |  |
| Creditors | 6,000 |  |  | 15,000 |  |  |
| Bank overdraft | – |  |  | 10,000 |  |  |
|  |  | 6,000 |  |  | 25,000 |  |
| **Working Capital** |  |  | 14,000 |  |  | 29,000 |
| **NET ASSETS** |  |  | 29,000 |  |  | 41,000 |
|  |  |  |  |  |  |  |
| **FINANCED BY** |  |  |  |  |  |  |
| **Capital** |  |  |  |  |  |  |
| Opening capital |  |  | 22,000 |  |  | 29,000 |
| Add net profit |  |  | 30,000 |  |  | 35 000 |
|  |  |  | 52,000 |  |  | 64,000 |
| Less drawings |  |  | 23,000 |  |  | 23,000 |
|  |  |  | 29,000 |  |  | 41,000 |

Notes:
- there were no purchases or disposals of fixed assets during the year
- during 20-5 and 20-6 selling prices were reduced in order to stimulate sales
- assume that price levels were stable

You are to use accounting ratios to analyse and assess the profitability, solvency/liquidity and asset utilisation of the business over the two years.

28.6* The final accounts for Springfield Limited for the years ended 30 June Year 8 and 30 June Year 9 are summarised below:

### TRADING AND PROFIT AND LOSS ACCOUNTS FOR YEARS ENDED 30 JUNE

|  | Year 8 | | Year 9 | |
|---|---|---|---|---|
|  | £000 | £000 | £000 | £000 |
| Sales |  | 4,800 |  | 5,500 |
| Less Cost of sales: |  |  |  |  |
| Opening stock | 220 |  | 360 |  |
| Purchases | 2,800 |  | 3,200 |  |
|  | 3,020 |  | 3,560 |  |
| Less Closing stock | 360 |  | 420 |  |
|  |  | 2,660 |  | 3,140 |
| Gross profit |  | 2,140 |  | 2,360 |
| Less Business expenses |  | 1,800 |  | 1,860 |
| Net profit |  | 340 |  | 500 |
| Proposed dividend |  | 200 |  | 300 |
| Retained profit for the year |  | 140 |  | 200 |

### BALANCE SHEETS AT 30 JUNE

|  | Year 8 | Year 9 |
|---|---|---|
|  | £000 | £000 |
| Called up Share Capital – £1 Ordinary shares | 1,300 | 1,300 |
| Profit and loss – retained profit | 540 | 740 |
| Proposed dividend | 200 | 300 |
| Creditors | 300 | 440 |
|  | 2,340 | 2,780 |
|  |  |  |
| Fixed assets | 1,380 | 1,750 |
| Stock | 360 | 420 |
| Debtors | 390 | 410 |
| Bank | 210 | 200 |
|  | 2,340 | 2,780 |

You are required to calculate the undermentioned ratios for each of Years 8 and 9, correct to two decimal places, in the format shown below:

| Ratio | Formula | Year 8 Calculation | Year 8 Answer | Year 9 Calculation | Year 9 Answer |
|---|---|---|---|---|---|
| (a) Rate of stock turnover | | | times | | times |
| (b) Gross profit to sales | | | % | | % |
| (c) Net profit to sales | | | % | | % |
| (d) Sales to capital employed at the year end | | | times | | times |
| (e) Return on capital employed at the year end | | | % | | % |
| (f) Current ratio | | | : 1 | | : 1 |
| (g) Liquidity ratio | | | : 1 | | : 1 |

*LCCI Examinations Board*

**28.7** The owners of Offiah Company and Robinson Company are having a friendly argument over the relative performance of their two similar businesses. The following information is available:

|  | Offiah Co | Robinson Co |
|---|---|---|
|  | £ | £ |
| Sales | 80,000 | 50,000 |
| Gross profit | 12,000 | 18,000 |
| Operating expenses | 4,000 | 12,000 |
| Opening stock | 5,200 | 8,800 |
| Capital employed | 100,000 | 75,000 |
| Creditors | 10,000 | 18,000 |
| Bank overdraft | nil | 400 |
| Closing stock | 5,800 | 10,000 |
| Debtors | 6,000 | 26,800 |
| Cash | 7,000 | nil |

You are required to:

(a)    for each company calculate to one decimal place:

(i)     gross profit margin

(ii)    stock turnover (use cost of goods sold divided by average stock)

(iii)   net profit margin

(iv)   return on capital employed

(v)    debtors' collection period

(vi)   current ratio

(b)    comment on the performance of each of the companies, using the ratios you have calculated

*Pitman Qualifications*

**28.8\***

J Stewart operates two departments, A and B, from which he sells goods that he has purchased. The departments incur their own specific costs as well as sharing costs that have been incurred for the business as a whole.

The following information is available for the year ended 31 December Year 7:

|  | £ |
|---|---|
| Sales | 900,000 |
| Purchases: |  |
| Department A | 160,000 |
| Department B | 240,000 |
| Rates | 81,000 |
| Sales staff salaries | 84,000 |
| Insurances | 36,000 |
| Vehicle running expenses | 7,000 |
| Advertising | 60,000 |
| Administration | 12,000 |
| Depreciation of fixtures and fittings | 9,900 |

Stock, valued at cost were:

|  | A | B |
|---|---|---|
|  | £ | £ |
| 1 January Year 7 | 12,000 | 22,000 |
| 31 December Year 7 | 14,000 | 18,000 |

Additional information is provided as follows:

(1) The number of sales people employed by each department is: Department A – 3, Department B – 4.

(2) The area occupied by each of the departments is as follows:

| | |
|---|---|
| Department A | 5,000 square metres |
| Department B | 4,000 square metres |

(3) The sales were divided between the departments as follows:

| | |
|---|---|
| Department A | 60% |
| Department B | 40% |

(4) The following bases are used for apportioning the expenses between the departments:

| Expenses | Basis of apportionment |
|---|---|
| Rates | area occupied |
| Sales staff salaries | number of sales people |
| Insurances | area occupied |
| Vehicle running expenses | sales value |
| Advertising | sales value |
| Administration | purchases |
| Depreciation of fixtures and fittings | area occupied |

You are required to prepare for J Stewart a columnar trading and profit and loss account for the year ended 31 December Year 7. Columns are required for Department A, Department B and for the total.

*LCCI Examinations Board*

# MULTIPLE CHOICE QUESTIONS

Read each question carefully.
Choose the one answer you think is correct (calculators may be needed).
The answers are on page 568.

1   The following information is available:

|  | £ |
|---|---|
| Sales | 200,000 |
| Purchases | 170,000 |
| Opening stock | 40,000 |
| Closing stock | 50,000 |

Gross profit percentage is:

A   10%
B   15%
C   20%
D   25%

2   The following information has been extracted from the accounts of Teme Traders Ltd:

|  | last year | this year |
|---|---|---|
| Sales | £300,000 | £350,000 |
| Gross profit percentage | 30% | 31% |
| Net profit percentage | 15% | 4% |

What conclusion do you draw?

A   buying prices have increased, but selling prices have not
B   expenses have increased greatly
C   closing stock has increased greatly
D   the company has paid too large a dividend

**3** The primary ratio is:

A      net profit % x asset turnover ratio  =  return on capital employed

B      gross profit % ÷ net profit %  =  operating profit %

C      liquid capital ratio x net profit %  =  asset turnover ratio

D      sales ÷ net assets  =  gearing ratio

**4** Which one of the following would you not take into account when calculating working capital?

A      machinery

B      cash

C      debtors

D      accruals

**5** Which one of the following would you not take into account when calculating the liquid capital ratio?

A      bank overdraft

B      prepayments

C      stock

D      creditors

**6** The following information is available:

| | £ |
|---|---|
| Sales for the year | 450,000 |
| Purchases for the year | 230,000 |
| Opening stock | 60,000 |
| Closing stock | 40,000 |

The stock turnover is:

A      73 days

B      41 days

C      58 days

D      88 days

**7** Which one of the following is the correct calculation for interest cover?

A      total debt/interest

B      interest/total debt

C      operating profit/interest

D      interest/operating profit

Multiple choice questions 8 to 11 relate to the the balance sheet of Mithian plc:

|  | £000 | £000 | £000 |
|---|---|---|---|
| **Fixed Assets** at net book value |  |  | 500 |
| **Current Assets** |  |  |  |
| Stock | 150 |  |  |
| Debtors | 95 |  |  |
| Bank | 5 | 250 |  |
| **Less Current Liabilities** |  |  |  |
| Creditors | 175 |  |  |
| Bank overdraft | 25 | 200 |  |
| **Working Capital** |  |  | 50 |
|  |  |  | 550 |
| **Less Long-term Liabilities** |  |  |  |
| Bank loan |  |  | 100 |
| NET ASSETS |  |  | 450 |
| **Capital and Reserves** |  |  |  |
| Ordinary share capital |  |  | 300 |
| Share premium account |  |  | 50 |
| Profit and loss account |  |  | 100 |
| SHAREHOLDERS' FUNDS |  |  | 450 |

**8** Which is the liquid (acid test) ratio for Mithian plc?

A  1.25:1

B  0.5:1

C  1:1

D  5:1

**9** Which is the calculation for the capital gearing ratio of Mithian plc?

A  300/450 x 100

B  350/450 x 100

C  125/450 x 100

D  100/450 x 100

**10** If Mithian plc's sales for the year are £405,000, which is the asset turnover ratio?

A  0.9:1

B  0.74:1

C  0.81:1

D  1.11:1

**11** Which is the debtors' collection period in days if the credit sales of Mithian plc are £405,000 for the year? (Round up to whole days).

A  86 days

B  68 days

C  158 days

D  61 days

# Computer Accounting

This final section of this book contains a series of four chapters which provide you with a practical 'hands-on' introduction to computer accounting, using Sage Line 50 software.

The four chapters contain text and Case Studies which explain how computer accounting works in practice. Most chapters conclude with an inputting exercise which enables you to enter accounting data into your computer and produce various print-outs.

The chapters are written around a single business – Pronto Supplies Limited – which buys and sells computer equipment and software. If you want to run the exercises 'for real' you will need to obtain from Osborne Books a 'Company' Sage file which has the company details set up on it. All you will have to do then is to enter details of invoices, credit notes and payments, and print out various daybooks, documents and reports.

The 'Company' file is available as a download in the Resources Section of www.osbornebooks.co.uk Back-up files for the inputting exercises are available on request to tutors. Please call Osborne Books on 01905 748071 if you would like further information.

# 29 SETTING UP THE COMPUTER FILES

This chapter explains how a business – Pronto Supplies Limited – sets up its accounting records on the computer.

It is important that you read the chapter carefully. It explains how the account and ledger structure of the Sage Line 50 software used here relates to the accounts and ledger system you have studied earlier in this book. You will see that there are great similarities.

You will not have to input the company details or the customer or supplier accounts – that is all done for you on the files provided by Osborne Books.

This chapter covers:

- the transfer of data from a manual accounting system to a computer accounting system
- the accounts in the Nominal Ledger
- the production of a trial balance from the Nominal Ledger

## technical note on setting up the files in Sage

### availability

The computer transactions contained in this chapter are contained in a file 'Company' , which is available direct from the Osborne Books website www.osbornebooks.co.uk

Please call 01905 748071 if you require further information.

### Sage compatibility

The software used for this backup is Sage Line 50, version 4, which can be read by any subsequent version of Sage Line 50. The version used for illustrating the text is version 7 of Sage Line 50.

### installation

Firstly install the file 'Company' on your computer system so that is accessible to the Sage application program. In order to activate the file, open up Sage Line 50 in the version that you are using. Go to 'Restore' in the main File menu and follow the instructions by locating 'Company'. Sage will then go through a conversion routine and produce a report. The Pronto Supplies Limited files should then be ready for the input exercises in the three chapters which follow this one.

## WHY SAGE AND WHICH SAGE?

Osborne Books (the publisher of this book) has chosen Sage software for this text for two very good reasons:

1 Sage software is widely used in business and is recognised as a user-friendly and reliable product.

2 Osborne Books has used Sage itself for over ten years and is well used to the way it works.

The Sage software used for illustrating this book is Sage Line 50 Accountant Plus (Version 7) for Windows. The screens displayed in this book are reproduced from this version by kind permission of Sage PLC.

### screen illustrations

It should be appreciated that some training centres and businesses may be using older (or newer) versions, and so some of the screens may look slightly different. This does not matter. Using Sage is like driving different models of car – the controls may be located in slightly different places and the dashboard may not look exactly the same, but the controls are still there and they still do the same thing. So if the screens shown here look unfamiliar, examine them carefully and you will see that they contain the same (or very similar) Sage icons and functions as the version you are using.

**Case Study**

# PRONTO SUPPLIES LIMITED: SETTING UP THE COMPANY IN SAGE

### the business

Pronto Supplies is a limited company run by Tom Cox who has worked as a computer consultant for over ten years. Pronto Supplies provides local businesses and other organisations with computer hardware, software and all the other computer 'bits and pieces' such as disks and ink cartridges needed in offices. It also provides consultancy for computer set-ups through its proprietor, Tom Cox. Pronto Supplies has eight employees in total. The business is situated on an industrial estate, at Unit 17 Severnvale Estate, Broadwater Road, Mereford, Wyvern, MR1 6TF.

### the accounting system

Pronto Supplies Limited started business on 1 January 2001. The business is registered for VAT (ie it charges VAT on its sales) and after a month of using a manual accounting system Tom has decided to transfer the accounts to Sage Line 50 software.

and sign up for a year's telephone technical support. Tom has also decided to put his payroll onto the computer, but this will be run on a separate Sage program.

Tom has chosen Sage Line 50 because it will enable him to:

- record the invoices issued to his customers to whom he sells on credit
- pay his suppliers on the due date
- keep a record of his bank receipts and payments
- record his income and expenses, business assets and loans in a main (nominal) ledger

In short he will have a computer accounting package which will enable him to:

- record all his financial transactions
- print out reports
- manage his business finances
- save time (and money) in running his accounting system

## TRANSFERRING DATA INTO SAGE

When a business first sets up a computer accounting system a substantial amount of data will need to be transferred onto the computer, even if the business is in its first week of trading.

A summary of this data is shown in the diagram opposite. This transfer is normally done manually, but certain data, eg names and addresses of customers and suppliers might be held already on a different computer program and can be transferred into Sage automatically.

As noted earlier, you will not have to do this data transfer yourself, as it has all been done for you on a file (prepared by Osborne Books) called 'Company'. You (or your teaching centre) can install this file on your computer, and this will enable you to get going in Sage and to input the transactions in the next chapter.

The images shown below and in the diagram are the icons on the Sage desktop which represent the different operating areas of the program. As you can see they very much relate to the ledger structure of the manual book-keeping system . . .

# from manual records to computer records - an overview

**manual records**

**Sage records**

---

**Sales Ledger**
(accounts of customers
who are given credit)
- names
- addresses
- balances (amounts owed)

→ **Customers**
the computerised
Sales Ledger

---

**Purchases Ledger**
(accounts of suppliers who
allow credit)
- names
- addresses
- balances (amounts owing)

→ **Suppliers**
the computerised
Purchases Ledger

---

**General (Nominal) Ledger**
accounts which record:
- income
- expenses
- assets (items owned)
- liabilities (loans etc)
- capital invested by owner
- control accounts

→ **Nominal**
the computerised Nominal
(Main) Ledger

Note that the bank
accounts are listed in
Nominal Ledger but are
operated through a
separate icon

**Cash Book**
accounts which record:
- money paid into the bank
- money paid out of the bank
- petty cash (office cash)

## setting up the organisation details

Setting up a computer accounting system – as seen in the diagram on the previous pages – involves a number of stages. Normally the organisation details are input first: the name, address, telephone, fax, email, and so on. Other details such the VAT registration and financial year-end are also input at this stage.

The screen below shows the details entered for Pronto Supplies Limited.

## SETTING UP THE SALES LEDGER

The next step is to input all the details of the customers to whom the business sells on credit. The type of details required include:

- customer name and address
- customer code (a coding reference used on the computer system)
- credit limit
- any discount terms (trade and settlement or cash discounts)
- any analysis code, eg type of customer, region of customer etc
- the balance of the customer's account

Study the input on the 'Customer Record' screen at the top of the next page.

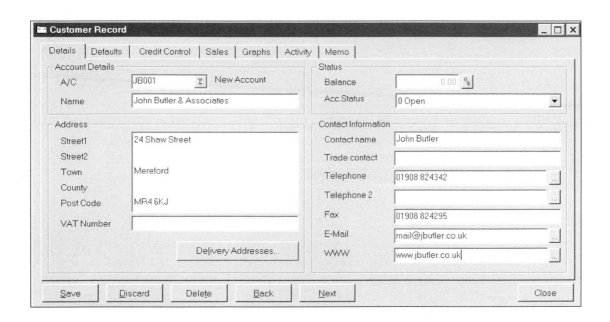

## SETTING UP THE PURCHASES LEDGER

The next step is to set up all the supplier accounts, including their opening balances, in the same way:

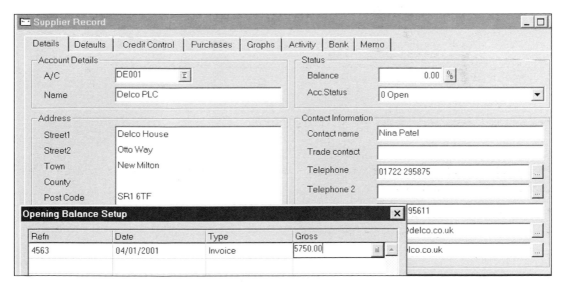

When this data has been input, the Sales and Purchases Ledgers – including the balances – will be set up on the system.

The next step will be to set up the General (Nominal) Ledger.

# NOMINAL (GENERAL) LEDGER ACCOUNTS

## nominal accounts

An account in a computer accounting system works as a 'running balance account' – it records financial transactions and has a running balance of what is left in the account at the end of each day. The nominal (general) ledger accounts in any accounting system are the accounts which are not subsidiary Ledger accounts, ie Customer accounts (Sales ledger) or Supplier accounts (Purchases ledger). Nominal accounts record income and expenses, assets, liabilities and capital.

## bank accounts

In a manual accounting system the bank accounts are kept in a separate Cash Book and are not strictly speaking part of the Nominal Ledger. In Sage the bank accounts of the business (including Petty Cash Account) are *listed* in NOMINAL, but they are *operated* from a separate BANK icon; just as in a manual accounting system the bank transactions are recorded in a separate Cash Book.

## the default Nominal accounts

When Tom Cox in the Case Study set up his company he chose the set of nominal accounts automatically provided by the Sage program. These 'default' accounts are common to most Sage systems, although they may vary slightly from version to version. If you click on the NOMINAL icon in the Sage opening screen the accounts are to be found in the nominal opening screen (see below). You can scroll down this screen to see the whole list. A typical SAGE nominal list is reproduced on the next page.

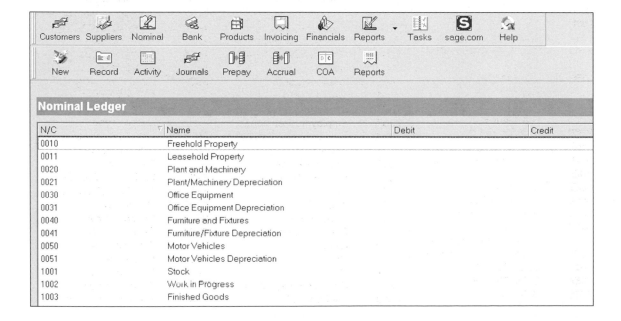

## Nominal Account List

| | |
|---|---|
| 0010 | Freehold Property |
| 0011 | Leasehold Property |
| 0020 | Plant and Machinery |
| 0021 | Plant/Machinery Depreciation |
| 0030 | Office Equipment |
| 0031 | Office Equipment Depreciation |
| 0040 | Furniture and Fixtures |
| 0041 | Furniture/Fixture Depreciation |
| 0050 | Motor Vehicles |
| 0051 | Motor Vehicles Depreciation |
| 1001 | Stock |
| 1002 | Work in Progress |
| 1003 | Finished Goods |
| 1100 | Debtors Control Account |
| 1101 | Sundry Debtors |
| 1102 | Other Debtors |
| 1103 | Prepayments |
| 1200 | Bank Current Account |
| 1210 | Bank Deposit Account |
| 1220 | Building Society Account |
| 1230 | Petty Cash |
| 1240 | Company Credit Card |
| 1250 | Credit Card Receipts |
| 2100 | Creditors Control Account |
| 2101 | Sundry Creditors |
| 2102 | Other Creditors |
| 2109 | Accruals |
| 2200 | Sales Tax Control Account |
| 2201 | Purchase Tax Control Account |
| 2202 | VAT Liability |
| 2210 | P.A.Y.E. |
| 2211 | National Insurance |
| 2220 | Net Wages |
| 2230 | Pension Fund |
| 2300 | Loans |
| 2310 | Hire Purchase |
| 2320 | Corporation Tax |
| 2330 | Mortgages |
| 3000 | Ordinary Shares |
| 3010 | Preference Shares |
| 3100 | Reserves |
| 3101 | Undistributed Reserves |
| 3200 | Profit and Loss Account |
| 4000 | Sales Type A |
| 4001 | Sales Type B |
| 4002 | Sales Type C |
| 4009 | Discounts Allowed |
| 4100 | Sales Type D |
| 4101 | Sales Type E |
| 4200 | Sales of Assets |
| 4400 | Credit Charges (Late Payments) |
| 4900 | Miscellaneous Income |
| 4901 | Royalties Received |
| 4902 | Commissions Received |
| 4903 | Insurance Claims |
| 4904 | Rent Income |
| 4905 | Distribution and Carriage |
| 5000 | Materials Purchased |
| 5001 | Materials Imported |
| 5002 | Miscellaneous Purchases |
| 5003 | Packaging |
| 5009 | Discounts Taken |
| 5100 | Carriage |
| 5101 | Import Duty |
| 5102 | Transport Insurance |
| 5200 | Opening Stock |
| 5201 | Closing Stock |
| 6000 | Productive Labour |
| 6001 | Cost of Sales Labour |
| 6002 | Sub-Contractors |
| 6100 | Sales Commissions |
| 6200 | Sales Promotions |
| 6201 | Advertising |
| 6202 | Gifts and Samples |
| 6203 | P.R.(Literature & Brochures) |
| 6900 | Miscellaneous Expenses |
| 7000 | Gross Wages |
| 7001 | Directors Salaries |
| 7002 | Directors Remuneration |
| 7003 | Staff Salaries |
| 7004 | Wages-Regular |
| 7005 | Wages-Casual |
| 7006 | Employers N.I. |
| 7007 | Employers Pensions |
| 7008 | Recruitment Expenses |
| 7009 | Adjustments |
| 7010 | SSP Reclaimed |
| 7011 | SMP Reclaimed |
| 7100 | Rent |
| 7102 | Water Rates |
| 7103 | General Rates |
| 7104 | Premises Insurance |
| 7200 | Electricity |
| 7201 | Gas |
| 7202 | Oil |
| 7203 | Other Heating Costs |
| 7300 | Fuel and Oil |
| 7301 | Repairs and Servicing |
| 7302 | Licences |
| 7303 | Vehicle Insurance |
| 7304 | Miscellaneous Motor Expenses |
| 7350 | Scale Charges |
| 7400 | Travelling |
| 7401 | Car Hire |
| 7402 | Hotels |
| 7403 | U.K. Entertainment |
| 7404 | Overseas Entertainment |
| 7405 | Overseas Travelling |
| 7406 | Subsistence |
| 7500 | Printing |
| 7501 | Postage and Carriage |
| 7502 | Telephone |
| 7503 | Telex/Telegram/Facsimile |
| 7504 | Office Stationery |
| 7505 | Books etc. |
| 7600 | Legal Fees |
| 7601 | Audit and Accountancy Fees |
| 7602 | Consultancy Fees |
| 7603 | Professional Fees |
| 7700 | Equipment Hire |
| 7701 | Office Machine Maintenance |
| 7800 | Repairs and Renewals |
| 7801 | Cleaning |
| 7802 | Laundry |
| 7803 | Premises Expenses |
| 7900 | Bank Interest Paid |
| 7901 | Bank Charges |
| 7902 | Currency Charges |
| 7903 | Loan Interest Paid |
| 7904 | H.P. Interest |
| 7905 | Credit Charges |
| 8000 | Depreciation |
| 8001 | Plant/Machinery Depreciation |
| 8002 | Furniture/Fitting Depreciation |
| 8003 | Vehicle Depreciation |
| 8004 | Office Equipment Depreciation |
| 8100 | Bad Debt Write Off |
| 8102 | Bad Debt Provision |
| 8200 | Donations |
| 8201 | Subscriptions |
| 8202 | Clothing Costs |
| 8203 | Training Costs |
| 8204 | Insurance |
| 8205 | Refreshments |
| 9998 | Suspense Account |
| 9999 | Mispostings Account |

We will now look at a Case Study showing how Pronto Supplies Limited sets up the nominal accounts and extracts an initial trial balance.

As mentioned before, all these transactions have already been input for you on the 'Company' file.

**Case Study**

# PRONTO SUPPLIES LIMITED: SETTING UP THE NOMINAL ACCOUNTS

Pronto Supplies Limited was set up in January 2001 and during that month operated a **manual** book-keeping system using hand-written double-entry ledger accounts.

It was a busy month for Tom Cox . . .

**financing**     Tom paid £75,000 into the bank as ordinary share capital (his 'capital') to start up the business.

Tom also raised a £35,000 business loan from the bank.

**assets**     The finance raised enabled Tom to buy:

| | |
|---|---|
| office machines | £35,000 |
| office equipment & computers | £15,000 |
| furniture for the office | £25,000 |

**purchases**     Tom bought in a substantial amount of stock during January for £69,100.

All of this stock was for resale by Pronto Supplies Limited.

**sales**     Tom divided his sales into three types:

Computer hardware sales

Computer software sales

Computer consultancy

**overheads**     Tom also had to pay expenses including:

| | |
|---|---|
| Wages | £16,230 |
| Advertising | £12,400 |
| Rent | £4,500 |
| Rates | £450 |
| Electricity | £150 |
| Telephone | £275 |
| Stationery | £175 |

## Pronto Supplies Trial Balance

At the end of January, Tom listed all the balances of his accounts in two columns, using a spreadsheet. This is his **trial balance** which will form the basis of the entries to the Sage system.

The columns are headed up Debit (Dr) and Credit (Cr) and they have the same total. In double-entry book-keeping each debit entry in the accounts is mirrored by a credit entry. If the book-keeping is correct, the total of debits should be the same as the total of the credits. The spreadsheet is shown below. Note that:

- The debtors control account (sales ledger control) shows the total amount owed by all Toms' customers; it is a debit balance because it is money owed to the business.

- The creditors control account (purchases ledger control) shows the total amount owed by Tom to his suppliers; it is a credit balance because it is money owed by the business.

- Tom is registered with HM Customs & Excise for Value Added Tax (VAT). This means that he has to quote his registration number on all his documents and also

  - charge VAT on his sales – this is due to HM Customs & Excise and so is a credit balance - Sales tax control account

  - reclaim VAT on what he has bought – this is due from HM Customs & Excise and so is a debit balance - Purchase tax control account

|  | A | B | C | D | E | F |
|---|---|---|---|---|---|---|
| 1 |  | Dr | Cr |  |  |  |
| 2 |  |  |  |  |  |  |
| 3 |  |  |  |  |  |  |
| 4 | Plant and machinery | 35000 |  |  |  |  |
| 5 | Office equipment | 15000 |  |  |  |  |
| 6 | Furniture and fixtures | 25000 |  |  |  |  |
| 7 | Debtors control account | 45500 |  |  |  |  |
| 8 | Bank current account | 12450 |  |  |  |  |
| 9 | Creditors control account |  | 32510 |  |  |  |
| 10 | Sales tax control account |  | 17920 |  |  |  |
| 11 | Purchase tax control account | 26600 |  |  |  |  |
| 12 | Loans |  | 35000 |  |  |  |
| 13 | Ordinary Shares |  | 75000 |  |  |  |
| 14 | Hardware sales |  | 85000 |  |  |  |
| 15 | Software sales |  | 15000 |  |  |  |
| 16 | Computer consultancy |  | 2400 |  |  |  |
| 17 | Materials purchased | 69100 |  |  |  |  |
| 18 | Advertising | 12400 |  |  |  |  |
| 19 | Gross wages | 16230 |  |  |  |  |
| 20 | Rent | 4500 |  |  |  |  |
| 21 | General rates | 450 |  |  |  |  |
| 22 | Electricity | 150 |  |  |  |  |
| 23 | Telephone | 275 |  |  |  |  |
| 24 | Stationery | 175 |  |  |  |  |
| 25 |  |  |  |  |  |  |
| 26 |  |  |  |  |  |  |
| 27 | Total | 262830 | 262830 |  |  |  |

## inputting the accounts into Sage Nominal

The date is 1 February 2001.

Tom uses his spreadsheet trial balance as the source document for inputting his nominal account balances. The procedure he adopts is:

1   He clicks on the NOMINAL icon on the opening screen and examines the nominal accounts list which appears on the NOMINAL screen. He allocates the accounts in his existing books with computer account numbers as follows:

| | |
|---|---|
| Plant and machinery | 0020 |
| Office equipment (photocopiers, computers) | 0030 |
| Furniture and fixtures | 0040 |
| Debtors control account | 1100 |
| Bank current account | 1200 |
| Creditors control account | 2100 |
| Sales tax control account | 2200 |
| Purchase tax control account | 2201 |
| Loans | 2300 |
| Ordinary Shares | 3000 |
| Computer hardware sales | 4000 |
| Computer software sales | 4001 |
| Computer consultancy | 4002 |
| Materials purchased | 5000 |
| Advertising | 6201 |
| Gross wages | 7000 |
| Rent | 7100 |
| General rates | 7103 |
| Electricity | 7200 |
| Telephone | 7502 |
| Stationery | 7504 |

2   Tom scrolls down the screen and clicks on all the accounts that he is going to need – they then show as selected.

But – importantly – he does not click on the following two accounts:

Debtors Control Account  (Sales Ledger Control Account)

Creditors Control Account  (Purchases Ledger Control Account)

This is because he has already input the debtors' (Customers') and creditors' (Suppliers') balances. If he inputs these totals now they will be entered into the computer twice and cause havoc with the accounting records!

The NOMINAL screen is shown at the top of the next page.

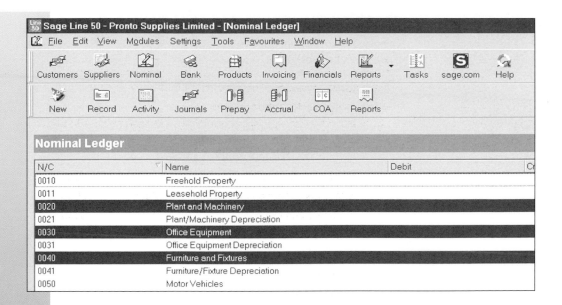

3 Tom is now ready to input the balances of these accounts. To do this he will

- Select the RECORD icon which will bring up a RECORD window.

- Click on O/B (Opening Balance) on the balance box which asks him to enter the date (01/02/2001) and the balance which must go in the correct box: debits on the left, credits on the right. He should ignore the 'ref' box.

The first account entry will look like this;

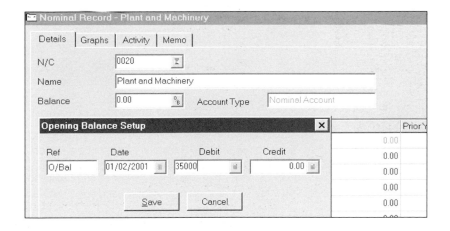

This record should then be saved.

Tom should repeat this for all the selected accounts, making sure that he is saving all the data as he goes along.

## checking the input – the trial balance

Tom needs to check that what he has input is accurate. He needs to check his original trial balance (see page 501) – against the computer trial balance.

The trial balance is produced through FINANCIALS by clicking on the TRIAL icon.

The printout produced is shown below.

**Pronto Supplies Limited**
**Period Trial Balance**

To Period:      Month 12, December 2001

| N/C | Name | Debit | Credit |
|---|---|---|---|
| 0020 | Plant and Machinery | 35,000.00 | |
| 0030 | Office Equipment | 15,000.00 | |
| 0040 | Furniture and Fixtures | 25,000.00 | |
| 1100 | Debtors Control Account | 45,500.00 | |
| 1200 | Bank Current Account | 12,450.00 | |
| 2100 | Creditors Control Account | | 32,510.00 |
| 2200 | Sales Tax Control Account | | 17,920.00 |
| 2201 | Purchase Tax Control Account | 26,600.00 | |
| 2300 | Loans | | 35,000.00 |
| 3000 | Ordinary Shares | | 75,000.00 |
| 4000 | Computer hardware sales | | 85,000.00 |
| 4001 | Computer software sales | | 15,000.00 |
| 4002 | Computer consultancy | | 2,400.00 |
| 5000 | Materials Purchased | 69,100.00 | |
| 6201 | Advertising | 12,400.00 | |
| 7000 | Gross Wages | 16,230.00 | |
| 7100 | Rent | 4,500.00 | |
| 7103 | General Rates | 450.00 | |
| 7200 | Electricity | 150.00 | |
| 7502 | Telephone | 275.00 | |
| 7504 | Office Stationery | 175.00 | |
| | Totals: | 262,830.00 | 262,830.00 |

Is the input accurate? Yes, because all the figures agree with the original trial balance figures (see page 501) and they are all in the correct column.

Tom is now ready to input February's transactions – new sales invoices, new purchase invoices and payments in and out of the bank. These will be dealt with in the chapters that follow.

**technical note**
The stage reached at the end of this Case Study is represented by the data on your 'Company' file, which should now be loaded onto your computer. The transactions in the chapters that follow should be input by you and checked by your tutor.

## CHAPTER SUMMARY

- When a business sets up its accounts on a Sage computer accounting package it will have to plan carefully how the data is to be transferred onto the computer.

- The first step in setting up the accounts on a Sage computer accounting package is to input the details of the organisation.

- The next stage will involve the inputting of the Customer and Supplier accounts – the basis of the Sales and Purchases ledgers.

- Lastly, the business will need to set up its Nominal (General) Ledger.

- Account numbers will be allocated to the nominal accounts, adopting the default list of accounts supplied by Sage in its 'chart of accounts' structure.

- If the business has already started trading it should input all its nominal account balances (except for the Debtors and Creditors control accounts).

- The input balances should be checked carefully against the source figures.

- The Sage program can then produce a trial balance which will show the balances that have been input.

**note**

There are no Questions in this introductory chapter.
The first set of inputting exercises is in the next chapter.

# 30 SELLING TO CUSTOMERS ON CREDIT

A business that sells on credit will invoice the goods or services supplied and then receive payment at a later date.

It is essential that details of the invoice are entered in the computer accounting records so that the sale can be recorded and the amount owed by the customer logged into the accounting system.

A credit note is dealt with by a computer accounting program in much the same way as an invoice (in terms of the input screens used.)

This chapter continues the Pronto Supplies Limited Case Study and shows how details of invoices and credit notes are entered into the computer accounting records.

The next chapter looks at how the invoices and credit notes issued by suppliers are dealt with by a computer accounting program.

## technical notes on setting up the files in Sage

### availability

The computer transactions contained in this chapter may be input into a Sage file called 'Company' which is available direct from the Resources section at www.osbornebooks.co.uk

Please call 01905 748071 for details.

### Sage compatibility

The software used for this backup is Sage Line 50, version 4, which can be read by any subsequent version of Sage Line 50. The version used for illustrating the text is version 7 of Sage Line 50.

### installation

Firstly install the file 'Company' on your computer system so that is accessible to the Sage application program. In order to activate the file, open up Sage Line 50 in the version that you are using. Go to 'Restore' in the main File menu and follow the instructions by locating 'Company'. Sage will then go through a conversion routine and produce a report. The Pronto Supplies Limited files should then be ready for the input exercises in the next three chapters.

## BACKGROUND TO FINANCIAL DOCUMENTS – REVISION

When a business sells goods or services it will use a number of different financial documents. A single sales transaction involves both seller and buyer. In this chapter we look at the situation from the point of view of the seller of the goods or services. Documents which are often used in the selling process for goods include:

- purchase order which the seller receives from the buyer

- delivery note which goes with the goods from the seller to the buyer

- invoice which lists the goods and tells the buyer what is owed

- credit note which is sent to the buyer if any refund is due

- statement sent by the seller to remind the buyer what is owed

- remittance advice sent by the buyer with the cheque to make payment

You will be familiar from your earlier studies with the way in which the documents 'flow' between buyer and seller.

## INVOICES, CREDIT NOTES AND SAGE

### the book-keeping background

The totals of invoices and credit notes have to be entered into the accounting records of a business. They record the sales and refunds made to customers who have bought on credit – the debtors of the business (known in Sage as Customers).

The amounts from these documents combine to provide the total of the Sales Ledger, which is the section of the accounting records which contains all the  debtor (Customer) balances.

The total of the debtor accounts is recorded in the Sales Ledger Control Account (known in Sage as Debtors Control Account). This tells the business how much in total is owing from customers who have bought on credit. The Sales Ledger Control Account is maintained in the General Ledger, known in Sage as the 'Nominal Ledger'.

### methods of recording invoices and credit notes

When a business uses a computer accounting program such as Sage, it will have to make sure that the details of each invoice and credit note issued are entered into the computer accounting records. Businesses using Sage accounting programs have two alternatives: batch entry and computer printed invoices.

# batch entry

The business produces the invoices independently of the computer program (ie it types or writes them out) and then enters the invoice details into the computer accounting program on a batch invoice screen. A 'batch' is simply a group of items (eg a 'batch' of cakes in the oven). The term is used in this context to describe a group of invoices which are all input at one time. This may not be on the day that each invoice is produced – it may be the end of the week, or even the month.

It is normal practice to add up the totals of all the actual invoices that are being input – the 'batch total' – and check this total against the invoice total calculated by the computer from the actual input. This will pick up any errors.

A batch invoice entry screen with three invoices input is shown below.

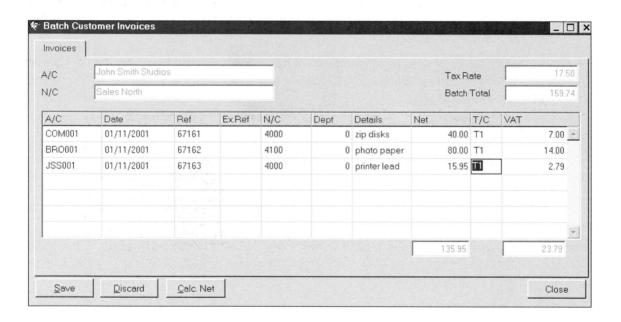

# notes on the data entry columns:

■  'A/C' column contains the customer account reference

■  'Date' is the date on which each invoice was issued

■  'Ref' column is the invoice number (note that they are consecutive)

■  'Ex.Ref' is optional – it could be used for the purchase order number

■  'N/C' column is the nominal account code which specifies which type of sale is involved

■  'Dept' is optional and is not used here

■  'Details' describes the goods that have been sold

- 'Net' is the amount of the invoice before VAT is added on

- 'T/C' is the tax code which sets up the VAT rate that applies – here T1 refers to Standard Rate VAT, and is a default rate set up in Sage.

- 'VAT' is calculated automatically

When the operator has completed the input and checked the batch totals with the computer totals, the batched invoices can be saved.

### computer printed invoices

Most versions of Sage include an invoicing function which requires the business to input the details of each invoice on screen. The computer system will then print out the invoices on the office printer – exactly as input. The invoices can either be for goods, or for a service provided. If the invoice is for goods, 'product' records with product codes will normally have to be set up in Sage, and the product code used each time stock is invoiced.

Service invoices do not require a product code, because no goods are involved in the transaction. An invoice input screen is shown below.

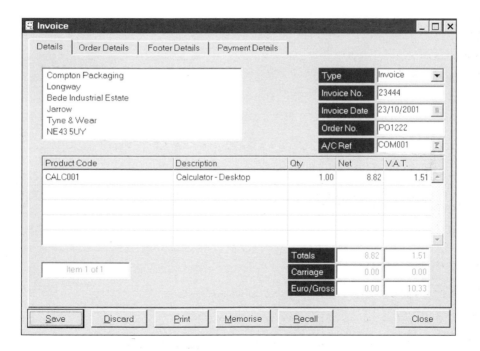

### important note: treatment of invoicing in this book

In these chapters we will concentrate on the batch entry method of recording invoices and credit notes. It is far simpler to operate and is common to all versions of Sage.

# PRONTO SUPPLIES LIMITED:
# PROCESSING SALES INVOICES AND CREDIT NOTES

Tom Cox runs Pronto Supplies Limited which provides computer hardware, software and consultancy services. At the beginning of February he input his Nominal accounts and his Customer and Supplier details and balances into his Sage accounting program. He has set up three Sales Accounts in his Nominal Ledger:

| | |
|---|---|
| Computer hardware sales | Account number 4000 |
| Computer software sales | Account number 4001 |
| Computer consultancy | Account number 4002 |

It is now 9 February, the end of the first full trading week. Tom needs to input

- the sales invoices he has issued to his customers
- the credit notes he has issued to his customers

He has the documents on file and has collected them in two batches . . .

**SALES INVOICES ISSUED**

| invoice | name | date | details | net amount | VAT |
|---|---|---|---|---|---|
| 10023 | John Butler & Associates | 5/02/01 | 1 x 17" monitor | 400.00 | 70.00 |
| 10024 | Charisma Design | 6/02/01 | 1 x printer lead | 16.00 | 2.80 |
| 10025 | Crowmatic Ltd | 6/02/01 | 1 x MacroWorx software | 100.00 | 17.50 |
| 10026 | Kay Denz | 8/02/01 | 2 hours consultancy | 120.00 | 21.00 |
| Subtotals | | | | 636.00 | 111.30 |
| Batch total | | | | | 747.30 |

**CREDIT NOTES ISSUED**

| credit note | name | date | details | net amount | VAT |
|---|---|---|---|---|---|
| 551 | David Boossey | 6/02/01 | Software returned | 200.00 | 35.00 |
| 552 | French Emporium | 6/02/01 | Disks returned (hardware) | 40.00 | 7.00 |
| Subtotals | | | | 240.00 | 42.00 |
| Batch total | | | | | 282.00 |

## batch invoice entry

Tom will start by opening up the CUSTOMERS screen in Sage and clicking on the INVOICE icon. This will show the screen shown on the next page. He will then

- identify the account references for each of the four customers
- enter each invoice on a new line
- take the data from the invoice: date, invoice no ('Ref'), product details and amounts
- enter the appropriate Sales account number ('N/C') for the type of sale

- enter the T1 tax code for standard rate VAT and check that the VAT amount calculated on screen is the same as on the invoice

When the input is complete Tom should check his original totals (Net, VAT and Batch total) against the computer totals. Once he is happy that his input is correct he should SAVE.

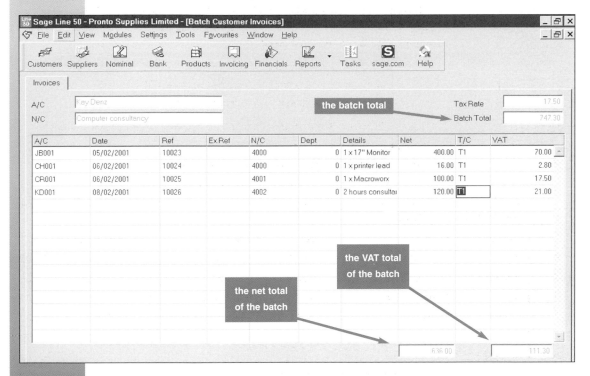

### checking the invoices are on the system

As a further check Tom could print out a Day Book Report. This can be obtained through the REPORTS icon on the CUSTOMER menu bar. The title of the report is 'Day Books: Customer Invoices (Summary)'. The report appears as follows:

Date: 01/11/2001     **Pronto Supplies Limited**     Page: 1
Time: 14:03:54

**Day Books: Customer Invoices (Summary)**

Date From: 05/02/2001
Date To: 31/12/2019

Transaction From: 1
Transaction To: 99999999

| Tran No. | Items | Tp | Date | A/C Ref | Inv Ref | Details | Net Amount | Tax Amount | Gross Amount |
|---|---|---|---|---|---|---|---|---|---|
| 54 | 1 | SI | 05/02/2001 | JB001 | 10023 | 1 x 17" Monitor | 400.00 | 70.00 | 470.00 |
| 55 | 1 | SI | 06/02/2001 | CH001 | 10024 | 1 x printer lead | 16.00 | 2.80 | 18.80 |
| 56 | 1 | SI | 06/02/2001 | CR001 | 10025 | 1 x Macroworx | 100.00 | 17.50 | 117.50 |
| 57 | 1 | SI | 08/02/2001 | KD001 | 10026 | 2 hours consultancy | 120.00 | 21.00 | 141.00 |
| | | | | | | Totals: | 636.00 | 111.30 | 747.30 |

### batch credit note entry

Tom will input the details from the two credit notes in much the same way as he processed the invoices. He will start by opening up the CUSTOMERS screen in Sage and clicking on the CREDIT icon. This will show the screen shown below. He will then identify the account references for each of the two customers and the Sales account numbers and input the credit note details as shown on the screen. When the input is complete he should again check his original totals (Net, VAT and Batch total) against the computer totals. Once he is happy that his input is correct he should SAVE.

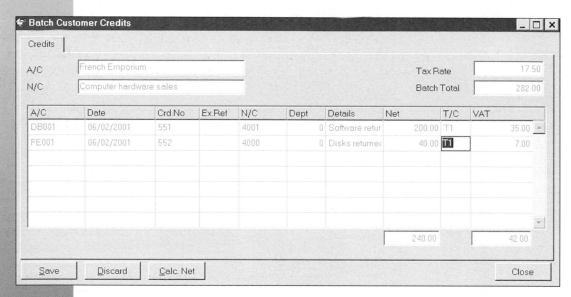

### checking the credit notes are on the system

As a further check Tom could print out a Day Book Report for credit notes. This can be obtained through the REPORTS icon on the CUSTOMER toolbar. The title of the report is 'Day Books: Customer Credits (Summary)'. The report appears as follows:

| Date: | 01/11/2001 | | **Pronto Supplies Limited** | | | | Page: | 1 |
|---|---|---|---|---|---|---|---|---|
| Time: | 14:06:17 | | **Day Books: Customer Credits (Summary)** | | | | | |

| Date From: | 05/02/2001 | | | Customer From: | |
|---|---|---|---|---|---|
| Date To: | 31/12/2019 | | | Customer To: | ZZZZZZZZ |

| Transaction From: | 1 |
|---|---|
| Transaction To: | 99999999 |

| Tran No. | Item s | Tp | Date | A/C Ref | Inv Ref | Details | Net Amount | Tax Amount | Gross Amount |
|---|---|---|---|---|---|---|---|---|---|
| 58 | 1 | SC | 06/02/2001 | DB001 | 551 | Software return | 200.00 | 35.00 | 235.00 |
| 59 | 1 | SC | 06/02/2001 | FE001 | 552 | Disks returned | 40.00 | 7.00 | 47.00 |
| | | | | | | Totals: | 240.00 | 42.00 | 282.00 |

Note: in the examples in this text, computer accounting does not use a separate 'returns' account; instead it automatically debits returns to sales account.

## producing statements

The Sage computer accounting system is set up to print out statements of account for customers. This will normally be done at the end of the month, but 'one-off' statements can be issued on any date.

In the example below, one of Tom's customers, David Boossey has asked for a statement of account as at 9 February. Tom selects the STATEMENT icon on the CUSTOMERS screen, follows the on-screen instructions and prints the statement for Customer code DB001 for the defined date range.

He prints onto A4 statement stationery which he has had printed by Sage.

The illustration below shows the text that is printed onto his stationery. The computer also prints a 'tear-off remittance advice which repeats the information shown on the statement. The amount at the bottom shows the total amount due to Pronto Supplies, ie an invoice total of £3,400 minus the credit note for £235 = £3,165.

| | | | | | | |
|---|---|---|---|---|---|---|
| Pronto Supplies Limited | | | | **STATEMENT** | | |
| Unit 17 Severnvale Estate | | | | | | |
| Broadwater Road | | | | | | |
| Mereford | | | | | | |
| Wyvern | | | | | | |
| MR1 6TF | | | | | | |

| | | | | |
|---|---|---|---|---|
| David Boossey | | | DB001 | |
| 17 Harebell Road | | | | |
| Mereford Green | | | 09/02/2001 | |
| MR6 4NB | | | | |

| | | | | |
|---|---|---|---|---|
| 10/01/01 | 10016 | Opening Balance | 3,400.00* | |
| 06/02/01 | 551 | Software returned | * | 235.00 |

| | | | | |
|---|---|---|---|---|
| -235.00 | 3,400.00 | 0.00 | 0.00 | 0.00 |

| | |
|---|---|
| **amount due** | **3,165.00** |

## CHAPTER SUMMARY

- Details of invoices and credit notes issued are entered into the accounting records of a business. When a computer program is used the details will be input on screen.

- Computer accounting programs will either print out the invoices and credit notes after input, or will need to have the details of existing invoices and credit notes input, commonly in batches.

- Computer accounting programs will also print out statements of account on demand.

- Organisations often have the stationery for financial documents preprinted. The computer then prints the accounting data on this stationery.

### technical note

Before starting the inputting tasks contained in the Student Activities you should ensure that the Sage file 'Company' (provided by Osborne Books) is loaded onto your computer.

# INPUTTING EXERCISES

## Task 1

Making sure that you have set the program date to 9 February 2001 (SETTINGS menu), enter the invoice details from the batch sheet below into the computer.

Check your totals before saving and print out a Day Books: Customer Invoices (Summary) Report to confirm the data that you have saved.

**BATCH SHEET**

**SALES INVOICES ISSUED**

| invoice | name | date | details | net amount | VAT |
|---|---|---|---|---|---|
| 10023 | John Butler & Associates | 5/02/01 | 1 x 17" monitor | 400.00 | 70.00 |
| 10024 | Charisma Design | 6/02/01 | 1 x printer lead | 16.00 | 2.80 |
| 10025 | Crowmatic Ltd | 6/02/01 | 1 x MacroWorx software | 100.00 | 17.50 |
| 10026 | Kay Denz | 8/02/01 | 2 hours consultancy | 120.00 | 21.00 |
| Subtotals | | | | 636.00 | 111.30 |
| Batch total | | | | | 747.30 |

## Task 2

Enter the following credit note batch details into the computer.

Check your totals before saving and print out a Day Books: Customer Credits (Summary) Report to confirm the data that you have saved.

**BATCH SHEET**

**CREDIT NOTES ISSUED**

| credit note | name | date | details | net amount | VAT |
|---|---|---|---|---|---|
| 551 | David Boossey | 6/02/01 | Software returned | 200.00 | 35.00 |
| 552 | French Emporium | 6/02/01 | Disks returned (hardware) | 40.00 | 7.00 |
| Subtotals | | | | 240.00 | 42.00 |
| Batch total | | | | | 282.00 |

## Task 3

It is now a week later and the date is now 16 February 2001. Change your program date setting (SETTINGS menu).

You have a further batch of invoices to process.

Enter the details into the computer. Check your totals before saving and print out a Day Books Summary Report to confirm the data that you have saved.

| account | invoice date | number | details | net | VAT |
|---|---|---|---|---|---|
| John Butler & Associates | 12/02/01 | 10027 | 2 hours consultancy | 120.00 | 21.00 |
| David Boossey | 13/02/01 | 10028 | 1 x EF102 printer | 200.00 | 35.00 |
| French Emporium | 14/02/01 | 10029 | 1 x QuorkEdit software | 400.00 | 70.00 |
| L Garr & Co | 16/02/01 | 10030 | 2 x Zap drive | 180.00 | 31.50 |
| Jo Green Systems | 16/02/01 | 10031 | 1 x Fileperfect software | 264.00 | 46.20 |
| Prism Trading Ltd | 16/02/01 | 10032 | 1 x 15" monitor | 320.00 | 56.00 |

## Task 4

You also on the same date have two credit notes to process. Enter the details into the computer. Check your totals before saving and print out a Day Books Summary Report to confirm the data that you have saved.

| account | date | reference | details | net | VAT |
|---|---|---|---|---|---|
| Jo Green Systems | 12/02/01 | 553 | 1 x printer lead | 16.00 | 2.80 |
| Mendell & Son | 13/02/01 | 554 | Zap disks (hardware) | 20.00 | 3.50 |

## Task 5

You have been asked to prepare an Aged Debtors Analysis. Run a debtor analysis report (as at 16 February) from REPORTS in Customers. Print it out.

## Task 6

Your customer David Boossey asks you for a statement of account as at 16 February.

Either print out a statement (account DB001) from CUSTOMERS, or email the same data and keep a printed copy.

## Task 7

Print out a Trial Balance as at 16 February 2001 to show the balances of the Nominal (Main) Ledger.

The figures should agree with the Trial Balance shown on the next page. If they do, your input is correct. If there are any discrepancies you will need sort them out before tackling the inputting exercises in the next chapter.

**Reminder! Have you made a backup?**

## Pronto Supplies, trial balance as at 16 February 2001

### Pronto Supplies Limited
### Period Trial Balance

**To Period:**     Month 2, February 2001

| N/C | Name | Debit | Credit |
|-----|------|------:|-------:|
| 0020 | Plant and Machinery | 35,000.00 | |
| 0030 | Office Equipment | 15,000.00 | |
| 0040 | Furniture and Fixtures | 25,000.00 | |
| 1100 | Debtors Control Account | 47,666.70 | |
| 1200 | Bank Current Account | 12,450.00 | |
| 2100 | Creditors Control Account | | 32,510.00 |
| 2200 | Sales Tax Control Account | | 18,242.70 |
| 2201 | Purchase Tax Control Account | 26,600.00 | |
| 2300 | Loans | | 35,000.00 |
| 3000 | Ordinary Shares | | 75,000.00 |
| 4000 | Computer hardware sales | | 86,040.00 |
| 4001 | Computer software sales | | 15,564.00 |
| 4002 | Computer consultancy | | 2,640.00 |
| 5000 | Materials Purchased | 69,100.00 | |
| 6201 | Advertising | 12,400.00 | |
| 7000 | Gross Wages | 16,230.00 | |
| 7100 | Rent | 4,500.00 | |
| 7103 | General Rates | 450.00 | |
| 7200 | Electricity | 150.00 | |
| 7502 | Telephone | 275.00 | |
| 7504 | Office Stationery | 175.00 | |
| | **Totals:** | 264,996.70 | 264,996.70 |

# 31 BUYING FROM SUPPLIERS ON CREDIT

This chapter should be read in conjunction with the last chapter 'Selling to credit customers' as it represents 'the other side of the coin' – invoices and credit notes as they are dealt with by the purchaser.

A business purchaser that buys on credit will receive an invoice for the goods or services supplied and will then have to pay at a later date.

Details of invoices and any credit notes received are entered by the purchaser into the account of the supplier in the computer accounting records. In this way the credit purchase and any credit due are recorded, and the total amount owing by the purchaser to the supplier logged into the accounting system.

This chapter continues the Pronto Supplies Case Study and shows how details of invoices and credit notes received are entered into supplier accounts in the computer accounting records.

## technical notes

### inputting exercises

It is rec ommended that the inputting exercises at the end of this chapter should follow on from the exercises at the end of the last chapter. The set-up files for these chapters are available for tutors direct from Osborne Books. The set-up file for this chapter is 'Customers'

Please call 01905 748071 for details.

### Sage compatibility

The software used for this backup is Sage Line 50, version 4, which can be read by any subsequent version of Sage Line 50. The version used for illustrating the text is version 7 of Sage Line 50.

## THE BOOK-KEEPING BACKGROUND

Details of invoices and credit notes received have to be entered into the accounting records of a business that buys on credit. These documents record the sales and refunds made by suppliers who have sold on credit – the **creditors** of the business, known in Sage as 'Suppliers'.

The amounts from these documents combine to provide the total of the Purchases Ledger, which is the section of the accounting records which contains all the supplier accounts and their balances.

The total of the Purchases Ledger is recorded in the Purchases Ledger Control Account (known in Sage as Creditors Control Account). This tells the business how much in total it owes to suppliers.

The documents received from the suppliers – invoices and credit notes – are recorded in the computer accounting system on the batch basis illustrated in the Case Study in the last chapter.

## PURCHASES AND EXPENSES AND CAPITAL ITEMS

One point that is very important to bear in mind is the difference between **purchases** and **expenses** and **capital items**, as it affects the nominal account codes used when inputting invoices and credit notes on the computer.

**Purchases** are items a business buys which it expects to turn into a product or sell as part of its day-to-day business. For example:

• a business that makes cheese will buy milk to make the cheese

• a supermarket will buy food and clothes to sell to the public

All these items are bought because they will be sold or turned into a product that will be sold. In Sage these purchases will be recorded in a **purchases account**, normally 5000, or a number in that category.

**Expenses**, on the other hand, are items which the business pays for which form part of the business running expenses (overheads), eg rent and electricity. Each expense has a separate nominal account number allocated in the Sage accounting system.

**Capital items** are 'one off' items that the business buys and intends to keep for a number of years, for example office equipment and furniture. These also have separate nominal account numbers in the Sage system.

The important point here is that all of these items may be bought on credit and each will have to be entered into the computer accounting records, **but with the correct nominal account number**.

# PRONTO SUPPLIES LIMITED: PROCESSING PURCHASES INVOICES AND CREDIT NOTES

It is now February 16 2001. Tom has a number of supplier invoices and supplier credit notes to enter into the computer accounting system.

He has the documents on file and has collected them in two batches.

---

**PURCHASES INVOICES RECEIVED**

| invoice | name | date | details | net amount | VAT |
|---|---|---|---|---|---|
| 11365 | Delco PLC | 9/02/01 | Desktop computers | 3,600.00 | 630.00 |
| 8576 | Electron Supplies | 9/02/01 | Peripherals | 2,000.00 | 350.00 |
| 2947 | MacCity | 12/02/01 | Powerbooks | 2,400.00 | 420.00 |
| 34983 | Synchromart | 14/02/01 | Software | 1,280.00 | 224.00 |
| Subtotals | | | | 9,280.00 | 1624.00 |
| Batch total | | | | | 10,904.00 |

---

**CREDIT NOTES RECEIVED**

| credit note | name | date | details | net amount | VAT |
|---|---|---|---|---|---|
| 7223 | Delco PLC | 6/02/01 | 1 x Computer | 480.00 | 84.00 |
| 552 | MacCity | 8/02/01 | 1 x optical mouse | 38.00 | 6.65 |
| Subtotals | | | | 518.00 | 90.65 |
| Batch total | | | | | 608.65 |

---

## batch invoice entry

Tom will start by opening up the SUPPLIERS screen in Sage and clicking on the INVOICE icon. This will show the screen shown on the next page. He will then

- identify the account references for each of the four customers

- enter each invoice on a new line

- take the data from the invoice: date, invoice no ('Ref'), product details and amounts

- enter the Materials Purchased account number 5000 under 'N/C'

- enter the T1 tax code for standard rate VAT and check that the VAT amount calculated on screen is the same as on the invoice – if there is a substantial difference (eg a mistake on the invoice) it should be queried with a higher authority*

When the input is complete Tom should check his original totals (Net, VAT and Batch total) against the computer totals. Once he is happy that his input is correct he can SAVE.

* Sometimes the VAT on the document will vary by a penny from the VAT on the screen. This is because Sage 'rounds' VAT up or down to the nearest penny, whereas the VAT authorities require that VAT is rounded down to the nearest penny. These one penny differences can be altered on the input screen to tally with the document VAT amount – normally without reference to a higher authority.

The batch suppliers' invoice screen will appear like this:

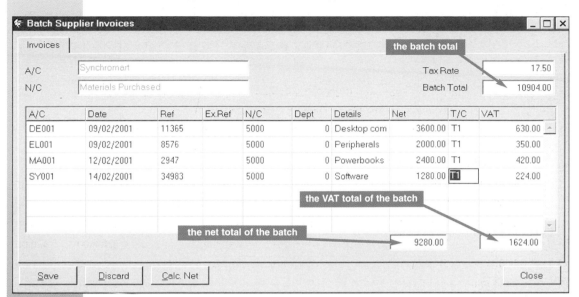

### checking the invoices are on the system

As a further check Tom could print out a Day Book Report. This can be obtained through the REPORTS icon on the SUPPLIER menu bar. The title of the report is 'Day Books: Supplier Invoices (Summary)'. The report appears as follows:

**Pronto Supplies Limited**                                    Page:    1

**Day Books: Supplier Invoices (Summary)**

Date From:        01/02/2001
Date To:          31/12/2019

Transaction From:    1
Transaction To:      99999999

| Tran No. | Item | Tp | Date | A/C Ref | Inv Ref | Details | Net Amount | Tax Amount | Gross Amount |
|---|---|---|---|---|---|---|---|---|---|
| 68 | 1 | PI | 09/02/2001 | DE001 | 11365 | Desktop computers | 3,600.00 | 630.00 | 4,230.00 |
| 69 | 1 | PI | 09/02/2001 | EL001 | 8576 | Peripherals | 2,000.00 | 350.00 | 2,350.00 |
| 70 | 1 | PI | 12/02/2001 | MA001 | 2947 | Powerbooks | 2,400.00 | 420.00 | 2,820.00 |
| 71 | 1 | PI | 14/02/2001 | SY001 | 34983 | Software | 1,280.00 | 224.00 | 1,504.00 |
| | | | | | | Totals | 9,280.00 | 1,624.00 | 10,904.00 |

### batch credit note entry

Tom will input the details from the two credit notes in much the same way as he processed the invoices. He will open up the SUPPLIERS screen in Sage and click on the CREDIT icon. This will show the screen shown on the next page. He will then identify the account references for each of the two customers and input the credit note details as shown on the screen. He will use the Materials Purchased account number 5000. When the input is complete he should again check his original totals (Net, VAT and Batch total) against the computer totals. Once he is happy that his input is correct he should SAVE.

The batch suppliers' credit note screen will appear like this:

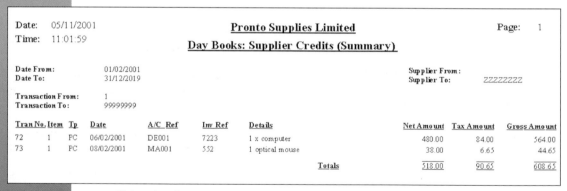

### checking the credit notes are on the system

As a further check Tom could print out a Day Book Report for Supplier Credit notes. This can be obtained through the REPORTS icon on the SUPPLIERS toolbar. The title of the report is 'Day Books: Supplier Credits (Summary)'. The report appears as follows:

| Date: | 05/11/2001 | | | | **Pronto Supplies Limited** | | | Page: | 1 |
|---|---|---|---|---|---|---|---|---|---|
| Time: | 11:01:59 | | | | **Day Books: Supplier Credits (Summary)** | | | | |

| Date From: | 01/02/2001 | | | Supplier From: | |
|---|---|---|---|---|---|
| Date To: | 31/12/2019 | | | Supplier To: | ZZZZZZZZ |

| Transaction From: | 1 |
|---|---|
| Transaction To: | 99999999 |

| Tran No. | Item | Tp | Date | A/C Ref | Inv Ref | Details | Net Amount | Tax Amount | Gross Amount |
|---|---|---|---|---|---|---|---|---|---|
| 72 | 1 | PC | 06/02/2001 | DE001 | 7223 | 1 x computer | 480.00 | 84.00 | 564.00 |
| 73 | 1 | PC | 08/02/2001 | MA001 | 552 | 1 optical mouse | 38.00 | 6.65 | 44.65 |
| | | | | | | Totals | 518.00 | 90.65 | 608.65 |

Note: the Sage accounting system does not use a separate 'returns' account for purchases returns; these items are credited to purchases account by the system.

### what next?

Tom has now entered into his computer:

- his company details and nominal (Main Ledger) accounts and balances
- customer and supplier details
- customer invoices and credit notes (in the last chapter)
- supplier invoices and credit notes (in this chapter)

The next chapter shows how he enters details of payments made to suppliers and payments received from customers.

## CHAPTER SUMMARY

- When a business buys on credit it will receive invoices and sometimes credit notes from its suppliers as part of the 'flow of documents'.

- The details of invoices and credit notes received must be entered into the accounting records of a business. If a computer program is used the details are input on screen and a report printed out.

- In the case of supplier invoices and credit notes it is important that the correct Nominal account number is used to describe whether the transaction relates to purchases, expenses or capital items.

- It is essential to check the details of invoices and credit notes before input and the details of input by printing out, for example, a day book report.

## technical note

Before starting the inputting tasks that follow you must ensure either that your input from the last chapter is correct or that the Sage file 'Customers' (provided by Osborne Books) is loaded or restored onto your computer.

# INPUTTING EXERCISES

## Task 1

Set the program date to 16 February 2001. Enter the following invoice details into the computer. Check your totals before saving and print out a Day Books: Supplier Invoice (Summary) Report to confirm the data that you have saved.

**PURCHASES INVOICES RECEIVED**

| invoice | name | date | details | net amount | VAT |
|---------|------|------|---------|-----------:|----:|
| 11365 | Delco PLC | 9/02/01 | Desktop computers | 3,600.00 | 630.00 |
| 8576 | Electron Supplies | 9/02/01 | Peripherals | 2,000.00 | 350.00 |
| 2947 | MacCity | 12/02/01 | Powerbooks | 2,400.00 | 420.00 |
| 34983 | Synchromart | 14/02/01 | Software | 1,280.00 | 224.00 |
| Subtotals | | | | 9,280.00 | 1624.00 |
| Batch total | | | | | 10,904.00 |

## Task 2

Enter the following credit note details into the computer. Check your totals before saving and print out a Day Books: Supplier Credits (Summary) Report to confirm the data that you have saved.

**CREDIT NOTES RECEIVED**

| credit note | name | date | details | net amount | VAT |
|-------------|------|------|---------|-----------:|----:|
| 7223 | Delco PLC | 6/02/01 | 1 x Computer | 480.00 | 84.00 |
| 552 | MacCity | 8/02/01 | 1 x optical mouse | 38.00 | 6.65 |
| Subtotals | | | | 518.00 | 90.65 |
| Batch total | | | | | 608.65 |

## Task 3

On the same day Tom receives two further supplier invoices in the post. He wants them to be input straightaway while the computer is up and running. He checks all the documentation and finds that the invoices are both correct. You are to input them, taking care to use the correct nominal code (0030 for Office Equipment). The computer and printer purchased are not for resale to customers but are to be used as office equipment at Pronto Supplies. When the input is complete the totals should be checked and a Day Book Summary Report printed (showing just the last two invoices, if possible).

| invoice | name | date | details | net amount | VAT |
|---------|------|------|---------|-----------|-----|
| 11377 | Delco PLC | 14/02/01 | Desktop computer | 400.00 | 70.00 |
| 8603 | Electron Supplies | 14/02/01 | Laser Printer | 360.00 | 63.00 |
| Subtotals | | | | 760.00 | 133.00 |
| Batch total | | | | | 893.00 |

**Reminder! Have you made a backup?**

**Task 4**

When you have completed tasks 1 to 3, print out a trial balance dated 16 February 2001.

Also run and print out an Aged Creditors Analysis from Reports in Suppliers to show the position of the Purchases Ledger as at 16 February 2001.

Check your trial balance against the figures shown below. If they agree, your input is correct. If there are any discrepancies you will need sort them out, or RESTORE from the file 'Suppliers' (from Osborne Books) before tackling the inputting exercises in the next chapter.

**Pronto Supplies, trial balance as at 16 February 2001**

**Pronto Supplies Limited**
**Period Trial Balance**

**To Period:**  Month 2, February 2001

| N/C | Name | Debit | Credit |
|-----|------|-------|--------|
| 0020 | Plant and Machinery | 35,000.00 | |
| 0030 | Office Equipment | 15,760.00 | |
| 0040 | Furniture and Fixtures | 25,000.00 | |
| 1100 | Debtors Control Account | 47,666.70 | |
| 1200 | Bank Current Account | 12,450.00 | |
| 2100 | Creditors Control Account | | 43,698.35 |
| 2200 | Sales Tax Control Account | | 18,242.70 |
| 2201 | Purchase Tax Control Account | 28,266.35 | |
| 2300 | Loans | | 35,000.00 |
| 3000 | Ordinary Shares | | 75,000.00 |
| 4000 | Computer hardware sales | | 86,040.00 |
| 4001 | Computer software sales | | 15,564.00 |
| 4002 | Computer consultancy | | 2,640.00 |
| 5000 | Materials Purchased | 77,862.00 | |
| 6201 | Advertising | 12,400.00 | |
| 7000 | Gross Wages | 16,230.00 | |
| 7100 | Rent | 4,500.00 | |
| 7103 | General Rates | 450.00 | |
| 7200 | Electricity | 150.00 | |
| 7502 | Telephone | 275.00 | |
| 7504 | Office Stationery | 175.00 | |
| | **Totals:** | 276,185.05 | 276,185.05 |

# 32 MAKING PAYMENTS

So far in this section of the book we have dealt with accounts for customers and suppliers and entered details of financial documents. But we have not covered the way in which the computer accounting system records the payment of money by customers to the business or by the business to suppliers.

The bank account is central to any accounting system. It is used not only for payments by customers and to suppliers (credit transactions), but also for transactions for which settlement is made straightaway (cash transactions).

The Case Study in this chapter – a continuation of Pronto Supplies Limited – explains how payments made and received are recorded in the computer accounting system.

The chapter concludes by illustrating other aspects of computer accounting payments:

- dealing with cash payments
- the setting up of a petty cash account and a rents receivable account on the computer
- journal entries
- bank reconciliation statements

## technical notes

### inputting exercises

It is recommended that the inputting exercises at the end of this chapter should follow on from the exercises at the end of the last chapter. The set-up files for these chapters are available to tutors direct from Osborne Books. The set-up file for this chapter is 'Suppliers'.

Please call 01905 748071 for details.

### Sage compatibility

The software used for this backup is Sage Line 50, version 4, which can be read by any subsequent version of Sage Line 50. The version used for illustrating the text is version 7 of Sage Line 50.

# THE BANK ACCOUNTS IN COMPUTER ACCOUNTING

The bank accounts and all the functions associated with them are found in Sage by clicking on the BANK icon in the main menu bar.

The BANK screen then appears as shown below.

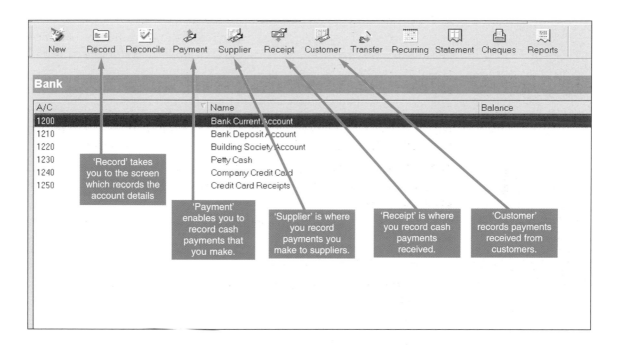

## types of bank account

The accounts listed above come from the default list provided by Sage for the Nominal (Main) Ledger. The business does not have to adopt all the bank accounts listed here, but may use some of them if it needs them:

- **bank current account** records all payments in and out of the bank 'cheque' account used for everyday purposes – it is the most commonly used account

- **bank deposit account** and building society account can be used if the business maintains interest-paying accounts for savings and for money that is not needed in the short term

- **petty cash account** can be used if the business maintains a petty cash system in the office for small purchases such as stationery and stamps

- **company credit card account** can be used if the business uses credit cards for its employees to pay for expenses

- **credit card receipts account** can be used if the business receives a significant number of credit card payments from its customers

## cash or credit payments?

The number of icons on the menu bar record payments which are either:

- **cash payments** – ie made straightaway without the need for invoices or credit notes
- **credit payments** – ie made in settlement of invoices

The problem is, which is which? The rule is:

=   **cash payments** (not involving credit customers or suppliers)

=   **credit payments** (payments from customers and to suppliers in settlement of accounts)

## bank account details

It must be stressed that if a Sage computer account number is listed on the BANK screen it does not have to be used. It is there so that it can be used if the business needs it. The Bank Current Account (here number 1200), for example, is always going to be used, assuming businesses always have bank current accounts!

When a business is setting up its bank accounts it should click on RECORD on the BANK screen to produce the bank account DETAILS screen . . .

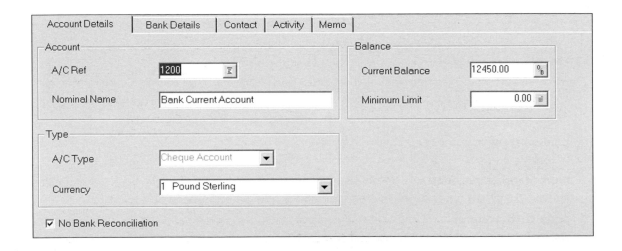

This screen enables the business to input details of the account, the bank and bank contact and to see the activity on the account. The unchecked box at the bottom left  in this example shows that the business will use the program to reconcile (tally up) the computer record of the bank account with the bank statement when it is received, to produce a bank reconciliation statement.

# RECORDING PAYMENTS FROM CUSTOMERS

## how do payments arrive?

When a payment arrives from a customer who has bought on credit it will normally arrive at the business in one of two ways:

- A cheque and **remittance advice**. A remittance advice is a document stating what the payment relates to – eg which invoices and credit notes.

- A remittance advice stating that the money has been sent direct to the business bank account in the form of a **BACS payment** (a BACS [Bankers Automated Clearing Services] payment is a payment sent direct between the banks' computers and does not involve a cheque).

Examples of cheque and BACS remittance advices are shown below:

| TO | **REMITTANCE ADVICE** | FROM |
|---|---|---|
| A B Supplies Limited<br>Unit 45 Elgar Estate,<br>Broadfield, BR7 4ER | | **Compsync**<br>**4 Friar Street**<br>**Broadfield**<br>**BR1 3RF**<br>Tel 01908 761234  Fax 01908 761987<br>VAT REG GB 0745 8383 56 |

| | | Account 3993 | 6 November 2003 | |
|---|---|---|---|---|

| date | your reference | our reference | payment amount |
|---|---|---|---|
| 01 10 03 | INVOICE 787923 | 47609 | 277.30 |
| 10 10 03 | CREDIT NOTE 12157 | 47609 | (27.73) |
| | | **CHEQUE TOTAL** | 249.57 |

### BACS REMITTANCE ADVICE

FROM: Excelsior Services
17 Gatley Way
Bristol BS1 9GH

TO
A B Supplies Ltd
Unit 45 Elgar Estate, Broadfield, BR7 4ER

06 12 03

| Your ref | Our ref | | Amount |
|---|---|---|---|
| 788102 | 3323 | BACS TRANSFER | 465.00 |
| | | TOTAL | 465.00 |

THIS HAS BEEN PAID BY BACS CREDIT TRANSFER DIRECTLY INTO YOUR BANK ACCOUNT AT ALBION BANK NO 11451226 SORT CODE 90 47 17

## customer payments and the accounting system

An incoming payment from a customer settling one or more invoices (less any credit notes) needs to be recorded in the accounting system:

■ the balance of bank account will increase (a debit in double-entry)

■ the balance of the customer's account (and the Sales Ledger Control Account ['Debtors Control Account' in Sage]) will decrease because the customer will owe less (a credit in double-entry accounting)

In computer accounting the payment is input once and the entries will be automatically made from the same screen. Any settlement discount involved will also be entered on the screen and the entries made automatically.

## the practicalities

The business will normally input a number (a 'batch') of payments at one time on a regular basis, eg every week, using the remittance advice as the source document. The remittance advice will have all the details on it (date, amount, invoices paid) and in the case of a BACS payment it is the only document from the customer relating to the payment the business will have.

The appropriate bank account should first be selected on the BANK screen and then the CUSTOMER icon selected to access the Customer Receipt input screen:

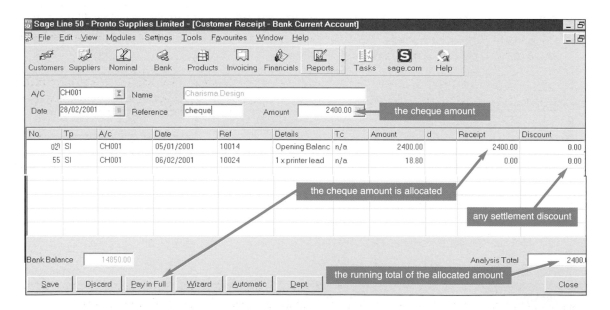

## processing the payments received

The procedure for recording the customer payment on this screen is to:

■ input the customer account reference – this will bring up on screen the account name and all the outstanding amounts due on invoices

- input a reference if required – for example you might key in 'cheque' or 'BACS' or the numerical reference relating to the payment

- input the amount of the payment in the Amount box

- click on the 'Receipt' box of the invoice that is being paid

- click on the 'Pay in Full' button at the bottom

- if there is more than one invoice being paid click on the items being paid as appropriate; the Analysis Total box at the bottom will shown a running total of the money allocated

- if there is a long list of invoices and a payment to cover them, click on 'Automatic' at the bottom and the computer will allocate the payment down the invoice list until the money amount of the payment runs out

- check that what you have done is correct and SAVE; details to check are:
  - customer, amount, invoices being paid and amount received
  - the amounts in the Amount box and the Analysis Total box should be the same (but see next point)

- if the amount received by way of payment is greater than the amount allocated to outstanding invoices the extra payment will show as a 'Payment on Account' after you have saved

- if the amount received by way of payment is less than the amount of the invoice(s) it is settling, the amount received will be allocated to the appropriate invoice(s) and the unpaid amount will show as outstanding on the Customer's account

- you should print out a Day Books: Customer Receipts (Summary) for these transactions from REPORTS in BANK to check that the total of the cheques (or BACS payments) received equals the total input

# RECORDING PAYMENTS TO SUPPLIERS

### what documents are involved?

A business pays its suppliers on the invoice due dates or after it receives a **statement** setting out the amounts due from invoices and any deductions made following the issue of credit notes.

Payment is often made by cheque, although some payments may be made by BACS transfer between the banks' computers. Payment is normally made in full, but occasionally a part payment may be made. A typical payment cheque, together with a completed counterfoil (cheque stub) is shown on the next page.

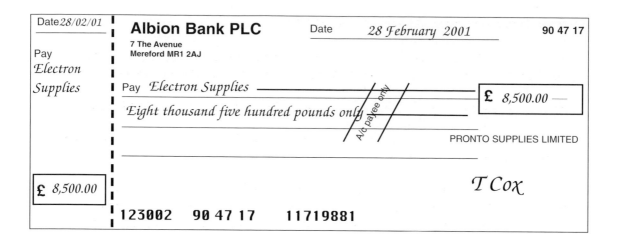

The business will send a **remittance advice** (see page 529) to the supplier with the cheque, or, if a BACS payment is being made, on its own. This, together with the cheque, will often provide the details for the input of the payment details on the computer.

Some programs can print remittance advices on the computer when the payment is processed. If the business decides to do this, the payment details are likely to be taken from the completed cheque and counterfoil. Some computer accounting programs which deal with long 'cheque runs' will also print the cheques themselves on special preprinted cheque stationery.

## supplier payments and the accounting system

Payment to a supplier settling one or more invoices (less any credit notes) needs to be recorded in the accounting system:

- the balance of bank account will decrease (a credit in double-entry)
- the balance of the supplier's account (and the Purchases Ledger Control Account ['Creditors Control Account' in Sage]) will decrease because the supplier will be owed less (a debit in double-entry accounting)

In computer accounting the payment is input once and the entries will be automatically made from the same screen. Any settlement discount received will also be entered on the screen and the accounts posted automatically.

## processing the payments

As with customer receipts, the business will normally input a number (a 'batch') of payments at one time on a regular basis, for example just after the cheques have been written out or the BACS payment instructions prepared.

The payments are input in Sage from the SUPPLIER icon on the BANK screen – after the appropriate bank account has been selected.

The procedure for recording the supplier payment is to:

- input the supplier reference in the box next to the word 'Payee' on the 'cheque' – this will bring up on screen the account name and all the outstanding amounts due on invoices

- input the cheque number on the cheque and alter the date if the cheque date is different

- input the amount of the payment in the amount box on the cheque; if it is a part payment the same procedure will be followed

- click on the Payment box of the invoice that is being paid – here it is the first one – and click on the 'Pay in full' icon at the bottom; if there is more than one invoice being paid click on the items being paid as appropriate; any part payment will be allocated to the appropriate invoice(s) in the same way

- check that what you have done is correct (ie supplier, amount, invoices being paid), print out a remittance advice if you want one by clicking on REMITTANCE, and SAVE

- print out a Day Books: Customer Payments (Summary) from REPORTS in BANK to check that the total of the cheques (or BACS payments) issued equals the total input on the computer

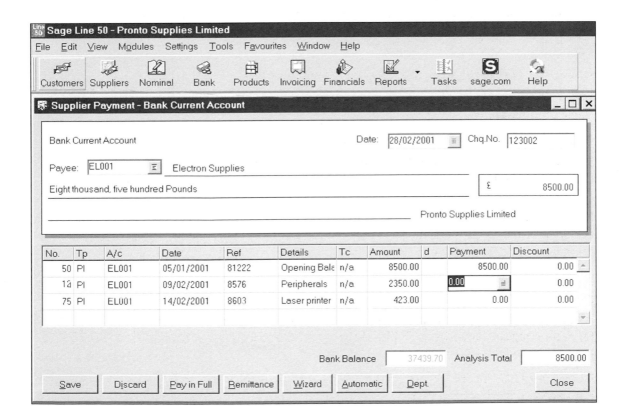

## printing remittance advices

As we have already seen, you can print out remittance advices to accompany cheques, or to advise BACS payments to the supplier.

Depending on the version of Sage you are using, the printing may have to be done when you have checked the payment details and before you Save the payment transaction. In Sage Line 50 Version 8 and later you have the facility to print the documents later, from an icon on the BANK toolbar.

In the version of Sage used to illustrate this book (Version 7) you click on the Remittance button at the bottom of the screen. This will bring up a screen for you to select a suitable remittance advice:

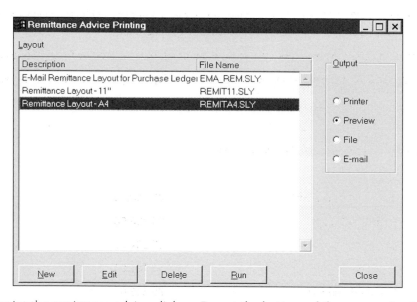

To print the remittance advice click on Run at the bottom of the screen. A printed remittance advice (extract) is shown below.

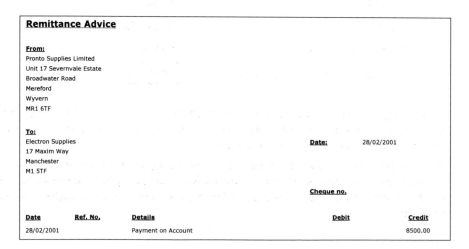

We will now look at the way in which Tom Cox's business, Pronto Supplies Limited, inputs its payments from customers and payments to suppliers on the computer.

**Case Study**

# PRONTO SUPPLIES LIMITED: PROCESSING PAYMENTS FROM CUSTOMERS AND TO SUPPLIERS

It is February 28 2001. Tom has received a number of cheques (with remittance advices) from his customers in settlement of invoices sent out in January.

Some of the cheques also take into account the credit notes issued by Pronto Supplies.

Tom also has a list of supplier invoices to pay, the money being due at the end of the month.

### receipts from customers

The list of cheques received is shown below.

| | |
|---|---|
| John Butler & Associates | £5,500.00 |
| Charisma Design | £2,400.00 |
| Crowmatic Limited | £3,234.00 |
| David Boossey | £3,165.00 |
| French Emporium | £5,553.00 |
| Jo Green Systems | £3,461.20 |
| L Garr & Co | £8,500.00 |
| Mendell & Son | £4,276.50 |
| Prism Trading Limited | £2,586.00 |
| Batch total of payments received | £38,675.70 |

These cheques are entered into the computer accounting system under CUSTOMER in the BANK section as shown on the screen shown at the top of the next page. This screen shows the second cheque on the list being input.

Tom then prints out a report 'Day Books: Customer Receipts (Summary)' which shows the transactions he has processed. This is also shown on the next page. He checks the total on the report against the batch total of the cheques (or remittance advices) he has received.

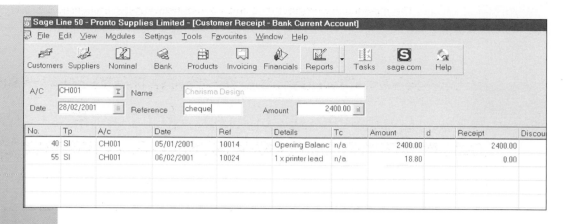

| | | | | | | | | | | | |
|---|---|---|---|---|---|---|---|---|---|---|---|
| No. | Tp | A/c | Date | Ref | Details | Tc | Amount | d | Receipt | Discou |
| 40 | SI | CH001 | 05/01/2001 | 10014 | Opening Balanc | n/a | 2400.00 | | 2400.00 | |
| 55 | SI | CH001 | 06/02/2001 | 10024 | 1 x printer lead | n/a | 18.80 | | 0.00 | |

Date:     09/11/2001                      **Pronto Supplies Limited**                              Page:     1
Time:     15:01:21            **Day Books: Customer Receipts (Summary)**

| Date From: | 28/02/2001 | | | | | Bank From: | |
|---|---|---|---|---|---|---|---|
| DateTo: | 28/02/2001 | | | | | Bank To: | 99999999 |

| Transaction From: | 1 | | | | | Customer From: | |
|---|---|---|---|---|---|---|---|
| Transaction To: | 99999999 | | | | | Customer To: | ZZZZZZZZ |

| No | Tp | Bank | A/C | Date | Refn | Details | Net | Tax | Gross | B |
|---|---|---|---|---|---|---|---|---|---|---|
| 76 | SR | 1200 | JB001 | 28/02/2001 | chq | Sales Receipt | 5,500.00 | 0.00 | 5,500.00 | - |
| 77 | SR | 1200 | CH001 | 28/02/2001 | chq | Sales Receipt | 2,400.00 | 0.00 | 2,400.00 | - |
| 78 | SR | 1200 | CR001 | 28/02/2001 | chq | Sales Receipt | 3,234.00 | 0.00 | 3,234.00 | - |
| 79 | SR | 1200 | DB001 | 28/02/2001 | chq | Sales Receipt | 3,165.00 | 0.00 | 3,165.00 | - |
| 80 | SR | 1200 | FE001 | 28/02/2001 | chq | Sales Receipt | 5,553.00 | 0.00 | 5,553.00 | - |
| 81 | SR | 1200 | JG001 | 28/02/2001 | chq | Sales Receipt | 3,461.20 | 0.00 | 3,461.20 | - |
| 82 | SR | 1200 | LG001 | 28/02/2001 | chq | Sales Receipt | 8,500.00 | 0.00 | 8,500.00 | - |
| 83 | SR | 1200 | ME001 | 28/02/2001 | chq | Sales Receipt | 4,276.50 | 0.00 | 4,276.50 | - |
| 84 | SR | 1200 | PT001 | 28/02/2001 | chq | Sales Receipt | 2,586.00 | 0.00 | 2,586.00 | - |
| | | | | | | **Totals:** | 38,675.70 | 0.00 | 38,675.70 | |

## payments to suppliers

Tom has made a list of the amounts he owes to his suppliers for goods sent to Pronto Supplies Limited in January.

The documents he has for this are his original purchase orders, invoices received and any credit notes issued by his suppliers.

The payment details are:

| | | |
|---|---|---|
| Delco PLC | £5,186.00 | Cheque 123001 |
| Electron Supplies | £8,500.00 | Cheque 123002 |
| MacCity | £4,455.35 | Cheque 123003 |
| Synchromart | £7,600.00 | Cheque 123004 |
| Tycomp Supplies | £6,160.00 | Cheque 123005 |
| Batch total of payments made | £31,901.35 | |

The cheques are prepared and entered into the computer accounting system under SUPPLIER in the BANK section as shown below. Tom also decides to print out remittance advices as he goes along.

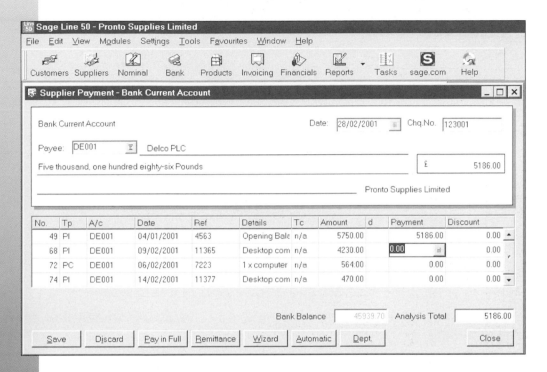

Tom then prints out a report Day Books: Supplier Receipts (Summary) which shows the transactions he has processed. He checks the total on the report against the total of the cheques he has issued.

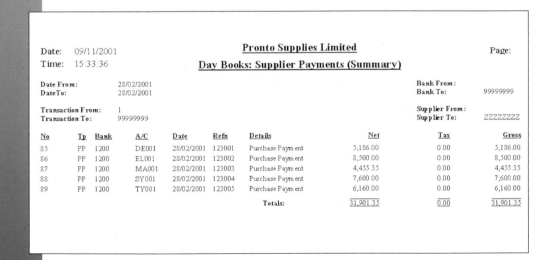

# DEALING WITH CREDIT NOTES

When inputting payments from customers and to suppliers in a program like Sage, you may encounter the situation where the amount received (or paid out) is not the same as the amount of the invoice being settled.

For example, if a customer is issued with an invoice for £1,000 and then issued with a credit note for £100 because some of the goods are faulty, the customer will only owe – and pay – £900. The computer screen, however, will show this £900 as two separate lines· an invoice for £1,000 and a credit note for £100. If the £900 cheque received is allocated against the £1,000, the computer will think a balance of £100 still needs to be paid against this invoice, even though the account balance is nil!

## the solution

The credit note, which is also outstanding on the computer screen needs to be allocated to the balance of the invoice. This is done by:

- clicking on the Receipt box on the credit note line
- clicking on 'Pay in Full' so that the analysis total shows a minus amount
- clicking on the Receipt box on the invoice line and then 'Pay in Full' so that the analysis box shows a nil balance

This tidying up procedure can be carried out before, during or after the payments received routine.

The procedure for allocating supplier credit notes to invoices works on exactly the same principles.

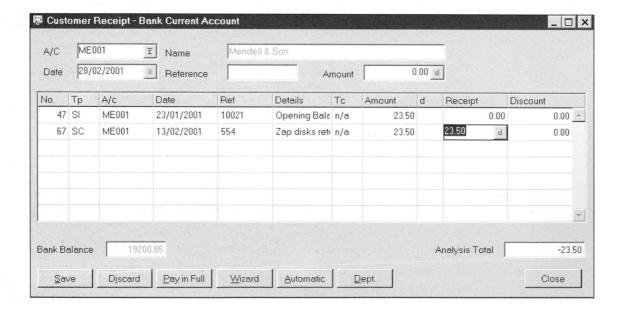

# CASH SALES

**Cash sales** made by a business are usually sales made 'over the counter'.

Cash sales can be made by cash, cheque or debit or credit card – they are not just notes and coins. The important point here is that the business should pay the money into the Bank Current Account as soon as possible – it will be safer in the bank and can be used to meet payments the business may have made.

The input screen for cash sales is reached from the RECEIPT icon on the BANK menu bar. It looks like this:

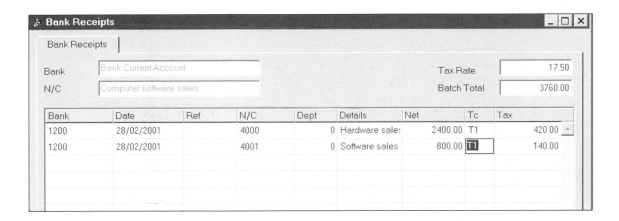

## inputting bank receipts

Cash sales paid straight into the bank may be input from the bank paying-in slips recorded in the handwritten business cash book or from a sales listing sheet. These receipts are known in Sage as Bank Receipts and are input as follows:

▨ input the computer bank account number

▨ enter the date (usually the date the money is paid into the bank)

▨ enter a reference (this can be the reference number of the paying-in slip)

▨ input the appropriate nominal code (N/C) for the type of sales involved

▨ enter a description of the payment (eg 'hardware sales') under 'Details'

▨ enter the net amount of the sales (ie the sales amount excluding VAT) and then click on T1 if the goods are standard rated for VAT – the computer will then automatically calculate the VAT amount for you and show it in the right-hand column

▨ check that the VAT amount shown agrees with your figure and change it on screen if it does not – there may be a rounding difference

▨ check the input details and totals and then SAVE

## Cash payments

Most credit payments made by businesses, as we saw in the last chapter, are to suppliers for goods and services provided and paid for on invoice. But businesses also have to make payments on a day-to-day and cash basis (immediate payment) for a wide variety of running costs such as wages and telephone bills.

These payments are input from the screen reached by clicking on the PAYMENT icon on the BANK menu bar. Study the example shown below. Here a telephone bill and wages have been paid from the Bank Current Account.

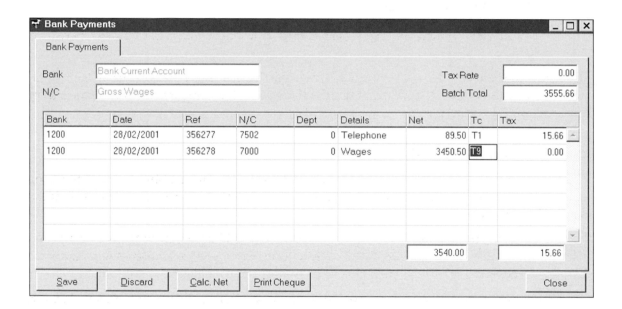

### inputting cash payments

Cash payments can be input from the handwritten business cash book (if one is used), or from the cheques issued and bills being paid (which should show any VAT element). The procedure for inputting is:

- input the computer bank account number

- enter the date (the date the payment is made)

- enter a reference (normally the cheque number or 'BACS' if the payment is a BACS payment)

- input the appropriate nominal code (N/C) for the type of payment involved

- enter a brief description of the nature of the payment (eg 'Telephone') under 'Details'

■ enter the net amount of the payment (ie the amount excluding VAT) and then click on T1 if the product is standard rated for VAT – the computer will then automatically calculate the VAT amount for you and show it in the right-hand column

■ check that the VAT amount shown agrees with your figure and change it on screen if it does not – there may be a rounding difference

## a note on VAT

The VAT rates used here are:

T1    the telephone bill is standard rated

T9    wages do not involve VAT

The code for a zero-rated item would have been T0. The code for a VAT exempt item would have been T2.

If you do not know what the VAT element of a payment figure is, enter the total figure in the 'Net' column and click on 'Calc.Net' at the bottom of the screen. The computer will then automatically calculate the VAT and adjust the Net figure accordingly.

## checking the input data

You will see that the screen on the previous page shows the Net, Tax and Batch totals. These will automatically update as you enter the transactions. It is important to check your input against the source data for your input.

If you are entering the data as a batch of entries you should add up the three totals (Net, VAT and Batch) manually and check them against the screen figures when you have finished your data entry, but before you Save.

As a final check you should print out a Day Book report (see example below) from Reports in BANK and check the entries against your handwritten records (your cash book, for example).

| Time: 14:36:46 | | | **Day Books: Bank Payments (Summary)** | | | | | |
|---|---|---|---|---|---|---|---|---|
| Date From: | | 01/02/2001 | | | | | Bank From: | |
| DateTo: | | 28/02/2001 | | | | | Bank To: | 99999999 |
| Transaction From: | | 1 | | | | | | |
| Transaction To: | | 99999999 | | | | | | |
| **No** | **Tp** | **Bank** | **Date** | **Refn** | **Details** | **Net** | **Tax** | **Gross** |
| 96 | BP | 1200 | 12/02/2001 | 122992 | Cash purchases | 15,500.00 | 2,712.50 | 18,212.50 |
| 97 | BP | 1200 | 14/02/2001 | 122993 | Advert | 10,200.00 | 1,785.00 | 11,985.00 |
| 98 | BP | 1200 | 15/02/2001 | 122994 | Furniture | 5,000.00 | 875.00 | 5,875.00 |
| 99 | BP | 1200 | 16/02/2001 | 122995 | Rent | 4,500.00 | 787.50 | 5,287.50 |
| 100 | BP | 1200 | 19/02/2001 | 122996 | Rates | 350.00 | 0.00 | 350.00 |
| 101 | BP | 1200 | 23/02/2001 | 122997 | RPower | 158.00 | 27.65 | 185.65 |
| 102 | BP | 1200 | 26/02/2001 | 122998 | ZipTelecom | 310.00 | 54.25 | 364.25 |
| 103 | BP | 1200 | 26/02/2001 | 122999 | Stationery | 340.00 | 59.50 | 399.50 |
| 104 | BP | 1200 | 28/02/2001 | 123000 | Wages | 16,780.00 | 0.00 | 16,780.00 |
| | | | | | Totals: | 53,138.00 | 6,301.40 | 59,439.40 |

# PRONTO SUPPLIES LIMITED:
# CASH RECEIPTS AND PAYMENTS

It is February 28 2001 and Tom has completed and checked his input of customer receipts and supplier payments.

He now has to input the various cash receipts and payments received and made during the month.

## cash receipts

Pronto Supplies Limited paid takings of cash sales into the bank current account three times during the month. The amounts recorded in the cash book are shown below. The reference quoted is the paying-in slip reference.

| Date | Details | Net amount (£) | VAT (£) | ref. |
|------|---------|---------------:|--------:|------|
| 9 Feb 2001 | Hardware sales | 12,500.00 | 2187.50 | 10736 |
| 9 Feb 2001 | Software sales | 4,680.00 | 819.00 | 10737 |
| 16 Feb 2001 | Hardware sales | 15,840.00 | 2,772.00 | 10738 |
| 16 Feb 2001 | Software sales | 3,680.00 | 644.00 | 10739 |
| 23 Feb 2001 | Hardware sales | 17,800.00 | 3,115.00 | 10740 |
| 23 Feb 2001 | Software sales | 4,800.00 | 840.00 | 10741 |
| | Totals | 59,300.00 | 10,377.50 | |

These sales receipts are entered into the computer accounting system on the RECEIPTS screen reached from the BANK menu bar. Note that the Bank Current Account and the appropriate nominal sales code (N/C) are used each time.

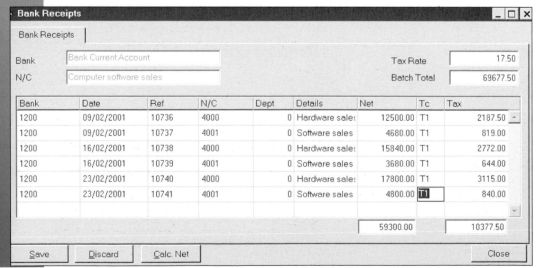

Tom then checks his listing totals against the on-screen totals for accuracy and clicks SAVE. He then prints out a report Day Books: Bank Receipts (Summary) as a paper-based record of the transactions he has processed. This is shown below. He again checks the totals on the report against the totals on his original listing.

**Pronto Supplies Limited**

**Day Books: Bank Receipts (Summary)**

Date From:    01/02/2001
DateTo:    28/02/2001

Transaction From:    1
Transaction To:    99999999

| No | Tp | Bank | Date | Refn | Details | Net | Tax | Gross |
|----|----|------|------|------|---------|-----|-----|-------|
| 90 | BR | 1200 | 09/02/2001 | 10736 | Hardware sales | 12,500.00 | 2,187.50 | 14,687.50 |
| 91 | BR | 1200 | 09/02/2001 | 10737 | Software sales | 4,680.00 | 819.00 | 5,499.00 |
| 92 | BR | 1200 | 16/02/2001 | 10738 | Hardware sales | 15,840.00 | 2,772.00 | 18,612.00 |
| 93 | BR | 1200 | 16/02/2001 | 10739 | Software sales | 3,680.00 | 644.00 | 4,324.00 |
| 94 | BR | 1200 | 23/02/2001 | 10740 | Hardware sales | 17,800.00 | 3,115.00 | 20,915.00 |
| 95 | BR | 1200 | 23/02/2001 | 10741 | Software sales | 4,800.00 | 840.00 | 5,640.00 |
| | | | | | **Totals:** | 59,300.00 | 10,377.50 | 69,677.50 |

## cash payments

Tom sees from the company cash book that Pronto Supplies Limited has made a number of cash payments – by cheque – during the month for a variety of purposes. They are listed below. They include:

- normal day-to-day running (revenue) expenses paid on a cash (immediate) basis
- the purchase of furniture (a capital item) for £5,000 on 15 February

| Date | Details | Net amount (£) | VAT (£) | chq no |
|------|---------|----------------|---------|--------|
| 12 Feb 2001 | Cash purchases | 15,500.00 | 2,712.50 | 122992 |
| 14 Feb 2001 | Advertising | 10,200.00 | 1,785.00 | 122993 |
| 15 Feb 2001 | Furniture | 5,000.00 | 875.00 | 122994 |
| 16 Feb 2001 | Rent | 4,500.00 | 787.50 | 122995 |
| 19 Feb 2001 | Rates | 350.00 | exempt | 122996 |
| 23 Feb 2001 | RPower (Electricity) | 158.00 | 27.65 | 122997 |
| 26 Feb 2001 | ZipTelecom (Telephone) | 310.00 | 54.25 | 122998 |
| 26 Feb 2001 | Stationery | 340.00 | 59.50 | 122999 |
| 28 Feb 2001 | Wages | 16,780.00 | no VAT | 123000 |
| | Totals | 53,138.00 | 6,301.40 | |

These sales payments are entered into the computer accounting system on the PAYMENTS screen reached from the BANK menu bar. Note that the Bank Current Account and the appropriate nominal code (N/C) is used each time. The reference in each case is the relevant cheque number.

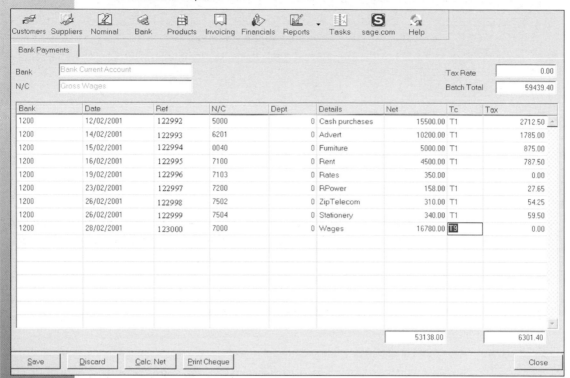

Tom then checks his listing totals against the on-screen totals for accuracy and clicks SAVE. He prints out a report Day Books: Bank Payments (Summary) as a record of the transactions he has processed. This is shown below. He compares the totals on the report against the totals on his original listing as a final check of input accuracy.

### Pronto Supplies Limited
### Day Books: Bank Payments (Summary)

Date From: 01/02/2001
DateTo: 28/02/2001

Transaction From: 1
Transaction To: 99999999

| No | Tp | Bank | Date | Refn | Details | Net | Tax | Gross |
|----|----|------|------|------|---------|-----|-----|-------|
| 96 | BP | 1200 | 12/02/2001 | 122992 | Cash purchases | 15,500.00 | 2,712.50 | 18,212.50 |
| 97 | BP | 1200 | 14/02/2001 | 122993 | Advert | 10,200.00 | 1,785.00 | 11,985.00 |
| 98 | BP | 1200 | 15/02/2001 | 122994 | Furniture | 5,000.00 | 875.00 | 5,875.00 |
| 99 | BP | 1200 | 16/02/2001 | 122995 | Rent | 4,500.00 | 787.50 | 5,287.50 |
| 100 | BP | 1200 | 19/02/2001 | 122996 | Rates | 350.00 | 0.00 | 350.00 |
| 101 | BP | 1200 | 23/02/2001 | 122997 | RPower | 158.00 | 27.65 | 185.65 |
| 102 | BP | 1200 | 26/02/2001 | 122998 | ZipTelecom | 310.00 | 54.25 | 364.25 |
| 103 | BP | 1200 | 26/02/2001 | 122999 | Stationery | 340.00 | 59.50 | 399.50 |
| 104 | BP | 1200 | 28/02/2001 | 123000 | Wages | 16,780.00 | 0.00 | 16,780.00 |
| | | | | | Totals: | 53,138.00 | 6,301.40 | 59,439.40 |

# USING A 'CASH' ACCOUNT

A business which holds substantial amounts of cash – eg shop 'takings' – may wish to operate a separate Cash Account on the computer, just as it may set up separate 'cash' columns in the manual Cash Book. If this is the case, it will open a separate account in BANK for this purpose. Any transfers to and from the actual bank Current Account will be made using the bank transfer screen. This transfer screen will also be used when making transfers to Petty Cash Account (see below).

# PETTY CASH

## petty cash and the accounting system

As you will know from your studies, **petty cash** is a fund of money kept in the business in the same way as the bank current account is a fund of money kept in the bank. A 'bank' account will be set up for petty cash on the computer which will handle all the transactions:

- payments of cash into petty cash from the bank current account
- payments out of petty cash to pay for small expense items

## payments into petty cash

The Sage computer system has a default Petty Cash Account which it classes as a bank account, although, of course, the money is not in the bank. The computer sees it as a 'money fund'.

When cash is needed to top up the petty cash, the business will normally cash a cheque at the bank and then put the money in the cash tin. The computer program requires the business to input the transaction as a TRANSFER from the BANK menu bar. In the screen below, a business has cashed a £100 cheque at the bank (using cheque 132003) to provide the cash.

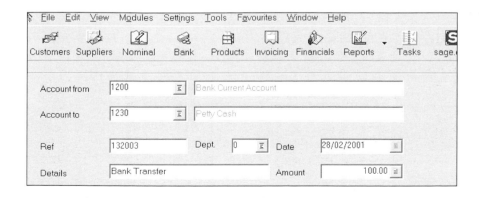

## payments out of petty cash

Payments out of Petty Cash Account are handled in exactly the same way on the computer as payments out of Bank Current Account.

The PAYMENTS screen is reached through the BANK menu bar. The details are then input from the petty cash vouchers or the petty cash book in which they are recorded.

The screen below shows a petty cash voucher and the input of the details into the Sage BANK PAYMENTS screen.

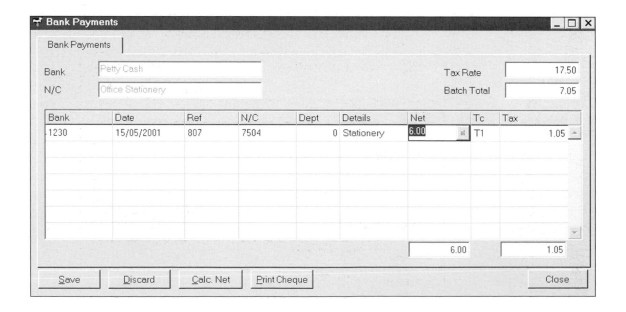

Points to remember are:

- the bank account number used is the Petty Cash Account number

- the reference is the petty cash voucher number

- petty cash vouchers and their receipts will not always show the VAT amount – the VAT and net amount can be calculated on the computer by inputting the full amount under 'Net' and then clicking on 'Calc.Net' at the bottom of the screen (using T1 code to denote standard rate VAT)

- when the details have been checked you should SAVE

- the details can also be checked against a Cash Payments Day Book printout if required (accessed through Reports in BANK)

**Case Study**

# PRONTO SUPPLIES LIMITED: SETTING UP THE PETTY CASH SYSTEM

At the beginning of February Tom Cox set up a petty cash system at Pronto Supplies Limited. The situation at 28 February is as follows:

- Tom notes that he cashed cheque no 122991 for £100 at the bank on 1 February.

- The £100 cash was transferred to the petty cash tin on 1 February.

- The tin contains three vouchers for payments made during the month – these are shown below and on the next page. They are ready for entry in the petty cash book as part of the month-end routine.

  Voucher PC101 shows the VAT included in the total (standard rate: T1)

  Voucher PC102 does not have any VAT in it (postage stamps are exempt:T2)

  Voucher PC103 does not show the VAT included in the total (standard rate: T1) because it was not shown separately on the original receipt.

**petty cash voucher**

Number *PC101*

date *7 Feb 2001*

| description | | amount | |
|---|---|---|---|
| | | £ | p |
| *Stationery* | | 36 | 00 |
| | VAT | 6 | 30 |
| *Receipt obtained* | | 42 | 30 |

signature *Nick Vellope*

authorised *Tom Cox*

**petty cash voucher**

Number *PC102*

date    *14 Feb 2001*

| description | | £ | p |
|---|---|---|---|
| *Postages* | | 25 | 00 |
| | VAT | | |
| *Receipt obtained* | | 25 | 00 |

signature    *R Patel*

authorised    *Tom Cox*

---

**petty cash voucher**

Number *PC103*

date    *20 Feb 2001*

| description | | £ | p |
|---|---|---|---|
| *Stationery* | | | |
| | VAT | | |
| *Receipt obtained* | | 18 | 80 |

signature    *B Radish*

authorised    *Tom Cox*

## the transfer to petty cash

Tom Cox first inputs the £100 transfer from the Bank Current Account to the Petty Cash Account. The screen is illustrated below. Note the use of the cheque number as the reference.

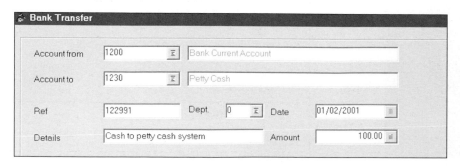

## inputting the vouchers

The petty cash payments are entered into the computer accounting system on the PAYMENTS screen reached from the BANK menu bar.

Note that the bank Petty Cash Account number and the appropriate nominal code (N/C) is used each time.

The postages nominal code was taken from the default nominal list.

The reference in each case is the relevant petty cash voucher number.

Postages are VAT exempt. The VAT on the third petty cash voucher was not on the receipt but has been calculated on-screen by inputting the total amount of £18.80 in the 'Net' column and clicking on 'Calc.Net' at the bottom of the screen:

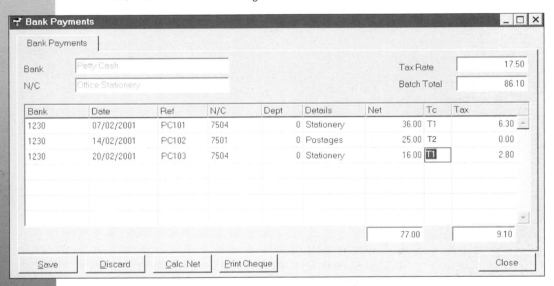

Tom then checks the batch total with the total of the vouchers and when he is happy that all the details are correct he will SAVE. The Day Book report will now show the petty cash payments. Note that the transaction code is 'CP' (second column from the left). This stands for 'Cash Payment'. This distinguishes the petty cash payments from payments by cheque (input through the same screen). These cheque payments have the code 'BP' which stands for 'Bank Payment'.

### Pronto Supplies Limited
### Day Books: Cash Payments (Summary)

| Date From: | 01/02/2001 | | | | | Bank From: | | |
| DateTo: | 28/02/2001 | | | | | Bank To: | 99999999 | |

| Transaction From: | 1 |
| Transaction To: | 99999999 |

| No | Tp | Bank | Date | Refn | Details | Net | Tax | Gross |
|----|----|------|------|------|---------|-----|-----|-------|
| 107 | CP | 1230 | 07/02/2001 | PC101 | Stationery | 36.00 | 6.30 | 42.30 |
| 108 | CP | 1230 | 14/02/2001 | PC102 | Postages | 25.00 | 0.00 | 25.00 |
| 109 | CP | 1230 | 20/02/2001 | PC103 | Stationery | 16.00 | 2.80 | 18.80 |
| | | | | | Totals: | 77.00 | 9.10 | 86.10 |

## JOURNAL ENTRIES

Journal entries enable you to make transfers from one nominal (General Ledger) account to another. Journal entries are used, for example, when you are completing a VAT return and need to transfer VAT amounts from one VAT account to another. It is also useful if an error needs to be corrected when an entry has been input to the wrong account.

Suppose you are inputting a batch of Bank Payments which include a number of bills that have to be paid. You have written out a cheque for £94 to RPower for a gas bill, but when inputting it you think it is for electricity and so post it to electricity (nominal account 7200) instead of gas (7201). You can correct your mistake using a journal entry. You bring up the screen by clicking on the JOURNALS icon on the NOMINAL menu bar:

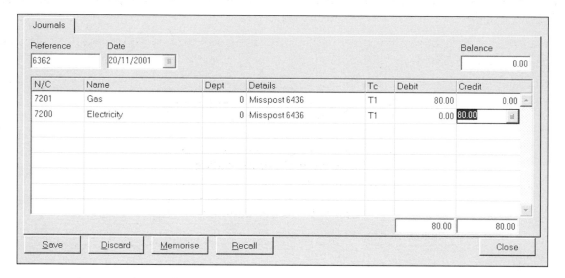

The procedure is:

▪ enter the reference (this could be the transaction number you can find by opening up the FINANCIALS screen and locating the transaction)

▪ enter the date

▪ enter the nominal code of the account to which you are going to post the debit; here it is Gas Account because you are recording an expense

▪ enter the reason for the transaction – here you are adjusting a mispost

▪ enter the VAT tax code input on the original (wrong) entry

▪ enter the net amount in the debit column (ie the amount before VAT has been added on) – here the net amount is £80 and VAT (here at standard rate) is £14 and the total is £94; note that neither the VAT nor the total appear on the screen because you are not adjusting the VAT; only the net amount has gone to the wrong account

- enter the nominal code of the account to which you are going to post the credit; here it is Electricity Account because you are effectively refunding the amount to the account – it is an income item and so a credit

- enter the remaining data as you did for the debit, but enter the net amount in the right-hand credit column

- make sure the Balance box reads zero – meaning that the debit equals the credit – and SAVE

## BANK RECONCILIATION ON THE COMPUTER

You should already know how to draw up a bank reconciliation statement. If you are not sure what this involves, you should first read Chapter 10 (page 132).

To recap, a bank reconciliation statement forms a link between the balances shown in the bank statement and the Bank Account in the cash book (or its computer equivalent).

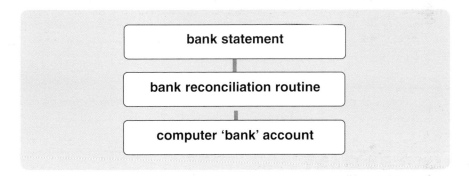

The Sage system allows you to carry out a bank reconciliation. The Bank Reconciliation screen, accessed through RECONCILE in BANK, is shown on the next page. The procedure is as follows:

**1** Enter the bank statement date and closing bank statement balance at the top of the screen and check that the opening balance is the same on the computer screen and on the bank statement.

**2** Compare the items on the screen with the bank statement – selecting them item by item – and update the computer with any items which appear on the bank statement and not on the computer screen (ie by inputting them, using the Adjustment button).

**3** When you have highlighted all the items on screen which are in the bank statement and updated the computer (see 2), check that the Sage 'Reconcile Balance' matches the bank statement closing balance and the Difference box shows zero. Reconciliation is then complete.

**4** Click SAVE – any unselected items (ie items on the computer but not in the bank, eg the £6,160 cheque on the screen on the next page) will appear again when you next carry out this bank reconciliation process.

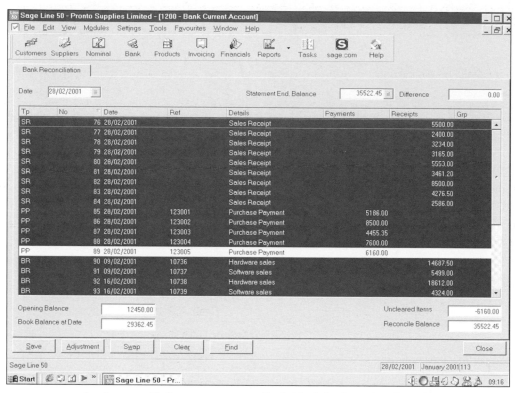

*a bank reconciliation screen – see Task 10 of the Inputting Exercises*

# CHAPTER SUMMARY

● A business can set up not only the bank current account in the computer accounting system, but also a number of other 'money' accounts. These, which include petty cash account, enable the business to keep track of the processing of money in a variety of forms.

● Payments received from customers who have bought on credit and payments to suppliers from whom the business has bought on credit can be processed through the computer accounting system.

● It is essential to check the input of payments from customers and to suppliers by obtaining a printout – such as a Day Book – from the computer.

● Petty cash transactions are processed on the computer through Petty Cash Account. Cash payments and receipts are either processed on the computer through the Bank Account, or through a special 'Cash' account which is the same as Cash Account in a manual accounting system.

● The computer accounting system also provides the facility for making adjustments with journal entries (eg for correcting errors), and reconciling the bank statement balances with the computer bank account.

# INPUTTING EXERCISES

## technical note

Before starting these inputting exercises you must ensure <u>either</u> that your input from the last chapter is correct <u>or</u> that the Sage file 'Suppliers' (provided by Osborne Books) is loaded or restored onto your computer.

**Task 1**

Set the program date to 28 February 2001. Enter the following customer cheques into BANK (CUSTOMER). Use the reference 'cheque'.

Print out a Day Books: Customer Receipts (Summary) Report from REPORTS in BANK. Agree the day book total with the batch total (below) to confirm the accuracy of your input.

| | |
|---|---|
| John Butler & Associates | £5,500.00 |
| Charisma Design | £2,400.00 |
| Crowmatic Limited | £3,234.00 |
| David Boossey | £3,165.00 |
| French Emporium | £5,553.00 |
| Jo Green Systems | £3,461.20 |
| L Garr & Co | £8,500.00 |
| Mendell & Son | £4,276.50 |
| Prism Trading Limited | £2,586.00 |
| Batch total of payments received | £38,675.70 |

**Task 2**

Enter the following cheques Tom is paying to suppliers into the computer (SUPPLIER in BANK). If you are able, print remittance advices for each payment (REMITTANCE button at the bottom of the screen). Print out a Day Books: Supplier Payments (Summary) Report from REPORTS in BANK. Agree the day book total with the batch total (below) to confirm the accuracy of your input. The cheques are dated 28 February.

| | | |
|---|---|---|
| Delco PLC | £5,186.00 | Cheque 123001 |
| Electron Supplies | £8,500.00 | Cheque 123002 |
| MacCity | £4,455.35 | Cheque 123003 |
| Synchromart | £7,600.00 | Cheque 123004 |
| Tycomp Supplies | £6,160.00 | Cheque 123005 |
| Batch total of payments made | £31,901.35 | |

## Task 3

If you have not already allocated your credit notes, check through your customer accounts by opening up the Customer Receipts screen for each one. You may find that some of them have a credit note outstanding and an invoice which has not been completely paid. You should in each case allocate the credit note to the appropriate invoice. Ensure in each case that the correct bank account is selected before you make the adjustment.

## Task 4

Repeat the procedure in Task 3 by opening up the Supplier Payments screen for each supplier. You should in each case allocate the credit note to the appropriate invoice.

## Task 5

Ensure the program date is set at 28 February 2001. Enter the following bank cash receipts into the computer. Check your totals before saving and print out a Day Books: Bank Receipts (Summary) Report to confirm the accuracy of your input. The nominal codes you will need are on the Trial Balance on page 557.

| Date | Details | Net amount (£) | VAT (£) | ref. |
|---|---|---|---|---|
| 9 Feb 2001 | Hardware sales | 12,500.00 | 2187.50 | 10736 |
| 9 Feb 2001 | Software sales | 4,680.00 | 819.00 | 10737 |
| 16 Feb 2001 | Hardware sales | 15,840.00 | 2,772.00 | 10738 |
| 16 Feb 2001 | Software sales | 3,680.00 | 644.00 | 10739 |
| 23 Feb 2001 | Hardware sales | 17,800.00 | 3,115.00 | 10740 |
| 23 Feb 2001 | Software sales | 4,800.00 | 840.00 | 10741 |
| | Totals | 59,300.00 | 10,377.50 | |

## Task 6

Keep the program date as 28 February 2001.

Enter the following cash payments into the computer. Take care over the nominal accounts that you choose and the VAT Tax codes used. T1 is the standard rate code, T2 is for exempt items and T9 is the code for transactions which do not involve VAT. You can find the nominal codes on the trial balance on page 557.

Check your totals before saving and print out a Day Books: Bank Payments (Summary) Report

| Date | Details | Net amount (£) | VAT (£) | chq no |
|---|---|---|---|---|
| 12 Feb 2001 | Materials purchased | 15,500.00 | 2,712.50 | 122992 |
| 14 Feb 2001 | Advertising | 10,200.00 | 1,785.00 | 122993 |
| 15 Feb 2001 | Furniture | 5,000.00 | 875.00 | 122994 |
| 16 Feb 2001 | Rent | 4,500.00 | 787.50 | 122995 |
| 19 Feb 2001 | Rates | 350.00 | exempt | 122996 |
| 23 Feb 2001 | Electricity (RPower) | 158.00 | 27.65 | 122997 |
| 26 Feb 2001 | Telephone (ZipTelecom) | 310.00 | 54.25 | 122998 |
| 26 Feb 2001 | Stationery | 340.00 | 59.50 | 122999 |
| 28 Feb 2001 | Wages | 16,780.00 | no VAT | 123000 |
| | Totals | 53,138.00 | 6,301.40 | |

## Task 7

Keep the program date as 28 February 2001.

On 1 February Tom cashed cheque 122991 for £100 at his bank to set up a petty cash system.

Carry out a bank transfer from Bank Current Account to Petty Cash Account for this amount.

## Task 8

Keep the program date as 28 February 2001. Tom has just authorised two more petty cash vouchers (shown below). Input these together with the three petty cash vouchers on pages 547 to 548 into Bank Payments, taking particular care with the VAT element on each one (postages are VAT exempt and stationery is standard-rated).

Print out a Day Books: Cash Payments (Summary) Report to confirm the accuracy of your input of the five vouchers.

Hint: remember to select the Petty Cash Bank account on the screen before running the report.

| petty cash voucher | | Number *PC104* |
|---|---|---|
| | date | *28 Feb 2001* |

| description | | amount | |
|---|---|---|---|
| | | £ | p |
| *Postage stamps* | | 5 | 00 |
| | VAT | | |
| *Receipt obtained* | | 5 | 00 |

signature  *R Cook*

authorised  *Tom Cox*

| petty cash voucher | | Number PC105 |
|---|---|---|
| | date | 28 Feb 2001 |

| description | | amount | |
|---|---|---|---|
| | | £ | p |
| Stationery | | | |
| | VAT | | |
| Receipt obtained | | 4 | 70 |

signature  R Patel

authorised  Tom Cox

## Task 9

Keep the program date as 28 February 2001.

Tom has been talking to his accountant about the categories of expenses which are recorded in his Nominal (General) Ledger. He finds that a payment of £100, made on 20 January, which appears under advertising (account 6201) was actually for office stationery (account 7504).

The accountant suggests that Tom makes a journal entry to adjust the position, debiting account 7504 and crediting account 6201. Make an appropriate journal entry, using the same VAT code (T1) as on the original transaction. The reference is 0041 and the current date 28 February 2001. The details are 'wrong post 20/01/01'. The JOURNALS screen is accessed through NOMINAL.

Print out a Day Books: Nominal Ledger Report dated 28 February 2001 from REPORTS in NOMINAL and check the details to confirm the accuracy of your input.

Print out a Trial Balance as at 28 February 2001 and check it against the Trial Balance shown opposite.

## Task 10

Enter a new program date of 6 March 2001.

Tom has an online facility with his bank and has just printed out his bank statement as at 5 March 2001. He decides to carry out a bank reconciliation on the computer, using the RECONCILE function through BANK.

The starting balance of the bank statement is £12,450, which agrees with the balance of account 1200 'Bank Current Account' on the computer, as shown on the opening trial balance (see page 504). The closing balance of the bank statement is £35,522.45.

All the items on the computer screen are on the bank statement apart from cheque 123005 for £6,160 which has not yet gone through the bank account.

When you have completed the reconciliation process, SAVE and run and print out a 'Bank Report: Reconciled and Un-reconciled' to show the items that have been reconciled and any that have not.

Note that some of the important figures for this Task are shown on the screen illustration on page 552.

## Task 11

Ensure the program date is still set at 6 March 2001.

Tom has decided to let out two small offices in his building. He wants to set up an account in NOMINAL to record the receipts of rent from the two tenants.

You are to set up a new account called 'Rents Receivable'. The account number allocated will be 4003.

When the account is set up, select account 4003 on the NOMINAL screen and print out a  Nominal List Report which will show that you have opened the account.

## Pronto Supplies, trial balance as at 28 February 2001

**Pronto Supplies Limited**
**Period Trial Balance**

**To Period:**    Month 2, February 2001

| N/C | Name | Debit | Credit |
|---|---|---|---|
| 0020 | Plant and Machinery | 35,000.00 | |
| 0030 | Office Equipment | 15,760.00 | |
| 0040 | Furniture and Fixtures | 30,000.00 | |
| 1100 | Debtors Control Account | 8,991.00 | |
| 1200 | Bank Current Account | 29,362.45 | |
| 1230 | Petty Cash | 4.20 | |
| 2100 | Creditors Control Account | | 11,797.00 |
| 2200 | Sales Tax Control Account | | 28,620.20 |
| 2201 | Purchase Tax Control Account | 34,577.55 | |
| 2300 | Loans | | 35,000.00 |
| 3000 | Ordinary Shares | | 75,000.00 |
| 4000 | Computer hardware sales | | 132,180.00 |
| 4001 | Computer software sales | | 28,724.00 |
| 4002 | Computer consultancy | | 2,640.00 |
| 5000 | Materials Purchased | 93,362.00 | |
| 6201 | Advertising | 22,500.00 | |
| 7000 | Gross Wages | 33,010.00 | |
| 7100 | Rent | 9,000.00 | |
| 7103 | General Rates | 800.00 | |
| 7200 | Electricity | 308.00 | |
| 7501 | Postage and Carriage | 30.00 | |
| 7502 | Telephone | 585.00 | |
| 7504 | Office Stationery | 671.00 | |
| | **Totals:** | 313,961.20 | 313,961.20 |

# Appendix 1

example layouts and accounting ratios

The layouts included here are:

- sole trader final accounts
- limited company final accounts
- cash flow statement

The Appendix also includes a worksheet which assists in the calculation of the main accounting ratios from a set of final accounts.

# sole trader final accounts

## TRADING AND PROFIT AND LOSS ACCOUNT OF ***name***
## FOR THE YEAR/PERIOD ENDED ***date***

| | £ | £ | £ | |
|---|---|---|---|---|
| **TRADING ACCOUNT** | | | | |
| Sales | | | x | |
| Less Sales returns | | | x | |
| *Net sales* | | | x | (a) |
| Opening stock | | x | | |
| Purchases | x | | | |
| Carriage in | x | | | |
| Less Purchases returns | x | | | |
| *Net purchases* | | x | | |
| | | x | | |
| Less Closing stock | | x | | |
| Cost of Goods Sold | | | x | (b) |
| **Gross profit** (a) – (b) | | | x | (c) |

| | £ | £ | £ | |
|---|---|---|---|---|
| **PROFIT AND LOSS ACCOUNT** | | | | |
| Add other income, eg | | | | |
| Discount received | | | x | |
| Reduction in provision for bad debts | | | x | (d) |
| Profit on sale of fixed assets | | | x | |
| Other income | | | x | |
| (c) + (d) | | | x | (e) |
| Less expenses, eg | | | | |
| Vehicle running expenses | | x | | |
| Rent | | x | | |
| Rates | | x | | |
| Heating and lighting | | x | | |
| Telephone | | x | | |
| Salaries and wages* | | x | | |
| Discount allowed | | x | | |
| Carriage out | | x | | |
| Other items, eg | | | | |
| Provision for depreciation | | x | | |
| Loss on sale of fixed assets | | x | | |
| Bad debts written off | | x | | |
| Increase in provision for bad debts | | x | | |
| | | | x | (f) |
| **Net profit** (e) – (f) | | | x | (g) |

\* Wages are sometimes listed as an expense in the trading account section

**BALANCE SHEET OF** \*\*\* name \*\*\* **AS AT** \*\*\* date \*\*\*

| | | £ | £ | £ | |
|---|---|---|---|---|---|
| **Fixed Assets** | | Cost (a) | Dep'n to date (b) | Net | (a) − (b) |
| | | | | | |
| *Intangible:* | Goodwill | x | x | x | |
| *Tangible:* | Premises | x | x | x | |
| | Equipment | x | x | x | |
| | Vehicles | x | x | x | |
| | etc | x | x | x | |
| | | x | x | x | (c) |
| **Current Assets** | | | | | |
| Stock (closing) | | | x | | |
| Debtors | | x | | | |
| Less Provision for bad debts | | x | | | |
| | | | x | | |
| Prepayments | | | x | | |
| Bank | | | x | | |
| Cash | | | x | | |
| | | | x | | (d) |
| **Less Current Liabilities** | | | | | |
| Creditors | | x | | | |
| Accruals | | x | | | |
| Bank overdraft | | x | | | |
| | | | x | | (e) |
| **Working Capital** (d)− (e) | | | | x | (f) |
| (c) + (f) | | | | x | (g) |
| **Less Long-term Liabilities** | | | | | |
| Loans | | | | x | (h) |
| **NET ASSETS** (g) − (h) | | | | x | (i) |
| | | | | | |
| *FINANCED BY* | | | | | |
| **Capital** | | | | | |
| Opening capital | | | | x | |
| Add Net profit (from profit and loss account) | | | | x | |
| | | | | x | |
| Less Drawings | | | | x | |
| | | | | x | (i) |

*Note:* Balance sheet balances at points (i)

Practical point: when preparing handwritten final accounts it is usual practice to underline all the headings and sub-headings shown in bold print in the example layout.

# limited company final accounts

### *** NAME OF COMPANY *** LIMITED
### TRADING AND PROFIT AND LOSS ACCOUNT FOR THE YEAR/PERIOD ENDED *** DATE ***

|  | £ | £ |  |
|---|---|---|---|
| Sales | x | (a) | |
| Opening stock | x | | |
| Purchases or production cost | <u>x</u> | | |
|  | x | | |
| Less Closing stock | <u>x</u> | | |
| Cost of Goods Sold | | <u>x</u> | (b) |
| **Gross profit** (a) − (b) | | x | (c) |
|  |  |  | |
| Less expenses: | | | |
| eg    Selling and distribution costs | x | | |
|        Administration costs | x | | |
|        Finance costs | <u>x</u> | | |
|  | | <u>x</u> | (d) |
| **Net profit for year before taxation** (c) − (d) | | x | (e) |
| Less corporation tax | | <u>x</u> | (f) |
| Profit for year after taxation (e) − (f) | | x | (g) |
| Less  interim dividends paid | | | |
|            ordinary shares | x | | |
|            preference shares | x | | |
|        final dividends proposed | | | |
|            ordinary shares | x | | |
|            preference shares | <u>x</u> | | |
|  | | <u>x</u> | (h) |
| Retained profit for year (g) − (h) | | x | (i) |
| Add balance of retained profits at beginning of year | | <u>x</u> | (j) |
| Balance of retained profits at end of year (i) + (j) | | <u><u>x</u></u> | (k) |

*Notes:*
- for a manufacturing business, production cost (ie the factory cost of manufacturing the products) is shown instead of purchases
- depreciation of fixed assets is included in the costs for production, selling and distribution, and administration, as appropriate
- directors' remuneration and debenture interest is included in the expenses

## *** NAME OF COMPANY *** LIMITED
### BALANCE SHEET AS AT *** DATE ***

| **Fixed Assets** | *Cost* (a) | *Dep'n to date* (b) | *Net* (a) − (b) |
|---|---|---|---|
| | £ | £ | £ |
| *Intangible* | | | |
| Goodwill | x | x | x |
| *Tangible* | | | |
| Freehold land and buildings | x | x | x |
| Machinery | x | x | x |
| Fixtures and fittings | x | x | x |
| etc | x | x | x |
| | x | x | x (c) |

| **Current Assets** | | | |
|---|---|---|---|
| Stock *(closing)* | | x | |
| Debtors | | x | |
| Bank | | x | |
| Cash | | x | |
| | | x | (d) |

| **Less Current Liabilities** | | | |
|---|---|---|---|
| Creditors | x | | |
| Bank overdraft | x | | |
| Proposed dividends | x | | |
| Corporation tax | x | | |
| | | x | (e) |

| **Working Capital** (d) − (e) | | | x (f) |
|---|---|---|---|
| (c) + (f) | | | x (g) |

| **Less Long-term Liabilities** | | | |
|---|---|---|---|
| Debentures | | | x (h) |
| **NET ASSETS** (g) − (h) | | | x (i) |

**FINANCED BY**

**Authorised share capital**

| | | |
|---|---|---|
| x (number) preference shares of £x (nominal value) each | | x |
| x (number) ordinary shares of £x (nominal value) each | | x |
| | | x |

**Issued share capital**

| | | |
|---|---|---|
| x (number) preference shares of £x (nominal value) each, fully/partly paid | | x |
| x (number) ordinary shares of £x (nominal value) each, fully/partly paid | | x |
| | | x |

**Capital reserves**

| | | |
|---|---|---|
| Share premium account | x | |
| Revaluation reserve | x | x |

**Revenue reserves**

| | | |
|---|---|---|
| Profit and loss account | x | |
| General reserve | x | x |
| **SHAREHOLDERS' FUNDS** | | x (i) |

*Note:* balance sheet balances at points (i)

# cash flow statement

## CASH FLOW STATEMENT FOR THE YEAR ENDED *** DATE ***

| | £ | £ |
|---|---|---|
| **Operating activities:** | | |
| Operating profit (note: before tax and interest) | x | |
| Depreciation for year | x | |
| Increase or decrease in stocks | (x) or x | |
| Increase or decrease in debtors | (x) or x | |
| Increase or decrease in creditors | x or (x) | |
| | | |
| *Net cash inflow from operating activities* | | x |
| | | |
| **Returns on investments and servicing of finance:** | | |
| Interest and dividends received | x | |
| Interest and dividends paid | | |
| (dividends on ordinary shares shown below) | (x) | |
| | | x or (x) |
| **Taxation:** | | |
| Corporation tax paid (note: amount *paid* during year) | | (x) |
| | | |
| **Capital expenditure and financial investment** | | |
| Payments to acquire fixed assets and investments | (x) | |
| Receipts from sales of fixed assets and investments | x | |
| | | x or (x) |
| **Acquisitions and disposals** | | |
| eg purchase of subsidiary undertakings | (x) | |
| eg sale of a business | x | x or (x) |
| | | |
| **Equity dividends paid:** (note: amount *paid* during year) | | (x) |
| *Cash inflow or outflow before use of liquid resources and financing* | | x or (x) |
| | | |
| **Management of liquid resources:** | | |
| eg purchase of treasury bills | (x) | |
| eg sale of treasury bills | x | |
| | | x or (x) |
| | | |
| **Financing:** | | |
| Issue of share capital | x | |
| Repayment of share capital | (x) | |
| Increase in loans | x | |
| Repayment of loans | (x) | |
| | | |
| | | x or (x) |
| **Increase or decrease in cash** | | x or (x) |

*Note:* money amounts shown in brackets indicate a deduction or, where the figure is a sub-total, a negative figure

# Accounting ratios worksheet

*This worksheet will assist in calculating the main accounting ratios from a set of final accounts. Use it as follows:*

- *enter the figures from the trading and profit and loss account and balance sheet against items 1 – 11*
- *calculate the ratios and percentages using the numbered figures, as indicated on the next page*

*Note that this will assist in the calculation of the main accounting ratios; but it will not provide the interpretative aspects.*

**FIGURES FROM FINAL ACCOUNTS**

| | | financial year-end | |
|---|---|---|---|
| | | previous year | current year |
| | | £ | £ |
| | **Trading and profit and loss account** | | |
| 1 | Sales (or turnover) | | |
| 2 | Cost of goods sold (or cost of sales) | | |
| 3 | Operating profit (or net profit + interest payable) | | |
| 4 | Net profit (or profit on ordinary activities) before taxation | | |
| | **Balance sheet** | | |
| 5 | Current assets sub-total | | |
| 6 | Stock | | |
| 7 | Debtors | | |
| 8 | Current liabilities sub-total (or creditors: amounts falling due within one year) | | |
| 9 | Trade creditors | | |
| 10 | Long-term liabilities (or creditors: amounts falling due after more than one year) | | |
| 11 | Capital and reserves total | | |

## ACCOUNTING RATIOS

| | | | previous year | current year |
|---|---|---|---|---|
| **Profitability** | *figures from the table on the previous page* | | | |
| Gross profit/sales percentage | $\dfrac{1-2}{1}$ | x $\dfrac{100}{1}$ | % | % |
| Operating profit/sales percentage | $\dfrac{3}{1}$ | x $\dfrac{100}{1}$ | % | % |
| Net profit/sales percentage | $\dfrac{4}{1}$ | x $\dfrac{100}{1}$ | % | % |
| Return on capital employed | $\dfrac{3}{10+11}$ | x $\dfrac{100}{1}$ | % | % |
| Return on equity | $\dfrac{4*}{11}$ | x $\dfrac{100}{1}$ | % | % |

\* less corporation tax, and preference dividend (if any)

| | | | previous year | current year |
|---|---|---|---|---|
| **Solvency/liquidity** | | | | |
| Working capital ratio | $\dfrac{5}{8}$ | | :1 | :1 |
| Liquid ratio | $\dfrac{5-6}{8}$ | | :1 | :1 |
| Capital gearing percentage | $\dfrac{10}{11}$ | x $\dfrac{100}{1}$ | % | % |

| | | | previous year | current year |
|---|---|---|---|---|
| **Asset utilisation** | | | | |
| Stock turnover (days) | $\dfrac{6\,*}{2}$ | x 365 | days | days |
|   \* ideally, this should be the average of opening stock and closing stock | | | | |
| Debtors' collection period (days) | $\dfrac{7}{1}$ | x 365 | days | days |
| Creditors' payment period (days) | $\dfrac{9}{2*}$ | x 365 | days | days |

\* ideally, this should be the purchases figure

# Appendix 2

## answers to questions

This appendix gives the answers to:

* multiple choice questions

* questions marked with an asterisk from the chapters

Where answers are given to questions from the past examination papers of examining boards, these answers are the responsibility of the author and not of the examining board.

# ANSWERS TO MULTIPLE CHOICE QUESTIONS

| question number | 1 | 2 | 3 | 4 | 5 | 6 | 7 | 8 | 9 | 10 | 11 | 12 |
|---|---|---|---|---|---|---|---|---|---|---|---|---|
| page 57 | A | C | D | C | A | A | D | B | A | A | C | D |
| page 88 | C | A | C | B | C | D | B | B | C | A | D | A |
| page 149 | B | C | B | D | D | A | D | B | C | A | D | B |
| page 215 | A | C | A | B | A | C | B | B | B | D | A | C |
| page 253 | A | B | C | D | C | B | B | C | C | A | C | B |
| page 315 | D | B | C | A | B | B | B | A | A | B | D | A |
| page 367 | A | D | A | A | C | D | D | C | B | B | B | A |
| page 417 | B | C | A | A | D | D | C | B | A | D | B | B |
| page 449 | A | B | C | C | D | D | D | C | A | B | B | C |
| page 488 | C | B | A | A | C | A | C | B | D | A | A | - |

# ANSWERS TO CHAPTER QUESTIONS

Answers to asterisked questions (*) follow in chapter order in this Appendix. Answers are given in fully displayed form: this will assist in showing the correct layouts – which is important in accounting.

Answers to the remaining questions are given in a separate *Business Accounts Tutor Pack* available to tutors. Please telephone Osborne Books (01905 748071) for further details.

# CHAPTER 1 What are Business Accounts?

**1.1**

(a) ledger
(b) debtor
(c) creditor
(d) sales day book
(e) cash book
(f) nominal ledger
(g) assets – liabilities = capital
(h) business entity
(i) auditors

**1.7**

| capital | £20,000 |
|---|---|
| capital | £10,000 |
| liabilities | £7,550 |
| assets | £14,100 |
| liabilities | £18,430 |
| assets | £21,160 |

**1.8**

(a) Owner started in business with capital of £10,000 in the bank
(b) Bought office equipment for £2,000, paying by cheque
(c) Received a loan of £6,000 by cheque
(d) Bought a van for £10,000, paying by cheque
(e) Owner introduces £2,000 additional capital by cheque
(f) Loan repayment of £3,000 made by cheque

# CHAPTER 2 Double-entry Book-keeping: First Principles

**2.2**

**Bank Account**

| Dr | | £ | Cr | | £ |
|---|---|---|---|---|---|
| 20-2 | | | 20-2 | | |
| 1 May | Capital | 6,000 | 4 May | Machinery | 3,500 |
| 12 May | L Warner: loan | 1,000 | 6 May | Office equipment | 2,000 |
| 17 May | Commission rec'd | 150 | 10 May | Rent paid | 350 |
| | | | 15 May | Wages | 250 |
| | | | 20 May | Drawings | 85 |
| | | | 25 May | Wages | 135 |

**Capital Account**

| Dr | | £ | Cr | | £ |
|---|---|---|---|---|---|
| 20-2 | | | 20-2 | | |
| | | | 1 May | Bank | 6,000 |

**Machinery Account**

| Dr | | £ | Cr | | £ |
|---|---|---|---|---|---|
| 20-2 | | | 20-2 | | |
| 4 May | Bank | 3,500 | | | |

**Office Equipment Account**

| Dr | | £ | Cr | | £ |
|---|---|---|---|---|---|
| 20-2 | | | 20-2 | | |
| 6 May | Bank | 2,000 | | | |

**Rent Paid Account**

| Dr | | £ | Cr | | £ |
|---|---|---|---|---|---|
| 20-2 | | | 20-2 | | |
| 10 May | Bank | 350 | | | |

**Lucy Warner: Loan Account**

| Dr | | £ | Cr | | £ |
|---|---|---|---|---|---|
| 20-2 | | | 20-2 | | |
| 12 May | Bank | 1,000 | 12 May | Bank | 1,000 |

**Wages Account**

| Dr | | £ | Cr | | £ |
|---|---|---|---|---|---|
| 20-2 | | | 20-2 | | |
| 15 May | Bank | 250 | | | |
| 25 May | Bank | 135 | | | |

**Commission Received Account**

| Dr | | £ | Cr | | £ |
|---|---|---|---|---|---|
| 20-2 | | | 20-2 | | |
| | | | 17 May | Bank | 150 |

**Drawings Account**

| Dr | | £ | Cr | | £ |
|---|---|---|---|---|---|
| 20-2 | | | 20-2 | | |
| 20 May | Bank | 85 | | | |

**2.4**

**Bank Account**

| Dr | | £ | Cr | | £ |
|---|---|---|---|---|---|
| 20-2 | | | 20-2 | | |
| 1 Mar | Capital | 6,500 | 4 Mar | Office equipment | 1,000 |
| 5 Mar | Bank loan | 2,500 | 7 Mar | Wages | 250 |
| 8 Mar | Commission rec'd | 150 | 10 Mar | Rent paid | 200 |
| | | | 12 Mar | Drawings | 175 |
| | | | 15 Mar | Van | 6,000 |

**Capital Account**

| Dr | | £ | Cr | | £ |
|---|---|---|---|---|---|
| 20-2 | | | 20-2 | | |
| | | | 1 Mar | Bank | 6,500 |

**Office Equipment Account**

| Dr | | £ | Cr | | £ |
|---|---|---|---|---|---|
| 20-2 | | | 20-2 | | |
| 4 Mar | Bank | 1,000 | | | |

**Bank Loan Account**

| Dr | | £ | Cr | | £ |
|---|---|---|---|---|---|
| 20-2 | | | 20-2 | | |
| | | | 5 Mar | Bank | 2,500 |

**Wages Account**

| Dr | | £ | Cr | | £ |
|---|---|---|---|---|---|
| 20-2 | | | 20-2 | | |
| 7 Mar | Bank | 250 | | | |

**Commission Received Account**

| Dr | | | Cr |
|---|---|---|---|
| 20-2 | £ | 20-2 | £ |
| | | 8 Mar Bank | 150 |

**Rent Paid Account**

| Dr | | | Cr |
|---|---|---|---|
| 20-2 | £ | 20-2 | £ |
| 10 Mar Bank | 200 | | |

**Drawings Account**

| Dr | | | Cr |
|---|---|---|---|
| 20-2 | £ | 20-2 | £ |
| 12 Mar Bank | 175 | | |

**Van Account**

| Dr | | | Cr |
|---|---|---|---|
| 20-2 | £ | 20-2 | £ |
| 15 Mar Bank | 6,000 | | |

## CHAPTER 3 Double-entry Book-keeping: Further Transactions

**3.2**

**Bank Account**

| Dr | | | | Cr |
|---|---|---|---|---|
| 20-1 | | £ | 20-1 | £ |
| 1 Feb | Capital | 3,000 | 3 Feb Purchases | 100 |
| 2 Feb | Sales | 250 | 5 Feb Wages | 150 |
| 7 Feb | Sales | 300 | 12 Feb Purchases | 200 |
| 15 Feb | J Walters: loan | 1,000 | 20 Feb Computer | 1,950 |
| 25 Feb | Sales | 150 | 27 Feb Wages | 125 |

**Capital Account**

| Dr | | | Cr |
|---|---|---|---|
| 20-1 | £ | 20-1 | £ |
| | | 1 Feb Bank | 3,000 |

**Sales Account**

| Dr | | | Cr |
|---|---|---|---|
| 20-1 | £ | 20-1 | £ |
| | | 2 Feb Bank | 250 |
| | | 7 Feb Bank | 300 |
| | | 25 Feb Bank | 150 |

**Purchases Account**

| Dr | | | Cr |
|---|---|---|---|
| 20-1 | £ | 20-1 | £ |
| 3 Feb Bank | 100 | | |
| 12 Feb Bank | 200 | | |

**Wages Account**

| Dr | | | Cr |
|---|---|---|---|
| 20-1 | £ | 20-1 | £ |
| 5 Feb Bank | 150 | | |
| 27 Feb Bank | 125 | | |

**J Walters: Loan Account**

| Dr | | | Cr |
|---|---|---|---|
| 20-1 | £ | 20-1 | £ |
| | | 15 Feb Bank | 1,000 |

**Computer Account**

| Dr | | | Cr |
|---|---|---|---|
| 20-1 | £ | 20-1 | £ |
| 20 Feb Bank | 1,950 | | |

**3.3**

**Bank Account**

| | | Debit | Credit | Balance |
|---|---|---|---|---|
| | | £ | £ | £ |
| 20-1 | | | | |
| 1 Feb | Capital | 3,000 | | 3,000 Dr |
| 2 Feb | Sales | 250 | | 3,250 Dr |
| 3 Feb | Purchases | | 100 | 3,150 Dr |
| 5 Feb | Wages | | 150 | 3,000 Dr |
| 7 Feb | Sales | 300 | | 3,300 Dr |
| 12 Feb | Purchases | | 200 | 3,100 Dr |
| 15 Feb | J Walters: loan | 1,000 | | 4,100 Dr |
| 20 Feb | Computer | | 1,950 | 2,150 Dr |
| 25 Feb | Sales | 150 | | 2,300 Dr |
| 27 Feb | Wages | | 125 | 2,175 Dr |

**3.4**

**Purchases Account**

| Dr | | | Cr |
|---|---|---|---|
| 20-1 | £ | 20-1 | £ |
| 4 Jan AB Supplies Ltd | 250 | | |
| 20 Jan Bank | 225 | | |

**AB Supplies Ltd**

| Dr | | | Cr |
|---|---|---|---|
| 20-1 | £ | 20-1 | £ |
| 15 Jan Bank | 250 | 4 Jan Purchases | 250 |

**Sales Account**

| Dr | | | Cr |
|---|---|---|---|
| 20-1 | £ | 20-1 | £ |
| | | 5 Jan Bank | 195 |
| | | 7 Jan Cash | 150 |
| | | 17 Jan L Lewis | 145 |

**Bank Account**

| Dr | | | | Cr |
|---|---|---|---|---|
| 20-1 | | £ | 20-1 | £ |
| 5 Jan | Sales | 195 | 15 Jan AB Supplies Ltd | 250 |
| 10 Jan | J Johnson: loan | 1,000 | 20 Jan Purchases | 225 |
| 29 Jan | L Lewis | 145 | 31 Jan Mercia Office Supplies Ltd | 160 |

## Cash Account

| Dr | | £ | Cr | | £ |
|---|---|---|---|---|---|
| 20-1 | | | 20-1 | | 125 |
| 7 Jan | Sales | 150 | 22 Jan | Wages | |

## J Johnson: Loan Account

| Dr | | £ | Cr | | £ |
|---|---|---|---|---|---|
| 20-1 | | | 20-1 | | 1,000 |
| | | | 10 Jan | Bank | |

## L Lewis

| Dr | | £ | Cr | | £ |
|---|---|---|---|---|---|
| 20-1 | | | 20-1 | | 145 |
| 17 Jan | Sales | 145 | 29 Jan | Bank | |

## Wages Account

| Dr | | £ | Cr | £ |
|---|---|---|---|---|
| 20-1 | | | 20-1 | |
| 22 Jan | Cash | 125 | | |

## Office Equipment Account

| Dr | | £ | Cr | £ |
|---|---|---|---|---|
| 20-1 | | | 20-1 | |
| 26 Jan | Mercia O S Ltd | 160 | | |

## Mercia Office Supplies Ltd

| Dr | | £ | Cr | | £ |
|---|---|---|---|---|---|
| 20-1 | | | 20-1 | | 160 |
| 31 Jan | Bank | 160 | 26 Jan | Office equipment | |

## CHAPTER 4    Business Documents

**4.1**

(a) purchase order  
(b) invoice  
(c) cash discount  
(d) trade discount  
(e) net  
(f) Value Added Tax  
(g) credit note  
(h) debit note  
(i) statement of account

**4.2**

- Net: £175 + £30.62 VAT = £205.62
- 2.5%: £175 + £29.85 VAT (£175 x 97.5% x 17.5%) = £204.85
- 5%: £175 + £29.09 VAT (£175 x 95% x 17.5%) = £204.09

## CHAPTER 5    Balancing Accounts – the Trial Balance

**5.3** (a)

### LORNA FOX
### Trial balance as at 31 March 20-2

| | Dr £ | Cr £ |
|---|---|---|
| Purchases | 96,250 | |
| Sales | | 146,390 |
| Sales returns | 8,500 | |
| Administration expenses | 10,240 | |
| Wages | 28,980 | |
| Telephone | 3,020 | |
| Interest paid | 2,350 | |
| Travel expenses | 1,045 | |
| Premises | 125,000 | |
| Machinery | 40,000 | |
| Debtors | 10,390 | |
| Bank overdraft | | 1,050 |
| Cash | 150 | |
| Creditors | | 12,495 |
| Loan from bank | | 20,000 |
| Drawings | 9,450 | |
| Capital | | 155,440 |
| | 335,375 | 335,375 |

(b) See Chapters 2 and 3 and page 65. The explanation should be appropriate for someone who does not understand accounting.

**5.4**

(a) principle  
(b) mispost  
(c) original entry  
(d) compensating  
(e) reversal of entries  
(f) omission

## 6.1

### Sales Day Book

| Date | Details | Invoice | Folio | Net | VAT | Gross |
|---|---|---|---|---|---|---|
| | | | | £ | £ | £ |
| 20-6 | | | | | | |
| 2 Feb | Wyvern Fashions | | | 200 | 35 | 235 |
| 10 Feb | Zandra Smith | | | 160 | 28 | 188 |
| 15 Feb | Just Jean | | | 120 | 21 | 141 |
| 23 Feb | Peter Sanders | | | 320 | 56 | 376 |
| 24 Feb | H Wilson | | | 80 | 14 | 94 |
| 26 Feb | Mercian Models | | | 320 | 56 | 376 |
| 28 Feb | Totals for month | | | 1,200 | 210 | 1,410 |

### Purchases Day Book

| Date | Details | Invoice | Folio | Net | VAT | Gross |
|---|---|---|---|---|---|---|
| | | | | £ | £ | £ |
| 20-6 | | | | | | |
| 1 Feb | Flair Clothing | | | 520 | 91 | 611 |
| 4 Feb | Modernwear | | | 240 | 42 | 282 |
| 18 Feb | Quality Clothing | | | 800 | 140 | 940 |
| 28 Feb | Flair Clothing | | | 200 | 35 | 235 |
| 28 Feb | Totals for month | | | 1,760 | 308 | 2,068 |

### GENERAL LEDGER
#### Value Added Tax Account

| Dr | | £ | | | Cr £ |
|---|---|---|---|---|---|
| 20-6 | | | 20-6 | | |
| 28 Feb | Purchases Day Book | 308 | 28 Feb | Sales Day Book | 210 |
| | | | 28 Feb | Balance c/d | 98 |
| | | 308 | | | 308 |
| 1 Mar | Balance b/d | 98 | | | |

## 6.4

### Sales Day Book

| Date | Details | Invoice | Folio | Net | VAT | Gross |
|---|---|---|---|---|---|---|
| | | | | £ | £ | £ |
| 20-2 | | | | | | |
| 5 Jan | Mereford College | 1093 | SL 201 | 3,900.00 | 682.50 | 4,582.50 |
| 7 Jan | Carpminster College | 1094 | SL 202 | 8,500.00 | 1,487.50 | 9,987.50 |
| 14 Jan | Carpminster College | 1095 | SL 202 | 1,800.50 | 315.08 | 2,115.58 |
| 14 Jan | Mereford College | 1096 | SL 201 | 2,950.75 | 516.38 | 3,467.13 |
| 20 Jan | Carpminster College | 1097 | SL 202 | 3,900.75 | 682.63 | 4,583.38 |
| 22 Jan | Mereford College | 1098 | SL 201 | 1,597.85 | 279.62 | 1,877.47 |
| 31 Jan | Totals for month | | | 22,649.85 | 3,963.71 | 26,613.56 |

### Purchases Day Book

| Date | Details | Invoice | Folio | Net | VAT | Gross |
|---|---|---|---|---|---|---|
| | | | | £ | £ | £ |
| 20-2 | | | | | | |
| 2 Jan | Macstrad plc | M:529 | PL 101 | 2,900.00 | 507.50 | 3,407.50 |
| 3 Jan | Amtosh plc | A7095 | PL 102 | 7,500.00 | 1,312.50 | 8,812.50 |
| 18 Jan | Macstrad plc | M2070 | PL 101 | 1,750.00 | 306.25 | 2,056.25 |
| 19 Jan | Amtosh plc | A7519 | PL 102 | 5,500.00 | 962.50 | 6,462.50 |
| 31 Jan | Totals for month | | | 17,650.00 | 3,088.75 | 20,738.75 |

### Sales Returns Day Book

| Date | Details | Credit Note | Folio | Net | VAT | Gross |
|---|---|---|---|---|---|---|
| | | | | £ | £ | £ |
| 20-2 | | | | | | |
| 13 Jan | Mereford College | CN109 | SL 201 | 850.73 | 148.87 | 999.60 |
| 27 Jan | Mereford College | CN110 | SL 201 | 593.81 | 103.91 | 697.72 |
| 31 Jan | Totals for month | | | 1,444.54 | 252.78 | 1,697.32 |

### Purchases Returns Day Book

| Date | Details | Credit Note | Folio | Net | VAT | Gross |
|---|---|---|---|---|---|---|
| | | | | £ | £ | £ |
| 20-2 | | | | | | |
| 10 Jan | Macstrad plc | MC105 | PL 101 | 319.75 | 55.95 | 375.70 |
| 12 Jan | Amtosh plc | AC 730 | PL 102 | 750.18 | 131.28 | 881.46 |
| 23 Jan | Macstrad plc | MC120 | PL 101 | 953.07 | 166.78 | 1,119.85 |
| 31 Jan | Totals for month | | | 2,023.00 | 354.01 | 2,377.01 |

### SALES LEDGER
#### Mereford College (account no 201)

| Dr | | £ | | | Cr £ |
|---|---|---|---|---|---|
| 20-2 | | | 20-2 | | |
| 1 Jan | Balance b/d | 705.35 | 13 Jan | Sales Returns | 999.60 |
| 5 Jan | Sales | 4,582.50 | 27 Jan | Sales Returns | 697.72 |
| 14 Jan | Sales | 3,467.13 | 31 Jan | Balance c/d | 8,935.13 |
| 22 Jan | Sales | 1,877.47 | | | |
| | | 10,632.45 | | | 10,632.45 |
| 1 Feb | Balance b/d | 8,935.13 | | | |

## Carpminster College (account no 202)

| Dr | | | £ | Cr | | | £ |
|---|---|---|---|---|---|---|---|
| 20-2 | | | | 20-2 | | | |
| 1 Jan | Balance b/d | | 801.97 | 31 Jan | Balance c/d | | 17,488.43 |
| 7 Jan | Sales | | 9,987.50 | | | | |
| 14 Jan | Sales | | 2,115.58 | | | | |
| 20 Jan | Sales | | 4,583.38 | | | | |
| | | | 17,488.43 | | | | 17,488.43 |
| 1 Feb | Balance b/d | | 17,488.43 | | | | |

## PURCHASES LEDGER
### Macstrad plc (account no 101)

| Dr | | £ | Cr | | £ |
|---|---|---|---|---|---|
| 20-2 | | | 20-2 | | |
| 10 Jan | Purchases Returns | 375.70 | 1 Jan | Balance b/d | 1,050.75 |
| 23 Jan | Purchases Returns | 1,119.85 | 2 Jan | Purchases | 3,407.50 |
| 31 Jan | Balance c/d | 5,018.95 | 18 Jan | Purchases | 2,056.25 |
| | | 6,514.50 | | | 6,514.50 |
| | | | 1 Feb | Balance b/d | 5,018.95 |

### Amtosh plc (account no 102)

| Dr | | £ | Cr | | £ |
|---|---|---|---|---|---|
| 20-2 | | | 20-2 | | |
| 12 Jan | Purchases Returns | 881.46 | 1 Jan | Balance b/d | 2,750.83 |
| 31 Jan | Balance c/d | 17,144.37 | 3 Jan | Purchases | 8,812.50 |
| | | | 19 Jan | Purchases | 6,462.50 |
| | | 18,025.83 | | | 18,025.83 |
| | | | 1 Feb | Balance b/d | 17,144.37 |

## GENERAL LEDGER
### Sales Account

| Dr | | £ | Cr | | £ |
|---|---|---|---|---|---|
| 20-2 | | | 20-2 | | |
| | | | 31 Jan | Sales Day Book | 22,649.85 |

### Purchases Account

| Dr | | £ | Cr | | £ |
|---|---|---|---|---|---|
| 20-2 | | | 20-2 | | |
| 31 Jan | Purchases Day Book | 17,650.00 | | | |

### Sales Returns Account

| Dr | | £ | Cr | | £ |
|---|---|---|---|---|---|
| 20-2 | | | 20-2 | | |
| 31 Jan | Sales Returns Day Book | 1,444.54 | | | |

## Purchases Returns Account

| Dr | | | £ | Cr | | | £ |
|---|---|---|---|---|---|---|---|
| 20-2 | | | | 20-2 | | | |
| | | | | 31 Jan | Purchases Returns Day Book | | 2,023.00 |

## Value Added Tax Account

| Dr | | £ | Cr | | £ |
|---|---|---|---|---|---|
| 20-2 | | | 20-2 | | |
| 31 Jan | Purchases Day Book | 3,088.75 | 31 Jan | Sales Day Book | 3,963.71 |
| 31 Jan | Sales Returns Day Book | 252.78 | 31 Jan | Purchases Returns Day Book | 354.01 |
| 31 Jan | Balance c/d | 976.19 | | | |
| | | 4,317.72 | | | 4,317.72 |
| | | | 1 Feb | Balance b/d | 976.19 |

### 6.5

| | Prime document | Primary Accounting Record | Account to be debited | Account to be credited |
|---|---|---|---|---|
| (a) | invoice received | purchases day book | purchases | A Cotton |
| (b) | invoice issued | sales day book | D Law | sales |
| (c) | cheque received | cash book | bank | sales |
| (d) | credit note received | purchases returns day book | A Cotton | purchases returns |
| (e) | cheque issued | cash book | gas | bank |
| (f) | credit note issued | sales returns day book | sales returns | D Law |

## CHAPTER 7   Value Added Tax

### 7.1 (a)

| Month | Purchases £ | VAT £ | Sales £ | VAT £ |
|---|---|---|---|---|
| April | 5,400 | 945 | 8,200 | 1,435 |
| May | 4,800 | 840 | 9,400 | 1,645 |
| June | 6,800 | 1,190 | 10,800 | 1,890 |

### (b) Value Added Tax Account

| Dr. | | £ | Cr. | | £ |
|---|---|---|---|---|---|
| 20-4 | | | 20-4 | | |
| 30 Apr | Purchases Day Book | 945 | 30 Apr | Sales Day Book | 1,435 |
| 31 May | Purchases Day Book | 840 | 31 May | Sales Day Book | 1,645 |
| 30 Jun | Purchases Day Book | 1,190 | 30 Jun | Sales Day Book | 1,890 |
| 30 Jun | Balance c/d | 1,995 | | | |
| | | 4,970 | | | 4,970 |
| | | | 1 Jul | Balance b/d | 1,995 |

(c) VAT account has a credit balance of £1,995: this means that Wyvern Computers owes the amount to HM Customs and Excise. The amount is payable not later than 31 July 20-4. The book-keeping entries for payment will be
– debit Value Added Tax Account
– credit Bank Account

If Wyvern Computers prepares a balance sheet at 30 June 20-4, the amount owing to HM Customs and Excise will be listed as a creditor.

**7.4** (a)

**Sales Day Book**

| Date | Details | Invoice | Folio | Net | VAT | Gross |
|---|---|---|---|---|---|---|
| 20-1 | | | | £ | £ | £ |
| 19 Aug | E Newman | SI 1547 | | 156.00 | 27.30 | 183.30 |
| 20 Aug | Wyvern Traders Ltd | SI 1548 | | 228.00 | 39.90 | 267.90 |
| 21 Aug | Teme Supplies | SI 1549 | | 350.00 | 61.25 | 411.25 |
| 22 Aug | Lugg Brothers & Co | SI 1550 | | 1,200.00 | 210.00 | 1,410.00 |
| 23 Aug | E Newman | | | 400.00 | 70.00 | 470.00 |
| 23 Aug | Totals for week | | | 2,334.00 | 408.45 | 2,742.45 |

**Sales Returns Day Book**

| Date | Details | Credit Note | Folio | Net | VAT | Gross |
|---|---|---|---|---|---|---|
| 20-1 | | | | £ | £ | £ |
| 22 Aug | Wyvern Traders Ltd | CN 121 | | 228.00 | 39.90 | 267.90 |
| 23 Aug | E Newman | CN 122 | | 78.00 | 13.65 | 91.65 |
| 23 Aug | Totals for week | | | 306.00 | 53.55 | 359.55 |

(b) *Sales Day Book:*
- The total of net sales is credited to sales account in the general ledger.
- The total of the VAT column is credited to the VAT account in the general ledger.
- The individual gross amounts for each customer are debited to the debtors' personal accounts in the sales ledger.

*Sales Returns Day Book:*
- The total of net sales returns is debited to sales returns account in the general ledger.
- The total of the VAT column is debited to the VAT account in the general ledger.
- The individual gross amounts for each customer are credited to the debtors' personal accounts in the sales ledger.

(c) Dr     **E Newman**     Cr

| Date | Details | £ | Date | Details | £ |
|---|---|---|---|---|---|
| 20-1 | | | 20-1 | | |
| 1 Aug | Balance b/d | 440.00 | 7 Aug | Bank | 440.00 |
| 19 Aug | Sales | 183.30 | 23 Aug | Sales returns | 91.65 |
| 23 Aug | Sales | 470.00 | 31 Aug | Balance c/d | 561.65 |
| | | 1,093.30 | | | 1,093.30 |
| 1 Sep | Balance b/d | 561.65 | | | |

---

# CHAPTER 8    Cash Book

**8.1** *Main responsibilities of the cashier*

- Recording receipts and payments by cheque and in cash in the firm's cash book
- Issuing receipts for cash (and sometimes cheques) received
- Making authorised cash payments (except for low-value expenses payments which are paid by the petty cashier)
- Preparing cheques and BACS payments for signature and authorisation
- Paying cash and cheques received into the bank
- Controlling the firm's cash, either in a cash till or cash box
- Issuing cash to the petty cashier who operates the firm's petty cash book
- Ensuring that all transactions passing through the cash book are supported by documentary evidence
- Checking the accuracy of the cash and bank balances at regular intervals
- Liaising with the other accounts staff – accounts clerks and petty cashier

*Qualities of a cashier*

- Accuracy – in writing up the cash book, in cash handling, and in ensuring that payments are made only against correct documents and appropriate authorisation
- Security – of cash and cheque books, and correct authorisation of payments
- Confidentiality – that all cash/bank transactions, including cash and bank balances, are kept confidential

**8.2**

**Cash Book**

Dr

| Date | Details | Folio | Discount allowed | Cash | Bank |
|---|---|---|---|---|---|
| | | | £ | £ | £ |
| 20-2 | | | | | |
| 1 Jun | Balance b/d | | | 280 | |
| 3 Jun | G Wheaton | | 5 | | 195 |
| 5 Jun | T Francis | | 2 | 53 | |
| 16 Jun | Bank | C | | 200 | |
| 18 Jun | H Watson | | 30 | | 640 |
| 28 Jun | M Perry | | 6 | | 234 |
| 30 Jun | K Willis | | | 45 | |
| 30 Jun | Balance c/d | | | | 1,904 |
| | | | 43 | 578 | 2,973 |
| 1 Jul | Balance b/d | | | 211 | |

Cr

| Date | Details | Folio | Discount received | Cash | Bank |
|---|---|---|---|---|---|
| | | | £ | £ | £ |
| 20-2 | | | | | |
| 1 Jun | Balance b/d | | | | 2,240 |
| 8 Jun | F Lloyd | | 10 | | 390 |
| 10 Jun | Wages | | | 165 | |
| 12 Jun | A Morris | | 3 | 97 | |
| 16 Jun | Cash | C | | | 200 |
| 20 Jun | R Marks | | | | 78 |
| 24 Jun | D Farr | | 2 | | 65 |
| 26 Jun | Telephone | | | 105 | |
| 30 Jun | Balance c/d | | | 211 | |
| | | | 15 | 578 | 2,973 |
| 1 Jul | Balance b/d | | | | 1,904 |

**Value Added Tax Account**

| Dr | | | £ | Cr | | | £ |
|---|---|---|---|---|---|---|---|
| 20-7 | | | | 20-7 | | | |
| 30 Apr | Cash Book | | 49 | 30 Apr | Cash Book | | 98 |

---

# CHAPTER 9  Petty Cash Book

**9.1**

Allow: (a), (b), (d), (f), (g), (h), (j) – all subject to an appropriate receipt being attached to the petty cash voucher, and payment being in accordance with the company's policies – eg amount, authorisation.

Refer:

(c) travel to work – not normally a business expense, except for emergency call-outs

(e) staff tea and coffee – check if it is company policy to pay for this personal expense of the office staff

(i) shelving for the office – this expense is, most probably, too large to be put through petty cash; check with the accounts supervisor who is likely to say that it should go through the main cash book

**9.5**

| | Expense (excluding VAT) £ | VAT £ | Total £ |
|---|---|---|---|
| (a) | 8.00 | 1.40 | 9.40 |
| (b) | 4.00 | 0.70 | 4.70 |
| (c) | 2.00 | 0.35 | 2.35 |
| (d) | 2.09 | 0.36 | 2.45 |
| (e) | 4.77 | 0.83 | 5.60 |
| (f) | 2.96 | 0.51 | 3.47 |
| (g) | 7.45 | 1.30 | 8.75 |
| (h) | 0.80 | 0.14 | 0.94 |
| (i) | 0.85 | 0.14 | 0.99 |
| (j) | 8.01 | 1.40 | 9.41 |

---

**Discount Allowed Account**

| Dr | | £ | Cr | |
|---|---|---|---|---|
| 20-2 | | | 20-2 | |
| 30 Jun | Cash Book | 43 | | |

**Discount Received Account**

| Dr | | £ | Cr | | £ |
|---|---|---|---|---|---|
| 20-2 | | | 20-2 | | |
| | | | 30 Jun | Cash Book | 15 |

**8.5**

**Cash Book**

| Date | Details | Folio | Disc allwd £ | VAT £ | Cash £ | Bank £ | Date | Details | Folio | Disc recd £ | VAT £ | Cash £ | Bank £ |
|---|---|---|---|---|---|---|---|---|---|---|---|---|---|
| 20-7 | | | | | | | 20-7 | | | | | | |
| 1 Apr | Balance b/d | | | | 85 | | 1 Apr | Balance b/d | | | | | 718 |
| 7 Apr | J Bowen | SL | 5 | | 85 | | 3 Apr | Travel exp | GL | | | 65 | |
| 10 Apr | Sales | GL | | 70 | | 470 | 4 Apr | Telephone | GL | | 35 | | 235 |
| 18 Apr | J Burrows | SL | 25 | | | 575 | 14 Apr | M Hughes | PL | 10 | | | 180 |
| 21 Apr | Sales | GL | | 28 | 188 | | 17 Apr | Purchases | GL | | 14 | | 94 |
| 22 Apr | Bank | C | | | 200 | | 22 Apr | Cash | C | | | | 200 |
| 30 Apr | Balance c/d | | | | | 627 | 24 Apr | Wilson Ltd | PL | 10 | | | 245 |
| | | | | | | | 25 Apr | Wages | GL | | | 350 | |
| | | | | | | | 30 Apr | Balance c/d | | | | 143 | |
| | | | 30 | 98 | 558 | 1,672 | | | | 20 | 49 | 558 | 1,672 |
| 1 May | Balance b/d | | | | 143 | | 1 May | Balance b/d | | | | | 627 |

**GENERAL LEDGER**

**Discount Allowed Account**

| Dr | | £ | Cr | |
|---|---|---|---|---|
| 20-7 | | | 20-7 | |
| 30 Apr | Cash Book | 30 | | |

**Discount Received Account**

| Dr | | £ | Cr | | £ |
|---|---|---|---|---|---|
| 20-7 | | | 20-7 | | |
| | | | 30 Apr | Cash Book | 20 |

**Miscellaneous Expenses Account**

| Dr | | £ p | | Cr £ p |
|---|---|---|---|---|
| 20-7 | | | | |
| 29 Aug | Petty Cash Book | 13.50 | | |

## CASH BOOK

**Cash book**

| Dr | | Cash £ p | Bank £ p | | | Cr Cash £ p | Bank £ p |
|---|---|---|---|---|---|---|---|
| 20-7 | | | | | 20-7 | | |
| | | | | | 29 Aug | Petty Cash Book 47.62 | |

**9.8**

| Receipts £ | Date | Details | Voucher No. | Total P'm't £ | VAT | Postages | Travel | Meals | Stationery |
|---|---|---|---|---|---|---|---|---|---|
| 150.00 | 20-1 | | | | | | | | |
| | 1 May | Balance b/d | | | | | | | |
| | 1 May | Postages | 455 | 7.00 | | 7.00 | | | |
| | 1 May | Travel | 456 | 2.85 | | | 2.85 | | |
| | 2 May | Meal allowance | 457 | 6.11 | | | | 6.11 | |
| | 3 May | Taxi | 458 | 4.70 | 0.70 | | 4.00 | | |
| | 4 May | Stationery | 459 | 3.76 | 0.56 | | | | 3.20 |
| | 7 May | Postages | 460 | 5.25 | | 5.25 | | | |
| | 8 May | Travel | 461 | 6.50 | | | 6.50 | | |
| | 9 May | Meal allowance | 462 | 6.11 | | | | 6.11 | |
| | 10 May | Stationery | 463 | 8.46 | 1.26 | | | | 7.20 |
| | 14 May | Taxi | 464 | 5.17 | 0.77 | | 4.40 | | |
| | 17 May | Stationery | 465 | 4.70 | 0.70 | | | | 4.00 |
| | 21 May | Travel | 466 | 3.50 | | | 3.50 | | |
| | 21 May | Postages | 467 | 4.50 | | 4.50 | | | |
| | 23 May | Bus fares | 468 | 3.80 | | | 3.80 | | |
| | 26 May | Catering | 469 | 10.81 | 1.61 | | | 9.20 | |
| | 27 May | Postages | 470 | 3.50 | | 3.50 | | | |
| | 27 May | Stationery | 471 | 7.52 | 1.12 | | | | 6.40 |
| | 28 May | Travel | 472 | 6.45 | | | 6.45 | | |
| | | | | 100.69 | 6.72 | 20.25 | 31.50 | 21.42 | 20.80 |
| 100.69 | 31 May | Cash received | | | | | | | |
| | 31 May | Balance c/d | | 150 00 | | | | | |
| 250.69 | | | | 250 69 | | | | | |
| 150.00 | 1 Jun | Balance b/d | | | | | | | |

**9.6**

## Petty Cash Book

| Receipts £ | Date | Details | Voucher No | Total Payment £ | VAT £ | Travel £ | Postages £ | Stationery £ | Meals £ | Misc £ |
|---|---|---|---|---|---|---|---|---|---|---|
| 75.00 | 20-7 | | | | | | | | | |
| | 1 Aug | Balance b/d | | | | | | | | |
| | 4 Aug | Taxi fare | 39 | 3.80 | 0.56 | 3.24 | | | | |
| | 6 Aug | Parcel post | 40 | 2.35 | | | 2.35 | | | |
| | 7 Aug | Pencils | 41 | 1.26 | 0.18 | | | 1.08 | | |
| | 11 Aug | Travel expenses | 42 | 5.46 | | 5.46 | | | | |
| | 12 Aug | Window cleaner | 43 | 8.50 | | | | | | 8.50 |
| | 14 Aug | Envelopes | 44 | 2.45 | 0.36 | | | 2.09 | | |
| | 18 Aug | Donation | 45 | 5.00 | | | | | | 5.00 |
| | 19 Aug | Rail fare/meal allow | 46 | 10.60 | | 5.60 | | | 5.00 | |
| | 20 Aug | Postage | 47 | 0.75 | | | 0.75 | | | |
| | 22 Aug | Tape | 48 | 1.50 | 0.22 | | | 1.28 | | |
| | 25 Aug | Postage | 49 | 0.55 | | | 0.55 | | | |
| | 27 Aug | Taxi fare | 50 | 5.40 | 0.80 | 4.60 | | | | |
| | | | | 47.62 | 2.12 | 18.90 | 3.65 | 4.45 | 5.00 | 13.50 |
| 47.62 | 29 Aug | Cash received | | | | | | | | |
| | 29 Aug | Balance c/d | | 75.00 | | | | | | |
| 122.62 | | | | 122.62 | | | | | | |
| 75.00 | 1 Sep | Balance b/d | | | | | | | | |

## GENERAL LEDGER

**Value Added Tax Account**

| Dr | | £ p | | Cr £ p |
|---|---|---|---|---|
| 20-7 | | | | |
| 29 Aug | Petty Cash Book | 2.12 | | |

**Travel Expenses Account**

| Dr | | £ p | | Cr £ p |
|---|---|---|---|---|
| 20-7 | | | | |
| 29 Aug | Petty Cash Book | 18.90 | | |

**Postages Account**

| Dr | | £ p | | Cr £ p |
|---|---|---|---|---|
| 20-7 | | | | |
| 29 Aug | Petty Cash Book | 3.65 | | |

**Stationery Account**

| Dr | | £ p | | Cr £ p |
|---|---|---|---|---|
| 20-7 | | | | |
| 29 Aug | Petty Cash Book | 4.45 | | |

**Meals Account**

| Dr | | £ p | | Cr £ p |
|---|---|---|---|---|
| 20-7 | | | | |
| 29 Aug | Petty Cash Book | 5.00 | | |

## 10.1

**TOM REID**

**BANK RECONCILIATION STATEMENT AS AT 31 DECEMBER 20-7**

| | £ | |
|---|---|---|
| Balance at bank as per cash book | | 200 |
| Add: unpresented cheque | | |
| B Kay cheque no. 345126 | | 20 |
| | | 220 |
| Less: outstanding lodgement | | |
| J Hill | | 13 |
| Balance at bank as per bank statement | | 207 |

## 10.2

**(a)**

**B Piper**

**Dr**      Cash Book (bank columns)      **Cr**

| | | £ | | | £ |
|---|---|---|---|---|---|
| 22 Nov | Balance b/d | 1,300 | 23 Nov | K Ferris | 300 |
| 23 Nov | Sales | 700 | 25 Nov | M Burgon | 246 |
| 25 Nov | O Dyer | 375 | 26 Nov | J Moon | 183 |
| 27 Nov | C Hinds | 422 | 27 Nov | D Lusky | 96 |
| | | | 30 Nov | Bank charges | 25 |
| | | | 30 Nov | Balance c/d | 1,947 |
| | | 2,797 | | | 2,797 |
| 1 Dec | Balance b/d | 1,947 | | | |

**(b)**

**B PIPER**

**BANK RECONCILIATION STATEMENT AS AT 30 NOVEMBER**

| | £ | £ |
|---|---|---|
| Balance at bank as per cash book | | 1,947 |
| Add: unpresented cheques | | |
| J Moon | 183 | |
| D Lusky | 96 | |
| | | 279 |
| | | 2,226 |
| Less: outstanding lodgement | | |
| C Hinds | | 422 |
| Balance at bank as per bank statement | | 1,804 |

## 10.6

**(a)**

**RECONCILIATION OF VANTAGE PRODUCTS' STATEMENT OF ACCOUNT AS AT 31 OCTOBER 20-8**

| | | £ | |
|---|---|---|---|
| Balance of account at 31 October 20-8 | | 2,545 | Cr |
| Add: payment sent on 28 October, not yet appearing on statement | | 1,570 | |
| cash discount received on 28 October, not yet appearing on statement | | 55 | |
| purchases returns on 30 October, not yet appearing on statement | | 105 | |
| invoice sent by Vantage Products on 28 October, not yet received | | 1,550 | |
| Balance of statement at 31 October 20-8 | | 5,825 | |

**(b)** (i)   £2,545 x 2.5%    = £63.62 cash discount

     (ii)   £2,545 − £63.62   = £2,481.38 amount of cheque

---

# CHAPTER 11  An Introduction to Computer Accounting

## 11.1

Explanation of two advantages out of the list on page 158. The most obvious advantages are speed of input, accuracy of transaction recording, accessibility of up-to-date information and document printing (eg invoices, credit notes and statements).

## 11.2

The main two advantages are that a spreadsheet saves time in calculation and secondly that if any of the figures should alter, the remaining dependent figures will automatically be recalculated.

## 11.3

Three from: ledger accounting, eg sales ledger, purchases ledger, cash book; payroll processing; management reports, eg aged debtors analysis, trial balance, profit and loss account and balance sheet. Other areas could include stock control and job costing.

## 11.4

Two from: hacking in from outside, hacking from the inside, theft from outside (or inside), computer breakdown when periodic back-ups have not been made, viruses, inefficient back-up policy.

## 12.1

### MATTHEW LLOYD
### TRADING AND PROFIT AND LOSS ACCOUNT
### FOR THE YEAR ENDED 31 DECEMBER 20-8

| | £ | £ |
|---|---|---|
| Sales | | 125,890 |
| Opening stock | – | |
| Purchases | 94,350 | |
| | 5,950 | |
| Less Closing stock | | |
| Cost of Goods Sold | | 88,400 |
| **Gross profit** | | 37,490 |
| Less expenses: | | |
| Rates | 4,850 | |
| Heating and lighting | 2,120 | |
| Wages and salaries | 10,350 | 17,320 |
| **Net profit** | | 20,170 |

### BALANCE SHEET AS AT 31 DECEMBER 20-8

| | £ | £ |
|---|---|---|
| **Fixed Assets** | | |
| Office equipment | 8,500 | |
| Vehicles | 10,750 | |
| | | 19,250 |
| **Current Assets** | | |
| Stock | 5,950 | |
| Debtors | 3,950 | |
| Bank | 4,225 | |
| Cash | 95 | |
| | 14,220 | |
| **Less Current Liabilities** | | |
| Creditors | 1,750 | |
| Value Added Tax | 450 | |
| | | 2,200 |
| **Working Capital** | | 12,020 |
| **NET ASSETS** | | 31,270 |
| **FINANCED BY** | | |
| **Capital** | | |
| Opening capital | | 20,000 |
| Add Net profit | | 20,170 |
| | | 40,170 |
| Less Drawings | | 8,900 |
| | | 31,270 |

## 12.3

| | |
|---|---|
| Business A: | gross profit £8,000, net profit £4,000 |
| Business B: | gross profit £17,000, expenses £7,000 |
| Business C: | sales £36,500, net profit £6,750 |
| Business D: | purchases £25,500, expenses £9,800 |
| Business E: | opening stock £8,350, net loss £1,700 |
| Business F: | closing stock £4,600, expenses £15,000 |

## 12.4

### JOHN ADAMS
### TRADING AND PROFIT AND LOSS ACCOUNT
### FOR THE YEAR ENDED 31 DECEMBER 20-7

| | £ | £ |
|---|---|---|
| Sales | | 259,688 |
| Opening stock | 14,350 | |
| Purchases | 114,472 | |
| | 128,822 | |
| Less Closing stock | 16,280 | |
| Cost of Goods Sold | | 112,542 |
| **Gross profit** | | 147,146 |
| Less expenses: | | |
| Rates | 13,718 | |
| Heating and lighting | 12,540 | |
| Wages and salaries | 42,614 | |
| Vehicle expenses | 5,817 | |
| Advertising | 6,341 | 81,030 |
| **Net profit** | | 66,116 |

### BALANCE SHEET AS AT 31 DECEMBER 20-7

| | £ | £ |
|---|---|---|
| **Fixed Assets** | | |
| Premises | | 75,000 |
| Office equipment | | 33,000 |
| Vehicles | | 21,500 |
| | | 129,500 |
| **Current Assets** | | |
| Stock | 16,280 | |
| Debtors | 23,854 | |
| Bank | 1,235 | |
| Cash | 125 | |
| | 41,494 | |
| **Less Current Liabilities** | | |
| Creditors | 17,281 | |
| Value Added Tax | 2,455 | |
| | 19,736 | |
| **Working Capital** | | 21,758 |
| | | 151,258 |
| **Less Long-term Liabilities** | | |
| Loan from bank | | 35,000 |
| **NET ASSETS** | | 116,258 |
| **FINANCED BY** | | |
| **Capital** | | |
| Opening capital | | 62,500 |
| Add Net profit | | 66,116 |
| | | 128,616 |
| Less Drawings | | 12,358 |
| | | 116,258 |

## 13.3 (a)

**Rent Received Account**

| Dr | | £ | | | | £ |
|---|---|---|---|---|---|---|
| 20-8 | | | 20-8 | | | |
| 30 Apr | Profit and loss account | 2,000 | 30 Apr | Balance b/d | | 1,675 |
| | | | 30 Apr | Balance c/d | | 325 |
| | | 2,000 | | | | 2,000 |
| 1 May | Balance b/d | 325 | | | | |

**Motor Expenses Account**

| Dr | | £ | | | | Cr |
|---|---|---|---|---|---|---|
| 20-8 | | | 20-8 | | | £ |
| 30 Apr | Balance b/d | 3,250 | 30 Apr | Profit and loss account | | 3,400 |
| 30 Apr | Balance c/d | 150 | | | | |
| | | 3,400 | | | | 3,400 |
| 1 May | Balance b/d | 150 | | | | |

**Insurance Account**

| Dr | | £ | | | | Cr |
|---|---|---|---|---|---|---|
| 20-8 | | | 20-8 | | | £ |
| 30 Apr | Balance b/d | 750 | 30 Apr | Profit and loss account | | 610 |
| | | | 30 Apr | Balance c/d | | 140 |
| | | 750 | | | | 750 |
| 1 May | Balance b/d | 140 | | | | |

**Wages Account**

| Dr | | £ | | | | Cr |
|---|---|---|---|---|---|---|
| 20-8 | | | 20-8 | | | £ |
| 30 Apr | Balance b/d | 3,750 | 30 Apr | Profit and loss account | | 3,940 |
| 30 Apr | Balance c/d | 190 | | | | |
| | | 3,940 | | | | 3,940 |
| | | | 1 May | Balance b/d | | 190 |

**Office Expenses Account**

| Dr | | £ | | | | Cr |
|---|---|---|---|---|---|---|
| 20-8 | | | 20-8 | | | £ |
| 30 Apr | Balance b/d | 1,000 | 30 Apr | Profit and loss account | | 950 |
| | | | 30 Apr | Balance c/d | | 50 |
| | | 1,000 | | | | 1,000 |
| 1 May | Balance b/d | 50 | | | | |

## (b)

### A BROWN
### PROFIT AND LOSS ACCOUNT FOR THE YEAR ENDED 30 APRIL 20-8

| | £ | £ |
|---|---|---|
| Gross profit | | 24,560 |
| Add Rent received | | 2,000 |
| | | 26,560 |
| Less expenses: | | |
| Rent paid | 2,500 | |
| Motor expenses | 3,400 | |
| Insurance | 610 | |
| Wages | 3,940 | |
| Office expenses | 950 | |
| Telephone | 860 | |
| | | 12,260 |
| **Net profit** | | 14,300 |

## 13.5

### DON SMITH
### TRADING AND PROFIT AND LOSS ACCOUNT FOR THE YEAR ENDED 31 DECEMBER 20-8

| | £ | £ |
|---|---|---|
| Sales | | 257,258 |
| Opening stock (1 January 20-8) | 18,471 | |
| Purchases | 138,960 | |
| | 157,431 | |
| Less Closing stock (31 December 20-8) | 14,075 | |
| Cost of Goods Sold | | 143,356 |
| **Gross profit** | | 113,902 |
| Add Discount received | | 591 |
| | | 114,493 |
| Less expenses: | | |
| Rent and rates | 10,612 | |
| Electricity | 2,164 | |
| Telephone | 1,695 | |
| Salaries | 56,256 | |
| Vehicle expenses | 10,855 | |
| Discount allowed | 478 | |
| | | 82,060 |
| **Net profit** | | 32,433 |

**13.5**   continued

## BALANCE SHEET AS AT 31 DECEMBER 20-8

| | £ | £ | £ |
|---|---|---|---|
| **Fixed Assets** | | | |
| Vehicles | | | 22,250 |
| Office equipment | | | 7,500 |
| | | | 29,750 |
| **Current Assets** | | | |
| Stock | | 14,075 | |
| Debtors | | 24,325 | |
| Prepayment | | 250 | |
| | | 38,650 | |
| **Less Current Liabilities** | | | |
| Creditors | 15,408 | | |
| Value Added Tax | 4,276 | | |
| Bank overdraft | 1,083 | | |
| Accruals | 475 | | |
| | 21,242 | | |
| **Working Capital** | | | 17,408 |
| **NET ASSETS** | | | 47,158 |
| | | | |
| ***FINANCED BY*** | | | |
| **Capital** | | | |
| Opening capital | | | 30,000 |
| Add net profit | | | 32,433 |
| | | | 62,433 |
| Less drawings | | | 15,275 |
| | | | 47,158 |

---

**14.1**   A letter incorporating the following points:

- Depreciation is a measure of the amount of the fall in value of fixed assets over a time period.
- It is a systematic method of charging against profits over the life of an asset.
- When the asset is sold, adjustments are made for over-provision or under-provision of depreciation.
- A recognised system which fits with the accounting concepts (see Business Accounts Chapter 17) of going concern, accruals, consistency and prudence.

**14.2**   (a)

**Provision for Depreciation Account – Car**

| Dr | | | £ | | | | Cr |
|---|---|---|---|---|---|---|---|
| 20-1 | | | | 20-1 | | | £ |
| 31 Dec | Balance c/d | | 3,000 | 31 Dec | Profit and loss account | | 3,000 |
| 20-2 | | | | 20-2 | | | |
| 31 Dec | Balance c/d | | 5,250 | 1 Jan | Balance b/d | | 3,000 |
| | | | | 31 Dec | Profit and loss account | | 2,250 |
| | | | 5,250 | | | | 5,250 |
| 20-3 | | | | 20-3 | | | |
| 31 Dec | Disposals account | | 6,937 | 1 Jan | Balance b/d | | 5,250 |
| | | | | 31 Dec | Profit and loss account | | 1,687 |
| | | | 6,937 | | | | 6,937 |

(b)

**BALANCE SHEET (EXTRACT) AS AT 31 DECEMBER 20-1**

| **Fixed Assets** | Cost | Dep'n to date | Net |
|---|---|---|---|
| | £ | £ | £ |
| Car | 12,000 | 3,000 | 9,000 |

**BALANCE SHEET (EXTRACT) AS AT 31 DECEMBER 20-2**

| **Fixed Assets** | Cost | Dep'n to date | Net |
|---|---|---|---|
| | £ | £ | £ |
| Car | 12,000 | 5,250 | 6,750 |

(c)

**Disposals Account**

| Dr | | £ | | Cr |
|---|---|---|---|---|
| 20-3 | | | 20-3 | £ |
| 31 Dec | Car account | 12,000 | 31 Dec   Provision for dep'n account | 6,937 |
| 31 Dec | Profit and loss account | 437 | 31 Dec   Bank | 5,500 |
| | (profit on sale) | | | |
| | | 12,437 | | 12,437 |

## 14.6
### HAZEL HARRIS
### TRADING AND PROFIT AND LOSS ACCOUNT FOR THE YEAR ENDED 31 DECEMBER 20-4

| | £ | £ |
|---|---:|---:|
| Sales | | 614,000 |
| Opening stock | 63,000 | |
| Purchases | 465,000 | |
| | 528,000 | |
| Less Closing stock | 88,000 | |
| Cost of Goods Sold | | 440,000 |
| **Gross profit** | | 174,000 |
| Add Discount received | | 8,140 |
| | | 182,140 |
| Less expenses: | | |
| Building repairs | 8,480 | |
| Vehicle expenses | 2,680 | |
| Wages and salaries | 89,240 | |
| Discount allowed | 10,610 | |
| Rates and insurance | 5,620 | |
| General expenses | 15,860 | |
| Provision for depreciation: vehicles | 2,400 | |
| furniture and fittings | 2,500 | 137,390 |
| **Net profit** | | 44,750 |

### BALANCE SHEET AS AT 31 DECEMBER 20-4

| | Cost £ | Dep'n to date £ | Net £ |
|---|---:|---:|---:|
| **Fixed Assets** | | | |
| Land and buildings | 100,000 | – | 100,000 |
| Vehicles | 12,000 | 4,800 | 7,200 |
| Furniture and fittings | 25,000 | 5,000 | 20,000 |
| | 137,000 | 9,800 | 127,200 |
| **Current Assets** | | | |
| Stock | | 88,000 | |
| Debtors | | 52,130 | |
| Prepayment | | 450 | |
| | | 140,580 | |
| **Less Current Liabilities** | | | |
| Creditors | 38,730 | | |
| Value Added Tax | 3,120 | | |
| Accrual | 3,180 | | |
| Bank | 2,000 | | |
| | | 47,030 | |
| **Working Capital** | | | 93,550 |
| | | | 220,750 |
| **Less Long-term Liabilities** | | | |
| Bank loan | | | 75,000 |
| **NET ASSETS** | | | 145,750 |
| **FINANCED BY** | | | |
| **Capital** | | | |
| Opening capital | | | 125,000 |
| Add Net profit | | | 44,750 |
| | | | 169,750 |
| Less Drawings | | | 24,000 |
| | | | 145,750 |

## 14.7 (a)

### Machines Account

| Dr | | | £ | | | Cr £ |
|---|---|---|---:|---|---|---:|
| Year 5/6 | | | | Year 5/6 | | |
| 1 Apr | Balance b/d (Machine E) | | 28,700 | 31 Mar | Balance c/d | 44,800 |
| | Bank (Machine E) | | 16,100 | | | |
| | | | 44,800 | | | 44,800 |
| Year 6/7 | | | | Year 6/7 | | |
| 1 Apr | Balance b/d (Machine F) | | 44,800 | 31 Mar | Disposals (Machine C) | 10,500 |
| | Bank (Machine F) | | 25,300 | | Balance c/d | 59,600 |
| | | | 70,100 | | | 70,100 |
| Year 7/8 | | | | Year 7/8 | | |
| 1 Apr | Balance b/d (Machine G) | | 59,600 | 31 Mar | Disposals (Machine D) | 18,200 |
| | Bank (Machine G) | | 5,400 | | Balance c/d | 46,800 |
| | | | 65,000 | | | 65,000 |
| Year 8/9 | | | | | | |
| 1 Apr | Balance b/d | | 46,800 | | | |

### (b)

### Provision for Depreciation Account – Machines

| Dr | | £ | | | Cr £ |
|---|---|---:|---|---|---:|
| Year 5/6 | | | Year 5/6 | | |
| 31 Mar | Balance c/d | 12,320 | 1 Apr | Balance b/d | 7,840 |
| | | | 31 Mar | Profit and loss account | 4,480 |
| | | 12,320 | | | 12,320 |
| Year 6/7 | | | Year 6/7 | | |
| 31 Mar | Disposals (Machine C) | *5,250 | 1 Apr | Balance b/d | 12,320 |
| 31 Mar | Balance c/d | 13,030 | 31 Mar | Profit and loss account | 5,960 |
| | | 18,280 | | | 18,280 |
| Year 7/8 | | | Year 7/8 | | |
| 31 Mar | Disposals (Machine D) | **7,280 | 1 Apr | Balance b/d | 13,030 |
| 31 Mar | Balance c/d | 10,430 | 31 Mar | Profit and loss account | 4,680 |
| | | 17,710 | | | 17,710 |
| Year 8/9 | | | Year 8/9 | | |
| | | | 1 Apr | Balance b/d | 10,430 |

* Machine C: £4,200 + £1,050 (depreciation for year ended 31 March Year 6)

** Machine D: £3,640 + £1,820 + £1,820 (depreciation for years ended 31 March Years 6 and 7)

**(c)**

| Dr | | Disposals Account – Machines | | Cr |
|---|---|---|---|---|
| | £ | | | £ |
| **Year 6/7** | | **Year 6/7** | | |
| Machines account | 10,500 | Provision for dep'n account | | 5,250 |
| Profit and loss account | | Bank (sale proceeds) | | 7,200 |
| (profit on sale of Machine C) | 1,950 | | | 12,450 |
| | 12,450 | | | |
| **Year 7/8** | | **Year 7/8** | | |
| Machines account | 18,200 | Provision for dep'n account | | 7,280 |
| | | Bank (sale proceeds) | | 9,000 |
| | | Profit and loss account | | |
| | | (loss on sale of Machine D) | | 1,920 |
| | 18,200 | | | 18,200 |

**(d)**

Balance sheet (extract) as at 31 March Year 8

| Fixed Assets | Cost | Dep'n to date | Net |
|---|---|---|---|
| | £ | £ | £ |
| Machines | 46,800 | 10,430 | 36,370 |

## CHAPTER 15 Bad Debts and Provision for Bad Debts

**15.2**

| Dr | | | Provision for Bad Debts Account | | | Cr |
|---|---|---|---|---|---|---|
| | | £ | | | | £ |
| **20-0/-1** | | | **20-0/-1** | | | |
| 30 Jun | Balance c/d | 400 | 1 Jul | Balance b/d | | 300 |
| | | | 30 Jun | Profit and loss account | | 100 |
| | | | | (increase in provision) | | |
| | | 400 | | | | 400 |
| **20-1/-2** | | | **20-1/-2** | | | |
| 30 Jun | Profit and loss account | 50 | 1 Jul | Balance b/d | | 400 |
| | (decrease in provision) | | | | | |
| 30 Jun | Balance c/d | 350 | | | | |
| | | 400 | | | | 400 |
| **20-2/-3** | | | **20-2/-3** | | | |
| | | | 1 Jul | Balance b/d | | 350 |

**20-1** *Extracts from final accounts produced for year ended 30 June:*
Profit and loss account: expense of £100
Balance sheet: debtors £8,000 - £400 = £7,600

**20-2** *Extracts from final accounts produced for year ended 30 June:*
Profit and loss account: income of £50
Balance sheet: debtors £7,000 - £350 = £6,650

---

**15.4**

### JAMES JENKINS

### TRADING AND PROFIT AND LOSS ACCOUNT FOR THE YEAR ENDED 30 JUNE 20-9

| | £ | £ | £ | £ |
|---|---|---|---|---|
| Sales | | | | 168,432 |
| Less Sales returns | | | | 975 |
| *Net sales* | | | | 167,457 |
| Opening stock | | | 9,427 | |
| Purchases | | 105,240 | | |
| Less Purchases returns | | 1,237 | | |
| *Net purchases* | | | 104,003 | |
| | | | 113,430 | |
| Less Closing stock | | | 11,517 | |
| Cost of Goods Sold | | | | 101,913 |
| **Gross profit** | | | | 65,544 |
| Add income: | | | | |
| Discount received | | | | 243 |
| Reduction in provision for bad debts | | | | 54 |
| | | | | 65,841 |
| Less expenses: | | | | |
| Discount allowed | | | 127 | |
| Wages and salaries | | | 30,841 | |
| Vehicle expenses | | | 1,076 | |
| Rent and rates | | | 8,521 | |
| Heating and lighting | | | 1,840 | |
| Telephone | | | 355 | |
| General expenses | | | 1,752 | |
| Bad debts written off | | | 85 | |
| Provision for depreciation: | | | | |
| vehicle | | | 1,125 | |
| shop fittings | | | 600 | |
| | | | | 46,322 |
| **Net profit** | | | | 19,519 |

| Description | Ledger balances | | Adjustments | | Profit and loss | | Balance sheet | |
|---|---|---|---|---|---|---|---|---|
| | Dr £ | Cr £ | Dr £ | Cr £ | Dr £ | Cr £ | Dr £ | Cr £ |
| Purchases and sales | 51,225 | 81,762 | | | 51,225 | 81,762 | | |
| Returns | 186 | 254 | | | 186 | 254 | | |
| Stock at 1 Jan 20-3 | 6,031 | | | | 6,031 | | | |
| Discounts | 324 | 438 | | | 324 | 438 | | |
| Motor expenses | 1,086 | | | | 1,086 | | | |
| Wages and salaries | 20,379 | | | | 20,379 | | | |
| Electricity | 876 | | 102 | | 978 | | | |
| Telephone | 1,241 | | | | 1,241 | | | |
| Rent and rates | 4,565 | | | 251 | 4,314 | | | |
| sundry expenses | 732 | | | | 732 | | | |
| Bad debts written off | 219 | | | | 219 | | | |
| Debtors and creditors | 1,040 | 7,671 | | | | | 1,040 | 7,671 |
| Value Added Tax | | 1,301 | | | | | | 1,301 |
| Bank | 3,501 | | | | | | 3,501 | |
| Cash | 21 | | | | | | 21 | |
| Motor vehicles | 15,000 | | | | | | 15,000 | |
| Prov for dep'n: vehicles | | 3,000 | | 3,000 | | | | 6,000 |
| Office equipment | 10,000 | | | | | | 10,000 | |
| Prov for dep'n: equipment | | 5,000 | | 1,000 | | | | 6,000 |
| Capital | | 25,000 | | | | | | 25,000 |
| Drawings | 8,000 | | | | | | 8,000 | |
| Provision for bad debts | | | | 52 | | | | 52 |
| | | | | | | | | |
| Closing stock: Profit & loss | | | | 8,210 | | 8,210 | | |
| Closing stock: Balance sheet | | | 8,210 | | | | 8,210 | |
| Accruals | | | | 102 | | | | 102 |
| Prepayments | | | 251 | | | | 251 | |
| Depreciation | | | 4,000 | | 4,000 | | | |
| Prov for bad debts:adjustment | | | 52 | | 52 | | | |
| | | | | | | | | |
| | | | | | | | | |
| | | | | | | | | |
| Net profit/loss | | | | | | 103 | 103 | |
| | 124,426 | 124,426 | 12,615 | 12,615 | 90,767 | 90,767 | 46,126 | 46,126 |

BALANCE SHEET AS AT 30 JUNE 20-9

| | Cost £ | Dep'n to date £ | Net £ |
|---|---|---|---|
| **Fixed Assets** | | | |
| Vehicle | 8,000 | 4,625 | 3,375 |
| Shop fittings | 6,000 | 3,000 | 3,000 |
| | 14,000 | 7,625 | 6,375 |

| | | | |
|---|---|---|---|
| **Current Assets** | | | |
| Stock | | 11,517 | |
| Debtors | 3,840 | | |
| Less Provision for bad debts | 96 | 3,744 | |
| Prepayments | | 275 | |
| Bank | | 21,419 | |
| Cash | | 155 | |
| | | 37,110 | |
| **Less Current Liabilities** | | | |
| Creditors | 5,294 | | |
| Value Added Tax | 1,492 | | |
| Accruals | 55 | 6,841 | |
| **Working Capital** | | | 30,269 |
| **NET ASSETS** | | | 36,644 |

| | | |
|---|---|---|
| **FINANCED BY** | | |
| **Capital** | | |
| Opening capital | | 36,175 |
| Add Net profit | | 19,519 |
| | | 55,694 |
| Less Drawings | | 19,050 |
| | | 36,644 |

## CHAPTER 17    The Regulatory Framework of Accounting

**17.2**

(a) Consistency concept: he should continue to use reducing balance method (it won't make any difference to the bank manager anyway).

(b) Prudence concept: stock valuation should be at lower of cost and net realisable value, ie £10,000 in this case.

(c) Business entity concept: car is an asset of John's firm, not a personal asset (in any case personal assets, for sole traders and partnerships, might well be used to repay debts of firm).

(d) Prudence concept: the bad debt should be written off as a bad debt in profit and loss account (so reducing net profit), and the balance sheet figure for debtors should be £27,500 (which is closer to the amount he can expect to receive from debtors).

(e) Accruals concept: expenses and revenues must be matched, therefore it must go through the old year's accounts.

(f) Going concern concept: presumes that business will continue to trade in the foreseeable future: alternative is 'gone concern' and assets may have very different values.

**17.3**

(a) Sales for February: 24 tables at £50 each = £1,200

(b) Closing stock at 28 February: 6 tables at £31 each = £186

(c) Cost of sales for February:

|  | £ |
|---|---|
| opening stock | 300 |
| plus purchases | 632 |
| less closing stock | 186 |
|  | 746 |

**17.5**

The closing stock is:

| units bought (20 + 10 + 10) | = | 40 |
|---|---|---|
| less   units sold (8 + 16) | = | 24 |
| equals   closing stock | = | 16 |

(a) FIFO

| 6 units at £3.50 | = | £21.00 |
|---|---|---|
| 10 units at £4.00 | = | £40.00 |
| 16 units closing stock | = | £61.00 |

(b) LIFO

| 16 units at £3.00 | = | £48.00 |

(c) AVCO

| 20 units at £3.00 | = | £ 60.00 |
|---|---|---|
| 10 units at £3.50 | = | £ 35.00 |
| 30 units at average cost of £3.17* | = | £ 95.00 |
| 8 units sold | = | £ 25.36 |
| 22 units at average cost of £3.17 | = | £ 69.64 |
| 10 units at £4.00 | = | £ 40.00 |
| 32 units at average cost of £3.43** | = | £109.64 |
| 16 units sold | = | £ 54.88 |
| 16 units closing stock | = | £ 54.76 |

*£95.00 ÷ 30 units

**£109.64 ÷ 32 units

*Note: some figures have been rounded to the nearest penny*

## CHAPTER 18    The Journal

**18.1**

| Date | Details | Folio | Dr £ | Cr £ |
|---|---|---|---|---|
| 20-8 |  |  |  |  |
| 1 May | Vehicle | GL | 6,500 |  |
|  | Fixtures and fittings | GL | 2,800 |  |
|  | Stock | GL | 4,100 |  |
|  | Cash | CB | 150 |  |
|  | Loan from husband | GL |  | 5,000 |
|  | Capital | GL |  | 8,550 |
|  |  |  | 13,550 | 13,550 |
|  | *Assets and liabilities at the start of business* |  |  |  |

**18.3**

| primary accounting record | debit | credit |
|---|---|---|
| (a) purchases day book | purchases account | Temeside Traders |
| (b) sales day book | Malvern Models | sales account |
| (c) journal | office equipment account | A-Z Computers Ltd |
| (d) sales returns day book | sales returns account | Johnson Bros |
| (e) cash book | bank account | Melanie Fisher |
| (f) cash book | cash account | sales account |
| (g) cash book | drawings account | cash account |
| (h) cash book | Stationery Supplies Ltd | bank account |
| (i) journal | bad debts written off account | J Bowen |
| (j) purchases returns day book | I Johnson | purchases returns account |

## 19.1

**ELAINE ROWE**
**TRIAL BALANCE AS AT 31 MAY 20-8**

|  | Dr £ | Cr £ |
|---|---|---|
| Equipment | 9,750 | |
| General expenses | 1,394 | |
| Sales £15,863 + £392 | | 16,255 |
| Purchases £7,590 – £196 | 7,394 | |
| Sales returns | 426 | |
| Purchases returns | | 674 |
| Creditors £2,095 – £196 | | 1,899 |
| Drawings £1,420 + £150 | 1,570 | |
| Debtors £3,738 + £392 – £545 | 3,585 | |
| Bank (£372) + £545 – £150 | 23 | |
| Capital | | 5,314 |
| | 24,142 | 24,142 |

## 19.3

(a)
| | |
|---|---|
| (1) | error of omission |
| (2) | error of principle |
| (3) | error of original entry |
| (4) | error of omission |
| (5) | error of principle |
| (6) | mispost/error of commission |

(b)

**Effect of errors on net profit**

| | Over-stated | No effect | Under-stated |
|---|---|---|---|
| (1) | ✓ | | |
| (2) | ✓ | | |
| (3) | | ✓ | |
| (4) | | ✓ | |
| (5) | | ✓ | |
| (6) | | | ✓ |

(c)

**JOURNAL**

| | Details | Dr £ | Cr £ |
|---|---|---|---|
| (1) | Stationery | 60 | |
| | Cash | | 60 |
| (2) | Repairs to premises | 715 | |
| | Premises | | 715 |
| (3) | Doogan Ltd | 470 | |
| | Office equipment | | 470 |
| | Office equipment | 420 | |
| | Doogan Ltd | | 420 |
| | | 890 | 890 |
| (4) | Drawings | 200 | |
| | Bank | | 200 |
| (5) | Office equipment | 630 | |
| | Purchases | | 630 |
| (6) | J Hailes | 320 | |
| | J Hales | | 320 |

**20.1**

### Sales Ledger Control Account

| Dr | | £ | | Cr | £ |
|---|---|---|---|---|---|
| 20-1 | | | 20-1 | | |
| 1 Jun | Balances b/d | 17,491 | 30 Jun | Sales returns | 1,045 |
| 30 Jun | Credit sales | 42,591 | 30 Jun | Payments received | 39,024 |
| | | | 30 Jun | Cash discount allowed | 593 |
| | | | 30 Jun | Bad debts written off | 296 |
| | | | 30 Jun | Balances c/d | 19,124 |
| | | 60,082 | | | 60,082 |
| 1 Jul | Balances b/d | 19,124 | | | |

**20.2**

### Purchases Ledger Control Account

| Dr | | £ | | Cr | £ |
|---|---|---|---|---|---|
| 20-2 | | | 20-2 | | |
| 30 Apr | Purchases returns | 653 | 1 Apr | Balances b/d | 14,275 |
| 30 Apr | Payments made to creditors | 31,074 | 30 Apr | Credit purchases | 36,592 |
| 30 Apr | Cash discount received | 1,048 | | | |
| 30 Apr | Set-off: sales ledger | 597 | | | |
| 30 Apr | Balances c/d | 17,495 | | | |
| | | 50,867 | | | 50,867 |
| | | | 1 May | Balances b/d | 17,495 |

**20.3** (a)

### S Day

| Dr | | £ | | Cr | £ |
|---|---|---|---|---|---|
| 1 Sep | Balance b/d | 6,000C | 4 Sep | Cash Book | 3,000 |
| 20 Sep | Sales Day Book | 1,400C | 23 Sep | Sales Returns Day Book | 140 |
| | | | 30 Sep | Balance c/d | 4,260 |
| | | 7,400 | | | 7,400 |
| 1 Oct | Balance b/d | 4,260 | | | |

### E Tait

| Dr | | £ | | Cr | £ |
|---|---|---|---|---|---|
| 15 Sep | Sales Day Book | 720 | 25 Sep | Cash Book | 200 |
| | | | 30 Sep | Balance c/d | 520 |
| | | 720 | | | 720 |
| 1 Oct | Balance b/d | 520 | | | |

**19.4**

| Date | Details | Folio | Dr £ | Cr £ |
|---|---|---|---|---|
| (a) | Office expenses | GL | 85 | |
| | Suspense | GL | | 85 |
| | *Omission of entry in office expenses account – payment made by cheque no .............. on ......(date)* | | | |
| (b) | Suspense | GL | 78 | |
| | Photocopying | GL | | 78 |
| | Photocopying | GL | 87 | |
| | Suspense | GL | | 87 |
| | | | 165 | 165 |
| | *Payment for photocopying £87 (cheque no .............. on ..............) entered in photocopying account as £78 in error* | | | |
| (c) | Suspense | GL | 100 | |
| | Sales returns | GL | | 100 |
| | *Overcast on ...(date)... now corrected* | | | |
| (d) | Commission received | GL | 25 | |
| | Suspense | GL | | 25 |
| | *Commission received on ............... entered twice in commission received account, now corrected* | | | |

### Suspense Account

| Dr | | £ | | | Cr | £ |
|---|---|---|---|---|---|---|
| 20-8 | | | 20-8 | | | |
| 30 Sep | Trial balance difference | 19 | (a) | | Office expenses | 85 |
| (b) | Photocopying | 78 | (b) | | Photocopying | 87 |
| (c) | Sales returns | 100 | (d) | | Commission received | 25 |
| | | 197 | | | | 197 |

**Dr**            **N Mack**           **Cr**

| | | £ | | | £ |
|---|---|---|---|---|---|
| 1 Sep | Balance b/d | 3,750 | 15 Sep | Cash Book | 1,750 |
| 30 Sep | Sales Day Book | 1,000 | 15 Sep | Cash discount allowed | 250 |
| | | | 30 Sep | Balance c/d | 2,750 |
| | | 4,750 | | | 4,750 |
| 1 Oct | Balance b/d | 2,750 | | | |

(b)

**Dr**       **Sales Ledger Control Account**       **Cr**

| | | £ | | | £ |
|---|---|---|---|---|---|
| 1 Sep | Balances b/d | 9,750 | 30 Sep | Cash Book | 4,950 |
| 30 Sep | Sales Day Book | 3,120 | 30 Sep | Cash discount allowed | 250 |
| | | | 30 Sep | Sales Returns Day Book | 140 |
| | | | 30 Sep | Balances c/d | 7,530 |
| | | 12,870 | | | 12,870 |
| 1 Oct | Balances b/d | 7,530 | | | |

(c) **Reconciliation of sales ledger control account with debtor balances**

| | 1 Sep | 30 Sep |
|---|---|---|
| | £ | £ |
| S Day | 6,000 | 4,260 |
| E Tait | — | 520 |
| N Mack | 3,750 | 2,750 |
| Sales ledger control account | 9,750 | 7,530 |

---

## CHAPTER 21   Incomplete Records

**21.1**

(a)
- receipts from sales
- add debtors at year end
- **sales for year**

| | £ |
|---|---|
| | 153,500 |
| | 2,500 |
| | 156,000 |

(b)
- payments to suppliers
- add creditors at year end
- **purchases for year**

| | £ |
|---|---|
| | 95,000 |
| | 65,000 |
| | 160,000 |

(c)
- payments for rent and rates
- less rent prepaid at 31 Dec 20-8
- **rent and rates for year**

| | £ |
|---|---|
| | 8,750 |
| | 250 |
| | 8,500 |

- payments for wages
- add wages accrued at 31 Dec 20-8
- **wages for year**

| | £ |
|---|---|
| | 15,000 |
| | 550 |
| | 15,550 |

---

(d)

**JANE PRICE**

**TRADING AND PROFIT AND LOSS ACCOUNT FOR THE YEAR ENDED 31 DECEMBER 20-8**

| | £ | £ |
|---|---|---|
| Sales | | 156,000 |
| Purchases | 160,000 | |
| Less Closing stock | 73,900 | |
| Cost of Goods Sold | | 86,100 |
| **Gross profit** | | 69,900 |
| Less expenses: | | |
| Advertising | 4,830 | |
| Rent and rates | 8,500 | |
| Wages | 15,550 | |
| General expenses | 5,000 | |
| Provision for depreciation: shop fittings | 10,000 | |
| | | 43,880 |
| **Net profit** | | 26,020 |

(e) **BALANCE SHEET AS AT 31 DECEMBER 20-8**

| | Cost | Dep'n to date | Net |
|---|---|---|---|
| | £ | £ | £ |
| **Fixed Assets** | | | |
| Shop fittings | 50,000 | 10,000 | 40,000 |
| **Current Assets** | | | |
| Stock | | 73,900 | |
| Debtors | | 2,500 | |
| Prepayment: rent | | 250 | |
| Bank* | | 19,900 | |
| | | 96,550 | |
| **Less Current Liabilities** | | | |
| Creditors | 65,000 | | |
| Accrual: wages | 550 | | |
| | | 65,550 | |
| **Working Capital** | | | 31,000 |
| **NET ASSETS** | | | 71,000 |
| **FINANCED BY** | | | |
| **Capital** | | | |
| Opening capital (introduced at start of year) | | | 60,000 |
| Add net profit | | | 26,020 |
| | | | 86,020 |
| Less drawings | | | 15,020 |
| | | | 71,000 |

\* Cash book summary:

| | £ |
|---|---|
| • total receipts for year | 213,500 |
| • less total payments for year | 193,600 |
| • **balance at year end** | 19,900 |

# CHAPTER 22   Club and Society Accounts

## 22.1

### WESTSIDE SPORTS CLUB
### INCOME AND EXPENDITURE ACCOUNT FOR THE YEAR ENDED 31 DECEMBER 20-8

|  | £ | £ | £ |
|---|---:|---:|---:|
| **Income** |  |  |  |
| Subscriptions |  |  | 1,460 |
| Competition entry fees |  |  | 498 |
| Sale of snacks |  | 1,108 |  |
| Purchase of snacks | 520 |  |  |
| Less Closing stock | 70 |  |  |
|  |  | 450 |  |
| Profit on snacks |  |  | 658 |
|  |  |  | 2,616 |
| **Less Expenditure** |  |  |  |
| Postage and stationery |  | 197 |  |
| Rent paid |  | 650 |  |
| Competition expenses |  | 320 |  |
| Provision for depreciation: equipment |  | 300 |  |
|  |  |  | 1,467 |
| **Surplus of income over expenditure** |  |  | 1,149 |

### BALANCE SHEET AS AT 31 DECEMBER 20-8

|  | £ | £ | £ |
|---|---:|---:|---:|
|  | *Cost* | *Dep'n to date* | *Net* |
| **Fixed Assets** |  |  |  |
| Equipment | 1,500 | 300 | 1,200 |
| **Current Assets** |  |  |  |
| Stock of snacks |  | 70 |  |
| Bank |  | 59 |  |
|  |  | 129 |  |
| **Less Current Liabilities** |  |  |  |
| Subscriptions in advance | 80 |  |  |
| Accrual for rent | 100 |  |  |
|  |  | 180 |  |
| **Working capital** |  |  | (51) |
| **NET ASSETS** |  |  | 1,149 |
| **REPRESENTED BY** |  |  |  |
| Accumulated fund |  |  | – |
| Surplus of income over expenditure |  |  | 1,149 |
|  |  |  | 1,149 |

## 22.3   (a)

### YESTERYEAR VINTAGE CAR CLUB
### ACCUMULATED FUND AS AT 1 JANUARY YEAR 46

|  | £ |
|---|---:|
| Subscriptions owing from Year 45 | 640 |
| Vintage cars | 124,000 |
| Bank | 7,266 |
| General expenses owing | (540) |
|  | 131,366 |

### (b)   INCOME AND EXPENDITURE ACCOUNT FOR THE YEAR ENDED 31 DECEMBER YEAR 46

|  | £ | £ | £ |
|---|---:|---:|---:|
| **Income** |  |  |  |
| Subscriptions |  |  | *21,140 |
| Social activities |  | 18,460 |  |
| Less expenses of social activities |  | 11,740 |  |
| Profit on social activities |  |  | 6,720 |
| Hire of cars |  |  | 8,600 |
|  |  |  | 36,460 |
| **Less Expenditure** |  |  |  |
| Heating and lighting |  | 3,606 |  |
| Hire of films |  | 620 |  |
| Administration and general expenses |  | **5,080 |  |
| Maintenance and servicing of cars |  | 9,165 |  |
| Repairs to cars |  | 3,856 |  |
| Promotional costs |  | 1,350 |  |
| Rent paid |  | 7,640 |  |
| Receipt from insurance company | 7,900 |  |  |
| Less Book value of vintage car | 9,800 |  |  |
| Loss on Vintage car |  | 1,900 |  |
|  |  | 33,217 |  |
| **Surplus of income over expenditure** |  |  | 3,243 |

*£21,700 – £640 (owing from Year 45) + £780 (in arrears) – £700 (in advance) = £21,140

**£6,040 – £540 (owing from Year 45) – £420 (prepaid) = £5,080

## BALANCE SHEET AS AT 31 DECEMBER YEAR 46

| | £ | £ |
|---|---|---|
| **Fixed Assets** | | |
| Vintage cars | | *126,300 |
| **Current Assets** | | |
| Subscriptions in arrears | 780 | |
| Prepayment | 420 | |
| Bank | 8,879 | |
| | 10,079 | |
| **Less Current Liabilities** | | |
| Subscriptions in advance | 700 | |
| Accruals | 1,070 | |
| | 1,770 | |
| **Working Capital** | | 8,309 |
| **NET ASSETS** | | 134,609 |
| **REPRESENTED BY** | | |
| Accumulated fund | | 131,366 |
| Surplus of income over expenditure | | 3,243 |
| | | 134,609 |

*£124,000 – £9,800 (car destroyed by fire) + £12,100 (addition) = £126,300

## CHAPTER 23    Partnership Accounts

### 23.1

**Partners' Capital Accounts**

| Dr | | Lysa £ | Mark £ | | | Lysa £ | Mark £ |
|---|---|---|---|---|---|---|---|
| 20-8 | | | | 20-8 | | | |
| 31 Dec | Balances c/d | 50,000 | 40,000 | 1 Jan | Balances b/d | 50,000 | 40,000 |
| | | | | 20-9 | | | |
| | | 50,000 | 40,000 | 1 Jan | Balances b/d | 50,000 | 40,000 |

**Partners' Current Accounts**

| Dr | | Lysa £ | Mark £ | | | Lysa £ | Mark £ |
|---|---|---|---|---|---|---|---|
| 20-8 | | | | 20-8 | | | |
| 31 Dec | Drawings | 13,000 | 12,250 | 1 Jan | Balances b/d | 420 | 1,780 |
| 31 Dec | Balance c/d | – | 830 | 31 Dec | Interest on capital | 2,500 | 2,000 |
| | | | | 31 Dec | Share of profits | 9,300 | 9,300 |
| | | | | 31 Dec | Balance c/d | 780 | – |
| | | 13,000 | 13,080 | | | 13,000 | 13,080 |
| 20-9 | | | | 20-9 | | | |
| 1 Jan | Balance b/d | 780 | – | 1 Jan | Balance b/d | – | 830 |

### 23.2    (a)

## JOHN JAMES AND STEVEN HILL TRADING AS "GRAPES"
## PROFIT AND LOSS ACCOUNT FOR THE YEAR ENDED 31 DECEMBER 20-1

| | £ | £ |
|---|---|---|
| **Gross profit** | | 89,000 |
| Less expenses: | | |
| Rent and rates | 7,500 | |
| Advertising | 12,000 | |
| Heat and light | 3,500 | |
| Wages and salaries | 18,000 | |
| Sundry expenses | 4,000 | |
| Provision for depreciation: shop fittings | 2,000 | |
| | | 47,000 |
| **Net profit** | | 42,000 |
| | | |
| Share of profits: | | |
| John James | | 21,000 |
| Steven Hill | | 21,000 |
| | | 42,000 |

## BALANCE SHEET AS AT 31 DECEMBER 20-1

| | Cost £ | Dep'n to date £ | Net £ |
|---|---|---|---|
| **Fixed Assets** | | | |
| Shop fittings | 20,000 | 2,000 | 18,000 |
| **Current Assets** | | | |
| Stock | | 35,000 | |
| Debtors | | 6,000 | |
| Bank | | 29,000 | |
| | | 70,000 | |
| **Less Current Liabilities** | | | |
| Creditors | 8,000 | | |
| Value Added Tax | 2,000 | | |
| | | 10,000 | |
| **Working Capital** | | | 60,000 |
| **NET ASSETS** | | | 78,000 |

| | | | Net £ |
|---|---|---|---|
| **FINANCED BY** | | | |
| **Capital Accounts** | | | |
| John James | | 38,000 | |
| Steven Hill | | 32,000 | |
| | | | 70,000 |
| **Current Accounts** | JAMES | HILL | |
| Opening balances | (3,000) | 1,000 | |
| Add share of profit | 21,000 | 21,000 | |
| | 18,000 | 22,000 | |
| Less drawings | 14,000 | 18,000 | |
| | 4,000 | 4,000 | 8,000 |
| | | | 78,000 |

## 24.3 (a)

**Dissolution (or Realisation) Account**

| Dr | £ | | Cr £ |
|---|---|---|---|
| Year 13 | | Year 13 | |
| 31 Dec Land and buildings | 901,080 | 31 Dec Meredew Limited | 1,030,000 |
| Equipment | 154,790 | Bank: debtors | 89,600 |
| Vehicles | 36,130 | Elm's capital account: vehicle | 8,000 |
| Stock | 74,000 | Loss on dissolution: | |
| Debtors | 102,000 | Cedar (one-third) | 47,300 |
| Bank: dissolution expenses | 1,500 | Elm (one-third) | 47,300 |
| | | Pine (one-third) | 47,300 |
| | 1,269,500 | | 1,269,500 |

## (b)

**Partners' Capital Accounts**

| Dr | Cedar £ | Elm £ | Pine £ |
|---|---|---|---|
| Current account | – | – | 6,130 |
| Dissolution account: | | | |
| vehicle | | 8,000 | – |
| loss | 47,300 | 47,300 | 47,300 |
| Deficiency of Pine | 7,600 | 3,800 | – |
| Meredew Ltd* | 95,100 | 26,900 | – |
| | 150,000 | 86,000 | 53,400 |

| Dr | Cedar £ | Elm £ | Pine £ |
|---|---|---|---|
| Balances b/d | 140,000 | 70,000 | 42,000 |
| Current accounts | 10,000 | 16,000 | – |
| Deficiency shared between: | | | |
| Cedar (two-thirds) | | | 7,600 |
| Elm (one-third) | | | 3,800 |
| | 150,000 | 86,000 | 53,400 |

\* The shares issued by Meredew Limited in part-consideration for the purchase of various assets are allocated as follows:

|  | £ |
|---|---|
| Cedar | 95,100 |
| Elm | 26,900 |
| | 122,000 |

## (c)

**Meredew Limited**

| Dr | £ | | Cr £ |
|---|---|---|---|
| Year 13 | | Year 13 | |
| 31 Dec Dissolution account | 1,030,000 | 31 Dec Bank | 908,000 |
| | | Capital accounts: | |
| | | Cedar | 95,100 |
| | | Elm | 26,900 |
| | 1,030,000 | | 1,030,000 |

---

## (b)

**Partners' Capital Accounts**

| Dr | James £ | Hill £ | | James £ | Hill £ |
|---|---|---|---|---|---|
| 20-1 | | | 20-1 | | |
| 31 Dec Balances c/d | 38,000 | 32,000 | 1 Jan Balances b/d | 38,000 | 32,000 |
| | | | 20-2 | | |
| | | | 1 Jan Balances b/d | 38,000 | 32,000 |

**Partners' Current Accounts**

| Dr | James £ | Hill £ | | James £ | Hill £ |
|---|---|---|---|---|---|
| 20-1 | | | 20-1 | | |
| 1 Jan Balance b/d | 3,000 | – | 1 Jan Balance b/d | – | 1,000 |
| 31 Dec Drawings | 14,000 | 18,000 | 31 Dec Share of profits | 21,000 | 21,000 |
| 31 Dec Balances c/d | 4,000 | 4,000 | | | |
| | 21,000 | 22,000 | | 21,000 | 22,000 |
| 20-2 | | | 20-2 | | |
| | | | 1 Jan Balances b/d | 4,000 | 4,000 |

## CHAPTER 24   Changes in Partnerships

### 24.1

**Partners' Capital Accounts**

| Dr | Jim £ | Maisie £ | Matt £ |
|---|---|---|---|
| 20-1 | | | |
| 1 Jan Goodwill written off | 24,000 | 16,000 | 8,000 |
| 31 Dec Drawings | 12,000 | 12,000 | 8,000 |
| 31 Dec Balances c/d | 82,800 | 51,200 | 22,000 |
| | 118,800 | 79,200 | 38,000 |
| 20-3 | | | |
| 1 Jan Goodwill written off | | 48,000 | 24,000 |
| 1 Jan Loan account: Jim | 118,800 | | |
| 1 Jan Balances c/d | | 27,200 | 10,000 |
| | 118,800 | 75,200 | 34,000 |

| Cr | Jim £ | Maisie £ | Matt £ |
|---|---|---|---|
| 20-1 | | | |
| 31 Dec Balances b/d | 60,000 | 40,000 | – |
| 20-2 | | | |
| 1 Jan Goodwill created | 28,800 | 19,200 | – |
| 1 Jan Bank | | | 28,000 |
| 31 Dec Share of profits | 30,000 | 20,000 | 10,000 |
| | 118,800 | 79,200 | 38,000 |
| 20-3 | | | |
| 1 Jan Balances b/d | 82,800 | 51,200 | 22,000 |
| 1 Jan Goodwill created | 36,000 | 24,000 | 12,000 |
| | 118,800 | 75,200 | 34,000 |
| 1 Jan Balances b/d | – | 27,200 | 10,000 |

(d)

| Dr | | | Bank Account | | Cr |
|---|---|---|---|---|---|
| **Year 13** | | £ | **Year 13** | | £ |
| 31 Dec | Meredew Limited | 908,000 | 31 Dec Balance b/d | | 613,300 |
| | Dissolution: debtors | 89,600 | Creditors | | 182,800 |
| | | | Loan: Cedar | | 200,000 |
| | | | Dissolution expenses | | 1,500 |
| | | 997,600 | | | 997,600 |

| | Cost £ | Dep'n to date £ | Net £ |
|---|---|---|---|
| **Fixed Assets** | | | |
| *Intangible* | | | |
| Goodwill | 20,000 | 6,000 | 14,000 |
| *Tangible* | | | |
| Premises | 175,000 | 10,500 | 164,500 |
| Office equipment | 25,000 | 5,000 | 20,000 |
| | 220,000 | 21,500 | 198,500 |
| **Current Assets** | | | |
| Stock | | 750 | |
| Debtors | | 42,500 | |
| | | 43,250 | |
| **Less Current Liabilities** | | | |
| Creditors | 7,250 | | |
| Bank overdraft | 13,950 | | |
| Proposed dividends | 40,000 | | |
| Corporation tax | 14,850 | | |
| | | 76,050 | |
| **Working Capital** | | | (32,800) |
| | | | 165,700 |
| **Less Long-term Liabilities** | | | |
| Bank loan | | | 55,000 |
| **NET ASSETS** | | | 110,700 |
| | | | |
| *FINANCED BY* | | | |
| **Issued Share Capital** | | | |
| 100,000 ordinary shares of £1 each | | | 100,000 |
| | | | |
| **Revenue Reserve** | | | |
| Profit and loss account | | | 10,700 |
| **SHAREHOLDERS' FUNDS** | | | 110,700 |

---

**CHAPTER 25   Limited Company Accounts**

25.2

JOBSEEKERS LIMITED

PROFIT AND LOSS ACCOUNT (APPROPRIATION SECTION)

FOR THE YEAR ENDED 31 DECEMBER 20-6

| | £ | £ |
|---|---|---|
| **Net profit for year before taxation** | | 68,200 |
| Less corporation tax | | 14,850 |
| Profit for year after taxation | | 53,350 |
| | | |
| Less interim ordinary dividends paid | 10,000 | |
| final ordinary dividend proposed | 40,000 | |
| | | 50,000 |
| Retained profit for year | | 3,350 |
| Retained profit at 1 January 20-6 | | 7,350 |
| Retained profit at 31 December 20-6 | | 10,700 |

## SIDBURY TRADING CO LTD
### TRADING AND PROFIT AND LOSS ACCOUNT FOR THE YEAR ENDED 31 DECEMBER 20-2

| | £ | £ | £ |
|---|---|---|---|
| Sales | | | 297,462 |
| Opening stock | | 42,618 | |
| Purchases | | 189,273 | |
| | | 231,891 | |
| Less Closing stock | | 47,288 | |
| Cost of Goods Sold | | | 184,603 |
| Gross profit | | | 112,859 |
| Less expenses: | | | |
| Provision for depreciation on vans | | 11,000 | |
| Rent and rates | | 3,600 | |
| General expenses | | 9,741 | |
| Wages and salaries | | 35,043 | |
| Bad debts written off | | 948 | |
| Increase in provision for bad debts | | 124 | |
| Directors' salaries | | 25,000 | |
| | | | 85,456 |
| **Net profit for year before taxation** | | | 27,403 |
| Less corporation tax | | | 12,000 |
| Profit for year after taxation | | | 15,403 |
| Less ordinary dividend proposed | | | 8,000 |
| Retained profit for year | | | 7,403 |
| Add balance of retained profits at beginning of year | | | 18,397 |
| Balance of retained profits at end of year | | | 25,800 |

## BRT LIMITED
### PROFIT AND LOSS APPROPRIATION ACCOUNT FOR THE YEAR ENDED 30 JUNE 20-7

| | £ | £ |
|---|---|---|
| **Net profit for year** | | 132,880 |
| Less preference dividend proposed | 1,800 | |
| ordinary dividend proposed | 15,000 | |
| | | 16,800 |
| | | 116,080 |
| Less transfer to general reserve | | 95,500 |
| Retained profit for year | | 20,580 |
| Retained profit at 1 July 20-6 | | 72,730 |
| Retained profit at 30 June 20-7 | | 93,310 |

### BALANCE SHEET AS AT 30 JUNE 20-7

| | £ | £ | £ |
|---|---|---|---|
| **Fixed Assets** | | | 447,000 |
| **Current Assets** | | 144,410 | |
| **Less Current Liabilities** | | | |
| Creditors | 55,800 | | |
| Preference dividend proposed | 1,800 | | |
| Ordinary dividend proposed | 15,000 | | |
| | | 72,600 | |
| **Working Capital** | | | 71,810 |
| **NET ASSETS** | | | 518,810 |
| | | | |
| *FINANCED BY* | | | |
| **Authorised Share Capital** | | | |
| 500,000 ordinary shares of £1 each | | | 500,000 |
| 50,000 6% preference shares of £1 each | | | 50,000 |
| | | | 550,000 |
| | | | |
| **Issued Share Capital** | | | |
| 300,000 ordinary shares of £1 each | | | 300,000 |
| 30,000 6% preference shares of £1 each | | | 30,000 |
| | | | 330,000 |
| | | | |
| **Revenue Reserves** | | | |
| General reserve | | 95,500 | |
| Profit and loss account | | 93,310 | |
| | | | 188,810 |
| | | | 518,810 |
| | | | |
| **SHAREHOLDERS' FUNDS** | | | |

**26.1**

| | | |
|---|---|---|
| (a) | manufacturing account | |
| (b) | manufacturing account | |
| (c) | manufacturing account | |
| (d) | profit and loss account | |
| (e) | profit and loss account | |
| (f) | manufacturing account | |
| (g) | profit and loss account | |

**26.2**

### BARBARA FRANCIS
### MANUFACTURING AND PROFIT AND LOSS ACCOUNT
for the year ended 31 December 20-8

| | £ | £ |
|---|---|---|
| Opening stock of raw materials | | 31,860 |
| Add Purchases of raw materials | | 237,660 |
| | | 269,520 |
| Less Closing stock of raw materials | | 44,790 |
| COST OF RAW MATERIALS USED | | 224,730 |
| Direct labour | | 234,630 |
| PRIME COST | | 459,360 |
| Add    Production (factory) overheads: | | |
|        Rent and rates | 24,690 | |
|        Power | 7,650 | |
|        Heat and light | 2,370 | |
|        Sundry expenses and maintenance | 8,190 | |
|        Depreciation of plant and machinery | 7,450 | |
| | | 50,350 |
| PRODUCTION (OR MANUFACTURING) COST OF GOODS COMPLETED | | 509,710 |
| | | |
| Sales | | 796,950 |
| Opening stock of finished goods | 42,640 | |
| Production (or manufacturing) cost of goods completed | 509,710 | |
| | 552,350 | |
| Less Closing stock of finished goods | 96,510 | |
| COST OF GOODS SOLD | | 455,840 |
| Gross profit | | 341,110 |
| Less Non-production overheads: | | |
|      Rent and rates | 8,230 | |
|      Salaries | 138,700 | |
|      Advertising | 22,170 | |
|      Office expenses | 7,860 | |
| | | 176,960 |
| Net profit | | 164,150 |

---

## BALANCE SHEET AS AT 31 DECEMBER 20-2

| | Cost £ | Dep'n to date £ | Net £ |
|---|---|---|---|
| **Fixed Assets** | | | |
| Land and buildings | 142,000 | — | 142,000 |
| Vans | 55,000 | 32,800 | 22,200 |
| | 197,000 | 32,800 | 164,200 |
| **Current Assets** | | | |
| Stock | | 47,288 | |
| Debtors | 26,482 | | |
| Less Provision for bad debts | 1,200 | 25,282 | |
| Prepayment (rates) | | 400 | |
| Bank | | 65,958 | |
| | | 138,928 | |
| **Less Current Liabilities** | | | |
| Creditors | 14,555 | | |
| Value Added Tax | 2,419 | | |
| Accrual (wages and salaries) | 354 | | |
| Corporation tax | 12,000 | | |
| Proposed ordinary dividend | 8,000 | 37,328 | |
| **Working Capital** | | | 101,600 |
| **NET ASSETS** | | | 265,800 |
| | | | |
| **FINANCED BY** | | | |
| **Authorised Share Capital** | | | |
| 300,000 ordinary shares of £1 each | | | 300,000 |
| **Issued Share Capital** | | | |
| 240,000 ordinary shares of £1 each, fully paid | | | 240,000 |
| **Revenue Reserves** | | | |
| Profit and loss account | | | 25,800 |
| **SHAREHOLDERS  FUNDS** | | | 265,800 |

## Memorandum

A manufacturing account has been prepared in order to show the main elements of cost which make up the manufacturing cost. In your business, the main elements of cost are:

- *direct materials* – the raw materials used to make the product
- *direct labour* – the wages of the workforce engaged in manufacturing the product
- *production overheads* – the other costs of manufacture; here rent and rates, power, heat and light, etc

The first two of these make up *prime cost*, the basic cost of manufacturing the product. Prime cost plus production overheads gives the production cost. The figure for production cost is carried down to the profit and loss account where it is used to calculate *cost of sales*. The profit and loss account then goes on to show *gross profit* and, after deduction of non-production overheads, *net profit*.

**26.3**

- opening stock, £10,000 plus factory profit (20 per cent) £2,000 = £12,000
- closing stock, £15,000 plus factory profit (20 per cent) £3,000 = £18,000

**Provision for Unrealised Profit Account**

| Dr | | £ | | | Cr £ |
|---|---|---|---|---|---|
| 20-9 | | | 20-9 | | |
| 31 Dec | Balance c/d | 3,000 | 1 Jan | Balance b/d | 2,000 |
| | | | | (adjustment in respect of opening stock) | |
| | | | 31 Dec | Profit and loss account | 1,000 |
| | | 3,000 | | | 3,000 |
| 20-0 | | | 20-0 | | |
| | | | 1 Jan | Balance b/d | 3,000 |

**27.1**

**CASH FLOW STATEMENT OF JOHN SMITH FOR THE YEAR ENDED 31 DECEMBER 20-2**

| | £ | £ |
|---|---|---|
| **Operating activities:** | | |
| Operating profit (before interest) | 11,250 | |
| Depreciation | 1,000 | |
| Increase in stock | (3,500) | |
| Increase in debtors | (800) | |
| Increase in creditors | 250 | |
| Net cash inflow from operating activities | | 8,200 |
| **Returns on investments and servicing of finance:** | | |
| Interest paid | (250) | |
| | | (250) |
| **Taxation:** | | |
| Corporation tax paid | | not applicable |
| **Capital expenditure and financial investment:** | | |
| Payments to acquire fixed assets | | (2,000) |
| **Equity dividends paid:** (drawings) | | (9,000) |
| Cash outflow before use of liquid resources and financing | | (3,050) |
| **Financing:** | | |
| **Decrease in cash** | | *(3,050) |
| | | – |
| * Bank balance at start of year | | 850 |
| Bank balance at end of year | | (2,200) |
| Decrease in cash | | (3,050) |

## LALLAN LIMITED
### CASH FLOW STATEMENT FOR THE YEAR ENDED 31 AUGUST 20-6

| | £000s | £000s |
|---|---|---|
| **Operating activities:** | | |
| Operating profit (see note 1) | 120 | |
| Depreciation for year | 440 | |
| Increase in stock | (50) | |
| Increase in debtors | (130) | |
| Increase in creditors | 110 | |
| Net cash inflow from operating activities | | 490 |
| **Returns on investments and servicing of finance:** | | – |
| **Taxation:** | | |
| Corporation tax paid (amount paid during year) | | (20) |
| **Capital expenditure and financial investment:** | | |
| Payments to acquire fixed assets | | (300) |
| **Acquisitions and disposals:** | | – |
| **Equity dividends paid:** (amount paid during year) | | (60) |
| Cash outflow before use of liquid resources and financing | | 110 |
| **Management of liquid resources:** | | – |
| **Financing:** | | |
| Issue of share capital | 100 | |
| Repayment of loans | (150) | |
| | | (50) |
| | | *60 |
| **Increase in cash** | | 60 |

| | | £000s |
|---|---|---|
| * | Cash/bank at start of year 20 + (20) | nil |
| | Cash/bank at end of year 10 + 50 | 60 |
| | Increase in cash | 60 |

Note 1: Calculation of operating profit for year:

| | £000s |
|---|---|
| increase in profit and loss account | 10 |
| current corporation tax at 31 August 20-6 | 30 |
| proposed dividends at 31 August 20-6 | 80 |
| operating profit for year ended 31 August 20-6 | 120 |

---

## CHAPTER 28   Interpretation of Accounts

**28.1**

| | A plc | B plc |
|---|---|---|
| • gross profit percentage | 11.85% | 54.26% |
| • net profit percentage | 2.87% | 21.08% |
| • operating profit percentage | 3.95% | 26.01% |
| • return on capital employed | 25% | 16.91% |

**28.2**

| | C plc | D plc |
|---|---|---|
| • working capital ratio | 1.51:1 | 1.04:1 |
| • liquid ratio | 0.82:1 | 0.65:1 |
| • debtors' collection period | 37 days | 3 days |
| • creditors' payment period | 57 days | 46 days |
| • stock turnover | 41 days | 18 days |
| • gearing ratio | 0.54:1 | 0.16:1 |

C plc is the chemical manufacturer, while D plc runs department stores.

All of the ratios for C are close to the benchmarks for a manufacturing business: eg working capital and liquid ratios, although a little low, are near the 'accepted' figures of 2:1 and 1:1, respectively. Debtors, creditors and stock turnover show quite a high level of stock being held; debtors' turnover indicates that most sales are on credit; creditors' turnover is rather high. The gearing ratio is acceptable – medium-geared.

For D plc, the ratios indicate a business that sells most of its goods on cash terms: low working capital and liquid ratios, with minimal debtors' turnover. The stock turnover is speedy, whilst creditors are paid after one-and-a-half months. The gearing ratio is low, indicating that there is scope for future borrowing should it be required.

**28.3**

| | ABC plc | XYZ plc |
|---|---|---|
| • dividend yield | 10% | 1.39% |
| • earnings per share | 30p | 36.67p |
| • earnings yield | 20% | 6.11% |
| • price/earnings ratio | 5:1 | 16.37:1 |
| • dividend cover | 2 times | 4.4 times |

XYZ plc is the better company for capital growth: less than a quarter of its earnings is paid out as dividends – the rest is retained in the company to build for the future, which should be reflected in its share price in the years to come.

ABC plc has a much higher dividend yield than XYZ and is the better company for income. Nevertheless, ABC retains half of its earnings, which should help its share price in the future.

# J STEWART
## DEPARTMENTAL TRADING AND PROFIT AND LOSS ACCOUNT
### FOR THE YEAR ENDED 31 DECEMBER YEAR 7

| | Basis of apportionment | Department A | | Department B | | Total | |
|---|---|---|---|---|---|---|---|
| | | £ | £ | £ | £ | £ | £ |
| Sales | Dept A 60%; dept B 40% | | 540,000 | | 360,000 | | 900,000 |
| Opening stock | | 12,000 | | 22,000 | | 34,000 | |
| Purchases | | 160,000 | | 240,000 | | 400,000 | |
| | | 172,000 | | 262,000 | | 434,000 | |
| Less Closing stock | | 14,000 | | 18,000 | | 32,000 | |
| Cost of Goods Sold | | | 158,000 | | 244,000 | | 402,000 |
| **Gross profit** | | | 382,000 | | 116,000 | | 498,000 |
| | | | | | | | |
| Less expenses: | | | | | | | |
| Rates | Area occupied | 45,000 | | 36,000 | | 81,000 | |
| Sales staff salaries | Number of sales people | 36,000 | | 48,000 | | 84,000 | |
| Insurances | Area occupied | 20,000 | | 16,000 | | 36,000 | |
| Vehicle running expenses | Sales value | 4,200 | | 2,800 | | 7,000 | |
| Advertising | Sales value | 36,000 | | 24,000 | | 60,000 | |
| Administration | Purchases | 4,800 | | 7,200 | | 12,000 | |
| Dep'n of fixtures and fittings | Area occupied | 5,500 | | 4,400 | | 9,900 | |
| | | | 151,500 | | 138,400 | | 289,900 |
| **Net profit/(loss)** | | | 230,500 | | (22,400) | | 208,100 |

**28.6**

*Note: all figures in £000s*

| | | Year 8 | Year 9 |
|---|---|---|---|
| (a) | Rate of stock turnover $\dfrac{\text{Cost of goods sold}}{\text{Average stock}}$ | $\dfrac{£2,660}{£290^*}$ = 9.17 times<br>$^*(£220 + £360) \div 2$ | $\dfrac{£3,140}{£390^*}$ = 8.05 times<br>$^*(£360 + £420) \div 2$ |
| (b) | Gross profit to sales $\dfrac{\text{Gross profit}}{\text{Sales}} \times \dfrac{100}{1}$ | $\dfrac{£2,140}{£4,800} \times \dfrac{100}{1}$ = 44.58% | $\dfrac{£2,360}{£5,500} \times \dfrac{100}{1}$ = 42.91% |
| (c) | Net profit to sales $\dfrac{\text{Net profit}}{\text{Sales}} \times \dfrac{100}{1}$ | $\dfrac{£340}{£4,800} \times \dfrac{100}{1}$ = 7.08% | $\dfrac{£500}{£5,500} \times \dfrac{100}{1}$ = 9.09% |
| (d) | Sales to capital employed $\dfrac{\text{Sales}}{\text{Capital employed}}$ | $\dfrac{£4,800}{£1,840^\dagger}$ = 2.61 times<br>$^\dagger$ share capital + profit and loss | $\dfrac{£5,500}{£2,040^\dagger}$ = 2.70 times |
| (e) | Return on capital employed $\dfrac{\text{Net profit}}{\text{Capital employed}} \times \dfrac{100}{1}$ | $\dfrac{£340}{£1,840} \times \dfrac{100}{1}$ = 18.48% | $\dfrac{£500}{£2,040} \times \dfrac{100}{1}$ = 24.51% |
| (f) | Current ratio $\dfrac{\text{Current assets}}{\text{Current liabilities}}$ | $\dfrac{£360 + £390 + £210}{£200 + £300} =$ $\dfrac{£960}{£500}$ = 1.92:1 | $\dfrac{£420 + £410 + £200}{£300 + £440} =$ $\dfrac{£1,030}{£740}$ = 1.39:1 |
| (g) | Liquidity ratio $\dfrac{(\text{Current assets} - \text{stock})}{\text{Current liabilities}}$ | $\dfrac{£960 - £360}{£500} =$ $\dfrac{£600}{£500}$ = 1.2:1 | $\dfrac{£1,030 - £420}{£740} =$ $\dfrac{£610}{£740}$ = 0.82:1 |

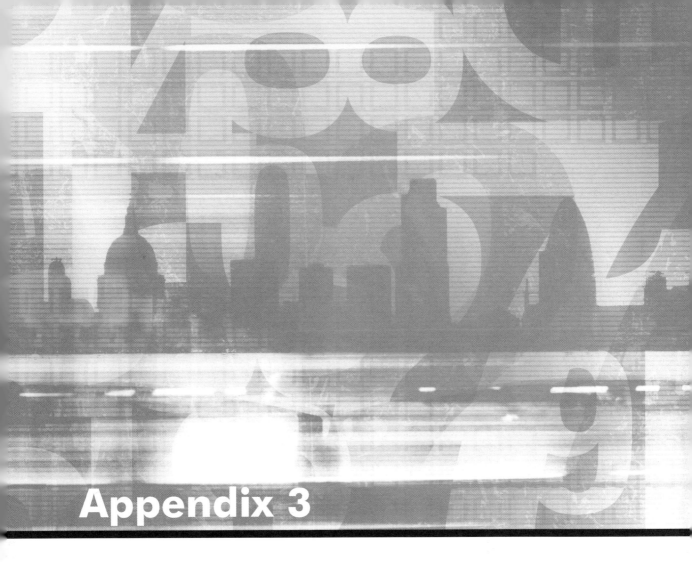

# Appendix 3

additional questions

# INTRODUCTION

This Appendix provides additional questions for most of the chapters in this text. These questions will provide useful extra practice and are ideal for homework.

Please note that in this edition the numbering of these questions follows on from the chapter questions. Chapter 1, for example, has eight questions at the end of the chapter text, so the first extra question in this Appendix is 1.9 which follows on from the last question (1.8) at the end of the chapter. This principle is followed in all of the chapters which have extra questions.

The answers to these questions are contained in the Business Accounts Tutor Pack which is available direct from Osborne Books. Please call 01905 748071 or visit www.osbornebooks.co.uk for further details.

Osborne Books is grateful to the following examination boards who have given permission for the reproduction of past examination questions: Association of Accounting Technicians, The Chartered Institute of Bankers, The Chartered Institute of Management Accountants, London Chamber of Commerce and Industry, Midland Examining Group, Pitman Examinations Institute, RSA Examinations Board, Southern Examining Group, Welsh Joint Education Committee.

The page references to the chapters are set out below.

**1.9** Write out the figures which make up the accounting equation (assets − liabilities = capital) after each of the following consecutive transactions (ignore VAT):

- owner starts in business with capital of £10,000 comprising £9,000 in the bank and £1,000 in cash
- buys office equipment for £2,500, paying by cheque
- obtains a loan of £2,000 by cheque from a friend
- buys factory machinery for £8,000, paying by cheque
- buys office equipment for £2,000 on credit from Wyvern Office Supplies

**1.10** Fill in the missing figures:

|     | Assets £ | Liabilities £ | Capital £ |
| --- | --- | --- | --- |
| (a) | 10,000 | 0 | .......... |
| (b) | 20,000 | 7,500 | .......... |
| (c) | 16,750 | .......... | 10,500 |
| (d) | .......... | 4,350 | 12,680 |
| (e) | 17,290 | .......... | 11,865 |
| (f) | .......... | 6,709 | 17,294 |

**1.11** The table below sets out account balances from the books of a business. The columns (a) to (f) show the account balances resulting from a series of transactions that have taken place over time. You are to compare each set of adjacent columns, ie (a) with (b) with (c), and so on, and state, with figures, what accounting transactions have taken place in each case. (Ignore VAT).

|  | (a) £ | (b) £ | (c) £ | (d) £ | (e) £ | (f) £ |
| --- | --- | --- | --- | --- | --- | --- |
| **Assets** | | | | | | |
| Office equipment | – | 5,000 | 5,000 | 5,500 | 5,500 | 5,500 |
| Machinery | – | – | – | – | 6,000 | 6,000 |
| Bank | 7,000 | 2,000 | 7,000 | 7,000 | 1,000 | 3,000 |
| Cash | 1,000 | 1,000 | 1,000 | 500 | 500 | 500 |
| **Liabilities** | | | | | | |
| Loan | – | – | 5,000 | 5,000 | 5,000 | 5,000 |
| **Capital** | 8,000 | 8,000 | 8,000 | 8,000 | 8,000 | 10,000 |

**2.7** The following are the business transactions of Andrew King (who is not registered for VAT) for the month of October 20-9:

1 Oct   Started in business with capital of £7,500 in the bank

4 Oct   Bought a machine for £4,000, paying by cheque

6 Oct   Bought office equipment for £2,250, paying by cheque

11 Oct   Paid rent £400, by cheque

12 Oct   Obtained a loan of £1,500 from a friend, Tina Richards, and paid her cheque into the bank

15 Oct   Paid wages £500, by cheque

18 Oct   Commission received £200, by cheque

20 Oct   Drawings £250, by cheque

25 Oct   Paid wages £450, by cheque

You are to:

(a)   write up Andrew King's bank account

(b)   complete the double-entry book-keeping transactions

**2.8** The following account appears in the books of Peter Singh:

| Dr | | | Bank Account | | Cr |
|---|---|---|---|---|---|
| 20-4 | | £ | 20-4 | | £ |
| 1 Jan | Capital | 10,000 | 2 Jan | Office Equipment | 3,000 |
| 4 Jan | Commission received | 500 | 3 Jan | Rates | 1,500 |
| 7 Jan | Bank Loan | 2,500 | 5 Jan | Cash | 250 |
| | | | 6 Jan | Drawings | 500 |
| | | | 8 Jan | Van | 7,500 |

Taking each transaction in turn, describe to Peter Singh the transaction undertaken by his business, and explain the other account in which each appears in his double-entry accounts.

**3.8** The following are the business transactions of Weston Traders for the month of May 20-2:

| | |
|---|---|
| 1 May | Started in business with capital of £7,500 in the bank |
| 3 May | Bought goods, £1,000, paying by cheque |
| 4 May | Sold goods, £750, a cheque being received |
| 6 May | Bought shop fittings for £2,000, paying by cheque |
| 7 May | Bought goods, £1,250, on credit from Bristol Supplies Limited |
| 10 May | Paid rent, £750, by cheque |
| 12 May | Sold goods, £1,500, on credit to Gordano Giftware |
| 14 May | Returned goods, £150, to Bristol Supplies Limited |
| 16 May | Paid wages, £1,500, by cheque |
| 18 May | Paid the amount owing to Bristol Supplies Limited by cheque |
| 21 May | Gordano Giftware returned goods, £250 |
| 24 May | Paid rent, £750, by cheque |
| 26 May | Sold goods, £550, a cheque being received |
| 28 May | Received a cheque from Gordano Giftware for the amount owing |

You are to record the transactions in the books of account.

**3.9** For each transaction below, complete the table to show the names of the accounts which will be debited and credited:

(a)   Bought goods on credit from Armscott Limited
(b)   Sold goods on credit to Orion Limited
(c)   Paid the carriage charge, by cheque, to deliver the goods to Orion Limited
(d)   Bought a photocopier for use in the business on credit from Office Products Limited
(e)   Returned unsatisfactory goods to Armscott Limited
(f)   Orion Limited returned unsatisfactory goods
(g)   Paid the amount owing to Armscott Limited by cheque
(h)   Received a cheque from Orion Limited for the amount owing

| Transaction | Account debited | Account credited |
|---|---|---|
| (a) | ........................... | ........................... |
| (b) | ........................... | ........................... |
| (c) | ........................... | ........................... |
| (d) | ........................... | ........................... |
| (e) | ........................... | ........................... |
| (f) | ........................... | ........................... |
| (g) | ........................... | ........................... |
| (h) | ........................... | ........................... |

**4.7**   Study carefully the following document received by W Hoddle Limited:

## STATEMENT OF ACCOUNT
### F. RAMSEY & SON
### 31 NORTH STREET
### LIVERPOOL

W Hoddle Ltd
Blackpool Road
Manchester

31 July 20-7

| Date | Reference | Dr | Cr | Balance |
|------|-----------|------|------|---------|
| July  1 | B/F | | | Dr    522.80 |
| July  8 | 62290 | 178.00 | | 700.80 |
| July 12 | 63492 | 132.80 | | 833.60 |
| July 14 | Cash & Disc | | 522.80 | 310.80 |
| July 17 | 89247 | 480.00 | | 790.80 |
| July 20 | 864 | | 58.00 | 732.80 |
| July 30 | 91082 | 347.20 | | 1,080.00 |

Cash Discount 5% if paid within ONE month of this Statement

(a)   In the above transactions, who is the supplier of the goods?

(b)   Explain the transactions that gave rise to the entries dated

(i)   12 July

(ii)   14 July

(iii)  20 July

(c)   If W Hoddle Ltd paid the above account on 18 August 20-7, how much cash discount did they receive?

(d)   Assume W Hoddle Ltd prepared a balance sheet on 31 July 20-7, state where, in the balance sheet, F Ramsey & Son's balance should have appeared.

(e)   In the ledger of F Ramsey & Son, show W Hoddle Ltd's account up to and including 14 July 20-7.

**4.8**   Compudisk sells computer disks and has a special sales offer.  A box of ten disks normally sells at £8.00 (excluding VAT).  Compudisk is offering a 20% trade discount for orders of ten boxes or more. It receives the following orders by e-mail:

(a)   20 boxes ordered by Osborne Electronics Limited

(b)   50 boxes ordered by Helfield College

(c)   5 boxes ordered by Jim Masters

(d)   1,000 boxes ordered by Trigger Trading Limited

(i)   calculate in each case

–   the total cost before discount

–   the discount

–   the cost after discount

–   the VAT at the current rate

–   the total cost

(ii)   Recalculate the totals for each order after allowing a cash discount of 2.5% for full settlement within 14 days.

**5.6** A Thompson commenced business on 1 February 20-0, paying £500 into a business bank account.

During the next two months the following transactions took place. All payments are made by cheque and all receipts are banked.

| February | | £ |
|---|---|---|
| 1 | Bought goods for resale | 150 |
| 5 | Paid rent | 50 |
| 10 | Business takings to date | 290 |
| 22 | Paid for advertising | 25 |
| 26 | A Thompson's drawings | 100 |
| 27 | Business takings | 240 |

| March | | |
|---|---|---|
| 2 | Bought goods for resale | 100 |
| 5 | Paid rent | 50 |
| 14 | Received a loan, L Lock | 450 |
| 16 | Business takings | 330 |
| 23 | A Thompson's drawings | 75 |
| 26 | Business takings | 180 |
| 29 | Paid for advertising leaflets | 30 |

You are required to:

(a) write up the bank account, balancing at the end of each month

(b) write up all the other accounts and balance the accounts at the end of the two month period

(c) extract a trial balance as at 31 March 20-0

**5.7** The following account appears in the ledger of Celia Donithorn:

| Dr | | | Georgina Harrison | | | Cr |
|---|---|---|---|---|---|---|
| | | £ | | | | £ |
| 1 Feb | Balance b/d | 200 | 3 Feb | Bank | | 190 |
| 6 Feb | Goods | 80 | 3 Feb | Discount | | 10 |
| | | | 10 Feb | Returns | | 15 |

(a) What is the meaning of each item recorded in the above account? 1 February has been completed as an example:

1 Feb Georgina Harrison owes Celia Donithorn £200

(b) What percentage cash discount was deducted on 3 February?

(c) Who owes whom how much at close of business on 10 February?

**5.8** Below are two ledger accounts in the books of Devenish Interiors. Study them carefully.

| Dr | | M Johnston | | | Cr |
|---|---|---|---|---|---|
| | | £ | | | £ |
| 1 Apr | Balance b/d | 150 | 10 Apr | Bank | 150 |
| 20 Apr | Sales | 200 | 22 Apr | Returns | 10 |
| | | | 28 Apr | Bank | 100 |
| | | | 30 Apr | Balance c/d | 90 |
| | | 350 | | | 350 |
| 1 May | Balance b/d | 90 | | | |

| Dr | | J Kelly | | | Cr |
|---|---|---|---|---|---|
| | | £ | | | £ |
| 7 Apr | Returns | 20 | 1 Apr | Balance b/d | 220 |
| 10 Apr | Bank | 200 | 6 Apr | Purchases | 110 |
| 15 Apr | Bank | 105 | 18 Apr | Purchases | 100 |
| 15 Apr | Discount received | 5 | | | |
| 20 Apr | Returns | 20 | | | |
| 30 Apr | Balance c/d | 80 | | | |
| | | 430 | | | 430 |
| | | | 1 May | Balance c/d | 80 |

Required:

(a) Explain the opening balance in the account of:
   (i) M Johnston
   (ii) J Kelly

(b) Which of the accounts is a debtor account on 30 April?

(c) Explain the 22 April entry in M Johnston's account.

(d) Explain the 15 April entries in J Kelly's account.

(e) What documents should have been received from J Kelly for 7 April and 20 April transactions?

**6.6**   The following invoices, in respect of purchases of goods for resale, have been received:
20-2

| | | |
|---|---|---|
| 2 January | T F Day | £850.45 |
| 10 January | B G Moon | £1,226.48 |
| 14 January | D S Cox | £912.14 |
| 18 January | T F Day | £1,009.63 |
| 25 January | B G Moon | £461.92 |
| 28 January | T F Day | £227.39 |
| 30 January | D S Cox | £1,013.27 |

*Note: ignore VAT*

Required:
(a)   rule up the purchases day book and enter the above invoices in it
(b)   total the purchases day book for the month
(c)   open the suppliers accounts and the purchases account
(d)   post the necessary entries from the day book to these accounts

**6.7**   C Emberson, a sole trader, buys and sells goods on credit. A bank account is kept through which all amounts received and paid are entered. On 30 November 20-8 the following balances remain in the books:

| | £ | £ |
|---|---|---|
| C Hills | | 154 |
| L Howe | | 275 |
| K Harris | 330 | |
| Bank | 740 | |
| Capital | | 641 |
| | 1,070 | 1,070 |

You are required to:
(a)   open appropriate ledger accounts for the above and enter balances as at 1 December 20-8
(b)   post the transactions indicated in the subsidiary books direct to the ledger and open any other accounts which may be required
(c)   balance the accounts where necessary and extract a trial balance on 31 December 20-8

| Purchases Day Book | | £ | VAT | Total |
|---|---|---|---|---|
| Dec | | | | |
| 13 | C Hills | 100 | 10 | 110 |
| 20 | C Hills | 150 | 15 | 165 |
| 21 | L Howe | 60 | 6 | 66 |
| | | 310 | 31 | 341 |

| Sales Day Book | | £ | VAT | Total |
|---|---|---|---|---|
| Dec | | | | |
| 11 | K Harris | 240 | 24 | 264 |
| 15 | K Harris | 80 | 8 | 88 |
| | | 320 | 32 | 352 |

| Payments Received | | £ |
|---|---|---|
| Dec | | |
| 16 | K Harris | 594 |

| Payments Made | | £ |
|---|---|---|
| Dec | | |
| 8 | C Hills | 154 |
| 15 | Printing expenses | 20 |

*Author's note: in this question a rate of VAT of 10 per cent has been used.*

**7.5**   Trix Traders Limited has the following transactions for the three months ended 31 December 20-5:

|  | Purchases | Expenses | Fixed assets | Sales |
|---|---|---|---|---|
|  | £ | £ | £ | £ |
| October | 7,200 | 2,360 | 3,200 | 12,800 |
| November | 7,600 | 1,920 | – | 14,000 |
| December | 8,400 | 3,640 | – | 15,600 |

All transactions are subject to Value Added Tax at a rate of 17.5 per cent; the company accounts for VAT on a quarterly basis, with the current quarter ending on 31 December 20-5.

You are to:

(a)   calculate the VAT amounts for each month

(b)   show the VAT account for the quarter as it will appear in the general ledger, and balance the account at 31 December 20-5 (note: assume a nil balance on the account at 1 October)

(c)   explain the significance of the balance of the VAT account at 31 December 20-5 and how it will be dealt with

**7.6**   The book-keeper of Priory Printers Limited has the following purchases invoices (PI) and sales invoices (SI) to enter into the accounts for the week commencing 10 June 20-2. All purchases and sales are subject to Value Added Tax at 17.5% and the amounts shown are the gross value (ie including VAT). None of the invoices for this week allows cash discount.

| Date | Number | Account name | Gross amount |
|---|---|---|---|
| 20-2 |  |  | £ |
| 10 Jun | PI 2472 | Paper Supplies Ltd | 470.00 |
| 10 Jun | SI 1347 | Wyvern Publishing | 622.75 |
| 11 Jun | PI 8771 | Severn Traders | 169.20 |
| 12 Jun | PI X244 | Computer Services Ltd | 195.05 |
| 12 Jun | SI 1348 | House of Cards Ltd | 298.45 |
| 13 Jun | PI 2491 | Paper Supplies Ltd | 559.30 |
| 13 Jun | SI 1349 | Lennox Publishers | 737.90 |
| 14 Jun | SI 1350 | House of Cards Ltd | 258.97 |
| 14 Jun | SI 1351 | Wyvern Publishing | 564.94 |

Required:

(a)   Write up and total Priory Printers Limited's purchases day book and sales day book for the week commencing 10 June 20-2.

(b)   Record the transactions in Priory Printers Limited's purchases ledger, sales ledger, and general ledger.

(c)   Balance the Value Added Tax Account at 14 June (other accounts need not be balanced) and explain the significance of the balance.

*Note: assume that all accounts have nil balances at 10 June 20-2.*

**8.7**  (a)  List *three* ways in which a trader can pay debts other than by cash or cheque.

  (b)  On 1 July year 7, the debit balances in the cash book of E Rich were:

Cash    £419

Bank   £3,685

His transactions for the month of July were:

| | |
|---|---|
| 2 July | Received cheque from A Wood £296 |
| 6 July | Paid wages in cash £102 |
| 9 July | Paid C Hill £211 by cheque in full settlement of his account of £224 |
| 12 July | Received £146 cash for sale of damaged stock |
| 12 July | Paid T Jarvis £1,023 by cheque in full settlement of his account of £1,051 |
| 13 July | Paid wages in cash £104 |
| 17 July | Received cheque for £500 from Atlas & Company |
| 19 July | Paid £21 in cash for postage stamps |
| 20 July | Paid wages in cash £102 |
| 23 July | Withdrew £200 from bank for office cash |
| 25 July | Paid W Moore £429 by cheque |
| 26 July | Paid wages in cash £105 |
| 28 July | Received £317 cash from T Phillips in full settlement of his account of £325, paid into bank the same day |
| 31 July | Paid £260 cash into bank |

Required:

Prepare the three-column cash book for the month of July year 7 and balance it at 31 July, bringing the balances down at 1 August.

608

**8.8** Choose from the statements **A-L** given below the **one** which you think best explains the meaning of each entry shown in the cash book. Enter the letter **A-L** of your choice in the space provided in the brackets at the side of each entry.

### CASH BOOK (credit side only)

|        |             | Discount | Cash | Bank |
|--------|-------------|----------|------|------|
|        |             | £        | £    | £    |
| 2 Jan  | Balance b/d |          |      | 380 (........) |
| 4 Jan  | M Hughes    | 30 (........) |   | 570 (........) |
| 9 Jan  | Bank        |          | 240 (........) | |
| 16 Jan | Motor van   |          |      | 5,850 (........) |
| 20 Jan | Purchases   |          | 735 (........) | |
| 31 Jan | Balances c/d |         | 25 (........) | 260 (........) |
|        |             | 30       | 1,000 | 7,060 |

A     Cash paid for the purchase of goods
B     The amount of the bank overdraft
C     Discount allowed by a creditor for prompt payment
D     Cheque received for the sale of a motor van
E     Cash withdrawn from bank
F     The balance in the firm's bank account
G     Value of a cheque received from a debtor
H     Cash paid into bank
I     Purchase of a motor van, paid for by cheque
J     Discount allowed to a debtor for prompt payment
K     Value of a cheque sent to a creditor
L     Cash in hand at the end of the month

**9.10**  You operate a petty cash book with an imprest of £150. The following expenses, supported by vouchers, were paid out of the petty cash:

*Voucher Nos*

| | | | |
|---|---|---|---|
| 1 | 3 February | Postage | £10.00 |
| 2 | 5 February | Travelling expenses | £6.50 |
| 3 | 9 February | Cleaner's wages | £25.00 |
| 4 | 12 February | Stationery | £7.20 |
| 5 | 15 February | Postage | £10.00 |
| 6 | 18 February | Travelling expenses | £7.30 |
| 7 | 20 February | Cleaner's wages | £25.00 |
| 8 | 24 February | Stationery | £4.75 |
| 9 | 26 February | T B Collins, a creditor | £3.90 |
| 10 | 27 February | Miscellaneous | £4.15 |
| 11 | 27 February | Postage | £10.00 |
| 12 | 28 February | Cleaner's wages | £25.00 |

At 1 February you had a balance of £18.26 and received cash on that date to make up the figure to the imprest amount.

Required:
Draw up the petty cash book for the month of February, including the balancing and the amount paid on 1 March year 7 to make up the imprest figure. The analysis column headings are postage, travelling expenses, stationery, wages, miscellaneous and ledger.

**9.11**  F Salmon keeps her petty cash book on the imprest system. The imprest figure was set at £350. On 1 November year 8 the balance of petty cash brought forward was £155. The following transactions took place during November year 8:

Year 8

| | |
|---|---|
| 1 Nov | Drew cash from the bank to restore the imprest |
| 4 Nov | Postage stamps £20 |
| 6 Nov | Train fare reimbursed £25 |
| 9 Nov | Petrol £15 |
| 10 Nov | Stationery £38 |
| 12 Nov | Bus fares £2 |
| 15 Nov | Paid £16 to P Gates – this was to refund an overpayment on his account in the sales ledger |
| 16 Nov | Stamps £30 |
| 18 Nov | Motor van repairs £35 |
| 20 Nov | Stationery £47 |
| 23 Nov | Petrol £28 |
| 25 Nov | Miscellaneous expenses £17 |
| 28 Nov | Parcel post charges £19 |
| 30 Nov | Travelling expenses £38 |

Required:
Draw up F Salmon's petty cash book, using the following analysis columns: postage; travelling expenses; motor van expenses; stationery; miscellaneous expenses; ledger accounts. Balance the account at 30 November, bring down the balance of cash in hand at that date, and show the amount of cash drawn from the bank to restore the imprest on 1 December year 8.

**10.7**   Below is the cash book (bank columns only) of Andrew Clark for the month of May 20-0 together with his bank statement for the same period.

**Andrew Clark**

| Dr | | | CASH BOOK | | Cr |
|---|---|---|---|---|---|
| 20-0 | | Bank | 20-0 | | Bank |
| | | £ | | | £ |
| 1 May | Balance b/d | 4,200 | 2 May | Cheque no 422 | 136 |
| 14 May | Sales | 1,414 | 7 May | Cheque no 423 | 204 |
| 21 May | Sales | 1,240 | 27 May | Cheque no 424 | 214 |
| 28 May | Sales | 1,160 | | | |

# BANK STATEMENT

Southern Bank plc
Northbrook Branch

In account with:
Mr Andrew Clark

| Date | Detail | Debit £ | Credit £ | Balance £ |
|---|---|---|---|---|
| 20-0 | | | | |
| 1 May | | | | 4,200 |
| 5 May | Cheque no 422 | 136 | | 4,064 |
| 10 May | Cheque no 423 | 204 | | 3,860 |
| 15 May | Counter credit | | 1,414 | |
| 15 May | National Insurance Company | 284 | | 4,990 |
| 22 May | Counter credit | | 1,240 | 6,230 |
| 31 May | Service charges | 100 | | 6,130 |

You are to:

(a)   rewrite the cash book making any adjustments you consider necessary

(b)   balance the cash book and bring the balance down

(c)   prepare a bank reconciliation statement as at 31 May 20-0

**10.8** Given below are the bank account and bank statement of C Cod for the month of May 20-9.

### C Cod's Bank Account

| | | £ | | | £ |
|---|---|---|---|---|---|
| 1 May | Balance | 144.00 | 9 May | M Roe | 108.00 |
| 10 May | Sales | 134.00 | 7 May | Drawings | 80.00 |
| 19 May | F Haddock | 300.00 | 18 May | Cash | 30.00 |
| 31 May | V Perch | 90.00 | 19 May | E Skate | 84.00 |
| 31 May | B Tench | 48.00 | 24 May | British Gas | 36.00 |
| | | | 29 May | N Fish | 108.00 |

**THE IZAAK WALTON BANK PLC**

**STATEMENT OF ACCOUNT**

C Cod
14 Pond Street
Banktown

123578

31 May 20-9

| Date | Detail | Debit | Credit | Balance |
|---|---|---|---|---|
| 1 May | Balance | | | 144.00 (cr) |
| 9 May | 00820 | 108.00 | | 36.00 |
| 10 May | Sundries | | 134.00 | 170.00 |
| 11 May | 00821 | 80.00 | | 90.00 |
| 18 May | 00822 | 30.00 | | 60.00 |
| 24 May | Cheque | | 300.00 | 360.00 |
| 24 May | 00823 | 84.00 | | 276.00 |
| 29 May | Mortgage SO | 90.00 | | 186.00 |
| 31 May | 00824 | 36.00 | | 150.00 |
| 31 May | Charges | 14.00 | | 136.00 |

You are to:

(a) Starting with the final balance on the bank account, which you have to calculate, bring the bank account up-to-date by referring to the bank statement of account

(b) Prepare a bank reconciliation statement for C Cod as on 31 May 20-9

**10.9** Kirsty McDonald has recently received the following bank statement:

**National Bank plc**
Kirsty McDonald Statement of Account

| Date | Details | Debits £ | Credits £ | Balance £ |
|---|---|---|---|---|
| 20-0 | | | | |
| 30 Oct | Balance | | | 841 |
| 31 Oct | 606218 | 23 | | 818 |
| 5 Nov | Sundry Credit | | 46 | 864 |
| 7 Nov | 606219 | 161 | | 703 |
| 9 Nov | Direct Debit | 18 | | 685 |
| 12 Nov | 606222 | 93 | | 592 |
| 15 Nov | Sundry Credit | | 207 | 799 |
| 19 Nov | 606223 | 246 | | 553 |
| 19 Nov | Bank Giro Credit | | 146 | 699 |
| 20 Nov | Bank Giro Credit | | 246 | 945 |
| 21 Nov | 606221 | 43 | | 902 |
| 21 Nov | Sundry Credit | | 63 | 965 |
| 22 Nov | Bank Giro Credit | | 79 | 1,044 |
| 23 Nov | Loan Interest | 391 | | 653 |
| 26 Nov | 606220 | 87 | | 566 |
| 26 Nov | Deposit A/C Interest | | 84 | 650 |
| 27 Nov | 606226 | 74 | | 576 |
| 28 Nov | Sundry Credit | | 88 | 664 |
| 30 Nov | 606225 | 185 | | 479 |

Her cash book showed the following details:

| 20-0 | | £ | 20-0 | | Cheque No | £ |
|---|---|---|---|---|---|---|
| 1 Nov | Balance b/d | 818 | 2 Nov | Rent | 219 | 161 |
| 5 Nov | B Mason | 46 | 5 Nov | H Gibson | 220 | 87 |
| 8 Nov | K Dean | 146 | 7 Nov | G Wise | 221 | 43 |
| 14 Nov | G Hunt | 207 | 8 Nov | T Allen | 222 | 93 |
| 16 Nov | C Charlton | 79 | 12 Nov | Gas | 223 | 246 |
| 19 Nov | D Banks | 63 | 15 Nov | F Causer | 224 | 692 |
| 26 Nov | P Perry | 88 | 19 Nov | M Lewis | 225 | 185 |
| 28 Nov | A Palmer | 29 | 23 Nov | G Bridges | 226 | 74 |
| 30 Nov | J Dixon | 17 | 29 Nov | L Wilson | 227 | 27 |
| 30 Nov | Balance c/d | 206 | 29 Nov | P Brown | 228 | 91 |
| | | 1,699 | | | | 1,699 |

Required:

(a)  Bring the cash book balance of £206 up-to-date as at 30 November 20-0

(b)  Draw up a bank reconciliation statement as at 30 November 20-0

**10.10** The following account appears in your purchases ledger:

### Convex Co Ltd

| 20-9 | | £ | 20-9 | | £ |
|---|---|---|---|---|---|
| 7 Oct | Bank | 711 | 1 Oct | Balance b/d | 776 |
| 7 Oct | Discount | 37 | 4 Oct | Purchases | 498 |
| 30 Oct | Bank | 1,235 | 25 Oct | Purchases | 1,022 |
| | Discount | 65 | | | |
| 31 Oct | Balance c/d | 248 | | | |
| | | 2,296 | | | 2,296 |
| | | | 1 Nov | Balance b/d | 248 |

During the first week in November a statement of account was received from Convex Co Ltd as follows:

| 20-9 | | £ | £ | £ |
|---|---|---|---|---|
| 1 Oct | Balance | | | 1,000 |
| 4 Oct | Sales | 498 | | 1,498 |
| 5 Oct | Bank | | 220 | |
| | Discount | | 4 | 1,274 |
| 10 Oct | Bank | | 711 | |
| | Discount | | 37 | 526 |
| 25 Oct | Sales | 1,022 | | 1,548 |

You are required to:

(a) reconcile the opening balance of £1,000 on the statement with that of £776 in your books

(b) reconcile the closing balance of £248 on your ledger account with that of £1,548 shown on the statement

**12.8** (a) Complete the table below for each item (1) to (7) indicating with a tick:

(i) whether the item would normally appear in the debit or credit column of the trial balance, and

(ii) in which 'final account' the item would appear at the end of the accounting period.

| | (i) TRIAL BALANCE | | (ii) FINAL ACCOUNTS | | |
| | Debit | Credit | Trading | Profit/Loss | Balance Sheet |
|---|---|---|---|---|---|
| 1. Rent paid | | | | | |
| 2. Van | | | | | |
| 3. Sales | | | | | |
| 4. Creditors | | | | | |
| 5. Purchases | | | | | |
| 6. Capital | | | | | |
| 7. Salaries | | | | | |

(b) Name one item not necessarily included in part (a), which could appear more than once in the final accounts at the year-end.

**12.9** The following trial balance was extracted from the books of Jane Walsh (who is the proprietor of a fabric shop) at the end of her financial year 30 April 20-0:

**Trial balance as at 30 April 20-0**

| | Dr £ | Cr £ |
|---|---|---|
| Sales | | 30,000 |
| Purchases | 15,700 | |
| Shop fittings | 13,000 | |
| Capital | | 15,000 |
| Opening stock | 4,700 | |
| Bank | 610 | |
| Cash | 100 | |
| Shop wages | 4,420 | |
| Debtors | 120 | |
| Drawings | 3,500 | |
| Creditors | | 2,030 |
| Light and heat | 260 | |
| Rent | 4,500 | |
| Insurance | 120 | |
| | 47,030 | 47,030 |

In preparing the year-end accounts, the following should be accounted for:
• the stock at the end of the year was valued at £4,400

You are required to:
(a) prepare Jane's trading account for the year ended 30 April 20-0
(b) prepare Jane's profit and loss account for the year ended 30 April 20-0
(c) draft Jane's balance sheet as at 30 April 20-0

**13.7**   The following trial balance was extracted from the books of Jane Osman who is the proprietor of a computer store, at the end of her financial year 31 March 20-2:

**TRIAL BALANCE**
**as at 31 March 20-2**

|  | Dr £ | Cr £ |
|---|---|---|
| Sales |  | 60,800 |
| Purchases | 31,400 |  |
| Shop fittings | 26,000 |  |
| Capital |  | 29,000 |
| Opening Stock (1 April 20-1) | 9,400 |  |
| Bank | 1,220 |  |
| Cash | 190 |  |
| Shop wages | 8,850 |  |
| Debtors | 230 |  |
| Drawings | 7,000 |  |
| Creditors |  | 4,550 |
| Light and heat | 520 |  |
| Rent | 8,500 |  |
| Insurance | 240 |  |
| Sales returns | 800 |  |
|  | 94,350 | 94,350 |

In preparing the year-end accounts, the following should be accounted for:
1.   the stock at the end of the year was valued at £8,800
2.   there is an accrual on shop wages amounting to £350
3.   the insurance is paid in advance by £60

You are required to:
(a)   prepare Jane's trading account for the year ended 31 March 20-2
(b)   prepare Jane's profit and loss account for the year ended 31 March 20-2
(c)   draft Jane's balance sheet as at 31 March 20-2

**13.8** Sandra Black operates a secretarial service to farmers and the following trial balance was extracted from her books on 31 May 20-0.

|                                | £      | £      |
|--------------------------------|--------|--------|
| Income from clients            |        | 32,500 |
| Commissions from other sources |        | 800    |
| Discounts received             |        | 150    |
| Stationery                     | 2,100  |        |
| Wages                          | 7,600  |        |
| Equipment                      | 4,500  |        |
| Vehicles                       | 6,500  |        |
| Rent and rates                 | 2,350  |        |
| Vehicle expenses               | 2,000  |        |
| Light and heat                 | 800    |        |
| Insurance                      | 850    |        |
| Telephone                      | 280    |        |
| Sundry expenses                | 175    |        |
| Drawings                       | 11,200 |        |
| Debtors                        | 760    |        |
| Creditors                      |        | 670    |
| Bank overdraft                 |        | 250    |
| Cash in hand                   | 175    |        |
| Capital                        |        | 4,920  |
|                                | 39,290 | 39,290 |

*Notes:*
(a)  At 31 May 20-0 there is an unpaid telephone bill of £52 and an unpaid electricity bill of £45.
(b)  Business rates prepaid at 31 May 20-0 are £120.
(c)  On 31 May 20-0 there is an unused stock of stationery valued at £150.

You are required to:
Prepare a profit and loss account for Sandra Black for the year ended 31 May 20-0 and a balance sheet as at that date, showing clearly therein the value of her capital, fixed assets, current assets and current liabilities.

**13.9** The trial balance of Bilton Potteries prepared after calculation of the gross profit is shown below:

**BILTON POTTERIES**
**Trial balance as at 31 January 20-2**

|  | Debit | Credit |
|---|---|---|
|  | £ | £ |
| Capital |  | 7,000 |
| Premises | 5,000 |  |
| Bank | 3,218 |  |
| Debtors | 434 |  |
| Stock (31 January 20-2) | 1,000 |  |
| Creditors |  | 870 |
| Drawings | 3,800 |  |
| Insurance | 450 |  |
| Rent receivable |  | 225 |
| Rates | 500 |  |
| Wages | 5,200 |  |
| Gross profit for year-ended 31 January 20-2 |  | 11,507 |
|  | 19,602 | 19,602 |

A detailed review by the accountant revealed that the following adjustments were outstanding:

(i)     Rates amounting to £100 had been paid in advance.

(ii)    Rent receivable of £75 was still outstanding at 31 January 20-2.

(iii)   The insurance total included the payment of £50 for private house contents insurance.

(iv)   Wages owing amounted to £300.

Requirements:

(a)   Open up the appropriate ledger accounts and post the above adjustments. Balance off these ledger accounts.

(b)   Prepare a profit and loss account for the year ended 31 January 20-2 and a balance sheet as at that date, after the above adjustments have been posted.

**13.10** A Bush is a sole trader who occupies rented premises. The annual rental is £2,400 which he pays quarterly. His lease and financial year commenced on 1 August year 1.

During his first financial year, A Bush made the following payments in respect of rent:

|        |             | £   |
|--------|-------------|-----|
| Year 1 | 1 August    | 600 |
|        | 4 November  | 600 |
|        |             |     |
| Year 2 | 31 March    | 600 |
|        | 8 August    | 600 |

He paid rates on the premises as follows:

| Year 1 | 31 August  | £75 for period 1 August to 30 September year 1   |
|--------|------------|--------------------------------------------------|
|        | 22 October | £220 for period 1 October to 31 March year 2     |
| Year 2 | 17 April   | £270 for period 1 April to 30 September year 2   |

He paid electricity bills as follows:

| Year 1 | 17 October | £310 |
|--------|------------|------|
| Year 2 | 21 January | £390 |
| Year 2 | 10 April   | £360 |

An electricity bill of £420 accrued due had not been paid.

Required:
(i)  Open the following accounts and, for the year ended 31 July year 2, enter the payments and make the necessary year-end adjustments for prepayments or accruals. Enter the transfers to profit and loss account and bring down balances at 1 August year 2.
   (a)  Rent payable
   (b)  Rates
   (c)  Electricity

(ii) Show the relevant extracts covering the above items from the balance sheet of A Bush as at 31 July year 2.

**14.8** Bert Greenwood bought a new vending machine for his business on 1 January 20-7 at a cost of £8,000. He intends to write off depreciation of the machine at the end of each business year which is 31 December. Greenwood however cannot decide whether to write off the depreciation by the straight-line method or the reducing balance method.

Required:
(a)  Prepare the provision for depreciation of machinery account as it should appear for the years 20-7 and 20-8 under:
   (i)   straight-line method at 12.5% per annum;
   (ii)  reducing balance method at 15% per annum.
(b)  The balance sheet extracts for the years 20-7 and 20-8 showing the book value of the machinery after depreciation by the reducing balance method.

**14.9** From the following trial balance extracted from the books of Paulo Gavinci, restaurateur, you are required to prepare the trading and profit and loss account for the year ended 30 April 20-0 and the balance sheet as at that date.

**Trial balance as at 30 April 20-0**

|  | Dr £ | Cr £ |
|---|---|---|
| Capital |  | 75,000 |
| Fixtures and fittings | 95,000 |  |
| Delivery vehicle | 8,000 |  |
| Opening stock | 2,000 |  |
| Cash | 450 |  |
| Bank |  | 4,300 |
| Bank loan (long-term) |  | 30,000 |
| Purchases | 190,250 |  |
| Sales |  | 300,000 |
| Creditors |  | 5,000 |
| Wages | 45,000 |  |
| Drawings | 25,000 |  |
| Purchases returns |  | 400 |
| Rent | 31,800 |  |
| General expenses | 17,200 |  |
|  | 414,700 | 414,700 |

You should also take the following additional information into account:
(a)   Closing stock at 30 April 20-0 was £1,600
(b)   Depreciation is to be provided as follows on a straight line basis:
      Fixtures and fittings – 20% on cost
      Delivery vehicle  – 25% on cost
(c)   Paulo took goods for personal use amounting to £250 at cost and an adjustment needs to be made for this
(d)   Provide for:
      Rent prepaid     £2,000
      Wages accrued  £1,000

**14.10** Colin and Reena Tan have run a small road haulage firm since 20-5, when they started the business with three transit vans which cost £30,000 each in 20-5.

The accounts relating to the transit vans have been lost and you are required to prepare and update the accounts from the following details and information available:

A charge of 20% depreciation has been charged on the vans using the reducing balance method On 1 January 20-8, a further transit van was purchased at a cost of £48,000 and on 30 June one of the original vans was sold for £10,000.

Depreciation is charged in the year of purchase but none in the year of sale.

You are required to prepare:

(a) vehicles account starting from 1 January 20-8;
(b) provision for depreciation of vehicles/transit vans;
(c) asset disposal account.

**14.11** The following table shows the cumulative effects of a succession of separate transactions on the assets and liabilities of a business:

| Transactions: | | A | B | C | D | E | F | G | H | I | J |
|---|---|---|---|---|---|---|---|---|---|---|---|
| | £000 | £000 | £000 | £000 | £000 | £000 | £000 | £000 | £000 | £000 | £000 |
| Assets: | | | | | | | | | | | |
| Property | 300 | 300 | 300 | 350 | 350 | 350 | 350 | 350 | 350 | 350 | 350 |
| Motor vans | 50 | 50 | 50 | 50 | 50 | 50 | 50 | 47 | 47 | 47 | 47 |
| Stock | 56 | 56 | 60 | 60 | 55 | 55 | 55 | 55 | 55 | 55 | 55 |
| Debtors | 65 | 65 | 65 | 65 | 72 | 72 | 72 | 72 | 72 | 72 | 65 |
| Prepayments | 10 | 10 | 10 | 10 | 10 | 10 | 10 | 10 | 10 | 10 | 10 |
| Bank | 17 | 47 | 47 | 47 | 47 | 44 | 34 | 38 | 33 | 32 | 39 |
| Cash | 2 | 2 | 2 | 2 | 2 | 5 | 5 | 5 | 5 | 5 | 5 |
| | 500 | 530 | 534 | 584 | 586 | 586 | 576 | 577 | 572 | 571 | 571 |
| | | | | | | | | | | | |
| Liabilities: | | | | | | | | | | | |
| Capital | 320 | 350 | 350 | 350 | 352 | 352 | 352 | 353 | 354 | 354 | 354 |
| Loan | 125 | 125 | 125 | 175 | 175 | 175 | 175 | 175 | 175 | 174 | 174 |
| Creditors | 42 | 42 | 46 | 46 | 46 | 46 | 46 | 46 | 40 | 40 | 40 |
| Accruals | 13 | 13 | 13 | 13 | 13 | 13 | 3 | 3 | 3 | 3 | 3 |
| | 500 | 530 | 534 | 584 | 586 | 586 | 576 | 577 | 572 | 571 | 571 |

Required:
Identify clearly and as fully as you can what transaction has taken place in each case. Do not copy out the table but use the reference letter for each transaction.

**15.6**   The following trial balance was extracted from the books of Paula Jones, a retail grocer, at the end of her financial year 31 March 20-0.

**Trial balance as at 31 March 20-0**

|  | Dr £ | Cr £ |
|---|---|---|
| Capital | | 200,000 |
| Debtors | 6,000 | |
| Creditors | | 4,000 |
| Drawings | 38,000 | |
| Cash in hand | 100 | |
| Bank | | 4,630 |
| Sales | | 168,000 |
| Purchases | 96,000 | |
| Opening stock | 6,400 | |
| Sales returns | 1,000 | |
| Carriage inwards | 400 | |
| Discount received | | 250 |
| Discount allowed | 380 | |
| Premises | 187,000 | |
| Fixtures and fittings (at cost) | 20,000 | |
| Provision for depreciation on fixtures | | 6,000 |
| Rates | 4,400 | |
| Insurance | 1,200 | |
| Wages and salaries | 22,000 | |
| | 382,880 | 382,880 |

In preparing the year-end accounts, the following should be accounted for:
1.   The closing stock was valued at £6,800
2.   Wages and salaries due but not paid amount to £1,000
3.   There is a prepayment on rates amounting to £600
4.   A debt amounting to £120 is considered irrecoverable
5.   Depreciation on fixtures is to be provided at the rate of 10% per annum on cost

You are required to:
(a)   prepare Paula's trading account for the year ended 31 March 20-0
(b)   prepare Paula's profit and loss account for the year
(c)   draft Paula's balance sheet as at 31 March 20-0

**15.7** The following trial balance was extracted from the books of Sandra Shenstone, a sole trader, as at the close of business on 30 June year 5:

|  | Dr | Cr |
|---|---|---|
|  | £ | £ |
| Capital account |  | 6,400 |
| Wages and salaries | 6,800 |  |
| Discounts allowed and received | 260 | 340 |
| Purchases and sales | 12,830 | 26,700 |
| Rent | 2,600 |  |
| Bad debts written off | 420 |  |
| Drawings | 2,450 |  |
| Delivery van | 1,800 |  |
| Bank overdraft |  | 2,200 |
| Returns inwards | 340 |  |
| Office furniture and equipment, at cost | 1,600 |  |
| Van running expenses | 780 |  |
| Rates and insurance | 760 |  |
| Debtors and creditors | 4,650 | 2,950 |
| General office expenses | 320 |  |
| Stock, 1 July year 4 | 2,930 |  |
| Cash in hand | 50 |  |
|  | 38,590 | 38,590 |

The following adjustments are to be made:
- Provide for depreciation as follows:
  Delivery van – £600
  Office furniture and equipment – 25% per annum on cost
- A provision of 2% of Debtors is to be created for doubtful debts
- Stock, 30 June year 5 – £3,160

Required:
Prepare a trading and profit and loss account for the year ended 30 June year 5, together with a balance sheet at that date.

**15.8** The following is the trial balance extracted from the ledger of Stamper, a sole trader who runs a shop, at 31 December 20-9:

|  | £ | £ |
|---|---:|---:|
| Capital 1 January 20-9 |  | 52,500 |
| Drawings | 20,000 |  |
| Sales |  | 150,750 |
| Purchases | 112,800 |  |
| Stock at 1 January 20-9 | 25,600 |  |
| Wages | 12,610 |  |
| Rent | 2,500 |  |
| Motor expenses | 1,240 |  |
| Motor vehicle: |  |  |
| at cost | 17,000 |  |
| accumulated depreciation at 1 January 20-9 |  | 3,000 |
| Equipment: |  |  |
| at cost | 15,000 |  |
| accumulated depreciation at 1 January 20-9 |  | 4,500 |
| Bank | 900 |  |
| Debtors | 9,950 |  |
| Creditors |  | 8,100 |
| Cash float | 250 |  |
| Insurance | 1,000 |  |
|  | 218,850 | 218,850 |

You are given the following additional information:
1.  Stock at 31 December 20-9 was valued at £27,350.
2.  Rent of £500 (included in the figure of £2,500 above) was prepaid at 31 December 20-9.
3.  Motor expenses of £140 are to be accrued at 31 December 20-9.
4.  A bad debt of £200 is to be written off.
5.  An invoice for insurance of £450 was wrongly recorded as purchases, and is included under purchases in the trial balance.
6.  The motor vehicle is depreciated on the straight line basis assuming a life of four years and a residual value of £5,000; the equipment is depreciated on the reducing balance basis using an annual rate of 30%.

Required:
Prepare the trading and profit and loss account of Stamper for the year to 31 December 20-9 and the balance sheet at that date.

**15.9** The following trial balance was extracted from the books of Percival Porteous at 31 May 20-0.

### Trial balance as at 31 May 20-0

| | £ | £ |
|---|---:|---:|
| Capital | | 54,960 |
| Drawings | 8,280 | |
| Premises at cost | 54,000 | |
| Sundry debtors and creditors | 7,500 | 6,228 |
| Opening stock | 11,100 | |
| Salaries | 5,280 | |
| Carriage inwards | 2,190 | |
| Carriage outwards | 2,340 | |
| Rates and insurance | 2,790 | |
| Purchases and sales | 102,000 | 145,185 |
| Returns inwards and outwards | 780 | 1,440 |
| Advertising | 1,041 | |
| Bad debts | 240 | |
| Rent receivable | | 960 |
| Office equipment at cost | 6,000 | |
| Shop fittings at cost | 18,000 | |
| Provision for depreciation: | | |
|     Office equipment | | 1,200 |
|     Shop fittings | | 4,800 |
| Cash in hand | 1,020 | |
| Bank overdraft | | 7,488 |
| Provision for bad debts | | 300 |
| | 222,561 | 222,561 |

You are given the following additional information:
(i)    Stock valued at 31 May 20-0 £12,600
(ii)    Salaries due but unpaid £1,800
(iii)    Rates and insurance prepaid £310
(iv)    The provision for bad debts is to be adjusted to 5% of debtors outstanding on 31 May 20-0
(v)    Depreciation is written off fixed assets as follows:
    Office equipment 10% per annum using the straight line basis
    Shop fittings 5% per annum using the reducing balance

You are required to:
Prepare Porteous's trading and profit and loss account for the year ended 31 May 20-0 showing clearly
(a)    the cost of goods sold
(b)    gross profit and net profit
and the balance sheet as at 31 May 20-0, highlighting the working capital.

**16.3** The following trial balance has been extracted by the book-keeper of Matt Smith at 31 December 20-8:

|  | Dr £ | Cr £ |
|---|---|---|
| Stock at 1 January 20-8 | 14,350 | |
| Purchases | 114,472 | |
| Sales | | 259,688 |
| Rates | 13,718 | |
| Heating and lighting | 12,540 | |
| Wages and salaries | 42,614 | |
| Motor vehicle expenses | 5,817 | |
| Advertising | 6,341 | |
| Premises | 75,000 | |
| Office equipment | 33,000 | |
| Motor vehicles | 21,500 | |
| Debtors | 23,854 | |
| Bank | 1,235 | |
| Cash | 125 | |
| Capital | | 62,500 |
| Drawings | 12,358 | |
| Loan from bank | | 35,000 |
| Creditors | | 14,258 |
| Value Added Tax | | 5,478 |
| | 376,924 | 376,924 |

Note: stock at 31 December 20-8 was valued at £16,280

You are to prepare the figures for the final accounts of Matt Smith for the year ended 31 December 20-8, using the extended trial balance method.

**16.4** The following trial balance has been extracted by the book-keeper of Jane Jones, who sells carpets, as at 31 December 20-9:

|  | Dr | Cr |
|---|---|---|
|  | £ | £ |
| Debtors | 37,200 | |
| Creditors | | 30,640 |
| Value Added Tax | | 4,280 |
| Bank | 14,640 | |
| Capital | | 50,500 |
| Sales | | 289,620 |
| Purchases | 182,636 | |
| Stock at 1 January 20-9 | 32,020 | |
| Wages and salaries | 36,930 | |
| Heat and light | 3,640 | |
| Rent and rates | 11,294 | |
| Vehicles | 20,000 | |
| Provision for depreciation on vehicles | | 4,000 |
| Equipment | 10,000 | |
| Provision for depreciation on equipment | | 1,000 |
| Sundry expenses | 1,690 | |
| Motor expenses | 3,368 | |
| Drawings | 26,622 | |
| | 380,040 | 380,040 |

Notes at 31 December 20-9:
- stock was valued at £34,000
- bad debts of £2,200 are to be written off and a provision for bad debts of 5% is to be created
- vehicles are to be depreciated at 20% per annum and equipment at 10% per annum (both using the reducing balance method)
- there are sundry expenses accruals of £270, and rates prepayments of £2,190

You are to prepare the figures for the final accounts of Jane Jones for the year ended 31 December 20-9, using the extended trial balance method.

**17.7**   The following information relates to Maynard Autos Limited:

|  | Purchases | Sales |
|---|---|---|
| June 20-1 | 800 units @ £6.00 | |
| July 20-1 | | 700 units |
| September 20-1 | 1,200 units @ £7.00 | |
| December 20-1 | | 600 units |
| February 20-2 | 1,000 units @ £8.00 | |
| April 20-2 | | 400 units |
| May 20-2 | 700 units @ £10.00 | |

You have been asked to value the stock:
(i)   using the FIFO method
(ii)   using the LIFO method

**17.8**   A and B are in business, buying and selling goods for resale. Neither of them are accountants but A has read a book on stock control whereas B has purchased a software package for daily stock records. During September 20-9 the following transactions occurred:

| 1 September | Balance brought forward:  NIL |
|---|---|
| 3 September | Bought 200 units @ £1.00 each |
| 7 September | Sold 180 units |
| 8 September | Bought 240 units @ £1.50 each |
| 14 September | Sold 170 units |
| 15 September | Bought 230 units @ £2.00 each |
| 21 September | Sold 150 units |

A prepares the stores ledger card using the LIFO method and B uses the same data to test the software package which uses the weighted average method of pricing.

You are required to:
(a)   show the ledger cards as they would appear for each method (calculations should be made to two decimal places of £1.00);
(b)   comment on the effect on profits of using each method of valuing stock.

**17.9** D Swift maintains manually prepared stock record cards for the recording of the receipts and issues of various items of stock held in the stores.

You are required to:
(i)     draw up a stock record card showing the following rulings and headings:

Item                                                               STOCK CARD

| Date | Details | Receipts | | Issues | | Balance | |
|---|---|---|---|---|---|---|---|
|  |  | Units | £ | Units | £ | Units | £ |
| 20-9<br>1 Sep | Balance |  |  |  |  | 12 | 144 |

(ii)    record the following movements of the item of stock reference number DW/04 for the month of September 20-9. The cost price of each item is £12 and there were 12 items in stock at 1 September 20-9.

*Receipts*

|  |  |  |
|---|---|---|
| 8 September | Invoice no 784 | 20 units |
| 15 September | Invoice no 847 | 48 units |
| 22 September | Invoice no 984 | 20 units |

*Issues*

|  |  |  |
|---|---|---|
| 6 September | Issue Note no A237 | 8 units |
| 17 September | Issue Note no D534 | 18 units |
| 24 September | Issue Note no B631 | 64 units |

On making a physical stockcheck on 30 September 20-9, Swift discovered that there were 8 units in stock. Adjust the stock record card for this difference and give some explanation.

**18.4**   On 1 May 20-0 the financial position of Carol Green was as follows:

|  | £ |
|---|---|
| Freehold premises | 45,000 |
| Fixtures and fittings | 12,500 |
| Motor vehicles | 9,500 |
| Bank overdraft | 2,800 |
| Cash in hand | 650 |
| Stock in hand | 1,320 |
| F Hardy (a trade debtor) | 160 |
| A Darby (a trade creditor) | 270 |

You are required to:
make a journal entry for the above showing clearly the capital of Carol Green on 1 May 20-0.

**18.5**   W E Carryit set up in business as a haulage contractor on 1 November 20-5. He decides to maintain his vehicle account at cost and to keep a separate provision for depreciation account. Vehicles are to be depreciated by 25% per annum using the reducing balance method. Depreciation is to be calculated on assets in existence at the end of each year, a full year's depreciation being charged in the year of purchase and none being charged in the year of disposal.

| 1 November 20-5 | Bought lorry costing £12,000, paying by cheque. |
|---|---|
| 6 December 20-6 | Bought lorry costing £18,000, paying by cheque. |
| 1 January 20-7 | The lorry bought on 1 November 20-5 was written off in an accident; the insurance company paying £8,450 in full settlement of the claim. |
| 7 March 20-8 | A new lorry costing £28,000 was bought on credit from Supatruks Ltd; they allowing £13,500 (ie its book value) in part exchange for the lorry bought on 6 December 20-6. The balance is to be paid in one year's time. |

You are required to:

(a)   prepare the vehicle accounts and provision for depreciation accounts for the years ended 31 October 20-6, 20-7 and 20-8, and to show how vehicles would have appeared in the balance sheet as at those dates.

(b)   give journal entries for the transactions which took place on 1 January 20-7 and 7 March 20-8.

*Note:* Disposal accounts are not required.

**19.6**   The Cashier extracts a trial balance which fails to agree; he then places the difference in a suspense account and tries to find the errors which have caused his trial balance to disagree.

The following errors are found:

(a)   Discount allowed to Forest and Company entered as £35 debited to their account.

(b)   Purchases of goods for £910 from Drystone Brothers posted to their account in error as £700.

(c)   Sales day book had been overcast by £70.

(d)   Balance on Clair and Sons' account of £245 in the sales ledger extracted in error as £385.

Show the suspense account after the above errors have been adjusted and the amount of the original error has been placed in the account.

**19.7**   Sally Jones was not able to balance her trial balance at 30 April 20-0 so she opened a suspense account to balance the trial balance.

Subsequently she discovered the following errors:

1.   the sale proceeds of an old delivery van amounting to £700 were placed to the sales account

2.   discount allowed amounting to £400 were entered as a credit balance in the trial balance

3.   debtors amounting to £500 had not been included in the trial balance total

You are required to:

(a)   make appropriate journal entries to rectify the errors

(b)   draft the suspense account after the errors have been corrected showing the original balance

Sally also wishes to create a provision for bad debts for £500 and write off a bad debt for Simon Joseph for £250

Draft the journal entry for these items.

**19.8** William Trent, in business as a dealer in hardware goods, found that his trial balance at 30 September year 12 did not agree and accordingly opened a suspense account. A subsequent search revealed the following errors or omissions:

1. Goods returned by F Mortimer £124 had been credited to his account and entered in the returns outwards book.
2. A cheque for £47 received from L Johnson had been dishonoured and posted in error from the cash book to the general expenses account. Trent had no intention as yet of treating the debt as irrecoverable.
3. Trent had taken goods, value £225 at cost, for his personal use: no entry had been made in the books.
4. A credit note for £850 in respect of a trade-in allowance obtained on one of the business motor vans had been incorrectly credited to both sales account and motor vans disposal account.
5. A payment by cheque of £45 for having the computer installation serviced had been posted to the computer asset account.

Required:
(i) Journal entries correcting these errors/omissions, including narrations.
(ii) The suspense account

   *Note:* If no entry is required in respect of any item, state this as a note beneath the account.
(iii) A statement, in the following form, showing the effect of each of these errors/omissions on the profit of the business:

|  | Profit under-stated £ | Profit over-stated £ |
|---|---|---|
| 1. | | |
| 2. | | |
| 3. | | |
| 4. | | |
| 5. | | |

**20.6** The sales ledgers of John Hine Limited were split into two sections and each section was balanced separately. Section 1 covered all dealings with food. Section 2 covered all dealings with clothing.

On 1 January the sales ledger balances were:

| | | | | |
|---|---|---|---|---|
| Section 1 | £84,200 debit | | Section 2 | £136,200 debit |
| Section 1 | £190 credit | | Section 2 | £1,260 credit |

During the twelve months to 31 December the books of original entry showed the following:

| | Section 1 | Section 2 |
|---|---|---|
| Sales | 678,672 | 497,285 |
| Cash received from debtors | 697,384 | 526,294 |
| Returns inwards | 3,475 | 1,226 |
| Discount allowed | 2,760 | 887 |
| Bad debts written off | 3,660 | 1,284 |

At 31 December the credit balances in the sales ledger were:

| | | | |
|---|---|---|---|
| Section 1 | £281 | Section 2 | £1,328 |

You are required to prepare control accounts for the two sections for the year ended 31 December and to carry down the balances as at that date.

**20.7** On 1 January 20-7, the balances in the bought ledger (purchases ledger) of John Matthews & Co, were £13,140.

During the half-year ending 30 June 20-7, transactions had taken place which resulted as follows:

| | £ |
|---|---|
| Purchases | 69,010 |
| Cash paid to creditors | 59,328 |
| Discount receivable | 2,472 |
| Purchases returns | 930 |
| Interest charged by creditors | 150 |
| Transfers to credit accounts in sales ledger | 220 |
| Cash overpaid returned | 20 |

(a) Prepare the bought ledger control account for the half-year.

(b) Give two reasons for keeping such an account.

**20.8** Rocker Ltd keeps control accounts for its sales and purchases ledgers which it balances at the end of each month. The balances on these accounts at 31 March 20-0 were:

|  | Debit £ | Credit £ |
|---|---|---|
| Purchases ledger | 782 | 78,298 |
| Sales ledger | 95,617 | 613 |

The following transactions and adjustments took place during April 20-0:

|  | £ |
|---|---|
| Sales on credit | 759,348 |
| Purchases on credit | 621,591 |
| Cash sales | 202,651 |
| Cash purchases | 7,985 |
| Returns from credit customers | 3,549 |
| Returns to credit suppliers | 4,581 |
| Cash received from credit customers | 703,195 |
| Cash paid to credit suppliers | 612,116 |
| Discounts received | 8,570 |
| Discounts allowed | 25,355 |
| Bad debts written off | 5,123 |
| Provision for doubtful debts increased by | 458 |

At 30 April 20-0, there were credit balances on the sales ledger totalling £161 and debit balances on the purchases ledger totalling £329.

Required:

Prepare the sales ledger control account and purchases ledger control account of Rocker Ltd for April 20-0, carrying down the balances as at 30 April 20-0.

**20.9** Mr James Ip keeps both sales and purchases ledgers. From the following details relating to his debtors and creditors, write up the sales ledger control account and the purchases ledger control account for the month of May 20-0. Explain why Mr Ip would prepare such control accounts and give two reasons for a credit balance on a customer's account.

| 20-0 |  | £ |
|---|---|---|
| 1 May | Sales ledger – debit balances | 9,134 |
|  | Sales ledger – credit balances | 44 |
|  | Purchases ledger – credit balances | 13,086 |
|  | Purchases ledger – debit balances | 53 |
| 31 May | Transactions for the month: |  |
|  | Sales (including cash sales of £2,794) | 14,318 |
|  | Purchases (including cash purchases of £3,122) | 24,677 |
|  | Cash received from debtors | 970 |
|  | Cheques received from debtors | 9,564 |
|  | Cheques paid out to creditors | 10,532 |
|  | Discount allowed | 382 |
|  | Discount received | 532 |
|  | Bad debts | 250 |
|  | Sales returns | 200 |
|  | Purchases returns | 908 |
|  | Dishonoured cheques | 58 |
|  | Transfer of a credit balance from the purchases ledger to the sales ledger | 160 |
|  | Sales ledger – debit balances | 9,226 |
|  | Sales ledger – credit balances | 80 |
|  | Purchases ledger – credit balances | 22,572 |
|  | Purchases ledger – debit balances | 116 |

**21.4**   James Harvey runs a stationery supplies shop. He is convinced that one of his employees is stealing stationery. He asks you to calculate from the accounting records the value of stock stolen. The following information is available:

- sales for the year, £180,000

- opening stock at the beginning of the year, £21,500

- purchases for the year, £132,000

- closing stock at the end of the year, £26,000

- the gross profit margin achieved on all sales is 30 per cent

You are to calculate the value of stock stolen (if any) during the year.

**21.5**   Bill Brown took out a statement of his financial position on 1 April 20-8 which showed the following:

|  | £ |
|---|---|
| Sundry creditors | 8,505 |
| Sundry debtors | 7,200 |
| Stock in trade | 1,350 |
| Cash and bank | 450 |
| Furniture and fittings | 2,655 |

After one year, during which Bill Brown introduced additional capital of £500 and withdrew £2,250 for his own requirements, his position was:

|  | £ |
|---|---|
| Sundry creditors | 6,831 |
| Sundry debtors | 5,400 |
| Stock in trade | 840 |
| Cash and bank | 1,350 |
| Furniture and fittings | 2,390 |

Required:

(a)   statements of affairs to show Bill Brown's capital position as at 1 April 20-8 and his new capital position one year later.

(b)   a statement showing the profit or loss made by Bill Brown for the year.

**21.6** Brian Withers runs a medium-sized family business as a general trader. He knows a great deal about selling but, sadly, very little about accounting. Brian is being very hard pressed to produce some trading results, and has asked your help in calculating his new profit or loss for the year to 30 April 20-8.

The only information available to you is a statement of his assets and liabilities at 1 May 20-7 and 30 April 20-8; details of these are given below:

|  | 1 May 20-7 | 30 April 20-8 |
|---|---|---|
|  | £ | £ |
| Cash at bank | 720 | 790 |
| Stock in trade | 6,400 | 6,700 |
| Trade debtors | 6,240 | 6,430 |
| Trade creditors | 1,330 | 1,450 |
| Fixed assets | 45,000 | 46,500 |
| Insurance paid in advance | 140 | 180 |
| Wages paid in arrears | 70 | 50 |
| Loan from father | 5,000 | 4,000 |

During the year Brian had taken monies from the business for his own private use to the value of £700 per month. During the financial year Brian had a small win on the football pools amounting to £2,000 which he paid into the business.

You are required to:

(a) prepare a statement of affairs at 1 May 20-7

(b) prepare a statement of affairs at 30 April 20-8

(c) calculate Brian's net profit or loss for the year

(d) give three advantages which a formal double-entry book-keeping system would have for Brian and his business

(e) explain why Brian should take account of payments in advance and payments in arrears

**21.7** D Bradley, a retailer, does not keep any books of account, but does operate a business bank account. A summary of the bank statements for the year ending 30 June 20-5 is given below.

| | £ | | £ |
|---|---|---|---|
| Receipts from customers | 22,820 | Opening balance | 2,025 |
| Additional capital paid in | 5,500 | Payments to creditors | 18,682 |
| | | Electricity | 1,825 |
| | | Rent and rates | 2,350 |
| | | Motor van | 2,400 |
| | | Closing balance | 1,038 |
| | 28,320 | | 28,320 |

During the year he paid expenses direct from cash received and these were estimated as £5,280 for wages and £1,250 for general expenses and D Bradley took drawings of £100 each week for himself.

D Bradley supplied the following details of his assets and liabilities at the year-end for the years 30 June 20-4 and 20-5:

| | 20-4 | 20-5 |
|---|---|---|
| | £ | £ |
| Fixtures at cost | 1,800 | 1,800 |
| Motor van at cost | | 2,400 |
| Stock | 13,680 | 12,790 |
| Debtors | 4,250 | 4,925 |
| Creditors | 2,575 | 3,520 |
| Accrued electricity | 485 | 520 |
| Prepaid rates | 280 | 340 |
| Cash in till | 120 | 210 |

| Depreciation is to be provided at | Fixtures 10% |
|---|---|
| | Motor van 25% |

You are required to prepare a trading and profit and loss account for the year ending 30 June 20-5 and a balance sheet as at 30 June 20-5.

**21.8** At 1 July year 6, the financial position of John Marcus, a dealer in fancy goods, was as follows:

| | £ | £ | | £ |
|---|---|---|---|---|
| Fixtures and fittings: | | | Capital account – J Marcus | 28,000 |
| At cost | 16,000 | | Trade creditors | 3,050 |
| *Less* aggregate depreciation | 6,400 | 9,600 | Electricity charges accrued | 290 |
| Stock-in-trade | | 12,400 | | |
| Trade debtors | | 2,900 | | |
| Prepayments (rates) | | 340 | | |
| Balance at bank | | 6,100 | | |
| | | 31,340 | | 31,340 |

Marcus does not keep a full set of account records but he was able to arrive at the following summarised data for the year which ended on 30 June year 7:

1. Sales for the year amounted to £117,460. Gross profit is 25% of sales.
2. Stock-in-trade, at cost, at 30 June year 7, has increased by 25% over the previous year.
3. Trade debtors at 30 June year 7 amounted to £5,200.
4. Trade creditors at 30 June year 7 amounted to £4,650.
5. Cash discounts for the year were as follows: allowed £720; received £560.
6. During the year he had acquired a motor van for £4,200 in cash.
7. Payments were made during the year as follows:
   Wages                        £12,680
   Rent, rates, electricity     £8,950
8. At 30 June year 7, electricity charges accrued were £260 and rent prepaid amounted to £520.
9. Marcus had written off bad debts amounting to £180 during the year.

Additional information:

- Depreciation was to be provided as follows:
  Fixtures and fittings    10% on cost
  Motor van                25% on cost

- Marcus wished to make a provision of 5% of debtors for bad debts at 30 June year 7. No such provision had been made at 30 June year 6.

Required:
Prepare for John Marcus:
(a) a trading and profit and loss account for the year ended 30 June year 7
(b) a balance sheet at 30 June year 7

**21.9** John Amos Limited (Wholesalers) had a fire at their warehouse on 30 November, the greater part of the stock being destroyed. Some stock was able to be salvaged and this was valued at £6,800.

The accounting records were kept in an office away from the fire and the accountant of John Amos was able to establish that in the last four months, sales were £251,200 and purchases £187,600.

The stock records showed that on 1 August stock had amounted to £94,300. The average gross profit on turnover during the last two years had been 22%. The business was fully insured against fire.

You are required to prepare the claim to be submitted to the insurance company in respect of stock destroyed by fire.

**22.5**  A group of young musicians intend to form a music society, meeting once a week commencing 1 September 20-0. They present the following financial estimates for your consideration:

1.  The club would expect 300 members, but only 50% of this target would be achieved in the first year. The membership fee would be £20 per annum.

2.  They can hire a hall for £20 per meeting, plus £5 weekly for light and heat.

3.  At the outset, they would need to buy stereo equipment costing £1,200.

4.  The equipment would be depreciated on a straight line basis over 4 years.

5.  The annual premium for all risks insurance will be £90 payable on commencement.

6.  Records costing £1,000 would be bought during the year. They would be treated as an expense of the society.

7.  It is estimated that each member would spend an average of £40 per annum on light refreshments. It is hoped to sell the refreshments at twice the purchase price.

You are required to:

(a)  Prepare an estimated receipts and payments account for the society's first year which would end on 31 August 20-1

(b)  Draw up an estimated income and expenditure account for the year ending 31 August 20-1

(c)  Draft the society's estimated balance sheet as at 31 August 20-1

**22.6**  The Secretary of the Greenroom Social Club issued the following receipts and payments account to members:

Receipts and Payments Account for the year to 30 June

|  | £ |  | £ |
|---|---|---|---|
| Cash balance | 1,620 | Wages | 15,300 |
| Subscriptions | 22,410 | Secretary's salary | 2,700 |
| Bank loan | 4,500 | Rent of hall | 900 |
| Games' fees | 270 | Printing and postage | 2,115 |
| Drink machine receipts | 936 | Purchase of new chairs | 3,240 |
|  |  | Loss on dance | 198 |
|  |  | Cash balance | 5,283 |
|  | 29,736 |  | 29,736 |

The Secretary gave the following information:

Subscriptions included £180 from previous year, £72 received in respect of advance payment for next year, and that £225 was due but unpaid.

Games' fees included £27 paid in advance for the following year's matches.

The cleaner had not been paid £108 for the month of June and was to be paid this amount in July.

Stationery purchased during the year and held in stock on 30 June was valued at £180. The furniture at 30 June was valued at £3,105 and this included what was purchased during the year. The accumulated fund at the previous 1 July was £1,800.

You are required to prepare an income and expenditure account for the club for the year ended 30 June and a balance sheet at that date.

**22.7** The assets and liabilities of the East Sutton Social Club as at 1 November 20-8 were:

Cash held at bank £380; furniture and equipment £420; bar stock £120; rent owing on premises £30.

The following is a summary of receipts and payments for the club for the year ended 31 October 20-9:

| Receipts | £ | Payments | £ |
|---|---|---|---|
| Balance 1 November 20-8 | 380 | Bar purchases | 1,485 |
| Subscriptions | 1,420 | Annual dance expenses | 580 |
| Annual dance | 750 | Rent of premises | 840 |
| Bar sales | 2,040 | Secretary's expenses | 225 |
| | | Purchase of furniture | 200 |
| | | Wages of caretaker | 580 |
| | | Balance 31 October 20-9 | 680 |
| | 4,590 | | 4,590 |

The following information was also available:

(i) Bar stock at 31 October 20-9 was £150

(ii) Rent for premises of £110 was owing at 31 October 20-9

You are required to:

(a) calculate the accumulated fund at 1 November 20-8

(b) prepare an income and expenditure account for the year ended 31 October 20-9, showing clearly the profit/loss on the bar and the dance

(c) prepare a balance sheet for the club as at 31 October 20-9

**22.8**   The honorary treasurer of the Capella Choir, a club for choral music enthusiasts, has prepared the following receipts and payments account for the year ended 31 May 20-8:

**Capella Choir**

*Receipts and Payments Account for the year ended 31 May 20-8*

| | £ | | £ |
|---|---|---|---|
| Cash and bank balances b/f | 410 | Secretarial expenses | 550 |
| Members' subscriptions | 1,480 | Rent of rehearsal room | 850 |
| Donations | 220 | Other rehearsal expenses | 350 |
| Sales of concert tickets | 2,680 | Fees and expenses | 2,870 |
| Grants and subsidies | 2,500 | Purchase of music | 1,300 |
| | | Travelling expenses | 490 |
| | | Stationery and printing | 670 |
| | | Cash and bank balances c/f | 210 |
| | 7,290 | | 7,290 |

The following valuations are also available:

| | 1 June 20-7 | 31 May 20-8 |
|---|---|---|
| | £ | £ |
| Subscriptions in arrears | 200 | 120 |
| Subscriptions in advance | 50 | 140 |
| Owing to suppliers of music | 510 | 660 |
| Stocks of music, at valuation | 6,160 | 7,100 |
| Grants and subsidies receivable | 950 | 1,400 |
| Travelling expenses accrued | 0 | 210 |

Required:

(a)   Prepare a calculation of the accumulated fund of the Capella Choir as at 1 June 20-7.

(b)   Draw up a summary subscriptions account for the year ended 31 May 20-8.

(c)   Prepare calculations of the following:

    1.   the depreciation charge on music for the year ended 31 May 20-8, and

    2.   grants and subsidies for the year ended 31 May 20-8.

(d)   Prepare the income and expenditure account for the Capella Choir for the year ended May 20-8 showing clearly the surplus or deficit for the year.

**23.5** Rexton, Sareeta and Sonia are in partnership, the capital invested in the partnership is £60,000, £35,000 and £20,000 respectively.

During the financial year ended 30 June 20-9 the partnership earned a net profit of £38,000.

The partners have agreed the following:
(i)   interest is to be allowed on capital at 12% per annum
(ii)  Sareeta and Sonia are to receive salaries of £10,000 and £8,600 respectively
(iii) profits and losses are to be shared in the ratio of 4:3:1

The partners had the following balances in their current accounts as at 30 June 20-9:

|         | £        |
|---------|----------|
| Rexton  | 1,400 Cr |
| Sareeta | 2,900 Dr |
| Sonia   | 1,165 Dr |

During the year to 30 June 20-9, the partners withdrew the following amounts from the partnership:

|         | £     |
|---------|-------|
| Rexton  | 6,300 |
| Sareeta | 4,700 |
| Sonia   | 9,800 |

You are required to prepare the appropriation account for the partnership and show each of the partner's current accounts as at 30 June 20-9.

**23.6**  D Brook and T Stream went into partnership on 1 January 20-2, each contributing £16,000 and £12,000 respectively as capital.

They agreed to share profits and losses equally and for T Stream to transfer £2,000 annually from 31 December 20-2 from his current account at each year end and until such time as his capital is the same as D Brook, the first payment being due on 31 December 20-2. Interest is to be allowed on capital at 10 per cent.

The following trial balance was prepared on 31 December 20-2:

|  |  | £ | £ |
|---|---|---:|---:|
| Capital accounts | D Brook | | 16,000 |
| | T Stream | | 12,000 |
| Drawings | D Brook | 3,500 | |
| | T Stream | 3,000 | |
| Purchases and sales | | 48,200 | 72,620 |
| Debtors and creditors | | 2,000 | 2,200 |
| Premises | | 25,000 | |
| Equipment and fixtures | | 7,000 | |
| Bank | | 1,260 | |
| Salaries | | 8,420 | |
| Rates | | 2,100 | |
| Advertising | | 320 | |
| Carriage inwards | | 180 | |
| Motor van rental | | 1,260 | |
| Discount allowed and received | | 320 | 480 |
| Bad debts | | 210 | |
| Heating and lighting | | 530 | |
| | | 103,300 | 103,300 |

The following information is available to complete the final accounts:

|  | £ |
|---|---:|
| • stock as at 31 December 20-2 | 6,280 |
| • a payment for advertising is due | 60 |
| • rates were paid in advance to 30 June 20-3 | 700 |

- equipment and fixtures are to be depreciated by 20 per cent per annum
- T Stream is to be given a commission of 2 per cent of the sales figure for the year but this is not in the accounts

You are required to prepare:

(a)  the partnership trading account for the year
(b)  the profit and loss account for the year
(c)  the appropriation account for the year
(d)  the current accounts for the year
(e)  a balance sheet of the partnership as at 31 December 20-2

**23.7** Gore and Pryor are in partnership with a partnership agreement which provides for the following:

(i)   Commission of 2% of sales to Gore

(ii)  Salary of £2,000 per annum payable to Pryor

(iii) Interest on partners' drawings: Gore £60; Pryor £50

(iv) Interest on capital at 10% per annum for each partner

(v)  Interest on Gore's loan at 12% per annum

(vi) Profit or loss sharing ratio: Gore 60%; Pryor 40%

The trial balance extracted from the partnership books at 31 December 20-9 was as follows:

|  | Dr | Cr |
|---|---|---|
|  | £ | £ |
| Premises | 29,600 |  |
| Equipment | 5,000 |  |
| Staff salaries | 4,200 |  |
| Administration expenses | 7,200 |  |
| Selling expenses | 5,400 |  |
| Bad debts written off | 300 |  |
| Provision for bad debts (1 January 20-9) |  | 100 |
| Debtors | 3,800 |  |
| Creditors |  | 4,900 |
| Stock (1 January 20-9) | 8,500 |  |
| Cash | 820 |  |
| Sales |  | 92,000 |
| Purchases | 53,000 |  |
| Carriage inwards | 500 |  |
| Gore – Capital at 1 January 20-9 |  | 12,000 |
| Gore – Current account at 1 January 20-9 |  | 900 |
| Gore – Drawings | 3,000 |  |
| Pryor – Capital at 1 January 20-9 |  | 8,000 |
| Pryor – Current account at 1 January 20-9 | 1,080 |  |
| Pryor – Drawings | 2,500 |  |
| Gore – Loan account |  | 7,000 |
|  | 124,900 | 124,900 |

Notes:

(i)    Stock at 31 December 20-9 was valued at £7,000

(ii)   Administration expenses paid in advance £400 and selling expenses outstanding at the year end £600

(iii)  Provision for doubtful debts at the year end to be adjusted to 5% of debtors

(iv)  Depreciation is charged on the book value of the equipment at 1 January 20-9 at the rate of 20% per annum

You are required to prepare from the information provided above, the

(a)   partnership trading and profit and loss account and appropriation account for the year ended 31 December 20-9

(b)   partnership balance sheet in vertical format as at 31 December 20-9

**24.4**  Rose, Tulip and Crocus are in partnership sharing profits and losses one-seventh, two-sevenths and four-sevenths respectively.

They are to dissolve the partnership and at the date of dissolution, the balances in the partnership books are:

|  |  | £ |
|---|---|---|
| Sundry creditors |  | 3,815 |
| Stock |  | 7,945 |
| Sundry debtors |  | 4,417 |
| Premises |  | 23,177 |
| Loan from Crocus |  | 2,450 |
| Capital accounts | Rose (credit) | 9,170 |
|  | Tulip (credit) | 10,290 |
|  | Crocus (credit) | 12,432 |
|  | Cash | 2,618 |

On sale of the assets the amount realised was:

| Stock | £7,812 |
|---|---|
| Premises | £21,000 |
| Debtors | £4,305 |

and the loan and all the creditors were paid off.

You are required to close all the above accounts and give the amounts each partner received.

**24.5** Alpha and Beta are in partnership. They share profits equally after Alpha has been allowed a salary of £4,000 pa. No interest is charged on drawings or allowed on current accounts or capital accounts. The trial balance of the partnership at 31 December 20-8 before adjusting for any of the items below, is as follows:

|  |  | Dr | Cr |
|---|---|---|---|
|  |  | £000 | £000 |
| Capital | – Alpha |  | 30 |
|  | – Beta |  | 25 |
| Current | – Alpha |  | 3 |
|  | – Beta |  | 4 |
| Drawings | – Alpha | 4 |  |
|  | – Beta | 5 |  |
| Sales |  |  | 200 |
| Stock 1 January 20-8 |  | 30 |  |
| Purchases |  | 103 |  |
| Operating expenses |  | 64 |  |
| Loan | – Beta (10%) |  | 10 |
|  | – Gamma (10%) |  | 20 |
| Land and buildings |  | 60 |  |
| Plant and machinery: |  |  |  |
|  | – cost | 70 |  |
|  | – depreciation to 31 December 20-8 |  | 40 |
| Debtors and creditors |  | 40 | 33 |
| Bank |  |  | 11 |
|  |  | 376 | 376 |

(i) Closing stock on hand at 31 December was £24,000.

(ii) On 31 December Alpha and Beta agree to take their manager, Gamma, into partnership. Gamma's loan account balance is to be transferred to a capital account as at 31 December. It is agreed that in future Alpha, Beta and Gamma will all share profits equally. Alpha will be allowed a salary of £4,000 as before, and Gamma will be allowed a salary of £5,000 pa (half of what he received in 20-8 as manager, included in operating expenses).

The three partners agree that the goodwill of the business at 31 December should be valued at £12,000, but is not to be recorded in the books. It is also agreed that land and buildings are to be revalued to a figure of £84,000 and that this revalued figure is to be retained and recorded in the accounts.

(iii) Interest on the loan has not been paid.

(iv) Included in sales are two items sold on 'sale or return' for £3,000 each. Each item had cost the business £1,000. One of these items was in fact returned on 4 January 20-9 and the other one was formally accepted by the customer on 6 January 20-9.

Required:

(a) Submit with appropriately labelled headings and subheadings:

    (i) partners' capital accounts in columnar form;

    (ii) partners' current accounts in columnar form;

    (iii) trading, profit and loss and appropriation account for 20-8;

    (iv) balance sheet as at 31 December 20-8

(b) Write a brief note to Gamma, who cannot understand why his capital account balance seems so much less than those of Alpha and Beta. Explain to him the adjustments you have made.

**25.7**   Swift Traders plc has an authorised share capital of £300,000 divided into 100,000 8% preference shares of £1 each and 200,000 ordinary shares of £1 each. All the preference shares have been issued at par and are fully paid: 150,000 of the ordinary shares have been issued at a premium of 25p per share and are fully paid.

The company also had loan capital consisting of £200,000 of 12% debentures.

On 1 November 20-8 the company's balance sheet showed retained profits of £12,890 and a general reserve of £22,760.

During the year ended 31 October 20-9 the company made a profit of £52,000 out of which the directors decided to:

(i)   transfer £5,000 to general reserve

(ii)   pay the preference dividend for the year

(iii)   declare an ordinary dividend of 12 pence per share

You are required to:

prepare the company's profit and loss appropriation account for the year ended 31 October 20-9 and the capital section of the balance sheet as at that date.

**25.8**   The authorised share capital of Highwood Co Ltd is 500,000 ordinary shares of £1 each. The following trial balance was extracted from the books of the company at the close of business on 31 December year 4.

|  | £ | £ |
|---|---|---|
| Issued and paid-up capital |  | 200,000 |
| Premises | 180,000 |  |
| Fixtures and fittings at cost | 70,000 |  |
| Purchases and sales | 327,000 | 509,000 |
| Debtors and creditors | 79,000 | 32,000 |
| Provision for depreciation on fixtures and fittings |  | 15,000 |
| Wages and salaries | 72,000 |  |
| Returns inwards | 7,000 |  |
| General expenses | 39,000 |  |
| Interest on debentures, half-year to 30 June year 4 | 3,000 |  |
| Insurance | 5,000 |  |
| Bad debts | 2,000 |  |
| Provision for bad and doubtful debts |  | 2,000 |
| Stock at 1 January year 4 | 28,000 |  |
| Bank balance | 23,000 |  |
| Profit and loss account at 1 January year 4 |  | 17,000 |
| 10% debentures |  | 60,000 |
|  | 835,000 | 835,000 |

Additional information:

1.   Stock at 31 December year 4 was valued at £29,000

2.   Wages due amounted to £2,000

3.   Insurance paid in advance amounted to £1,000

4.   The provision for doubtful debts is to be increased to £3,000

5.   The provision for depreciation on fixtures and fittings is to be increased by 10% of the cost pric

6.   A dividend of £0.15 per ordinary share is proposed for year 4

Required:

(i)   A trading and profit and loss account for the year ended 31 December year 4

(ii)   A balance sheet in vertical form as at 31 December year 4

**25.9** The following balances remain in the books after the completion of the profit and loss account of Maginn Company Ltd for the year ended 31 December 20-9.

|  | £ |
|---|---|
| Profit and loss account balance (1 January 20-9) | 17,400 |
| Net profit before tax and dividends (31 December 20-9) | 36,720 |
| Authorised Share Capital: |  |
| 175,000 £1 ordinary shares | 175,000 |
| 50,000 8% preference shares of £1 each | 50,000 |
| Issued Share Capital: |  |
| 150,000 £1 ordinary shares | 150,000 |
| 37,500 8% preference shares of £1 each | 37,500 |
| Premises at cost | 112,500 |
| Fixtures and fittings at cost | 60,000 |
| Office equipment at cost | 6,750 |
| Motor vans at cost | 30,000 |
| Provisions for depreciation (31 December 20-9): |  |
| Fixtures and fittings | 28,500 |
| Office equipment | 2,550 |
| Motor vans | 18,750 |
| Share premium account | 15,000 |
| 12.5% £1 mortgage debentures | 13,975 |
| Interim dividends: |  |
| Preference shareholders | 1,500 |
| Ordinary shareholders | 7,500 |
| Reserves | 15,000 |
| Debtors | 60,375 |
| Creditors | 38,400 |
| Stock at 31 December 20-9 | 59,730 |
| Expenses outstanding | 1,365 |
| Expenses prepaid | 1,800 |
| Bank balance | 35,005 |

The directors decide to recommend to:
(i)  transfer £7,500 to the reserves
(ii) provide for the final preference dividend and for a recommended final ordinary dividend of 7.5 pence in the £

From the information provided, you are required to prepare:
(a) Maginn Company Ltd's profit and loss appropriation account for the year ended 31 December 20-9
(b) the company's balance sheet in vertical format as at 31 December 20-9

*(Note: Ignore taxation)*

**26.6** The balances shown below are from the books of the Protem Manufacturing Company as at 30 September year 9:

|  | £ |
|---|---|
| Stocks at 1 October year 8: | |
| Raw materials | 39,000 |
| Work-in-progress at prime cost | 8,100 |
| Finished goods | 51,930 |
| Purchases of raw materials for the year | 214,760 |
| Sales | 365,752 |
| Returns outwards – raw materials | 1,350 |
| Plant and machinery, at cost | 93,000 |
| Office equipment | 19,800 |
| Factory wages | 33,560 |
| Factory    – lighting and heating | 13,700 |
| – power | 7,600 |
| – rates and insurance | 3,800 |

The following details are also available:

1.   Stocks at 30 September year 9:

| Raw materials | £43,630 |
|---|---|
| Work-in-progress at prime cost | £5,160 |
| Finished goods | £57,400 |

2.   Factory lighting and heating expenses
accrued at 30 September year 9          £760

3.   Factory rates and insurance paid in advance
at 30 September year 9          £240

4.   Depreciation is to be provided on plant and machinery at the rate of 15% per annum on cost

Required:

Prepare the manufacturing and trading account of Protem Manufacturing Company for the year ended 30 September year 9.

**26.7**  Chesterton Plc are manufacturers.
At the end of their accounting year, 30 April 20-9, the following information was available:

|  | £ |
|---|---:|
| Stocks, 1 May 20-8: | |
| raw materials | 17,500 |
| finished goods | 24,800 |
| work-in-progress | 15,270 |
| Wages and salaries: | |
| factory direct | 138,500 |
| factory indirect | 27,200 |
| Purchases of raw materials | 95,600 |
| Power and fuel (indirect) | 18,260 |
| Sales | 410,400 |
| Insurance | 3,680 |
| Returns inwards (finished goods) | 5,200 |
| Stocks, 30 April 20-9 | |
| raw materials | 13,200 |
| finished goods | 14,600 |
| work-in-progress | 15,700 |

*Notes:*

- The company's machinery cost £82,000 and the provision for depreciation on 1 May 20-8 was £27,000. Machinery is to be depreciated by 20% per annum using the reducing balance method.

- Fuel and power £390 is in arrears at 30 April 20-9; at the same date insurance £240 is prepaid.

- Insurance is to be allocated 5/8ths factory; 3/8ths administration

Required:

For Chesterton Plc

(a)  A manufacturing account for the year ended 30 April 20-9, showing clearly

    (i)  cost of raw materials consumed

    (ii)  prime cost

    (iii)  total cost of production

(b)  A trading account for the year ended 30 April 20-9 showing clearly

    (i)  cost of sales of finished goods

    (ii)  gross profit

**26.8** Makit is in business as a manufacturer and the following balances were extracted from his books on 31 October 20-9:

| | £ | £ |
|---|---:|---:|
| Stocks at 1 November 20-8: | | |
|    Raw materials | 2,400 | |
|    Finished goods | 16,750 | |
|    Work-in-progress | 4,500 | |
| Purchases raw materials | 87,900 | |
| Manufacturing wages | 94,000 | |
| Factory expenses | 22,670 | |
| Rent and property insurance | 6,780 | |
| Carriage on raw materials | 650 | |
| Plant and machinery at cost | 85,000 | |
| Office equipment at cost | 9,500 | |
| Motor vehicles at cost | 14,500 | |
| Provision for depreciation: | | |
|    Plant and machinery | | 22,000 |
|    Office equipment | | 3,400 |
|    Motor vehicles | | 4,500 |
| Light and heat | 6,000 | |
| Office salaries | 22,000 | |
| Office expenses | 7,800 | |
| Selling and distribution costs | 28,000 | |
| Sales | | 300,000 |
| Drawings | 18,000 | |
| Cash in hand | 780 | |
| Bank | | 8,680 |
| Capital | | 89,280 |
| Debtors | 6,400 | |
| Creditors | | 5,770 |
| | 433,630 | 433,630 |

You are required to:
Prepare the manufacturing, trading, profit and loss account for the year ended 31 October 20-9 and a balance sheet as at that date, after giving effect to the following adjustments:

(i) The stocks on 31 October 20-9 were:

| | |
|---|---|
|    Raw materials | £2,870 |
|    Finished goods | £14,600 |
|    Work-in-progress | £4,750 |

(ii) Light and heat and rent and insurance are to be apportioned three-quarters to manufacturing account and one-quarter to profit and loss account.

(iii) At 31 October 20-9 manufacturing wages of £600 were unpaid and rent had been prepaid by £380

(iv) Depreciation is to be written off fixed assets as follows:

| | £ |
|---|---:|
|    Plant and machinery | 8,500 |
|    Fixtures and fittings | 950 |
|    Vehicles | 2,500 |

**27.6**

The following are the balance sheets of Jane Clark's business for 20-3 and 20-4:

### BALANCE SHEET AS AT 30 SEPTEMBER

| | | 20-3 | | 20-4 |
|---|---|---|---|---|
| **Fixed Assets** | £ | £ | £ | £ |
| Machinery at cost | 20,000 | | 20,000 | |
| Less depreciation to date | 11,000 | | 13,500 | |
| | | 9,000 | | 6,500 |
| Vehicles at cost | 80,000 | | 100,000 | |
| Less depreciation to date | 25,000 | | 40,000 | |
| | | 55,000 | | 60,000 |
| | | 64,000 | | 66,500 |
| **Current Assets** | | | | |
| Stock | 22,500 | | 33,000 | |
| Debtors | 18,000 | | 27,500 | |
| Bank | 6,250 | | − | |
| | 46,750 | | 60,500 | |
| **Less Current Liabilities** | | | | |
| Creditors | 14,250 | | 25,350 | |
| Bank | − | | 9,600 | |
| | 14,250 | | 34,950 | |
| **Working Capital** | | 32,500 | | 25,550 |
| | | 96,500 | | 92,050 |
| **Less Long-term Liabilities** | | | | |
| Bank loan | | 12,500 | | − |
| **NET ASSETS** | | 84,000 | | 92,050 |
| *FINANCED BY* | | | | |
| **Capital** | | 76,050 | | 84,000 |
| Add Net profit | | 25,450 | | 33,250 |
| | | 101,500 | | 117,250 |
| Less Drawings | | 17,500 | | 25,200 |
| | | 84,000 | | 92,050 |

*Note:* Loan and overdraft interest paid in 20-4 was £2,250.

Jane Clark asks you to explain how, despite her increased profits in 20-4, a healthy bank balance at the start of the year has been turned into an overdraft.

You are to prepare a cash flow statement for the year ended 30 September 20-4.

**27.7** The balance sheets of Simplex Limited are shown below.

## BALANCE SHEETS AS AT 31 DECEMBER

| | 20-6 £ Cost | 20-6 £ Dep'n | 20-6 £ Net | 20-7 £ Cost | 20-7 £ Dep'n | 20-7 £ Net |
|---|---|---|---|---|---|---|
| **Fixed Assets** | | | | | | |
| Land and buildings | 100,000 | 10,000 | 90,000 | 100,000 | 12,000 | 88,000 |
| Plant and equipment | 51,400 | 8,400 | 43,000 | 70,300 | 14,300 | 56,000 |
| | 151,400 | 18,400 | 133,000 | 170,300 | 26,300 | 144,000 |
| **Current Assets** | | | | | | |
| Stock | | 44,000 | | | 61,000 | |
| Debtors | | 28,000 | | | 32,000 | |
| Bank | | - | | | 5,000 | |
| | | 72,000 | | | 98,000 | |
| **Less Current Liabilities** | | | | | | |
| Creditors | 23,000 | | | 27,500 | | |
| Bank overdraft | 6,500 | | | - | | |
| Corporation tax | 13,500 | | | 16,000 | | |
| Dividend proposed | 10,500 | | | 15,000 | | |
| | | 53,500 | | | 58,500 | |
| **Working Capital** | | | 18,500 | | | 39,500 |
| | | | 151,500 | | | 183,500 |
| **Less Long-term Liabilities** | | | | | | |
| Debentures | | | 30,000 | | | 40,000 |
| **NET ASSETS** | | | 121,500 | | | 143,500 |
| | | | | | | |
| ***FINANCED BY*** | | | | | | |
| **Shareholders' Funds** | | | | | | |
| Share capital | | | 110,000 | | | 130,000 |
| Retained profits | | | 11,500 | | | 13,500 |
| | | | 121,500 | | | 143,500 |

Notes
- interest paid on the debentures and bank overdraft in 20-7 was £2,850
- you should show your calculation of profit (before tax and interest)

You are to prepare a cash flow statement for the year-ended 31 December 20-7.

**28.9** The summarised balance sheets of Ritt Ltd at the end of two consecutive financial years were as shown below.

### SUMMARISED BALANCE SHEETS AS AT 31 MARCH

| 20-6 £000 | 20-6 £000 | | 20-7 £000 | 20-7 £000 |
|---|---|---|---|---|
| | | **Fixed Assets** (at written down values) | | |
| 50 | | Premises | 48 | |
| 115 | | Plant and equipment | 196 | |
| 42 | | Vehicles | 81 | |
| | 207 | | | 325 |
| | | **Current Assets** | | |
| 86 | | Stock | 177 | |
| 49 | | Debtors and prepayments | 62 | |
| 53 | | Bank and cash | 30 | |
| 188 | | | 269 | |
| | | **Current Liabilities** | | |
| 72 | | Creditors and accruals | 132 | |
| 20 | | Proposed dividends | 30 | |
| 92 | | | 162 | |
| | 96 | **Working Capital** | | 107 |
| | 303 | **NET ASSETS EMPLOYED** | | 432 |
| | | *FINANCED BY* | | |
| 250 | | Ordinary share capital | 250 | |
| 53 | | Reserves | 82 | |
| | 303 | Shareholders' funds | | 332 |
| | – | Loan capital: 7% debentures | | 100 |
| | 303 | | | 432 |

Turnover was £541,000 and £675,000 for the years ended 31 March 20-6 and 20-7 respectively. Corresponding figures for cost of sales were £369,000 and £481,000, respectively.

At 31 March 20-5, reserves had totalled £21,000. Ordinary share capital was the same at the end of 20-5 as at the end of 20-6.

Required:
(a)  Calculate, for each of the two years, the ratios listed below:
   gross profit/turnover percentage
   net profit/turnover percentage
   turnover/net assets employed
   net profit/net assets employed percentage
   current assets/current liabilities
   quick assets/current liabilities
   (Calculations should be correct to one decimal place)

(b)   Comment on each of the figures you have calculated in (a) above, giving probable reasons for the differences between the two years.

**28.10** Martin and Helen Jarvis own and manage a retail store under the trade name of 'Life & Leisure'. It is run as two departments: (G) Games, etc, managed by Martin, and (B) Books, etc, managed by Helen.

The following trial balance was extracted from the books of Life & Leisure at 31 March year 8, the accounting year end:

|  |  | £ | £ |
|---|---|---:|---:|
| Sales: | G |  | 240,000 |
|  | B |  | 360,000 |
| Stock at cost at 1 April year 7: | G | 42,000 |  |
|  | B | 14,000 |  |
| Purchases |  | 422,600 |  |
| Sales expenses: | G | 33,400 |  |
|  | B | 45,700 |  |
| Administrative expenses |  | 7,300 |  |
| Establishment expenses (rates, insurance, etc) |  | 16,600 |  |
| Advertising campaign |  | 8,500 |  |
| Debtors |  | 3,200 |  |
| Creditors |  |  | 8,300 |
| Bank and cash balances |  | 14,900 |  |
| Ten year lease on business premises, at cost |  | 66,000 |  |
| Fixtures and fittings, at cost |  | 18,000 |  |
| Motor van at cost |  | 9,000 |  |
| Provisions for depreciation at 1 April year 7: |  |  |  |
| Amortisation* of lease |  |  | 13,200 |
| Fixtures and fittings |  |  | 8,000 |
| Motor van |  |  | 3,600 |
| Joint capitals at 1 April year 7 |  |  | 68,100 |
|  |  | 701,200 | 701,200 |

*Author's note: amortisation is the term used to depreciate a lease.*

The following additional information was available:
1.  The analysis of purchases over the year had been inadequate and only an aggregate figure was available.
2.  Gross profit as a percentage of sales is earned on average as follows: G 37%; B 24%.
3.  Stock-in-hand, valued at cost, 31 March year 8: G £41,400; B £12,400.
4.  Establishment expenses, administrative expenses, and cost of the advertising campaign were all to be apportioned in proportion to the sales of each department.
5.  Establishment expenses prepaid at 31 March year 8: £400.
6.  Sales expenses accrued at 31 March year 8: G £730; B £490.
7.  Commission to sales staff was to be allowed in respect of each department, calculated as 4% of each department's gross profit.
8.  Depreciation was to be provided as follows, based on the cost of the asset held at the year end:
    Fixtures and fittings – 15% per annum
    Motor van – 20% per annum
9.  The fixed asset depreciation was to be apportioned to departments as follows:

|  | G | B |
|---|---|---|
| Lease on business premises | 50% | 50% |
| Fixtures and fittings | 40% | 60% |
| Motor van | 80% | 20% |

Required:
(i)   Prepare columnar departmental trading and profit and loss accounts for Life & Leisure for the year ended 31 March year 8.
(ii)  (a) Calculate the ratio of aggregate net profit to the amount of capital at 1 April year 7.
      (b) No provision has been made in the figures for a payment to either Martin or Helen for the time they have devoted over the year to managing the business. Explain briefly whether you consider this to be reasonable.

# Index